SIOUX
WAR
Dispatches

SIOUX WAR Dispatches

Reports from the Field, 1876–1877

Marc H. Abrams

WESTHOLME
Yardley

Frontispiece: A line of mounted Sioux warriors photographed by Edward Curtis in 1906. This image recreates what a U.S. Cavalryman may have seen during the Sioux War. (*Library of Congress*)

Westholme Publishing, LLC
904 Edgewood Road
Yardley, Pennsylvania 19067
Visit our Web site at www.westholmepublishing.com

First Printing May 2012
10 9 8 7 6 5 4 3 2 1

ISBN: 978-1-59416-156-8

Also available as an eBook.

Printed in the United States of America.

In loving memory of my dad,
Joseph L. Abrams

CONTENTS

List of Maps

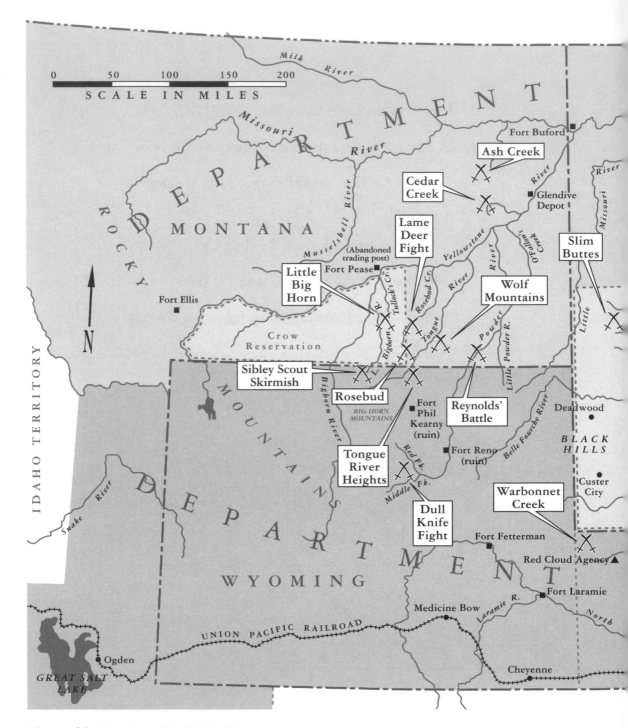

Theater of the Great Sioux War, 1876–1877.

OF DAKOTA

DAKOTA

NORTH DAKOTA

Missouri River

■ Fort Stevenson

NORTHERN PACIFIC RAILROAD

Fort Abraham Lincoln ■

Heart River

Bismarck

■ Fort Rice

Cannonball River

▲ Standing Rock Agency

TERRITORY

Grand River

MINNESOTA

Moreau River

St. Paul

Great

SOUTH DAKOTA

River

Cheyenne

▲ Cheyenne River Agency

N

Sioux

▲ Crow Creek Agency

White River

▲ Lower Brule Agency

Reservation

Fort Randall

Yankton

▲ Spotted Tail Agency

OF THE PLATTE

IOWA

NEBRASKA

Platte River

Omaha

Sidney

River

UNION PACIFIC RAILROAD

Platte River

FOREWORD

The Indian Wars of the American West were, in the contemporary public mind, akin to the foreign wars of later centuries. Far distant readers were both thrilled and horrified at the drama being played out in the vast unsettled regions of our country. The only practical medium of mass communication was the printed word. The public relied upon the dispatches of war correspondents in the field (and on inflammatory editors ensconced safely behind their desks) to gain their information. In addition to professional writers, some correspondents were the soldiers themselves. Their dispatches have added meaning, for they did not always agree with the policies that had sent them into the field.

When attempting to reconstruct and understand events from our past, the most vital source material is, of course, that which is closest to the event in time and place. These correspondents were there, in the heat and cold, in the dust and mud, and some of them never returned from their assignments. Their words and unique perspectives still resonate as human and historical documents.

Marc Abrams has provided an invaluable service to scholars and lay readers in compiling this treasure trove of primary information. Not content with merely gathering the reports, Marc offers hundreds of detailed annotations to provide deeper background and understanding of the events and people involved in them. Like the correspondents he has come to know through his research, Marc has done the hard work; we need only read in comfort and benefit from his efforts.

Douglas W. Ellison,
author of *Sole Survivor: An Examination of the Frank Finkel Narrative* and *Mystery of the Rosebud*.

INTRODUCTION

The story of the Sioux War of 1876–1877, also known as the Great Sioux War, has been told hundreds of times, and, no doubt, will continue to be told and retold for many hundreds more. The story endures largely because of our interest in George Armstrong Custer's larger-than-life persona, his larger-than-life last battle, and his larger-than-life death along the Little Big Horn River in June 1876 (along with some 210 men from the five companies who perished with him). Of course, the story of the Little Big Horn itself (or the Sioux War as a whole) would not be complete without acknowledging the two thousand or three thousand Sioux and Cheyenne fighters, the last holdouts of a warrior race in a quickly fading era who, for a brief moment, ruled the day. After all, they, too, have captured our imaginations. But this book goes well beyond just the battle of the Little Big Horn. It picks up with the Black Hills dilemma (that is, following the discovery of gold in 1874, the US government wanted control of the hills despite the fact that they were legally held by the Sioux under treaty) and the issue of the unceded territory (the disputed hunting lands adjacent to the Great Sioux Reservation), and continues through to spring 1877 and the surrender of Oglala Sioux Chief Crazy Horse.

The main narrative is told through the extensive use of contemporary newspaper reports written by civilians and military personnel who accompanied the various army columns into Indian country. These include dispatches from Reuben Davenport, Robert Strahorn, Joe Wasson, John F. Finerty, James J. O'Kelly, Jerry Roche, Major Thaddeus Stanton, Major James Brisbin, and others. Without their words, this book would not exist. When it was necessary to use material from outside of the newspapers, I tried to use official reports or first-person accounts, such as the wonderful diaries of John Gregory Bourke, the longtime lieutenant of the Third Cavalry and aide to General George Crook. As much as possible, I attempted to tell the story of the Sioux War strictly through the words of those who were there, but again, the bulk of the material was drawn from period newspapers.

Following the death of *Bismarck Tribune/New York Herald* reporter Mark Kellogg in the battle of the

Little Big Horn, the *Herald* paid tribute to him and printed the following thoughts about civilian war correspondents in its issue of July 10, 1876:

The army correspondent often holds the post of honor in journalism because he holds the post of danger. It is his duty and his privilege to share the risks of battle, and for the sake of the pen to defy the dangers of the sword. His services are not merely those of a historian, but are rendered to the power which now makes history possible. Caesar wrote his own commentaries and Napoleon dictated his own memoirs, but the correspondent must record the fight the moment it is fought, nor wait for the slow official reports. The anxious eyes that watch a distant army where every soldier is a husband, brother or son, the impatient heart of the country that beats for victory, cannot wait till the government chooses to give its cold, calm despatches. The press must speak, and it is the press, and through it the nation, that the war correspondent serves.

At least two other civilian correspondents almost paid the ultimate price during the Sioux War, Davenport and Finerty, but you will have to read the text to find out the circumstances. The fact of the matter was that unless the correspondents chose to remain behind with the slower moving wagon train and/or infantry, they often found themselves in the midst of the action and had to take part in the fighting to survive. As far as the Indian warriors were concerned, they made no distinction between soldier and correspondent.

Whether you are new to the Sioux War or well-versed in these events, I hope you find this book an exciting and informative read. Some items will certainly be new to most or all readers, such as a description of the battle of the Little Big Horn by Brule Sioux warrior Black Bear and the description of General Crook by Captain Harry Cushing.

I

Black Hills Gold Seekers

"The policy of the government in recognizing the right of the Indians to any portion of the soil is a mistake. . . . The red devils have no more right to an acre of land than have the coyote or the rattlesnake, and the Indian's chances for heaven after death are about as good as those of the animals above named."—Editorial, "Who Killed Custer?," *Daily Colorado Chieftain*, July 7, 1876

"We have not more than three hundred thousand Indians within the borders of the Republic. This is less than the population of Brooklyn. Brooklyn is content to live on a few square miles—there to live in peace. Yet three hundred thousand Indians demand more space than the German Empire."—Editorial, "The Indian Question—Let Us End It Now and Forever," *New York Herald*, July 9, 1876

"The whole Sioux nation, taking the largest estimate, is not larger than one of our city wards. We could put them on a tract of land not larger than Rhode Island and keep them there."—Editorial, "The Indian Question," *New York Herald*, August 7, 1876

On August 18, 1875, the *New York Herald* printed a lengthy dispatch from its young correspondent Reuben Briggs Davenport, then about twenty-three, under the bold-print headline, "The Black Hills." Davenport's dispatch included a proclamation from General George Crook, commander of the Department of the Platte, dated July 29, 1875. Speaking for the president of the United States, Crook announced that all miners and other "unauthorized citizens" had until August 15, 1875, to leave the "Indian reservation of the Black Hills" and the unceded territory on its western boundary, "until some new treaty arrangement" was in place. In the meantime, Crook was ordered to occupy the "reservation and territory with troops and to remove all miners or other unauthorized citizens" in the area "in violation of treaty obligations." After August 15, the troops would have to use force to evict the offending whites. However, Crook's closing statement gave the miners some hope for their future operations:

It is suggested that the miners now in the Hills assemble at the military post about to be established at Camp Harney, near the stockade on French Creek, on or before the 10th day of August; that they there and then hold a meeting and take such steps as may seem best to them by organization and drafting of proper resolutions to secure to each, when this country shall be opened, the benefit of his discoveries and the labor he has already expended.

Of course, even in the best of times it is not easy to suppress a gold rush, and the summer of 1875 could hardly be considered the best of times. America and Europe were then in the midst of a six-year economic depression, and when it was reported in the newspapers that Lieutenant Colonel George Armstrong Custer's expedition to the Black Hills in July 1874, the primary mission of which was to locate a suitable site for a new military post, had discovered gold in the "grass roots," the lure of quick riches was irresistible.[1] And the draw of the Black Hills was only increased the following year when an expedition under geologist Walter P. Jenney confirmed the previous reports.[2] But there was a legal problem with this new influx of gold seekers and adventurers into the Black Hills, and it was article 2 of the Sioux Treaty of 1868.[3] This clause essentially set aside the western half of present-day South Dakota, everything west of the Missouri River, which included the Black Hills,

for the absolute and undisturbed use and occupation of the Indians herein named[4] . . . ; and the United States now solemnly agrees that no persons except those herein designated and authorized so to do, and except such officers, agents, and employés of the Government as may be authorized to enter upon Indian reservations in discharge of duties enjoined by law, shall ever be permitted to pass over, settle upon, or reside in the territory described in this article, or in such territory as may be added to this reservation for the use of said Indians.[5]

In other words, the miners were in the Black Hills illegally. Additionally, article 16 covered what was known as the "unceded Indian territory," an area mostly west and adjacent to the Great Sioux Reservation. It stated: "The United States hereby agrees and stipulates that the country north of the North Platte River and east of the summits of the Big Horn Mountains shall be held and considered to be unceded Indian territory, and also stipulates and agrees that no white person or persons shall be permitted to settle upon or occupy any portion of the same."

This clause was soon to present two additional difficulties. First, this "unceded" area was intended to serve as a "seasonal hunting" ground, not a permanent home, although many Indians used it as such.[6] In fairness, however, many of those who did so had not signed the treaty and therefore were not legally bound by its specifications. Second, the words "east of the summits of the Big Horn Mountains" were somewhat vague (how far east?), and there was no mention of a northern boundary, which was implied but not explicitly stated, and therefore made it open to interpretation too. Geographically, the Big Horn Mountains start to break down just north of the Montana border, finally coming to an end at the Big Horn River, just south of present-day Fort Smith-Yellowtail Dam.[7] The upper reaches (that is, the southern extremities) of the Big Horn River run west of the Big Horn Mountains, and the upper reaches of the Little Big Horn run east. By the time they join, the distance is about thirty-eight miles north of the mountain range.[8] Article 16 used the words "east of the summits of the Big Horn Mountains." Considering that the Big Horn Mountains start to break down just north of the Montana border, the northern boundary of the unceded territory can be considered to be in close proximity to the Wyoming-Montana state line. And it just so happens that the Wyoming-Montana state line formed the southern boundary of the Crow Reservation (and still does). This interpretation would make things nice and neat: the northern boundary of the unceded territory ends right where the Crow Reservation starts. The eastern boundary of the Crow Reservation as stated in the Crow Treaty of 1868 was the "107th degree of longitude west of Greenwich," stretching from the Montana state line north to the Yellowstone River. The battle of the

Cartoon lampooning the negotiations between the Grant Administration and the Indians over the Black Hills. (*Library of Congress*)

Little Big Horn took place about twenty-one miles *west* of the 107th degree of longitude. That is, the most famous battle of the Indian Wars was fought on land that was part of the Crow Reservation. On the other hand, if you wish to interpret "east of the summits of the Big Horn Mountains" as including the lower reaches of the Little Big Horn River, then the battle of the Little Big Horn took place on land that was mistakenly assigned to more than one tribe at the same time.[9] And that analysis may be more viable than you think. Keep in mind, we don't know how the treaty stipulations were explained to the Sioux (and their allies), or how accurately they were interpreted. In all likelihood, their understanding of the treaty was that the western terminus of the unceded territory extended (in a north-south line) from the Big Horn Mountains all the way to the Yellowstone, following the course of the Big Horn River. This is borne out by a statement made in the late 1920s by Wooden Leg, an old-time Cheyenne warrior and veteran of the Great Sioux War. In speaking of a raiding party in which he participated in 1876 against the Crow Indians, he stated [italics mine]: "Our sixth sleep was on *the west side of the Bighorn river*, just below the place where in past times had been the soldier fort [C. F. Smith]. *We were now in Crow land.*"[10]

Clearly, Wooden Leg's understanding was that Crow territory started west of the Big Horn River, and it is safe to say that this meant from the northern end of the Big Horn Mountains all the way north to its junction with the Yellowstone. In fact, this was the understanding of a correspondent of the *New York Tribune* who stated in April 1876 that the unceded lands included "all the country north of the North Platte River to the Yellowstone River, and west to the summit of the Big Horn Mountains."[11]

The fact that the Sioux may not have understood the treaty was illustrated in a *New York Herald* article on May 20, 1876:

The treaty of 1868 was explained to the Indians in one way and was written, signed and sealed in another. As a consequence the Indians, in supposed conformity with their stipulations, early found themselves violating the letter of the document. They have always repudiated representations of their culpability,

and have been surprised in turn by aggressions of the whites, which have been in contravention of both the written and the spoken treaty.[12]

Even prior to General Crook's July proclamation, the army had been making an effort to keep prospectors out of the Black Hills, as illustrated in this clipping from Denver's *Weekly Rocky Mountain News* on April 7, 1875:

"California Joe" and two other characters, who left Denver about a week ago, were seen forty miles beyond Cheyenne, Monday, pulling out for the Black Hills. Their outfit consisted of one horse and a wagon, a lot of provisions, blankets, a few mining tools, and guns, revolvers, and ammunition. Close in their rear was a company of cavalry from Fort Russell, under command of Major Whitney. The Major had instructions to follow along after the Denver outfit, and if they crossed the line of the reservation, at Fort Laramie, to arrest them. "California Joe" said they were going to the Black Hills, and a host as big as the old army of the Potomac wouldn't stop them.

Contemporary readers would have come across other newspaper accounts of soldiers trying to keep miners out of the Black Hills. According to a report in the *Weekly Colorado Chieftain*, May 20, 1875, Lieutenant Robert G. Armstrong of the First Infantry had apprehended "the Andrews-Wharton party, en route to the Black Hills from Sioux City, consisting of forty-two men, six wagons and twenty-two horses. Eleven of the party had reached to within sixty miles of Harney's Peak." A dispatch in the *New York Herald*,

June 23, 1875, stated that Captain John Mix of the Second Cavalry had brought in a party of miners.[13] On August 18, 1875, the same paper reported that Captain Anson Mills of the Third Cavalry had intercepted another band of would-be mining enthusiasts.

An editorial in the *New York Herald* the following summer, July 7, 1876, pointed out that the army had made an honest, if not a disagreeable, effort to keep gold-hungry whites out of the Black Hills:

The government, feeling that public opinion . . . would not countenance the abrogation of the Indian treaty by utterly disregarding its stipulations, issued orders to the commanders of the military posts that covered the approaches to the Black Hills to stop all parties of miners and others who would attempt to enter the region for any purpose. This order was rigorously carried out for some time, but was eventually allowed to lose its force, until the territory that had been guaranteed to the Indians by treaty was occupied by large parties of miners and the military, who took actual possession of it. At first alarmed at the inroads of the whites, the Indians solemnly protested against the invasion of their lands, but without avail, for what rights does the Indian possess that the civilized white man is bound to respect?[14]

As noted in the above quote, the order to keep whites out of the Black Hills eventually lost its force. This was visibly demonstrated by the fact that, in early November 1875, President Ulysses Grant had withdrawn all troops from policing the Black Hills: "[The] President decided that the orders heretofore issued for-

bidding the occupation of the Black Hills country by miners should not be rescinded, still no fixed resistance [by the army] should be made to the miners' going in, it being his belief that such resistance only increased their desire and complicated the troubles."[15]

That is, the miners were now expected to stay out of the Black Hills by the force of words only. Of course, nobody could have seriously entertained the thought that they would. This change in policy was clearly reflected in an article from the *New York Times*, January 25, 1876, which stated, "Twelve hundred men are now in that portion of the Black Hills through which Rapid Creek runs." It continued: "The average diggings are $1 per hour to each man, and $137 were taken out in six hours by four men. The next day the same force took out in the same time $112. 'California Joe' saw $34 taken out of one pan, there being one nugget worth $20."

And the following news clipping appeared in the *Deseret News* out of Salt Lake City on February 2:

Cheyenne, Wyo., 14—A hundred and fifty men left here today for the Black Hills. A party came in last night, and reports that during the eight days of their trip from Custer City [in the Black Hills] they counted 185 wagons en route for the Hills. Two hundred men are outfitting here now and will start this week. The incoming trains bring scores of gold-seekers daily.

As may be expected, the search for gold yielded mixed results. Many prospectors, perhaps expecting easy pickings, were quickly disillusioned; however, some accounts did report moderate success. A report out of Yankton, in present-day South Dakota, in early June declared that a "large party of men returned today from the Black Hills, bringing $20,000 in [gold] dust."[16] A dispatch out of Bismarck, in present-day North Dakota, told of one party that had arrived with $15,000, four men that earned $3,600 in one day, and of a claim that was yielding from $1,800 to $2,800 per day, with two "gangs of men of ten each being employed mining night and day."[17]

Despite these and other success stories, a review of newspaper accounts gives the impression that these reports were the exception, not the rule. One man expressed the frustration that many felt when he wrote:

I have noticed in a number of our leading papers, accounts of the richness of the Black Hills and the abundance of gold to be found there. These reports are calculated to send a large majority of people there who can just raise money enough to get there, thinking when there, that they could make a fortune in a short time. This is all a mistaken idea, for I have been there with a party and if there was so much gold to be found I think I and my friends would have found some of it.[18]

Interestingly, individuals trying to make heads or tails of the situation in the Black Hills from reading newspaper accounts during 1875–76 would have been perplexed by the lack of consensus in those accounts. The *Weekly Colorado Chieftain* of April 6, 1876, summed up the confusion best

when it stated:

Reports from the Black Hills continue to come in. There is not a particle of gold in the country. The diggings are all panning out finely, and rich finds being made every day. Anybody who goes there is sure to starve to death unless he returns with all speed. Vast fortunes may be made there in a few weeks or even days. No living thing grows there. It is a land flowing with milk and honey.

And the *Weekly Rocky Mountain News* voiced similar sentiments:

The gold in the Black Hills seems more than ever of the now-you-see-it-and-now-you-don't order. No two persons tell the same story about it, or see it with the same eyes. Even the Denverites that have been there do not agree in their several statements, and not a correspondent but contradicts all the rest. It is very bewildering, all this.[19]

Some of the comments that made their way into the papers were comedic in nature. One editorial suggested that the wisest policy for the government to follow was to let the troops stand by while "the Indians and miners shoot and scalp each other until both sides were satisfied and ready to quit."[20] And the *Brooklyn Daily Eagle* offered prospective Black Hillers the following three humorous observations:

—Strange to say nobody has yet come out with the "Black Hills' Hair Restorative."
—No one should start for the Black Hills without a wig and some mucilage.
—There may not be gold, but there's no question about the quantity of lead in the Black Hills. Every Indian has a gun full of it and isn't stingy.[21]

The *Deseret News* voiced an interesting perspective, pointing out one of the positive side effects of the Black Hills gold rush:

The police business has been remarkably dull lately, which is an evidence that the moral tone of the city has considerably improved, owing doubtless, to considerable of the scum of society floating off to the Black Hills. Should Sitting Bull or any of his adherents get after members of the disreputable class alluded to with the scalping knife society will be none the worse off.[22]

In the last days of May 1876, William T. Sherman, commanding general of the army, took part in a meeting that included President Grant and Wyoming Governor John M. Thayer. Writing to General Philip H. Sheridan, commander of the Military Division of the Missouri, afterward, Sherman quoted the president as saying

the people who had gone to the Black Hills in Dakota, inside the Sioux reservation, or who may hereafter go there, are there wrongfully, and that they should be notified of the fact. But the Government is engaged in certain measures that will probably result in the opening up of the country to occupation and settlement. Meantime the Indians should not be allowed to scalp and kill anybody, and you are authorized to afford protection to all persons who are coming away or who are conveying goods and stores for those already there.[23]

And what were those "certain measures" that the president mentioned? Military operations had been under way for several months against

A party of miners heads out from Deadwood, South Dakota, to search for gold in the Black Hills in 1876. (*Library of Congress*)

the various bands of Sioux, and their Cheyenne allies, who resisted reservation life and preferred to roam free in the aforementioned "unceded territory," and points beyond. If those Indians could be defeated and contained, the balance of power in the region would swing drastically in favor of the United States. As it was now, the nontreaty (or nonreservation) Indians, sometimes referred to as "winter roamers" by historians, made "the agencies their base of supplies" and "their recruiting and ordnance depots,"[24] while many of the reservation Indians found it necessary to travel to the unceded territory in order to hunt and supplement insufficient government rations.[25] The winter roamers were devoted to the traditional ways of their ancestors, "subsisting by the chase and trade."[26]

Those who made a habit of living on the reservation during the winter, then reverting to the old free life for several months every spring and summer, are generally referred to as the "summer roamers." All in all, the government found it a chaotic system.

By spring 1876, the danger of traveling from points south into the Black Hills had become dire enough that Sheridan called for troops to patrol and protect the primary routes leading from Cheyenne, Wyoming, and Sidney, Nebraska, into the Hills, the initial troop deployments occurring during May and June.[27] Roving bands of Sioux and Cheyennes were making travel rather dangerous. One man from Milwaukee, Herman Ganzio, lived to tell of this danger, coming within seconds of losing his scalp entirely. He related his horrifying (hair-raising?) experience to a reporter from the *Kansas City Times*:

A few hundred yards further on I looked down a ravine to the right and saw five mounted Indians ride across the valley. I started to go back to the train, when at least a dozen Indians ran at me out of the brush and you bet I ran and hollered for help. In a minute more two or three of them shot at me. I felt a sharp, stinging pain in my left leg and another in my left shoulder, and I fell. Then they were upon me in a minute, and one of them put his knee in my back, while another hit me a clip with a club or a butt of a gun, I don't know which. I had no time to think. All I knew was I was being scalped. My hair was held tight; I felt a hot, a red-hot stinging sort of pain all around the top of my head—being torn out by the roots, it was too much; I

couldn't stand it; I died—at least I thought I did. But my scalp was saved just as it was being torn off. The boys at the wagon had seen me running; saw the Indians and came on—13 of them—and got up just in time to prevent the red devils [from] finishing their work. The Indians, as well as my friends, thought I was dead. But I came to again, and my scalp was laid back again. It was only half torn off, as you will see, and is growing again nicely.[28]

One party of gold seekers out of Boulder, Colorado, knowing they were headed into an area considered dangerous due to Sioux and Cheyenne hostility, adopted the motto "Black Hills, or scalped."[29]

But Indians were not the only danger to the mining population. According to Sherman, a good portion of the killing and robbing in and around the Black Hills was due "to some bad white men of the desperado class."[30] One officer suggested, "Lynching is the only cure for such rascals."[31] Even Sitting Bull was quoted as saying, "The whites kill themselves, and make the Black Hills stink, there are so many dead."[32]

Perhaps the most famous of this outlaw class was William F. Chambers, better known as "Persimmon Bill." Bill was involved in the killing of a sergeant from the Fourth Infantry in the first days of March 1876.[33] His reputation was so bad that "Captain Jack" Crawford, the "Poet Scout," reported he had joined Sitting Bull in the wake of Custer's defeat.[34]

The Black Hills situation, and by extension the Great Sioux Reservation, was representative of a larger problem that was then on the minds of many citizens and government officials. As stated in an editorial from the *New York Herald* on June 25, 1876: "It is inconsistent with our civilization and with common sense to allow the Indian to rove over a country as fine as that around the Black Hills, preventing its development in order that he may shoot game and scalp his neighbors. That can never be. This region must be taken from the Indian even as we took Pennsylvania and Illinois."[35]

The issue was summed up succinctly by US Senator Timothy O. Howe of Wisconsin. He said the Sioux had a reservation large enough for a small empire but didn't cultivate it, and therefore it was of no use to them. Additionally, the government had to feed them. In the end, it would be cheaper to collect them on a smaller reservation.[36]

Howe's statement is telling. His sole concern was agriculture. He dismissed, or was unaware of, the fact that the Cheyennes, Arapahoes, and, most strongly, the Sioux, held the Black Hills to be sacred land, a view that was certainly understood by whites at the time. For instance, an editorial in the *Chicago Journal* in spring 1874 said, "The Sioux will not give up the Black Hills, which are held by them in the most sacred relations, without a severe struggle."[37]

One old-time frontiersman weighed in on the subject. He claimed to know of gold in the Black Hills since 1858, and did not think the Sioux would give up the region so easily: "The question in my mind is, will the Indians cheerfully give up the [Black Hills] country, even if they are well paid? I fear not. Hence here is the trouble. The whites must have this country, and it is proper they should. Time only will tell."[38]

And so the stage was set. The Black Hills were rich in gold—although it took some effort to retrieve it, more than most were willing to give—but the Indians were spiritually attached to the land. The US government had tried to buy the land in a series of councils held in late September 1875, in Nebraska (proceedings that the nontreaty Indians unsuccessfully tried to interfere with), but the sides could not agree on a price.[39] When US senator William Allison of Iowa suggested to the Indians that the government could lease the land instead, just long enough to remove the gold and other precious minerals, the response was not quite what he expected: "When this seductive proposal was translated to the chiefs, instead of hearing a chorus of approving 'hows,' he was greeted with shouts of uncontrollable laughter from the whole body of aboriginal dignitaries. The idea of the white men ever consenting to surrender to the Indians a territory in which they had once gained a foothold struck these not entirely unsophisticated children of nature as a tremendous joke, and it proved altogether too much for their proverbial gravity."[40]

And so the matter remained unsettled for the time being.[41]

But buying the Black Hills was only one part of the problem for the government; it was glaringly obvious that something had to be done about the nonreservation Indians, a perpetual thorn in the side of manifest destiny. In fact, the nontreaty bands had contested the advance of the Northern Pacific Railroad in 1873, the surveyors plotting a course up the Yellowstone Valley in Montana, directly through territory the Sioux long considered to be their hunting ground. However, the best resistance the Sioux had been able to muster was two skirmishes, August 4 and 11, with troops under Custer that were serving as an escort for the surveyors.[42]

In a letter dated November 9, 1875, Indian inspector Erwin C. Watkins surmised that the Indians causing the government so much frustration numbered "but a few hundred warriors," a mere "drop in the bucket in number compared to the great body of Indians who have accepted the peaceful policy." In his judgment, one thousand soldiers "sent into their country in the winter, when the Indians are . . . most helpless, would be amply sufficient for their capture or punishment."[43] Indeed, steps toward that end were already in motion (and will be discussed in chapter two).

Following are several engaging newspaper accounts related to the Black Hills excitement during winter and spring 1876; also included is a brief account of a prospecting trip to the Powder River region by way of Bozeman, Montana, seemingly written in

May 1876. In this latter account, the prospectors were accompanied by a party of Crow Indians on a horse-stealing expedition against the Sioux, and some scalp-taking if the scalps were not too hard to come by.

The Daily Colorado Chieftain (Pueblo)
Tuesday, March 7, 1876

The Black Hills.

The Opinion Of One Who Is Posted On The Hills Country—Scarcity Of Water—Many Returning From The Hills.

Editor Chieftain—Black Hills or burst, that is the cry in this, the great Key City of Union Pacific Railroad notoriety. In order that your numerous readers may know a little about the country and the prospects of those going, I will give you a little insight into the trunk of the "Elephant."

Probably on an average of fifty men per day leave this place for the hills, some of these take grub enough to last them through, having nothing left after they arrive there, but very few take enough for thirty days after they get there. There is another class and they are not few, that start out without any blankets, grub, or war tools. Now how any sensible person can be so foolhardy as to go into an Indian country where there is a space one hundred and seventy miles, without a single habitation, without money or anything eatable, is more than I can conjecture. The prices of provisions at the mines inside of thirty days will be doubled as the Spring advances, the danger of the loss of stock and scalps will raise the price of freight and it must be put on the goods, and inside of sixty days the government will be called upon to aid the starving and disgusted crowd that are flocking from all points to the

Hills, at the rate of hundreds per day. There is no doubt but that there will be twenty thousand persons in the Black Hills within ninety days, and of that amount nine tenths have all they have in the world in the investment, and as a general thing they are persons that have had no experience in mines. There has been, to my certain knowledge, gold taken in there to "Salt" with, and what pilgrims are in there will find out the meaning of that word (Salt).

General Crook left Fort Laramie the 24th of February for the Big Horn and Powder River, and for Sitting Bull, and he will find warm work.[44] Sitting Bull's band is composed of refugees of all the different bands of Indians, and also includes many white men and deserters from the army. It is part of the Indian nature to fight, and when they get fairly at work, the pious, well-behaved and well-fed government pets about the Spotted Tail and Red Cloud agencies will put in an appearance on the Black Hills road, and those footsore and weary half-starved gold seekers will most of them learn what the Sioux war whoop means. It is very pretty and entertaining to read Longfellow and look at the noble red man in the picture books, but when you see him on his own ground in war costume, you see a different breed of dogs, and when armed as they are now with improved Winchester and Sharp[s] rifles, the picture of Bright Juniata with her arrow and quiver gives place to something whistling at long range.

The mines about Custer Gulch, are, as a general thing, very flat, and for water, a three months' supply is all that can be relied upon; the ground is deep, say from eighteen to thirty-five feet, and heavy gold at the bedrock. It will take three or four months to open a dam at Custer, and that is what the miners know, therefore there is no opening and no work on

mines in progress but all attention is taken up in building cabins and speculating lots, the mines being a secondary consideration. There is no denying that in a very few instances pay has been found, but not in such quantities as has been represented, in fact the country has great drawbacks in regard to successful mining and it will be several years before any great quantity of precious metals will be mined. What impressed me most was that all the old miners were wanting to sell, and they don't seem to be excited at all, but those of the pilgrims who are taking their lessons in the business are the only ones excited. Most of the old timers that I saw wanted to sell their claims and go farther prospecting.

The great cry of too early for mining is played out, when you consider the low altitude and the fine weather. To be sure it requires running water for successful mining, but a frost of a few inches does not stop successful prospecting and the opening of claims.

At Deadwood, about ninety miles north of Custer, are probably the best diggings found and the best results obtained that are reliable.[45] I got from the owner of the claim, on which three men worked two-thirds of a day with two sluices, and the result was fourteen dollars. Now, I would ask any experienced miner if that is a very heavy result for a claim that required four foot of stripping. We can beat that every day in Colorado with thousands of acres to go on.

I have traveled through the Indian country pretty extensively, and I pity the immigrants who are caught out when the grass grows, for the Sioux mean business. It has begun with horse stealing from the Hillers and will lead to a few being killed on both sides, and when the ball is fairly opened Uncle Sam will have to step in and bring his children home, and a greater portion of them will be found worse off than they were at starting, and [will] find out that distance lends enchantment to the view—but enchantment is poor stuff to thicken soup with.

The return has commenced, and several miners from Montana and the west traveled with us on the return road, and the parts visited by them that I had not seen fully convinced me that, take the whole thing together, there is no foundation in the excitement now existing.

Several poor but respectable young men who were away from home and without money had diverse and sundry gold nuggets that were made into breast pins, and sold the same to the Cheyenneites, who being kind hearted to the strange miners, paid for them the full value of the trinkets as a reminder of Black Hills prosperity, and they were rich for a time, until an honest jeweler of that burg pronounced them to be made of worthless brass.

Jolly Traveler, Cheyenne, Wy.,
March 3, 1876.

New York Times
Friday, March 24, 1876

HUNTING FOR GOLD.

BLACK HILLS NUGGETS OF NEWS.

WORK ENOUGH BUT POOR PAY—THE RICH DISCOVERIES ALWAYS "SOMEWHERE ELSE"—THE MINERS DETERMINED TO FIND SOMETHING—THE BIG HORN BASIN FRUITFUL—GEN. CROOK'S EXPEDITION.

Cheyenne, Wyoming, Friday, March 17, 1876—There is no abatement in the Black Hills furore. The rush for the "diggings" seems to have but fairly begun. From fifty to seventy-five men and boys leave this place every day for the front. Yesterday 130 outfitted, and went forward, in several different parties, the most of them well supplied and armed, but some few on foot with packs on their backs and with scarcely enough "hard tack" for their ten or twelve days' tramp to Custer City. The weather still remains good, and there has been no suffering either along the road or in the various camps. Violent wind and snow storms are likely to come up though at any time from now until the 1st of May, and all who have started out scantily provided are running a great risk. The liability, too, of being attacked at any moment by hostile bands of Indians ought to deter prudent men from venturing away from the larger and well-armed parties.

The scramble is wonderful. Nobody has yet arrived at Cheyenne who could show anything great in the way of "colors," and there are small knots of returning pilgrims coming in here almost every day. The only thing at all tempting is a nugget or two displayed on the counters of one of the saloons here, and which every Black Hiller bound for the front is invited in to see. There are some, however, who say that these "specimens" were brought in from one of the old Sweetwater camps. This much must be said, the most of the emigrants arriving here seem to be fairly infatuated. They are ready and eager to listen to the most wonderful tales of discoveries with which the people here are careful to fill their ears. They scarcely deign to interview the returning prospectors, and if any of them bring discouraging news it is at once inferred that the parties have a "good thing," and want to keep all the prospectors they can out of the Hills.

There are now about two thousand people at Custer City, and half that number at Hill City. And yet the records show that fully 5,000 men have left

Cheyenne for these points during the past four months. Fully as many have gone in by the other routes, via Bismarck, Yankton, Sidney, and Fort Pierre. So, either these fortune-seekers must have scattered over different portions of the 100 square miles that this gold region is supposed to occupy, or they have come out again and gone home. They have done both. The larger portion are no doubt yet in the Hills. Probably there are now as many as 8,000 in that country. How many more there will be in the next two or three months, it is hard to say. If the Indian outbreak daily looked for, and the fierce storms, keep off, the numbers will in all probability be doubled.

A gentleman who reached here last night from Custer City, through in six days, reports that by actual count he met 978 men on the road to the "diggings." The roads are in prime condition, and weather clear and warm. There is said to be plenty of money in circulation at the new camps, as there always is in every miners' camp. The dream of a golden harvest at hand makes everybody a spendthrift. Custer City is orderly and quiet. Some families have already arrived, exercising a due restraint on the gold hunters. A Methodist preacher is already on the ground, and has organized a church. A printing office is en route. There are no regular mails, and communication with the outside world is by whatever scraps of information the daily arriving pilgrims may bring. There is the old-time heartiness in camp, and every new band of prospectors is received with cheers and vigorous hand-shaking, and they in turn are expected to stand treat. Many reach the camp wholly out of money or provisions, but they are hospitably treated, and the prevailing disposition seems to be to "give every man a chance." There is no class of men so san-

guine as these gold-seekers, and while many have spent weeks and months running up and down the gulches, but failing as yet to "pan out" even a fair day's wages, they are serene as millionaires, and talk of bonanzas which they are sure to strike. Large numbers have quietly pushed out westward into the headwaters of Wind River, Owl Creek Mountains, Powder River and Clark's Fork of the Yellowstone. It will be remembered that the "Big Horn Expedition" which fitted out at Cheyenne in 1870, discovered gold on Owl Creek and rich diggings on Clark's Fork, and also made some fine discoveries in the old Sweetwater region at the head of one of the branches of the Big Horn. They were at that time driven out by the military, and the frequent incursions of the savages seems to have kept miners away until this time.

DOUBTS ABOUT THE HILLS.

It is believed by those who have examined this whole region thoroughly—I refer to Northern Wyoming and Montana—that the Black Hills will not prove the richest gold region; that in fact it will in a short time be almost wholly deserted, and there will ensue a stampede for the Big Horn Mountains and Clark's Fork, to the westward. This region, too, is readily accessible by small steamboats up the Yellowstone as far as the mouth of Clark's Fork, bringing prospectors almost into the heart of the new gold district. The Crescent Mountain, which incloses the Big Horn River Basin on the east, north and west, is nearly five hundred miles in length, and according to Surveyor General Reed, of Wyoming, is gold bearing in its whole extent. The only quick and practicable route at this season of the year to the Big Horn Mountains is from Cheyenne via Fort Fetterman.

In conversing with parties just returned from the Black Hills, your correspondent noticed that a large proportion—though they had nothing to show for their three or four months' prospecting—express themselves satisfied with that country, and intend to return again after taking in fresh supplies or stocking up with goods to go into trade at one of the mining camps. All have much to say of the beauty and fertility of the region about Custer City. Farming can be carried on with much success, as a few ranches show by their last year's product. In the western portion of the hills are fine groves of pine, in some places dense forests of large trees covering hillside and valley. Heavy forests of hardwood cover the eastern slope of the hills.

But the existence of gold in paying quantities in the Black Hills region, after all the prospecting of the past few months, seems still a matter of doubt. Of all the returning pilgrims no one has been able to show any large nuggets, or to give any satisfactory account of his success. Some of those who are still in the Hills, in writing back to friends, express their determination to "see it out," but as yet cannot report anything big. Some appear to be making fair days' wages, say from two dollars to three dollars, but it costs them nearly this to live, even under a blanket and on bacon and hard tack. One report has just come in from an apparently trustworthy source, that a party of five sluiced in fifteen hours $250 in gold dust. But such reports as this are rare, and it is evident that no fortunes are yet being made by any of the vast throng who occupy the Black Hills. Those few who claim to have washed out $10 or $20 per day for a week or more at a time, forget to say that these claims do not hold out, and generally after a few days have to be abandoned, not paying enough to work

them. Then, again, must be considered the weeks and months that are wasted, and nothing obtained. These few pay streaks do not begin to make up the expense and time consumed in prospecting. They are too few and far between.

REPORTS FROM THE MINERS THEMSELVES.

An old friend writes to your correspondent that his party, who have been in the Hills some two months, have sunk fourteen or fifteen holes going to bed-rock, and in all cases getting some gold, but not in paying quantities. His emphatic testimony is as follows: "As to advising others to come here, I cannot; but as for myself, I am content to stay a few months longer and see what will turn up. Where gold is so universally found in small quantities there must be a rich pay streak in some place. As yet there are not twenty men in the Hills who are mining enough gold to pay for what they eat." A former resident of Golden City, near Denver, who has been operating on Spring Creek, near Hill City, for two months, writes that he has located four claims that may pay four to five dollars per day to the man in the summer, but not now. As much drainage and other work has to be done in opening claims he does not think that anything less than ten-dollar diggings will pay. He adds: "No one is making money here now, and can't this winter. It is too cold to open new claims. I think we can make some money here next summer."

There are new discoveries reported almost daily in some distant field, resulting in a grand stampede for the new "diggings." So the people that inhabit the different camps are in a constant strain of excitement, ready to "pull up" at any moment and rush forward for some new Eldorado. It is said that rich discoveries some fifty miles north of Spring

Creek are just now drawing together quite a throng. The dirt at the new camp is said to yield pay from the grass roots down, and at the rate of $20 per day to the man. Another returned miner, with whom we have conversed, says: "If there are any mines in the Black Hills that will warrant a stampede like the present one, I have failed to find them; and that is the honest verdict of all the parties with whom I have talked. Rich diggings may possibly be discovered yet, but the chances for another California are not good. My advice is that if a man can get a good chance to make board and clothes where he is, he had better give the Black Hills a wide berth. My belief is that before summer an army of disgusted prospectors will be pouring out of the Black Hills."

The Means Of Transportation.

While there are opportunities for parties to get transportation almost any day from Cheyenne or Denver to Custer City, there is as yet no regularly organized stage line. The teams that go in are generally freighting teams, taking from eight to twelve days for the trips from Cheyenne. There is quite an active demand for passengers, and, as a consequence, fares have come down some in the past two or three weeks. Parties have been taken with ordinary miners' outfit[s] for from $15 to $20. The rate from Denver is generally $25. A regularly equipped stage line, however, will be in operation between Cheyenne and Custer City daily after the 1st of April. It will be equipped with Concord overland coaches and fast horses, and make the run in between two and three days. In connection with this a freight line to carry miners' outfits, supplies, and second and third-class passengers, will be established. The first-class fare will be put at $20; second-class at $15, and

third-class $10. Good eating stations, at convenient places along the route, will be opened. Considerable cutting of rates among the railroad companies bidding for the Black Hills travel is already noticeable. St. Louis papers advertise the fare from that point to Cheyenne at $25, distance 1,015 miles; and the through fare to the Hills $35, distance 1,260 miles. This is cheap traveling for this Western country, where railroad fares generally run from six to eight and stage fares from ten to fifteen cents per mile.

An expedition is now en route from St. Louis to the Hills, and another leaves that city on April 6. A large colony is forming in Chicago, and will shortly leave for the "diggings." There is no doubt that these expeditions, which seem to be forming in most of the principal cities and in some of the smaller towns, are got up by speculators who circulate glowing reports of the country. They arrange with the railroad companies to charter one or more cars at a special rate and charge their own prices for passengers, which, although low, enables them to make a handsome thing. There is considerable rivalry—it might be called hostility—between the different outfitting points, which has now reached such a pitch that agents are employed at the principal cities where there is any Black Hills excitement to herald forth the advantages of one place and the miserable disadvantages of another. The St. Louis and Chicago press seem to be opening their columns pretty liberally to the quarrel.

Gov. [John L.] Pennington, of Dakota, who, of course, feels interested in having the few settlements of that Territory reap all possible advantage from the Black Hills furor while it lasts, declares that the best route is via Yankton, Fort Randall, and old Fort Pierre, and thinks that "any person who does not know this, and is fool enough to go all the way to Cheyenne and then come back to the Black Hills, ought not to go at all." In the private letter, from which we quote, the Governor also lets off a blast against the Union Pacific Railroad Company and the people of Cheyenne. But so far as the railroad company is concerned it must be admitted that they have placed their fares very low, and so long as people are bound to go to the Black Hills, they can scarcely get cheaper riding toward their destination.

The denizens of many of these frontier towns seem to feed on excitement. So every few days a rumor will reach town that a party of Black Hillers has been overtaken by the Indians and scalped. Such stories as these, always applied to some well-known parties who have left the community and are en route to the Hills, has the effect for a time to get up an intense feeling, and scouting parties to go to the rescue are got together upon the spur of the moment, and as suddenly disbanded.

Gen. Crook's Movements.

The movements of Gen. Crook's command, which left Cheyenne for the north three weeks ago, have been watched and speculated upon with considerable interest. The destination and purpose were kept secret so far as possible, and whatever the outcome it is evident that the Black Hills pilgrims have taken it to mean protection for them, and this may in a measure account for the rapidly-swelling hegira to the mines. Gen. Crook's command is finely mounted on picked horses, and in every way splendidly equipped with commissary, arms, ammunition, &c. So far as can be ascertained from hints thrown out it is settled that the Indians roaming throughout the Big Horn and Powder River regions are to be removed east-

ward, leaving Wyoming and large portions of Montana and Dakota free. The "Big Horn Expedition," as this is called, consists of five battalions of cavalry and one of infantry. A band of picked scouts, whose lives have been spent on the frontier and in the Rocky Mountains, accompanies the expedition. There are 650 picked cavalry horses, 480 mules for the wagon train, and 400 pack mules. It is apparent that, although Gen. Crook expected to take the Indians by surprise, they have already anticipated the movement, and sent couriers to inform all the Northern tribes. While in camp at Fort Fetterman [in February], an Arapahoe chief [Plenty-of-Bears], with several lodges, approached and wanted to "talk peace." When questioned about the Indians in the country to the northward, he replied, "Minneconjou heap braves. Many lodges. Makum tired count 'um." It is believed that the combined hostile tribes in the country enumerate 20,000 and that they can muster about four thousand warriors. The next two or three weeks will doubtless develop something more of the plans of this expedition. The Indians are in a fighting mood, and have already attacked small settlements, threatened the mining camps in the Black Hills, driven off considerable stock, and committed other depredations.[46]

New York Times
Sunday, April 30, 1876

A Vain Search For Gold.

Over The Hills And Far Away.

The Champion Swindle Of The Centennial Year—Black Hills Miners Find Plenty Of "Scenery" And "Climate" But Little Gold— Expenses Heavy And Money

SCARCE—A BETTER PROSPECT IN THE BIG HORN MOUNTAINS.

Custer City, Dakota, Thursday, April 13, 1876.—We had a rough tramp of it between Cheyenne and this place. The weather was tolerably fine when we started out, but just before reaching Fort Laramie we encountered a furious snowstorm, and the last 150 miles was made through snow, sleet, drifts, high winds, and, at times, bitter cold weather. Though we did not lay aside for this—we were not in a condition to—yet some days it was with the greatest difficulty that we made over six or eight miles. Had it not been for our guide, an old plainsman, who had been over the ground several times before, we must have lost our way. We got through safe at last, however, sixteen days out from Cheyenne. We expected to get through in ten. The distance is said to be from 250 to 270 miles, but it seemed to us much farther. In fact, one of our party had a readometer, and according to his measurement the distance is not far from 330 miles. Very few parties make it in less than thirteen days. We met a great many coming out of the mines. Only a few had any "colors" to show. Many were a good deal "down in the mouth" and demoralized. We saw some who were scantily clad, and out of provisions. They expected to get through by foraging on the parties they would meet. We were called upon several times to share with such.

There are ranches and stations every ten or twelve miles apart, where the pilgrim can get a fair meal at $1. As a matter of interest to those who think of going into the Hills I have made a note of the stations and distances from Cheyenne:

[Fred] Schwartze's Ranch	18
Horse Creek [Fagan's Ranch]	28
Bear Springs	38
Chugwater [Phillips' Ranch]	52
Chimney Rock	62
Jack Hunton's	66
Chug Springs	70
Eagle's Nest	77
Six-Mile Ranche	87
Fort Laramie	95
Government Bridge	97
Government Farm	109
Raw Hide	125
Raw Hide Springs	138
Running Water	146
Hat Creek	165
Indian Creek	175
Cheyenne River	230
Red Cañon	250
Last Water	265
Pleasant Valley	300
Custer City	310
Hill City	325
Rapid City	365

A great many are now coming into the Hills by other routes. I think the majority are outfitting at Yankton. A large party arrived a day or two ago from that place. They came from Chicago, thence to Sioux City and Yankton by rail. The route is up the Missouri River to Brule City, and thence via the valley of the White Earth River. The distance is about the same from Yankton as from Cheyenne. Since the steamers have resumed their trips on the Upper Missouri, I hear that the most of the travel is coming in that direction. The boats start from St. Louis, taking in Kansas City, St. Joseph, Omaha, Sioux City, and Yankton, and run up as far as Fort Benton. Smaller boats run from Yankton to the head of navigation beyond Fort Benton. Fort Pierre and Fort Sully become the best places to strike out for the Hills, the route lying via the south fork of the Cheyenne River. But a number of prospecting parties have taken the boats that go to Fort Buford,[47] and thence to the mouth of the Big Horn, the head of navigation on the Yellowstone, determined to be among the first to reach the new gold land, the Big Horn Mountains. All the miners hereabout are getting worked into fever-heat on the glittering prospects of this new El Dorado, and several parties have struck over the rugged country in that direction. There seems no doubt but that the Big Horn region is rich in gold, and before the Black Hills have been prospected sufficiently to find whether there is gold in paying quantities they stand a chance of being deserted in a grand stampede for the Big Horn country. The reports of officers and scouts who accompanied Gen. Crook's late Indian campaign have heightened the interest, I might almost say the excitement, for that is what it amounts to. Probably the stories in passing from mouth to mouth have been considerably colored. But there are credible reports that both quartz and gulch deposits of great richness have been found there.

The Indians have frequently brought nuggets to the military posts, and point toward the Big Horn Mountains as the source, declaring by significant shrugs that there is plenty more and better where that came from. Exploring parties and prospectors have from time to time brought further evidence of the great wealth of this new gold and silver region. But the presence of the hostile Sioux and other tribes, who look upon the country as their best hunting ground, has prevented its occupation. Should Crook's second expedition, upon which he is soon to enter, result in removing the Indians from the Big Horn country, there is every reason to believe that there will be a great rush that way, and before the year is through that now almost for-bidden section may be the new California.

At Fort Laramie, on my way to this place, I fell in with one of the scouts who led the way for Gen. Crook's troops. He has spent years in the mountains of Montana, Wyoming, and Dakota, and probably knows the Big Horn and Wind River country as well as any white man. He has seen among the Indians five nuggets and colors, and they regard the Big Horn Mountains as their treasure land. From him I obtained a description of the route and distances to the point nearest where the best indications of gold were found. As he was with Gen. Crook's Big Horn expedition from the time the officers of that command left Cheyenne, the [mileage] table is from that place. As far as [Jack] Hunton's Ranch, sixty-six miles from Cheyenne, the route is the same as by the table given elsewhere for the Black Hills. Following on, to Phillips' Ranch[48] is eighty-eight miles from Cheyenne—

Cottonwood Ranch	108
Elkhorn	133
Wagon Hound	148
Fort Fetterman	164
Sage Creek	179
South Fork Cheyenne River	197
Buffalo Wallow	218
Dry Fork Powder River	241
Old Fort Reno	256
Crazy Woman's Fork	284
Clear Fork	304
Old Fort Phil Kearny	324
North Goose Creek	344
Bear Creek	365
Grass Lodge Creek	388
Old Fort C. F. Smith	407

This latter point is on the Big Horn River. The reported gold mines of the Rosebud are about twenty miles to the southeast, and distant from the Yellowstone River to the north from fifty to sixty miles. There is a trail striking off from Old Fort Reno westward around the lower end of the Big Horn Mountains, and then to the north, down No Wood Creek to a point west of the base of Cloud Peak, where it runs up a small creek, in the bed and gulches of which, it is said, some of the best prospects on record for fine gold exist. The gulches have the advantage of swift and never-failing streams from the adjacent high peaks, which tower to the height of 13,000 feet, giving the miner every advantage for washing out and sluicing. Capt. [William F.] Raynolds, of the Topographical Engineers, says in one of his reports that very decided evidences of gold were discovered in the Big Horn Mountains. Gen. Sheridan seems to have had good reasons for believing that the Big Horn country was a valuable gold region, for in his annual report of 1874 he says:

"I have for five or six years past believed that there was extensive deposits of gold in the country west of the Black Hills, extending as far west as the old Crow Reservation in Montana, and as far south as the Wind River Mountains in Wyoming, embracing the valleys of Powder River, Tongue River, Big Rosebud, Little Rosebud, Big Horn, and Wind River. It is possible that it may exist in quantities to be of national importance; and the valleys of some of the rivers named, especially of Wind River and the Big Horn, are of great agricultural importance, having good soil and the greatest abundance of timber and water."

Before reaching Custer City your correspondent noticed that returning Black Hillers had very little gold to show, and very little to say about gold. They could, however, dilate on scenery, climate, timber, and farm facilities. I do not so much wonder at it now. We all like to make the best of everything, and he who has run the risks and had the hardships of a trip to this El Dorado against the remonstrance of friends, hates to own up that the country is not only not golden, but utterly barren. I find it pleasanter to think that we shall find our golden fleece, at length, in the Big Horn Mountains, than to confess that we all have been shorn in the Black Hills. However, let us come down to where we are, and describe our surroundings and prospects.

Custer City is not only a bustling camp, but a regular frontier city. It seems strange to find here, 300 miles from civilization, a metropolis, with its mayor and councilmen, courts, policemen, pawnbrokers, coroners, and its Custer, Crook, and Harney avenues. But here it is—a city, and yet it has no charter; holds no allegiance to any State or Territory, has no regular mail service, no newspaper (though the outfit for one has arrived), no churches, no schools, and no homes. It is a place of pine shanties, and none of its inhabitants talk or act as if they were here for good. They are drifting away to Deadwood, Rapid Creek, or to the newest "diggings" as fast as they arrive. The court-house is a log cabin, sixteen feet square, pine pole and dirt roof, no floor, and a foot-square window. The hotel—there is but one now, though two more are going up—is of hewn logs, about twenty feet square and one story high. The cheapest board is $10 to $12 per week, and the accommodations are a cot on the ground and hard tack. If a man runs out of provisions and is obliged to stock up anew he finds prices a little stiff. Flour, $10 to $12 per 100 pounds; bacon twenty-five cents per pound; sugar forty cents; tobacco, $1.50; potatoes, ten to fifteen cents per pound—and everything else in like proportion. If a man must drink, he pays twenty-five to fifty cents for a "swig"; a bungling barber will shave him for thirty cents. Nothing short of ten cents is recognized here. Yet money is very scarce. The majority are hard up. There is no chance to get work. And so the hundreds have had to idle the winter through waiting for spring to open so that they could hunt for gold.

It is now getting near the time when active mining may be begun. The snow is nearly gone, the streams are thawed out, and the frost in many places out of the ground. The "diggings" on the east side of the Hills, consisting of French Creek, Spring Creek, and Castle Creek, are deep and will require months to get them open for thorough hydraulic mining. On the north side of the Hills the "diggings" are more shallow, being from two to eight feet on Iron, Sand, and Bear creeks. As to the results of mining, from all that I can see and hear, a man by diligent work can take out from $1 to $2 per day. The washings are seldom higher than three cents per pan, and often not over half a cent. Now this is not quite up to the representations of interested parties who told us at Chicago that the gold washings paid as high as $20 per day to the man, and would average $2 per hour to any man at all used to placer mining. To be sure there are exceptional cases. I have heard that a party got $2.75 out of seven pans of dirt on French Creek, some ten miles below here, and that some parties in Deadwood diggings have averaged $4 per day to the man. On Deadwood Creek, they claim to be taking out from fifty cents to $1 per pan, and on Iron Creek about the same. This is on the north side of the Hills. Some are said to be taking out $10 per day per man.

All this, however, is a rumor. As far as Custer City and vicinity are concerned, I must say that we are greatly deceived. I do not wonder everybody is just ready to make a rush for the Big Horn, or any other region that promises gold, in spite of the dangers that threaten. I am fully persuaded that those most active in inciting this Black Hills furor have been perpetrating a great swindle and see what means they use.

Among the flaming Black Hills pamphlets which have been scattered through the East I remember the testimony of Gen. Crook and Prof. Jenny [Walter P. Jenney] quoted to support the Munchausen stories about the gold mines of this section. Crook is reported to have washed out one pan of dirt that yielded seventy cents, and obtained $6 in gold from one cubic foot of sand. Prof. Jenny is reported to have said that the diggings will pay $4 per day and upward to the man, and that gold exists, not only in paying quantities, but in "almost incredible profusion."

A man who has half a chance to make a fair living back in the States would be very foolish, in my opinion, to "pull up" and start for this country. There may be good diggings found yet, and the new mines to the north and west of us may turn out to be very rich. But it is all uncertain. And there are chances that the Indians will play the mischief with us all this summer. They have been hovering around, stealing our stock and threatening to destroy every camp in the Black Hills and drive all the miners out. But if they [the prospectors] are bound to come, and there still seem to be thousands, if I may judge from what those arriving here every day tell, it is well to be fully prepared, and to come with one's eyes wide open. Take plenty of provisions. A party of two, with pack animals, will want to take about the following rations for a prospecting trip through this country: 200 pounds of flour, 100 pounds bacon, 100 pounds sugar, 50 pounds beans, 25 pounds coffee, 20 pounds butter, 20 pounds dried apples, 10 pounds soap, 4 pounds tea, 2 pounds pepper, 6 pounds baking powder, 1/2 pound mustard, 1 gallon vinegar, 10 pounds salt, 2 picks, 2 gold pans, 2 shovels, 2 pair rubber boots, 1 tent, 1 bread pan, 1 camp kettle, 1 box cinnamon, 1 coffee mill. This outfit will cost about $100.

New York Tribune
Thursday, April 27, 1876

THE BLACK HILLS.

THOUSANDS SEARCHING FOR GOLD.

AN INDIAN RESERVATION INVADED—NON-INTERFERENCE BY THE GOVERNMENT—THE ROAD TO THE HILLS—NOT MUCH GOLD YET SENT TO THE SETTLEMENTS.

Cheyenne, Wy. T., April 22—One of the most curious examples of the manner in which the Government observes or neglects its treaty obligations with the Indians is apparent in the history of the rapid settlement of the Black Hills. The larger portion of the Hills lies in the Territory of Dakota, and is on the only well-defined Indian reservation mentioned in the Treaty of 1868. The smaller but perhaps equally rich area lies in Wyoming Territory, and this, with all the country north of the North Platte River to the Yellowstone River, and west to the summit of the Big Horn Mountains, in this territory, was set aside by the terms of the above-mentioned treaty for the use of the Indians, under the title of "unceded lands." White people were strictly prohibited from encroaching upon this region, and it is scarcely a year ago that, in pursuance of orders from Gen. Sheridan, the military forces of this department were actively engaged in

capturing trains bound for the Black Hills and turning them back, even going so far as to carry out the letter of the order, and burn and destroy property in some instances. Emphatic warnings were sent out from Washington to the effect that this country was guaranteed to the Indians by treaty obligations, and must be held for them until such time as it could be obtained by purchase, or by the modification of existing law.

The orders of the departments and of the military commanders have not been revoked, but stand today in as much force as ever.[49] But no one hears of interference with the thousands who are pouring into the new gold fields; the military authorities have ceased to trouble them; even the Interior Department is silent. Yet the Government has not purchased the Black Hills nor any other portion of the unceded lands from the Indians, nor has the treaty been modified in the slightest degree. Thousands of people are wending their way to join the thousands already in the new Eldorado. Towns are being built, daily stage lines from Cheyenne to Custer City are carrying hundreds of persons northward; mail routes are established by act of Congress itself, and the people of the United States are snatching away from the Indians the richest portion of their unceded lands, and even part of their reservation, without so much as a "Thank you"—all this, too, in spite of treaty obligations which have the force of law.

On the other hand, it may be stated that an effort was made to purchase the Black Hills, which was unsuccessful, and bills have been introduced in Congress to extinguish the Indian title thereto. Moreover, there is the old story of non-observance of the requirements of the treaty on the part of the Indians; of raids and murders along the frontier, and of numberless depredations committed by them. These are given as reasons why the treaty should no longer be observed. In other words, then, the United States makes treaties with a people who it is very sure will observe them only so long as the treaties please, and which it breaks itself whenever it finds new gold-diggings. It treats with beggarly tribes whom it taxes its people to feed. It steals half the money appropriated to feed them, and if the Indians object to this and make up from the frontier settlers the deficiency, it sends troops to thrash them into making another treaty, which is observed in the same way as was the one preceding it.

The Black Hills country we have occupied. It is no longer barred to the people, though under the treaty we have no right to it. How rich in gold it is cannot yet be determined. It has valuable timber, excellent pasturage, and no small area of arable lands. If the mines should prove not worth the working, there is still room for many other industries in that region sufficient to employ a considerable population profitably. This population it will certainly very soon have, if one judges by the numbers journeying in that direction through Cheyenne. The unusually wintry weather of March and April seems to have had no effect in retarding the advance of the constantly enlarging column. The Indians occasionally make a descent upon straggling travelers, but so far they have not checked the movements of a single party from this direction. This is doubtless due in no small degree to the nearness of the military posts of Fort Laramie and Camp Robinson. The road hence to Custer City, by way of Fort Laramie, Rawhide, Running Water, Cheyenne River, and Red Canyon, is much of the way over high natural divides and is generally almost equal to a turnpike. The distance is 228 miles, and the stages, which now

leave here tri-weekly, make it in five days. Stations have been established at convenient distances, and accommodation, such as one usually finds on the frontier, is provided for the traveler. It is not always equal to that found in the Eastern States, but what difference does it make to a man on the way to the mines with visions of golden wealth in his head? A blanket, a piece of fried bacon, a cup of muddy coffee, and a hot and heavy biscuit are luxuries enough to satisfy the most exacting. Most people go in their own conveyances and carry their own provisions. Many go out in fast freight teams hired here for the purpose. Sawmills, printing-offices, stocks of goods of all kinds, and even a variety theater have already gone to Custer City, together with gambling outfits and the usual crowds which flock from one mining camp to another.

Thus far little gold has been brought here, but owing to heavy snows and cold weather no mining could be done, and it will be midsummer before we hear what the result of all this search for gold is going to be. The present indications are that this region will be a good place for poor men. The gold is found in gulches and in quantities to pay the laborer all the way from $2 to $10, and even more, per day. The quartz loads have scarcely been prospected yet, and even if they are found to be rich in gold it will require capital to work them. Gulch-mining requires no capital but the pick and pan, and the possibility of "pockets" from which a fortune may be extracted in a day is a very attractive thing to the "pilgrim." New discoveries are reported almost daily along the eastern or Dakota side of the Hills, while on the western or Bear Lodge side, which has not been as yet so extensively prospected, there come reports of nuggets and "finds" that indicate an equally valuable district.

Altogether there is no lack of encouraging reports, but a year will tell us what there is in the Black Hills.

Gen. Crook continues making preparations for his next expedition against the Indians. It is expected to start about the middle of May, and will be strong enough in numbers to permit of the division of the command into two or three flying columns which can follow the Indians with safety. A summer camp will probably be established at old Fort Phil Kearney, in charge of a force of infantry, and from this base, which is to be kept well supplied, rapid movements can be made through every part of the hostile country.

Weekly Rocky Mountain News (Denver), Wednesday, May 17, 1876

RAIDING REDSKINS.

THE SCALP-RAISING SEASON OPENING IN THE BLACK HILLS.

STRAGGLING GOLD HUNTERS GREETED BY SHOWERS OF BULLETS.

LATEST NEWS FROM THE INDIAN OUTBREAK IN THE NORTH.

[Written by Robert E. Strahorn]

Fort Laramie, Wyoming,
May 6, 1876.

From returning Black Hillers who reached this post last evening, I have obtained late advices in regard to the upper country. There are now some two hundred men on the road leading to the northern Eldorado, eighty of whom [from Pennsylvania] are going north, sixty-five coming southward, and the remainder are to camp on Hat Creek, seventy-five miles distant, awaiting the arrival of more emigrants, so that greater safety will be insured during their future progress.

All of these trains were attacked simultaneously by a large band of Indians, on last Tuesday morning [May 2], while they were quietly traveling along, eight miles beyond Hat Creek. The train of May & Parrott, of Cheyenne, consisting of twenty men, was first attacked and a running fight kept up for a distance of three miles, when the outfit reached the top of a high bluff. There the whites were compelled to halt, and, amid the

YELLS OF THE SAVAGES

who surrounded them, corralled their wagons and horses and continued the defense for three or four hours. About that time the train of L. R. Gwin, a Californian, consisting of sixty-five men with wagons, etc., came up, and, thus strengthened, the gold seekers pushed on to Hat Creek, some four miles further, and made camp for the night. They had scarcely turned their stock down to water before the savages again appeared and commenced firing from three directions. So determined was this attack that the whites were soon in imminent danger of losing their stock. To avert this catastrophe, and at the same time put a bold face on matters, Mr. Gwin, at the head of a small detachment of mounted men, made a circuit around the besiegers, and dashed in upon them from the rear. The savages

BROKE AND FLED IN DISMAY,

and as the brave little party who made the sally returned to camp another party of some thirty men joined the camp. All came to the conclusion, however, that the top of a neighboring hill would make a far safer camp ground, and, moving thither, remained undisturbed during the night.

As these trains pulled away from the eighty Pennsylvanians referred to above, they heard heavy firing in the vicinity of the latter's position, but of the result none could tell, as the parties were going in opposite directions, and saw each other no more. The Pennsylvanians had only thirty poor, old-fashioned guns among them, and from the brisk fusillade heard in their direction, it is believed that they were roughly handled.

During the fight the Indians generally kept behind shelter and did very wild shooting. Only one white man was injured, he receiving a bullet through the ankle. Fourteen animals belonging to the different trains were shot and the wagons were pretty well

Perforated By Bullets.

When the first fire was delivered by the savages, the train was pretty badly "strung out" and the last wagon composing it, belonging to the husband of the negro woman who was killed in the late Red Cañon massacre, was closed in upon and captured.[50] Its occupants, by dint of some hard running, made their escape to the balance of the train, which was quickly "closed up."

It is now feared that the two men who went out to secure the bodies of the massacred Metz family, about a week ago, have been waylaid and killed by the Indians. They have not been seen by any of the incoming gold hunters, and have not even been heard of since leaving the fort.

Indians In The Black Hills.

Bands of the hostile Sioux are continually moving over the different roads and trails in the Black Hills, and have often come in sight of Custer City. They have even run off stock from the town site of Custer, and have been equally rampant in the neighborhood of Hill City. My informant left Custer one week ago, and he says the inhabitants were then building stockades and otherwise fortifying the town, being really afraid of an attack upon that metropolis in miniature. Late

arrivals in Custer bring tidings of numerous petty depredations in the northern districts of the Hills, such as running off small bands of stock, and the occasional massacre of straggling miners. At Custer they have organized two or three bands of volunteers to pursue and chastise the redskins, but thus far no favorable results have accrued to the citizens, aside from their being prepared to better resist future incursions.

More Killing And Stealing.

The garrison was startled last evening by the news that Indians had, the evening before [May 5], visited Hunton's ranch, on the Chugwater, twenty-six miles south of this post, and stolen thirty head of horses. Besides this, James Hunton, a well known frontiersman, was supposed to have been killed, from the fact that his horse came galloping into the ranch without the rider. Twenty men, under Lieutenant [James N.] Allison [Second Cavalry], were immediately started in pursuit of the marauders, and it soon after transpired that the report was only too well founded. Mr. Hunton had rode out into the hills in search of stray stock, and when some five or six miles from the ranch was evidently surprised by about thirty Indians. From the appearance of the ground in the vicinity it is believed that his horse, in making some terrific bounds to escape, unfortunately stumbled and threw his rider; that Mr. Hunton regained his feet and ran some fifty yards, when he, catching his foot in a vine, also stumbled. There he was surrounded, and the savages amused themselves by firing eight bullets into his head and body, almost any one of which would have proved fatal. The ground in the vicinity of where the body was discovered was literally covered with moccasin tracks.[51]

The savages then endeavored to catch his horse, which is known all over this frontier as being a very superior animal. They ran him until arriving in sight of the ranch, and finding their endeavors vain in that direction, remained lying concealed until night, when they broke into a corral and pasture field near the house and rescued the thirty horses already referred to. Their trail leads in the direction of Red Cloud Agency, and owing to a "cut off" made by Lieutenant Allison, it is not unlikely that he will either strike them before they reach that hive of rascally bees, or else make the pursuit so hot that they will be glad to relinquish their booty and scatter to the four winds. I am reminded here that on the morning after the attack upon the wagon train, narrated in this letter, the southward bound emigrants struck a fresh trail of about sixty of the Indians coming directly from the location of Red Cloud Agency. They at once came to the conclusion that the trail was made by their besiegers, and thus consistently furnished another link in the chain of evidence that is now condemning the unruly braves, who draw their rations at that point.

Paying Their Compliments to the Fort.

Emboldened by their success all around the horizon the cheeky braves are now occasionally coming to the tops of the bluffs, a mile or two distant, and taking observations of this staunch old fort. Fresh trails of small war parties have been found within the past few days in different directions from five to fifteen miles distant. If the barbarians can safely run in upon settlements as secure as we had all fancied that on the Chugwater, and carry out their designs by the side of the telegraph and stage line now, it is difficult to say what they will not do when

the "grass grows green," and when balmy nights woo sleepless "reds" to the chase.

Meantime 340,000 pounds of toothsome bacon and snowy flour and fragrant "Rio," with other odds and ends as appetizers—to say nothing of the numerous herds of swine awaiting slaughter—are going forward to refresh the poor Indian when he returns exhausted from such a foraging trip as his last. And then, alas for the inconsistency of human charity, a batch of over a million pounds of hard hard-tack and salt pork, with a wicked ballast of powder and lead, is also going forward to supply the soldiers who hunt the Indians who have been refreshed, from a well filled larder, through the Quaker policy that Grant built.

Alter Ego.

New York Herald
Thursday, May 18, 1876

The Black Hills.

Sorry Condition Of The Seeking Miners—Want And The Tomahawk Thinning Them Out—The People Fleeing For Safety—Movements Of The Military Expedition.

Cheyenne, Wy. T., May 17, 1876. Parties of frightened miners, who have hastily left the Black Hills and pushed southward with all convenient speed, daily arrive here, bringing melancholy stories. The mining settlements will soon be deserted unless the terror of returning across the open plains, which are now infested by bands of bloodthirsty Sioux, should counterbalance in the minds of the unfortunates the hardships and perils of remaining where they are. Food and ammunition they report to be very scanty there and held by the traders at fabulous prices. Many of

The Repentant Emigrants

suffer from enforced fasting, except when they may chance to secure small supplies of wild game, which has become very shy. The majority of them have ventured and lost their all in seeking the fancied El Dorado. They are depleted not only in purse but in health and spirits. Those who have reached this point say that

The Sioux

are in the heart of the Black Hills skulking among the rocks and in the canyons, and opening a treacherous fire upon white men whenever they can reach them. They can neither hunt nor dig for fear of the unseen enemy. John Kelly, Martin Dean and John Golden, members of a party of ninety which escaped from the Hills, relate their discovery of three white men on their outward way

Dead And Scalped

near Mountain City, twenty-five miles north of Custer. One of them had been tomahawked, and their wagon was riddled with balls. Dead horses and mules lie along the trail. In Cold Springs Canyon they found the corpse of another invader killed by a wound given behind and scalped. Today it is reported that Jim Sanders, a gallant scout and hunter, has been

Butchered By The Sioux

near Iron Creek, in the Black Hills. The returned miners, who are of course terrified by their experience, say it is impossible for the squatters to hold out against want and the Indians long. There are only two alternatives, to

Risk A Massacre

on the Plains or to submit to be picked off and starved to death in the Hill country. The settlements have already lost by departure and demise two-thirds of their inhabitants. Custer City once claimed 1,200 souls and has now only 300. Hill City has 200 empty cabins and twenty miners; Mountain City has six cabins and two inhabitants. The Deadwood and Whitewood gulches, where there were 1,000 people, contain now but 200; Little Beaver and Potato gulches have about twenty-five men; in Bear Gulch there are two women. This census was taken by Allen Haight, who was mail carrier for the miners.

The Military Expedition.

The Big Horn and Yellowstone expedition cannot be too early in the field in order to cow the Sioux before they have committed more butchery. The troops are rapidly concentrating at Fort Fetterman. Some of them move tomorrow, others on Thursday; the last companies leave Medicine Bow[52] for the north on Saturday. General Crook will try to incite Indians against Indians; if not [a]ranging the Brule Sioux[,] Spotted Tail's band[,] on his side, at least enlisting the Crows. Severe fighting or a long and arduous chase will ensue. There was never a prospect of a more bitter frontier struggle.

Weekly Rocky Mountain News (Denver), Wednesday, May 31, 1876

The Black Hills.

The Advantages And Disadvantages Of That Indian-Infested Region.

Judge Kuykendall, of Cheyenne, writes as follows from Custer City, under recent date: "I have been north to Sand, Bear, Potatoe, Iron, Deadwood and Whitewood Creeks. Of course I had to take desperate chances, as men were killed in front, rear and on both flanks; but I am bound to give this country a thorough investigation and shall follow the tide wherever it may go.

"Custer City is a 'dead duck' for the present. Indians and white thieves are stealing all the stock; one or the other got away with my ponies. One man was shot half a mile from town yesterday, not seriously, however. I came along a few minutes afterwards, looking for the ponies, but the thieves had run off five of them. We know of about forty men being killed, and many have left for Cheyenne through fear alone. Are we never going to get mail facilities? Troops should be stationed at the Cheyenne River, Custer City, Cold Springs, Camp Crook on Rapid Creek, Crook City on Whitewood, Spear Fish Creek, and at the crossing of the Cheyenne on the Fort Pierre road. All we want to make everything successful is protection for mails and transportation; it is next to impossible to do business under the present state of affairs. Cheyenne must adopt some plan to get freight through quicker and cheaper to compete with other routes, and that without delay. Deadwood, Whitewood and the tributary gulches are very rich, and they are overrun with men; there must be two or three thousand men in that locality. Gold is coming out of the ground and will do so in abundance.

"It seems strange to us in the Hills that the government will persist in feeding Indians in their idleness, at least the old men, squaws, boys and papooses at the agencies, when it is perfectly patent that the young bucks and warriors from there are committing most, if not all, the depredations. Crook's first expedition was certainly bad for the Hills; but if he goes north again with a good force, it will be the means of either controlling the Indians in that vicinity or their entire annihilation. In either case the occupation of that country by whites will be immediate.

"I consider the Deadwood and Whitewood country much safer than here; for the reason that there are and will be more men in these newly discovered, rich gulches, which are densely timbered.

"Many men, in my opinion, have returned to Cheyenne who will, within twelve months, curse themselves for fools; at the same time many of us who stay may by that time sleep under the sod in some silent valley. It would take a long letter to describe this whole country; the Hills are putting on their mantle of green, which is refreshing to the eye, and beauty will soon unfold itself upon every side.

"Give my respects to all friends, and tell them I am on foot in a strange country; but am not like Richard, for I have no kingdom to squander on a 'plug.'"

W. [William] L. Kuykendall.

Colorado Springs Gazette
Saturday, June 3, 1876

THE BLACK HILLS COUNTRY.

The following article presents a rather discouraging view of the mining and other interests in the Black Hills country:

A reaction of feeling against the Black Hills mining has set in, and it appears to be supported by facts, though there is no doubt that some of the stories told by returning adventurers were invented purely for a story's sake. A specimen case of the kind is that of a party lately returned to Denver from the mining country with their wagon riddled with bullet-holes, and with one of their number so wounded that his arm was carried in a sling. This they said was the work of Indians, but it afterwards came out that they did not meet with a single Indian;

that they shot their own bullets through the wagon for the sake of making a sensation, and that the wounded man was accidentally hurt during this operation. Yet there is doubtless great danger to life and property in the Black Hills region, and the enthusiasm awakened by General Custer's report of a rich gold country was caused by a very exaggerated idea of the value of the gold diggings. Reports by way of Cheyenne from returning miners say that the number of murders committed by the Indians has not been fully told. The Indians are said to harass the miners constantly, and among the whites themselves there are so many desperate men that life is quite insecure. The miners number about twenty-five hundred, but they are distrustful of each other, inharmonious and broken into small parties, and are easily exposed to the mercies of the Sioux. They are frightened at their danger, and propose to organize a volunteer force to fight the Indians by Indian tactics, who are said to be growing worse and worse every day.

Gold in paying quantities is found in some places, but the expectations of a few months ago are far from realization, and it is said to be the opinion of California miners that there is little foundation for them. Few miners are finding enough gold to pay their expenses, and many are leaving the diggings. Now that the character of the region is so well known, where is the wisdom of an Indian war to punish these murderous red men? It sounds finely to talk of asserting the dignity of the government and inflicting righteous retribution upon the raiders, but the true policy of the government is to take the course which will ultimately tend best to secure the peace of the frontier; and how the proposed expedition of Gen. Crook will do that is clear only to those who believe in the policy of extermination. The exploration of the Black Hills region has not been a felicitous event and any further disturbance of the Indians there, so long in advance of the needs of civilization, with so slight inducements for the miner or farmer, would seem a mistaken course. Let the Indians remain undisturbed as long as their lands are not wanted, and let all dealings with them be by honest men, and both Indians and whites will be gainers.

Weekly Rocky Mountain News (Denver), Wednesday, June 7, 1876

The Powder River Expedition.

It Has Done Much Traveling And But Little Prospecting.

A letter from a member of the Powder River Expedition supplies the following interesting intelligence:

"The Powder River Expedition, which left Bozeman on or about April 1, is now 220 miles from Bozeman. We are 202 in number, have 38 wagons, and a number of packers and pack animals. The horses have not been counted. In addition to the above there is a party of Crow Indians traveling with us. They often leave us for a short time and go ahead of the outfit. They are on a horse-stealing expedition, and would be pleased to procure a scalp or two from the Sioux, providing the white men would first capture them. Our captain is William Langston, a very good man for the position, one who believes the great secret of Indian warfare is in having strong guards. He puts on 48 guards every day, consisting of 32 for picket duty, and 16 mounted. All hands are called up at daybreak, and the horses which have been corralled during the night are turned out, and every one in camp is ready for an attack.

So far we have not seen a Sioux or a sign of one. The Crows make medicine each night in our camp, and then have to use flour and sugar to properly season it.

"The country we have passed through I cannot praise. It is destitute of timber, excepting cottonwood on some of the streams, and there is not enough of this to fence the bottoms surrounding. The Stillwater and Pryor Creek valleys are good, but a scarcity of timber is noticed even there. The Big Horn valley at Fort Smith[53] is a good one, and timber is available in the mountains both for fencing and building purposes. For forty or fifty miles west from Fort Smith, on the Big Horn, the country is on the Bad Lands order, and the water alkaline. Game is plentiful. We have buffalo, elk, antelope, sheep and white and black tail deer and bear.

"Thus far but little prospecting has been done, nor have we seen any good prospecting country until we came to Fort Smith. There the men prospected and found fine colors on the bars and in the gravel of the river, but not enough to stay on. No one felt elated over it, but many said that it indicated good ground higher up at the source. Yesterday we camped on Soap Creek, prospected, and found nothing.

"We have but two guns poorer than the old style Winchester rifle, and all but three have rifles, and about half pistols of the best pattern. We only fear the stampeding of our stock. We hear of an expedition of sixteen men in our rear from Helena. I think they will turn back, but they could soon overtake us, for we travel slow on account of our stock, which is on the thin order, and the grass is poor. From now on the outfit will prospect more than heretofore.

"The Rosebud, Stillwater, Boulder and Big Horn rivers are very difficult to ford on account of the large boulders in the bed of the streams. We came near losing a man by drowning on the Big Horn. The water was up to the wagon boxes at the best ford.

"The Crows have been ahead to Tongue River and report no Sioux. We expect to make Goose Creek [a tributary of the Tongue], our main prospecting point, soon."

W. C. Boyd.

2

The Battle of Powder River

"There was evidently fighting to be done; when and where nobody knew. It was General Crook's desire to move quickly and secretly. His destination was the Big Horn region. The soldiers imagined the rest."—Special Correspondent, Cheyenne, April 8, 1876, *New York Times*, April 15, 1876

"[The present Indian war] would have come on just the same had the Black Hills never been heard of, though that affair has undoubtedly aggravated it."—Cuthbert Mills, In Camp at Fort Fetterman, July 23, 1876, *New York Times*, August 3, 1876

With treaty proceedings for the Black Hills having produced no results in September 1875, and troops being recalled from patrolling the region in early November, events were quickly coalescing toward a violent confrontation. As one newspaper phrased it, "there are to be stirring times ahead in the Indian country this spring."[1] Even prior to these events, in an interview with Reuben Davenport in the Black Hills on August 2, 1875, General George Crook had stated: "There is undoubtedly to be a great fight yet. The government has to whip the Sioux. The sooner it is done the better."[2]

Writing from Cheyenne, Wyoming, on February 23, 1876, twenty-three-year-old correspondent Robert E. Strahorn informed readers of the *Weekly Rocky Mountain News* that General Crook's "suddenly organized expedition" was the result of events that started back in December 1875. It was then that

an order was issued by proper authorities, the disobeying of which by the Indians was the direct cause of this campaign. The order was to the effect that all the tribes of the Sioux then off their reservation should immediately repair thereto, and that if they failed to obey by the 31st of January [1876] they would be considered common enemies, and thoroughly chastised.[3]

The order Strahorn was referring to was written by Secretary of the Interior Zachariah Chandler on December 3, 1875. It was one of a series of communiqués that set in motion a chain of events that reverberates to this day.

As a result of the directive, Indian runners were sent from the agencies to notify those tribes living outside the Great Sioux Reservation to report to their respective agencies no later than the January deadline,[4] but General Sheridan had serious doubts that the order would be obeyed: "The matter of notifying the Indians to come in is perhaps well to put on paper, but it will in all probability be regarded as a good joke by the Indians."[5]

Sheridan was incorrect. It was not that the Indians laughed at the order, it was that they did not understand the weight of such an ultimatum, assuming they even received it, and, even if they intended compliance (which they probably did not), their sense of time and urgency was far removed from that of the white world, one ruled by clocks and calendars.[6] As illustration, on February 12, 1876, agent H. W. Bingham of the Cheyenne River Agency in Dakota Territory reported the following to Commissioner of Indians Affairs John Q. Smith:

I have the honor to report the return on yesterday of one of the delegations sent from this agency some time ago to the camps of Sitting Bull and other wild bands, to invite them to come on the reservation or be considered enemies.

From the statements of these messengers, the "hostile" Indians received the above invitation and warning in good spirit, and without any exhibition of ill-feeling. They answered that, as they were now engaged in hunting buffalo, they could not conveniently accept my invitation at present, but that early in the spring they will visit this agency to dispose of their robes and skins, when the question as to their future movements can be thoroughly discussed. They are now camped on the Yellowstone River, and my informants say they are not only peaceably inclined, but deny the statements, so extensively circulated, that they intended to make war on the frontier on the approach of spring.[7]

Whether this message, or others like it, ever passed Sheridan's desk is unknown, but in all probability it would not have altered his plans for a military campaign. The deadline for Sitting Bull and the other "wild bands" to report to their respective agencies had passed almost two weeks before, and on February 1, responsibility for the so-called hostile Indians was transferred from the Interior Department to the War Department. The war had already started, only the nonreservation Indians did not know it. However, Sheridan's plan to have troops ready for a winter campaign from the Departments of the Platte and Dakota failed to materialize. By the end of February, only General Crook, Commander of the Department of the Platte, was ready to take the field. General Alfred H. Terry reported he could not have Custer's Seventh Cavalry ready for action before spring.[8]

Crook's headquarters and jumping off point was Fort Fetterman, Wyoming Territory, about eighty miles northwest of Fort Laramie, and it was here that his command was busy gathering and organizing during the closing days of February. The column, once complete, would consist of five companies each from the Second and Third cavalry regiments,[9] two companies of the Fourth Infantry, twenty-five to thirty scouts, plus about 150 men hired to work the pack train and wagon train, altogether about 870 strong.[10] According to Strahorn, based upon the "best authority," the Sioux and Cheyennes numbered twelve thousand to fifteen thousand, of which "at least three thousand can be counted upon as being first class fighting braves, almost as well armed as troops could possibly be. Knowing their country thoroughly, and with an attachment for it second only to the love of life itself, they certainly are not to be despised as enemies, and it needs no prophet to foretell serious times, if they fight as they can reasonably be expected to."[11]

The scouts were organized by Major Paymaster Thaddeus H. Stanton,[12] chief of scouts, and they included some impressive names, such as Ben Clark, Baptiste "Big Bat" Pourier, Baptiste "Little Bat" Garnier, Louis Richard, Louis Archambeau, Edouard Lajeunesse, Jack Russell ("Buckskin Jack"), Speed Stagner, Frank Grouard, and Jules Ecoffee.[13]

Crook was known for being reserved and uncommunicative, so it was no wonder that Strahorn wrote that there was "a tantalizing air of mysteriousness about some of the details and objects" of the campaign.[14] However, he soon learned that the general had three objectives for the expedition:

First, that he is determined to strike a blow at once which will demoralize the savages from the start; second, that a winter campaign, although terribly arduous in that region, will have thrice the terror that one would be likely to influence two months later; third, because everything points to a general Indian war in the section adjacent to the Black Hills, even in advance of the advent of spring, and to make the small force at his command adequate to the demands of next summer's serious task, General Crook sees the prime necessity of immediately crushing out the more Western tribes, at the same time showing all others that the Big Horn and Powder River regions are not to be made the hiding place of the whole Sioux nation in case of its general defeat.[15]

On February 27, Colonel Joseph J. Reynolds, Third Cavalry, assumed command of the expedition;[16] Crook would ride along, supposedly as an observer, though for all intents and purposes, he retained command. About the same time, ten or twelve lodges of Arapahoes under Plenty-of-Bears passed by Fort Fetterman on the way to Red Cloud Agency. Upon being questioned on the number of Indians roaming the northern country, the chief informed the soldiers, "Minneconjou heap braves. Many lodges. Makum tired countum."[17] An even larger party of Arapahoes under Black Crow passed by shortly after. Strahorn noted that [Black Crow] "is very much afraid something unpleasant is about to happen, and says he is on his way to the agency. He intimates that Indian runners have already conveyed intelligence of an anticipated move by the military from this point to the northern tribes."[18]

The Crook-Reynolds column departed Fort Fetterman on the morning of March 1, following north along the traces of the old Bozeman Trail. After crossing the North Platte, they were officially on "Indian ground."[19] One correspondent commented:

Exciting times may be expected, unless the weather, which has been remarkably spring-like and mild throughout the winter, interferes with the progress of the campaign. The troops are provided with shelter tents only, and considerable suffering is apprehended. Pack-mules furnish the entire transportation, the necessity for rapid marching rendering any other impracticable.[20]

Much to the delight of the troops, their departure that morning was accompanied by a "bright and cheering" sun. However, the previous night the snow had come down heavily, and the men were expecting about a foot before it let up. Despite the difficulties of traveling in blizzard conditions and marching in deep snow, General Crook considered nasty weather an ally: "The worse it gets the better; always hunt Indians in bad weather," he was quoted by Strahorn.[21]

The column marched north for fifteen miles that first day, camping at Sage Creek at 1 p.m. According to Strahorn, the line, when closed, was about two miles long. The adventurous newsman rode up front with the "rollicking, keen-eyed band of scouts," followed by the cavalry, infantry, ambulances, transportation wagons, pack trains, and last, about sixty to seventy head of beef cattle "to

General George Crook in the 1870s. (*National Archives*)

be slaughtered along the way as occasion demanded."[22]

The best laid plans often go awry, and so it was with Crook's marching food supply. In the early morning hours of March 3, on the south fork of the Cheyenne River, Indians stampeded the cattle. As Strahorn aptly described it: "There were a number of unearthly yells as if from a man surprised, several rifle shots in quick succession, an Indian whoop, a cloud of dust, and a man was dangerously wounded, a herd of fifty cattle and a horse vanished, and that is what we know of a stampede."[23]

The wounded man was herder Jim Wright. The stampeded cattle were trailed for six miles by a search party that returned without them, stating the animals were headed in the direction of Fort Fetterman, about thirty-two miles away.[24]

The command continued north that day, and signs of Indians picked up in frequency and freshness. After marching twenty-one miles and getting its first view of the Big Horn Mountains, the column made camp at a point called Buffalo Wallow, well aware they were being watched.[25] The next day's march of twenty-three miles was relatively uneventful, but that night there was some excitement in camp when a sentry fired on several Indians creeping through the grass.[26]

On March 5, amid blizzard conditions, the troops reached Powder River and the "ghostly relief of old Fort Reno," abandoned eight years earlier as part of the Fort Laramie Treaty of 1868. Although several Indian trails were plainly visible during the day, none were followed. As General Crook expressed it, he was not after the "small fry" but hoped to surprise the main camp of Indians in their mountain fastness.[27]

At about eight o'clock that night, a sentry observed three mounted Indians coming toward him. Not waiting to find out if they were friend or foe, he fired. An exchange of shots immediately followed, which picked up in intensity when additional warriors began firing from two ends of the encampment. Priority number one was to extinguish the campfires, which were speedily "kicked to smithereens."[28] Hiding behind trees and sagebrush, "the Indians did their usual skulking, and rendered the whole affair very tantalizing, and all that could be done in the way of returning their fire was to watch the flashes of their guns and send a bullet after the flash; it was about as "sure a thing" of hitting the flash as the Indian."[29]

Though others showed alarm, Crook remained calm throughout the encounter:

He was reclining quietly upon a few robes [in his tent], evidently in deep thought, when the firing commenced. Without glancing upward to see where it came from, he waited until excited officers commenced rushing forward with versions of the affair and asking for instructions. He coolly replied that the plan of the Indians was simply to stampede a portion of our stock. . . . He said the early firing of the sentry had completely frustrated their scheme by placing our entire command in a state of preparation, and concluded by remarking that we would hear no more of the Indians that night. . . . [A]nd as the general suggested, there was not another shot fired during the night.[30]

A march of twenty-six miles on March 6 brought the command to Crazy Woman's Fork of Powder River. At dusk Crook summoned all of the officers to his tent to dispense final instructions before they should break away from the pack train:

Gathered in a semi-circle around Generals Crook and Reynolds, the ten or a dozen veterans listening respectfully to their leaders, with the confusion and bustle incident to the move all about, furnished a picture long to be remembered. In a few plain sentences General Crook made known his wishes and expectations from each one in authority.[31]

Crook's primary instruction was for the troops to travel light. In addition to the clothes on their backs, the men

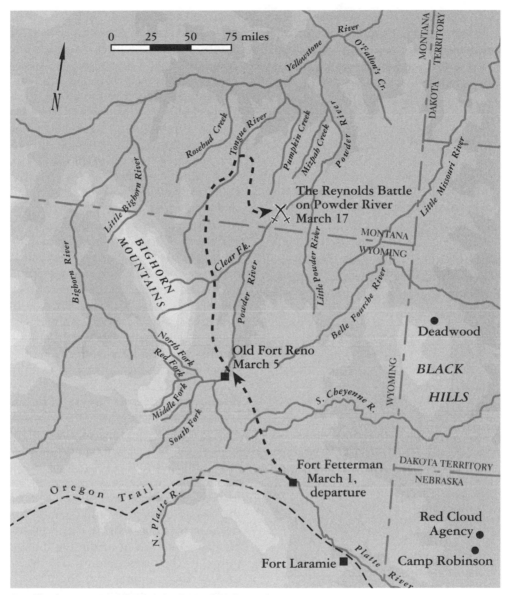

Crook's advance toward the Powder River, March 1876.

were allowed either two blankets or one buffalo robe each. They would live on hardtack, coffee, sugar, and half-rations of bacon for the next fifteen days. The horses would have to make do with one-sixth their regular feed of grain. Each man was to carry one hundred rounds of ammunition, the same allowance per man being carried on the pack train. The men could carry shelter tents, and the officers could bring along fly tents.[32]

The two companies of the Fourth Infantry, under Captain Edwin M. Coates, were ordered back to Fort Reno with the wagon train to await the return of the attack force. Campaign preparations kept the officers and men busy on March 7. Strahorn closed his dispatch that day: "We are to start north at dark, our scouts having already picked a trail."[33]

At this time we turn our narrative over to Major Stanton and correspondent Strahorn, each of whom takes us up to and through the battle of Powder River, March 17, 1876. Also included is a brief report from Crook to Sheridan written shortly after the fight. This encounter set the tone for much of the war that was to follow; however, it did not quite have the upbeat cadence that Sheridan was looking for.

New York Tribune,
Tuesday, April 4, 1876

The Big Horn Expedition.

An Indian Encampment Destroyed.

Gen. Crook's Line Of March Down Tongue River Toward The Yellowstone—Intensely Cold Weather—A Night March—Fight With The Indians On Powder River—Crazy Horse's Village Surprised—Killed And Wounded—Return Of The Troops To Fort Reno—Result Of The Expedition.

[Written by Major Thaddeus H. Stanton]

Old Fort Reno, Wy. T., March 21—The Big Horn expedition returned to this point today, after marching over 400 miles in 14 days, encountering unusually severe weather, and destroying an active and pestilent Indian village which has troubled the Wyoming frontier. The details of each day's marching, and the results of the expedition, as well as the character of the country through which the troops moved, are given herewith. The Indians who have caused the most mischief along the frontiers of Nebraska and Wyoming, who have stolen the greatest number of horses and committed the largest number of murders, have been badly punished on the Powder River, and their families are left without shelter, provision[s], or clothing. Moreover, immense quantities of powder, caps, and other ammunition have been destroyed, so that they have little material wherewith to go to war again. Each tepee in the encampment which was surprised was a small arsenal, in which was stored a large supply of war material. This was all obtained from the worthy agents and traders at the various Indian agencies, especially at Red Cloud and Spotted Tail. The expedition has demonstrated that the number of hostile Indians in this northern country has been greatly overestimated. Instead of 15,000 or 20,000, there are probably not over 2,000 all told. This command, in the country which was covered by its marches and which was supposed to be the seat of powerful warlike tribes, has not seen over 600 Indians. These probably constitute half of the hostile Indians now off their reservations. Doubtless during the summer this number is increased by young bucks whom the agents permit to leave their agencies, and who materially assist the predatory excursions of the openly hostile; but that there is in this region a warlike population large enough to endanger the general peace of the frontier is one of those humbugs which Indian agents find profitable to perpetuate.

At Reno the wounded were transferred to ambulances, and the whole command took a breathing spell. In two days the column will set out for Fort Fetterman, whence the troops will return to their posts to prepare for other campaigns during the summer.

MARCH TO THE ENCAMPMENT.

In Camp, Tuesday Night, March 7—Just after dark the ten companies of cavalry which comprise the active force of this command moved out of the camp on Crazy Woman River, followed the old road to Fort Phil Kearney for three miles, and then took a course due north. All tents, except shelter tents for the men and tent flies for the officers, had been left with the wagons, to be sent back to Powder River. Cooking outfits had been surrendered; extra bedding and clothing had been packed up and left, and nothing but the most absolutely necessary articles were retained. The ration itself was confined to the essentials; that is, to hard bread, bacon, sugar and coffee, and half rations of bacon. Capt. Coates of the 4th Infantry was intrusted with the duty of taking the train back to the Powder River. Goodbyes were said, and we were off. The moon shone brightly, and the night was warm and pleasant. The great Big Horn range was visible from our line of march, Cloud Peak, especially, towering above all its comrades, the one giant of the mountains. The column wound its way sinuously across the plains, and looked like an immense black serpent.

Wednesday, March 8—The march lasted till 5 a.m., today—10 hours—during which time the column marched 35 miles, the pack trains being close up when the final halt was ordered. The camp was pitched on the Clear Fork of the Lodgepole River, a tributary of Crazy Woman River. This stream has its sources in the mountains, and the water is therefore clear and excellent. The bed is about 40 yards in width. Very little wood could be found, and this was from willow and box elder trees. The grass was much better than at our last camp, and our animals cropped the brown bunches eagerly. For an hour before reaching camp the air had been growing colder, and a keen north wind had sprung up. Scarcely had the horses and mules been picketed and sentinels posted when officers and men threw themselves upon the ground with the hope of wresting a little sleep from the last hour of the night. This attempt was a complete failure, as the air kept growing colder every moment, and a cold northeast snowstorm swept down from the great mountain ridges into the valley. Not an officer or man had enough bedding to make him even passably comfortable, and it was not cheerful to walk through the camp and see them lying on the ground with heads and bodies covered, while their feet, encased in boots, were sticking out in the storm.

At 10 a.m. the command moved five miles further down the stream to its junction with Piney Creek. The two streams are thence known as Lodgepole. The weather remained bitterly cold, and the animals having only half forage its effect on them was very obvious. Wood was also very scarce here, and it was difficult to get enough to cook the food and partially warm the soldiers. Places under banks where a blanket could be spread and some shelter secured, were searched for actively, and as night fell one could not have told, from anything he heard, but that the troops were as comfortable and contented as if they had been in the best garrison quarters. The ridges along the valley of the Lodgepole River almost assume the magnitude of mountains, lacking, however, their rocky character. They seem to partake of the bad-land features so common in this country, and show [illegible] from which are visible red and yellow arenaceous clays, with outcroppings of coal and lignite, and here and there a layer of limestone. The low temperatures of the atmosphere and the probable proximity of Indians were considered sufficient reasons for not making an effort to see if these hills possess any fossiliferous deposits.

Thursday, March 9—This morning broke with snow falling fast over our little camp in the willows, and under the banks looked anything but cheerful. The sky was so dark and the air so full of snow that the high ridges were shut out and nothing could be seen a hundred yards distant. The work of loading the pack-mules was not complete until 10 o'clock, and so severe was the cold and storm that it was a work difficult to accomplish at all. At 10 a.m. the command moved out, and again faced the storm. Crossed the Piney Fork River four miles from camp, and then bore north over a high and terribly rough country for 13 miles, bringing us to a small stream called by the Indians Prairie Dog Creek, where we found wood and water enough for camp, which was accordingly pitched at 4 p.m. The snow ceased falling about noon, but the air remained bitterly cold. The snow was a foot deep in many places, and traveling was very exhausting to the animals, the crust on the old snow being too thin to bear them up, and making the journey exceedingly tiresome work. About our camp, on the side of the mountain, the fall of snow was much lighter, and the grass was of excellent quality. Instead of half rations of forage, I find we only have about one-sixth full forage, and we shall in a few days be entirely dependant upon grass for the sustenance of the animals.

Friday, March 10—Daylight found snow still falling and the air very sharp, the thermometer marking 6 degrees below zero. Moved out at 8:30 a.m., and followed the creek 22 miles to near its junction with Tongue River, and went into camp at 5 p.m., though the pack-train did not come in until an hour later. The north hillsides and banks were covered with ice under the snow, so that horses and mules frequently fell, and sometimes slipped from the top of a hill to the bottom. We have lost only one animal as yet, however, that being a mule, which fell down a steep hillside and was found at the foot literally smashed to pieces. About noon the sun came out, and we could see the Big Horn range on our left some 20 or 30 miles distant. Our march is nearly parallel with that range so far, and usually in a northerly direction. Today's march makes 80 miles from our camp on Crazy Woman River. Scouts sent out yesterday to go to the forks of the Tongue River, 10 miles west of where we are now, killed a black-tail deer about dark, and immediately went into camp to have a feast, displaying the true Indian character. We passed their camp this morning, about 10 miles from our own, and found a hindquarter awaiting the General. It was frozen hard, but we found that, cut in thin slices and broiled on the coals, it was very delicious. The party came in this evening and reported finding a recently abandoned camp of about 60 lodges at the forks of the Tongue River. The snow was so deep that they could not tell which way the Indians had gone. Wood is plenty at our camp here, but the water is alkaline, and the grass poor. The country, so far, seems absolutely worthless for the use of civilized men.

Saturday, March 11—At 7 o'clock this morning the thermometer marked 22 degrees below zero, and as that was the full capacity of the instrument, we had no means of telling how much colder it was. Notwithstanding the severity of the weather, the animals fed all night on such grass as they could get from under the snow, which was thin and poor at best. They remained free until 8 o'clock, and then the packers began loading the mules. By 10 o'clock, the hour of starting, the weather had moderated several degrees, and the march was down Prairie Dog Creek to Tongue River, four miles, and down this latter stream four miles further, where good grass and plenty of wood were found, and Gen. Crook decided to go into camp and give the animals a chance to graze the remainder of the day.

Sunday, March 12—This morning was the coldest we have yet experienced, the mercury in the thermometer dropping into the bulb—the same experience as yesterday—but the air was much sharper, and Dr. [Charles E.] Munn decided that the degree of cold would be properly expressed by - - 30. The command marched at 9:30 a.m., and proceeded down Tongue River. Five miles out Tongue River cañon was entered, and we traveled in it throughout the day, or until 5 p.m., when camp preparations were ordered. Fifteen miles of the 20 miles marched today were down the cañon, which is narrow, irregular, full of sharp elbows, and has walls of red sandstone and conglomerate 350 to 500 feet in height. We crossed the river 19 times on the ice, and the entire command marched for considerable distances down the river on its thick, icy covering. About midway in the cañon we found a piece of buffalo skin on a stick with a note which ran thus: "Up to right buffalow." The scouts had killed an enormous bull bison, and stripped all the best parts of the flesh from him, and packed it on their horses, so there was little left worthy of our attention. Louis Richard with his party of eleven half-breeds was sent over to Rosebud Creek this morning

to look for Indians, and Ben Clark with Frank Grouard, the Kanaka,[34] and about twenty others, went down the river about fifteen miles below our present camp to reconnoiter near the mouth of Hanging Woman Creek. Both parties returned late in the evening, having seen no sign of Indians.

Monday, March 13—Thermometer stood at zero this morning, with a cold northwest wind, and about four inches of snow. Left camp at 9 o'clock, and continued our march down Tongue River. Passed several lately abandoned Indian encampments, and at 2 p.m. captured a handsome mule, which had evidently strayed from some village not far ahead of us. Many indications served to satisfy us that we were not far from Indians, and we went into camp at 2:30 p.m. under some small bluffs, having marched 13 miles. Scouts were sent three miles further down stream to waylay the trail of the mule, and instructed to kill any Indian who might be following it up. At dark the scouts were sent down the river to reconnoiter, with instructions to follow it, if necessary, to the Yellowstone, about 50 miles distant, and report what they may find. At the mouth of Hanging Woman River today we saw six buffaloes, and killed one of them, the meat of which was distributed through the camp. We also passed a cave which had been excavated into the bank by the Indians to get red clay for paint. Crossed the river seven times on the ice, and at our camp find plenty of wood, principally dry cottonwood. The Indians have cut down enormous quantities of this tree, almost destroying the principal timber these valleys afford. The bluffs on each side have a dark, irregular fringe of scrub pine, cedar, and juniper, and greasebrush flourishes in the bottom. The guides relate that there are innumerable trout in the Tongue River, and many of the soldiers have been endeavoring to entice these finny delicacies to bite at bait suspended through holes cut in the ice. I have not heard that a fish has been caught as yet. Our food is all frozen hard, and has to be thawed before it can be eaten. Much of the time the column looks like a procession of Santa Clauses, so heavily are beards and mustaches covered with ice. To march into battle with banners flying and drums beating, to the roar of artillery and the rattle of musketry, does not call for half the nerve and determination that must be daily exercised to pursue mile after mile in such inhospitable weather over a wild and rugged country, a savage foe, whose presence one is likely to first know of by a fatal bullet.

The scouts are well into harness and do good work. But there is no concealing the fact that some of them, who have Indian wives, are not half as eager to encounter the enemy now as when they were at Fort Fetterman. As each mile brings them nearer to the hostile savages their courage seems to wane. Among these cowards, however, are not such men as Ben Clark, Frank Grouard, Louis Richard, Little Bat, and others. They display the qualities of courage, judgment, and coolness that highly recommend them, and Colonel Reynolds finds their services of great value. The weather in this region, 400 miles north of Cheyenne,[35] seems to be utterly unpredictable, and would certainly puzzle a meteorologist. If we go to bed at night with a clear sky and bright moon, we generally awake in a snowstorm.

Tuesday, March 14—Snowing this morning lightly, and has continued all day, with thermometer −5 degrees. Broke camp at 9 o'clock, and marched 10 miles down the river, camping near the mouth of Otter Creek,[36] a small stream emptying into the Tongue River

on the south side. Crossed the latter stream five times today. Saw four buffaloes at head of the column, and so badly wounded one that a detachment was sent out to overhaul and bring him in.[37] Gen. Crook, who is a crack shot, killed six pin-tailed grouse as we came into camp, with his Springfield musket, taking off the head only in each case. Camp was pitched in a grove of dead cottonwood and ash, which make splendid fires, and the stock finds fair grass on the bluffs overlooking the river, though they have to get it from under the snow as best they can. The Little Panther Mountains extend along both sides of the [Tongue] river, and consist of high tower-shaped and castellated hills, crowned with a dark fringe of pine trees. The formation consists exclusively of red and yellow sandstone, as far as we can discover, no quartz, granite or other Paleozoic rocks being visible. Evidently this is not a gold-bearing region, the cheap maps to the contrary notwithstanding.

The soldiers found a frozen arm in camp, chopped off at the elbow. The flesh was perfect, and showed a number of buckshot holes. Apparently it had not been long detached from the Indian who had worn it. One of the guides thinks it was a Crow Indian, killed by the Sioux, with whom they are continually at war, and he also says it is the custom to mutilate the bodies of those they take or kill in battle on both sides. Our scouts, sent out last night to thoroughly explore the lower part of this stream and Rosebud, have not yet returned, and we will wait to hear from them before moving the command further.

Wednesday, March 15—Scouts returned this evening, having reconnoitered the lower portions of the valleys of the Tongue River and the Rosebud to the Yellowstone without finding Indians.

The signs seemed to indicate that all the villages have moved over to Powder River, and thither, accordingly, we shall take up our march tomorrow. Weather clear and pleasant today, after seven days of storm. Animals have had a day's good grazing, which they much needed. Many of the pack-mules are terribly sore, the flesh being worn away to the ribs and backbone in patches as large as two hands. It takes about 36 mules to a company of cavalry, including those ridden by the packers, so that we have 360 mules to carry provisions, ammunition, bedding, &c., for the expedition. Of the meat ration for the troops, only one-half supply was brought. The good mule-packer is hard to find, and out of a hundred men who pretend to know something about it, not ten will generally be employed by an experienced pack-master. Of those we have, many have seen service with Gen. Crook in Idaho, Montana, Oregon and Arizona, and may be classed among the best. Yet even some of these are pretty well tired out by the hard work and severe weather. I heard one of them say last night, "Well, boys, I think if next summer is a good season for washing, my mother can make enough to keep me at home. I don't want no more of this." One of our pack-masters named [Dick] Closter has been at the business for 25 years. His hair and beard are perfectly white, or the latter would be except for a path of tobacco juice down through the middle of it. He has a kindly face, and is a man of a great deal of originality and native force of character. They are all of them hard-fisted, honest, and blunt-speaking fellows, and are in excellent repute throughout the command. Pack-mules and good packers are a necessity for any successful campaigning in a region as rough and nearly impracticable as this. Expeditions will undoubtedly be required to follow this one, as it does not now seem probable that we shall succeed in finding and removing the hostile Indians from this country. For all of these [future expeditions] pack-trains will be the only means of transporting the supplies of the army.

BATTLE OF POWDER RIVER.

In Camp, Saturday, March 18— Thursday last [March 16] the command moved across country to the headwaters of Otter Creek, 18 miles, over rough, broken mesas, and on descending into the creek the scouts saw two Indians. A halt was called here, the command was divided, quarter forage issued to the animals and one day's rations to the men. Colonel Reynolds, with six companies of cavalry[38] and half the scouts, moved from camp at 10 p.m. and marched towards Powder River, leaving four companies and the pack-train behind. These Gen. Crook was to bring to the same stream at the mouth of Lodgepole Creek. The night was bitterly cold, and on the high mountain ridges snow lay a foot deep. Light snow fell during the first part of the night, but not enough to prevent the scouts from following, dark as it was, a fresh Indian trail leading towards Powder River. The country was terribly rough and broken, so that the companies experienced much difficulty in keeping the column in good order. At 4:20 a.m. we had marched 30 miles, and were, as near as we could tell, near the Powder River breaks. A halt was called here, and the column took shelter in a ravine. No fires were allowed to be kindled, nor even a match lighted. The cold was more intense than we had yet felt, and seemed to be at least 30 degrees below zero. The command remained here till about 6 o'clock, doing their utmost to keep from freezing, the scouts meantime going out to reconnoiter. At this hour they returned, reporting a larger and fresher trail leading down to the river, which was about four miles distant. The column immediately started on this trail. The approach to the river seemed almost impracticable. Before reaching the final precipices which overlooked the riverbed, the scouts discovered that a village of about 100 lodges lay in the valley at the foot of the bluffs.

It was now 8 o'clock. The sun shone brightly through the cold, frosty air. The column halted, and Capt. [Henry E.] Noyes's battalion, 2d Cavalry, was ordered up to the front. It consisted of Company I, 2d Cavalry, Capt. H. E. Noyes and Lieut. C. [Christopher] T. Hall, and Company K, 2d Cavalry, Capt. James Egan. This battalion was ordered to descend to the valley, and while Capt. Egan charged the camp, Capt. Noyes was to cut out the herd of horses feeding close by and drive it up the river. With this column Lieut. Bourke of Gen. Crook's staff and R. E. Strahorn went as volunteer aids. Capt. Moore's battalion, consisting of Company F, 3d Cavalry (Capt. Alex Moore and Lieut. Bainbridge Reynolds) [the Colonel's son] and Company E, 2d Cavalry (First Lieut. W. C. Rawolle and Lieut. F. W. Sibley) was ordered to dismount and proceed along the edge of the ridge to a position covering the eastern side of the village, opposite that from which Capt. Egan was to charge. Major Stanton accompanied this column. Capt. Mills's [Anson Mills, Third Cavalry] battalion was ordered to follow Egan, dismounted, and support him in the engagement, which might follow the charge. These columns began the descent of the mountain, through gorges which were almost perpendicular, and it seemed almost impossible that horses could be taken through them. Nearly two hours were occupied in getting the horses of the charging column down

these rough sides of the mountain, and even there, when a point was reached where the men could mount their horses and proceed toward the village in the narrow valley beneath, Moore's battalion had not been able to gain its position on the eastern side, after clambering along the edges of the mountain. A few Indians could be seen with the herd, driving them to the edge of the river, but nothing indicated that they knew of our approach.

Just at 9 o'clock Capt. Egan turned the point of the mountain nearest the river, and first in a walk and then in a rapid trot started for the village. The company went first in column of twos, but when within 200 yards of the village the command "Left front into line" was given, and with a yell they rushed into the encampment. Capt. Noyes had in the mean time wheeled to the right and started the herd up the river. With the yell of the charging column the Indians sprang up as by magic, and poured in a rapid fire from all sides. Egan charged through and [again] through the village before Moore's and Mills's battalions got within supporting distance, and finding things getting very hot, formed his line in some high willows on the south side of the camp, from which point he poured in rapid volleys upon the Indians. Up to this time the Indians supposed that one company was all they had to contend with, but when the other battalions appeared, rapidly advancing, deployed as skirmishers, and pouring in a galling fire of musketry, they broke on all sides and took refuge in the rocks along the side of the mountain. The camp, consisting of 110 lodges, with immense quantities of robes, fresh meat, and plunder of all kinds, with over 700 head of horses, was in our possession. The work of burning began immediately, and soon the whole encampment was in flames. Large quantities of ammunition, especially powder, were stored in the tepees, and explosions followed the burning of every tent. The camp was well supplied with bedding, cooking utensils and clothing, all from Red Cloud Agency, while fixed ammunition, percussion caps, lead and powder were in great abundance.

While the work of demolition was going on under the direction of Colonel Reynolds, the Indians poured in a well-directed fire from the sides of the mountain and from every available hiding place. Not satisfied with this, they made a determined attack on the troops about noon, with a view to regaining possession of the camp. Capt. Mills, who had charge of the skirmish line, perceived their movement, and asked for additional men. These were sent in promptly from Egan's, Noyes's, Lieut. J. B. Johnson's, Lieut. Rawolle's and Capt. Moore's companies, and the attack was quickly and handsomely repulsed, the Indians retiring in disorder.

After the work of destruction had been completed, the withdrawal of the troops began, Lieut. C. T. Hall, 2d Cavalry, drawing in the last line of skirmishers, and the whole command moved rapidly up the river, 20 miles, to the mouth of Lodgepole Creek, where it went into camp, after two days and one night of constant marching.

The camp attacked was that of Crazy Horse, who is chief of the only remaining band of Ogalalla Sioux now openly hostile.[39] The usual estimate employed in numbering Indians is seven persons to a lodge or tepee. This would give over 700 Indians in the encampment, but there did not seem to be over five hundred in this one. Probably several war parties were out on plundering expeditions at the time of the attack. What the Indian loss was could not be ascertained,

but about 30 were killed near the camp, and doubtless many more fell under the sharpshooting of the troops.[40] Our casualties were as follows:

KILLED.

Sergeant Peter Dowdy, Co. E, 3d Cavalry.
Private George Schneider, Co. K, 2d Cavalry.
Private Michael McCannon, Co. F, 3d Cavalry.
Private George E. Ayres,[41] Co. M, 3d Cavalry.

WOUNDED.

Artificer Patrick Goings, Co. K, 2d Cavalry, flesh wound, left shoulder, slightly.
Private Edward Egan, Co. K, 2d Cavalry, right lower part of chest, dangerously.
Private John Droege, Co. K, 2d Cavalry, through left arm.
Corporal John Lang, Co. E, 2d Cavalry, through right ankle.
Sergeant Charles Kaminski, Co. M, 3d Cavalry, left knee, slightly.

Lieut. Bourke, Mr. Strahorn, and Hospital Steward W. C. Bryan went with Egan on the charge, and behaved with decided gallantry.[42] The last named had a horse killed under him, and Lieut. Bourke had his bridle-rein shot away. Capt Egan's horse was shot through the neck, and most of the horses in his company were wounded, and nearly every man had bullet-holes through clothing or equipments. Lieut. Bourke and Mr. Strahorn were conspicuous for their coolness and courage throughout the engagement.

The Indians occupied what seemed to them an impregnable camp. The walls of the mountains on both sides of the river were of great height, precipitous, and full of gorges. The descent made by the troops was over these obstacles, and of course from a point where an enemy was least expected. If Capt. Moore's battalion had reached the position assigned to it, scarcely an Indian could have escaped. That it did not, was one of the mistakes which possibly could have been foreseen and provided for, but was not. As it was, a band of the most troublesome Indians on the whole Wyoming frontier received a severe chastisement, and is so badly crippled that it will probably now go to Red Cloud Agency, and remain. At all events it is certain that such a result cannot be long delayed, for other expeditions will soon follow this one, and the country will be made so hot for them that they will have to abandon it. The material found in this camp proves conclusively that these Indians, though openly hostile, obtain ammunition, arms, and supplies of all sorts from the agency at Red Cloud. This agency should at once be moved to the Missouri River and the most important bases of supply for hostile Indians be broken up. It is hardly fair that the Indian Department should be permitted to furnish arms and powder to hostile Indians; but as long as there is money to be made in this way and thieving agents are to be supported the system will probably continue.

After the fighting was over the troops marched rapidly up the river [20 miles] to the mouth of Lodgepole Creek. This point was reached at nightfall [March 17] by all except Moore's battalion and Capt. Egan's company. Company E, 2d Cavalry, was the rear guard, and assisted Major Stanton and the scouts in bringing up the herd of horses. Many of these were shot on the road, and the remainder reached camp about 9 p.m. The troops had been in the saddle for 36 hours, with the exception of five hours during which they were fighting, and all, officers and men, were much exhausted.

The horses had had no grazing, and began to show signs of complete exhaustion. Upon arriving at Lodgepole, it was found that Gen. Crook and the other four companies and pack-train had not arrived, so that everybody was supperless and without a blanket. The night, therefore, was not a cheerful one, but not a murmur was heard. The wounded men lay upon the snow or leaned against a tree, and slept as best they could on so cold a night.

Owing to some misunderstanding, our four dead men were left on the field to be mutilated by the Indians. How this occurred is not fully explained, and may be the subject of investigation. These men could have been removed easily, but they were not, and that they were not caused a great deal of dissatisfaction among the troops.

Today (Saturday) [March 18] at noon Gen. Crook and the remainder of the command arrived. In the meantime a portion of the herd of ponies had straggled into the ravines and fallen into the hands of the Indians. The village was very rich in plunder—the accumulations of a great many stealing expeditions. This was all effectually destroyed, not enough being left to make a respectable bed for a papoose.

It does not seem probable that there are half as many hostile Indians in this northern country as the War Department has supposed. For nearly two weeks this command has been marching through the best part of the whole unceded Sioux lands, and it has not seen 1,000 Indians in all. I doubt if there are 3,000 hostile people south of the Missouri and east of the Big Horn Mountains. Other military expeditions will soon follow this one, and in the end all these tribes will be glad to take agency rations, poor and insufficient as they generally are, for the rest of their days.

The scene of this engagement is on the left bank of the main Powder River [facing north], about 85 miles north of old Fort Reno, very near the southern boundary of Montana. This region is terribly rough and sterile, and only the narrow riverbed, running deep down in the cañons, affords water and limited pasturage. It has scarcely ever been visited by white men since [Captain William F.] Raynolds made his reconnoissance in 1855 [1859]. On every side the country is broken up into barren "bad lands," with high buttes, almost attaining the magnitude of mountains, overlooking the general plain. These buttes are composed of clays and sands, with coal seams frequently visible, but do not afford fossil remains of any value, so far as we could discover. The country has no attractions for a civilized man, and can offer nothing in mitigation of its general sterility and worthlessness. I must decidedly agree with Gen. Hazen in his view of the barrenness and utterly valueless character of this whole region of country, in respect to its adaptability to agricultural and pastoral uses. As a fastness for a few wretched Indians it has its advantages. Even these can only live in it by stealing from the frontiers and the agencies. To rely upon game would be to embrace starvation, for there is very little to be found.

It is hardly proper to close this sketch of the engagement without referring more particularly to those causes which prevented its complete success. First among these was the failure of Capt. Moore's battalion to reach the position assigned it in the rear of the village, or a point covering the rear, before the charge was made by Capt. Egan. This failure allowed the Indians to make good their escape to the rocky fastnesses of the mountains overlooking the valley, from which they subsequently poured in a galling fire upon our troops. Moore's battalion was a strong one in numbers, and needed only to be led to the front where it could be effective to do good service. When it was discovered that the battalion would not be at the place assigned it, and that its commander did not apparently intend to put it there, Major Stanton and Lieut. Sibley, with five men, left it and went on, taking up the position which the battalion should have occupied, and gave the flying savages the best enfilading fire they could. But they were too few to prevent the escape of the Indians. This was the first serious blunder. The next was that after the herd of ponies, numbering over 700, had been captured, driven twenty miles from the scene of action, and turned over to Colonel Reynolds, commanding the troops, he failed to place a guard around them, so that the greater portion of them strayed off during the night and were picked up by the Indians. When informed next morning that the herd had escaped, and the scouts reported that it was being driven off by Indians, only two or three miles from camp, he positively declined to send a man or horse to recapture them, thus allowing the most substantial fruits of the victory to be taken away without an opposing effort.

The next blunder was in leaving his dead upon the field and directing that they be so left, when it was perfectly easy to have thrown them upon horses and borne them away for burial. It was even stated that one wounded man had been left behind in the village, belonging to Company M, 3d Cavalry, and that the line of skirmishers covering the withdrawal of the troops saw the Indians rush into camp and scalp him. If these statements are true (and all except the last undoubtedly are) they should lead to an investigation. If they were the result of incompetency and inefficiency it should be known. Furthermore, there were large quantities of buffalo meat and venison in the village, which Gen. Crook had directed, in case of capture, to be brought out for the use of the troops, who were on half rations of fresh meat. This was not done, and as a result, the soldiers have had no fresh meat except ponies since that time.

I cannot omit in this account of our long march and the fight on Powder River to mention the gallantry and soldier-like conduct of Capt. Egan, 2d United States Cavalry. For skill in the management of his company, which is composed of excellent men, for coolness and daring and all the qualities of a good soldier, commend me to him every time. Frank Grouard, too, the Society Island[43] scout, has proved by his courage, boldness, quickness and accuracy of perception in hunting Indians, as well as his unfailing knowledge respecting the country through which we have operated, a guide of the very first quality. Gen. Crook has found his services of great value, and will undoubtedly give him more work to do before long. Such men are not picked up every day.

Weekly Rocky Mountain News (Denver), Wednesday, April 12, 1876

THE FIGHT WITH CRAZY HORSE.

HONORABLE NIGHT MARCH TO THE CHIEFTAIN'S VILLAGE.

A GALLANT ONSLAUGHT AND A STUBBORN RESISTANCE.

SOME FOOD FOR UNPLEASANT REFLECTION.

[Written by Robert E. Strahorn]

Camp on Powder River, Montana, March 18, 1876.

Without doubt the most remarkable event of General Crook's present campaign was the night march commenced early on the evening of the 16th inst. As a matter of history it well deserves a place by the side of any similar incident known to frontier service; and if the three hundred gallant and uncomplaining spirits who participated in its thrilling scenes had nothing more whereof to tell in future bivouacs around more peaceful fires, this would be enough. A hard day's march had just been accomplished, man and beast had earned the hardy fare, and the bed of frozen ground that usually were their lot; but the circumstances narrated in my last [dispatch] changed the aspect of affairs. A leader like General Crook was in search of just such circumstances, and if there were any complaints heard in connection with the swiftness of his movements, they came from those whose lot it was to remain behind. Therefore, in about two hours after reaching Otter Creek, with darkness already

SHADOWING THE GULCHES,

the three squadrons pushed swiftly and silently forward. A cutting breeze, with its usual perversity in these parts, drove the falling snow directly in our faces. The storm, with not even a moonlit sky above, served to deepen the gloom so rapidly that we were little more than out of sight of the campfires left behind until the blackest of nights was upon us.

Riding at the head of the scouts, in company with Major Stanton and Lieutenant J. G. Bourke—the latter aidde-camp to General Crook—I had, during the night, an excellent opportunity of witnessing the truly remarkable achievement of Frank Gruard [Grouard], our principal guide and trailer. His knowledge of the country had been noteworthy ever since the opening of the campaign, but the duty he was now called upon to perform was of just the nature that would have bewildered almost any one in broad daylight. He had orders to follow the "back trail" of the two Indians we had seen early in the evening, lead where it would. This he did through the entire night, in the face of a storm that was constantly rendering the pony tracks of the two savages less distinct, while it was also hourly increasing the tedium of travel. Over rugged bluffs, up narrow valleys, through gloomy defiles and down break-neck declivities, plunged

THE INDOMITABLE FRANK;

now down on his hands and knees in the deep snow, scrutinizing the faint foot prints, then, losing the trail for an instant, darting to and fro until it was found, and again following it up with the keenness of a hound, and a fearlessness that would have imbued almost any one with fresh vim and courage. Nor should we forget his valuable assistants, Baptiste Garnier, Jack Russell, Baptiste Pourier, Louis Gingras and others of our keen-eyed scouts, who were practically indispensable. With such unfailing celerity was this trailing accomplished that during almost every hour of the long night orders would come from the rear to halt in order that the command might be kept "closed up."

Toward morning the clouds commenced breaking, and soon the sky was almost clear. But with the change came the most intense cold we had ever experienced, and were it not that the almost exhausted men were compelled to walk and lead their horses much of the way, on account of the roughness of the country, many cases of freezing must have been recorded. And the worst was yet to come. At four in the morning we halted upon what seemed the apex of this entire region. We had at least been ascending quite rapidly nearly all night, and, now,

Frank Grouard, one of General Crook's most important scouts. (*Missouri Historical Society*)

by the aid of the dim starlight, and through the thick, frosty atmosphere, we could look down, down, as far as the strained vision would reach, into a wilderness of mountain, forest and vale. How to get down, and at the same time be morally certain of striking the Indians at once, was then the question—for we knew that somewhere through that mass of rocky upheavals must flow the Powder. Again the ever ready scouts were to show us their true worth, and, with Frank in the lead, off they bounded to find or make a way.

"WAITING FOR THE SCOUTS."

Near the summit upon which we had thus briefly halted was a deep, narrow ravine, and in order to have his men as well sheltered as possible while waiting, Colonel Reynolds ordered the command to take position therein and dismount. Here a scene was presented which we can never forget. The cold grew in intensity, and exert ourselves as we would to keep up our circulation, it seemed almost unendurable. The fatiguing marches of the day and night, the great strain upon the nerves caused by the loss of sleep and the continuous cold, the hunger, too, making itself felt, and our not being permitted to enkindle a single fire, however small, on account of the danger of alarming the foe—all of these influences combined told severely upon the strongest physiques. Making my way up and down the gulch in which the shivering men and horses were crowded like bees in a hive, I had no trouble in discovering how they were bearing up under such difficulties. There were very few complaints, but every few moments some poor fellow would drop into the snow, "just for a minute, you know," and when at once shaken up by his more determined comrades, would make all sorts of excuses to be allowed to enter that sleep which, if undisturbed, would have known no waking. Officers were everywhere on the alert to keep their men upon their feet, and, thanks to this general watchfulness, no cases of amputation are yet known to be necessary on account of freezing, although nearly all of us are now nursing frost-bitten feet, faces, or ears. At daylight the returning scouts reported the discovery of a trail leading down to the river, and that the stream was yet some three or four miles distant. An advance was at once ordered—an order that was obeyed with more than usual willingness.

Discovery Of The Village.

In less than an hour the scouts, who had again been pushed far in advance, came back with the pleasing intelligence that the encampment of Crazy Horse, consisting of over a hundred lodges, lay under the shelter of the mountain we were then descending. They described its situation as best they could and advised that in making the attack the command separate, as two gulches leading down into the valley admitted of an approach from two directions. A short consulta-

tion was held which resulted in plans for an immediate attack, Colonel Reynolds detailing the Egan Grays, Company K, 2nd Cavalry, Capt. James Egan, to charge through the village from the upper end, to, if possible, thoroughly demoralize the foe from the start and drive him out of the brush; Companies F, 3rd Cavalry, and E, 2nd Cavalry, Captain Moore, battalion commander, and Lieutenant W. C. Rawolle, to dismount, take a position on the left of the village and thus prevent the escape of the savages; Company I, Second Cavalry, Captain H. E. Noyes, to cut out the ponies and drive them from the field; and Companies M and E, Third Cavalry, Captain A. Mills and Lieutenant J. B. Johnson, to act as reserve. These preliminaries being arranged and a

Thorough Understanding

arrived at by the various officers they at once proceeded toward the positions assigned, each headed by about an equal number of the fifteen or twenty scouts. Major Stanton, having virtually finished his duties as chief of scouts by piloting the command to the camp of the foe, could have consistently remained at headquarters, but, dismounting, shouldering his long rifle, and advancing at the head of Captain Moore's column, it was quite evident that he didn't propose to stop until the fight ended, at least. Lieutenant Bourke, also detached from any command, and myself, cast our fortunes with Captain Egan, by whose side we remained during the continuance of the fight.

Separating a mile or more from the village, both divisions had an extremely serious time of it getting over the ground—more especially the one with which we were connected, because we were compelled to take our horses while the others left theirs behind under a suitable guard. The Indians had good reason to wonder at the idea of a command of cavalry coming from that direction, considering the terrible plunges our horses were compelled to make down icy cañons, through fallen timber and over dangerous rock-strewn chasms. However, Captain Egan does not believe in impossibilities, and in less than thirty minutes we had floundered to the bottom. Here, securely hid by a low bluff, we could look over and see

The Village

spread out in full view, yet nearly a mile distant. Its position was such as a more civilized chieftain might have selected, and crafty Crazy Horse rose considerably in our estimation as with one long, eager look we took in those points which particularly interested us now—its adaptability for speedy abandonment rather than its strength. Looking down the valley, between us and the camp, lay a long, wide stretch of bench land, a natural pasturage; meeting this, and with an elevation from ten to twelve feet lower, was a narrow belt of bottom land, with the river washing it on the right. At the limit of this view, where the river swept quite closely around the base of a high and very rugged mountain, and on our side of the stream, lay the object of so much toil and search. The hundred and odd tepees were nestled quite cozily in a grove of large cottonwoods, and on the lower and river side were sheltered by a dense growth of willows. Scattered here and there, quietly feeding along both banks of the stream, were bands of

Hundreds Of Ponies.

Not the slightest mistrust or alarm was apparent in this forest home, and it was undoubtedly as clear a case of surprise as there is on record. Arms were hastily inspected, belts filled with cartridges, overcoats and other impediments to ease of movement strapped to the saddles,

and, after a thorough inspection of the ground lying between us and the village to aid an undiscovered approach, the eager little squad was ordered to creep forward to cover, a little farther on, before mounting. That point reached, a few brief instructions were given by Captain Egan to the effect that the horses should be trotted slowly over the ground until it was certain that we were discovered, then, drawing our revolvers, we should put the steeds to the full gallop, dash into the village with as much force, and with as terrific yells as possible, and when once among the savages, to empty our six-shooters "where they would do the most good." Obtaining cover by winding down around the back of the bench land referred to, and securing good ground on the edge of the river bottom, the order to "fall in for [the] charge" was soon given by the clear-headed captain. In a twinkling the company, with only half its complement of men, swung beautifully forward with one solid front for

The Charge.

Revolvers were drawn with a grip that meant something more than parade, the pace was slightly accelerated, and, when within less than two hundred yards of the nearest tepee, the first terror stricken savage was seen to run and loudly whoop the alarm. "Charge, my boys!" came like an electric flash from the dauntless leader, and giving their magnificent gray steeds rein and spur, and yelling like so many demons, the gallant "forty-seven" bounded into the village with the speed and force of a hurricane. With the savages swarming out of their tepees and scattering almost under our feet, we fired right and left at their retreating forms, our horses meanwhile worked into such a frenzy by the din of whoops and yells and discharging arms that they fairly flew over the ground. The demoralization of the foe seemed to last but an instant. A majority of the redskins

SNATCHED THEIR ARMS

as they ran, dropped as though shot, behind a log or stump, in the tall grass, or took temporary refuge in the thickets of willow and plum. Bullets and casualties were then bestowed upon us with a will that showed plainly we were not to sweep the field without paying a penalty. The beautiful gray horses were a splendid mark for the Indians, and four or five dropped before we got through the village, Captain Egan's own animal being among the number.[44] Then, with the desperate foe pouring in bullets from behind every convenient cover in the shape of rocks, trees, thickets, etc., we were ordered to dismount, turn our horses over to every fourth man, and continue the fight with our carbines. Our position was now indeed a critical one. In vain did we scan the face and foot of the bluffs which Captain Moore was

ORDERED TO OCCUPY.

No troops were in sight, and the savages, evidently believing no other force at hand, must have thought it an easy matter to annihilate us in a very short course of events. But Captain Egan did not seem to think the case quite so desperate and soon ordered a charge through the brush on foot. While advancing, the savages resisting at every step, a small detachment of troops was seen running down the hill to the left of where we had looked for the command of Captain Moore, but instead of that officer we afterward learned that it was Major Stanton, who, finding that Captain Moore was not endeavoring to get into position, secured half a dozen men and advanced to the scene of action. Soon after, Captain Mills and Lieutenant

Johnson, with companies M and E, 3rd Cavalry, came forward and did excellent service in assisting to drive the enemy from the field and in destroying the village. I am informed that Captain Moore also finally followed in the wake of Captain Mills, after the Indians had taken advantage of the loophole left in their rear and escaped.

The Indians, severely punished and driven from their village, took refuge in the mountain thus unguarded, and from that time forward, aside from the destruction of their property, had a positive advantage over the troops. Scattered all over this almost impregnable mountainside, and secreted behind its numerous walls of rock, they could pick off our men without running the slightest risk of losing their own lives. Therefore, the more the engagement was prolonged after the prime object of the expedition was accomplished, the more serious and useless were our losses. Realizing this, Colonel Reynolds, at 2 p.m., after a five hours' engagement, ordered the command to abandon its position and to at once proceed toward the mouth of Lodge Pole—the rendezvous appointed by General Crook—some twelve [twenty] miles up the river, which point was reached at dark.

LOSS TO THE INDIANS.

With all the scenes of native splendor and luxury our fancy had pictured, this Powder River reality yet excels, yet astonishes. In the more than one hundred large tepees totally destroyed were beds of furs and robes that, to a soldier, looked simply fit for savage gods; war bonnets and squaw dresses, regal in their construction and decoration, requiring months for making and worth from five to ten ponies each; cooking utensils that an ordinary housewife would not be ashamed of; tons of dried and fresh meats, and occasionally dried fruits; every tepee an arsenal within itself, with its kegs and canisters of powder, its large supply of bar lead, caps and fixed ammunition; and then piles of such miscellaneous articles as axes, knives, saddles— over 125 of these—buckskin clothing of every description, moccasins, beautifully ornamented saddle bags, sewing outfits, and really everything any frontiersman would need to insure his comfort. With the exception of a few robes and other trinkets removed by the troops, these vast stores, in many instances the accumulation of a lifetime, were piled upon the dismantled tepees and the whole reduced to ashes. In the case of the generous piles of nicely dried meat, this action was particularly unfortunate, as the troops needed such provender badly, and General Crook had especially impressed upon the minds of the officers the importance of saving it.

But the grand item in this connection was the capture of a herd of 700 ponies, horses and mules, many of which were of the best class, and identified as belonging to various stock men on the Colorado and Wyoming frontier. These were gathered and driven a short distance from the battlefield by the command of Captain Noyes, assisted by the scouts. However, this triumph was of

COMPARATIVELY SHORT DURATION,

as a few of the never-sleeping Indians swooped down upon the herd this morning [March 18] and recaptured nearly the entire band. Leaving no orders for the disposal of the ponies yesterday on the field, Colonel Reynolds also neglected to place a guard around them last night, when Major Stanton—who, with a few scouts, had taken it upon himself to drive them twenty miles to their camp—turned them over to him. Also, when at daylight this morning, the ponies were reported as being driven off by the Indians, the colonel declined sending a force in pursuit, although they could easily have been recovered.

The loss of the savages in killed and wounded cannot even be approximated, although men who were on the skirmish line during the engagement state it all the way from thirty to fifty.[45] Retreating slowly, as they did after our first onslaught, and nearly always close to cover of some kind, they had no difficulty in removing every body from one position to another.

LOSS OF THE COMMAND.

The command suffered a loss of four killed and four wounded. The killed were Privates Peter Dowdy, Company E., Third Cavalry; Michael McCannon,[46] Company I, Second Cavalry; Lorenzo E. Ayers, Company M, Third Cavalry; George Schneider, Company K, Second Cavalry. Wounded: Patrick Goings, artificer, Company K, Second Cavalry, seriously; Edward Egan, private (same company), seriously; John Lang, corporal, Company E, Second Cavalry, slightly; Charles Kaminski, sergeant, Company M, Third Cavalry, seriously. It was noticed that at the opening of the fight the shooting of the Indians was very mild, but a marked improvement in their aim was manifested toward the close. Bows and arrows were used in exceptional cases, but no wounds inflicted by them.

INCIDENTS OF THE FIGHT.

In charging into one of the tepees a man received a bullet through his cap. It just grazed his head, and as himself and a comrade or two rushed in to wreak their vengeance on the redskin who had fired, what was their astonishment at seeing three or four squaws, armed with revolvers, in the act of slipping through the opposite side of the wigwam, by way of a hole they had just carved with butcher knives.

These Indians may be cowardly, but they have a queer way of showing it. While in the extreme front we noticed a small band of ponies on our right that had been overlooked by the men detailed to gather them in. The main body of Indians was then on our left, and we were amazed to see a gaudily dressed warrior, well mounted, emerge from behind a clump of bushes, tauntingly brandish his weapons, and start with break-neck speed toward the ponies, with the evident intention of making off with them. To accomplish this he was compelled to ride within two hundred yards of fifteen or twenty of us, and just before reaching the goal, faithful horse and reckless rider fell riddled with bullets.

Steward Bryan,[47] of the Fort Fetterman hospital, who was with us on the charge, just after dismounting discovered a young warrior but a few yards distant with revolvers leveled over the top of a stump and in the act of shooting at him. The steward dodged behind his horse's head and the poor animal received the bullet in his brain. That Indian, it is generally believed, belonged to Lieutenant Bourke—although he denies the soft impeachment—as he was seen to look over the sights of his revolver in that direction about the time the audacious brave disappeared.

The village contained about 700 people, of whom the greater number were Sioux, who steal ponies from the frontier, go to the northern agencies and draw supplies, and also trade ponies there for arms and ammunition. There were also a few lodges of renegade Arapahoes.

Private [Theodore] Gouget, a Frenchman, of Captain Egan's company, while charging over rough ground on foot, fell, unnoticed, into a deep narrow pit. He was just tall enough to level his gun over the edge, and although the position was swept by the enemy's fire from three directions and there was no one to keep him company, he thought that a good place from which to fire some sixty rounds.

Private [Jeremiah J.] Murphy, Company M, Third Cavalry, had his gunstock shattered in his hands, and a pair of pantaloons ruined by the same ball. He now prefers carrying that broken gun and wearing those punctured pantaloons to getting a new outfit.

We failed to see the white girl who is known to be with this tribe. She was captured when only two or three years old, from Mormon emigrants, it is believed, and is now about twenty years of age. Frank Gruard, who, while a prisoner here saw her daily, says she is quite handsome, has a very pleasant disposition, and is esteemed and guarded as the richest treasure by her dusky companions. He never knew them to insult [rape] or mistreat her, and she is not obliged to perform any of the common labor of the squaws, most of her time being spent in doing fancy bead work, embroidery, etc. Yet, not knowing a word of English, and having no knowledge of a more convenient sphere, she often, by her listless and unsatisfied manner, betrays a desire to leave the tribe, or at least to make some change for the better.

Among the domestic animals about the village we noticed several broods of chickens and a number of fine dogs. The conduct of several of the latter seemed particularly strange. Lying by the sides of their masters' tepees when we arrived, they would not change their position one iota. As the domicile was torn down and it with its effects set on fire, the great faithful fellow would still remain motionless as a statue, heedless of coaxing, gazing wistfully and without a growl at the bands of destroyers.

AN ABRIDGED SYNOPSIS.

General Crook, in ignorance of what has transpired, has failed to meet us here as yet, and while waiting we have time to take a hasty glance at the work of the last twenty-four hours. In spite of the fact that we have, in the midst of winter, thus found and routed from his stronghold the second savage chieftain in importance, perhaps, in the whole western country, and have utterly wiped out his village and supplies, a number of very unpleasant conclusions here force themselves upon us. And it is only due the people who support the army and pride themselves in its efficiency, as well as to the brave and true soldier, who otherwise would suffer with the coward and the pretender, that these conclusions take the shape of words. Disguise it as we may, the fact still remains that owing to the failure yesterday of Captain Moore to take the position assigned him, a large proportion of the Indians were permitted to escape, thus rendering the victory incomplete in its most important detail; and further, that through this same tardiness, the situation of his brother officer, Captain Egan—who had charged into the heart of the enemy, in obedience to orders, with but a handful of men—was greatly imperiled. Then, in view of the fact that the troops were on half rations of meat, and that General Crook had instructed the officer in command to save all that could be carried off, the destruction of the large quantities of buffalo and venison not only deprived the troops of that which rightfully belonged to them, but also withheld from them that of which they now stand in great need. Also, the leaving of the bodies of the dead and one wounded man upon the field to fall into the hands of the red

monsters, who, no doubt, immediately swept over it after our departure, seems utterly inexcusable, as there was no obstacle in the way of their prompt removal that could not have been surmounted by a battalion of troops. This grave oversight sounds all the worse from the fact that during the latter part of the engagement, one battalion or squadron [under Capt. Noyes] was permitted to unsaddle its animals, make coffee, and partake of lunch in the very sight of the battlefield. Another point and I am done. After having captured some 700 ponies—by all odds the most important fruits of the victory—Colonel Reynolds, in neglecting to either place a guard over them, or to order their recapture when informed that the Indians were driving them away, certainly allowed the savages to equip themselves with the most important auxiliary to their future predatory incursions upon our frontier.

Alter Ego.

New York Times
Sunday, March 26, 1876

A FIGHT WITH SIOUX INDIANS.

CRAZY HORSE'S VILLAGE ON POWDER RIVER CAPTURED AND BURNED BY A DETACHMENT OF GENERAL CROOK'S EXPEDITION.

Fort Reno, March 22—A detachment of Gen. Crook's expedition against the hostile Sioux, consisting of Mills', Noyes', and Moore's squadrons, numbering about three hundred and thirty men and officers, under command of Colonel Reynolds, captured and burned Crazy Horse's village on the morning of the 17th. It was on Powder River, twenty miles below the mouth of Clear Fork, and had about one hundred lodges. The village was charged by Capt. Egan's company with pistols, Capt. Noyes' "C" Company stampeding and running off the herd of ponies, numbering five or six hundred. The other troops quickly followed Capt. Egan's attack, which had driven the Indians from their village. Mills' and Moore's squadrons went in, dismounted, and the Indians retreated to the bluffs and ravines back of their camp, and from secure shelter harassed the troops while the work of destroying the village went on. It was burned, with large quantities of ammunition, robes, meat, and other things valuable to Indians. Our loss was four enlisted men killed and seven wounded. No casualties occurred among the officers. The loss among the Indians is not known. At 2 p.m., when the work of destruction was complete, the troops marched for the mouth of Clear Fork, where they expected to meet Gen. Crook, with supplies. They arrived there at dark, and Gen. Crook arrived the next day at noon. The command engaged in this affair marched seventy-five miles from 8 a.m. on the 16th to dark on the 17th, with but three hours' rest in the afternoon of the 16th. Both men and horses were very much exhausted from the tax on their endurance.

Chicago, March 25—The following telegram was received at Gen. Sheridan's Headquarters this morning:

Fort Reno, March 22—We cut loose from the wagon train on the 7th inst., and scouted the Tongue and Rosebud rivers until satisfied that there were no Indians upon them; then struck across the country toward Powder River. Colonel Reynolds, with part of the command, was pushed forward [March 16] on a trail leading to the village of Crazy Horse, near the mouth of Little Powder River. This he attacked and destroyed on the 17th inst., finding it a perfect magazine of ammunition, war material, and general supplies. Crazy Horse had with him the Northern Cheyennes and some of the Minneconjous, probably in all one-half of the Indians off the reservations. Every evidence was found to prove these Indians [were] in co-partnership with those at the Red Cloud and Spotted Tail agencies, and that the proceeds of their raids upon the settlements had been taken to those agencies and supplies brought out in return. In this connection I would again urgently recommend the immediate transfer of the Indians of those agencies to the Missouri River. I am satisfied that if Sitting Bull is on this side of the Yellowstone, that he is camped at the mouth of Powder River. We experienced severe weather during our absence from the wagon train, snow falling every day but one, and the mercurial thermometer on several occasions failing to register.

George Crook, Brigadier General.

3

The Skirmish at
Tongue River Heights

"The campaign promises to be an important one. An old forty-niner of California, and one who has for nineteen years been mining in Colorado and the [Black] Hills, said yesterday that there were at least 30,000 Indians between the Big Horn and Black Hills ranges, and unless the whites took care they would likely be beaten."—Dispatch from Fort D. A. Russell, Wyoming Territory, May 20, 1876, *New York Daily Graphic*, May 25, 1876

"We are at the threshold of a great struggle, and although it is out of any one's power to avert it now, a false impression as to its leading causes should not be suffered to remain. That 'Injuns is pisen' [poison] may be an excuse for all that is done to the Sioux, but history will not give much credit to excuses that are selfishness; for where the red man takes a scalp the white man takes the land."—Editorial, "The Hostile Sioux," *New York Herald*, May 29, 1876

"The campaign . . . against the Sioux originated in the refusal of that nation to leave their camps on the Big Horn and Tongue rivers, in the valley of the Yellowstone, and enter upon a reservation which the Government had set apart for them. After the Sioux leader, Sitting Bull, had scornfully disregarded the orders of the Government, troops were directed to enter the country and to expel the Indians."—Editorial, "End of the Campaign," *New York Tribune*, September 18, 1876

Following the battle of Powder River, the Cheyennes, destitute, set out to find the winter village of Crazy Horse. Realizing there was safety in numbers, the combined tribes—Crazy Horse's Oglalas and Old Bear's Cheyennes—sought a union with Sitting Bull's Hunkpapas.[1] Sitting Bull was a well known "spiritual leader" whose "distinguishing characteristic" was "unre-lenting hostility to the white race"; he never acquiesced to the whites, signed a treaty, lived on a reservation, or put his hand out for government rations. This was the beginning of a temporary alliance in which the tribes would travel together for mutual security.[2] As winter gave way to spring, the alliance would attract additional support from other roving bands of Sioux, such as the Sans Arcs and Minneconjous, not to mention the summer roamers.

General Crook's column returned to Fort Fetterman on March 26, nine days after the lackluster partial victo-ry over the Cheyennes and Sioux at Powder River. Writing one day after the fight, correspondent Robert Strahorn was quick to point out why he believed the attack had been botched.[3] However, by the time of his next dispatch from old Fort Reno on March 22, he surprisingly shied away from any critical comments: "Over one hundred large tepees, with the accumulations of years in the shape of arms, ammunition, clothing, robes, blankets and cooking utensils, and tons of fresh and dried meat, were reduced to ashes. This reduced the foe to absolute want, and rendered his demoralization all the more complete from the fact that it took place in the heart of his own country, far from any supply post, and with most vigorous winter weather upon him."[4]

Several lines later he added: "The soldiers displayed great fortitude and gallantry; especially the Egan Grays, consisting of forty-seven men under the command of Captain James Egan, who charged through the Indian village, and for a time with-stood the entire fire of the enemy poured in from the cover of under-brush and rocks on all sides."[5]

The most negative comment he had was about the weather, which had been "extremely disagreeable during the entire campaign." Indeed, the temperature had invariably been well below zero, accompanied by the usual hazards and discomforts of icy conditions.

Be that as it may, it could not be denied that because of Reynolds's hasty withdrawal from the village, four dead troopers had been left behind.[6] Even worse, if true, was the accusation that a wounded trooper had been left behind to the mercies of the Indians, which would have been anything but tender.[7] On top of that, he torched the food supplies, against Crook's wishes.[8] With freezing tem-peratures and insufficient provisions, Crook gave up the idea of continuing on to the mouth of the Powder River, where he expected to find Sitting Bull.[9] As Major Stanton expressed it:

Gen. Crook proposed to push boldly down the Powder River to its mouth, and attack Sitting Bull's band before the latter could possibly escape him. This would have ended the war, and prevent-ed the necessity of sending other expedi-tions. Col. Reynolds neglected to obey [Crook's instructions] . . . and burned, destroyed, and left enough meat there to have fully enabled Gen. Crook to carry out the plan of the campaign. But with this failure, and only partial rations for four days left, it was impossible to take the command further, and the only thing left to do was to return to Reno.[10]

If that was not enough, the Cheyennes recaptured most of their horses the morning after the fight, a detail that certainly reflected negatively on the ranking officer.[11] With Crook turning back to Fort Reno to regroup, Sheridan's plans for a winter conquest over the recalcitrant and defiant Sioux and Cheyennes were dashed.

Dashed, too, were the military careers of two officers: Colonel Reynolds and Captain Moore. Crook preferred courts-martial charges against them for "misbehavior before the enemy."[12] The trials took place in January 1877, and both men were found guilty. Reynolds was suspended from rank and command for one year. Moore was sentenced to suspension from command for six months and confinement to his post, Fort Laramie. President Grant remitted both sentences in honor of their past service, but neither man fared well afterward. Reynolds retired on June 25, 1877, and Moore resigned his commission on August 10, 1879.[13] A third officer, Captain Noyes, was also court-martialed, the charges filed by Reynolds being for "conduct to the prejudice of good order and military discipline." Holding the captured horse herd a short distance from the village, Noyes had allowed his company to unsaddle their tired mounts while the men made coffee. With the results of the fight being less than expected, it just did not look good. The trial took place in late April 1876. Though found guilty, Crook let him off easy, stating it was punishment enough that he was censured by

his fellow officers, essentially chalking the incident up to an "error in judgment."[14] Noyes was back in action with the Second Cavalry in time for Crook's spring-summer campaign.

And this new campaign was to be quite different than its predecessor. Instead of just one column in the field, there would be three. As one correspondent explained: "There is a sort of anaconda combination planning for the purpose of crushing Sitting Bull, Gen. Crook's troops forming this part of the circle. The troops of Gen. Terry and Col. [John] Gibbon[15] are already under way from Minnesota [Dakota Territory][16] and Montana. . . . The movement of the troops of Gen. Terry and Col. Gibbon, it is expected, will drive the Indians into the grasp of Gen. Crook's troops."[17]

This strangulation-style strategy, as devised by Sheridan, was the same used against the Southern Plains tribes in 1868–69 and 1874–75. It was a simple idea that had worked effectively in the past. Three or more army columns would converge upon a common area, making it difficult for the Indians to escape.[18] As Sherman expressed it, "We conquered the Kiowas and the Comanches in the same way. We hemmed them in and caught them by finding their camps."[19] If the Indians evaded one column, they were bound to run into another. As applied to the current campaign, if the Sioux and Cheyennes somehow avoided one or all of the army columns, there were not too many options available; continuously hard pressed with no time to replenish food stores, they could either escape to Canada or sue for peace and surrender at the agencies.[20] The biggest problem for the army was coordination among the columns, and, consequently, much was left to chance. That is why it was important that each column be relatively strong enough to fend for itself.

In this new campaign, Sheridan's strategy called for three simultaneous columns. General Crook would advance from Fort Fetterman, Wyoming Territory, in the south; General Terry from Fort Abraham Lincoln, Dakota Territory, in the east; and Colonel Gibbon, Seventh Infantry, from Forts Shaw and Ellis, Montana Territory, in the west. Gibbon's column, operating under Terry's orders, was the smallest of the three units, and therefore more of a "supporting force."[21] The region they were to converge upon was west of the Great Sioux Reservation, south of the Yellowstone and east of the Big Horn Mountains, including the valleys of the Powder, Tongue, Rosebud, and Big Horn rivers. On May 29, Sheridan wrote a letter to Sherman, explaining his loosely styled strategy and how he envisioned it would play out in the military campaign that was just then getting under way:

As no very accurate information can be obtained as to the location of hostile Indians, and as there would be no telling how long they would stay at any one place, if it was known, I have given no instructions to Generals Crook or Terry, preferring that they should do the best

they can under the circumstances, and under what they may develop, as I think it would be unwise to make any combinations in such a country as they will have to operate in.[22] As hostile Indians, in any great numbers, cannot keep the field as a body for a week, or at most ten days, I therefore consider—and so do Terry and Crook—that each column will be able to take care of itself, and of chastising the Indians, should it have the opportunity.

The organization of these commands and what they expect to accomplish has been as yet left to the department commanders. I presume that the following will occur:

General Terry will drive the Indians toward the Big Horn Valley, and General Crook will drive them back toward Terry; Colonel Gibbon moving down on the north side of the Yellowstone to intercept, if possible, such as may want to go north of the Missouri to the Milk River.[23]

It sounded good on paper. It should have worked. In most cases it probably would have worked. But this year proved to be different.

Generals Crook and Terry fronted the two primary commands. Crook had about 1,000 men and Terry about 930. Colonel Gibbon led about 425, including 196 cavalry. That's a fighting force close to 2,350 men, including some 1,770 cavalry.[24] During the winter of 1875–76, the nontreaty Indians were thought to number between eight hundred and one thousand fighting men.[25] Regardless of the accuracy of this estimate, their numbers had increased considerably as winter turned to spring. Based on newspaper reports between March and late July 1876,

Sitting Bull's legions had grown to between two thousand and four thousand.[26] One newspaper story in late May 1876 clearly illustrated the uncertainty regarding the number of "hostile" Indians, declaring one total, then changing it in the very next sentence:

In all there are of Cheyennes, Sioux and others, some 3,000 ready to fight out this campaign against Gen. Crook. They have numerous allies, and well-informed people place the actual hostile Indian camp at from 7,000 to 8,000 first-class fighting men, armed with the best rifles and plentifully supplied with ammunition furnished by post traders and speculators who grow rich on helping to shed the blood of the regular army. . . . They are commanded by Sitting Bull and Crazy Horse [who are] eager to signalize themselves by slaughtering the whites.[27]

Despite the planned three-pronged assault, one reporter was not too optimistic about the upcoming expedition. Recognizing the inherent difficulty of trying to find the Indians during the warmer months, he wrote:

From June until October they will wander from pasture to pasture and hunting ground to hunting ground, and the probability of entrapping them again into a fair engagement is very faint. The fruit of the present enterprise, therefore, is more likely to be the ashes of wasted gunpowder alone than anything else, while the Sioux may stealthily add many scalps to their blood encrusted trophies.[28]

As Reuben Davenport (now about twenty-four) documented, many on the frontier were unable to sympathize with a people that glorified in "blood encrusted trophies." The fact

A Meeting with the Crows

New York Herald,
Wednesday, May 3, 1876

Bozeman, Montana
April 14, 1876

A council with the Crow Indians was held at their agency near the mouth of Stillwater on the 9th of April, and Colonel Gibbon called on the Crows to give him such aid as they could in subduing the Sioux. Chiefs claiming to represent 3,000 Crows were present at the council, and great excitement prevailed, many of the chiefs declaring it was the duty of the Crow Nation to aid the whites, who had always been their friends, against their ancient and inveterate enemies, the Sioux. The Crows asked time to consider, and it was believed most of the young men would go to war against the Sioux. Lately the Sioux have been hunting on the Crow reservation, and have killed several Crows. The Crows say they cannot hunt the buffalo on their own land for fear of the Sioux, and only a few weeks ago asked the whites to come and help them drive the enemy beyond the Yellowstone. All the Big and Little Horn country is included in the Crow reservation, and game is plenty near the mouth of the Big Horn River, but the Sioux occupied the country and the Crows could not hunt. The Sioux have whipped the Crows so often that they were completely cowed, but the troops coming into the country have put a new spirit in them, and it is believed they will seize upon this opportunity to revenge themselves upon the Sioux for past injuries.

is that the majority of westerners viewed the Indians as being less than human: "The men of the Territories and ultra-Missouri States look upon the Indian, as he now exists on the plains of Dakotah and Wyoming, as human only in his strictly physical traits of form, anatomy and physiology. It is impossible, after having some experience of frontier life, not to join, partially at least, in this belief."[29]

One frontiersman explained to the *Herald* correspondent the opinion held by many on the frontier that the romantic version of the Indian was far from the reality:

People who have not personally become acquainted with the Sioux, Arapahoe or Cheyenne races may be amused by romances setting forth the nobility of the red man as he appears in the classic literature of the past 300 years, but they have very dim ideas of the animal in his real state. . . . The mould of man is only a disguise [for the Indian]. . . . Vengeance being his creed, a process of extermination to be enforced so long as he remains unsubjected would be justifiable.[30]

To Davenport's credit, he did not entirely buy what the man was selling (although he was not above referring to the Sioux as savages in his dispatches), and acknowledged that the views expressed were likely the result of ulterior motives:

The view of the situation on this frontier just reproduced illustrates much of the public sentiment. The horror of the Sioux, however, in my opinion, is exaggerated. It is noticeable that those who express it most strongly are those "honest" miners who have been most eager to invade the Black Hills.[31]

On the road from Cheyenne to Fort Fetterman, Davenport observed that dejected parties of miners were leaving the Black Hills, at the same time capturing for posterity a sample of the wordplay then in vogue:

They are returning to civilization in swarms, panic stricken by the crack of Indian rifles and disgusted with fortune. . . . When asked, "Did you find any gold?" the reply usually was of the purport, "Yes, but a darned sight too many Indians."

Some satirical "boy in blue" in repartee applied to them the contemptuous sobriquet which they had previously freely bestowed on Eastern men who have been attracted hither by the rumor of gold. "So you've turned tender-feet, 'ave ya? Don't like the Black 'ills 'swell's ye did, do ye?"[32]

A few days later, at Fort Fetterman, he learned from a man named Murphy that the people occupying Custer City, in the Black Hills, "live in constant terror; all who can are abandoning the country."[33]

On May 16, General Crook visited the Red Cloud Agency hoping to acquire scouts for the forthcoming campaign, but the trip did not go as planned due to the interference of agency officials. Davenport sarcastically noted: "The Indian agents have prevented the Sioux from joining General Crook, but they do not seem to be able to restrain them from joining the bands now engaged in hostilities."[34]

To back up that claim, the same report declared that one thousand agency Sioux were then on their way to join Sitting Bull. In fact, reports of

Indians leaving their reservation to join the "hostiles" had become quite commonplace during spring 1876.

According to Davenport, Red Cloud also gave Crook a warning:

The Gray Fox [Crook] must understand that the Dakotas, and especially the Ogallalas, have many warriors, many guns and ponies. They are brave and ready to fight for their country. They are not afraid of the soldiers nor of their chief. Many braves are ready to meet them. Every lodge will send its young men, and they all will say of the Great Father's dogs, "Let them come!"[35]

For Crook, the day almost turned out to be his last. About four or five warriors from the agency had planned to ambush him on the road back to Fort Laramie, but when the general's military escort turned out to be stronger than expected, they turned their deadly attention to a local mail carrier named Charles Clark. A telegram out of Fort Laramie on May 17 reported the unfortunate incident:

General Crook narrowly escaped an ambuscade on his return to this post. When he reached a point fifteen miles this side of Red Cloud, he met Charles Clark, the stage driver and mail carrier. The latter proceeded toward the agency, and when within ten miles of there, a war party, which had been lying in ambuscade, attacked and killed him, took the four horses he had been driving and decamped, leaving the body, stage, and mails on the road. The corpse and mail were taken to Camp Robinson today by a detachment of troops sent out by the commanding officer. Clark was one of the best men in the employ of the stage company. He had been tending stock here, and this was his first trip with the mails, he having taken the place [of the former mail carrier] of his own accord and because his predecessor had refused to again carry the mail through, being afraid of the Indians.[36]

That Crook had indeed been the target was confirmed shortly afterward by a Sioux named Rocky Bear.[37] Not able to secure the services of Red Cloud's followers, Crook now turned his attention to enlisting the Crows and Shoshones, both tribes being hereditary enemies of the Sioux. "This plan of making Indians fight Indians," a correspondent was to record in May 1877, "is the keystone of the wonderful success General Crook has met with in his management of the wild tribes."[38]

Shortly thereafter it was arranged that three hundred Crow Indians would join the command at the ruins of Fort Reno on the Powder River, ninety miles north of Fort Fetterman, on May 30.[39] Lieutenant Bourke considered the Crow scouts to be "equal to that of an additional Regiment,"[40] but high water was making the North Platte difficult to cross,[41] on top of which the ferry boat cable snapped several times,[42] and Crook, knowing he would not be able to make the rendezvous on time, was concerned that the Crows would not wait for him. On May 27, Davenport wrote from Fort Fetterman: "[It] is feared that the Crows will disperse when they do not find the army at the trysting place. General Crook has, therefore, ordered two companies of the Third Cavalry, commanded by Captain

[Frederick] Van Vliet and Lieutenant [Emmet] Crawford, to set out today with supplies for eight days to meet the Indian allies, and remain in camp with them until the coming up of the main force."[43]

On May 29, for the second time in three months, Crook departed Fort Fetterman at the head of a large military command, once again moving north along the Bozeman Trail. This time his force, officially named the Big Horn and Yellowstone Expedition, consisted of ten companies of the Third Cavalry, five companies of the Second Cavalry, three companies of the Ninth Infantry, and two companies of the Fourth Infantry. In all, there were about 825 cavalry, 185 infantry, some 200 "well-armed" teamsters and packers, 100 wagons (pulled by six mules each), and about 320 pack mules, not to mention enough ammunition to wipe out the Sioux nation several times over.[44] As laid out in General Orders No. 1, May 28, Lieutenant Colonel William B. Royall, Third Cavalry, was placed in charge of the cavalry, and Major Alexander Chambers, Fourth Infantry, was given command of the infantry.[45] Royall, previously in the Fifth Cavalry, had served with Crook in Arizona against the Apaches, and was "an officer of acknowledged courage and judgment," while Chambers had "studied the Indian for years on the frontier, and brings excellent executive ability to the aid of a thorough education in the art of frontier warfare."[46] Civilian Tom Moore, who was with Crook during the winter campaign, was back as chief packer.[47]

With Crook transferred to the Department of the Platte from Arizona in April 1875, hopes were running high in the nation's capital and on the frontier that he would be able to duplicate his success against the Apaches by subduing the Sioux and Cheyennes. The consensus on the frontier was that relations between the government and the Sioux had

reached at last the crisis which military men on the frontiers of Nebraska, Dakota and Wyoming have predicted so long. . . . [Crook's] ability in warfare with the Indians has been so well demonstrated in the country of the Apaches . . . that it needs no eulogy. In the War Office it is held in high esteem and has caused the giving to him of the task of reducing to submission the wild bands of the Sioux. No brigadier in the army could have inspired the people of this department with more confidence in the efficacy of his protecting power. His intention of fully exerting it is determined. The measures to that end are to be offensive as well as defensive until the enemy of the miner and settler shall have recognized the futility of further attempts at aggression and independence.[48]

According to Strahorn, Crook was planning for "brisk operation[s] during the entire summer, if necessary."[49]

[The] cavalry and pack trains will be pushing into any region of country an Indian can and does penetrate. Returning to the supply camp when supplies give out, the sallies will continue to be made as often as necessary. General Crook sets no date upon which to return, but quietly says he wishes to stay out until he can once and forever settle the Sioux problem. How long this will take is little more than a matter of conjecture, although it is generally believed that the entire summer will be required.[50]

Strange to say, but some of the people Strahorn met while on the trip to Fort Fetterman thought a summer campaign against the Sioux actually sounded like fun: "Interested friends at the different forts . . . usually said, 'Oh, you will have a holiday trip this summer. So different from our last winter's campaign, you know, nice warm days and pleasant nights. Really I wouldn't mind going along myself.'"[51]

The first day's march was a short one, and the command camped for the night at Sage Creek, about twelve miles northwest of Fort Fetterman. The next day it reached the south fork of the Cheyenne River where, as one officer jokingly noted, Crook's "last expedition issued all their fresh beef to Sitting Bull."[52] Three days later, on June 2, Crook's force arrived at the ruins of old Fort Reno; it found Van Vliet and Crawford, but no Crows, and no sign of the Sioux. Wasting no time, Crook dispatched his three main guides, Grouard, Richard,[53] and Pourier on an important mission: [They were to go] "north to the Big Horn River, 150 miles distant, to meet the Crows there, or to swim the stream and go on to their agency if unsuccessful in finding them sooner. The brave scouts started at night, and expected to make the ride from the Powder [River] to Big Horn Cañon and back to Fort Kearney in seven or eight days."[54]

Five days later, the command made camp at the junction of Prairie Dog Creek and Tongue River, deep in enemy territory, about 190 miles, as the crow flies, from Fort Fetterman. Late that night, they received a visit from "a solitary Sioux [who] came to the top of a neighboring bluff and created no little amusement by asking impertinent questions and hurling braggadocio at our devoted heads in true savage style. One of our men who speaks the Sioux tongue kept up a conversation with him for some time, but nothing satisfactory was elicited."[55]

Also on June 7, the command laid to rest its first fatality, Private Francis Tierney, Third Cavalry. Tierney had accidentally shot himself with his revolver on May 30, "the ball entering his thigh and passing upward into the abdomen, inflicting a mortal wound." He died the night of June 6, after "great suffering."[56] The same day Tierney died, Sergeant Andrew J. O'Leary, Ninth Infantry, broke his arm when an ambulance tipped over.[57] Such was life on an Indian campaign.

Although Grouard, Richard, and Pourier were not due back for another day or two, Strahorn no doubt spoke for Crook when he wrote: "Their return is looked for with unfeigned anxiety, as well it may be. Without the Crows or some other trusty Indian scouts to follow the Sioux—on the principle that it 'takes a thief to catch a thief'—there must be much bewilderment and unnecessary traveling to find the savages in their own haunts."[58]

Unless, of course, they found the troops first. Now we turn to four exciting narratives about the skirmish at Tongue River Heights, June 9, 1876, just south of the Montana line. Two of the reports are from correspondent Joe Wasson[59] (who had previously accompanied Crook on his 1867 campaign against the Paiute Indians in Oregon), one is from Reuben Davenport, the *New York Herald* correspondent, whose dispatches were soon to take aim at General Crook as if they were fired from a Sioux rifle, and lastly, there is a little-known account by Charles St. George Stanley, the mysterious artist-correspondent for *Frank Leslie's Illustrated Newspaper*.[60]

Daily Alta California (San Francisco), Thursday, July 6, 1876

Gen. Crook's Expedition.

The Big Horn And Yellowstone Country—The Route From Fort Fetterman To The Scene Of The Late Engagement—Our Correspondent's Description Of The First Brush With The Indians.

[Written by Joe Wasson]

In Camp, Forks Tongue River and Prairie Dog Creek, Wyoming Territory, June 9—I sent you a few items from Sage Creek, twelve miles this side of Fort Fetterman, May 30, since which time Crook's command has pulled along to this place, in the heart of the Indian country 187 miles, or 232 miles from the nearest point on the Union Pacific Railroad. As yet, not a hostile shot has been fired, though we have lost one man by accident; and of the 2,300 horses and

mules, only nine have failed to connect since they left Cheyenne and Medicine Bow, and the general health of both men and beasts has been better than expected. Three or four cases of mumps and one of scarlet fever are all that have been reported among the soldiers or citizen employes. The weather has been cool and favorable for marching as a general thing. On the 30th of May, Francis A. Tierney, private in Co. B, Third Cavalry, accidentally shot himself with his revolver, and lived until the night before our arrival here (the 7th inst.), where he was buried about sundown with all the military honors possible. Captain [Guy V.] Henry [Third Cavalry] read the burial service, after which three volleys were fired over the grave; flat stones laid therein, his name inscribed, etc. He was a native of New York, aged twenty-eight years. It was something as impressive and lonely almost as a funeral at sea.

The Country.

From Fort Fetterman, on the North Platte, to old Fort Reno, on Powder River, the distance is 90 miles; the road is an excellent natural one, over a rolling, grassy country. The water, at convenient distances, was too much tinctured with alkali to be very acceptable. The several little streams were headwaters of the Cheyenne and Powder rivers; one or two had considerable cottonwood timber adjacent. Deer, elk, antelope, sage hens, grouse, etc., added variety to the bill of fare. On the morning of June 1, there was a slight fall of snow to grace and purify the scene—and also cause the hair to fall. Fort Reno was located on the west bank of Powder River and was the first of a line of three posts, reaching through to the Big Horn River—Forts Kearney [Kearny], and C. F. Smith being the other two—all of which were abandoned under the Treaty of Laramie of 1868,

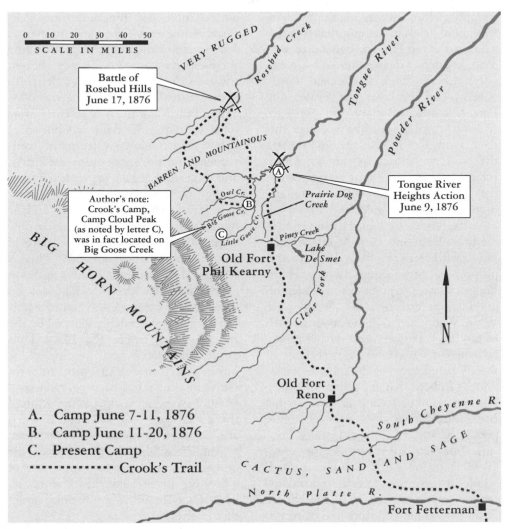

Crook's Advance Toward Tongue River Heights and Rosebud Creek, June 1876. This map is based on one that was used to illustrate Lt. James E. H. Foster's dispatch published in the July 13, 1876 edition of the *New York Daily Graphic*, see page 92.

and which treaty was the result of the celebrated Fetterman Massacre, in December 1866, at Kearney. These posts were all burned by the Indians after the treaty, and only the stone chimneys and desecrated graveyards remain to tell the sickening story. Powder River is over one hundred feet wide, three feet deep, and its bottom lands well timbered with cottonwood.

From the second day after leaving the Platte, the Big Horn range loomed up as majestic and bold as the Sierra Nevada, looking west from about Virginia City. It is called Big Horn because of the Indian name for mountain sheep. It is 150 miles long by 50 broad, and at least 50 miles of it is covered with snow, culminating in Cloud Peak. It is also heavily timbered, and is a powerful watershed to the eastward. Big Horn River is practically Wind River, and heads in the mountains to the westward. From Powder River north, our road crossed Crazy Woman's Creek, Clear Creek, Rock Creek and Piney [Creek]—on the latter was located old Fort Kearney. All these are excellent streams, coming out from under the road. From Reno to Kearney (63 miles), the road was closer to the Big Horn Range, over a magnificent grazing country. The mountains evidently contain more or less placer gold, and a party of 60 men, headed by John H. Graves, formerly of Diamond City, Montana, had just arrived from the Black Hills for the purpose of prospecting the Big Horn Range. Graves reports a few miles of good diggings on Dead Wood and White Wood creeks, in the northern part of the Black Hills, but no paying mines elsewhere to speak of. Custer City is merely hanging on by the eyebrows; it is not the Indians that are killing the place, but the want of paying ground. If the Big Horn Range does not contain a goodly breadth of paying deposits, outside appearances are very deceptive, to say nothing of the frequently reported good prospects. These mountains remind one very much of the Boise Basin Mountains of Idaho, and being on the line of the Montana diggings, gold will certainly be found—whether in paying quantities remains to be seen. I hope to be able to go over the ground myself, after taking a turn at Indian scouting.

MASSACRE HILL.

At old Kearney the long mound containing the remains of the Fetterman Massacre is yet plainly visible, and about three miles north of the post, on the road we traveled, the place where the affair occurred was pointed out. It is called Massacre Hill, a point to where the doomed party retreated, after seeing the trap laid for them. But their want of ammunition and breech-loading guns made it impossible for them to escape. Not a man of the ninety odd, including three citizens, but was literally shot or speared in cold blood. Capt. Fetterman, Lieutenants Brown and Greenwood,[61] and the entire company of infantry, were piled up along the road and buried as before said. Colonel Carrington commanded the post and heard the firing, and it is said that he was prevented from going to the scene by his wife [Margaret], who has since died; and he has also married the widow Greenwood,[62] who called him all sorts of names during the massacre. This is Richard the Third enacted over again on a small scale. I wish you would look up the Treaty of Laramie, and consider how often it has been brutally violated by the Indians, long before the Black Hills excitement. Had it been the English, or most any other but our tolerant Government, the Fetterman Massacre would have been avenged to the death of the last savage engaged therein. But it is as it is, and here we are, Mr. Merryman, as the circus has it, going over the ground in battle array, for the purpose of enforcing the so-called treaty aforesaid. The savages have had a soft thing under that idiotic stipulation.

It is to be hoped that the Black Hills and Big Horn expeditions of last year and this will compel the Government to gather in all the Sioux scalawags if it takes the entire U. S. army to do so. The Red Cloud and Spotted Tail agencies should be moved eastward to the Missouri River, and this vast and valuable country secured to civilization at once.

THE CAMP.

This camp is pleasantly situated on the south bank of Tongue River—the chief haunt of the hostile Sioux—at an elevation above the sea of 3,750 feet.

Medicine Bow, on the Union Pacific Railroad, is 6,500 feet. There is quite a forest of cottonwood and box elder on the bottom land. The river is about 200 feet wide and three deep, and contains a variety of fish. The grazing is good, and there are plenty of buffalo, deer, etc., round about, and hostile Indians spying around, so that altogether the place is quite interesting. Until we reached here Indian "sign" was singularly scarce, but enough was visible to give us to know that we were continually watched, and the night after our arrival here[63] a band of eight mounted Sioux came to the edge of the high bluff overlooking our camp from the north side of the river, and called out, asking various questions, regarding the Crow Indians and half-breeds, as if the former had come here direct from the Red Cloud Agency. You will remember that Crook sent to Montana for a band of Crow allies, and expected to meet them at old Fort Reno, but failing to connect he sent his three chief scouts on ahead to Montana to see about it. As yet we have not received any news from them, although it is now about time. Their services are in demand here, as a party of about twenty-five hostiles crossed the river last night just below Prairie Dog Creek, showing that we are watched in some force. But this morning the gratifying intelligence came in from Fetterman, in despatches for General Crook, to the effect that one hundred Snake [Shoshone] Indians were due at old Fort Kearney, 35 miles back, on yesterday, so that they may be expected in now every hour. They come from Fort Stambaugh, near the South Pass, on the Sweetwater River. Even should the Crows fail to appear at all, and the Snake allies come to hand all right, the command will soon leave here for the war path. A base of supply will be established at this or some other point on Tongue River, the wagons sent back to Fetterman for more rations, etc. The several companies of infantry will be detailed for these duties. The rest here is very refreshing, indeed. There is a general cleaning up of clothes, guns, etc., overhauling of stock on hand, horses shod, etc.

First Hostile Demonstration.

Saturday, June 10—Our camp on Tongue River was the scene of considerable variety of entertainment yesterday afternoon and evening. Before dinner we had two horse races and one foot race. Captain Burt's charger won the two former, and the poor animal had scarcely cooled off, when his left fore-leg was broken by a bullet fired from the bluff north of the river, and heretofore described. The pickets on the receding bluffs, east of Prairie Dog Creek, sounded the alarm, which was soon followed by a raking, random volley from a party of well-mounted Indians, estimated all the way from 25 to 100, as seen from different stand-points. The distance from the edge of the bluff to the outer edge of camp is 500 to 700 yards, and the enemy's guns were of much longer range. The bullets "zipped" in among our tents, horses, and wagons, in a way extremely interesting. The soldiers, teamsters, etc., returned the fire at once; but General Crook put a stop to that as soon as possible, considering it a causeless waste of ammunition, and calculated to convey to the enemy a poor opinion of our coolness. Three companies of the Ninth Infantry—Captains Burroughs, Burt and Munson[64]—were sent across the creek to guard the approaches from the east, and four of the Third Cavalry—Captains Mills, Lawson, Sartorius and Andrews[65]—were ordered to ford the river and ascend the bluff. All this was done in good time and shape. The Indians, in the meantime, kept up their fire on our camp until the cavalry got within shooting distance, when they fell back into the higher hills and ravines, occasionally coming forward, circling about and returning the fire of the soldiers. It was a full hour and nearly dark before peace once more prevailed on Tongue River. It is singular that no more damage was done to camp, which is concentrated into a small space. At least three hundred shots were fired into it, and no man was seriously hurt; two cavalrymen were bruised by spent balls.[66] One mule was fatally wounded, and besides Burt's, Lieutenant Robertson's[67] horse was shot in the leg. One or two other animals were reported slightly hurt. There is no satisfactory evidence that the enemy was damaged in the least. He was very chary of his sacred person, except in one or two instances, where a bold warrior dashed to the edge of the bluff, presenting a tempting mark on the horizon. The marks of their long-range guns, as furnished by the government and agents, are here and there visible in tent-poles, wagon-beds, etc. Gen. Crook thinks this impudent demonstration in broad daylight was done for the purpose of covering the retreat of an entire village not far off, and regrets that his expected Indian allies were not on hand ere this to do scouting duty. As it is, we are in a state of suspense; we will probably have to move up or down the river for grass ere the arrival of either the Crows or Snakes. It is feared that the warrior element of the enemy will mostly cross the Yellowstone, and give much trouble to catch ere winter.

Jose.

New York Tribune,
Saturday, July 1, 1876

THE SIOUX WAR.

GEN. CROOK'S EXPEDITION.

AN ATTACK BY THE SIOUX.

[Written by Joc Wasson]

Camp on Tongue River, June 10—The expedition of Gen. Crook has remained in camp here for several days, waiting the arrival of the Crow and the Snake Indians, who will act as scouts. Yesterday afternoon the hostile Indians first made their appearance. The camp is surrounded by bluffs, bold or receding, and the pickets, wherever placed, are plainly visible from almost any point. About 6 p.m. those on the receding bluffs below the mouth of a creek, half a mile to the eastward, were seen firing in the air and making demonstrations to attract our attention. Scarcely had this occurred when firing commenced on a high bluff on the north side of the river, where no pickets were placed in the day time, and bullets began to "zip" overhead among the tents, horses, and wagons throughout the camp, and all hands soon realized that a party of hostile Indians had begun an attack. On the impulse of the moment the fire was returned from almost every portion of our side, but owing to the extreme distance—500 to 800 yards—to where the Indians were, Gen. Crook ordered all firing to cease, as it was a mere waste of ammunition. The pickets having discovered the Indians, unexpectedly so the latter, prevented the sneaking wretches from doing more than fire at random. They were mounted, and some of them rode up to the edge of the bluff in very plain sight for an instant, only to turn and fall back out of range, on the whole, it must be said, affording a very pretty sight. In the mean time three companies of the 9th Infantry, C, H, and G, Capts. Munson, Burt, and Burroughs, with Lieuts. Capron,[68] Robertson, and Carpenter,[69] were formed under the fire and hurried across the creek to guard the approaches from the east, while Col. Royall of the 3d Cavalry dispatched companies M, A, E and I of his regiment across the river to engage the enemy or drive them away. The water came up to the horses' flanks, but all were over and up the bluff in short order. Perhaps 100 shots were exchanged between the cavalry and the Indians, but at too long range to effect anything serious. The Indians would keep falling back and circling round in such fashion that it was useless to follow them, especially so late in the evening.

The firing altogether lasted about one hour—from 6 to 7 o'clock p.m. The casualties and injuries sustained on our side were few and almost unworthy of mention considering the number of shots fired into the camp—at least 250. Two cavalrymen were slightly wounded by spent balls. Gen. Crook thinks the enemy consisted of the inhabitants of a single village, and the object of their attack was to cover their change of camp.

New York Herald,
Friday, June 16, 1876

An Indian Battle.

The Warring Sioux Attack General Crook's Command.

Tongue River Camp Surprised At Midnight.

A Sharp Fusillade.

Charging The Red Enemy From A Dangerous Position.

[Written by Reuben B. Davenport]

General Crook's Big Horn Expedition, Camp on Goose Creek, June 11, via Fort Fetterman, June 15.

This body of troops had marched 190 consecutive miles on [through] June 7, when Tongue River was reached, and then they rested three days. Until then no unequivocal signs of Indians had been seen, although puffs of smoke rose above the eastern horizon. Part of these signals were made by a party of miners from Montana, who were examining gulches in search of gold near Pumpkin Butte and removing toward the Black Hills. Their recent camping grounds were found, where they had erected redoubts for defense against Indians, with whom they had probably had skirmishes.

Dusky Warriors Eloquent At A Distance.

On the night of our arrival at Tongue River Camp [June 7] we were aroused at twelve o'clock by a loud declamation delivered by a sombre figure walking on the top of the bluffs on the north bank, opposite General Crook's headquarters. Other figures from time to time appeared and harangued successively during an hour. As nearly as could be comprehended, they announced the destruction of the invading force if not withdrawn, and warned us of a formidable attack before two suns should roll around. They asked us, as if in irony,

If The Crows Had Joined

the troops; and now some fear is felt lest harm may have come to the guides[70] sent to Montana Agency [Crow Agency] to gain their alliance, who have not yet returned. After this visitation the camp was strongly picketed, but a day and night succeeded the savage menaces with only a slight false alarm. The day before yesterday, at about four o'clock in the afternoon, the infantry picket saw about fifty Indians on the bluff opposite the camp, stealing to positions behind the rocks.

THE INFANTRY FIRED

upon them and the camp was alarmed. Though surprised they immediately returned the fire with yells. A hundred flashes were instantly seen along the crest of the ridge, and several mounted warriors rode out in full view, circling rapidly, and there was instantly heard another sharp fusillade. A volley from the camp was poured into the bluff. The pickets on every side were strengthened and the herd secured, in anticipation of any attempt that might be made to capture it. Half a mile up the river

A BAND OF SIOUX

tried to cross, but were driven back by the prompt attention of the pickets. Indians were seen at the same time on the south side of the camp, but they remained distant. A battalion, under the command of Captain Mills, Third Cavalry, advanced rapidly across the river, dismounted in a grove under the bluff and charged up the deep ravine. The first man to reach the top saw

TWO HUNDRED INDIANS,

moving incessantly on ponies, but slowly receding. The troops, stretching out in a skirmish line, drove them back in the face of a brisk fire, which they answered wherever the redskins were visible above the sagebrush, behind which they sought to screen themselves. They seemed bold and confident, and when a feint of retiring was executed by the troops they quickly changed their retreat to an advance. It is supposed they had a large reserve massed in the ravines and expected to entice the small party into a pursuit, so as to

SURROUND AND ANNIHILATE THEM.

When they saw the full strength of the cavalry they finally retreated. One of the party of Indians, on attempting to cross the river, was shot, and was lifted from his seat by his companions. Those on the bluff led off the riderless pony.

It was supposed that two Indians were wounded or killed, at least. No soldier engaged in the fight was injured, but two in the camp suffered contusions from spent balls. Three horses and one mule were killed.

SHOSHONE AUXILIARIES.

Intelligence has been received by our commander of the probable coming of 120 Shoshones as auxiliaries, under Washakie, the chief. Their arrival is expected every day, and active aggressive operations only await the coming of these Indian allies.

THREE THOUSAND MORE WARRIORS PAINTED.

General Crook is informed that 3,000 more warriors have deserted the Red Cloud Agency, proceeding north on the warpath. It will probably be his policy to prevent them finding refuge there again if whipped, until they sue for peace and surrender their arms. The presence of the Fifth Cavalry there is to enforce this plan.

In consequence of the unsafe position of the camp on Tongue River the expedition marched today sixteen miles to this point, which will be made the base of supplies. The Herald courier with this despatch makes a most perilous journey through a region alive with Sioux guerillas.[71]

Colorado Miner (Georgetown), Saturday, June 15, 1878

[Written by Charles St. George Stanley][72]

Returning to camp [June 9], I found that a horse race was upon the tapis, and turned aside to witness it. Of course it was not perhaps as au fait [up to the standard] as the affairs at Jerome Park, or the Derby, don't you know? but still we

enjoyed it. After the horse race, the packers got up a foot race and this athletic
exhibition was witnessed by a large portion of the command. Returning slowly
to our tents I noticed that the clouds
hanging in the west began to assume all
the beautiful tints of a glorious sunset, a
thing of almost daily occurrence.

Supper was ready and we arranged
ourselves around the mess table, with the
frugal meal (beans and bacon) before us.
Jokes were cracked and we were merry
with strophe and antistrophe of conversation, when a sharp report broke upon
the evening air, followed by the vengeful
hiss of a bullet. Then another and another report and finally a regular volley.
"Indians!" was the cry and away we
dashed to secure our weapons. It was
some time before order was brought out
of the confusion, and then along the
whole line the rattle of musketry told
that the enemy were being answered.
The firing by this time had become so
general across the river, and the passage
of bullets so rapid, that the air seemed
alive with bees as the leaden hail whizzed
over and around us.

Volley answered volley and the
evening breeze drifted clouds of smoke
redolent of powder through the trees.
The yelling of the savages was something
horrible, and the wild, painted forms of
the Dakotas, darting here and there
upon the bluffs opposite, firing at every
plunge of their ponies, gave the scene a
sinister appearance. One warrior in particular, attracted attention. He was
mounted upon a white war pony,
smeared with great bands of vermillion,
and his head adorned with a coffee pot,
brightly burnished and decorated with
eagle plumes. This individual rejoiced in
the sobriquet of "The man with the Tin
Hat," and it was his business to pass rapidly backwards and forwards upon the
side of the ridge, in order to draw the fire
of the troops, thus enabling his comrades

to fire into us with impunity. His
appearance was so striking that he naturally attracted the attention as well as the
fire of the command, although without
effect, as the confounded rascal seemed
to bear a charmed existence.[73] At this
juncture some of the packers displayed
an utter disregard for personal safety, and
running to the river bank at a point
where the vegetation ceased, and a small
stretch of sward intervened, turned
handsprings and somersaults, yelling at
the top of their voices, "head him off!"
"hobble him!" "nosebag him!" and other
kindred expressions peculiar to their profession, until the thing became really
amusing.

For one hour the firing continued and
some of us, especially those under fire for
the first time, felt unusually blue. I must
confess that the horrible whizzing of rifle
balls was most demoralizing, and I for
one, managed to keep well behind a
large cottonwood tree, although for
appearance sake, I blazed away with a
vengeance until the atmosphere around
that tree resembled a foretaste of the
hereafter (the other place). Tom Cooper,
a reckless sort of a fellow, and one of
Closter's train, passing by, remarked: "I
thought you'd find a tree rather convenient," and away went all my grand ideas
of bravery, and the humiliation of the situation burst upon me in all its vividness.

It seemed impossible to dislodge the
enemy, by platoon or any other kind of
firing, and it was at last determined by
the General, that a charge would effect
the purpose. Ordering companies M, A,
I, and E, out upon this duty, the little
party, under command of Capt. Mills,
swam the river, and picketing their horses upon the other bank, stormed the hill
with decided success.

In a few moments they had driven the
enemy beyond the bluff and into the valley upon the other side, without loss,
and it was now safe to leave our shelter,

as the hiss of bullets had ceased. It is of no use talking; a fight with the possibilities of you don't know what, before you, is anything but pleasant, and upon the battlefield, the beauties of peace are greatly enhanced.

Thus ended our first brush with the enemy, and taking into consideration the fact that our loss was only in wounded, we got off very well. Of the enemy, it is always an almost impossibility to tell their loss, as they bear off their dead and wounded in a remarkably rapid manner. We lost several animals, and this with a few wounded, included our casualties, although during the fight, or skirmish rather, the firing was hot enough to have occasioned a heavy list of killed. I think it was due to the fact of abundant shelter at hand that our casualties were so slight, for upon an open field, I am confident we would have suffered severely, as the enemy were almost all of them armed with Winchester repeating rifles.

Sitting Bull. (*Library of Congress*)

INTERLUDE

Sitting Bull
"A unique power among the Indians"

Sitting Bull in his own words:

I never taught my people to trust Americans. I have told them the truth—that the Americans are great liars. I have never dealt with the Americans. Why should I? The land belonged to my people. I say I never dealt with them—I mean I never treated with them in a way to surrender my people's rights. I traded with them, but I always gave full value for what I got. I never asked the United States government to make me presents of blankets or cloth or anything of that kind. The most I did was to ask them to send me an honest trader that I could trade with, and I proposed to give him buffalo robes and elk skins and other hides in exchange for what we wanted. I told every trader who came to our camps that I did not want any favors from him—that I wanted to trade with him fairly and equally, giving him full value for what I got—but the traders wanted me to trade with them on no such terms. They wanted to give little and get much. They told me that if I did not accept what they would give me in trade they would get the government to fight me. I told them I did not want to fight.[74]

From Major James M. Walsh of the Northwest Mounted Police:

In point of fact he is a medicine man, but a far greater, more influential medicine man than any savage I have ever known. He has constituted himself a ruler. He is a unique power among the

Indians. . . . Sitting Bull has no traitors in his camp; there are none to be jealous of him. He does not assert himself over strongly. He does not interfere with the rights or duties of others. His power consists in the universal confidence which is given to his judgment, which he seldom denotes until he is asked for an expression of it. It has been, so far, so accurate, it has guided his people so well, he has been caught in so few mistakes, and he has saved even the ablest and oldest chiefs from so many evil consequences of their own misjudgment, that today his word, among them all, is worth more than the united voices of the rest of the camp. He speaks. They listen and they obey.[75]

In the words of Abbot Martin Marty, a missionary:

Sitting Bull was proud that he knew nothing of the language and customs of the pale face, and avoided learning them. He obtained and maintained supremacy over his tribe simply by superior natural cunning. He was essentially a demagogue, following the will of the majority instead of shaping their opinions. He was originally a medicine man, and the warriors rallied around him because they discovered in him the qualities of personal courage and shrewdness. He was never chosen chief, nor do the Sioux ever elect a chief. They simply follow the man they believe to possess superior wisdom until they lose faith in him, when they rally around some other person who happens to have the ascendancy in their good opinions. One secret of Sitting Bull's long continued popularity is his extreme reserve and apparent humility. He is among the poorest of his tribe. . . . He was also very devout, according to the savage idea of devotion, and this quality won him respect. He observed with strict fidelity all the ceremonies of his pagan religion, such as the sun dance and the new moon dance. He worships the sun, the moon and earth, and believes that he hears the voice of God in the wind and the roar of waters. His personal habits are simple by choice as well as by necessity. He despises the costumes of civilization. A shirt, a pair of leggings, moccasins and a coarse blanket is all he wants. Buffalo meat is all the food he will eat. Whiskey he looks upon as the drink of evil spirits and will not taste it. He is as unostentatious in his manner as he is simple in his habits. He exacts no deferential treatment and lays no claim to being chief, though he is implicitly obeyed.[76]

And lastly, President Grant:

Correspondent—Mr. President, do you share the general admiration for Sitting Bull as a tactician—as an Indian Napoleon?
The President—Oh no! He is just as wily as most of the Indians who will never fight our troops unless they have them at a decided disadvantage.[77]

4

The Battle of the Rosebud

"It looks as if wars with the Indians are unavoidable, and that the summer is to be occupied by the troops in killing off the restless Sioux. General Crook's command is on the march, and the plains ere long will be the scene of more bloodshed and more extermination. Another Centennial year will see the Indians entirely off the face of this continent, and their wars of today but a memory to the descendants of those who are now engaged in the work of fighting them."—Untitled clipping, *Brooklyn Daily Eagle*, May 30, 1876

"The Indian allies filed forward in a quiet, dignified manner and I noticed the war coloring of black and red upon their faces lending a sinister expression to their stern, dark appearance."—Charles St. George Stanley's recollection of the Indian scouts on June 16, *Colorado Miner*, June 29, 1878

The skirmish at Tongue River Heights, twelve days out from Fort Fetterman, served as a good training exercise for the troops. At least that was the opinion of Lieutenant John G. Bourke, Third Cavalry, who was General Crook's aide-de-camp. As a matter of fact, he wished the Sioux and Cheyennes would "make attacks of this kind every night." He wrote, "No greater advantage can accrue to young troops than to keep them constantly under fire; they learn the importance of implicit obedience to authority, of keeping constantly in readiness for instant attack or defense and above all things of saving their ammunition."[1]

The fight also demonstrated one of the problems of Indian warfare, a problem that would plague participants throughout the Indian Wars, and particularly survivors of the battle of the Little Big Horn: the frequent inability to get a semiaccurate count of their Indian foes. As pointed out in the last chapter, estimates of the number of warriors engaged on June 9 ranged from twenty-five to one hundred, with one man claiming he saw an improbable two hundred who were "moving incessantly." A difference of twenty or twenty-five would be reasonable, but a difference of seventy-five or one hundred is hard to reconcile. The Indians who mixed it up with Crook at Tongue River Heights turned out to be a party of Cheyennes led by Little Hawk. They were from a village at the confluence of Muddy Creek and the Rosebud, looking to run off horses, not for a fight, so in all probability their numbers were on the low side.[2]

Two days after the Tongue River affair, Crook dropped back sixteen miles south to the mouth of Goose Creek. As Wasson recorded, the mood of the command was somewhat uneasy. The general and others were "in the throes of anxiety over the non-arrival of the Crow and Snake allies [and the three scouts who had gone to meet them]."[3]

However, on June 14, the mood of the bivouac brightened when the Indian allies, in company with Captain Burt, who had gone out to meet them, rode into camp. Wasson described the afternoon's events:

About 2 p.m. the camp was awakened from its sleepy condition by the sudden appearance of Gruard [Grouard] and Richard, scouts, accompanied by Mountain Feather, one of the leading Crow Indians, and bringing the joyful intelligence that in a very few hours over 170 Crow warriors would arrive.[4] A deputation was detailed to go out and meet them. By 6 o'clock the party, headed by Capt. Burt, came into camp, stacked their arms about 100 yards south of headquarters, proceeded to erect tepees, and generally settle down as part and parcel of the expedition. The motley group was the center of curious interest on the part of soldiers, teamsters and packers. These Indians all have good arms of their own, mostly Sharps car-bines, with a few Springfield needle-guns and other breech-loaders, besides revolvers.[5] They are generally well supplied with ammunition. The terms on which they join the expedition are economical enough for the Government; the latter is to furnish them with rations, and their wages are to consist of what they capture from the enemy. Rations of hard bread, sugar and coffee were dealt out to them at once, and it was an interesting ceremony to see the head men serve out the supplies to their companions. Most of the Crows are large and of good physique, and the tribe is noted for a comparatively light complexion and its boast of never having killed any white men. By sundown the same day the Snakes, 86 in number, rode up to headquarters.[6] The Crows bring the report that a part or all of Gen. Gibbon's command had reached the Yellowstone River opposite the Sioux village, but had not succeeded in getting across the river.[7] Nothing has yet been heard of Gen. Terry's command. Gen. Crook has decided to cut loose from both wagons and packs, mount every available man on horses and mules, and seek the Indians. It is 90 miles at least to where the Sioux camp is, or was lately; and only by the most rapid and desperate of marches can the village be reached and surprised under the most favorable conditions.[8]

Correspondent Strahorn offered this interesting sketch of the arrival of the Crows and Shoshones, noting not only their importance to the campaign, but the importance of the commissary department to the Indian scouts:

Gen. Crook's long looked-for Indian allies, numbering 180 Crows and 80 Snakes, arrived in camp on the evening of the 14th inst. The event was hailed with more rejoicing than would have been the arrival of thrice the number of regular troops, and it was looked upon as marking a most auspicious era—the beginning of the end of a strangely thrilling war of races. The friendly red men came charging and whooping toward the General's headquarters as though their lives depended upon the earnestness of their demonstrations. Many of them were rigged out in war costumes of the most extravagant character, looking quite singular in their blotches of paint, their other wild adornments, and still wilder gyrations. To be a Crow or Snake just then was evidently better than to be a savage King, and to watch each individual as Gen. Crook came forward to extend a cordial greeting was worth more than a view of a modern hippodrome. But to have been a Crow or Snake Indian an hour later would have been only one step more glorious than to have been a gorged anaconda or a stuffed bear, for an attack upon the commissary department was what these gallant braves had long been riding for.[9]

That night there was a big council between Crook and the leading men of the Crows and Shoshones. Many of the whites looked on, fascinated by their new allies. The spectacle caused Davenport to write that the Crows and Shoshones "are eager for Sioux scalps and plunder."[10] Strahorn left behind this vivid description of the proceedings:

Quite late in the evening a council of war was held near the General's headquarters, which was attended not only by all the chiefs and "head soldiers" of the friendly bands, but also by nearly all of the commanders of battalions and companies composing the expedition. A huge council fire was built, the chieftains and officers forming a large circle around it, and Gen. Crook, with his aides and interpreters, standing within the cordon near the allies. The usual expressions of good-will and eternal fealty were indulged in by the Indians, as were also their boasts of bravery and prowess in battle. They would hunt the Sioux as the bloodhound tracks the refugee, and, once found, they would teach our soldiers how to fight, and how to steal ponies. They were informed by the General that all they were expected to do was to find the villages of the common enemy; he would attend to the fighting; they might have the ponies. Returning to their camp near by, a scene as weird as any ever witnessed took place. Many of them stripped to the skin, with huge daubs of paint all over their bodies and limbs, others in their startling and devilish attire of war, and still others in a ludicrous combination of savage and civilized dress, took part in the oddest of odd dances and contortions. Whether flitting and whooping singly around among the dozens of bright camp fires or dancing hand in hand in groups of a dozen or more, the joyful, yelling, chanting mass resembled more a panorama of thrilling phantasies than aught of natural earth-life, phantasies infernal rather than those of another sphere. The inky darkness preceding a thunder storm, and the occasional flashes of lightning giving it birth, heightened the wondrous effect as only such elements can. It must have been well on toward dawn when the last of these thoroughly exhausted natives crept off to his robe or blanket, and more than one good round denunciation did the zealous braves get during the night from neighboring white men who could not sleep for the terrible din.[11]

Crook was now ready for his next move, a bold strike against the Sioux, who, according to a report from the Crows, were camped some ninety miles north on the Tongue River.[12] Wanting to move quickly with as mobile a force as possible, he mounted 175 infantrymen and 20 of the packers on mules pulled from the pack train and wagon train.[13] In fact, Crook, revealing his appreciation for infantry, had expressed his desire to mount the "walk-a-heaps," as the Indians called them, about ten days prior, in conversation with Strahorn:

General Crook has quite a fancy for infantry, and told me the other day that it was quite likely that a company or two of the "long guns" would be mounted on mules this summer and kept right up with the cavalry. Dismount a cavalryman in battle—as he often must be in this kind of warfare—and you have him out of his element, because he will naturally feel that he is lost, and that his sole means of locomotion are gone; but start out an infantryman and he goes ahead with the perfect realization that there is but one way to get out of a difficulty, and that is to fight [his way] out.[14]

But there was a problem. The infantrymen were unaccustomed to riding mules, and the mules were unaccustomed to being ridden. The amusing scene on June 15, as infantryman and mule met for the first time, was humorously captured by Strahorn in the *New York Times*:

The animals were chosen from the wagon and pack trains, bridled, saddled, and in a manner "broken in" during the day. There may have been riders, ancient or modern, more famous than these, but

if due weight were given to the ludicrous aspect of the undertaking we, who were eye-witnesses to this tumultuous affair under the shadow of the Big Horn Mountains, can never imagine a spectacle more novel in itself. Mules and men were green and stubborn alike. There were mules that had never seen a saddle and men who had never seen a mule— only to wish him further off. Slow, momentous mountings and quick, disgraceful dismountings were the order of the hour. Thus 200 gallant infantrymen were either dashing hither and thither upon 200 kicking mules or else a fair proportion were nervously endeavoring to do so. But fortunately there were no serious mishaps, and night found every man ready with his mule and little bundle, anxious for the start that the end might sooner come.[15]

As was Crook's custom, the supply wagons were to be left behind and the men were stripped down to the bare essentials: four days' rations of hard bread and bacon, one blanket, one saddle blanket, the clothes on their backs, and one hundred rounds of ammunition.[16] With the infantry mounted, the command marched about thirty-five miles on June 16 before camping. However, they were no longer pursuing a course down the Tongue, but had marched north and west to the headwaters of the Rosebud, the next river west. Crook explained the reason for the change of plans, rather vaguely, in his official report:

Marching [toward the Yellowstone] from our camp on the South Fork of Tongue River, or Goose Creek, . . . on the evening of the first day's march we came to a small stream near the divide that

GENERAL CROOK'S ARMY CROSSING THE WEST FORK OF GOOSE CREEK THE DAY BEFORE THE BATTLE OF THE ROSEBUD, JUNE 16TH, 1876.

General Crook's column crossing Goose Creek on the day before the battle of the Rosebud. (*Library of Congress*)

separates the waters of the Tongue and Rosebud. We discovered that a small party of [Sioux] hunters had seen us. We crossed the divide that evening and camped on the headwaters of a small stream, laid down on the maps as Rosebud Creek, and about 35 or 40 miles from our camp on Tongue River.[17]

That night the troops formed "in a hollow square in anticipation of a night attack, as the Crows had reported fresh signs of Sioux."[18]

Earlier that day, the Indian allies had taken part in a buffalo hunt,[19] an incident that undoubtedly irked Crook, who certainly did not want to go out of his way to alert the Sioux of his presence. However, as reporter John F. Finerty noted, the general was having a hard time keeping his "wild allies under discipline."[20] They had gorged themselves on so much buffalo meat that they were "rendered utterly useless as scouts for the time being."[21] When Crook requested that they "go forward that night and post him on the exact location of Sitting Bull's camp . . . the savages refused, and, instead, chanted some of their infernal war songs—"melodies" that combine the braying of a mule, the neighing of a horse and the roaring of a bull—to the annoyance of the whole camp, for our men were tired after their long march and wanted to sleep. But nobody could stop their mouths and we were forced to submit."[22]

Crook was in a difficult situation. Fearing the scouts would just up and leave or hang around in a sullen mood, he held his tongue.[23]

The next morning, June 17, the column was moving near sunrise, about 5:30 a.m.

(Davenport:) "The day was bright and keen, a perfect calm pervading earth and air, and the dark pine bluffs in the north, at the near extremity of the Rosebud Mountains, seemed like smouldering embers, a murky haze enveloping them."[24]

(Strahorn:) "The line of march followed the Rosebud—a small, sluggish, almost lifeless stream—with the mountains of the same name immediately on the left and the Wolf Mountains stretching off to Tongue River on the right. Our allies were far out on either flank and ahead so as to, if possible, spy the Sioux village, or at least guard against an ambush."[25]

Now it is time to hand the reins over to correspondents Robert Strahorn and Reuben Davenport, and Lieutenant James E. H. Foster of the Third Cavalry, as they take us through the largest-scale battle ever between Indian and soldier during the Plains Indian Wars: the battle of the Rosebud.

Weekly Rocky Mountain News (Denver), Wednesday, July 5, 1876

CROOK.

THE BATTLE OF ROSEBUD.

AN ABSORBING PEN PICTURE OF GENERAL CROOK'S LITTLE DIFFICULTY WITH MR. SITTING BULL.

[Written by Robert E. Strahorn]

Big Horn Expedition, Camp Cloud Peak, Wyoming, June 20, 1876. The startling boast of Sitting Bull that General Crook need not procure scouts to find him, as he was ready and anxious for an encounter, has already been most strikingly fulfilled—even twice in less than a month after its utterance. And it has been fulfilled by the savage chieftain almost before the General has had a simple opportunity to hunt him. While we have been casting around for a supply depot S. B. has been fixing up his commissary with buffalo, laying in a good supply of ammunition, and fattening his fleetest ponies. While we were starting for his lair, he was also setting out for us, and he was even accommodating enough to meet our entire column half way.

THE BATTLE OF ROSEBUD.

We had made a hard day's march from this camp on mule and horseback, and were just nicely started down the Rosebud next morning (some twenty miles north of the Montana line), when Sitting Bull extended his second welcome. It was about 8 a.m. on the 17th of June, when our Crow scouts, who had been far ahead and on either flank, sent in a few runners with the information that the Sioux were in sight. No particulars were given, but believing it to be only a small hunting party discovered, General Crook ordered horses unsaddled and picketed upon the luxuriant grass to await further reports. We had hardly stretched out for a little rest before brisk firing was heard on our left and the friendly Indians came dashing in with wild whoops, with hundreds of Sioux following to within half a mile of our position. Here the hostiles gathered along the summit of a long rocky ridge, evidently thinking to hold it against any onslaught the troops might make. Three companies of infantry were instantly thrown forward in that direction as skirmishers, while the remaining two companies soon followed. Several companies of cavalry were at the same time ordered to turn the left flank of the foe by making a circuit to their position in that direction. But few moments elapsed before nearly the entire cavalry force was advancing, and a brisk charge directly in the face of the Sioux was being made by the friendly Indians and infantry. There was no such thing as hesitation in the part here performed, and the precipitous heights were carried under a perfect rain of bullets. The summit gained and the Indians swept off in wild confusion, it was for the first time really evident against what fearful odds our brave officers and men had to struggle, while the field was yet not half won.

From here a perfect view of

THE WELL CHOSEN FIELD

could be obtained and a thorough realization of its wonderful advantages to the foe entered into. From the summit of this mile-long bluff or mountain, at many different points, protruded almost vertical ledges of rocks. They were from two to five feet in height and formed a barricade which human hands could not have rendered more effective and secure. Here was a place for the display of true courage both upon the part of besieged and besiegers, and it is one of the anomalies of an Indian's character of bravery to see him so reckless in open fight, and to see him abandon a position so near approaching the impregnable when steadily approached by a foe far his inferior in numbers. Stretching off for dozens of miles in every direction were the pine-covered Rosebud mountains— every mountain its own perfect fortress of rocky heights and cañon creased sides. Below us, on the left, now retreating before the cavalry, were the enemy, and just beyond was a mountain similar to that upon which we stood. Their advance guard of gallant retreaters had already reached its heights and were pouring in a fire at long range both at us and the advancing cavalry. At this

moment the eye could not cover a single mountain near enough to have objects upon it distinguishable without resting upon a band of approaching savages. Right, left, front and rear alike were faced by the incoming braves, and it seemed as though the whole surface of the country for miles around was one vast skirmish line, with its own natives of the forest as skirmishers. It was a general uprising, and mounted upon splendid ponies the Sioux concentrated with great rapidity. Still the General believed that it was only a fight made to prevent our advancing upon the village until it too could be put upon wheels of Sioux invention and silently stolen away. He determined to sweep the field and then make a bold dash at full speed for the tepees of the warriors, which he thought could not be far off. The entire line of the foe, now extending in a semi-circle for a distance of three or four miles, was therefore again sent reeling and scattered for shelter. But concentrating the troops for a charge on the Indian's home

WAS NO EASY MATTER.

No sooner would the commander order one position abandoned than the savages, evidently regarding it as a retreat, would swarm forward from hidden recesses in the hills and rocks, and harass those who covered the withdrawal with wonderful recklessness, courage or whatever it might be called. Nearly three hours had passed in carrying out these advances, counter-movements, etc., when it was finally apparent that nothing but a complete repulse, well followed up, would allow a change of either flank to be made in safety. Thus, while about half of the cavalry force was under full headway down toward where the village was believed to be located, the remainder, supported by the infantry, made a steady advance upon the main body of

Indians, pouring in quick volleys at every opportunity. The overthrow was soon final and complete, the Sioux scattered in every direction, their firing was entirely silenced, and no more seen of them during the day.

ORIGINAL PURPOSE ABANDONED.

General Crook now found a large number of wounded upon his hands who must be cared for; his ammunition supply had been greatly diminished; his rations could not hold out until the Yellowstone was reached if he was delayed by even only one more such an engagement, and for these and other reasons he at once determined to camp on the battlefield for the night and return to this, the regular "home camp," during the two days following. It is plain that to care for the wounded alone would have necessitated a division of the column—which, under such circumstances, was inexpedient—to say nothing of the trouble and disaster which might follow the other exigencies named. The division which had started for the village was therefore recalled and the homeward movement inaugurated as indicated.

HOW THE TROOPS BEHAVED.

Unimportant delays and misunderstandings occurred during the day, as they always will occur in an engagement covering so much ground and requiring so much discretion at the hands of subalterns, but taken from beginning to end the battle was remarkable for display of courage and fortitude on the part of men and officers as well as for a lack of jealously and a general determination to carry the one great end. Time and space will not allow me to particularize now, but the part taken in action by the different battalions must not go unnoticed. The Third Cavalry did noble service under the leadership of Major A.

[Andrew] W. Evans and with Captain Anson Mills as commander of its second battalion. It will be remembered that this is the regiment which unjustly suffered by its record in the Crazy Horse fight last March, because one or two of its battalion commanders failed to carry positions assigned them. The brilliant service rendered by it on the 17th of June only verifies our position that men are moulded by their officers, and will follow an intelligent and courageous leader into destruction itself. The five companies of the Second Cavalry, under Captain H. E. Noyes, reflected nothing but credit upon their regiment so far as they had opportunity to participate in the thrilling scenes of the memorable day. Their entire force, led by Colonel W. B. Royall, can point with pride to its part in what we now believe to be the turning point of the Sioux Indian war.

As for the infantry, composed of two companies of the Fourth and three of the Ninth regiment, commanded by Major Alexander Chambers, it can be truly said that the service of no arm of the expedition could have come in better play. The long rifles in steady hands carried more terror for the savages than carbines could, as the range could be made long and effective as well.[26] Of course this branch did most of its service on foot, but one gallant charge was made by the boys on "mule-back" that was as little relished by the Sioux as it was enjoyed by our own eager watchers. Instances of personal bravery were very numerous. Captain Nickerson[27] and Lieutenant Bourke, of General Crook's staff, were especially notable for their gallantry. The former received General Crook's order to have the large battalion of cavalry on the way to the village recalled when that force was already some three or four miles out, and all communication with headquarters cut off. Every moment was widening the breach; some one of known responsibility must go and as at once without an escort, as troops were needed in the opposite direction. Mounting his horse the brave captain instantly determined to carry the message himself, and carry it he did across three miles of country that had been swarming with redskins only an hour before, and was entirely unprotected then.[28] Lieutenant Bourke led a company of cavalry on a handsome and decisive charge where the foe was to be dislodged from a valuable position, and afterward, far out on the skirmish line, saved the life of a man who had been shot through both arms, and was about to fall into the hands of the bloodthirsty Sioux. Lieutenant Chase,[29] of Colonel Royall's staff, also accomplished some very dangerous rides across exposed positions while in performance of his duty, and evinced no little courage and ability in various ways. In fact there were few of the officers who did not distinguish themselves, because it was a desperate struggle, and to be at the post of duty at all was sufficient to entitle one to endearing credit.

INDIAN RECKLESSNESS.

The Sioux were all splendidly mounted, and so long as pressed did much of their firing on horseback. Some of the most reckless feats of equestrianism imaginable were performed by them within range of the broadsides of an entire company. In numerous instances one or two warriors dashed out from behind their cover of rocks, hugged close to the neck of the pony and half bounced, half tumbled down the nearly vertical banks after a bold Crow, Snake or white skirmisher, delivered a shot or two and like a flash disappeared in spite of volleys sent after them. Up hill or down, over rocks, through cañons and in every conceivable

dangerous condition of affairs their breakneck, devil may care riding was accomplished. One reckless brave got badly pressed by the cavalry, at a certain point in the field, and jerking out his bowie knife he slashed apart his saddle girt, slipped it with all of its trappings from under him while his pony was at full speed, and thus unencumbered made his escape. So closely did the Indians approach our skirmishers at times that they inflicted several wounds with battle axes, lances and arrows, and in one or two instances they closed in upon a brave soldier and got his scalp before his comrades could rush forward to the rescue. They repeatedly courted death by endeavoring to secure the bodies of their own dead. One instance of this kind was plainly visible to many of us. An Indian riding along the edge of a bluff was, with his pony, made the target for dozens of rifles, and rider, pony and all finally tumbled head over heels down the hillside. Two braves immediately sallied forth for the body of their defunct brother, but one of these also fell before it was reached. The other seemed to think one live Indian better than two dead ones, and hastily scrambled heavenward. Another warrior met him, however, and persuaded him to go along on a second trial. About the time the bodies were reached a pony was shot, and both Indians, then thoroughly demoralized, made for cover and reached it in safety. One thing is an absolute certainty, and that is the fact that the Sioux had staked a great deal on this battle and that their fighting was consequently little less than savage frenzy or the fighting of demons.

THE CROWS AND SNAKES AS FIELDERS.

The friendly Indians are blamed for not discovering the Sioux village the night before the battle, and thus losing to our column the grand opportunity of a surprise. They certainly manifested much carelessness and apathy previous to the fight, having their war dances and infernal noises around camp at night, and firing at buffalo and other game to a sufficient extent to alarm the country, in the day time. But a hostile volley once fired and they were different beings. They manifested the greatest delight at speedily meeting their old foes. They threw aside extra luggage, some even stripping to the simple breech-clout, and fairly flew to the hills occupied by the enemy, when Captain Randall,[30] their leader, indicated the time to start. The Snakes were evidently the better Indians from the beginning to the close, exercising more judgment, displaying more real courage, and effecting as much as the Crows, or more, considering the disparity in numbers in favor of the latter. Nevertheless, they all would go as far as a soldier dared, and the Sioux seemed to have a very wholesome dislike of such a combination. As expert as the hostiles on horseback, far more intelligent and fully as well skilled in this kind of warfare, and possessing any quantity of "grit," so long as well backed, these allies were to be compared to nothing so much as a pack of human blood hounds. One of the Crow chiefs rescued a dismounted cavalryman from falling into the hands of the pursuing hostiles by galloping up at the critical moment and fairly jerking him up on his pony, the soldier of course aiding him by doing any amount of hasty climbing.[31] The stout pony carried both men off in safety. A hand-to-hand encounter was also witnessed between a Crow and a Sioux, the latter being quickly disarmed by his antagonist and brained with the butt end of a carbine.

The "Packers,"

some twenty in number, detailed from the pack train and led by Thomas Moore, have received much praise for the share they took in the engagement. They were armed principally with the Sharps sporting rifle and were essentially the sharpshooters for the day. More than a few hostiles owe their death to the great proficiency and careful aim of the gallant little body of civilians. One robust old gentleman among them, Mr. [Dick] Closter, whose hair and beard are white as snow, is said to have made wonderful shots at very long range—from ten to twelve hundred yards.

"Hospital Gully."

Near by the heaviest firing, but more sheltered than points far distant, were the headquarters of the medical corps. The spot was a grassy little gully or nook just below the brow of the hill first assaulted. On one edge of the pretty basin a cluster of small but rich green bushes gave to the place an air of refreshment as the hot June sun added heat to over heated brows. Happening there just as the final repulse of the enemy was made, I saw most of the poor sufferers who were brought in at that time of severe loss. Fifteen or twenty of the wounded were carried there, arranged around the common center, and horses led close beside them to afford even only a little precious shade. Captain Guy V. Henry, of the Third Cavalry, was brought in during my brief stay, his wound being a very dangerous one through the face by a bullet, and at the same time it was reported that General Crook was wounded—a report which grew out of his having his horse shot from under him while the General was at the front directing the movements of the troops. From this point the wounded were removed down by the side of the Rosebud during the afternoon, and every comfort at hand afforded them by Medical Director [Albert] Hartsuff and

Surgeons [Julius H.] Patzki and Stevens [Charles R. Stephens]. In bringing them back to this camp travois were construct-ed in the usual Indian fashion and care-fully lifted over rocks or rough ground. The nine dead were buried there close by the Rosebud in one large grave. The ground was carefully replaced from where it was taken, and then a large fire built over the spot to mislead the savages who would ask nothing better than to know where our silent dead lie.

The Waste Of Ammunition.

Our troops fired over ten thousand rounds of ammunition, and it is believed the Sioux discharged from a third to a half more. Behind a ledge of rocks from where a band of them fired for a little over half an hour, a peck of cartridge shells were found, and other places of concealment were strewn with them almost as thickly. Many of these were the long, hard shooting Sharps, which show another decided advantage they have over our troops. But the marvel of it is how so much ammunition could be expended with so little loss of life to our force. Dodging, and skulking, and scat-tering out, as the savages always do, we could not expect to hand them a very long mortality list, but not possessing that snake-like, weasel-like faculty of being where we are not, or not being just where we are supposed to be, it is hard to see why an average Indian marksman could not kill but once in a thousand shots.

Loss To The Command.

There were nine of our soldiers killed outright, and nineteen severely wound-ed. Besides this there were a dozen or more slightly scratched with spent bul-lets, battle-axes, lances and arrows. The latter are already fit for duty and are not reported in the official list. Our Indian allies lost one [Shoshone] killed and seven wounded.

Indians Sent To Their Happy Hunting Grounds.

Thirteen Sioux scalps dangled from diverse and sundry belts of friendly Indians at the close of the battle. As many more of the enemy killed by our troops were not reached by the allies, and a number were plainly seen slung over the backs of ponies and carried off. The lowest possible estimate to be made of the loss of the hostiles in killed and wounded would therefore be over one hundred, and some of our more san-guine officers place it at one hundred and fifty. The Sioux also lost many ponies that were either shot or captured through their reckless riding. If this does not prove the most bitter pill for Sitting Bull he has ever swallowed, and one which does not result in a severe attack of mental as well as physical dyspepsia, we shall lose all faith in Indian signs.

Sitting Bull's Army And "Dead Cañon."

The number of [hostile] warriors who were detailed to escort us through "Dead Cañon"—of which more anon—is vari-ously estimated at from twelve hundred to two thousand. As four or five hundred either way would hardly have effected a change in the result, we will strike the happy medium and call it sixteen hun-dred. When this regiment and a half of northern braves were first discovered by our friendly Indians they were fixing up a nice mess for us on the castellated walls of "Dead Cañon." This gash with such an ominous name, is situated three or four miles below the battleground and cuts deep and abruptly through quite high mountains. On our course north-ward we would have been filing between the gloomy walls in about an hour from the time of our first alarm, had the alarm never reached us. The cañon is just long enough to comfortably admit the whole column in regular line of march, and whether the game of the Sioux was to playfully roll down rocks from those dizzy heights, or to consume enough ammunition to shoot us down in detail it matters not, since they were discovered and found it necessary to give us a more open fight.

Alter Ego.

New York Herald,
Thursday, July 6, 1876

BATTLE OF ROSEBUD CREEK.

FIRST FIGHT OF THE CAMPAIGN AGAINST THE SIOUX.

THE ATTACK AND RETREAT AS DESCRIBED.

HOW GENERAL CROOK WAS FORCED INTO ACTION.

WONDERFUL BRAVERY OF THE TROOPS.

WHAT THE FAILURE OF THE CROWS COST.

THE RESULT OF THEIR POW-WOW.

A TERRIBLE SLAUGHTER OF THE SIOUX WARRIORS.

THE SCALPING OF UNITED STATES SKIRMISHERS TOLD BY AN EYE WITNESS.

[Written by Reuben B. Davenport]

Military Camp on South Fork of Goose Creek, Wyoming, June 20, 1876. Three days ago the first fight of the campaign against the Sioux in this military department took place. The fighting column marched from the camp, situated at the fork of Goose Creek, on June 16, accompanied by the 250 Indian auxiliaries who had arrived on the preceding day [that is, *two days prior*], and numbered about 1,300 men. The infantry were mounted upon mules borrowed from the pack trains. Twenty mounted packers were also allowed to go, and carried carbines. The cavalry battalions contained 832 able soldiers. The friendly Indians were loaned firearms belonging to the government and their belts filled with cartridges. Old Crow was the principal leader of the Crows and Medicine Crow and Good Heart his lieutenants. Louissant, called by his tribe "Weesaw," was the chief of the Snakes, or Shoshones, who are divided into two companies, regularly disciplined in imitation of the white soldiers.[32] Louissant is captain of one and Cosgrove, a white man, commands the other. They march sometimes in column, and nearly every Shoshone in going to war, carries a long white wand ornamented with pennants or streamers of fur, hair and red cloth. They wear earth-colored blankets and ride usually either white or spotted ponies, whose tails and manes they daub with red or orange paint. Nothing could be more bright and picturesque than the whole body of friendly Indians as they galloped by the long column of the expedition early in the first morning of the march as it wound around the bases of the low foot hills called the Chetish or Wolf Mountains, which were traversed in moving toward the headwaters of Rosebud Creek. Several of the Snakes still carry their ancient spears and round shields of buffalo horn and elk hide, besides their modern firearms. Imagination did not require more than the presence of the brown arid hills and the distant snow-capped mountains to convert them into a cavalcade of Bedouins.

After crossing the sterile hills and leaving behind those stunted thorns and cedars the column stretched like a giant serpent over a green divide, whose surface is undulating as billows of mid-ocean, and which separates the water sheds of the Tongue River and the Rosebud Creek. The country is beautiful. The march was silent as possible, and the column was dispersed so as to avoid raising dust, which might give warning to the enemy. It was hoped to approach within thirty miles of the Sioux village and then to advance on it during the night.

After a weary march of thirty-five miles the column bivouacked at the head of the valley of the Rosebud on June 16. The soldiers placed their blankets so that in sleeping their lines formed a hollow square, inside of which the animals were picketed.

The Signal Of Battle.

On the morning of June 17 the command moved at five o'clock. The Crow scouts went in front and on the flanks, but they had omitted to send forward their spies during the night, although on the previous day they had found indubitable signs that the Sioux were then engaged in hunting the buffalo southward. About half-past seven an advance of ten miles had been made, when, suddenly, Old Crow appeared on a hill near the stream and gave a signal. Soon other scouts dashed into the valley. Meanwhile the Crows were catching their war ponies, stripping off their superfluous garments, and some of them had formed in line and were singing their war song. A halt had been made at the first signal of the scouts, and the order was given to unsaddle the animals, it being supposed that they had merely seen some of the Sioux, near their village upon the hills, engaged in herding their ponies. The two battalions of the Third Cavalry [under Captains Mills and Henry] were resting on the south side of the creek and

the one of the Second [under Captain Noyes] on the north side. Suddenly yells were heard beyond the low hill on the north, and shots were fired, which every moment were becoming more frequent. The Crows were wild with excitement, and shouted to the interpreters that their scouts were being killed and that they must go to join them. After circling on their ponies in the valley for ten minutes they dashed over the hill and disappeared. The firing became more and more rapid. The cavalry were making ready to mount, when scouts came galloping back again, hallooing that the Sioux were charging.

The First Charge.

General Crook rode to the first crest and saw that they were coming forward to attack the whole command in the valley. Orders were given Colonel Royall to lead the battalions of the Third Cavalry across the stream, deploy his troops as skirmishers, and occupy the hills in the possession of the enemy. Captain Henry's battalion of the Third Cavalry, consisting of Companies D, B, L and F, advanced northward up a series of ridges occupied by the Indians, who retired before the steady charge from point to point. At last was reached the top of a ridge adjacent to the highest crest, but separated from it by a deep ravine. The Sioux were in front and were promptly attacked. They occupied also a palisade on the left, about 800 yards distant.

Captain Andrews' company [of the Third Cavalry] had become detached from its battalion and had advanced on the extreme left, and it was employed in checking an early flanking movement of the Indians. Colonel Royall, in advancing, had crossed and left behind him the deep hollow west of the main ridge on which the Sioux first appeared and back over which they had been driven by a line of infantry to a higher crest, stopping [at] its northern extremity.

The troops were going forward with an ardor and enthusiasm which found vent in cheers and their officers were surprised to observe that they were receiving no support from the centre, which was yielding ground and permitting the enemy to turn their fire against the right flank. After checking the advance behind a friendly crest behind which his soldiers lay while pouring into the Sioux a hot answering fire, Colonel Royall was expectant of seeing the advance on his right resumed, as the latter were then apparently beginning to feel a panic. Seeing the long gallant skirmish line pause, however, they [the Indians] dashed forward on the right and left, and in an instant nearly every point of vantage within, in front and in the rear, and to the flank of the line, was covered with savages wildly circling their ponies and charging hither and thither, while they fired from their seats with wonderful rapidity and accuracy.

At this moment the loss to the troops commenced. They opened a severe fire upon the Indians, which was seen to have instant effect, but a cry arose that they were the Crows, and immediately it was checked. Thus was lost an excellent opportunity for punishing them severely. They screened themselves behind elevations and continued a harassing fire. Still the troops on the right did not advance, and the suspense grew terrible as the position was every moment more perilous as the Sioux appeared at intervals on the left flank, charging on their ponies and each time further toward the rear. In the meantime they swept down into the valley where the command had halted in the morning at the first alarm, directly behind the left wing, and, killing a Snake, captured a small herd of ponies which he was guarding. Lieutenant Foster,[33] with a squad of men from Captain Andrews' company, was sent to cut off the Sioux and recapture the ponies. He dashed after them two miles and only halted when he found the enemy springing up so thickly around him that he feared it would be impossible to fight his way back. In rejoining the left wing he rode through a series of ravines, and in emerging from them at full gallop was unfortunately mistaken for a party of the enemy and three volleys were fired at him by the troops. No damage was done to his men.

THE ORDER TO FALL BACK.

As Colonel Royall was determining to make a rapid charge on the heights held by the Sioux, and by desperately dislodging them, extricating himself from his exposed position, Captain Nickerson, aide-de-camp, having made a wide circuit around the hollow lying between the General's headquarters and Colonel Royall's line, dashed down a steep side hill under a concentrated fire, the bullets making the dust fly under his horse's hoofs, and delivered the unexpected order to fall back. The line on the main ridge, backed by a mass of cavalry and infantry, still remained stationary. To retreat into the hollow on the right, which would be necessary in order to form a junction with the centre, was to risk the certain loss of nearly the whole battalion. Colonel Royall, however, obeyed his order to extend his line in that direction by sending Captain [Charles] Meinhold's company of the Third Cavalry around by such a route as saved it from much exposure and then slowly receded from crest to crest, keeping a strong line of skirmishers continually deployed to amuse the enemy. As the retreat progressed they obtained better range upon the troops at every moment, but the skirmishers did their utmost in

firing coolly and with steady aim. It cannot be doubted that their bullets took
effect among the savages crowded on the
high point of the main ridge. Many were
seen to fall and subsequently several dead
ponies strewed the ground. The horses
belonging to the dismounted cavalrymen were led first into the small ravines
in the bottom of the valley.

A DEADLY FIRE.

At this juncture the soldiers felt great dis-
couragement, but preserved their coolness, although death had just begun his
work among them, a murderous enfilading fire causing them to drop every
moment. Captain [Peter] Vroom,
Lieutenant [Charles] Morton and
Lieutenant [Henry R.] Lemly, of the
Third Cavalry, took places in the skirmish line when the enemy were within
range and used their carbines with effect.
Unwilling to let slip an opportunity for
helping the extrication of the left line,
with which my own fate was identified
by the chance of battle, I dismounted at
several points during our retreat and
fired with the skirmishers. At last, when
the receding line reached the last ridge
next to the fatal hollow, it became evident that the sacrifice of a few lives was
inevitable for the salvation of many
more. Colonel Royall sent his adjutant,
Lieutenant Lemly, through the storm of
bullets to ask a support of infantry to
protect his retreat. About the same
moment Captain Guy V. Henry, who
had remained at the head of his battalion
under the hottest fire, was horribly
wounded in the face. He was lifted from
his horse and led to the rear by two of his
soldiers. The tide of retreat now grew
more excited and turbulent, and I was
pressed back with the soldier attending
me, over the rearward crest upon the
slope, which was raked by an oblique fire
from the north.

The infantry which was expected to
relieve this line was not in position soon
enough to check the wild advance of the
Sioux, who, observing the retiring body
becoming crowded together on the edge
of the gap which it must cross under fire,
rushed both down and up the valley on
the right while they poured their fire
from the high bluff across the low elevation, rendering it utterly untenable,
while they were charging at the same
time to prevent its abandonment. A
swarm of Sioux were within 1,000 yards
of me in front and I heard their shots in
the rear as they murdered the poor soldiers of the rear guard of the retreat.[34] I
was obliged either to take the chance of
death then or wait to cross with the battalion, which would attract a still more
fatal fire, because it would form a large
mark for the aim of the enemy. The hill
where the General's headquarters were
and a large body of troops which had not
yet been engaged was more than half a
mile distant. I chose the converging
ravines and rode through them a greater
part of the way, but as I galloped up the
slope opposite the one I had left I heard
the yells of the savages close behind, and
the reports of their rifles, as I emerged
from the safer ground, sounded remarkably near and loud.

BUTCHERING THE TROOPS.

Looking behind I saw a dozen Sioux surrounding a group of soldiers who had
straggled behind the retreat. Six were
killed at one spot. A recruit surrendered
his carbine to a painted warrior, who
flung it to the ground, and cleft his head
with a stroke of the tomahawk.[35]
William W. Allen [Third Cavalry], a
brave, old soldier, who had been twenty
years in the army, fought with magnificent courage, and was killed. The Sioux
rode so close to their victims that they
shot them in the face with revolvers and

Charge of the Sioux on Colonel Royall's position. (*Library of Congress*)

the powder blackened the flesh. Captains Burrowes and Burt's companies of [Ninth] infantry by this time were firing well directed volleys from a position half way down the west side of the high bluff, and just after my escape the Snake Indians, gallantly led by their chiefs, Louissant and Cosgrove, dashed with thrilling shouts into the hollow, among the Sioux who were on the rear of the cavalry, and drove them back. Captain Henry, weak from the bleeding of his wound, had been unable to keep up with the retreat and had sunk on the ground. Louissant put himself astride the body and for five minutes kept the Sioux off, when some soldiers of his company rushed back and rescued him. About the same time a corporal of F Company, of the Third Cavalry, made a last charge, with three men, and captured from the enemy the bodies of their comrades, thus saving them from the scalping knife. The Snakes took two scalps from the Sioux whom they killed in the hollow, and swung them, fresh and bleeding, with gleeful triumph above their heads as they returned. The infantry under Captains Burrowes and Burt executed their part admirably.

It remains to be said of the portion of the engagement which I have thus far described that it was the most important and dangerous, and that in it Captain Henry's battalion of the Third Cavalry and Captain Andrews' company of the Second [Third] Cavalry, with all their officers, displayed a most honorable degree of fortitude and bravery. They had a more arduous duty and suffered more severely than any other portion of the command. Colonel Royall was circumscribed by orders in every one of his movements, and the disaster attending the retreat would have been much greater had it not been so skillfully directed by him. On the left of his line was a lofty crescent-shaped palisade, toward which, early in the morning, he deployed skirmishers. Had the order to fall back [as ordered by General Crook] been a little later this [position] would have been occupied [by soldiers]. It would then have been impossible for the Sioux to have circled around to the rear, and a fire could have been turned upon the last high point held by them, which would have compelled them to hide behind it, while the cavalry could have charged up the hollow and reached them before they could realize their predicament. Then the soldiers could have dismounted and fired such volleys as would have ended the fight and made it a chase.

The Fight On The Right.

It is now time to glance at the other portions of the field, where there were three times as many troops as were on the left, and yet where there was hardly any fighting, except that done by successive lines of skirmishers, which held the southern end of the great ridge.

In the morning, after the Crows and Snakes had rushed forward to meet the Sioux, Captain Kane's[36] company of infantry was first ordered forward to the top of the nearest hill. From that point it commenced firing. The Sioux were seen in great numbers beyond, covering every summit, and were engaged with the friendly Indians in a warm fusillade. The infantry advanced toward the high ridge, resting upon each successive elevation, which they mounted to discharge volleys into the groups of the enemy occupying still higher points. Captain Noyes, in command of the battalion of the Second Cavalry, composed of companies A, B, D, E and I, saw the importance of carrying a portion of the main ridge immediately before the Indians could advance further south and attack the column in

the valley, where a portion of the cavalry was not yet mounted. He, therefore, advanced before receiving any orders, passed the right flank of the infantry and took a knoll beyond them.

The friendly Indians had been carried by the impetuosity of their first charge far beyond the front of the infantry, and a party of the Snakes seemed to be fighting independently on a cone-shaped mound, just visible two miles away. As the sequel showed, they killed and scalped a small party of Sioux there, and held their ground until the troops advanced beyond them. The Crows and the rest of the Snakes were between the troops and the Sioux, and it was feared that the bullets intended for the latter would strike our allies. After great shouting by the interpreters of General Crook's wishes they retired running, as if in flight. The Sioux, as well as the cavalry on the left, mistook the movements, and the former became extremely bold and advanced in swarms. It was then that Colonel Royall's line found itself too far ahead in the very midst of the enemy. Captain Mills' battalion of the Third Cavalry, composed of companies A, E, I and M, which had been ordered to make the first charge, now advanced through the battalion of the Second Cavalry, deployed in a skirmish line and charged the point above where the smoke of the Indian rifles was growing dense. It was carried with inspiriting shouts, and the Sioux ran back to another, still higher, apex. The hostile lines were here face to face, although each availed itself of the protection of the stony summits. Volley after volley was exchanged between them, and the Sioux lost several of their warriors. General Crook saw thirteen of them fall.

Early in the engagement a squadron of the Third Cavalry, comprising companies C and G, under command of

Captain Van Vliet, had occupied a steep bluff on the south side of the stream to protect the troops in the bottom while they were saddling their horses. It was withdrawn as soon as the whole command was engaged in the forward movement, and was now posted on the high ridge, dismounted and ready for action in the rear of Captain Mills' line. The Indians meanwhile were flocking to a butte northeast of this position, and had opened fire upon it.

The Order To Destroy The Village.

Captain Mills received an order to wheel his battalion to the right, advance a furlong, then wheel to the left and charge the steep incline. It was executed with rapidity, and the summit carried, but not until the enemy before dispersing had delivered three heavy volleys at the advancing line. The battalion, after halting on the bluff, was ordered by General Crook to advance directly through the canyon of the stream northward, toward the supposed locality of the Sioux village. By transposition of the forces it now formed the right of the command, and the Second Cavalry battalion was ordered to follow it as a support. The General directed that the battle in progress should be ignored by this wing of the command and that it should capture and destroy the village. Frank Gruard was ordered to ride in the front and select the route of march. It was expected that the tepees of the bands of Sitting Bull and Crazy Horse would be found only ten miles distant. Hardly had the first battalion moved away when Captain Noyes was sent a counter order, based upon a new report brought to General Crook by a Crow, that the village was in an exactly opposite direction. Captain Nickerson, aide and acting assistant adjutant general, was despatched at full gallop to check

Captain Mills' advance, and overtook him only after a chase of five miles, during which he was accompanied by a solitary orderly. The two battalions recalled were ordered to positions to protect the rear and command the valley where the morning halt had been made.

The Last Effort Of The Sioux.

The Indians, after the withdrawal of Captain Mills' battalion from the long ridge, had regained the crest which he evacuated, and engaged Van Vliet's squadron at the same time that they poured a terrible fire into Colonel Royall's line on the left, compelling him, after holding his position at a disadvantage so long and with such brave retaliation, to order at last a rapid retreat across a deep defile, with the enemy charging both flanks and the rear. This was the last effort of the Sioux. The infantry and Snakes drove them steadily back from the moment that the left wing emerged from its race of the gauntlet.

The Disconsolate Crows.

After the firing had ceased the whole force was concentrated, and it advanced in pursuit of the Indians. It was observed, however, that the Crows remained behind on the summit of a hill, where they were holding a pow-wow. They had captured a pony from the Sioux, which they had left at home in their village and they feared lest it had been attacked during their absence. They also desired to take back two of their braves who were wounded, and to condole with the squaw of a young Snake who belonged to their band and who was killed. General Crook, on learning of their disaffection, determined to return to the point where the battle began and to rest there until evening, so that the Crows might fully determine what they would do. They told him, at length, that they could not stay, but must have their war dance at home over the scalps which they had won. Believing that the Sioux village had been removed during the fight, and dreading to march forward through so rough a country after the desertion of his scouts, General Crook determined in the morning to move back toward Goose Creek. The object of the scout, which was so unsuccessful and yet not without an encouraging result, was to discover and destroy the village of the Sioux, which the guides, white, half-breed and Indian, agreed in declaring to be on the Yellowstone River, between the mouths of the Rosebud and the Tongue. It proved to be nearer the base of the expedition than was believed, and General Crook's ignorance of its proximity, due to the negligence and inactivity of the Crow allies, who were entrusted with the work of scouting, is the cause of the failure of the movement. The Sioux were certainly repulsed in their bold and confident onset, and lost many of their bravest warriors, but, when they fled, could not be pursued without great danger in the rough country through which their way lay.

THE CAUSE OF THE FAILURE.

Had his scouts proved faithful, so that he could have been prepared to occupy the commanding positions with infantry in advance of the main column, he would have had warning of the concentration of the enemy to impede his course, and could have driven him back into his village and ended the campaign by destroying it. It will be seen that the blame of the miscarriage of the scout belongs to the Crows, whose instincts, vigilance and knowledge of their own country was relied upon to render every move of the force intelligent. On the contrary, their undisciplined frenzy and failure to discover the lodgment of the enemy in time to frustrate their meditated attack precipitated a battle which began with a stupendous advantage on his side and in a spot of his own choice naturally suitable to the success of their method of warfare. The Sioux's strength was masked, except when, emboldened by the disastrous withdrawal of the left wing of the cavalry, they made a dash from both ends of a deep hollow which lay in its way and exposed it to a murderous fire, and suddenly swarmed on the front, left and rear. Then it was that the timely fire of the infantry upon their main body, the charge of the Snakes into the hollow and a rapid pursuit of them for three miles, dismayed them utterly and they fell back and disappeared. Had it not been for their occupation, unperceived by the General, of positions from which they could pour an enfilading fire upon both flanks of the body of cavalry on the left, they would not have stood in the face of the troops a moment after their first charge. The injury inflicted upon them must have been much greater than that which we suffered. Their loss of lives is estimated at about one hundred. There is no doubt that all the northern Sioux warriors were engaged in the battle, and it is believed that they have been severely crippled.

New York Daily Graphic,
Thursday, July 13, 1876

BATTLE OF THE ROSEBUD.

A THRILLING DESCRIPTION OF GENERAL CROOK'S BRAVE FIGHT BY AN OFFICER OF HIS COMMAND— WONDERFUL BRAVERY OF THE TROOPS.

[Written by Lieutenant James E. H. Foster][37]

Camp on Goose Creek, June 20—From Crook's camp on Goose Creek to the point on the Rosebud where he first struck the river it is upwards of forty miles, and the command made the march in about fourteen hours, and one-half of the route was over a country that for ruggedness and utter sterility almost equals the worst part of the Bad Lands. Upon going into camp on the night of the 16th the command was formed in a hollow square, with the animals in the centre. The morning broke without incident worthy of special mention, and at six o'clock the column—the Third Cavalry on the left bank and the Second Cavalry and infantry on the right—began its march down the stream. The Crows and Snakes deployed in the advance and on the flanks. After marching about three miles in this order the command was halted, unsaddled, and ordered to graze their horses, it being understood that the Crows and Snakes had found signs indicating that we were in the vicinity of the large village that we were in search of.

At this time the common opinion was that we were to remain where we were all day in bivouac and at night make a swift march on the enemy, attacking at daybreak in the morning. But Sitting Bull, whom we afterwards found was then waiting for us to enter the narrows of the Rosebud a few miles further down, he having occupied the crests of the precipices on either side, finding that we had halted and evidently intended to remain where we were for the present, gathered his warriors and, sending a large body around to occupy the bluffs south of us, made a strong push with the main force right for our camp, evidently hoping to be upon us before we could saddle up and to sweep the field in one grand rush.

A dropping, desultory fire on our right first announced that the Sioux were in the vicinity, and this rapidly swelling to a heavy skirmish fire, together with the return of the Snakes and Crows who came rushing pell-mell into camp closely pursued, showed that we had before us one day earlier than we had anticipated a fight with the main fighting force of the Sioux nation. In the mean time we had all saddled up. The Second Cavalry dismounted, and the infantry—all deployed as skirmishers—pushed for and recaptured the heights north of camp, and the infantry swinging to the left gallantly carried the high hill marked "A" in the sketch of the field [see map on page 95]. Van Vliet, with his own and Crawford's troops of the Third, charged for the bluffs south of the camp, reaching them just in time to repulse a strong body of the enemy who had been sent to occupy them, and held the position until ordered positively to withdraw by General Crook, who desired to concentrate the whole command on the hill and ridge marked "A," in order to make a dash at the village, which was said to be seven miles further down the creek.

Colonel Royall, with Mills's battalion, consisting of Mills's, Sutorius's, Andrews's, and Lawson's troops of the Third, pushed into the valley between the ridges marked respectively "B" and "C," and going left front into line at a gallop, ordered Andrews, with I Troop, to carry the ridge on the left, and Mills, with the remainder of his battalion, to take the one on the right, both of them being held by a strong body of the enemy. The plateau was gained, and reforming, the charge was sounded and the crests cleared with a dash and spirit worthy of all praise, the officers riding gallantly in advance of the platoons, although the retreating enemy were all the time delivering a sharp fire on the advancing line.

Mills pushed on to the point marked "B," when he was ordered to halt and hold the ground won. This he did until ordered by General Crook to join him on the hill occupied by the infantry. Andrews, after detaching his subaltern, Lieutenant Foster, with the second platoon, to charge a body of the enemy further to the left, dashed on under a strong fire with the remainder of I Troop and carried the point marked "C," holding it until peremptory orders came to fall back and rest his left at the point marked "E." The point taken so gallantly by Andrews is a natural redoubt, commanding everything within range, and the enemy afterwards occupied it and annoyed Royall's first line terribly by an enfilading fire.

In the meanwhile Foster, in accordance with his orders, led his platoon, charging as foragers over the valley to the left, and gaining the crest of the ridge marked "H," drove a body of the enemy that held it pell-mell from their position. Continuing his charge, the next ridge was carried in the same style, when wheeling to the right in order to conform to the general direction of the main line, he swept along the plateau, the enemy, though superior in numbers, running before him, firing from their ponies as they gave way. The rocky knoll marked "I" was next charged for and taken, and a sharp fire coming from a timber-clad point of a ridge marked "K," the plucky little party—numbering less than twenty men—was placed under cover behind the knoll marked "I," from whence issued some of the best shots fired on the enemy occupying the point "K." With an abiding faith in his men and horses Foster again advanced, charging and carrying the point "K" and following the retreating enemy along the crest of the ridge, both pursuers and pursued firing rapidly as the movement was executed. Occupying the end of this ridge (D) it was determined to halt and

await the advance of the line, but finding that a body of the enemy were moving along the ridge on his right (L) with the evident intention of intercepting the party the retreat was ordered. The moment this retreat began the Indians followed rapidly, delivering a heavy fire as they advanced, but they were kept at a respectful distance by the fire of the retreating platoon, who fell back deliberately and in perfect order to a point just south and east of "K," which position it was determined to hold. At this moment an orderly from Colonel Royall, and Private [Herbert] Weaver, of I Troop, from Captain Andrews, came up, after running the gauntlet of a sharp fire from the enemy, with peremptory orders to fall back at once and as rapidly as possible, as the Indians were trying to cut off the platoon. Starting at a trot down the hill, at the base of which ran the dry bed of a stream about eight feet wide and as many deep, with steep banks on either side, the platoon had gotten half way to the bottom when the advance of the pursuing Indians reached the crest just abandoned and poured a scattering volley into the party. The order was given to take the charging gait and make for our own lines. A broad valley had to be crossed to reach the left of Royall's first position, and in doing so two men, Privates [James] O'Brien and Stewart [Charles Stuart], and one horse were wounded. The platoon now joined their troop on the left about the point marked "E."

In the meanwhile Henry's battalion, consisting of his own, Meinhold's, Vroom's, and [Lieut. Bainbridge] Reynolds's troops of the Third, had occupied this line, but Meinhold being ordered back to report to General Crook, I Troop extended their line, and the ridge was held as before. The left now suffered from a front fire from the

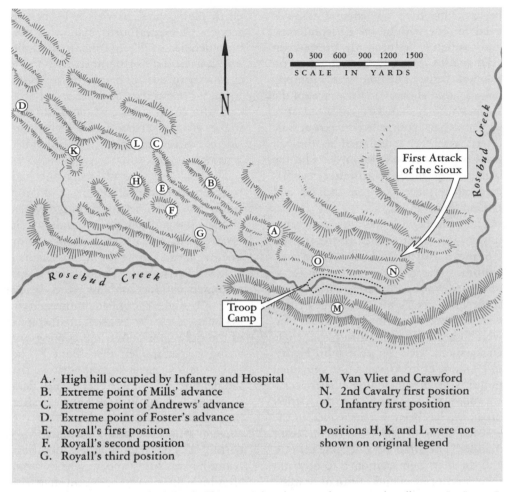

A. High hill occupied by Infantry and Hospital
B. Extreme point of Mills' advance
C. Extreme point of Andrews' advance
D. Extreme point of Foster's advance
E. Royall's first position
F. Royall's second position
G. Royall's third position

M. Van Vliet and Crawford
N. 2nd Cavalry first position
O. Infantry first position

Positions H, K and L were not
shown on original legend

The battleground along Rosebud Creek. This map is based on one that was used to illustrate Lt. James E. H. Foster's dispatch published in the July 13, 1876 edition of the *New York Daily Graphic.*

ridge "B" and a fire by the Indians that occupied "L" and "C." At one time a number of men in this part of the line started to go back. Being strongly appealed to by the officer in charge, one of them turning about said: "All right, Lieutenant, if you say stay, we'll stay." They went back and remained without a murmur until the positive order came to abandon the position and fall back.

This retrograde movement was made on foot, and the enemy, occupying the position just abandoned, fired steadily and heavily on our retreating line. Occupying the second line, the enemy not only pressing us in front but getting on our flanks, Royall refused the left of his line and held on stoutly against from 500 to 700 Indians, until again the order came to fall back from the commanding general. The men and officers, not knowing the object of the withdrawal and knowing well that Royall's immediate command were not whipped, naturally supposed that some disaster had happened on the right. Again the retreat began. This time the enemy, emboldened by our withdrawal a second time and evidently reinforced, pressed on even harder than before, coming in on the left flank. The line was promptly halted, faced about, and the braver of the savages who had pressed on in advance of the others compelled to retire. The retreat was then continued to the last position, which was destined to be the scene of the fiercest encounter that has ever taken place between Indians and United States troops.

The officers with the four companies under the immediate command of Colonel Royall—Henry, Andrews, Vroom, Reynolds, and Foster— remained mounted, and, although a conspicuous mark for the enemy's rifles, were on the line with their men, who were fighting on foot, during the whole engagement. First Sergeant John Henry, of I Troop, Third Cavalry, also remained mounted in the line doing efficient service and displaying courage of the highest order. He has been recommended to the consideration of the department commander. The affair now became serious, and the men were cautioned to husband their ammunition and to fire only when they had a fair assurance of hitting their man. A few minutes had only elapsed when, with their wild yell[s], firing as they came, a vast mess of savages dashed at the line. The men received them steadily and, pouring in volley after volley, drove them back in confusion to their cover in the rocks and ravines beyond the slope. One warrior was left dead on the field within fifty yards of the line, the others that were hit either holding on to their ponies or being carried back by their companions. By this time the four companies, that had averaged about forty men each at the opening of the fight, were so depleted by casualties and details necessary to carry the wound-ed to the hospital, as well as losing the services of every fourth man who had been detailed in the morning to hold the lead horses, did not number in all more than sixty or seventy men, whilst in their front, if the estimate of experienced officers who could see the whole field from higher ground further back is to be considered, there were upwards of 700 Sioux warriors.

The Indians, who all the while had kept up a steady rolling fire from the front, now extended their line down a ravine on our right flank, rendering it necessary to refuse that portion of our line, which was done promptly. Colonel Guy V. Henry, of the Third Cavalry, was wounded by this enfilading fire, being shot through the head immediately below the eyes, the ball striking the apex of the right cheek bone and coming out at the apex of the left cheek bone.[38] The gallant fellow never lost his seat in the saddle, but rode slowly back to the field hospital, and would have returned after having the wound dressed but that the surgeon in charge positively refused to permit it. Poor Henry knew not how badly he was hurt, and was ready even after his wound to go back and share the then probable fate of Royall and the battalion of the gallant Third horse. The slanderous assertions that were made in regard to the regiment for the alleged acts of one of its companies at the affair of Powder River, which assertions had been published in journals like the New York *Tribune*, induced the line officers with Royall to expose themselves unnecessarily—facing death with a laugh and a passing joke, and with an utter recklessness that may be charming to those who admire high courage and unquenchable pluck, but that induced General Crook to say that he did not desire that *such* officers should throw their lives away. He knew the stuff they were made of and felt satisfied that they would "stay put" wherever they might be ordered. And so it can be said of the balance of the Third and the gallant old Second Dragoons. If either had been on "Royall's line" that day they would have behaved as bravely as the men who, with their brave commands, so nobly held their position against ten to one.

The firing was now terrific, the repeating rifles used by the Indians enabling them to make it one continuous volley. Officers who were through the war and were there say that they never in their experience saw anything hotter. Again the Sioux advanced. With their "Yip! yip! hi-yah! hi-yah!" urging their ponies to their utmost speed, they came in myriads from the ravine on our right. Facing by the right flank and breaking to the right and left in open order the men gallantly poured in volley after volley, and again the pride of the Sioux nation were dragged in the dust and drenched with their best blood. Returning to their cover, they again endeavored to shake the everlasting courage of the gallant little band by their scorching fire. Men, brave men and true, were falling every moment. The wounded were carried back to the hospital by details called from the line, which, growing thinner and thinner, seemed to be dwindling so constantly that annihilation was apparently but a question of time.

"Better to die right here than back in the ravine," said one officer to another. "It's only a question of cartridges," said a soldier to his comrade, who stood by him in the line.

Royall sent Lieutenant Lemly, of his staff (who already had a horse shot), at a gallop back to General Crook asking for help. Already the order had come to retire, but seeing no way to withdraw he asked for assistance to cover the retreat of his men to their horses. Morton, acting adjutant of the Third Cavalry, after carrying orders all day through the hottest of the fight, as calmly as though on a pleasure ride, now took charge of the headquarters escort and with them did good service.

At last the supreme moment arrived. The Sioux, massing in all their strength, charged with a yell on the right flank and on the front. For an instant it looked as through Royall and his little band were doomed. The Indians never flinched under our fire, but pressed on, and the worn-out, harassed little battalion gave way. The officers with one accord dashed forward. Sergeant [John] Henry's clear, ringing voice was heard high above the tumult shouting, "Face them, men! [D]——them, face them!" whilst some officers, calling out, "Great God, men; don't go back on the old Third!" raised a cheer, and the line faced about, fired into the enemy at such short range as to almost burn the noses of their ponies, and drove them back almost 200 yards over the slope on their front, the officers riding with and ahead of the charging line.

A lull followed—a season of rest thankfully welcomed by the officers and men. Again it was broken by the enemy, who opened fire as before from the rocks and ravines on our front and right. The order was given to make for the horses and mount in the ravine below, and then fall back rapidly to the hill on which the field hospital had been established and that was now occupied by the infantry and C, G, and B troops, Third Cavalry. This movement was executed at once, Burt and Burrowes, of the Ninth Infantry, coming down from the hill and each firing a volley into the mass of savages that had again advanced when they saw our line withdraw. This aid, though late in coming, checked the main body who were rushing over the crest, but a party of Sioux that had started down the ravine killed and wounded a number of our men while [they were] mounting.

In the meanwhile, before Royall's first position had been abandoned, Mills, with M, E, and a part of A troop, of the Third—twenty men and the first sergeant of A Troop having been detached to act with the friendly Indians—and the battalion of the Second Cavalry, consisting of Noyes, Wells, Dewees, Rawolle, and Swigert's troops,[39] was sent down the Rosebud to march on and charge the village which was supposed to be located seven or eight miles below. They had gone five or six miles when they were overtaken by Captain Nickerson, with orders from General Crook to change direction to the left, come out of the creek valley, and by a detour regain the main body, which was done.

Having assembled the whole command on the hill and ridge to the eastward, marked "A," General Crook started with the cavalry down the stream, but arriving at the head of the canyon or narrows of the Rosebud the Crows and Shoshones lost their courage and refused to go further, saying that the Sioux were as many as the blades of grass on the prairies and would destroy them if they entered the canyon. The column then returned to the hill on which the field hospital, guarded by the infantry, still was, and from thence marched to the old camp, each company burying its dead that evening.

The loss of the enemy can only be estimated. The Crows and Shoshones took fourteen scalps, but as the enemy, owing to our continued withdrawal after Royall's gallant advance in the morning, had every opportunity to get their dead and wounded off the field, their loss in killed alone must number not less than fifty, and perhaps will reach 100.

The ground in front and on the flanks of Royall's last stand was found to show unmistakable signs of the rough handling that the enemy had undergone. Clotted pools of blood back behind the rocks showed where their killed and wounded had been carried before final removal from the field. Sitting Bull evidently intended to have another Phil Kearny massacre; but the breech-loading rifles and the pluck of the officers and men, who fought with such magnificent courage under Royall's able command, gave him a setback.

Colonel Royall has highly commended the gallant conduct of the officers who were with his immediate command, and personally complemented Lieutenants Reynolds and Foster on the evening after the engagement. There can be no doubt that any portion of the command similarly situated would have behaved as well, but as troops D, I, L and F happened to have the opportunity and fought throughout with such splendid courage they certainly deserve and will doubtless receive the honors for the affair of Rosebud Hills. The Third Cavalry have in this affair sustained the ancient reputation of the "Old Mounted Rifles." Soldiers who, when in full retreat before an enemy superior in force, with advantage of position and in arms, will face the foe and fire as steadily and deliberately as though on the drill ground when an officer rides out and commands, "Skirmishers, halt!" must be imbued with the very highest grade of soldierly discipline. Men who will turn again and charge the advancing enemy when to all appearances all is lost and everything in confusion at a simple appeal to their regimental pride cannot be lacking in esprit de corps. Both these things this noble little battalion did.

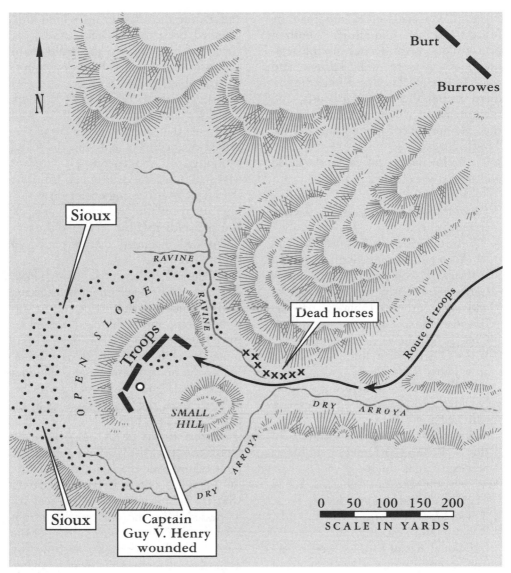

The Battle of the Rosebud, June 17, 1876. This map is based on one that was used to illustrate Lt. James E. H. Foster's dispatch published in the July 13, 1876 edition of the *New York Daily Graphic*.

That evening the sad duty of committing the bodies of the dead to the earth was performed. Fires were built over their last resting places in order that the savages might not find where they had been buried. The night passed without incident and in the morning the column began its march up the Rosebud, it having been determined to return to the wagons [on Goose Creek] in order that our wounded might be taken care of and that additional supplies might be procured. A feeling of sadness seemed to spread over the companies whose ranks had been depleted of some gallant spirits. Especially were Allen, of I Troop, and

Sergeant Marshall, of F, mourned by officers and men. Old soldiers—both of over twenty years' service in the regiment—they were well known and respected by all. They died like true soldiers, facing the enemy gallantly, and their memories will long be green among the commissioned and enlisted of the Third Horse.

The following is a full list of the killed and seriously wounded:

Third Cavalry, D Troop— *Wounded*—Colonel Guy V. Henry, seriously, head.

I Troop—*Killed*—Privates William W. Allen and Eugene Flynn.

Wounded—Sergeant Andrew Groesch, seriously, head, arm, chest, and leg; Corporal Tobias Carty, leg; Privates Francis Smith, breast and leg; Charles W. Stewart, hand and arm; James O'Brien, arm; John Losciborski, arm; James Riley, chest.

L Troop—*Killed*—Sergeant Antoine Neukirchen; Privates Potts, Bennett, Mitchell and Conner.

Wounded—Trumpeter Edwards, side; Private Kramer, shoulder; Sergeant Cook, thigh.

F Troop—*Killed*—Sergeant David Marshall, Private Gilbert Rowe.

Wounded—Privates Town, side; Robeson and Featherly.

Individual acts of heroism were of frequent occurrence during the progress of the action, among which was the feat performed by Old Crow, chief of the Crows, who with his people did good service during the day. First Sergeant Van Moll, of A Troop, Third Cavalry, being detached with twenty men to act with the friendly Indians, was left at one time far in advance of our own people, dismounted and exhausted. A party of the enemy seeing his desperate position made a dash at the sergeant, when Old Crow, with great heroism rushed down and, taking the sergeant up behind him, galloped back to our lines amidst the cheers of the troops, the triumphant shouts of our allies, and the disappointed yells of the enemy.[40]

Farrier [Gerald] O'Grady, of F Troop, Third Cavalry, accompanied by a small party of that gallant command, displayed great courage in dashing back and bringing off the corpse of Sergeant Marshall in a shower of bullets from the then rapidly advancing enemy, thus saving from mutilation the remains of a gallant old soldier whose service in the regiment had extended over a period of twenty-five years.

William W. Allen, of I Troop, Third, died as such a soldier might be expected to. His horse was shot twice and he was dismounted, and being hard pressed by the enemy he turned upon them, determined to sell his life as dearly as possible. Nobly the brave fellow fought, standing all the while and firing coolly with his carbine, until the Sioux, coming in on either side, shot him down. Allen then tried to draw his pistol, but one of the Sioux, clubbing his carbine, struck the poor fellow over the head, thus ending the unequal contest. Sergeant Groesch, who lay desperately wounded near by, witnessed this scene, and was saved from a similar fate by the timely arrival of the Crows and Shoshones, accompanied by a number of men of his own company, who took him back to the hospital.

Private Herbert W. Weaver, of I Troop, displayed high courage in carrying the order for Lieutenant Foster to withdraw, as in doing so he had to pass over open ground commanded by the rifles of the enemy, thus running the gauntlet of their fire at the imminent risk of his life.

Trumpeter [Elmer] Snow, of M Troop, having both hands disabled by a bullet through the wrists, rode his horse for the hospital. The animal becoming frightened at the balls striking around him broke into a run, and the trumpeter being afraid he would carry him too far and into the enemy's lines threw himself off as he passed near the hospital on the hill.

Private [Michael] McMahon, of I Troop, also deserves special mention. He was in the charge made by the Second Platoon on the extreme left in the morning, and when the third and last charge was made, rode alongside of the chief of platoon, and was first on the ridge just abandoned by the enemy. McMahon was reprimanded for riding ahead of an officer whilst he was leading a charge and complimented for his courage at the same time.

Z.

5

Rallies, Repulses, and "Villainous Falsehoods"

"The battle was a surprise, and the one thing which the whole history of Indian warfare proves is that it is the supreme duty of a commander to guard against a surprise. . . . General Crook had no idea of fighting a battle until the enemy were unexpectedly upon him in full force."—Editorial, "Details of General Crook's Battle with the Sioux," *New York Herald*, July 6, 1876

"There is little rear or front in the usual Indian fight. In fact it is all front, for they circulate on all sides, and shoot from every point which offers a place of concealment. When the Sioux attacked General Crook in the valley of the Rosebud . . . the firing opened in rear, front, and flanks within five minutes of the time the first shots were heard. There are no non-combatants in such affairs as this. One place is as safe, or unsafe, as another, and every man who has a gun goes in to use it, if he wishes to save his scalp."—Cuthbert Mills, In Camp at Fort Fetterman, July 23, 1876, *New York Times*, August 3, 1876

"Crook was met by the entire force [of Indians] on the Rosebud, but by his great foresight and good fortune, escaped a trap which Custer fell into a week later."—Joe Wasson, In Camp at Junction of Yellowstone and Powder Rivers, August 18, 1876, *Daily Alta California*, September 26, 1876

"[The battle of the Rosebud] was a surprise to all as no one anticipated the fact of Indians meeting a large command half way, but then there is no telling what they will not do, and the theory that one white man is as good as half a dozen Indians in vogue on the frontier, in the past, is now exploded, for armed as the savages are with the Winchester repeating rifle, and Sharps (90 grain), they are not an insignificant foe."—Charles St. George Stanley, *Colorado Miner*, June 29, 1878

Following the battle of the Rosebud, it seemed that everyone but George Crook could give an estimate of the number of Indians engaged. Writing to Sheridan on June 19, Crook stated: "They displayed a strong force at all points, occupying so many and such covered places that it is impossible to correctly estimate their numbers. The attack, however, showed that they anticipated that they were strong enough to thoroughly defeat the command."[1]

In contrast, most other participants and eyewitnesses had no trouble giving estimates:

The story in the *Times* carried a dateline of June 27, and Crook's letter to Sheridan was dated June 19, so at some point between the two reports, he finally decided on a number. When he did, his assessment was considerably higher than that of anyone else.

One of the interesting sidelights that developed after the battle of the Rosebud concerned Reuben Davenport, the correspondent for the *New York Herald*, which had described him as having "a quick eye, a clear head and steady nerves."[4] Davenport submitted three articles to the *Herald* detailing the action at the

Correspondent	Newspaper	Estimate of Indians
Unknown	*Cheyenne Daily Leader*, June 24, 1876	1,500
Davenport	*New York Herald*, June 24, 1876	2,500
Strahorn	*Weekly Rocky Mountain News*, June 28, 1876	1,200–1,500
Wasson	*New York Tribune*, July 6, 1876	1,000
Lieutenant Foster	*New York Daily Graphic*, July 13, 1876	500–700[2]
Strahorn	*New York Times*, July 13, 1876	1,400–1,500

Strahorn probably summed up the number of Indians best when he wrote in the *New York Times*:

The number of Sioux engaged is estimated at all the way from twelve hundred to two thousand. Allowing amply for exaggerated ideas, the number can safely be placed at fourteen or fifteen hundred, which would be quite a respectable increase over our own force of a little above one thousand fighting men.[3]

A little later in the same dispatch he added a detail learned in a recent conversation with Crook: "Gen. Crook is now satisfied that he has opposed to him no less than 3,000 well-armed, superbly mounted warriors."

Rosebud, and some of his comments were critical of Crook's generalship. For instance, his June 19 dispatch from Goose Creek stated that Royall "manipulated his men under the difficult and conflicting orders from his superior with consummate skill, although he could not prevent unnecessary sacrifice of life without risking the penalty of disobedience."[5]

And his June 20 dispatch added insult to injury: "Colonel Royall was circumscribed by orders [from Crook] in every one of his movements, and the disaster attending the retreat would have been much greater had it not been so skillfully directed by him."[6]

But it was not until his June 22 dispatch that the reason for his censure and indignation became fully evident. Here we learn that Royall's battalion, which was fighting on the left of the line and with whom Davenport had thrown in, was in the most "dangerous portion of the field" during the battle:

[They] bore the brunt of the boldest and most destructive sallies of the Sioux, without the support from the main portion of the command, [who were] most of the time unengaged, which they sorely needed, until too late to prevent the sacrifice of nine soldiers who were killed and nineteen who were wounded. All of the losses were sustained on the left excepting the disabling of three infantrymen by chance balls on the high bluff in the middle of the field.[7]

And Davenport was in the thick of the action, dismounting several times to take his place on the skirmish line with the troops. He may have been a reporter, but this distinction was irrelevant to the Sioux. His perilous escape from the left of the line was printed in the *New York Herald* on July 6, 1876.[8] Naturally, Crook was less than pleased at being disparaged in the pages of a major newspaper. In a letter to Sheridan on July 23, Crook wrote: "The *New York Herald* has published [the] most villainous falsehoods from the correspondent with this command in regard to the Rosebud fight . . . which are intended to do the command and myself great injustice."[9]

In Crook's defense, Royall must take some of the blame for separating himself too far from the rest of the command to receive prompt support, chasing the Indians from ridge to ridge. From Royall's official report:

I now found myself upon the extreme left with Captain Andrews' company and Captain Henry's battalion of the Third Cavalry (consisting of companies D, B, L and F commanded respectively by Captains Henry, and Meinhold and Lieutenants Vroom and Reynolds of that regiment), the Indians occupying the series of ridges in our immediate front. They were steadily charged and retreated from one crest to another, my instructions at this time being to slowly advance.[10]

His instructions may have been to advance slowly, but he still ended up a mile or more from the rest of the command.[11]

Getting back to Davenport, Lieutenant John Bourke, Crook's aide, referred to him as a "whipped cur" skulking about the camp because of his lack of popularity stemming from his dispatches that found their way back to the bivouac. But Bourke also pointed out that, despite Crook's anger, the scorned reporter was still permitted to remain with the command, receiving all the "same privileges as the other correspondents."[12]

On August 3, the *New York Herald* published another of Davenport's dispatches, this one dated July 23, in which the reporter again voiced his displeasure with the commanding general:

Since June 19 General Crook's force has been idle. But little scouting has been done except in the most desultory manner, and it has been supplemented by no

active movement of the main body looking to the terminating of the campaign.
All the plans of the commander have
apparently hung upon the prospective
accession of reinforcements.
Opportunities for definitely ascertaining
the position and movements of the
enemy have not been improved.[13]

And this criticism was followed
soon after by another in the same
report:

Ever since its departure from Fort
Fetterman [May 29] the conduct of this
expedition has been remarkable for the
contempt shown by the general commanding for many of the fundamental
principles of military policy. One might
have inferred that the enemy against
whom we were moving was impotent
and harmless. The march was unguarded; the camps have not been compact
enough for the most advantageous
defense; the scouting has been without
system; the troops, although many of
them were the rawest recruits, have
scarcely been drilled, notwithstanding
that they have been languishing in indo-
lence for nearly two months,[14] and the
proximity of Indians has not been taken
advantage of to strike them a blow.

At this point the *Cheyenne Daily
Leader* entered the fray. In an editorial on August 9, Davenport was
referred to as "asinine" and his statements as "severely" abusive. But wishing to be helpful, the paper also
offered the following suggestion:

[Davenport] should be sent home at
once, but as it is not probable that this
will be done, we suggest that Gen.
Sherman promote Field Marshal
Davenport, the correspondent, to the
command of the Department of the
Platte.[15] It may be urged that Davenport

is too young to command, but as he is
not too young to criticize, this objection
would not hold water.

In fact, when it came to the battle
of the Rosebud, Davenport's criticisms were not entirely incorrect. His
error was in not showing the proper
tact when expressing them. Reporter
John Finerty also acknowledged that
mistakes were made, but he exhibited
greater diplomacy in expressing it,
and avoided finger pointing and calling out the general by name: "Some
mistakes, perhaps, were committed,
but in a fight which was next door to
a surprise, these were inevitable."[16]

And Strahorn weighed in on the
matter, too, deflecting some of the
criticism from Crook and placing it
on his subordinates instead:
"Unimportant delays and misunderstandings occurred during the day, as
they always will occur in an engagement covering so much ground and
requiring so much discretion at the
hands of subalterns."[17]

As for the battle of the Rosebud,
General Crook would probably be
the first to admit that it was a difficult battle to manage, made even
more so by the fact that, as Finerty
noted, he *was* caught by surprise.
This detail is made clear in several
accounts, all of which make a point
of stating that the cavalry was unsaddled when the bullets started flying.[18]
One anonymous story out of Helena,
Montana, was particularly damning:

[Crook's] camp was surprised in the early
morning after the pickets had been
called in by about 1,000 Sioux . . . under
Crazy Horse. . . . The cavalry were watering their horses and some of the men

were having their breakfast when the attack was made. . . . It was a complete surprise. About a hundred horses belonging to the Third Cavalry were stampeded and fell into the hands of the Indians, including their equipments. . . . The troops . . . fought under a sense of disadvantage all the time . . . and the principal fighting was done by the Snakes.[19]

And it wasn't just the suddenness of the attack that made matters difficult. According to more than one account, the battle stretched in a semicircle for some three to four miles.[20]

The overall style of fighting was best summed up by Strahorn, who described it as a series of "rallies and repulses."[21] The Sioux and Cheyennes would stand united one moment, then "fly to pieces" the next.[22] They "would flee before a steady assault" but "turn with light-ning-like rapidity and plunge into death's very jaws in endeavors to cut off detached parties of troops or [Indian] allies."[23]

Strahorn also recorded some examples of Indian prowess during the fight:

In one case a soldier was scalped before his comrades, a few yards distant, could rush to his rescue, and in another the Indians had killed a cavalryman in a hand-to-hand fight, plundered his body of watch, gun, clothing, &c., and were just about to scalp him as neighboring skirmishers reached the spot. In charging from or back to cover, down terrific stretches of descent, these matchless riders would swing low on one side of their ponies, quickly change position at an opportunity to fire, and again squirm almost out of sight, with evidently no

Fighting from Horseback

New York Times,
September 16, 1876

On the Yellowstone River Near Glendive Creek, September 6, 1876. To any man, unless really an old cavalry soldier, the management of our high-bred American horses under fire and amid the excitement of the battlefield requires almost undivided attention, and the delivery of an effective fire, or indeed any fire approaching to accuracy, from the back of his horse, is a clear impossibility. In several Indian affairs I have observed that the Indians, as a general rule, dismount before firing, or if they do not, their ponies will so quietly stand that the rider may aim and deliver his fire without deranging his piece. The rapid firing from the back of his pony as he gallops around or past an adversary, now erect and in an instant half-concealed as he turns himself on his pony's flank, is of little account and only so much ammunition wasted, except from the usual damage from all wild shooting or chance shots.

—Unknown

thought of being unhorsed. If the ground was extremely rough or ordinarily smooth, the Indian used it to advantage all the same.[24]

One eyewitness was impressed with the swiftness and agility of the warriors when taking the scalp of a fallen foe:

During the progress of the battle I had for the first time in my life occasion to witness how Indians scalp their fallen foe, and it is quite impossible to relate how quick it is done. A warrior, struck by the deadly bullet, drops from his horse. The victor in rapid course runs toward his victim. The docile warhorse stops; dismounting and remounting are performed in no time; the victor warrior touching the ground with one foot only, the other leg resting still on the saddle. A grip for the scalp, a flash of the knife or tomahawk, and a jerk. The warrior is remounted, an unearthly cry is uttered, and a bloody scalp of long jet black hair fastened to the lance and raised high above the victor's head tells that one more redskin has gone to the happy hunting ground.[25]

Contrasting the equestrian skills of the soldiers and their Indian foes, it was Wasson's opinion that: "The average soldier on horseback is a most helpless mortal alongside of the most insignificant savage. The latter will manage his horse without bits, and shoot from the animal with effect, while, were the soldier to attempt it, he would shoot off his horse head-over-heels."[26]

Who won the battle of the Rosebud? Strahorn, after pointing out that the Indians had better arms, not to mention hardy ponies that could "scale heights and descend depths" with ease, thought the soldiers won. After all, the "troops swept everything before them" and drove the Sioux and Cheyennes from the battlefield, pursuing them for several miles. Continuing, he commented: "It will not be difficult to realize what terror this blow carries to the heart of the braves who have never before known absolute defeat."[27]

However, he followed this up a little later with: "If their village was

near, of which we have little proof, their desperate struggle, even if it was not crowned with victory, was to answer the purpose of covering its removal.[28]

That is, even though the Indians gave up the fight and left Crook in possession of the field, practically speaking, they accomplished their goal—they stopped Crook. Of course at the time, neither Crook nor the Indians had any idea that it would be for more than six weeks.

Despite Davenport's criticisms mentioned above, he, too, declared that the troops were the victors: "The Sioux were certainly repulsed in their bold and confident onset, and lost many of their bravest warriors."[29]

Wasson took a different angle. He didn't know who won; he wasn't even sure it was a battle. He wrote:

The battle had lasted over three hours, resulting in nine soldiers killed and twenty wounded; one Snake Indian killed, three wounded, and four Crows wounded. It can hardly be called a battle, although there was ammunition enough expended on our side to have killed the entire Sioux race, and the circle of fire was at one time at least three miles in length.[30]

The final word on this topic goes to Crook himself. In an interview with Finerty on October 26, he said that, notwithstanding that his command was outnumbered: "[T]he troops under my command, about one-thousand in actual strength[31] . . . thrashed these Indians on a field of their own choosing and completely routed them from it."[32]

Crook's report to Sheridan stated nine soldiers were killed and twenty-one wounded.[33] Bourke wrote that ten men were killed, forty-seven wounded, four of them mortally.[34] That would bring the number of killed up to fourteen. Accounts generally agree that the Sioux and Cheyennes lost at least one hundred in killed and wounded.[35] Considering that Strahorn estimated the troops fired more than ten thousand rounds,[36] that's a fairly low hit rate; even lower if you use Finerty's estimate of twenty-five thousand shots fired.[37] On the other hand, the Indians didn't exactly win any awards for accuracy either. Strahorn credited them with firing thirteen thousand to fifteen thousand rounds and was surprised that "so much ammunition could be expended" by their opponents yet so few soldiers killed.[38] It is not known how many scalps the Sioux and Cheyennes proudly waved that day, but at battle's end, the Indian scouts had collected thirteen, eight of which, according to Davenport, were taken by the Shoshones.[39]

The Crows, fearing that the Sioux may have attacked their village in their absence, left Crook the day after the fight,[40] but not before venting their grief from past confrontations on a wounded combatant they found on the battlefield. Davenport described the scene that ensued:

On the morning following the fight, as the column was moving from the place of bivouac, there suddenly arose among the red allies a singular excitement. One of them had ridden up to a dark object lying beside the stream and sat and gazed at it, and after others had joined him, they all chattered wildly together as the South American monkeys when they discover the propinquity of a snake. After gestures and yells they dismounted and brandished knives. Approaching them, I beheld lying on the fresh, dewy grass, under the gentle shadow of a stooping willow, the most horrible object that could meet the eye. A dusky human form, nude and blood-besmeared, was writhing under the knives of the merciless victors. The object was a Sioux who, in the latter part of the fight, had been wounded by a Snake, scalped and left for dead. In tearing the tuft of raven hair from his head a portion of the bone, fractured with a stroke of the tomahawk, had clung to the flesh, and the brain was laid bare. And yet, in the morning the savage was still alive, and hearing the tramp of horses and believing his tribe had beaten the whites, he had crawled out of the gully in which he lay and called, "Minne!" (water) to a Crow who had passed and who he undoubtedly thought was a Sioux. The Crow turned, and his face kindled with a fearful joy. Six shots were fired into the prostrate figure. The head and limbs were severed from the body and the flesh hacked and the bones hewn until there was nothing about it recognizable as human. Infamies too shameful and disgusting for record completed the ghastly climax of horror. It was an illustration of the fiendish ferocity of all the Plains Indians toward their foes. The Sioux practice even more refined barbarities, torturing their victims in the most exquisite manner and making them more dreadful by deferring, by every art in their power, the welcome relief of death.[41]

Undoubtedly, the sight was more than a little repulsive to the observing whites. An unknown onlooker reporting for the *New York Times* recorded:

I observed lying on the field of battle the trunk of a Herculean Sioux, who when alive must have stood between six and seven feet high. His head was missing, his legs were cut off at the knees, his arms at the elbows. But mutilated as it was this gigantic corpse still seemed to ridicule the slender-built pale-face looking down on him. Indian war is terrible.[42]

Another spectator was Charles St. George Stanley, the self-proclaimed "Bohemian of Frank Leslie's staff." Stanley wrote that the scene "beggared description for bloodthirsty cruelty and savage joy," then added: "To witness the scene was horrifying enough, but to watch the diabolical expression of delight with which they dissected the body of the Sioux and heaped upon it every indignity, was terrible in the extreme, and to say the least one can but deplore such passions in the higher animal—man."[43]

After this incident Lieutenant Bourke recorded in his journal (June 18): "The sooner the manifest destiny of the [white] race shall be accomplished and the Indian as an Indian cease to exist, the better. After contact with civilization of nearly 300 years, the American tribes have never voluntarily learned anything but its vices."[44]

Private Richard Bennett, Company L, Third Cavalry, fared no better than this unnamed Sioux warrior. During the battle his "body was disemboweled by the savages and the hands and feet cut off."[45] Another soldier was

"hacked into small pieces" while another was "found with a bowie knife buried into his skull up to the hilt."[46]

No doubt the unidentified *New York Times* correspondent spoke for many of the whites when he wrote, "Indian war is terrible."

On June 21, three days after the Crows departed for home, all but five of the Shoshones followed suit.[47] St. George Stanley recorded: "Their destination was the valley of the Great Popoagie, and their professed reason for going, a fear that in their absence stray bands of Sioux might have played havoc in their villages."[48]

Even though there was talk of them returning at some future date, the fact was that, after just one battle, Crook had lost practically every Indian scout. Writing from Camp Cloud Peak on June 27, Strahorn explained why this was a serious setback to the campaign: "The greatest of all needs is an adequate corps of competent scouts; to move in the dim sight of our present knowledge of the actual whereabouts and numbers of the foe would only be time worse than wasted."[49]

Without Indian scouts, Frank Grouard became even more important to the success of the expedition. Grouard had lived with the Sioux for about six years, originally as a prisoner, and possessed valuable knowledge of the lay of the land and probable camping places.

Early on June 21, the same day the Shoshones said their good-byes, the supply train, under Captain John V. Furey, a quartermaster, set out for

Fort Fetterman, transporting the wounded from the late battle.[50] It was expected back in about three weeks with fresh supplies, ammunition, and five companies of infantry that Crook had requested.[51] About the infantry, Wasson explained: "Gen. Crook believes in having plenty of infantry for hunting the savages out of the rough places. A foot soldier can crawl where an Indian can, and is not bothered in battle with a clumsy American horse."[52]

In a follow-up dispatch written several weeks later, Wasson further detailed Crook's high opinion of infantry: "Gen. Crook values a soldier of infantry, armed with the long Springfield needle-gun, rightly maneuvered, as equal to six mounted Sioux; hence his desire for more infantry before again marching into the enemy's strongholds."[53]

Writing from Camp Cloud Peak on June 28, Robert Strahorn aptly wrapped up the current situation of General Crook's Big Horn and Yellowstone Expedition:

We have settled down to quiet, though really not to contented waiting, for more force, more scouts, more powder and lead, and more "grub." We have felt the strength of Sitting Bull sufficiently to know that this campaign is a far more serious matter than we had even imagined at the start. Three thousand desperate, well armed, superbly mounted warriors, in their own country, are odds our little force of eleven hundred strong might struggle against if necessary, but more troops now best at hand may well be used at such a critical hour.[54]

More troops now best at hand . . . at such a critical hour. A certain flamboyant hero of the Civil War was soon to share those thoughts exactly.

INTERLUDE

"Poor fellows, I'm really sorry for them"

Two days after the battle of the Rosebud, General Crook sent a dispatch to department headquarters in Omaha requesting additional troops, particularly infantry. His message was relayed from Fort Fetterman on June 22, and action was swift, as illustrated below. The following letter was originally printed in the *New York Tribune* on July 7, 1876.

A PROPHETIC LETTER

The following communication from a young New York gentleman in business in Salt Lake City to his sister in this city seems, in view of occurrences since it was written, to be almost prophetic:

Banking-House of Walker Brothers, Salt Lake City, June 23, 1876. My Dear Jennie: This is rather a stirring day among the soldiers and officers here at Camp Douglas, and a sad day for the wives of those who are unfortunate enough to be married, for this morning orders came from Gen. Sheridan to Gen. Smith to start three companies of the 14th for the Black Hills at once. They leave on the 7 o'clock train, and officers and men have been rushing around town today vainly endeavoring to remember everything they need for their outfit. Poor fellows, I'm real sorry for them, for it is more than probable that many of them will lose their scalps before this miserable war is over.

It is reported that Gen. Crook is having a big fight with the Sioux, and that his troops have been very severely handled. I am afraid it is true, too, for the miserable economy of our Government only gave Crook 1,500 men to fight 5,000 Sioux, the fiercest warriors on the continent. They are beginning to see the folly of sending such a handful into that wild country, and troops are being ordered there from all directions. If anybody but Crook had the command, every scalp would be raised before the reinforcements arrived; fortunately, however, he is the best Indian fighter in the army, and will probably hold his own until more troops arrive.

Those miserable Eastern papers who have been yelling "Reduce, reduce the army" will have to change their tune now, for there are hardly men enough in the whole army to whip these Sioux. I suppose that you folks in the East don't pay much attention to the Indian war, but when one sees men leaving their families and starting out to fight these red devils, and knows that the chances are even whether they ever come back or not, it is almost impossible to keep from worrying about them as much as if they were kin. Then you see the Black Hills are only about 500 miles east of this place, and as many Salt Lakers are up there mining, we are always hearing from them, and consequently feel interested, and I have taken it for granted that you are too; but I must not bore you too much, especially as Gen. Crook's fate will be decided long before this reaches you.

6

The Battle of
the Little Big Horn

Q. "Is the steady fire of dismounted troops greatly superior in its execution to that of savages mounted on horseback?"
A. "Yes, but if the Sioux can surround a smaller body they surely will annihilate it. The Fort Phil Kearney massacre, in which the brave Fetterman fell, illustrates their prowess."—Interview with a newspaper editor, "An Editor's Sentiments," *New York Herald*, May 20, 1876

"When Crook, with thirteen hundred men, was unable to follow up a fight with Sitting Bull we may well be anxious over the fate of either of Terry's detachments, numbering less than seven hundred men, if they should meet the Sioux single handed."—Editorial, "The Hide and Seek for Sitting Bull," *New York Herald*, June 27, 1876

"Custer was a well-made man, rather lean and lithe, with clean limbs and strong hips, and a slender, almost womanly body. His yellow hair, generally worn long, gave him the appearance of a Danish or Norwegian hero— some Viking's son. Few men had less of military hauteur and more military chivalry."—Unknown, "Reminiscences of Custer," *New York Daily Graphic*, July 7, 1876

"[Major] Reno was already engaged in the valley below, and as Custer rode along the ridge above him he raised his hat, and a cheer to their comrades burst from the throats of the 250 men who were following the standard of their beloved commander. On down the ridge with Custer they rode, over a little ridge, disappeared from sight, and we never saw them again alive. That cheer was the last sound we ever heard from their lips."
—Anonymous soldier with the Seventh Cavalry (In Camp at the Mouth of the Big Horn), July 5, 1876, *New York Herald*, July 30, 1876

"Sitting Bull is regarded as a very able leader and skillful evolutionist. His tribe is as thoroughly trained as any civilized crack corps. In past seasons he has been drilling his braves, imitating the movements of our men while at parade or practice. The way he surrounded Custer was masterly."
—Interview with Thomas Harrington, late of the Seventh Infantry, *New York Herald*, August 21, 1876

"Custer alone, with half a dozen men, was making his last stand. Then Custer remained alone for a moment, finally falling, pierced by numerous bullets and lying undisturbed among that yellow horde, which regarded him with awe as some powerful agency of the Evil Spirit. There he lay, even as did the Custer of a quarter of a century ago, his yellow locks undisturbed, his face marred only by the battle smoke, and his sword in his hand even in death. Such was the mimic battle given at Sheridan last Friday, at once the first and the most lifelike attempt to reproduce the Custer massacre."—"Reproduction of the Custer Massacre," *New York Times*, July 6, 1902

"Permit me to be very plain. . . . There was no massacre. There was no killing of defenseless people. The Little Big Horn affair was a real fight in which the whites were badly worsted. They were out to get the Indians, and the Indians turned the tables and got the whites."—Historian Patrick Edward Byrne, Bismarck, North Dakota, January 2, 1924, *New York Times*, January 13, 1924

On July 6, 1876, the headlines in the *New York Herald* abruptly announced details about a deadly Indian battle that had taken place in the western territories not even two weeks before:

"A BLOODY BATTLE"

"AN ATTACK ON SITTING BULL ON THE LITTLE HORN RIVER"

"NARROW ESCAPE OF COLONEL RENO'S COMMAND"

Some of the headlines were hard to believe:

"GENERAL CUSTER KILLED"

"A HORRIBLE SLAUGHTER PEN"

"OVER THREE HUNDRED OF THE TROOPS KILLED"

On June 25, 1876, the same day that Lieutenant Colonel George A. Custer and five companies of the Seventh Cavalry were engaged in the fight of their lives on the bluffs overlooking the Little Big Horn River, the *New York Herald* printed an editorial with the headline "The News from the Frontier—A Centennial War." Ironically, considering what was then taking place one thousand seven hundred miles to the west, it stated:

The Indian, even now, is as much of a romance to us as the caliphs of the "Arabian Nights." We do not know him. We never see him. We are indifferently acquainted with his manners or customs. We question if one in twenty, even of our educated people, could tell where the Apaches, the Utes or the Sioux inhabit. We know in a vague, half-informed way, that out in the vast expanse beyond the Mississippi there still wanders a remnant of those savage men who once ruled and dwelt here.

As hinted at in the editorial's headline, the United States was then celebrating one hundred years of independence, and Philadelphia was playing home to the colossal anniversary bash. Its theme was "A Century of Progress," and on display were the latest technological advancements. Some ten million visitors got their first look at Alexander Graham Bell's newly patented telephone, a mechanical calculator with more than fifteen thousand moving parts, an early version of a dentist drill, and a cable made by the Roebling brothers, a prototype of the one to be used in the construction of the Brooklyn Bridge. Some even tasted Heinz ketchup for the first time.[1]

General Sheridan, who was in Philadelphia to visit the Centennial Exposition and to speak at a meeting of the Army of the Cumberland, told a *New York Herald* reporter that the story of the death of Custer and three hundred soldiers at the hands of the Sioux, news of which was received that morning, July 6, was "so horrible that he could only accept it when it came officially." It was also his belief that when the truth of the story was

known, "it would be found less alarming" than what was first reported.[2] Outrageous stories of Indian battles were nothing new, and rumors spread quickly. However, to Sheridan's chagrin, news of the disaster was confirmed later that afternoon. Meeting with the journalist once again, he was asked if he "had any information as to the cause or the responsibility of the disaster. . . . The General said, with sorrowful feeling, that it was too soon to pass any judgment upon an action of this extent. It would be unfair to the memory of Custer or of any soldier who loses his life in battle to pass an opinion until the whole story was known."[3]

As part of Sheridan's grand strategy to entrap the nontreaty Sioux somewhere south of the Yellowstone and west of the Great Sioux Reservation, the Dakota Column[4] marched out of Fort Abraham Lincoln early on May 17, 1876, to the tune of "The Girl I Left behind Me."[5] Their course was due west along the Heart River. Led by Brigadier General Alfred H. Terry, the column consisted of all twelve companies of the Seventh Cavalry, under Lieutenant Colonel George A. Custer, "the fighting force of the expedition,"[6] (the next two senior officers after Custer were Major Marcus A. Reno and Captain Frederick W. Benteen) two companies of the Seventeenth Infantry, one of the Sixth Infantry, and three Gatling guns, attended by a small crew from the Twentieth Infantry. They totaled roughly 930 men, about 750 of which were cavalry. There were also 150 wagons with teamsters, 200 pack mules, and about 40 Indian scouts, most of whom were from the Arikara tribe.[7] The wagons were carrying supplies for thirty days, by which time the command should have reached the supply depot known as "Stanley's Stockade," several miles above the mouth of Glendive Creek, one of the southern tributaries of the Yellowstone.[8] The depot was under the command of Major Orlando H. Moore, Sixth Infantry.

Custer was lucky to be riding along, or so he must have thought at the time. He almost missed the expedition, one he was supposed to lead until he was replaced by Terry at Grant's behest. Custer had brought the president's wrath down upon himself for what was regarded as hearsay testimony in Washington on the selling of post traderships. The *Doylestown Democrat* of Pennsylvania effectively summed up the situation:

The meanest act of President Grant is the removal of General Custer from his command because he went to Washington in obedience to a subpoena and testified before the Committee on Expenditures in the War Department. His testimony was strongly against Grant's friends [including the recently resigned secretary of war, William W. Belknap], the post traders, and their swindling go-betweens. This displeased the President and he takes his revenge on General Custer.[9]

Commenting on the quality of Custer's testimony, another newspaper remarked: "He . . . testified vaguely and interviewed copiously."[10]

The newspapers had a field day with the entire fiasco, with editorials appearing almost daily under headlines such as "Custer Sacrificed," "Grant's Revenge," and "Grant's Cruelty to Custer."[11]

As the headlines illustrate, most of the press was less than favorable to Grant, who was referred to as a "modern Caesar" and a despot.[12] The *Hartford Daily Times* stated: "The sudden and rude displacement by the President of General Custer looks. . . very much like a mere act of personal vengeance."[13]

And from the *New York World*: "The removal of General Custer from his command by the President is a scandalous performance. There is, unfortunately, every reason to put the worst construction upon it."[14]

And an editorial in the *New York Herald* declared: "Nothing that the President has done of late proves as this 'disgracing' of Custer does how utterly committed he is to the programme of standing by his friends, and it also shows how unfitted he is for the trust reposed in him by the people."[15]

But Custer had his detractors too. The *Troy Times* of New York commented:

General Custer, upon being sworn, stated no single fact of his own knowledge relative to the alleged corruption. His whole testimony was a glib, bitter partisan repetition of camp stories, colored in the manner best designed to injure the administration, and based upon nothing but the silly twaddle of a Western camp. Many of the stories that he told have been disproved by credible witnesses.[16]

And this from the *New London Telegram* of Connecticut:

General Custer was a brilliant and dashing cavalry officer during the war, but his distinguishing characteristic is his egotism. His testimony before the Congressional committee in the matter of the post traderships, when boiled down, amounted to little. It was made up of assertions and opinions and had no foundation of facts to rest upon. The witness went out of his way to slur the administration and his main object seemed to be to draw public attention to himself. The President's course toward him seems to have had the approval of General Sherman and the Secretary of War, and that this is the case furnishes very strong proof that the President did nothing which he was not fully justified in doing. General Custer is one of that class of men who are better fitted for a time of war than for a time of peace. The time of peace furnishes him but little opportunity to gain the notoriety that he craves. When he was called to Washington as a witness, he thought he saw an opportunity for notoriety, and he made the most of it; and in doing this he made a very unpleasant and ridiculous exhibition of himself.[17]

However, the *Milwaukee Commercial Times* gets credit for the biggest miscalculation of the century when it wrote, "General Custer won't get scalped by anybody but the President this year."[18]

On May 6, Custer sent a letter to Grant—ghostwritten by Terry—pleading to be allowed to join his regiment when it was due to take the field shortly.[19] It was accompanied by an endorsement from Terry. In fact, Terry, who had no experience fighting Indians, was keen for Custer to participate in the expedition. As hard-nosed as Grant had been on the issue, he finally relented (but requested that Custer take along no newspapermen, "who always make mischief").[20] Perhaps the negative press also played a role in Grant's decision. Terry and Custer received the news two days later, after which it was telegraphed from St. Paul (where Terry had his headquarters) across the country. The *New York Herald* printed the notice of the president's sudden turnabout on May 10:

President Grant has partially abandoned his original determination not to permit General Custer to accompany his command in their intended campaign against the Indians. Orders permitting General Custer to take the field were received . . . from Washington . . . [on May 8], but General Custer is not to be allowed to go in command of the column, but in a subordinate capacity. It is well known, however, that but for President Grant's interference General Custer would have gone in command of the expedition.

This dispatch was followed up with an editorial from the *Herald*, which included some additional swipes at Grant:

The outrage on General Custer continues to excite the attention of newspapers everywhere. At least three-fourths of them bitterly denounce the President for his cruel and autocratic action against the gallant Indian fighter. Even the papers friendly to the President speak of the affair as one which need not have occurred, and are sorry that he should have been injudicious at a moment when his party depended upon him for wisdom. Something was due to public opinion, which is just now very sensitive to any needless exposure of private spleen in its servants. There are a few papers which defend the President on technical grounds, but the people will not easily be convinced that in punishing General Custer the President did not really commit an outrage on themselves. President Grant is not at this day in a position to put himself in contrast with any faithful military or civil officer before popular opinion. The odds are against him, and he will suffer with little effort on his own part. That he acted angrily and unwisely seems to be his own late opinion for as will be seen from our St. Paul despatch, he will permit General Custer to accompany the expedition, not as its commander, but as a subordinate—that is, General Custer goes in disgrace, being permitted to fight, but to fight only under punishment. This last bit of news shows weakness and apology on the part of the President, but it does not wipe out the stain with which he has covered himself.[21]

In reality, for Custer, ever the optimist, riding along "in a subordinate capacity," that is, second in command, was not such a bad deal. That same day he allegedly told an old friend that he would "cut loose" from Terry as soon as opportunity offered.[22] All things considered, Custer must have regarded this as good news.

Fort Abraham Lincoln, established in June 1872, near the confluence of the Missouri and Heart rivers, was all bustle and activity in the weeks preceding the departure of the Dakota

> ## A Classic View Of Custer
> *Bismarck Tribune*, May 17, 1876
>
> In Camp [at Fort Lincoln],
> May 14, 1876.
>
> Gen. George A. Custer, dressed in a dashing suit of buckskin, is prominent everywhere. Here, there, flitting to and fro, in his quick eager way, taking in everything connected with his command, as well as generally, with the keen, incisive manner for which he is so well known. The General is full of perfect readiness for a fray with the hostile red devils, and woe to the body of scalp-lifters that comes within reach of himself and brave companions in arms.
> —Reporter Mark Kellogg

Column. An anonymous dispatch to the *New York Herald* dated April 30, stated:

The grounds surrounding Fort Lincoln recall vividly the scenes witnessed during the [Civil] war. They are dotted with different camps, made by the companies reporting for duty with the expedition. In one portion the cavalry is located, in another the battery of Gatling guns; then there is the infantry camp, and last the immense wagon train with its numerous attendants. Orderlies and messengers may be seen galloping in all directions, seemingly intent on business of some kind; teamsters earnestly arguing with refractory mules and the general condition of the atmosphere surrounding the fort would convince an outsider most thoroughly that the dogs of war were about to be let loose.[23]

The dispatch also detailed the reasons behind the expedition:

To cause certain bands of the Sioux nation to curb their warlike propensities and go to the reservations set apart for them is the purpose of an expedition now being organized at Fort Abraham Lincoln, Dakota Territory. In the fastnesses of the mountains on either side of the Big Horn River and in the country adjacent thereto there have been encamped for a number of years bands of Indians who have declined the aid offered them by the government, preferring to maintain an independent life and support themselves rather than submit to the care of agents appointed to exercise a kindly surveillance over their welfare. Unfortunately, however, they have not confined themselves entirely to the chase, but have made raids on the settlers of Montana and Dakota, stealing stock, plundering ranches and killing the inhabitants, until they have inaugurated such a reign of terror that their numbers are popularly supposed to be hundreds of thousands instead of two or three thousand.

At all of the agencies on the Missouri River there are numbers of dissatisfied Indians, whom it would be impossible to please under any circumstances. Then there are certain young men anxious to make a name for themselves in order to gain influence in their tribe, and which, should they remain quietly on the reservation, they could not accomplish. From these classes the hostile Indians receive their recruits, and as they are generally desperate characters, without much to lose but everything to gain, they make good fighting men. In addition to these fighting qualities they are well armed with the improved fire arms, have plenty of ammunition, obtaining these from unscrupulous traders, and living as they

do in a section of the country but very little known, it is not to be wondered at that they are feared by the poor settlers of the frontier.[24]

According to forty-five-year-old reporter Mark Kellogg (who was accompanying the Terry-Custer column against Sheridan's orders to not bring along any newspapermen), when the command departed Fort Lincoln on May 17, it was expecting to meet Sitting Bull somewhere near the Little Missouri River, about 130 miles due west of its current position. This was based on the "latest information brought in by scouts from the hostile camps."[25]

But in fact, this information was already outdated. Just seven days earlier, the *New York Herald* had printed a dispatch from Omaha, dated May 9 (eight days prior to Kellogg's report), that stated, "Sitting Bull's village is reported to be on the Yellowstone, at the mouth of Powder River." That's an additional ninety-five miles, more or less, west of the Little Missouri. It is hard to believe that Terry was not aware of this latest information. Additionally, it was reported as far back as January that Sitting Bull had "removed from the Little Missouri some time ago."[26] And that report had been addressed to the head of the Department of Dakota—General Terry.

Kellogg's dispatch from the *Herald* on May 18 went on to say that Sitting Bull had one thousand five hundred lodges and three thousand warriors, typical of the numbers that were making the rounds in the newspapers at the time.[27] "By some this estimate is considered large, but there is no doubt that more hostile Indians can be concentrated between the Little Missouri and Yellowstone rivers than at any other point in the country."[28]

Even if there were three thousand warriors in the region they were marching toward, no one expected to meet them all at the same time. Sitting Bull's name was frequently used synonymously as representing all of the "hostiles," and this often created false impressions of his/their fighting strength. After all, if Terry really expected to find Sitting Bull on the Little Missouri, or elsewhere, with such a large number of warriors, then he marched out of Fort Lincoln believing he was already outnumbered three to one.

The way the rain had been coming down in Dakota Territory, it may not have mattered. The ground had turned into a muddy quagmire, the mules couldn't find their footing, and the command made no more than forty miles in the first four days. Despite the fact that they were still so close to Fort Lincoln and there was no sign of Indians, precautions still had to be taken while on the march. As the contemporary frontier expression had it, "When you see no Indians be on your guard, for they are waiting for a chance to catch you napping."[29] Accordingly, every morning Custer would take three companies and ride ahead.[30] (Not too bad for someone who two weeks earlier had been banned from the expedition.) Additional companies of the Seventh Cavalry rode on either flank.

The Dakota Column finally reached the Little Missouri River on May 29, almost two weeks after starting. The following day Terry wrote to Sheridan: "Contrary to all the predictions of the guides and scouts, no Indians have been found here, and there are no signs that any have been in this neighborhood within six months or a year. . . . Our progress has heretofore been slower than I could have wished, but the force is in excellent condition."[31]

That same day Terry gave Custer permission to take four companies of the Seventh Cavalry, C, D, F, and M, and some Indian scouts, to search for Indian trails south along the Little Missouri River Valley. A dispatch, possibly written by Custer, declared:

Custer's scouting party rode fifty miles in about twelve hours, thoroughly examining the valley of the river. . . . Custer states that not only were no signs discovered indicating the presence of Indians in the valley, but . . . that no considerable body of Indians have visited or passed through the valley within a period of six months.[32]

As if they knew where the Indians were all along, a few lines later the same article stated: "Rumor . . . now places Sitting Bull and all his followers snugly in their villages on Powder River, one of the eastern tributaries of the Yellowstone, and distant from this point about 100 miles."

But one thing was for certain: with three columns now in the field, "gradually converging upon Sitting Bull's strongholds in the Big Horn and Powder River countries," the net was tightening around the nontreaty

Indians and the many dissatisfied Indians who were leaving the Great Sioux Reservation to join them.[33]

A freak June 1 snowstorm kept the command in camp for two days several miles southeast of Sentinel Buttes, in present-day North Dakota, but on June 3 they were once again trekking west. That morning three horsemen were seen approaching in the distance, but no one could make out who they were. As reported in the *New York Herald* on June 27 (again, possibly written by Custer):

The quick eye of Custer was the first to solve the problem. "They are scouts from the stockade," was his remark to Terry. [Terry:] "What makes you think they are scouts from the stockade?" [Custer:] "We have no men so far to our front as those are; two are dressed in citizens' clothes and one of them is riding a white horse. We have no parties with the expedition answering that description; besides they are approaching us at a gallop, and are coming from the right direction to be from the stockade."[34]

The scouts delivered a dispatch from Gibbon to Terry. The news from Gibbon was that he was camped at the mouth of the Rosebud River, that three of his men had been killed on May 23 while out hunting, that Indians had stolen the horses of his Crow scouts, and, almost as an afterthought, that a village was reported "some distance up the Rosebud."[35] For whatever reason, the writer of the dispatch in the *Herald* included all these details except for the story about the village on the Rosebud. Nevertheless, on two separate occasions, May 16 and May 27, Lieutenant James H. Bradley,

Seventh Infantry, from Gibbon's command,[36] had led scouting expeditions that discovered a large Sioux village, first on the Tongue, then on the Rosebud.[37] In other words, the village (or one of the villages) that the three commands were seeking had been located, and it was moving west.

At this point, with the Indians clearly not between the Dakota Column and the supply depot on Glendive Creek (about thirty to forty miles to the northwest), or along the Yellowstone at all, Terry deemed it best to continue southwest from their current position, Beaver Creek, until reaching the Powder, then strike north, downriver, until they reached the Yellowstone. Though unstated, it was a reconnaissance in force. In the meantime, the scouts were told to return to the Glendive Depot with instructions for Major Moore to reload the supplies on the steamer *Far West* and to set up a new depot at the mouth of the Powder River (a.k.a. the Yellowstone Depot).[38] Terry also offered two of the scouts an extra two hundred dollars each if they would continue on and deliver a message to Gibbon: to halt wherever he was on the river and await further instructions.[39]

On the night of June 6, the command camped on the South Fork of O'Fallon's Creek. By the following night it could be at Powder River— that is, if someone knew the best route. Even Charley Reynolds, their thirty-four-year-old guide, was unfamiliar with this territory.[40] Opportunity knocked, and Custer answered:

Taking with him a sufficient number of troops to make a trail, as well as to enable him to leave men on prominent points as guides to the main column, the General started at five o'clock in the morning [June 7], and after a most laborious day and a ride of probably fifty miles, he marked out through the Bad Lands that border Powder River a practicable route for wagons, the distance over which from the camp of the preceding night was thirty-two miles. Custer reached Powder River about half-past three p.m. The main column, under Terry, arrived and was snugly in camp on the right bank of Powder River before sundown. General Terry congratulated Custer immediately upon his arrival upon his success as a guide, and remarked that, in coming along through the Bad Lands, he had not believed it possible that a practicable route could be found to Powder River valley. The point reached on this latter [river] was about twenty-five miles from its mouth.[41]

On the 8th, taking companies A and I of the cavalry as an escort, under Captains Myles Moylan and Myles Keogh, respectively, Terry trekked down the valley of the Powder River to its mouth. He needed to satisfy his mind. Had the steamer and supplies arrived safely? Had the scouts succeeded in reaching Gibbon? While Terry was checking on these points of interest, Custer was left in temporary charge of the encampment, "Grant's positive orders to the contrary notwithstanding."[42]

Terry returned to his command late on June 9 with the latest news (the same day that Crook had had his first skirmish with the "hostiles" at Tongue River Heights). The supplies from the stockade had been transported safely by the *Far West* to the Powder River; the two scouts he had wanted to reach Gibbon near the Rosebud had turned back after running into a party of Indians (what good is two hundred dollars if you lose your hair or worse?[43]); Terry had taken the *Far West* thirty-five miles up the Yellowstone and met Gibbon; and he had instructed Gibbon to retrace his steps to the Rosebud in order to prevent the Sioux from crossing to the north at that point[44] (assuming they had not already). Terry also brought back the newest member of the expedition, on loan from Gibbon, a thirty-nine-year-old half-Sioux guide named Mitch Bouyer.

Furthermore, the next day, June 10, Terry would send half the cavalry on a scout south along the Powder River "to clear it of any small detached bands of Indians who might be lurking away from the larger village."[45]

[For this purpose] a column was organized, commanded by Major [Marcus A.] Reno, consisting of Keogh's, Yates', MacDougall's, Smith's, Calhoun's, and Harrington's companies of the 7th Cavalry, constituting the right wing, a Gatling gun under Lieut. [Frank X.] Kinzie, and a detachment of [seven] Indian scouts [plus Bouyer], to proceed on a reconnaissance up the Powder River and then to strike across to the mouth of Tongue River.[46]

While the Powder River scout was in progress, the rest of the command would push on to the mouth of the Tongue River and there await Major Reno's return. Upon that event, Terry had still other plans, these involving his "disgraced" subordinate:

Custer will select nine companies of his regiment and a detachment of Indian scouts, and with a large train of pack mules, loaded with supplies for at least fifteen days, proceed up the valley of Tongue River some distance; then striking west will move quickly to the Rosebud River, upon which stream the Indians are reported to be in heavy force [as seen by Lieutenant Bradley on May 27]; then down the valley of the Rosebud.[47]

In the interim, the remaining three companies of the Seventh Cavalry, perhaps with Gibbon's four companies of the Second Cavalry, would scout west along the Yellowstone, from the Tongue to the Rosebud, then up the Rosebud until they met Custer's command coming from the opposite direction. A letter sent to the *New York Herald*, possibly written by Custer, stated: "By these arrangements it will be seen that if the Indians are anywhere in the vicinity where they are reported to be the prospect of discovering them is excellent, or to express it as I heard an Irish cavalryman put it the other day, 'There's a moighty foin chance for a fight or a foot race.'"[48]

Regarding the latest whereabouts of the Sioux, an anonymous dispatch to the *New York Tribune* dated June 12 stated: "It is generally supposed that the hostile Sioux are encamped on the south side of the Yellowstone, between the Tongue and Big Horn rivers.[49]

The question now was, with Crook coming from the south and Terry probing from the north, would the Indians hang around long enough until the net was securely in place and there was no chance of escape?

Terry's column reached the mouth of the Powder River at about 6 p.m. on June 11 and set up camp for several days. The next stop was the Tongue River. Terry would travel on the steamer *Far West*, while Custer went by land, some thirty-five miles west. He departed the morning of June 15 and arrived the morning of the seventeenth, right about the same time of day that the battle of the Rosebud was getting under way. Now there was nothing to do but wait for Reno, word from whom was received two days later:

On the evening of June 19 scouts came in from Major Reno. They said he had reached the Yellowstone some few miles above the Tongue River. He had made a march of about 250 miles, scouted some distance up the Powder River, then crossed the country, and discovered a heavy Indian trail, consisting of nearly 400 lodges, near the Rosebud. Its age was supposed to be about 10 days. . . . The whole command then marched for the Rosebud.[50]

Reno's orders had called for him to advance no farther than the Tongue River, but he pushed on to the Rosebud, the next river west of the Tongue, striking it about twenty-three miles above its mouth on June 16. Here he followed a large Indian trail up the valley for about ten miles—three and a half miles that night and six and a half miles the next morning (the Indian scouts advanced even further). Most certainly Bouyer, being familiar with the land and believing he could help provide valuable information on the whereabouts of the Indian village, influenced Reno's decision to deviate from his orders.[51] After all, the primary need was to locate the village. As it turned out, Terry did not approve of Reno's initiative. It was feared that his actions may have prematurely "flushed the covey" in the Rosebud and Big Horn valleys, that by "deviating from the route prescribed in his orders he incurred the risk of alarming the Sioux and enabling them to escape."[52]

The *New York Herald* carried a scathing dispatch about the incident, allegedly written by Custer:

Reno, after an absence of ten days, returned, when it was found, to the disgust and disappointment of every member of the entire expedition, from the commanding general down to the lowest private, that Reno, instead of simply failing to accomplish any good results, had so misconducted his force as to embarrass, if not seriously and permanently mar, all hopes of future success of the expedition. He had not only deliberately, and without a shadow of excuse, failed to obey his written orders issued by General Terry's personal directions, but he had acted in positive disobedience to the strict injunctions of the department commander.[53]

After detailing the route Reno followed, the dispatch went on to say:

An abandoned camp ground of the Indians was found [on the Rosebud], on which 380 lodges had been pitched. The trail led up the valley of the Rosebud. Reno took up the trail and followed it

Major Marcus A. Reno. (*National Archives*)

about twenty miles, but faint heart never won fair lady, neither did it ever pursue and overtake an Indian village. Had Reno, after first violating his orders, pursued and overtaken the Indians, his original disobedience of orders would have been overlooked, but his determination forsook him at this point, and instead of continuing the pursuit and at least bringing the Indians to bay, he gave the order to countermarch and face his command to the rear, from which point he made his way back to the mouth of Tongue River and reported the details of his gross and inexcusable blunder to General Terry.

His commanding officer informed Reno in unmistakable language that the latter's conduct amounted to positive disobedience of orders, the sad consequences of which could not yet be fully determined. The details of this affair will not bear investigation. A court martial is strongly hinted at, and if one is not ordered it will not be because it is not richly deserved. . . . Few officers have ever had so fine an opportunity to make a successful and telling strike and few ever so completely failed to improve their opportunity.[54]

It was a strange twist in logic. Since Reno had already disobeyed orders, he should have taken things one step further, pursued the Indians and defeated them in battle. Had he done so, his original disobedience would have been forgiven. The ironic part is that the writer (Custer?) was probably right.

Despite the fact that Terry apparently steamrolled Reno for moving on to the Rosebud, the latter's disobedience turned out to be useful. As one officer expressed it in his dispatch of June 28: "It was now known no Indians were on Tongue River or Powder River, and the net had narrowed down to the Rosebud, Little Horn and Big Horn rivers."[55]

Accordingly, Terry updated his plan, thus saving time and energy that would otherwise have been wasted. There was no need to send Custer up the Tongue River and then have him cross over to the Rosebud. Instead, the column would continue on to the mouth of the Rosebud, from which point Custer could repeat the now well established pattern: march up one river, cross over to the next river west, then down that river toward the Yellowstone. Except in this case, Gibbon's column, accompanied by Terry, was going to take a more active role: they would continue up the Yellowstone to the mouth of the Big Horn, then up that river to the Little Big Horn looking for Custer coming down. If all went well, they would crush Sitting Bull's army between them. Unless, of course, Custer found them first. As a matter of fact, it was pretty much expected that he would. Major James S. Brisbin, of the Second Cavalry, stated:

It was announced by General Terry that General Custer's column would strike the blow, and Colonel Gibbon and his men received the decision without a murmur. There was great rivalry between the two columns, and each wanted to be in at the death. Colonel Gibbon's cavalry had been in the field since the 22nd of last February,[56] herding and watching these Indians, and the infantry had been in the field and on the march since early last March. They had come to regard the Yellowstone Indians as their peculiar property, and have worked and waited five months until the Indians could be concentrated and Generals Crook and Terry could get into position to prevent their escape. The Montana column felt disappointed when they learned that they were not to be present at the final capture of the great village, but General Terry's reasons for according the honor of the attack to General Custer were good ones. First, Custer had all cavalry and could pursue if they attempted to escape, while Gibbon's column was half infantry, and in rapid marching in approaching the village, as well as in pursuing the Indians after the fight, Colonel Gibbon's cavalry and infantry must become separated and the strength of the column be weakened. Second, General Custer's column was numerically stronger than Gibbon's, and General Terry desired the strongest column to strike the Indians; so it was decided that Custer's men were, as usual, to have the post of honor, and the officer's and men of the Montana column cheered them and bid them God speed.[57]

Additionally, Lieutenant Edward J. McClernand, Second Cavalry, noted in his journal on June 24: "The plan of the campaign seems to be for us [Gibbon's command] to move to the Little Big Horn, and thus get below the village supposed to be on that stream, while General Custer strikes them from above."[58]

On June 22, 1876, a buckskin-clad Custer, at the head of all twelve companies of the Seventh Cavalry, which now numbered some 600 men,[59] plus 35 Indian scouts, a handful of guides and packers, and 185 pack mules carrying 15 days' rations,[60] departed up the Rosebud. If there was ever going to be a chance for Custer to "cut loose" from Terry, this was it, gift wrapped, and he was going to make the most of it:

Custer advised his subordinate officers . . . in regard to rations, that it would be well to carry an extra supply of salt, because, if at the end of the fifteen days the command should be pursuing a trail, he did not propose to turn back for lack of rations, but would subsist his men on fresh meat . . . if the country provided it; pack mules if nothing better offered. The *Herald* correspondent will accompany Custer's column, and in the event of a "fight or a foot race," will be on the ground to make due record thereof for the benefit of the *Herald* readers.[61]

On June 21, Mark Kellogg, the correspondent for the *Bismarck Tribune* (with an occasional article in the *New York Herald*) and the only official journalist to accompany the expedition, wrote, "I have the liberty of the entire column, headquarters and all, and will get down to bottom facts in all matters connected with

---

Riding Off Into History

New York Herald, July 8, 1876

Custer's Battle Field, Little Horn, June 28, 1876.

The men were in the best of spirits, [on the afternoon of June 22] and mounted on the finest horses that could be bought in the East. General Custer, dressed in a suit of buckskin and mounted on a magnificent blooded mare, rode proudly at the head of his regiment, and looked every inch a soldier. The last good-by[e] was said, the officers clustered around General Terry, their idolized department commander, for a final shake of the hand, and, in the best of spirits, filled with high hopes, they galloped away to their death.

General Custer lingered behind a little for General Terry's instructions, and, with a grip like iron and a "God bless you," Terry turned back to the boat.

Custer was proud of his regiment, but his face wore a sad expression. I have known him for sixteen years, and I never saw Custer so nervous and sad as he was when we last met. I fear the displeasure of the President weighed heavily on his mind and had much to do with his untimely death.

—Major James S. Brisbin

---

the expedition."[62] In another dispatch he jotted down the now famous, and hugely ambiguous, line: "I go with Custer and will be at the death."[63]

Writing of Terry, Kellogg noted: "Brigadier General A. H. Terry, in command of this expedition, I find to be my ideal of a commanding general—large brained, sagacious, far-reaching, cool under all circumstances and with rare executive abilities. He is besides genial, courteous, frank and manly."[64]

But he saved his best for last. His description of Custer is grandiloquent, and reads more like a paid advertisement. On the other hand, Kellogg may have hit it on the head:

And now a word for the most peculiar genius in the army, a man of strong impulses, of great hearted friendships and bitter enmities, of quick, nervous temperament, undaunted courage, will and determination; a man possessing electric mental capacity and of iron frame and constitution; a brave, faithful, gallant soldier, who has warm friends and bitter enemies; the hardest rider, the greatest pusher, with the most untiring vigilance, overcoming seeming impossibilities and with an ambition to succeed in all things he undertakes; a man to do right, as he construes the right, in every case; one respected and beloved by his followers, who would freely follow him into the "jaws of hell." Of Lieutenant Colonel G. A. Custer I am now writing. Do not think I am overdrawing the picture. The pen picture is true to the life, and is drawn not only from actual observation, but from an experience that cannot mislead me.[65]

Terry's written orders to Custer were printed in the *New York Tribune* on July 7, 1876:

Camp at the Mouth of Rosebud River,
June 22, 1876.

Lieut. Col. Custer, 7th Cavalry.

Colonel: The Brigadier General commanding directs that as soon as your regiment can be made ready for the march you proceed up the Rosebud in pursuit of the Indians whose trail was discovered by Major Reno a few days since. It is, of course, impossible to give any definite instructions in regard to this movement, and, were it not impossible to do so, the Department Commander places too much confidence in your zeal, energy, and ability to wish to impose upon you precise orders which might hamper your action when nearly in contact with the enemy. He will, however, indicate to you his own views of what your action should be, and he desires that you should conform to them unless you shall see sufficient reason for departing from them. He thinks that you should proceed up the Rosebud until you ascertain definitely the direction in which the trail above spoken of leads. Should it be found, as it appears to be almost certain that it will be found, to turn toward the Little Big Horn, he thinks that you should still proceed southward perhaps as far as the head waters of the Tongue, and then turn toward the Little Big Horn, feeling constantly, however, to your left so as to preclude the possibility of the escape of the Indians to the south or southeast by passing around your left flank. The column of Col. Gibbon is now in motion for the mouth of the Big Horn. As soon as it reaches that point it will cross the Yellowstone and move up at least as far as the forks of the Big and Little Big Horn. Of course its future movements must be controlled by circumstances as they arise; but it is hoped that the Indians, if upon the Little Big Horn, may be so nearly inclosed by the two columns that their escape will be impossible. The Department Commander desires that on your way up the Rosebud you should thoroughly examine the upper part of Tulloch's Creek [a tributary of the Big Horn River], and that you should endeavor to send a scout through to Col. Gibbon's column with information of the result of your examination. The lower part of this creek will be examined by a detachment from Col. Gibbon's command. The supply steamer [*Far West*] will be pushed up the Big Horn as far as the forks of the river are found to be navigable for that space,[66] and the Department Commander, who will accompany the column of Col. Gibbon, desires you to report to him there not later than the expiration of the time for which your troops are rationed [15 days], unless in the mean time you receive further orders.

Respectfully, &c.,
E. W. Smith, Captain 18th Infantry,
Acting Assistant Adjutant General.

Although unstated in Terry's wordy instructions, much of which can be construed as suggestions, he verbally informed Custer that Gibbon's column would be at the mouth of the Little Big Horn on June 26 (barring any unforeseen circumstances). However, it should be understood that this date had nothing to do with a predetermined time of attack. After all, when Custer departed the Rosebud on June 22, no one knew exactly where the Indian village was located, other than that it *may have been* somewhere along the Little Big Horn. The June 26 date and Gibbon's expected position thereon were stated so that Custer, or one or more couriers from Custer, would know when and where to find him.[67] The number of Indians that Custer expected to meet, should he find them, was about fifteen hundred.[68]

The courier/scout that Custer was supposed to "endeavor to send" through to Terry with information about the upper part of Tullock's

Creek was George Herendeen, a twenty-nine-year-old civilian trader and former occupant of abandoned Fort Pease (a short-lived trading post), who was transferred from Gibbon to Custer specifically to carry out this task. As Gibbon explained:

General Terry expressed a desire that Custer should communicate with him by sending a scout down the valley of Tullock's Fork, and send him any news of importance he might have, especially as to whether or not any hostiles were on that stream. . . . Herendeen stipulated that in case he was called upon to incur the additional risk of carrying dispatches his compensation should be increased. This was agreed to, and he accompanied General Custer's troops.[69]

Herendeen went on to write two detailed accounts of the part the Reno battalion played in the battle of the Little Big Horn, both of which were printed in the *New York Herald*. The first appeared on July 8, 1876, and the second on January 22, 1878.[70] We will quote from both of these accounts, labeling them "H1" and "H2," respectively. We pick up his narrative at noon on June 22, at the start of Custer's historic ride to the Little Big Horn:

(H2) We started out on the 22nd about noon and traveled up the Rosebud. [Mitch] Boyer and Bloody Knife, a Ree [Arikara] Scout, had the lead and Custer traveled with them. Lieutenant [Charles] Varnum with his scouts followed Custer in advance of the column. We marched about twelve miles and went into camp at five p.m.

General Custer ordered reveille to be sounded at four and the command to be ready to march at five o'clock next morning. This was the morning of the 23rd, and we marched promptly at five a.m. Our course led up the stream four or five miles, when we struck an Indian trail which Reno had followed a few days before. We followed the trail until five p.m., when we encamped for the night and in the evening Custer sent the Crow scouts who were with us on in advance to see what they could find out.

On the morning of the 24th we broke camp at five o'clock and continued following the trail up the stream. Soon after starting Custer, who was in advance with Boyer, called me to him and told me to get ready, saying he thought he would send me and Charlie Reynolds to the head of Tulloch's Fork to take a look. I told the General it was not time yet, as we were then traveling in the direction of the head of the Tullock, and I could only follow his trail. I called Boyer, who was a little ahead, back, and asked him if I was not correct in my statement to the General, and he said, "Yes, further up on the Rosebud we would come opposite a gap, and then we could cut across and strike the Tullock in about fifteen miles' ride." Custer said, "All right, I could wait."

We had not proceeded far when the Crows came in on the run and reported the trail was getting fresh ahead, and that they had seen some fresh pony tracks. . . . Custer, on receiving the above intelligence halted his command, dismounted the men and had the officers' call sounded. He held a council with his officers, but I was not near enough to hear what passed. . . .

At this point, with the village seemingly close at hand, Herendeen's mission to Terry fell by the wayside, although it is still unclear to this day precisely why. According to Lieutenant Edward S. Godfrey,

Seventh Cavalry, the Crow scouts who were riding in advance of the main column "seemed to be doing their work thoroughly, giving special attention to the right, toward Tulloch's Creek."[71] Perhaps Custer considered this sufficient, and since nothing of special note was discovered, decided not to send Herendeen to scout the area for himself and never bothered to send him to Terry. However, there are two problems with this scenario. First, Godfrey's statement lacks any positive knowledge that the headwaters of Tulloch's Creek were indeed scouted at all. Secondly, if Herendeen made the ride, it was extra money in his pocket. Would Custer have purposely denied the scout a chance to earn this extra money? Perhaps Custer left the decision up to Herendeen, who, sensing the coming conflict and not wanting to miss out on the action, chose to stay with the command. Another possibility is that he considered it too dangerous to attempt such a ride at this time. Unfortunately, Herendeen's two accounts are silent on the matter.[72]

It was at this juncture that Custer made a fateful choice that would forever cement his place in history. The fresh trail that the Crows reported was headed west toward the Little Big Horn. But what about Terry's orders: If the trail is found to turn toward the Little Big Horn, Custer "should still proceed southward perhaps as far as the head waters of the Tongue."

For Custer there was only one thing to do. He would succeed where Reno failed. Still feeling the sting of

Captain Francis M. Gibson remembers Custer, Reno, and Benteen

Francis M. Gibson (1847–1919) was a lieutenant in Company H, Seventh Cavalry, at the time of the battle of the Little Big Horn. He was appointed captain in February 1880, and retired from the army in December 1891, after which he became the deputy commissioner of the Street Cleaning Department in New York City. His entire army career, more than twenty-four years, was spent with the Seventh Cavalry. In an article Gibson wrote more than twenty years after the memorable events of 1876, the former cavalryman recalled the three senior officers of the regiment:

New York Evening Post,
February 20, 1897

[Custer, Reno and Benteen] possessed very different characteristics. Custer's gallantry and dash have gone down to history. He was also a man of extreme nervous energy: his untiring activity was boundless, and so also was his intensity of purpose.

He was utterly fearless, always sanguine of success, had an abiding faith in the ability of his regiment to succeed when others would fail, and reposed absolute confidence in his chosen friends. His daring exploits attest his bravery, and his fighting qualities should stamp him an able officer. He was a thorough cavalryman from top to toe.

Major Reno was regarded an able officer, but he lacked the dash, the energy, the determination, and the ambition of Custer. Benteen is a man of many noble characteristics. He is as brave as was Julius Caesar, and as cool under fire as the proverbial cucumber. In a tight place his coolness is reassuring, and his judgment can always be depended upon, and all the survivors of the battle of the Little Big Horn are very glad he was there to exercise his superior judgment. Captain Benteen is a man of stolid determination, and when he takes up a position, either on the field of battle or in the midst of peaceful pursuits, it is next to impossible to move him. He is generous to a fault, and most charitable, and places his principles of honor on the very highest plane.

the president's anger, this was his chance to show that he was the right man for the job, to show that he was the key to victory, that without his services, the army would not fare as well, to "redeem himself in public opinion," "to retrieve his standing by some splendid act of successful daring."[73] In fact, his motivation aside, Custer did what just about any other cavalry leader would have done at that time and under those circumstances. He followed the trail. Herendeen again:

(H2) Toward evening the trail became so fresh that Custer ordered flankers to be kept well out and a sharp lookout had for lodges leaving to the right or the left. He said he wanted to get the whole village, and nothing must leave the main trail without his knowing it. About dusk we halted and went into camp on the trail. It was then very fresh and the General sent Varnum, Boyer and some scouts on ahead to examine the trail and adjacent country. The men were given orders to graze their animals, get supper and be ready to start at eleven p.m. Everybody rested until ten p.m., when we packed up again and moved out. The night was very dark and our progress slow. After marching some ten miles about two a.m. we halted; the horses were unsaddled and the men lay down to rest. The packs were taken off the mules and everything done to rest and recuperate the animals.

Some time during the night the scouts came in and reported to Custer that the Indian camp was found. We packed up and moved forward at early light. Mitch Boyer and Reynolds, who had been out, said the camp was very large. Boyer said it was the biggest village he had ever seen.[74] Reynolds said there was a heap of them, and Custer replied "he could whip them." Reynolds said it would take six hours hard fighting to whip them.

About nine o'clock on the morning of the 25th of June, and the last day of our march, Custer halted his troops and concealed them as well as he could. He then took an orderly and rode up on the Divide about four miles to where Lieutenant Varnum and Boyer were. The General was trying to get a look at the village, which was over on the other side of the divide on the Little Big Horn.

(H1) In about an hour Custer returned [from the lookout] and said he could not see the Indian village, but the scouts and a half-breed guide, "Mitch Boyer," said they could distinctly see it some fifteen miles off. While General Custer was looking for the Indian village the scouts came in and reported that he had been discovered, and that news was then on its way to the village that he was coming.[75] Another scout said two Sioux war parties had stolen up and seen the command; and on looking in a ravine near by, sure enough fresh pony tracks were found. Custer had "officers' call" blown, gave his orders and the command was put in fighting order.

By "fighting order," Herendeen was referring to Custer's division of the command into three fighting battalions. Captain Frederick Benteen was given companies H, D, and K, about 115 men. Major Reno was placed in charge of companies M, A, and G, roughly 140 men. Custer took control of the largest battalion, companies C, E, F, I, and L, totaling some 212 men. Company B, under Captain Thomas McDougall, was detailed to guard the pack train, the cavalry escort totaling 132 men. Shortly after making these designations, Custer ordered Benteen on a scout to the left in search of Indians,[76] while he and Reno continued along the creek they were following (since named Reno Creek). Once again, Herendeen continues the narrative:

(H2) As soon as the orders were issued we started up the Divide at a fast walk and traveled about three or four miles, when we came to the top. The scouts, under Lieutenants Varnum and Hare, then pushed on ahead at a lope and the command followed at a trot. I was with the scouts, and we kept down a creek which led toward the Little Horn. When we got near the mouth of the creek we saw a lodge standing on the bank. We rode up on a hill, so as to flank and overlook the lodge, and soon saw it was deserted. From the top of the hill we looked ahead down the Little Big Horn and saw a heavy cloud of dust and some stock apparently running. We could see beyond the stream a few Indians on the hills riding very fast, and seemingly running away. I said the Indians were running and we would have to hurry up, or we would not catch them. Lieutenant Hare wrote a note to Custer, but I do not know what he reported. I presume he thought as the rest of us did, that the Indians were getting away. Custer was near at hand, and was riding at a fast trot.

The scouts charged down on the abandoned lodge, cut it open, and found in it a dead Indian. Custer came up while we were at the lodge, Major Reno having the advance. I heard Custer say to Reno, "Reno, take the scouts, lead out, and I will be with you."[77] Reno started at a gallop, and as he rode called out, "Keep your horses well in hand." My horse fell and for a few moments I was delayed, but I caught up with Reno at the ford.

As we were crossing I heard the Crow scouts call out to one another, "The Sioux are coming up to meet us," and, understanding their language, I called to Reno, "The Sioux are coming." Reno waited a few moments until the command closed up, then crossed the Little Big Horn and formed in line of battle on the prairie, just outside some timber. The formation was made without halting, and the line kept on moving, first at a trot and then at a gallop.

We could see a large body of Indians just ahead of us and apparently waiting for us. We advanced probably half a mile, the Indians setting fire to some timber on our right and in our front. A few Indians were in the timber and we fired on them, but no shots were returned. Very soon we dismounted, and the soldiers formed a skirmish line, facing the hills.

Captain Frederick Benteen. (*Wyoming Historical Society*)

On events up to this time, Lieutenant Charles DeRudio, Seventh Cavalry, afterward remarked:

Having reached the river we forded, and on reaching the plain beyond the opposite bank we were ordered into line of battle. Everything being as was ordered, we started on a gallop, and for two miles pursued close on the verge of an immense and blinding cloud of dust raised by the madly flying savages ahead of us. The dust cloud was so dense that we could distinguish nothing, so Reno halted the battalion, and, after dismounting, formed a skirmish line, the right flank resting on the edge of a dry, thickly wooded creek. While the horses were being led to shelter in the wood the Indians opened a galling fire on us, which was immediately responded to, the skirmish continuing for about half an hour.[78]

A report in the *New York Herald*, based on the testimony of battle participants, declared:

The fire was terrific, and reminded those present at that engagement of the Wilderness [May 1864]. Reno says he never heard firing more terrific. In a moment his command was completely surrounded with the howling devils on every side, firing at short range. Charley Reynolds, the well-known scout, afterward killed, exclaimed: "We are gone up. There is no hope for us."[79]

Next, Herendeen takes us from the skirmish line to a command decision that was to have deadly consequences for more than thirty men:

(H2) The [skirmish] line extended to the left and front, and firing almost immediately began, the Indians being near the foot hills of the little valley. In a short time the firing became quite heavy, the Indians moving to the left and working to our rear. The horses were now led into the timber on our right and rear, and the soldiers fell back to cover among the bushes and small trees. There was a little park or meadow just within the timber, and on this the command formed and mounted. I was one of the last men to get into the timber and halted at the edge of the bushes to fire at some Indians who were coming into the timber on our left and rear. I got my horse and joined the command, which I found mounted and sitting in line of battle in the park or open space among the bushes. There was little firing for some minutes, and then we received a volley from the bushes. Bloody Knife was just in my front at the time, and Reno on my left. The volley killed Bloody Knife and one soldier. I heard the soldier call out as he fell, "Oh! my God, I have got it."

Reno gave the order to dismount, and almost immediately gave the order to mount again. The soldiers were not all on horseback when Reno started out of the timber toward the prairie, the men following him. The men scattered, getting out of the woods as best they could. They ran quartering toward the Little Big Horn. I had started out of the timber when the command did, about half of it being ahead of me and the other half in my rear. There was such a cloud of dust no one could see where he was going; just as I got out on the edge of the prairie my horse fell, throwing me off and running away. I ran back to the timber about 150 yards and took cover among the bushes. Just as I turned back I heard some officer call out: "Halt men! halt! let us fight them!"

As soon as the troops led by Reno emerged from the timber the Indians closed down upon them, some ahead, some alongside and some in the rear of them.

(H1) The command headed for the ford, pressed closely by Indians in large numbers, and at every moment the rate of speed was increased, until it became a dead run for the ford. The Sioux, mounted on their swift ponies, dashed up by the side of the soldiers and fired at them, killing both men and horses. Little resistance was offered and it was a complete rout to the ford.[80]

As described by Herendeen, Reno's retreat from the timber was nothing more than a headlong, every-man-for-himself race for life to the Little Big Horn. By all accounts, it was disorganized and lacked military discipline, and at least thirty-two men were killed.[81] To the enraged Indians, it was a good old-fashioned buffalo hunt. Certainly, there were soldiers who knew it didn't have to be that way. Recollect Lieutenant Foster's pride-filled description (at the end of chapter four) of how a battalion of the Third Cavalry retreated from a larger force of Indians at the battle of the Rosebud:

Soldiers who, when in full retreat before an enemy superior in force, with advantage of position and in arms, will face the foe and fire as steadily and deliberately as though on the drill ground when an officer rides out and commands, 'Skirmishers, halt!' must be imbued with the very highest grade of soldierly discipline. Men who will turn again and charge the advancing enemy when to all appearances all is lost and everything in confusion at a simple appeal to their regimental pride cannot be lacking in esprit de corps. Both these things this noble little battalion did.[82]

Based on conversations with men from Reno's battalion, Major James S. Brisbin, Second Cavalry, with Gibbon's command, assembled the following description of their madcap charge from the timber to the river:

A wild scramble for life now began. It was every one for himself. Indians on every side rose up and fired at the flying horsemen, and hundreds mounted on swift ponies pursued the soldiers, easily enough coming up with the heavy American horses. It was a hand to hand fight, one trooper often having as many as five Indians after him. The troops used their revolvers at short range, emptying an Indian saddle at every shot. At the ford, about a mile distant, a strong force of Indians was found holding it. But the troopers dashed over them, crossed the river, and began to ascend the high bank opposite.[83] It was a mere Indian trail leading up the face of a bald hill. The Indians rallied and, taking shelter in the bushes about the ford, opened a deadly fire on the soldiers as they forded and ascended the opposite bank.

Major Reno's Race For Life

New York Tribune, July 13, 1876

Camp at Mouth of the Big Horn, M. T., July 3, 1876.

Reno advanced along the plain, meeting with no opposition until he reached a little grove. Here his line was attacked. He immediately deployed his skirmishers and dismounted. The horses were led into the wood[s] and the cavalrymen engaged the enemy. The Indians appeared in immense numbers. They attacked him fiercely in front, and at the same time turned his left flank and compelled his force to retreat into the woods. The Indians followed in hordes and drove the force before them to the river. The bluffs on the opposite side were steep and high, but the water in the river was low. The Indians, flushed with success, rushed upon our men and a hand-to-hand conflict ensued. Here McIntosh was shot. Hodgson was shot midway in the stream and fell before he could reach the opposite bank. Dr. DeWolf crossed in safety, but was killed on the bluffs. The rest of the command fought their way up the heights, with the Indians in hot pursuit. Death seemed to stare every man in the face, when suddenly Benteen came to the rescue.

—As told to
a special correspondent

On account of the narrowness of the ford a great crowd soon collected about the crossing and became jammed there; and into this mass of men and horses the Indians fired at short range. The loss of life here was fearful. Lieutenant Hodgson fell while gallantly endeavoring to get his men across the stream. Hodgson had already crossed the ford himself and was ascending the opposite bank when his horse was shot and rolled down the bank with him. Detaching himself from the fallen animal he grasped the stirrups of a passing soldier to help himself up the bank, and had nearly reached the top when a shot struck him and he fell back, rolling down the bank into the water. As soon as the soldiers reached the hill overlooking this ford they dismounted and opened fire on the Indians to cover the crossing of their comrades.[84]

As Reno's men were treacherously making their way across the river and up the opposite precipitous bluff, they were met by Benteen's three companies approaching the same bluff from the south. It was a lucky turn for Reno that Benteen had abandoned his fruitless scouting mission and arrived on the scene just when he did. Captain Gibson later recounted his part in Benteen's unproductive search for Indians:

[Captain] Benteen ordered me to select half a dozen men on the best horses, get ahead of the battalion, and proceed as rapidly as possible to the valley, and report to him without delay what I found there; at the same time he handed me his field-glasses. His object in sending me was to save unnecessary fatigue to both horses and men in case nothing was there. I got to the valley and found it as quiet as the grave itself. Up the valley I could see a long distance, but in the direction of the village only a short one, owing to the turn in the valley and the broken character of the country. I hurried back to Benteen, and told him there was no use going any further in that direction. Therefore, in compliance with

Gen. Custer's orders, in case no Indians were seen in the valley, we were to return by the shortest route to the trail of the main command, and follow it up.[85]

While following in the wake of the Seventh Cavalry's tracks, he was met by two couriers from Custer's command; first by Sergeant Daniel A. Kanipe, Company C, sent back to hurry up the pack train (a few miles in the rear of Benteen's battalion),[86] then, shortly after, by trumpeter John Martin, Company H (Benteen's own company). Martin, who turned out to be the last white man to see Custer alive, was serving as Custer's orderly trumpeter that day. He carried an urgent message from his commander, quickly scrawled by the regimental adjutant, Lieutenant William W. Cooke: "Benteen. Come on. Big Village. Be Quick. Bring Packs. W. W. Cooke. P. bring pacs."[87]

Whether Benteen moved with as much haste as possible after receiving Custer's message has been a matter of debate since the day of the battle. Nevertheless, once he reached Reno's position on the bluff, his search for Custer ceased (a point of contention among many battle students who feel he should have continued on without Reno, or that the combined battalions should have moved out briskly in the apparent direction Custer most likely traveled), and the reunited battalions looked to prepare themselves for a siege. At the moment, Reno was in no mood for advancing; besides, Custer was supposed to be supporting him, not the other way around. According to Gibson, Reno told Benteen that "the last he saw of

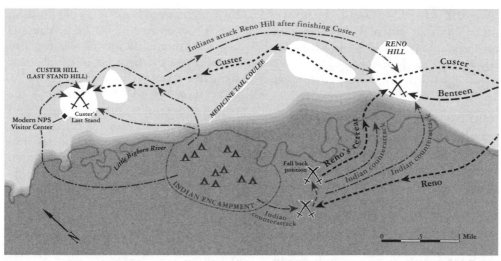

The Battle of the Little Big Horn, June 25, 1876, showing the general movements of the opposing forces.

Custer was on the crest of the hill we were then on, but that his [Custer's] troops must have been behind the slope, as he did not see them."[88]

Continuing now with Herendeen's narrative, the scout found himself in a perilous situation, left behind in the timber, along with about twelve other men:

(H1) I did not see the men at the ford, and do not know what took place further than a good many were killed when the command left the timber. Just as I got out my horse stumbled and fell and I was dismounted, the horse running away after Reno's command.

(H2) When I went back to the timber, after my horse threw me, just as I reached the cover I met Lieutenant DeRudio and stopped to talk to him.[89] As we spoke together about a dozen soldiers, some on foot and some on horseback, came along and I called to them to come into the timber and we could stand

the Indians off. The soldiers joined us at once and we concealed ourselves, tying the horses to the trees. Just as we got settled down firing below us opened up and we knew Custer was engaged. The Indians had been leaving Reno and going down the valley in considerable numbers at full speed.

Of this part of the fight, Red Horse, a Sioux Indian, recalled:

After driving this party [Reno] back the Indians corralled them on the top of a high hill [on the other side of the river] and held them there until they saw that the women and children were in danger of being taken prisoners by another party of troops [under Custer] which just then made its appearance below. The word passed among the Indians like a whirlwind and they all started to attack this new party, leaving the troops on the hill.[90]

An anonymous trooper who clawed his way up to that hill, known today as Reno Hill, afterward reflected:

"We did not understand the movement [of the Indians] then, but we
understand it now, and while we
stood on the hill wiping the sweat
from our brows and waiting to catch
our breath, we could hear faintly the
sound of volleys in the direction in
which Custer had gone. In an hour
they ceased and all was still."[91]

Herendeen again, from his position
in the timber:

(H2) The firing down the valley [in
Custer's direction] was very heavy. There
were about nine volleys at intervals and
the intermediate firing was quite rapid.
The heavy firing lasted from three-quarters of an hour to an hour and then it
died away.

I said to the men who were with me,
"Boys, we had better get out of this." I
told them that the fight below had
stopped, and it was a guess how it had
gone, but I thought likely in favor of the
Indians, and we had better get away
before they came back up the valley. I
started out and the men followed me.[92]

(H1) I deployed the men as skirmishers
and we moved forward on foot toward
the river. When we had got nearly to the
river we met five Indians on ponies, and
they fired on us. I returned the fire and
the Indians broke and we forded the
river, the water being breast deep. We
finally got over, wounded men and all,
and headed for Reno's command, which
I could see drawn up on the bluffs along
the river about a mile off. We reached
Reno in safety. We had not been with
Reno more than fifteen minutes when I
saw the Indians coming up the valley
from Custer's fight. Reno was then moving his whole command down the ridge
toward Custer.[93] The Indians crossed the
river below Reno and swarmed up the
bluff on all sides. After skirmishing with

them Reno went back to his old position
which was on one of the highest points
along the bluffs. It was now about five
o'clock, and the fight lasted until it was
too dark to see to shoot.

As soon as it was dark Reno took the
packs and saddles off the mules and
horses and made breastworks of them.
He also dragged the dead horses and
mules on the line and sheltered the men
behind them. Some of the men dug rifle
pits with their butcher knives and all
slept on their arms.

"The situation where the command made its final stand was peculiar," Private Jacob Adams of
Company H later stated. "We were in
a large basin, at the center of which
we had our horses. Along the outer
edges of the basin, at the top of the
ridges, we lay, for the Indians had us
surrounded and fought us from every
quarter."[94] Captain Gibson later
recalled:

Troop H . . . was posted along the crest
of a hill that overlooked the rest of the
command, which was located about
three hundred yards away, across a broad
slope [basin], which was somewhat protected, but very little, from the constant
and heavy cross-fire of our wily foe. In
this slope our horses, pack mules, supplies, and extra ammunition found such
poor shelter as it afforded. Many of our
animals were killed, and as the weather
was hot they decomposed rapidly, which
by no means added to our comfort.[95]

That night the men on Reno Hill
wondered what had happened to
Custer. Despite what many had earlier seen from Weir Peak (Indians
shooting into objects on the ground),
the thought that he was killed, along
with all five companies of their com-

rades, seemed an unlikely development. More likely the five companies had been bested in battle and were holed up somewhere like they were,[96] or perhaps Custer had (temporarily) deserted them in favor of reuniting with Terry and Gibbon. Best-case scenario, Custer would come to their rescue the next day. Worst-case scenario, with sunrise the fight for life would start again.

(H1) At the peep of day the Indians opened a heavy fire, and a desperate fight ensued, lasting until ten o'clock [a.m.]. The Indians charged our position three or four times, coming up close enough to hit our men with stones, which they threw by hand. Captain Benteen saw a large mass of Indians gathering on his front to charge, and ordered his men to charge on foot and scatter them. Benteen led the charge and was upon the Indians before they knew what they were about, and killed a great many. They were evidently much surprised at this offensive movement, and I think in desperate fighting Benteen is one of the bravest men I ever saw in a fight. All the time he was going about through the bullets, encouraging the soldiers to stand up to their work and not let the Indians whip them. He went among the horses and pack mules and drove out the men who were skulking there, compelling them to go into the line and do their duty. He never sheltered his own person once during the battle, and I do not see how he escaped being killed.

About ten o'clock in the forenoon, and soon after Benteen made his charge, the men began to clamor for water. Many of them had not tasted water for thirty-six hours, and the fighting and hot sun parched their throats. Some had their tongues swollen and others could hardly speak. The men tried to eat crack-ers and hardtack, but could not raise enough saliva to moisten them. Several tried grass, but it stuck to their lips, and not one could spit or speak plainly. The wounded were reported dying for want of water, and a good many soldiers volunteered to go to the river to get some or perish in the attempt. We were fighting on the bluffs, about 700 yards from the river, and a ravine led down from the battlefield close to the river's edge. The men had to run over an open space of about 100 yards to get into the head of the ravine, and this open space was commanded by the Indians on the bluffs. The soldiers, about fifty strong, dashed over the open plateau, and entered the ravine. They rushed down it to the mouth and found it closely guarded by a party of Indians posted in the timber across the river. The water could be approached to within about thirty feet under cover; but then one had to step out on the river bank and take the Indians' fire. The boys ran the gauntlet bravely. Some would dash down to the river with camp kettles, fill them, and then take shelter in the bend of the ravine, behind the rocks, and there canteens were filled and carried up the hill. Before all the men and wounded were supplied one man was killed and six or seven wounded in this desperate attempt. One man had the bone of his leg shattered by a ball, and it has since been amputated.[97] About two o'clock the Indians began drawing off but kept skirmishing until late in the afternoon, and near dark all drew off. We now got water for the animals, many of them being almost dead, and they were put out to graze on the hillside.

On June 24, Gibbon's command—five companies of infantry,[98] four companies of cavalry, a battery of Gatling guns, and a mule train carrying about one week's rations[99]—were ferried to the south side of the Yellowstone, at the mouth of the Big Horn. Their destination was the mouth of the Little Big Horn, about thirty miles south as the crow flies, which point they hoped to reach two days later. On the morning of June 26, Lieutenant Bradley, riding in advance with a handful of Crow scouts, came across the trail of four Indians that the scouts assumed to be Sioux. Following their tracks for several miles they discovered an abandoned horse and several personal items, which were quickly recognized as belonging to some of the Crow scouts that had been sent with Custer several days before. Shortly after this they spotted three Indians a couple of miles away, and after signaling with blankets for "a long time to no purpose,"[100] they were finally able to convey that they were friends. As expected, the three men they were trailing turned out to be Crow scouts who had been transferred to Custer's command back at the Rosebud: White Man Runs Him, Goes Ahead, and Hairy Moccasin. What they reported to their fellow tribesmen was the first news of Custer's massive defeat at the Little Big Horn. Bradley wrote:

It was a terrible, terrible story, so different from the outcome we had hoped for this campaign. . . . My men listened to . . . [the news] with eager interest, betraying none of the emotion of the Crows, but looking at each other with white faces in pained silence, too full of the dreadful

recital to utter a word. Did we doubt the tale? I could not; there was an undefined vague something about it, unlooked for though it was, that commanded assent, and the most I could do was to hope that in the terror of the three fugitives from the fatal field their account of the disaster was somewhat overdrawn. But that there had been a disaster—a terrible disaster—I felt assured.[101]

Major Brisbin added:

[The Crows] said they had been with Custer until the day before—the 25th— when, while near a village, he had been surprised and his regiment cut to pieces. They said this had happened at about twenty miles from where they then were. They were at the junction of the Little Horn with the Big Horn. They reported the Sioux as "covering all the plain"—a force too numerous to count. . . . Upon full consideration of the story of the Crow scouts it was not believed to be altogether true. It was, however, conceded on all hands that some event of grave import had happened, but the worst that any one conceived as the possible fate of the gallant Seventh Cavalry and its dashing leader was that it had been repulsed and compelled to retire for support.[102]

General Terry and Colonel Gibbon were especially incredulous of the news: "Their story was not credited [by the commanding officers]. It was supposed that some fighting, perhaps severe fighting, had taken place, but it was not believed that disaster could have overtaken so large a force as twelve companies of cavalry."[103]

As the column advanced "every eye [was] bent upon a cloud of smoke resting over the southern horizon, which was hailed as a sign that Custer was successful and had fired the village," or, as another expressed it, "[we] felt sure that Custer was ravaging the valley."[104]

Brisbin picks up the narrative once more:

It was now 11:00 a.m. of the 26th, and Gibbon's command was closed up and a forced march was made toward a heavy smoke seen on the Little Horn about fifteen miles away. By 1:00 p.m. the command had reached the Little Horn, six miles distant. The command was put over in deep water, but on a good ford, and by 5:00 p.m. was again in motion. Two scouts with messages for Custer were sent out, one to the right and the other to the left, but both returned in an hour and reported the hills full of Indians, who had pursued them. One scout, named [Muggins] Taylor, had over a hundred shots fired at him while thus pursued.

Indians now began to appear on the bluffs to our right, and the column was closed up and prepared for battle. Lieutenant [Charles F.] Roe, with Company F of the Second Cavalry, was sent out to feel the enemy, and exchanged shots with the Indian scouts, who fled before his advance.[105]

Our line of march was in a level bottom land of considerable width, with the Little Horn on our left and steep blufflike hills at a distance on our right. In these hills we had seen Indians for some time; the scouts reported them very numerous and at nightfall a large body of them was visible. Colonel Gibbon therefore halted [after a march of twenty-nine miles], formed a square, and encamped in the center of the bottom or prairie, well out of rifle range from both the river and the bluff. All night the men lay on their arms, and were prepared to move forward with daylight.[106]

An anonymous officer achieved the dramatic when he wrote: "We lie down full of anxiety for Custer; many think he has been defeated, but will not acknowledge it even to themselves. I hope that tomorrow will answer all our queries."[107]

He was right; the next day would bring answers, and as history will bear witness, a whole lot more questions. From the field diary of an unknown officer (as printed in the *New York Herald*):

Tuesday, June 27—Broke camp at twenty minutes past seven a.m. and started for the smoke seen yesterday. Quite a number of ponies were picked up. Upon reaching the top of a bluff about two miles from last night's camp we could plainly see two skin lodges and a number of horses in the bottom timber. . . . I have had some little experience in Indian matters, but I could not understand the state of things that appeared to exist here. Nearing the two lodges we found the ground strewn with Indian camp equipage, piles of lodge poles tied together ready for trailing, buffalo robes, cavalry saddles, cooking utensils, coffee mills, China dishes, new spades, axes, guns, pistols, horn spoons, wooden soup bowls, all lying scattered about in the utmost confusion, and a great many Indian dogs that fled like wolves at our approach.

Arriving at the lodges we found a number of fine ponies lying in a circle around them shot dead, and in one of the lodges were three dead warriors and five in the other one, all laid out in state, wrapped in beautifully dressed robes, headdresses, leggings and embroidered moccasins.

Moving on I picked up a pair of pants that had evidently belonged to a cavalry officer; another picked up a buckskin coat, with "Porter, Seventh Cavalry," marked in the lining, a bullet hole through the right breast, passing out under the right shoulder. It was very much blood-stained. Now we began to find cavalry saddles and to realize that there must be truth to the report of the Crow scouts, and that Custer's force had been severely punished. Just then, like a thunderbolt, came a report from Lieutenant Bradley, who was on the hills on the opposite side of the river, that he had discovered the dead bodies of 196 white men.[108]

Bradley's news hit hard, and Terry called a halt. Brisbin wrote that the report "might well have been called incredible, but that the statement was of so clear a matter of fact, reported so directly, that doubt was not possible."[109] Soon the entire column was passing through the "ruins or remains of an immense Indian village." Continuing, Brisbin recalled:

Evidences that it had been hastily abandoned were seen on every hand. Buffalo robes, elk skins, kettles, camp utensils generally, such as are used by Indians, were scattered on the ground in every direction[110]—wounded Indian ponies struggled here and dead ones lay quietly there. Dead horses, branded "Seventh Cavalry," were seen. Then we saw the head of a white man, but could nowhere find his body; and, a moment later, we came upon a dead cavalryman with an arrow sticking in his back and the top of his skull crushed in.

An officer picked up a shirt, deeply stained with blood, and a pair of drawers. On the waistband of the drawers was written "Lieutenant Sturgis, Seventh Cavalry." This news spread through the column, and it was readily comprehended that this well known and favorite young officer was no more. He was the son of the Colonel of the Seventh Cavalry.

That a battle had been fought near by was plain, but what the result had been we could as yet only conjecture. That it had been severe was amply attested by the bodies Bradley had found. Some believed that Custer, in a desperate fight, had captured the village and was in pursuit of the foe; others furtively surmised that Custer and his whole command were destroyed. If he had been defeated only why had he not retreated to the mouth of the Little Horn, where he was sure to meet Gibbon's column? But if he was alive and victorious why had he not sent his messengers, as directed, to the same point?[111]

As the troops were trying to make sense of the chaotic and ghastly scene, Lieutenant Joshua W. Jacobs, Seventh Infantry, galloped in with the news that Major Reno and about three hundred men were on the hills to the left. They "knew nothing of Custer; did not know that he had had a fight."[112]

Brisbin again:

On we went, therefore, till we came upon Reno's battlefield [at the southern end of the village][113] and marched among the bodies of fallen soldiers and their horses. All the bodies were horribly mutilated, offensive from the heat and covered with swarms of flies. An officer recognized the body of Lieutenant [Donald] McIntosh, of the Seventh Cavalry, and of a soldier of McIntosh's company. McIntosh was himself part Indian, a highly educated gentleman and a fine officer. He has fallen in battle with his face toward the enemy, and it is hoped the government will remember his widow and his little children at Fort Lincoln.

Reno's battlefield was a dreadful place—horses and ponies, white men and Indians, all dead together, and their bodies mingled as if they had died where they fought in all the wild confusion of the melee.[114]

Another eyewitness noted:

At every step we found tokens of the dreadful carnage. Here was brave McIntosh; here lay Isaiah [Dorman], our Negro scout; close by, Charley Reynolds, the chief scout had bravely met his fate; and here, close together, were the bodies of our cavalrymen and their horses.[115]

Soon two mounted officers crossed the river and approached Gibbon's column. They turned out to be Lieutenants George Wallace and Luther Hare of the Seventh Cavalry. To the question, "Where is Custer?" they replied: "He left us Sunday morning with five companies, and we have heard nothing from him since."

[Shortly afterward,] Our commander with a small escort forded the stream, and scaling the almost perpendicular bluffs joined Reno's force. He was greeted with cheer upon cheer. Stout-hearted soldiers who had not flinched in the hour of peril now wept like children, and smiles returned to the wan faces of the wounded men. The Indians had retreated when they saw our line of infantry approaching. We had rescued these despairing soldiers.[116]

An anonymous observer on Reno Hill recalled: "General Terry was with Colonel Gibbon, and when he rode into our works many a gallant fellow did not feel ashamed to let his general see tears of heartfelt gratitude rolling down his cheeks for deliverance from a horrible death. The General was also deeply affected, and

did all that was possible for our speedy relief and comfort."[117]

Brisbin also recorded the historic scene:

Reno was found on a high hill, and when the officers of our column made their way up the officers of the Seventh grasped them by the hand and shed tears. Reno came forward, and, for the circumstances, was wonderfully calm and at ease.[118] He said he wanted doctors and medicines and canvas to shelter the wounded from the sun, and wished to have his wounded men helped down into the valley. He would have moved them several hours before, as he felt sure that the Indians were gone and help was near, but thought it better to avoid even the possibility of having to move them twice. They were all got down before night, but it was then too late to move his camp, and he passed another night there. But in the cool air of night the odors were less unendurable.[119]

Surviving with Reno were the remnants of seven companies of cavalry: 328 men, including 51 on the wounded list. Over the next couple of days, many of the survivors traversed the battlefield, identifying the remains if possible and burying the dead, where Custer and some 210 soldiers fought their last fight.[120] "All the officers' graves," wrote Brisbin, "were marked by hollow sticks, sunk deep in the ground, containing the names of the dead."[121]

If the following descriptions are any indication, Custer's battlefield was a sight they would never forget:

The battlefield looked like a slaughter pen . . . the dead were much mutilated.[122]

Many of the men found dead on Custer's field were horribly mutilated and most

GENERAL CUSTER'S DEATH STRUGGLE.
The Battle of the Little Big Horn.

One of many romantic and inaccurate depictions of the combined Indian force overwhelming the
Seventh Cavalry that were popular following the battle. (*Library of Congress*)

had their skulls smashed by stone mallets. This was the work of the squaws, who swarmed to the battlefield robbing and mutilating the bodies of the dead and killing the dying and wounded.[123]

Many were gashed with knives and some had their noses and other members cut off. The heads of four white soldiers were found in the Sioux camp that had been severed from the trunks, but the bodies could not be found on the battlefield or in the village.[124]

The remains bear many evidences of torture. The heads of nearly all had been crushed with stone clubs, while in other cases their heads were severed from the bodies. The entrails in many cases had been taken out, and from many the limbs were chopped off. Other bodies were partially burned, a few were not found, but clothing belonging to them was found and recognized.[125]

Across Custer's breast laid, face downward, the semi-nude corpse of a sergeant of the Seventh Cavalry. . . . This poor fellow was robbed of everything but his undershirt; the crown of his skull was knocked away, his ears cut off, his left leg chopped asunder, and the rest of his frame perforated with rifle balls. . . . Tom Custer's heart was literally dug out. The red devils appeared to have vented their savagery upon his remains. We could barely lift them up intact, they were so hacked up with knives. . . . Very few of the slain had hair long enough to scalp. We noticed that those who had hair enough were scalped, while those whose hair was too short were either beheaded or else brained. The savages must have been exasperated where scalping was an impossibility. They varied the monotony by cutting off noses, ears, limbs and perpetrating other indignities, and conducted the butchery with method at times, for we would come across a pile of heads here, or stack of arms and legs there, and so on. As a rule, however, noses, ears, heads and limbs were scattered all over the battleground. Some of the heads were impaled on poles stuck into the ground for that purpose. In three or four cases the amputations were performed with surgical neatness; in all others mere chopping was the manner. . . . The beheaded privates we had considerable difficulty in identifying, their heads being mixed up and scattered around; only privates were beheaded.[126]

It is sickening to look at the bodies stripped. Here a hand gone, here a foot or a head, ghastly gashes cut in all parts of the body, eyes gouged out, noses and ears cut off and skulls crushed in. One sees at a distance a dead horse lying on the plain or near the river, and upon a near approach the gleaming white skin of a naked cavalry soldier, the body cut and mangled beyond description, is brought into view.[127]

The men, horses and mules were piled up, over and across and under each other, presenting one of the most horrible sights I ever saw.[128]

It makes one heart sick to look over the battleground and see the poor fellows, some of them with their entrails cut out, others with their eyes dug out and hearts laid across their face. They even stopped to cut their pockets to get their money and watches. The most fearful sight was Lieutenant Cook[e]. He was a splendid looking man, with long dark whiskers. They dug his face all out so as to get his fine beard, it is supposed.[129]

We found a man's head with a lariat attached. The Indians had dragged the body around until the head had become detached.[130]

Sitting Bull's Description of Custer's Last Stand

New York Herald,
November 16, 1877

Fort Walsh, Northwest Territory,
October 17, 1877.

"The trouble with the soldiers," [Sitting Bull stated] "was they were so exhausted and their horses bothered them so much that they could not take good aim. Some of their horses broke away from them and left them to stand and drop and die. When the Long Hair, the General, found that he was so outnumbered and threatened on his flanks, he took the best course he could have taken. The bugle blew. It was an order to fall back. All the men fell back fighting and dropping. They could not fire fast enough, though. But from our side it was so," said Sitting Bull, and here he clapped his hands rapidly twice a second to express with what quickness and continuance the balls flew from the Henry and Winchester rifles wielded by the Indians. "They could not stand up under such a fire," he added.

—As told to reporter
Jerome B. Stillson

The Indians had taken all the soldiers' clothing, guns and ammunition, and the bridles and saddles from the dead horses. Many of the men were so mutilated and so changed by the two days of hot sun that they could not be recognized. Those who were only wounded at first were cut in the face and on the body with the tomahawk. Some had their bodies shot full of arrows, others were scalped.[131]

However, when it came to describing Custer's remains, "the *beau sabreur* of the Army of the Potomac,"[132] the grisly descriptions, as if by the mutual consent of all involved, were transformed into the comforting image of a man sleeping peacefully or portrayed rather innocuously, undoubtedly for the benefit of his widow, Elizabeth Custer:

Near the top of a little knoll . . . lay Custer himself, and it touched my heart to see that the savages, in a kind of human recognition of heroic clay, had respected the corpse of the man they knew so well. . . . He lay as if asleep, his face calm and a smile on his lips.[133]

Poor Custer's troubles in this world are over. He fell like a gallant soldier as he was, and the savages recognizing him as a "great brave" refused to scalp or otherwise mutilate his person.[134]

Custer seemed to be sleeping: his attitude was natural, his expression sweet and serene.[135]

All but Custer himself are brutally mutilated. He is stripped only.[136]

Custer's [body] was not mutilated. He was shot through the body and through the head.[137]

They did not disfigure General Custer in any way.[138]

Custer's expression was serene.[139]

Even some fifteen years later, an eyewitness declared:

All the bodies were entirely naked and nearly all were horribly mutilated. Custer's, however, was not disturbed.[140]

The truth of the matter is that, in addition to suffering two bullet wounds, one to the left side of his forehead and one near his heart, Custer's thigh was slashed, a finger severed and an arrow shoved into his penis.[141]

One anonymous writer likely summed up everyone's feelings after looking at the bloody battlefield when he declared: "The ghastly detail[s] would seem to court oblivion, if it were in the nature of things possible to forget or cloak them up."[142]

As far as the author can tell, the first mention of there being a "last stand" was in the following paragraph from an anonymous writer in a dispatch dated "Mouth of the Big Horn, July 1," and printed in the *New York Herald* on July 8:

At the highest point of the ridge lay Custer, surrounded by a chosen band. Here were his two brothers and his nephew (Mr. Reed), Colonels Yates and Cooke, and Lieutenant [Algernon E.] Smith, all lying in a circle of a few yards, their horses beside them. Here, behind Yates' company, the last stand had been made, and here, one after another, these last survivors of Custer's five companies had met their death. The companies had successively thrown themselves across the path of the advancing enemy and had been annihilated. Not a man has escaped to tell the tale, but it was inscribed on the surface of the barren hills in a language more eloquent than words.[143]

A few days later, a similar description appeared in the *New York Tribune*:

Lieutenant Smith fought his way to a peak, where a last stand was made. They must have known that their hour had

Statement of Little Buck Elk about the Battle of the Little Big Horn

New York Times, October 19, 1876

Washington, Oct. 18—The Commissioner of Indian Affairs today received a letter from Indian Agent Mitchell, dated Fort Peck, Montana, September 25. Agent Mitchell writes as follows:

"Little Buck Elk, an Uncapapa, Chief of the Soldiers' Band, arrived here on the evening of the 23rd. . . . Little Buck Elk stated that he was in the fight in which Gen. Custer and all his men were slaughtered, and that eleven different tribes were engaged in the fight. He said the Indians were as thick as bees at the fight, and that there were so many of them that they could not all take part in it; that the soldiers were all brave men and fought well; that some of them, when they found themselves surrounded and overpowered, broke through the lines and tried to make their escape, but were pursued and killed, miles from the battleground. One soldier, who had a faster horse than the rest, made his escape into the bad lands, and after he had ridden seven or eight miles accidentally ran into a war party of Indians and was killed by them. This soldier rode a big horse with flaxen mane, and had a Government saddle and gray saddle blanket, but it was not known whether he was an officer or not. He also stated that they captured six battle flags, and that no soldiers were taken alive; but after the fight the women went among the dead bodies and robbed and mutilated them. There were plenty of watches and money taken from them, which the young warriors are now wearing on their shirts and belts. Little Buck Elk promised me that if the watch belonging to Lieutenant [John J.] Crittenden [20th Infantry] could be found he would bring it to the agency."

come. Here were Custer and his brother, Adjutant Cook[e], Capt. Yates, Lieut. Riley, Lieut. Smith, and a few soldiers. Making ramparts of their fallen horses, they fought to the end.[144]

"At the highest point of the ridge lay Custer, surrounded by a chosen band. . . . these last survivors of Custer's five companies . . . Not a man escaped to tell the tale." "They must have known that their hour had come. . . . Making ramparts of their fallen horses, they fought to the end." "[T]he last stand had been made." The imagery was fantastic. There were no survivors to tell the tale. Our fascination with death, and on such a grand scale, is piqued. Custer was a charismatic frontier personality. The Indian warriors were colorful, capable of horrific savagery on the battlefield, and represented the last holdouts of a dying era. Mix up the ingredients and you have the recipe for a legendary battle that has remained in the public consciousness since the day it occurred.

According to Lieutenant John Carland, Sixth Infantry, when Terry arrived on the battlefield, he looked down at the lifeless Custer and, with teary eyes, said, "The flower of the army is gone at last." And if Carland is to be believed, there were "seventeen cartridge shells by Custer's side, where he had kept them off until the last moment."[145]

"The flower of the army is gone at last." But how did it happen? What went wrong? How could this modern army, led by one of its top commanders, fall to a technologically inferior, some would say Stone Age, foe? Was it simply a matter of overwhelming numbers? One contemporary writer thought the odds were satisfactory, or would have been under "ordinary circumstances":

Information derived from many sources, including . . . the observations of officers engaged in the battle, leads to the conclusion that 2,500 or 3,000 Indians composed the fighting force arrayed against Custer and his 600. Still, these were odds which any officer of the Seventh Cavalry would have unhesitatingly accepted for his regiment under any ordinary circumstances of Indian warfare.[146]

But this view was too simplistic. Yes, technically, the twelve companies of the Seventh Cavalry numbered about six hundred soldiers at the time of battle, but they were divided into four battalions (including McDougall's company with the pack train) that made each segment unable to properly defend itself, even if confronted by no more than half the estimated total of Indians. And when the horse holders are subtracted from the number of men available to fight, generally one man for every four horses, the odds are even more staggering.[147] But what if Custer had kept all twelve companies together?[148] Dr. Henry R. Porter, the only one of three surgeons to survive the battle, believed that "the result would have been the same . . ., only the massacre would have been more terrible."[149] Lieutenant Carland echoed this sentiment when he wrote:

There can be no blame attached to any one for this fearful slaughter. If Custer had had the whole regiment [together] it would only have been worse as the Sioux were too many. Of course there will be some blamed by Eastern papers, but as an eyewitness of the whole battle[field] I cannot censure any one.[150]

Sherman, based on the earliest of reports, conjectured that "Gen. Custer attempted a battle without reconnoitering the position, and that he was too bold."[151] Following the same line of thought, Lieutenant Alfred Johnson, Seventh Infantry, wrote, "I am clearly of the opinion that General Custer did not know the extent of this camp."[152]

One writer blamed Custer's defeat on the fatigue of the troops, and then followed it up with a healthy dose of speculation:

While Reno was attacking the village from the south Custer's force would assault the Indians on the flank and in the rear. It was a shrewd plan, but he overrated the endurance of his soldiers; they were faint and weary; they had been in the saddle 24 hours. . . . [Custer] had gone around the bluffs and had attempted to ford the river at the northern end of the village.[153] The Indians were massed in his front and on his flanks. The whole command dismounted and made a determined resistance, which checked momentarily the onset of the Indians. Then Custer ordered a retreat, his force dividing in order to take advantage of two ravines on the left flank. The enemy had already appeared in large force on the right and closed the door of escape in that direction. At the head of the upper ravine Calhoun's company was apparently thrown out as skirmishers to defend the entrance. Here their bodies were found after the battle; the skirmish lines were clearly marked by the rows of the slain with heaps of empty cartridge shells; Calhoun and Crittenden were in their places—in advance of the files.[154]

Perhaps the one theory that hit closest to the truth, and that embraced the lack of advance surveillance guessed at by Sherman, was that expressed in the *New York Tribune* on July 7, 1876: "Custer underestimated the enemy, separated his force, and was defeated in detail." He also misjudged the time necessary to find a suitable fording place downstream to make a simultaneous attack, thus "losing the moral effect."[155]

An article appeared in the *New York Herald* on July 26 based upon statements of the Crow scout Curley.[156] Possibly written by Major Brisbin, the scenario was, for the most part, reasonable, and still holds up today:

Custer had to go further down the river and further away from Reno than he wished on account of the steep bank along the north side; but at last he found a ford and dashed for it. The Indians met him and poured in a heavy fire from across the narrow river. Custer dismounted to fight on foot, but could not get his skirmishers over the stream. Meantime hundreds of Indians, on foot and on ponies, poured over the river, which was only about three feet deep, and filled the ravines on each side of Custer's men. Custer then fell back to some high ground behind him and seized the ravines in his immediate vicinity. The Indians completely surrounded Custer and poured in a terrible fire on all sides. They charged Custer on foot in vast numbers, but were again and again driven back.[157]

Based on the available evidence, an anonymous report printed in the *New York Herald* on July 8 also laid out a logical outline of events:

At a point about three miles down the right bank of the stream [from Reno Hill] Custer had evidently attempted to ford and attack the village from the ford. The trail was found to lead back up to the bluffs and to the northward, as if the troops had been repulsed and compelled to retreat and at the same time had been cut off from regaining the forces under Reno. The bluffs along the right bank come sharply down to the water and are interspersed by numerous ravines all along the slopes and ridges, and in the ravines, lying as they had fought, line behind line, showing where defensive positions had been successfully taken up and held till none were left to fight, there, huddled in a narrow compass, horses and men were piled promiscuously.[158]

After Crazy Horse surrendered in May 1877, he and Horned Horse suggested to a reporter that Custer's

downfall was in misreading the situation as it unfolded:

The attack was a surprise and totally unlooked for. When Custer [Reno] made the charge the women, papooses, children, and in fact, all that were not fighters, made a stampede in a northerly direction. Custer, seeing so numerous a body, mistook them for the main body of Indians retreating and abandoning their villages [in the face of Reno's charge], and immediately gave pursuit. The warriors in the village, seeing this, divided their forces into two parts, one intercepting Custer between their noncombatants and him, and the other getting in his rear. Outnumbering him as they did, they had him at their mercy, and the dreadful massacre ensued.[159]

It was an ironic twist of fate: despite launching a surprise attack, the attackers were the ones who were surprised. Instead of scattering to avoid a pitched battle, as everyone expected the Indians to do (if experience was any indication), they responded with an even stronger offensive than the one launched against them. The troops, having been separated into smaller fighting units, were soon battling for their lives. Custer's battalion was particularly in a bad way: not only was it separated from Reno and Benteen, but it was itself separated into two battalions (under Captains Myles Keogh and George Yates). And the hilly terrain was not conducive to cavalry tactics.

On June 28, while many of the men were engaged in burying the dead, Gibbon's cavalry was sent on a reconnaissance to determine where the Indians had gone:

Colonel Gibbon's cavalry followed the Indians for about ten miles, and ascertained that they had moved to the south and west by several trails. A good deal of property had been thrown away by them to lighten their march, and was found scattered for many miles over the prairies. Many of their dead were also discovered secreted in ravines a long distance from the battlefield. Among them were Arapahoes and Cheyennes as well as Sioux.[160]

While it is impossible to know just how many Indians were killed in the fights with Reno and Custer, some historians believe the number may be as low as forty-three.[161] According to Red Horse, the Indians suffered 136 killed and 160 wounded. Of course, this suggests that the Indians laid out all of their dead and counted them, which is not likely. Another report from an Indian source claimed that only thirty-one Indians were killed.[162] Whatever the number, it seems likely that others died in the following days and weeks from wounds received in the battle. According to John W. Smith, a frontier trader "who speaks Sioux fluently," reliable Indians at Standing Rock Agency told him that forty Indians were killed in the Custer battle, and that twenty more had later died of their wounds.[163] Of the Indian casualties, an undetermined number were the result of friendly fire:

Horned Horse says the smoke and dust was so great that foe could not be distinguished from friend. The horses were wild with fright and uncontrollable. The Indians were knocking each other from their steeds, and it is an absolute fact that the young bucks in their excitement and fury killed each other, several dead Indians being found killed by arrows. Horned Horse represented this hell of fire and smoke and death by interturning his fingers and saying: "Just like this, Indians and white men."[164]

As is usual with such disasters, the need to assign blame quickly followed. An anonymous dispatch to the *New York Herald* gave voice to one or more officers who wished to remain anonymous:

Whether Custer did right or wrong in attacking as he did, your correspondent does not pretend to say. An officer informs me General Terry did not expect or desire General Custer to attack the Indians until he [Terry] should reach the Little Horn and gain a position from which he could support him. Custer attacked forty-eight hours [!] in advance of the time Terry was to reach that point. An officer informs your correspondent when Custer came in sight of the 1,800 lodges, a village of upward of 7,000 Indians, he swung his hat and said— "Hurrah! Custer's luck! The biggest Indian village on the American continent!"[165]

A dispatch out of Chicago, printed in the *New York Times* on July 7, stated: "Gen. Custer was directed by Gen. Terry to find and feel of the Indians, but not to fight unless Terry arrived with infantry and with Gibbon's column."[166]

However, as previously noted, Custer's column *was* expected to "strike the blow." Writing to Sheridan on July 2, Terry composed a letter to clear himself of any wrongdoing in the loss of almost half of the Seventh Cavalry:

Camp Big Horn, July 2. I think I owe it to myself to put you more fully in possession of the facts of the late operations. While at the mouth of the Rosebud [June 21] I submitted my plan to Gen. Gibbon and Gen. Custer. It was that Custer, with his whole regiment, should move up the Rosebud till he should meet a trail Reno had discovered a few days before, but that he should not follow it directly to the Little Big Horn; that he should send scouts over it and keep his main force further toward the south, so as to prevent the Indians from slipping in between himself and the mountains. He was also to examine the head waters of the Tullock's Creek, as he passed it, and send me word of what he found there. A scout [Herendeen] was furnished him for the purpose of crossing the country to me. We calculated it would take Gibbon's column until the 26th to reach the mouth of the Little Big Horn, and that the wide sweep I had proposed Custer should make would require so much time that Gibbon would be able to cooperate with him in attacking any Indians that might be found on the stream.[167] I asked Custer how long his marches would be. He said they would be at the rate of about thirty miles a day. Measurements were made and calculations based on that rate of progress. I talked with him about his strength and at one time suggested that perhaps it would be well for me to take Gibbon's cavalry and go with him. To the latter suggestion he replied: that, without reference to the command, he would prefer his own regiment alone. As a homogenous body, as much could be done with it as with the two combined. He expressed the utmost confidence that he had all the force that he could need, and I shared his confidence. The plan adopted was the only one which promised to bring the infantry into action, and I desired to make sure of things by getting up every available man. I offered Custer the battery of Gatling guns, but he declined it, saying that it might embarrass him, and that he was strong enough without it.

The movements proposed by Gen. Gibbon's column were carried out to the letter, and had the attack been deferred until it was up, I cannot doubt that we should have been successful. The Indians had evidently prepared themselves for a stand, but as I learned from Capt. Benton [Benteen] that on the 22nd the cavalry marched twelve miles; on the 23rd, twenty-five miles; from 5 a.m. till 8 p.m., of the 24th, forty-five miles, and then after night ten miles further, resting, but without unsaddling, twenty-three miles, to the battlefield. The proposed route was not taken, but as soon as the trail was struck it was followed. I cannot learn that any examination of Tullock's Creek was made. I do not tell you this to cast any reflections upon Custer, for whatever errors he may have committed Custer's action is unexplainable in the case.

A. H. Terry, Brigadier General.[168]

As noted earlier in this chapter, on July 6, Sheridan was unwilling to make any public statements to a *New York Herald* reporter about the military disaster that befell Custer until more of the facts were learned. And he was right; it would have been "unfair to the memory of Custer." The most the reporter could get out of him was that "Custer was a gallant, daring man, who knew the Indian country well, who had served against various tribes, and who, in addition to his natural ability and courage, had special experience."[169] As right as

Sheridan was in holding his tongue, especially if his comments would have reflected negatively on Custer, it makes for boring history. Luckily, when Sheridan left the room, one of his subalterns opened up to the *Herald* correspondent:

The truth about Custer is that he was a pet soldier who had risen not above his merit but higher than men of equal merit. He fought with Phil Sheridan and through the patronage of Sheridan he rose, but while Sheridan liked his valor and his dash he never trusted his judgment. . . . While Sheridan is always cool, Custer was always aflame. He was like a thermometer. He had a touch of romance about him, and when the war broke out he used to go about dressed like one of Byron's pirates in the Archipelago, with waving, shining locks and a broad, flapping sombrero. Rising to high command early in life he lost the repose necessary to success in high command. Why, I remember when we were chasing Lee and had him up against Appomattox, Custer rushed into the rebel lines and wanted Longstreet to surrender the whole army to him. You see Custer imagined that if he could frighten Longstreet into a surrender all he would have to do would be to turn over the whole rebel gang to Grant, but Longstreet, who had wonderful sense, quietly told the furious young man that he did not command the army to surrender it, and that Lee was off to see Grant on that same business.

Then Custer must rush into politics, and went swinging around the circle with [President] Johnson. He wanted to be a statesman, and but for Sheridan's influence with Grant the republicans would have thrown him; but you see we all liked Custer and did not mind his little freaks in that way any more than we

would have minded temper in a woman. Sheridan, to keep Custer in his place, kept him out on the Plains at work. He gave him a fine command, one of the best cavalry regiments in the service. The colonel, Sturges [Sturgis], was allowed to bask in the sunshine in a large city while Custer was the real commander. In this service Custer did well, and indicated the partiality of Sheridan as well as the kind feelings of his friends. But Grant's administration began to go down, and it looked like a new deal. The old spirit which sent Custer swinging around the circle revived in him. He came East and took a prominent part in reforming the army. Well, that is all right in theory; but, you see, when a soldier goes out of soldiering he is sure to blunder.

Then he must write his war memoirs. Sherman did it, and Frederick and Napoleon, and why should not Custer? So people began to cry 'Dime novel!' at him. Well, in these memoirs he began to write recklessly about the army. He took to praising McClellan as the great man of the war. Probably he was; but it was no business of Custer, and, coming as it did when the democrats began to look lively, it annoyed the administration. Grant grew so much annoyed that even Sheridan could do no good, and Custer was disgraced. Instead of commanding the Yellowstone expedition . . . he was made a subordinate. . . . Custer felt . . . [disgraced] and went out to the field to do some tremendous thing, astonish the country and overwhelm the administration. So, when he saw some Sioux camps, instead of waiting for Gibbon or for Terry, who would have shared or usurped his honors, he rushed in without knowing or caring. It reminds me very much of the charge of the Light Brigade at Balaklava. . . . Custer's glorious death and the valor of his men will become a legend in our history. . . . We all think, much as we lament Custer and much as we respect his generous, brave nature, that he sacrificed the Seventh Cavalry to his ambition and wounded vanity. He played an appalling stake and lost. As the great commander said of Cardigan's charge of the light brigade—'It is superb, but it is not war.'

I liked Custer so well that I wish I could throw only laurels on his grave. But one must think of those who died with him, of the dishonor to our flag, of the exultant frenzy this will inspire in the Indians, of the more combats to come. The defeat of Custer—God knows only what it means. It may unite the Indians as they were under Tecumseh, and while in the end we shall conquer that league, it will require blood and treasure that might have been saved but for these mad doings on the Yellowstone.[170]

On July 7, the same day it ran the interview with Sheridan, the *New York Herald* melodramatically asserted:

Had Custer been in command of the campaign a sense of responsibility would have restrained and tempered his impetuosity. But this brave soldier had been rendered desperate by ill usage, and when "death was set in one eye and honor in the other" he courted a heroic death rather than endure the disgrace which the cold malignity of the President had attempted to put upon him. It would be hardly too severe to say to President Grant, "Behold your hands! They are red with the blood of Custer and his brave three hundred."[171]

On July 8, Sheridan sent a communication to Sherman calling for calm, control, and cash:

I think it premature to think of asking for volunteer cavalry, with the attendant expense. . . . We are all right; give us a lit-

tle time. I deeply deplore the loss of Custer and his officers and men. I fear it was an unnecessary sacrifice due to misapprehension and a superabundance of courage—the latter extraordinarily developed in Custer. . . . [I]f Congress will give the $200,000 which I have asked for the past two years, for the establishment of the posts at Tongue River and the mouth of the Big Horn, it will be in the interest of economy and will settle the Sioux question.[172]

Back in Montana and Wyoming, the Indian campaign had come to a crushing halt. Crook was waiting for reinforcements in northern Wyoming, and Terry, after sending about three dozen wounded men back to Fort Lincoln on the steamer *Far West*, had to regroup on the Yellowstone. And he, too, would request reinforcements. Both columns would remain virtually inactive until the first days of August.

In a dispatch to the *New York Herald* dated July 1, an anonymous writer with the expedition left his readers with this thought:

In closing my hasty narrative of this affair, in certain respects the most remarkable in modern history, I purposely refrain from comment. The naked facts, so far as they are known, must guide your readers to a conclusion as to the causes of the calamity.[173]

In a letter to his father on July 2, Lieutenant George D. Wallace, Seventh Cavalry, wrote:

Our noble regiment is almost obliterated, but a merciful God has spared a few. Of the five companies that were with General Custer not one man is left to tell the story of the massacre.[174]

Lieutenant Johnson of the Seventh Infantry, also writing to his father, expressed the hope that the Sioux would soon get their comeuppance: "Generals Terry, Gibbon and Crook are old campaigners and will strike a telling blow with an iron hand should an opportunity present itself."[175]

In closing this chapter, let us give the final word to one of the warriors who fought on that hot June day in 1876. Describing his pictographic depiction of the battle of the Little Big Horn twenty-five years after the event, Black Bear, a Brule Sioux warrior, recalled:

I was in that fight. I was a young man then, and I remember it was the biggest thing in my life. I think I make a picture of it, so that all my people know about it.

That man in the middle on the horse, see him? That is 'Long Hair.' See how his hair wave[s] out behind.[176] He ride[s] alone. There is one of his men dead (pointing to a figure of a man in a slouch hat lying down). There is another. Indians are killing them.

There are Indians on horses. They ride round and round Long Hair. They ride fast, and every time they pass they kill some of his men. Indians can ride fast and they can shoot. Long Hair know that and he fight well, but Indians were like the dust the wind blows. No man can count them. Long Hair must die and he knows it.[177] That horse he rides, it is killed, but he fights on. I know that because I see it.

(Around the edge of the picture are rows of Indians holding rifles to their shoulders and all aiming at the center, where Custer stands alone.) "These men all Sioux but they are different tribes. The Ogalalas stand here. The Brules

Superhuman Indian Warriors

In the weeks following the battle of the Little Big Horn, the Sioux were sometimes transformed into a race of superhuman fighting men, as illustrated in this clipping from the *Cheyenne Daily Leader* on August 17, 1876:

The Savage Sioux—The Sioux are among the very best fighters in the world. They possess union and self-reliance, cunning without equal, a personnel in which every man is an athlete capable of super-eminent feats of endurance, horsemanship and agility. Further, they possess the vast advantage of fighting on ground of their own selection, in their own country, and with whose resources, either for supplies or defense, they have a perfect familiarity. It affords them too, at every step, natural fortifications equal—for purposes of concealment or defense—to the most elaborate work possible to engineering skill. Well mounted, armed with the very best of modern small arms, ever alert and tireless, regarding death in battle as an honor to be sought rather than as a calamity to be avoided, they are practically as effective as a civilized army of 20,000 men operating in an open country and according to the rules of modern warfare.

here. They sometimes fight each other, but now they all fighting against Long Hair.[178]

Black Bear's interviewer added:

Crude as the picture is, it conveys an admirable idea of a multitude against a handful. Nothing could better illustrate the force of superior numbers than the circle of feather-bedecked savages closing in relentlessly on the one brave man who is given the place of importance in the center. The artist is a good-natured Brule, who is more than six feet tall. The cordial way in which he shakes hands with strangers, and his habitual smile did not bear out his story, which he tells proudly, of how he participated in the Custer massacre and "kill heap white men."[179]

INTERLUDE

Thoughts on Custer and the Battle of the Little Big Horn

"To make General Custer a scapegoat would be to place upon his head iniquities for which he is no more responsible than were the brave men who charged at Balaklava for the policy which brought on the Crimean War."
—*Brooklyn Daily Eagle*, July 7, 1876

"The magnetism of the man discovered for him a warm sympathy among the people so that in his cruel end thousands recognized a personal loss as well as a national disaster."
—*New York Herald*, July 7, 1876

"The country will give him its admiration, its tears, its regrets; it will pardon his error, if he committed one, and inscribe his name in bright letters on the roll of fame. For the planning of this mismanaged, ill-starred campaign he was not responsible."
—*New York Herald*, July 7, 1876

Major Robert E. A. Crofton: "I have seen a little Indian fighting, and I tell you that it is the worst business a man can engage in. Here is General Custer,

one of the bravest of men and one of the best Indian fighters that ever lived, after years of successful experience, beaten and cut down and all of his command with him. He who had so often baffled the wiles of the Indian and overmatched them in cunning, at length falls a victim to Indian strategy. I can look at it in no other manner, and I am pretty sure that when we get official reports we shall learn that the unfortunate General fell into a trap."
—*New York Times*, July 7, 1876

"The precise particulars of that horrible catastrophe will never be known. There are no survivors. The course of the detachment, after it began the attack, is traced only by the bodies of the slain."
—*New York Times*, July 7, 1876

"If such a catastrophe should provoke the people into demanding a speedy and complete revision of our Indian policy, the blood of our soldiers will not have been shed entirely in vain."
—*New York Tribune*, July 7, 1876

"Death came to him as he would have wished, at the head of his column, on the field of honor."
—*Colorado Springs Gazette*, July 8, 1876

"All we know of this harrowing massacre is learned by an inspection of the dead. General Custer and his brave five companies advanced to the attack, were veiled in the smoke of murderous muskets, and none escaped to tell the tale."
—*New York Herald*, July 8, 1876

"The mysterious silence which reigned over those mutilated dead must have been more eloquent than any words, because amid such surroundings conjecture, aided by imagination, must have drawn a more dreadful picture of the battle than the tongues of the dead could

have given had they been able to speak. All that we are ever likely to know of the immediate circumstances of the battle is mere inference from the position and appearance of the corpses. A dark pall of mystery hangs over the scene and will hang forever."
—*New York Herald*, July 8, 1876

Major General Thomas L. Rosser: "As a soldier I would sooner today lie in the grave of General Custer and his gallant comrades alone in that distant wilderness, that when the 'last trumpet' sounds I could rise to judgment from my post of duty, than to live in the place of the survivors of the siege on the hills. I knew General Custer well . . . and, being on opposite sides during the late war, we often met and measured strength on the fields of Virginia; and I can truly say now that I never met a more enterprising, gallant or dangerous an enemy during those four years of terrible war, or a more genial, whole-souled, chivalrous gentleman and friend in peace than Major General George A. Custer."
—*New York Herald*, July 11, 1876

"Had Custer let Sitting Bull escape after so much pains to find him, he would have incurred the indignant censure of every army officer and of the whole country. Inconsiderate and ungenerous minds have blamed him for not awaiting the arrival of Terry and Gibbon before making the attack. But if he had waited and given the Indians an opportunity to run away, what would have been said of him?"
—*New York Herald*, July 11, 1876

"This slaughter of General Custer and his troops is one of the most remarkable events of modern times. . . . It is very unusual for the attacking party to be annihilated by the party of the defense.

It looks very much as if Custer had greatly underrated the fighting capacity of his foe. The victory of the Sioux . . . is not very likely to inspire the troops with an extraordinarily ardent desire to get into close quarters with the Red Men, who are becoming 'exceedingly angry.'"
—*Deseret News*, July 12, 1876

"If Custer was too weak without the support of Terry and Gibbon why was he sent away from them on an errand where they could not support him, and when he might have met the Indians at any time?"
—*New York Herald*, July 13, 1876

"A deed like this on the Yellowstone will shine out in our history with the splendor of Thermopylae in the history of Greece. The courage of Custer was as high as that of Leonidas. . . . Custer's death has all the romance, all the beauty of high achievement. It has no parallel in our history, and few, indeed, in the history of other nations."
—*New York Herald*, July 14, 1876

Gen. Andrew T. McReynolds: "General Custer may have been too impulsive, but, after all, the great forte of cavalry is reckless dash. Custer's only fault, if fault it may be termed, consists in failure. If it had been a success, as doubtless he had every reason to anticipate, imperishable laurels would have crowned his brow."
—*New York Tribune*, July 15, 1876

"Enclosed please find $1 toward the Custer monument in commemoration of the greatest cavalry officer ever born—a man who always rode at the head of his men. I hereby suggest that the United States government should keep in its possession the plot of ground where Custer and his comrades were found riddled with the bullets of the

cursed Sioux, and that it would be no more than right for them to erect a monument on the spot, so as to show future generations how she remembered her sons."
—*New York Herald*, July 17, 1876

"Those who knew Custer do not wonder that he tried to make the most of it and hazarded all in an attempt to conquer the Sioux without assistance. . . . [F]aith in his own fortune and the chafing he had received at the hands of the President . . . was the immediate cause of the disaster."
—*New York Herald*, July 18, 1876

"Brave Custer's memory will ever be enshrined in the hearts of the pioneers of the west, and the Great West will now see to it that Custer's last battle shall be made the 'beginning of the end' of the Indian troubles on the frontier."
—*Weekly Rocky Mountain News*, July 19, 1876

"The criticism of Major Reno that he did not go to the relief of Custer fails when the fact is stated that he had a narrow escape from Custer's fate whose command was five miles away. It was more than the gallant Reno could do to take care of himself."
—*Daily Colorado Chieftain*, July 20, 1876

"Indians who believe that God punishes men for their wickedness and regards them for their good work will very certainly look upon their success in killing General Custer and his troops while invading the Sioux country for no better a purpose than the protection of whites who were violating law and justice as being significant of the will of the Great Spirit."
—*New York Herald*, August 3, 1876

"The fate of the brave and gallant Custer has deeply touched the public heart, which sees only a fearless soldier leading a charge against an ambushed foe, and falling at the head of his men and in the thick of the fray."
—*Harper's Weekly*, August 5, 1876

"We can hardly doubt that the disaster to our arms on the sad occasion of Custer's last attack was in some measure caused by a total absence of experience in horsemanship or the use of arms on the part of our troops, who were largely made up of recent recruits. It is well to understand that such recruits, who represent as good material for rank and file as is possessed by any country in the world, are not given the opportunities of serviceable drill, that any other country would furnish. . . . Let us, then, take the recruit in the field. If his horsemanship be on a par with his rifle practice imagine him in action, with one hand grasping the pommel of his saddle, striving to retain his stirrupless and uncertain seat, while Sioux warriors in front dash toward him, yelling and waving their blankets, scaring horse and man, until the latter has his brains knocked out while looking round helplessly for succor."
—*New York Herald*, August 5, 1876

Major General Thomas L. Rosser: "Custer did that which in ninety-nine cases out of 100 will succeed, but this by chance was the fatal exception, yet the result does not impair the value of the rule."
—*New York Herald*, August 22, 1876

President Grant: "I regard Custer's massacre as a sacrifice of troops, brought on by Custer himself, that was wholly unnecessary—wholly unnecessary."
—*New York Herald*, September 2, 1876

"There is only one sure way to kill Indians, and that is to go where they are and kill them before they can kill you. Custer had the correct idea, but an insufficient force and an excess of bravery."
—*Weekly Rocky Mountain News*, September 13, 1876

INTERLUDE

"He was the personification of bravery and dash"

As a one-time correspondent for the *New York Tribune*, Samuel J. Barrows (1845–1909) accompanied Colonel David S. Stanley's Yellowstone Expedition of 1873 (in which Custer participated) and Custer's Black Hills Expedition of 1874. Upon Custer's death, Barrows wrote the following tribute to his old friend, which was printed in the *Tribune* on July 10, 1876:

New York Tribune,
Monday, July 10, 1876

REMINISCENCES OF GENERAL CUSTER.

A BORN CAVALRYMAN—COURAGE AND ENDURANCE—LOVE OF DISPLAY—HIS WRITINGS.

Cambridge, Mass., July 8, 1876.
To the Editor of the Tribune—
Sir: I accompanied Gen. Custer on the Yellowstone and Black Hills expeditions. He was a born cavalryman. He was never more in his element than when mounted on Dandy, his favorite horse, and riding at the head of his regiment. He once said to me, "I would rather be a private in the cavalry than a line officer in the infantry." He was the personification of bravery and dash. His most bitter enemies never accused him of cowardice. If he had only added discretion to his valor he would have been a perfect soldier. His impetuosity very often ran away with his judgment. He was impatient of control. He liked to act independently of others and take all the risk and all the glory to himself. He frequently got himself into trouble by assuming more authority than really belonged to his rank. It was so on the Yellowstone expedition, where he came into collision with Gen. [David S.] Stanley, his superior officer, and was placed under arrest and compelled to ride at the rear of his column for two or three days, until Gen. [Thomas L.] Rosser, who fought against Custer in the Shenandoah Valley during the war,[180] but was then acting as engineer of the Northern Pacific Railroad, succeeded in effecting a reconciliation. Custer and Stanley afterward got on very well, and perhaps the quarrel would never have occurred if the two generals had been left alone to themselves without the intervention of camp gossips, who sought to foster the traditional jealousy between infantry and cavalry. For Stanley was the soul of generosity, and Custer did not really mean to be arrogant; but from the time when he entered West Point to the day when he fell on the Big Horn, he was accustomed to take just as much liberty as he was entitled to.

For this reason, Custer worked most easily and effectively when under general orders, when not hampered by special restrictions, or his success [not] made dependent on anybody else. Gen. Terry understood his man when, in the order directing him to march up the Rosebud, he very liberally said: "The Department Commander places too much confidence in your zeal, energy, and ability to wish to impose upon you precise orders which might hamper your action when nearly in contact with the enemy." But Gen. Terry did not understand Custer if he thought he would wait for Gibbon's support before attacking an Indian camp. Undoubtedly he ought to have done this; but with his native impetuosity, his reckless daring, his confidence in his own regiment, which had never failed him, and his love of public approval, Custer could no more help charging this Indian camp than he could help charging just so many buffaloes. He had never learned to spell the word "defeat"; he knew nothing but success, and if he had met the Indians on the open plain, success would undoubtedly have been his; for no body of Indians could stand the charge of the 7th Cavalry when it swept over the plains like a whirlwind. But in the Mauvaises Terres [Bad Lands] and the narrow valley of the Little Big Horn he did it at a fearful risk.

With all his bravery and self-reliance, his love of independent action, Custer was more dependent than most men on the kind approval of his fellows. He was even vain; he loved display in dress and in action. He would pay $40 for a pair of troop boots to wear on parade, and have everything else in keeping. On the Yellowstone expedition he wore a bright red shirt, which made him the best mark for a rifle of any man in the regiment. I remonstrated with him for this reckless exposure, but found an appeal to his wife more effectual, and on the next campaign he wore a buckskin suit. He formerly wore his hair very long, letting it fall in a heavy mass upon his shoulders, but cut if off before going out on the Black Hills [expedition], producing quite a change in his appearance.

But if vain and ambitious, Custer had none of those great vices which are so common and so distressing in the army. He never touched liquor in any form; he did not smoke or chew or gamble. In early life he had been addicted to some of these habits, but was entirely won from them by the loving, purifying influence of his devoted wife. He was a man of great energy and remarkable endurance. He could outride almost any man in his regiment, I believe, if it were put to a test. His men had many nicknames for him, which celebrated this hardihood. When he set out to reach a certain point at a certain time, you could be sure that he would be there if he killed every horse in the command. He was sometimes too severe in forcing marches, but he never seemed to get tired himself, and he never expected his men to be so. In cutting our way through the forests of the Black Hills, I have often seen him take an ax and work as hard as any of the pioneers. He was never idle when he had a pretext for doing anything. Whatever he did he did thoroughly. He would overshoot the mark, but never fall short. He fretted in garrison sometimes, because it was too inactive; but he found an outlet here for his energies in writing articles for the press. He made some enemies in the army by the freedom with which he wrote and criticized. I think it was not Custer's habit to add to his fame by disparaging the reputation of others. As he loved praise himself, so he liked to award it to others whenever it was due.

He had a remarkable memory. He could recall in its proper order every detail of any action, no matter how remote of which he was a participant. He was rather verbose in writing, and had no gifts as a speaker; but his writing interested the masses from their close attention to details, and from his facility with the pen as with the sword in bringing a thing to a climax. As he was apt to overdo in action, so he was apt to exaggerate in statement, not from any willful disregard of the truth, but because he saw things bigger than they really were. He did not distort the truth; he magnified it. He was a natural optimist. He took rose-colored views of everything, even of the miserable lands of the Northern Pacific Railroad. He had a historical memory, but not a historical mind. He was no philosopher; he could reel off facts from his mind better than he could analyze or mass them. He was not a student, nor a deep thinker. He loved to take part in events rather than to brood over them. He was fond of fun, genial and pleasant in his manner; a loving and devoted husband. It was my privilege to spend two weeks in his family at one time, and I know how happy he was in his social relations. His loss will be felt by those who had learned to know him through the productions of his pen; by the remnant of the famous Seventh he had so often led to victory; but by none more than by those who had won a place in his affection.

Lieutenant Calhoun, his brother-in-law, was a young man [thirty years old] equally temperate and exemplary. He served on the Black Hills expedition as adjutant.

Captain Thomas Custer was distinguished for the same daring and the same recklessness as his brother. He was a hard rider, a great hunter, and had often distinguished himself in action.

Lieutenant Hodgson was a brave young man from Philadelphia, an excellent officer who knew how to keep his company in fine order whether in garrison or on the march. He was generous to a fault and more than once has your correspondent shared his tent and his mess when prevented from reaching his own quarters. He was unmarried.

Lieutenant Algernon E. Smith was in command of Company E, one of the finest companies in the regiment. He was formerly on Gen. Custer's staff and

was an excellent commissary. He leaves a wife, but no children.

Captain George W. Yates was one of the best-hearted men in the regiment. He had had long experience as a cavalry officer and knew every detail of the service. He was a good companion at the campfire and a brave man in the field. He leaves a wife and two children.

Lieutenant McIntosh, also married, was a half-breed who had received a fine education. His father was a member of the Hudson Bay Company. He knew nothing of Indian life in its wilder forms except as he met it while serving with his regiment.

S. J. B.

INTERLUDE

"The calamity is one of those things that could not be prevented"

This interesting interview with John Hobart Walker was printed in the *New York Daily Graphic* on July 11, 1876. Walker, a Civil War veteran and "prominent Brooklyn Grand Army Man," had retired from the Twenty-third Infantry in March 1869 "after having been injured." On June 6, 1891, he was confronted by Alfred Hull, who accused the retired captain and brevet major of "paying too close attention to Mrs. Hull." A fight ensued and Walker, badly injured with kicks to the head and body and two fractured ribs, died five nights later. His death was reported in the *New York Times* on June 12, 1891.

New York Daily Graphic,
Tuesday, July 11, 1876

AN INDIAN FIGHTER'S VIEWS.

"FIGHTING CAPTAIN JACK WALKER" ON THE RECENT MASSACRE AND THE METHODS OF THE RED MAN.

There is now engaged in business on Wall Street, a quiet, unassuming gentleman about thirty-five years old, physically light and lithe, with an open, intelligent countenance and agreeable manners. As far as appearance goes he would be one of the last men who would be selected as having endured the hardships incident to active military duties on the frontier. This gentleman is ex-Captain and Brevet Major John H. Walker, of the Fourteenth United States Infantry—known in the west, on account of his many successful encounters with the redskins as "Fighting Captain Jack Walker." This officer was prominent in the campaigns during 1865–69 against the Pi Ute and Snake Indians, under command of General Crook and others, when the Pi Utes and Snake Indians far west of the Black Hills, in Idaho, Nevada, and Oregon, were whipped into their places after many sanguinary conflicts. Lieutenant Calhoun,[181] the correspondent of The Graphic who was slain with Custer, was formerly a member of Major Walker's command, and was subsequently promoted to the Seventh Cavalry.[182]

A reporter of *The Graphic* called upon Major Walker to ascertain his views regarding recent disasters and the general conduct of the Indian conflict. Among many other interesting details, Major Walker stated that the criticisms of the course of General Custer in forcing the fighting were out of place. His own plan, and that of all successful Indian fighters, was always to attack the Indians whenever they were found, and to do the best, regardless of their numbers. If such tactics were not pursued the Indians dispersed rapidly and were hard to hunt up again in sufficient bodies to allow of any severe punishment being inflicted upon them. General Custer had always held this view and practice in Indian warfare, and, until his last fatal battle, had been remarkably successful.

Major Walker's opinion of this final event is that Custer discovered the trail of the Indians and followed it energetically in the belief that he would not have time to communicate with Terry or receive reinforcements before the Indians got away; that he found them in his front rather suddenly, and thinking he would not have such an opportunity again, pitched in to do his best to whip them. Major Walker does not believe that General Custer had any correct knowledge of the force he was attacking, and thinks he must have been badly informed by his scouts. In all such campaigns much depends upon the scouts, and if they are poor or do not do their work thoroughly the commander is very apt to be misled. It is also his opinion that General Custer had a perfect right to make an attack without waiting for General Terry, as, by the latter's own report, he had instructed Custer to make such changes as his discretion suggested under extraordinary circumstances.

Major Walker also believes that in the battle recently fought by General Crook the Indians were found in larger numbers than was expected. "The fact is," he said, "the Indians have left the reservations in very large numbers, going out with no other purpose than to join the hostile bands, and our army officers did not expect to find such large bodies of them. General Crook is a good and a stubborn fighter and will keep after them until he finds and whips them." The Major was of the opinion that the effect of the Indian successes thus far will be to draw all the fighting Indians from the reservations, together with those known as renegades. The renegades are chiefly remnants of broken-up tribes, and leave the reservations for the sole purpose of plunder. "I have fought them," said Major Walker, "when they would shake in the faces of my men the red blankets that had been issued to them on the reservations hundreds of miles distant. There are always plenty of white men who are ready to furnish arms and supplies to the Indians, and there is no law against their doing so. The Indians trade the stock they steal 400 or 500 miles away to these bad white men, and in this manner they get all the arms and ammunition they need."

Major Walker is also of the opinion that the result will very soon demonstrate the wisdom of General Sheridan's application for money to establish posts on the Yellowstone. He says that at least two posts are needed there as points from which to carry on operations against the Indians whenever it becomes necessary, and he thinks the great mistake made by Congress for the last two years in refusing to appropriate $200,000 for this purpose will cost the country, besides the valuable lives already lost, many more and a vast amount of money. He states that the Indian war will last for many months, but does not believe that the Indians will keep together in large bands. They know the white men so well and their capability of putting a large force in the field, that they will scatter and divide. The Indians have remarkable facilities for concentrating at short notice. "They have," says Major Walker, "as perfect a system of signals as any in existence. Fires on the tops of hills, lighted and extinguished in a certain way, and, when marching, leaving along their route piles of stones indicating their direction and

numbers, are some of the means of communicating with each other."

Regarding the composition of the armies for Indian warfare, Major Walker was emphatic in stating that both cavalry and infantry are needed, even if the cavalry does sometimes get ahead. He advocates the filling up of the cavalry companies to the maximum number of 100 men and then backing them with infantry, but does not think any more regiments are needed, especially if the trouble is not settled prior to the setting in of winter. It has always been General Crook's idea that the winter months, after all, are the best in which to deal with the redskins. They remain more in their camps in winter, and in consequence are more easily found. They cannot hunt as in summer, and have their supplies more concentrated.

"The Indians have 40,000 square miles to scatter about in," said the Major, "but for all practical purposes the Government force will be large enough if the cavalry companies are filled up to 100 men each."

Major Walker said: "After all, when we look squarely at the question, the Indians have some cause of complaint, and it is a fact that they believe they fight in defense of an inalienable right—certain rights which they will never yield until they are so subdued and annihilated as to render them glad to stay in any one locality where the march of civilization shall crowd them. We have marched so far in that direction and the necessity for opening up the wild lands is so great that our people will not, even with a semblance of justice to back the Indians, be dictated to by them. Hence they are bound to go under at no distant day and a large proportion of them will be killed in their resistance."

Major Walker instanced the Nez Perces tribe of Idaho in connection with the belief held by the Indians generally that they were the owners of the country. This tribe of Indians has many educated men among their number, and the chief, Lawyer, speaks fluently four different languages. Their children have been educated at the East. Yet, with all this civilization, one branch of the tribe, under War Eagle, refused to sign the treaty, the chief proudly pointing to the history of the tribe that records no instance of resistance to a white man, and as proudly asserting that he would sign no treaty as he was one of the original owners of the soil.

In conclusion Major Walker said: "It is foolish for any one to think that General Custer could have waited for reinforcements. The calamity is one of those things that could not be prevented."

INTERLUDE

Was the Battle of the Little Big Horn a "Massacre"?

In the days and weeks following the battle of the Little Big Horn, it was not uncommon to find the fight referred to as a massacre in the daily papers. However, just as quickly, an alternate view took shape, which objected to the term massacre. Although the *New York Times* was not above using the word, that didn't stop it from printing the following editorial on July 12:

If it is unreasonable to lay at the door of the peace policy results due strictly to deviations from it, there is a like lack of reason in the anger which styles Sitting Bull's recent victory a "fiendish massacre." Custer went out to beat the Sioux. Had he succeeded, would he have been guilty of a "fiendish massacre"? The soldier has blows to take as well as to give, and there is no justice in styling the defeat of an attacking force "a fiendish massacre," when its success would have been called a glorious victory. We did not fancy that the Southern people deserved extermination because we were beaten at Bull Run, nor did the rebels call the defeat at Gettysburg a "fiendish massacre."

Three days later, the *Brooklyn Daily Eagle* took up the cause:

There appears to have been no treachery in this encounter. The Indians were not the attacking party. They were acting on the offensive against their pursuers, and the fearful execution of their arms was wrought in actual combat on the field. Had they been found in smaller force, and had a few hundred of them been cut down by our gallant soldiers, no particular animosity would have been felt, and new laurels would have been given to the brave commander.

It wasn't long before Wendell Phillips, a well known humanitarian, joined the dispute.[183] On July 19, the *New York Herald* reprinted one of his letters to the *Boston Transcript*:

Will you please explain why even your columns talk of the "Custer Massacre"? The Sioux war, all confess, is one that our misconduct provoked. During such a war General Custer has fallen in a fair fight, simply because the enemy had more soldierly skill and strategy than Custer had. What kind of war is it, where if we kill the enemy, it is death; if he kills us it is a massacre? When the farmers of Concord and Lexington, in 1775, shot the British invaders of their villages was it a massacre? When the

Southerners mowed us down at Bull Run and Ball's Bluff, there was no talk of massacre. When the North paid them in their coin at Gettysburg and Antietam, there were no [newspaper] columns with staring capitals "Gettysburg Massacre." The general use of this abusive term betrays the unfairness of the American press."

On August 2, 1876, the *Deseret News*, a long-time champion of Indian rights, reprinted an editorial that first appeared in the *Sacramento Record-Union*:

A curious instance of the ease with which an improper use of any word or term is accepted has occurred recently in connection with the destruction of Custer's command. From one end of the country to the other the event has been spoken of as a "massacre." Perhaps a definition in the dictionaries may appear to warrant the employment of such a term, but if we wish to perceive how unjustifiably it is used in this connection we have only to inquire: Supposing the case had been reversed, and Custer's command had killed all the Sioux—as they assuredly would have done had they been able—should we have called the event a "massacre" of the Indians? Most assuredly we should have done nothing of the kind, but, instead, it would have been designated a "crushing defeat," a "terrible blow," a "glorious victory," and so forth. The simple truth is that General Custer went out to slaughter the Indians, and the Indians slaughtered him, in a square, standup fight. No doubt he was outnumbered, but he knew that the odds were against him when he charged down upon the village, and he took his chance with his eyes open. It is just as well to call things by their right names, for presently Custer may be avenged upon the

A Titled British Ass

Daily Colorado Chieftain, July 23, 1876

In the house of commons on July 21, one Sir Edward Watkin, who appears to be one of those far-away-from-home philanthropists whose sight is too distant to observe any trouble going on under his nose, but can distinctly see that which is five thousand miles away, has turned his attention to the Custer massacre, and sympathizes deeply with the unfortunate and downtrodden Sioux, whose last little playful prank was to murder a gallant officer of the United States army and some two hundred and fifty of his men. Had Custer and his men been killed in a fair fight with civilized people their death would not have created so much indignation, but when surrounded by four times their number and every man butchered, scalped and mutilated, the indignant people of the United States are not in a condition to listen calmly to the unmelodious braying of this titled British ass. . . . Sir Edward should remember the homely proverb to the effect that advice unasked for has a disagreeable odor, and also that those who poke their noses into the affairs of others sometimes get those noses smashed.

—Editorial

Sioux, and then it will be awkward to have to talk of the "Sioux massacre," and might seem like disparaging the bravery of our gallant boys in blue.

Thomas Harrington, late a trooper with the Seventh Infantry, helped clarify the issue when he stated that

Sitting Bull "might have taken high rank as a military genius" if not for "the butchery that ensued [after the battle]," then added, "if he whips us [again] there will be a second massacre."[184] In other words, it was not the battle itself that was considered a massacre, but the extensive and deliberate mutilations that came afterward. So yes, there was a battle and there was a massacre of sorts that followed, but they were two separate issues, even if the newspapers did not always take the time to make the distinction.

INTERLUDE

A Father's Accusations and
a Veteran's Rebuttal

Among the slain on Custer's battlefield was twenty-two-year-old Lieutenant James G. Sturgis, son of Colonel Samuel D. Sturgis, the commanding officer of the Seventh Cavalry. Several days after learning of his only son's death, he was interviewed by a St. Louis reporter. Basing his statements on early reports of the battle, from which he tried to re-create the order of events, Colonel Sturgis made some wild accusations against Custer, accusing him of purposely sacrificing his son and another young lieutenant, twenty-nine-year-old James E. Porter, while he held back with the older, more experienced, officers as a personal guard. On July 17, 1876, his allegations were printed in the *New York Times*, in an article headlined "Gen. Custer's Death—An Interview

with Colonel Sturgis," part of which stated:

Why was not Gen. Custer at the head of his troops instead of a long distance in the rear of them? Why was not his body found where the hottest fight occurred, instead of back on that knoll? No officers were found dead at the front but those young lieutenants who had been sent there to die as a sacrifice. . . . And it is proposed to erect a monument to the memory of Gen. Custer! What for! Monuments commemorate deeds worthy of emulation by after generations. Is such conduct as Custer's to be held up to our youth as a bright example to follow? He was guilty of disobedience and of sacrificing good men's lives to win notoriety for himself.

The elder Sturgis was understandably distressed and clearly grieving for his son, and Custer was the obvious and easy target for his anger. However, such public statements, especially those tainted with absurdity, were likely to stir a retort, and that is exactly what Sturgis drew forth in a lengthy and detailed response from Edwin A. Sherburne, a veteran of the Civil War. Sherburne's letter, originally published in the *Chicago Tribune*, was reprinted in the *New York Herald* on July 26:

New York Herald,
Wednesday, July 26, 1876

GENERAL STURGIS.

AN IOWA VOLUNTEER PAYS HIS RESPECTS
TO CUSTER'S TRADUCER.

Chicago, July 22, 1876.
To the Editor of the Chicago Tribune—
Your daily of July 19 contains a letter from your St. Louis correspondent relat-

ing what General Sturgis said to him on the 18th about General Custer. The substance of Sturgis' remarks is an insinuation that General Custer was a coward, because (as he avers) "the bodies of 300 or more soldiers were found piled up in a little ravine, while behind were found those of Custer and his 'chosen officers.' What a spectacle," he says, "it would have been to find 300 soldiers collected on one side, and, in the rear, the commander of the little force surrounded by its officers! Mind, I don't want to impugn their bravery!" Oh, no! But he means for every one else to. He then flings in the assertion that "Custer was insanely ambitious of glory," and that "Custer's luck affords a good clue to his ruling passion," criticizes "Custer's want of judgment, which drew these men into a trap," and then says that "the records" show him (Sturgis) to have been one of the "most successful Indian fighters," that "in 1860 he followed the Kiowas and Comanches so that their camps were entirely broken up and they caused no further trouble." He also says that he told somebody in St. Paul two years ago that he "didn't believe Custer knew sufficient of the Indian character to fight them to advantage, that he was liable to be led into a trap, in which case I (Sturgis) told the gentleman there would be no one left to tell the tale." And then he congratulates himself that now, at the first important attack, "the prophecy is fulfilled," and winds up by asserting that General Custer was unpopular with his troops, was a tyrant, and had no regard for the soldiers under him. Now, Mr. Editor, cowardice in the face of the enemy is, under the laws of war, punishable with death. It ought also to be the law that a cowardly attack on the reputation of a dead soldier should meet the same fate.

We regard with contempt the man who strikes a woman or a child, or any one much weaker then he, and not able to defend himself. We call the Indian a fiend and dastard because he mutilates the dead bodies of his helpless victims, and yet these acts are brave and honorable compared with rending by falsehood or cunning innuendo the soldiery character of one who, so far as we know, died fighting with his face to the enemy, with flashing blade and straining nerve to the very last. "But," says General Sturgis, "mind, I don't want to impugn their bravery!" To add that remark to what he had already said was like styling a man a thief and in the next breath averring that he did not want to impugn his honesty! Now, sir, General Custer was bound by no ties to me other than those which knitted him to every soldier of our country. But, as soldiers, we do claim him as a comrade and a brother, of whose every record we are proud; and, sir, in the name of the comrades with whom he fought, and to whom his presence at the head of their column was an inspiration which told like a lightning flash on the enemy in many a charge and battle, I deny that he was a "tyrant" or regarded "unkindly by his men." The attempt to stain him with cowardice needs no denial. The unanimous testimony of all who served with him and of all who ever heard of him refutes that, and "Custer's luck," as General Sturgis sneeringly styles Custer's success, was what naturally resulted to a soldier whose heart was a stranger to fear, who went to battle with an eye gleaming like a blazing star, and whose arm was ever found in the thickest of the fight, dealing blows both well directed and resistless.

General Sturgis' object seems to be to get before the mind of his listener a comparison of his "record" with that of the dead General, which shall be injurious to the latter. To assist General Sturgis' memory in this laudable effort, I would suggest to your correspondent in his next interview to ask General Sturgis if, in the summer of 1864, he did not march out of Memphis, Tenn., at the head of a fine division of from 7,000 to 10,000 men to attack General Forrest (a rebel cavalry general known to be near and supposed to have about the same number of men), and if he did not march with the most indifferent ignorance right into "a trap" set for him by Forrest, get caught by surprise so completely that his entire command, without striking a blow, was broken and scattered in utter rout and confusion,[185] and what were not captured sent flying back to Memphis in little detached parties, like a flock of scared sheep before a pack of wolves, minus guns, knapsacks, artillery, baggage and wagons? And ask him if he and a "few of his chosen officers" were not among the first to arrive in Memphis, and if he was not seen the next day after his return playing billiards in a saloon there, while his weary, hunted soldiers were straggling into town every now and then in little detached parties, while their wounded and dead comrades still lay on the field of rout (not battle). And if he did not remain "behind" in Memphis while General A. J. Smith went, with no greater number of men, and administered a sound drubbing to Forrest on the field of Tupelo [July 14-15, 1864]. And, when this "successful Indian fighter" has answered these questions, ask him if he remembers winning the regard of his soldiers by ordering a private of the Second Kansas Volunteers to be lashed to the wheel of a cannon and scourged with twenty lashes on his bare back, and, when he failed to find a man in that regiment who would execute the sentence, ordering two "regulars" from his own regiment to come and do the job, while

he stood by to see that it was well "laid on"; and if, when all things were ready, an officer of the Second Kansas, at the head of his battalion, under arms, did not step forward and tell General Sturgis that the sound of the first blow on their comrade's back was the signal for his battalion to riddle the "generous, beloved General" with bullets, and if the said General's cheek didn't blanch with fear when he cast his eyes down the constantly lengthening line of stern frontiersmen who faced him, and if he didn't walk off, leaving them to free their unwhipped comrade. When he shall have answered all this to the satisfaction of your correspondent and the readers of his vituperative story, and then pointed to any authenticated instance where he has been entitled to the name of warrior, it may be a little less indecent for him to make comparisons between himself and General Custer. But until then he should "lay his mouth in the dust."

E. A. Sherburne, formerly of the
27th Iowa Infantry Volunteers.

7

General Crook's Problems

"All other Indian wars sink into insignificance compared with this."
—Reuben B. Davenport, Camp Cloud Peak, July 12, 1876, *New York Herald*, July 16, 1876

"No artillery has been ordered [by General Crook], which most of the officers consider a very unfortunate omission, as, after poor Custer's experience, the passion for charging into Indian villages has somewhat subsided."—Unknown, Camp Cloud Peak, July 16, 1876, *Daily Alta California*, July 24, 1876

"So far as definite damage to either side is concerned, the advantages thus far are in favor of the savage; and both big and little events have conspired to render the future of operations impossible to foresee."—Joe Wasson, Camp at South Fork of Tongue River, July 22, 1876, *Daily Alta California*, August 1, 1876

Writing from Crook's bivouac on Goose Creek on June 27, in the shadow of the Big Horn Mountains, Cloud Peak rising "cold and stern" in the distance, Reuben Davenport expressed concern about the future of the campaign because of goings-on some sixteen hundred miles to the east:

Rumors reach us here, at the outskirts of the populous world, of the influences made to work at Washington to force a negotiation for peace upon the Sioux. To us the phrase has a ludicrous sound, as we have certain knowledge that no peo-

ple ever were more nerved to desperate war or less open to soft seductions of pacific benevolence than they who await the soldiers of the United States with the bold spirit and prowess which they showed on the 17th of June in the Rosebud Hills.[1]

It was Davenport's opinion that if the army did not finish the job now, it would only be putting off the inevitable:

Unless [the Sioux and Cheyennes] were injured by the fire of General Crook's command in the battle of that day much more severely than we conceive, it is preposterous to prate of counseling with Sitting Bull or any of his breech-clouted minions. Should this campaign be checked at its beginning . . . it will merely procrastinate the inevitable taming which the Sioux must undergo. . . . A treaty constructed of expedients will be of no value.[2]

But tidings of a peace initiative were not the only rumor buzzing about Crook's camp:

A rumor of a battle between the hostile Sioux and the force of cavalry commanded by General Custer, of General Terry's column, has reached us. It came from the Red Cloud Agency, by way of Forts Laramie and Fetterman, brought thither by the friendly Sioux, "Hand," who last year served the Herald as a courier. He was told the news by a runner from the band of Sitting Bull, who said that many were killed on both sides, and that neither won an advantage.[3]

Whether this rumor of a battle with Custer was really nothing more than that, which by some uncanny coincidence turned out to be true shortly afterward, is unknown. After all, these types of rumors were nothing new. Back on June 9, there was a report in the *New York Herald*, based on the tale of an Indian courier two days previous, that Custer's troops had had a big battle with the Sioux and many were killed on both sides. On the other hand, if the rumor reported by Davenport was based in fact, then it was really quite an amazing feat. It would mean that news of the legendary fight somehow reached two forts and Red Cloud Agency and made its way back to Crook's camp all within forty-eight hours.

In addition to these two items, Davenport noted that the battle of the Rosebud was a hot topic around the camp: "Gossip and comparison of observations regarding the engagement of June 17 are not yet done. It has already been fought over a thousand times by the light of the camp fires, and the lines of advance and retreat marked as often in the ashes with rude gravers of cottonwood faggots."[4]

According to Robert Strahorn, each cavalry company was exercising its horses "briskly every day," and a general inspection of the troops was slated for the last day of the month:

On the 30th inst., there will be a regular muster and inspection of the entire force composing the infantry and cavalry battalions, together with all the miscellaneous equipage of the expedition. There will be the usual parade, reviews and evolutions, and to us who have so little to break the monotony while in camp, the affair is looked forward to with no little interest.[5]

In the first eight days since Crook had returned to his supply base on Goose Creek, the camp had been moved three times "in order to allow the pack and saddle animals new pasture."[6] According to the few Shoshone scouts who remained behind with the command, "Sioux spies" were watching their every movement, hoping to catch camp stragglers unawares. Rumors and gossip, frequent changes of camp, skulking Sioux, pending troop inspections, not to mention the beautiful mountain scenery, were not enough to keep Davenport absorbed. After sitting around for one week, the *Herald* correspondent was bored: "Idleness in camp is the most irksome experience in the world, as the chroniclers of war have oftentimes remarked, but it is especially so 200 miles from the telegraph and 300 from the railroad. Isolation is nearly as complete here as within the walls of a prison."[7]

Trying to find something to fill out his dispatch, Joe Wasson wrote about the boredom:

With the single interval of the big skirmish on Rosebud Creek, June 17 . . . Crook's campaign has been thus far little else than a picnic excursion. The longer I put it off the more difficult it is to start up the scribbling machine. . . . During this tedious interval, various attempts were made to break the monotony. Books were almost unknown in camp, and the newspapers were invariably from twenty days old to one month. Cards became stale amusement.[8]

Lucky for Davenport and Wasson, Crook was planning "to break the monotony of waiting for supplies" with a little exploring expedition into the unknown recesses of the Big Horn Mountains, "to explore the deep valleys beyond in search of the rumored indications of gold, which scouts and troopers have long been so fond of depicting in their tales."[9] According to Davenport, it was an area "where white men had never entered and where there is no evidence that the Indian had ever gone."[10]

Strahorn was looking forward to the trip too; in addition to demonstrating "the existence or non-existence of gold" in the region directly to the west, the "excitement of the chase and the satisfaction of viewing the fresh and novel scenes inside those rocky barriers, promise double rewards for the undertaking."[11]

Accompanying Crook were Lieutenant Colonel William Royall, Captains Anson Mills and Andrew Burt, Lieutenants William Carpenter, Walter Schuyler, Henry Lemly, and John Bourke, six to eight packers, plus correspondents Davenport, Strahorn, Finerty, and Wasson. They were all mounted on mules, and each man carried four days' rations of hard bread, bacon, coffee, and sugar in his saddlebag.[12]

After ascending the nearby heights for two miles on the first of July, Crook's party of adventurers was about one thousand feet above the bivouac. Davenport described the scene:

We looked back at the white spots upon the table land by the stream, which were our canvas dwellings, and they were so small and filled so little space that the army of the Big Horn seemed to have dwindled to less than a battalion. In the vast plain it seemed like a mere fleet of petrels on the ocean.[13]

Davenport marveled at the sight of Cloud Peak and its surroundings:

We were then probably nearer it than any white man had ever been before us. Travelers have agreed that it is the highest mass of the Big Horn Mountains, but they have never described its peculiar outlines. We, for the first time, realize its great superiority of height and the abruptness and grotesqueness of the contour of the topmost crag. This is the feature by which Cloud Peak should hereafter be known. Its sister peaks are more symmetrical; no other in the whole range is so ragged and broken in form.[14]

Wasson was also impressed with the bivouac's namesake:

The summit is bare granite piled on granite again, till it culminates in one grand and rugged elevation known as Cloud Peak—a cluster of rim-like cliffs, as if the remains of an old volcano, and adapted to the business of gathering and holding the clouds. This mountain is over 11,000 feet high.[15]

The four-day trip was a memorable experience for all who took part, but as far as gold was concerned, there was practically nothing to report. The best Davenport could write was that the packers "found the 'color of gold,' a single flake, in the soil on the margin of No Wood Creek."[16]

Between the battle of the Rosebud on June 17 and Crook's recommencing of the stalled campaign more than six weeks later, the most noteworthy incident that occurred to any part of his force was the Sibley Scout, a three-day luckless affair in all but the fact that no member of the scouting party was killed. The lone correspondent to accompany Lieutenant Sibley and his specially selected group of men was John F. Finerty, correspondent for the *Chicago Times*. His thrilling adventure tale was first published in the newspaper on July 26, and was picked up by the *New York Herald* three days later. Here is Finerty's story of the Sibley Scout, from the *Herald*:

New York Herald,
Saturday, July 29, 1876

SIBLEY'S ESCAPE.

GRAPHIC STORY OF THE FIGHT IN THE BIG HORN RANGE.

A FORTY-FIVE MILE RACE.

WONDERFUL ADVENTURES OF THE SCOUTS.

FRANK GROUARD.

Camp Cloud Peak, Wy. T.,
July 11, 1876.

The day after Crook's party returned from their hunt, the General, expecting the wagon train every moment, determined to send out a reconnoitering party along the base of the mountains, northwest, to discover where the Indians were and to take a general observation of the country. Lieutenant Frederick W. Sibley, of Company E, Second Cavalry, with twenty-five picked men drawn from the regiment, was detailed to accompany the scouts, Frank Grouard and Baptiste Pourier, on the reconnoissance. John Becker, a mule packer, who had some experience as a guide, was also of the party. The scouts had ventured forward some twenty miles two nights before, but saw Indians and returned. An officer came around to my tent on the morning of July 6 and informed me of the plan. He said the party were going in the direction of the Little Big Horn River, northwest, and if no Indians were discovered they would proceed still further. As I was sent out here

TO SEE THE COUNTRY

and not to dry-rot around camps I made up my mind to go with Sibley, who is a fine young officer and a son of the late Colonel Sibley, of Chicago. I obtained Crook's permission, which he appeared rather reluctant to give, and was ready to start when the party mustered at noon. Each of us carried 100 rounds of ammunition and enough provender to last a week. The scouts led us to camp on Big Goose Creek, but thirteen miles from Camp Cloud Peak, where we remained until night. When evening had sufficiently advanced our little party, thirty men, all told, moved forward for the most part on the old Fort C. F. Smith road, Grouard keeping a sharp lookout from every vantage point ahead. The full moon rose upon us by eight o'clock, and we continued our ride along the foot of the mountains until two o'clock that morning. Then we halted at a point seven miles from the Little Big Horn, in Montana, and fully forty miles from our permanent camp, half-corralled our horses and slept until daylight, our pickets

Keeping Watch From The Bluffs

above our encampment.

At half-past four o'clock on the morning of Friday, July 7, we were again in the saddle, pressing on toward where the scouts supposed the Indian village to be. Reaching the foot of a rocky mound Grouard told us to halt while he took observations. By this time we had moved about four miles from our late bivouac. We observed Grouard's movement with some interest, as we knew we were in the enemy's country, and might encounter Indians at any moment. Scarcely had the scout taken a first look from the crest of the ridge when a peculiar motion of his hand summoned Baptiste to his side. Both left their ponies below the bluff and observed the country from between the rocks on the summit. A minute afterward they had mounted their horses, and came galloping back to us. "Quick, for your lives!" cried Grouard. We mounted immediately and followed him. He led us among hills of red sandstone, the footstool of the mountains, and we were

obliged to make our horses leap down on rocky ledges as much as six or seven feet to follow his course. Within fifteen minutes we reached a hill sufficiently large to conceal our horses, while those of us who were furnished with glasses—namely, Grouard, Pourier, Lieutenant Sibley and myself—went into the rocks and waited to see what was coming. "What did you see, Frank?" asked Sibley of the scout. "Only Sitting Bull's war party," Frank replied. "Knew they were up here without coming at all." We did not have long to wait for the confirmation of his words. Almost at the same instant

Groups Of Mounted Savages

appeared on every hill north and east of us. Every moment increased their numbers, until they seemed to cover the country far and wide. "They have not seen us yet," said the scout. "Unless some of them hit upon the trail we are comparatively safe."

Gradually the right flank of the Indians approached the ground over which we had come that morning and the previous night. We watched their movements with breathless interest. Suddenly an Indian attired in a red blanket halted, looked for a moment at the earth, and began to ride round in a circle. "Now look out," said Grouard, "that fellow has found our trail and they will be after us in five minutes."

"What are we going to do?" asked the young officer.

"Well, we have but one chance of escape," said Grouard; "let us lead our horses into the mountains and try to cross them. Meanwhile

Prepare For The Worst."

Then we left the rocks and went down among the soldiers. Lieutenant Sibley said to them: "Men, the Indians have discovered us. We will have to do some fighting. If we can make an honorable escape all together we shall do it. If retreat is impossible let no man surrender.

Die In Your Tracks,

for the Indians show no mercy."

"All right, sir," said the men, and the whole party followed the scouts and the officer up the steep mountain side, which at that point was steep to a discouraging extent. The Indians must have seen us, they were scarcely more than a mile distant, for hundreds of them had halted and appeared to be in consultation. We continued our retreat until we struck an old Sioux trail on the first ridge. "This path leads to the snowy range," said Grouard. "If we can reach there without being overtaken or cut off our chances are pretty fair." Most of the road was rather good and we proceeded in a northwestern direction at a brisk trot. Having gone five miles and seeing no Indians on our track Grouard concluded that they had abandoned the pursuit or else did not care about attacking us in the hills. The horses were

Badly Used Up

and many of the men were suffering from hunger; so we halted to make some coffee and to allow our animals to recuperate. This occupied about an hour, when we again mounted and set forward. We crossed the main branch of the Tongue River, flowing through the mountains, and were in full view of the snowy range. The same splendid scenery that I had observed when out with Crook's party was visible on every side. The trail led through natural parks, open spaces bordered by rocks and pine trees on the mountain sides. Here the country was comparatively open. Suddenly John Becker, the packer, and a soldier rode up, exclaiming,

"The Indians! The Indians!"

Grouard looked over his shoulder and saw some of the red devils riding on our left flank. We had reached a plain on the mountain range, timber on our left, timber on our front, and rocks and timber on our right, at about 200 yards distance. "Keep to the left along the woods," said the scout. Scarce were the words uttered when from the rocks there came a ringing volley. The Indians had fired upon us, and had struck my horse and two others. Fortunately, the scoundrels fired too low, miscalculating the distance, and not a man was wounded. Our animals, after the manner of American horses, stampeded and nearly

Dashed Out Our Brains

against the trees on our left. The savages gave us three more volleys, wounding more of our horses, before we got the beasts tied to the timber. We gave them a volley back to keep them in check, and then formed a circular skirmish line in the woods. We could see the Indian leader, dressed in what appeared to be white buckskin, directing the movements of his men. Grouard recognized him. He is a Cheyenne called White Antelope, famed for his enterprise and skill. The Cheyennes and Sioux are firm allies and always fight together. White Antelope led one charge against us, but our fire sent himself and his warriors back in quick time. Then the Indians laid low in the rocks and kept up an incessant fire on our position, filling the trees around us with lead. Not a man of us ever expected to leave that spot alive. They evidently aimed at our horses, thinking that by killing them all means of escape would be cut off from us.

Meanwhile their numbers continued to increase. The open slopes swarmed with Indians, and we could hear their savage, encouraging yells to each other. Cheyennes and Sioux were mixed together and appeared to be in great glee.

They had evidently recognized Grouard, whom

They Mortally Hate,

for they called out to him in Sioux, "Standing Bear (the name they give him), do you think that there are no men but yours in this country?" We reserved our fire until an Indian showed himself. They were prodigal of their ammunition, and fired wildly. But they were fast surrounding us. We had fought them and kept them at bay for two hours, from half-past eleven until half-past one o'clock, but they were twenty to our one, and we knew that unless a special Providence interposed, we could never carry our lives away with us. We were looking Death full in the face, and so close that we could feel his cold breath upon our foreheads and his icy grip upon our hearts.

"No Surrender!"

was the word passed from man to man. Each one of us would have blown out his own brains rather than fall alive into Indian hands. A disabling wound would have been the same as death. I had often wondered how a man felt when he saw inevitable sudden doom before him. I know it now, for I had no idea of escape, and could not have suffered more if an Indian knife or bullet had pierced my heart. So it was with all of us. It is one thing to face Death in the midst of excitement. It is quite another thing to meet him in almost cold blood, with the prospect of your dishonored carcass being first mutilated and then left to feed the fox and the vulture. After a man once sees the skull and crossbones as our party saw it on the afternoon of July 7 no subsequent glimpse of grim mortality can possibly impress him in the same manner. Well, the eternal shadows were fast closing around us, the bullets were hitting nearer every moment, and

The Indian Yell

was growing stronger and fiercer, when a hand was laid on my shoulder, and a soldier named [Valentine] Rufus, my neighbor on the skirmish line, said, "The rest are retiring. Lieutenant Sibley tells us to do the same." I quietly withdrew from the friendly pine tree which had kept at least a dozen bullets from making havoc of my body. "Go to your saddle bags and take all your ammunition," said Sibley as I passed him. "We are going to abandon the horses. The Indians are all around us, and we must take to the rocks on foot. It is

Our Only Chance."

I did as directed, but felt a pang at leaving my noble beast, which was bleeding from a wound in the side. We dared not shoot our horses, for that would discover our movement to the enemy. Grouard advised this proceeding. With a celerity which was only possible to men struggling for life, and to escape a dreadful fate, our party obeyed their orders, and, in Indian file, retired through the wood and fallen trees in our rear toward the east, firing a volley and some scattering shots before we moved out, to make the Indians believe we were still in position. Our horses were evidently visible to the savages—a circumstance that facilitated our escape. We ran for a mile through the forest, waded Tongue River (the headwaters) up to our waists and gained the rocks of the mountain ridge, where no Indian pony could follow us, when we heard five or six scattering volleys in succession. It was the final fire of the Indians before they made their charge at our "late corral" to get our scalps. "We are safe for the present," said Grouard, with a grim smile, "but let us lose no time in putting more rocks between us and the White Antelope."[17] We followed his advice with a feeling of thankfulness which only men in such trials can ever know. How astonished the Indians must have been when they ran in upon the maimed horses and

Did Not Get A Single Scalp!

Even under such circumstances as we were placed in we had a little laugh at their expense. But we had escaped one danger only to encounter another. Fully forty-five miles of mountain, rock and forest lay between us and Crook's camp. We could not carry a single particle of food, and had to throw away everything superfluous in the way of clothing. With at least 500 Indians behind us and uncounted precipices before us we found our rifles and 100 rounds of ammunition each a sufficient load to carry. The brave Grouard, the ablest of scouts, conducted our retreat, and we marched, climbed and tumbled over places that at other times would have been impossible to us, until midnight. Then we halted under an immense pile of rocks on the top of a mountain, and there witnessed one of the most terrible wind storms that can be imagined. Long before dawn we were again stumbling through the rocks and forest, and at daylight reached

The Tremendous Canyon

cut in the mountain by what is called the eastern fork of Tongue River. Most of our men were too exhausted to make the descent of the canyon, so Grouard led us through an open valley down by the river, on the left bank, for two miles as hard as we could go, for if discovered there by the savages we could only halt and die together. Fortune favored us, and we made the right bank of the stream unobserved, being then about twenty-five miles from Crook's headquarters. In our front were the plains of the eastern slope, full of hostile Indians, while our only avenue of escape was to climb over the tremendous precipice

which formed the right side of the canyon. But the dauntless Grouard was equal to the crisis. He scaled that gigantic wall diagonally, and led us along a mere squirrel path not more than a foot wide with an abyss 500 feet below, and a sheer wall of rock 200 feet high above us. After an hour's Herculean toil we gained the crest and saw the point of the mountain, about twenty miles distant, where lay our camp. This, as may be imagined, was a blissful vision, but we were

Half Dead With Fatigue,

and some of us were almost famine stricken. Yet the indefatigable Grouard would not stop until we reached the eastern foot hills, where we made a dive into the valley to obtain water, our only refreshment on that hard, rugged road. Scarcely had we slaked our thirst when Grouard led us up the hills again, and we had barely reached the timber when, around the rocks at the point we had doubled shortly before, appeared another strong party of Sioux. This made us desperate. Every man examined his rifle and looked to his ammunition. We all felt that life would be too dearly purchased by further flight, and following the example of

The Brave Young Sibley

and the two gallant scouts, we took up our position among the rocks on a knoll we had reached, determined to sell our lives as dearly as possible. "Finerty," said Sibley to me, "we are in hard luck, but damn them, we'll show the red scoundrels how white men can die. Boys (turning to the soldiers), we have a good position; let every shot dispose of an Indian."

At that moment not a man among us felt any inclination to get away. Desperation and revenge had usurped the place of the animal instinct to preserve our lives. In such moments mind is superior to matter and soul to the nerves.

But we were spared the ordeal. The Sioux failed to observe us, as, very fortunately, they did not advance high enough to find our trail, but kept eastward on the lower branch of Tongue River. Thoroughly worn out we all fell asleep, excepting the tireless scouts, and awoke at dark somewhat refreshed. Not a man of us, Sioux or no Sioux, could endure the mountain journey longer, so we took our thirty jaded, hunted lives in our hands and struck along the valley, actually wading Big Goose Creek up to our armpits, at three o'clock Sunday morning, the water being cold as the mountain snow could make it. Two men, Sergeant [Oscar R.] Cornwell and Private [Harry G.] Collins, were too exhausted to cross, so they hid in the brush until we sent two companies of cavalry after them when we reached camp. After crossing Big Goose we were nearly a dozen miles from our camp on Little Goose Creek, and you may judge how badly we were used up when it took four hours to make six miles. The rocks had skinned our feet and starvation had weakened our frames. Only a few were vigorous enough to push on. At five o'clock we saw

A FEW MORE INDIANS,

but we took no pains to conceal ourselves further. They evidently mistook us for a camp outguard, and, being only a handful, kept away. At seven o'clock we met some cavalry out hunting and we sent into camp for horses, as most of the men could walk no further. Captain DeWees and Rawolle, of the Second Cavalry, came out to us with led horses, and we reached camp at ten o'clock Sunday morning [July 9] amid congratulations from every side. The men who remained at Goose Creek were brought in some hours later. Thus, after passing

through incredible danger and great privation, every man of our thirty, unwounded as by a miracle, found himself safe in Camp Cloud Peak, surrounded by comrades. For conducting this retreat with such consummate success Frank Grouard deserves the highest place among the scouts of the American continent.

The oldest of our Indian fighters, including Colonel Royall, concur in saying that escape from danger so imminent and appalling in a manner so successful

IS UNPARALLELED

in the history of Indian warfare. It was fortunate for the party that an officer possessing the coolness and good sense of Lieutenant Sibley commanded it. A rash, confused, bull-headed leader would have disregarded Grouard and brought ruin upon us all.

We found on getting in that General Crook was up in the mountains on another hunting expedition. A messenger was sent for him at once, but did not find him. News reached our camp by the scout, Louis Richard, from Fort Fetterman, on Monday, to the effect that General Custer, with five companies of the Seventh Cavalry,

HAD BEEN MASSACRED

in an Indian village not far from where Crook encountered the Sioux on June 17.[18] This led Colonel Royall, who feared that Crook might be waylaid in the mountains by Indians, to send four companies of cavalry to his rescue. They met the General coming back with some officers and packers, having killed about twenty elk—a great boon to the camp, as we had been living chiefly on bacon for a month. Crook said very little when he heard of our adventure and Custer's disaster, but

HE KEPT UP A BIG THINKING.

J. F. Finerty.

✳

About three and a half weeks after Sibley's misadventure with the Sioux and Cheyennes, a party of Shoshone and Ute scouts was examining the area where the fight took place and came across the bodies of two Indians likely killed at the time. Davenport recorded the incident in a dispatch dated August 4:

Seemingly as if by instinct a Ute, who rode into the ravine, stumbled upon a putrid corpse in a thicket of wild cherry. The resounding blood-curdling yell which then arose cannot be imagined by the reader nor described by me. It was such as many who have perused Cooper have dreamed of in a shuddering nightmare but have never heard. A sickening stench attracted the Utes to a narrow gully, and there they beheld another mass of mortality. The body first found was wrapped in costly cerements, bedecked with ornaments and accompanied by the full paraphernalia of the mighty and revered warrior. The headdress and other portions of the costume betokened that the dead once bore the rank of a high chief. The friendly Indians stripped it and tore off the rotting scalp, and then cut it barbarously with their knives. The second body was evidently that of a common Sioux soldier. It was covered by only a blanket and a breechclout. The death wounds of both were easily found and had been caused by bullets. . . . Despite the fact that the trophies [scalps and accoutrements] they had secured were not won by their own valor the Utes and Snakes performed a hideous war dance around them, not ceasing their horrible minstrelsy until long after midnight.[19]

The body of the "revered warrior" mentioned by Davenport may have been that of White Antelope (also known as High Bear/Tall Bear). He had been shot in the head and instantly killed during the clash with Sibley's scouting party.[20]

Other than providing a great story, the Sibley Scout was a complete disaster; the entire party of thirty men was almost killed, and they lost all of their horses and possessions, retaining only the clothes on their backs and their firearms. Davenport, suggesting that Sibley's party had been followed from the moment they left camp, wryly noted: "The handful of men [had] left our camp in broad daylight [on July 6], with a strange absence of precaution, for which somebody superior to Sibley in rank is responsible, it being usual to disguise such movements under the shelter of darkness."[21]

The next bit of excitement occurred on Tuesday, July 11, when 213 Shoshones, under Chief Washakie, joined Crook at his bivouac. In a dispatch dated July 23, Davenport described the distinguished Indian leader:

Washakie, the chief of all the Northern Shoshones, is a man of handsome features and imposing stature. His form is massive, but symmetrical. His face in profile resembles that of [Henry Ward] Beecher, the emotionalist; in front it resembles that of Spotted Tail, the chief of the Brules, and his eyes have the same bright and intelligent twinkle, mingled with gleams of benevolent humor. Contact with civilization seems to have ripened his originally noble nature. He is a true friend of the white man, and one who makes his acquaintance cannot help believing in a kinship of mind between him and paler sages of the more fortunate Caucasian race. . . . His hair is silvered with the hoary dust of sixty years,[22] but he looks as young as if he had found in the Shoshone Sierra Mountains the fountain which Ponce de Leon sought in vain in the land of flowers.[23]

Davenport also noted that the Shoshones brought along quite a few of their women: "Twenty of the warriors are accompanied by their squaws, and there are three maidens who will probably bestow themselves upon the bravest trio of young braves, so proven in battle."[24]

The following day, Crook's camp received three unexpected visitors from Colonel Gibbon's command at the confluence of the Big Horn and Yellowstone rivers:

Three couriers, James Bell, William Evans, and Benjamin Stewart, arrived in this camp this morning from General Terry's camp on the Yellowstone, near the mouth of the Big Horn River [one hundred miles to the north]. They started on the 9th and made the most daring ride on record, through the stronghold of the Sioux, in three nights and two days. They brought a dispatch from General Terry to General Crook recounting the details of the massacre of General Custer and his command on the 25th and Major Reno's fight and rescue.[25]

Lieutenant Bourke, Crook's aide, recorded Terry's July 9 dispatch in his journal:

On the 25th ult. General Custer, crossing over from the valley of the Rosebud to the Little Big Horn found on the last named stream an enormous Indian village. He had with him his whole Regiment and a strong detachment of scouts. At the time of the discovery of the Indians he had but eight companies close at hand but with these he attacked in two detachments, one, under himself, of five companies; the other under Major Reno, of three companies. The attacks of these two detachments were made at points nearly, if not quite, three miles apart. I greatly regret to say that Custer, and every officer and man under his immediate command, were killed. . . . Two hundred and sixty-eight officers, men and civilians were killed and there were fifty-two wounded. . . . It is estimated that not less than twenty-five hundred warriors were in the fight. Besides the lodges in the village, a vast number of temporary shelters were found, showing that many Indians were present there, besides those who properly belonged to the village. . . . This morning, I received from General Sheridan a copy of your dispatch to him, giving an account of your fight of the 17th ultimo, and as it gives me information of your position at that time, I hope that the bearers of this may be able to find your train and reach you. The great and, to me, wholly unexpected strength which the Indians have developed seems to make it important and indeed necessary that we should unite or at least act in close cooperation. In my ignorance of your present position and of the position of the Indians, I am unable to propose a plan for this, but if you will devise one and communicate it to me, I will follow it. . . . I hope that it is unnecessary for me to say that should our forces unite, even in my own Department, I shall assume nothing by reason of my seniority, but shall be prepared to cooperate with you in the most cordial and hearty manner, leaving you entirely free to pursue your own course. I am most anxious to assist you in any way that promises to bring the campaign to a favorable and speedy conclusion.[26]

Clearly, Terry did not want to be in charge when it came to fighting the Sioux. It was the reason he petitioned Grant to reinstate Custer as a member of the Dakota Column, and it was the reason he was now so willing to relinquish command and planning to Crook.[27] Crook's response to Terry, written July 16, was probably not phrased exactly the way the latter general wished to hear it: "If you think the interests of the service will be advanced by combination I will most cheerfully *serve under you*"[28] (italics mine). It appears that Terry tried to pass off responsibility for the campaign to Crook, who was only too happy to pass it right back to Terry. It was as if neither man wanted the responsibility at this particular time. From Crook's perspective, first there was the failed winter campaign, then a massive confrontation/standstill at the Rosebud, which now began to look more like one heck of a close call considering what happened to Custer's command eight days later,[29] and most recently Sibley's hapless and near-fatal scouting expedition. The thought must have passed through Crook's mind that events were not supposed to be playing out this way. Trying to get inside the general's head, Davenport speculated:

He seems to have formed his estimate of the Sioux from his experience of the Apaches, and the surprise which he suffered on June 17 was the first awakening from this delusion. Nothing is more certain than that Apaches are insignificant and contemptible in comparison with the Sioux.[30]

As alluded to by Davenport, it was not likely that Crook's experience fighting Apaches was going to be very useful in his battles against the Sioux. The Apaches were not considered horse Indians and fought in relatively small groups or raiding parties. The Sioux (and their Cheyenne allies) were capable of gathering in much greater numbers and were expert horsemen. According to Davenport, Crook failed to make himself familiar with his new enemy:

Although a stranger to the Sioux at the beginning of his administration in this department, General Crook, as well as I can learn, consulted none of his subordinates regarding their knowledge of the enemy whom he was about to fight. Many of these gallant gentlemen had been constantly engaged in dealing with the Sioux in their military capacity since 1866.[31]

Late night "visits" from the Sioux and Cheyennes kept the pickets extra busy and extra vigilant. Still, the cunning warriors managed to steal a couple of horses, as one correspondent noted in his dispatch on July 12:

Our camp has been sadly harassed during the past week, and it is simply wonderful how we have managed to escape injury and loss so far. For four or five consecutive nights the savages have sent over detachments to pay us midnight visits, invariably coming around at a time and in a manner alarmingly suggestive of "churchyards yawning." The first night they were noticed by infantry pickets, who saw a dozen or so of them crawling stealthily in the direction of the horses; but a few hurried shots scattered them. They came again, however, and it was only last night they succeeded in get-

ting away with a couple of cavalry horses. The bold fellows crept within the
picket lines of the cavalry camp, cut the
lariats with scalping knives, took a pair
of patent hobbles from one of the animals, and left a hair lariat of their own
behind as a memento. The place was visited this morning by a few of us, and we
found a couple of Indian scalping knives,
and a few insignificant trinkets belonging to the savages, on the spot.

On the night of the 10th they made a
desperate effort to smoke us out, by firing the prairie grass, and succeeded in
doing so, causing us the loss of two mess-
chests and a few other heavy and immov-
able articles. Our companies had formed
a hollow square around the camp and
were sleeping on their arms, and the savages, finding it impossible to force [their
way] through the camp, had recourse to
the fire and smoke process. Early this
morning we had to beat a hasty retreat
out of the burning grass to save [our]
quarters.[32]

One day after receiving Terry's letter, the long-awaited wagon train
made its welcome appearance:

The wagon train arrived on the 13th
inst. from Fort Fetterman, with fresh
supplies for sixty days[33] for 1,800 men
and five additional companies of
infantry [219 men and 11 officers][34] as
follows: Companies B, C, F, and I of the
Fourteenth, from Camp Douglas, Utah
Territory, and Company G, of the
Fourth Infantry, from Fort Sanders,
Wyoming.[35]

Crook had been planning to
resume his pursuit of the Sioux upon
the arrival of the infantry reinforcements (his current force then consisted of fifteen companies of cavalry
and five of infantry, totaling some

Colonel Wesley Merritt. (*National Archives*)

one thousand men), but now, as
reported by Wasson, Terry's message
of dread had caused him to change
the program. Writing from the South
Fork of the Tongue River, the veteran
correspondent explained the details
in his July 22 dispatch to the *Daily
Alta California*:

Crook got a despatch from General
Terry on July 12, which prompted him
to send for the eight companies of the
Fifth Cavalry [about four hundred men]
under Colonel [Wesley] Merritt, near
Laramie, hence instead of Crook starting
on the war path on the return of the
wagons, he has delayed accordingly. . . .
Orders were already issued for the pack-
train to be all ready, and but for Terry's
almost imploring despatch, this command would have been making more
history of some kind or other ere this.[36]

In a letter to Assistant Adjutant
General Richard Drum on June 12,
Crook wrote that, despite being out-

numbered three to one, he had "no doubt" of his ability "to whip" the Sioux with his present force, however, "the victory would be barren of results." Instead, it would be "better to defer the attack until I can get the Fifth here, and then end the campaign with one crushing blow."[37]

Crook thought the eight companies of cavalry reinforcements would reach him by the end of July.[38] However, as luck would have it, just as Merritt was about to start for Crook's camp on Goose Creek, some 800 Indians, mostly Cheyennes, including perhaps 150 warriors, fled from Red Cloud Agency to join the hostiles.[39] Sheridan had no choice but to redirect Merritt's cavalry to cut them off, an order that resulted in the famous skirmish at Warbonnet Creek. Lieutenant Charles King's stirring account of that skirmish, including a most fortuitous incident in the life of William F. "Buffalo Bill" Cody, showman and scout, was published in the *New York Herald* on July 23, 1876, and follows here:

New York Herald,
Sunday, July 23, 1876

DETAILS OF COLONEL MERRITT'S CHARGE ON THE CHEYENNES.

A SHORT STRUGGLE—THE INDIANS, UTTERLY SURPRISED, RUSH BACK IN DISORDER.

Fort Laramie, July 22, 1876. At noon on Saturday, the 15th inst., the Fifth Cavalry, under General Merritt, were bivouacked on Rawhide Creek, eighteen miles from Fort Laramie, to which point they were ordered in from the Cheyenne River, 100 miles to the north, en route to join Crook. A courier suddenly appeared from the [Red Cloud] agency with despatches stating that 800 Cheyennes were making preparations to leave at once for the Northwest to join Sitting Bull; that he was to throw himself across their line of march in time to intercept them. Merritt had to make eighty miles before they could make thirty, but off he went, and Sunday night [July 16] found him with seven companies [totaling about 335 men and 16 officers] hiding under the bluffs on War Bonnet or Hat Creek, square up their front.

THE INDIANS APPEAR.

At daybreak Monday morning Lieutenant King commanding the outposts to the southeast, sent in word that the war parties were coming over the ridge from the direction of the reservation. Joining him at the advanced post, General Merritt found the report correct. The command noiselessly mounted and was massed under the bluffs, a quarter of a mile to the rear, out of sight of the Indians. At the same time

THE WAGON TRAIN

was some six miles off to the southwest, slowly approaching, and the Indians were closely watching it, but keeping concealed from the view of its guard. The two companies of infantry with it were riding in the wagons. At six o'clock the Indians were swarming all along the ridge to the southeast, some three miles away. Suddenly a party of eight or ten warriors came dashing down a ravine which led directly under the hill where Lieutenant King, with his six men, were watching.

WAITING FOR SCALPS.

The object was as suddenly apparent. Two horsemen, unconscious of the proximity of the foe, had ventured out ahead of the train and were making rapidly for the creek. They were couriers with despatches to the command. The Indians, utterly ignorant of the rapid move of the Fifth, were simply bent on jumping on the couriers and getting their scalps. "Buffalo Bill," chief of the scouts, lay on the hill with King, and instantly sprang to his horse down off the hill.

"All of you keep out of sight," said the General. "Mount now, and when the word is given off with you."

Then, turning to the officer of the picket, he said: "Watch them, King. Give the word when you are ready."

Crouching behind the little butte, Bill and his party of two scouts and six soldiers were breathlessly waiting; half way up was the General with all of his staff. The Lieutenant lay at the crest watching the rapidly advancing foe. Down they came nearer and nearer, the sun flashing from their brilliantly painted bodies and their polished ornaments. Then, just as they are dashing by the front of the hill, King shouts, "Now, lads, in with you."

With a rush and yell the troopers are hurled upon the Indians' flank, not fifty yards away.

The First Redskin Shot.

General Merritt springs up to see the attack just as a tall Indian reeled in his saddle, shot by Corporal [Thomas W.] Wilkinson, of K Company. An answering bullet whistled by the General's head, when King—still on the watch—sung out, "Here they come by the dozens."

The reserve Indians came swarming down from the ridge to the rescue. Company K was instantly ordered to the front. But before it appeared from behind the bluff the Indians, emboldened by the rush of their friends to the rescue, turned savagely on Buffalo Bill and the little party at the outpost.

Cody Kills Yellow Hand.

The latter sprang from their horses and met the daring charge with a volley. Yellow Hand [Yellow Hair], a young Cheyenne brave, came foremost, singling Bill as a foeman worthy of his steel. Cody coolly knelt, and, taking deliberate aim, sent his bullet through the chief's leg and into his horse's head. Down went the two, and, before his friends could reach him, a second shot from Bill's rifle laid the redskin low.

A Grand Surprise.

On came the others, bent on annihilating the little band that opposed them, when, to their amazement, a long blue line popped up in their very front, and K Company, with Captain [Julius W.] Mason at its head, dashed at them. Leaving their dead, the Cheyennes scattered back, helter skelter, to the ridge, but their fire was wild and their stand a short one. Company after company debouched from behind the bluff, and, utterly disheartened, the Indians rushed for the reservation. General Merritt pursued them till night, when the whole command went into camp at the agency.

The Indian Losses.

The Indians left their dead and admit having more wounded. They also lost six ponies. Their friends at Red Cloud say they never dreamed the Fifth Cavalry could get there in time to head them off. The regiment sustained no loss. It arrived at Laramie yesterday and leaves for Crook's camp tomorrow.

Unstated by King was the fact that Cody took Yellow Hair's scalp and, holding it high for everyone to see, declared it was, "The first scalp for Custer."[40] Cody went on to perform the feat numerous times in his stage show and later in the arena, expanding somewhat on the details, which had been transformed into a deadly duel, but that's show business. In 1890, King, who retired in 1879 at the rank of captain, wrote an account of the 1876 campaign, aptly titled *Campaigning with Crook*. In this latter version, Corporal Wilkinson's shot misses its mark (unlike the newspaper story) as the bullet merely "whistles by" the tall Indian at whom he fired.[41] Modern accounts of the skirmish at Warbonnet Creek invariably state that Yellow Hair was the sole casualty, but that is not what was reported in the newspapers at the time. According to a clipping in the *Cheyenne Sun*, reprinted in the *Weekly Rocky Mountain News* on July 26, three Cheyennes were killed in the skirmish. According to James Hastings, the agent at Red Cloud Agency, the Indians told him "that some of their number had been killed."[42] Lastly, Surgeon Robert B. Grimes stated in a letter to his brother, "We afterward found other dead Indians—four in all. They were in full war dress, feathers, bonnets, and all the savage paraphernalia."[43] The problem is that Grimes was not there,[44] and the other reports are unsubstantiated. On the other hand, Merritt's official report, written one day after the incident, only mentions one Indian killed.[45] Merritt's report was likely correct.

In conversation with a correspondent a week after the death of Yellow Hair, one of the officers who witnessed the action at Warbonnet Creek said the soldiers were "mightily amused" at the way the "Indians had scattered when the cavalry made a charge on them," and the "whole affair was exactly like a play which he was watching from a proscenium box."[46] As for Yellow Hair, if the report was even half-accurate, he was armed to the teeth:

From him as he lay dead on the field, was taken, first, a Winchester repeating rifle of the latest and most improved pattern, with a full supply of ammunition for it; second, the newest style of Smith & Wesson navy revolver, with ammunition; a Colt's old-style navy revolver, with ammunition; a heavy knife, shield, and spear.[47]

With the situation at Red Cloud Agency now under control, Merritt was back on the road to Crook on July 23. Five days later he was joined by two additional companies of the Fifth Cavalry, making ten in all, a total of 550 men, not including officers.[48]

For Crook, Merritt's arrival could not come soon enough. In a dispatch on July 16, he had informed Sheridan:

It is my intention to move out after the hostiles as soon as Merritt gets here with the Fifth. . . . I am getting anxious about Merritt's ability to reach me soon, as the grass is getting very dry and the Indians are liable to burn it any day.[49]

The same day that Merritt departed Red Cloud Agency, Wasson was putting together his next dispatch for the *New York Tribune*. Commenting on the supposed whereabouts of the hostiles he wrote:

The Sioux are either scattered already or are in force on the headwaters of the Little Big Horn and Ash Creek, near the Montana line, not more than 40 miles distant. . . . A small party of Snake scouts will be sent out tonight and endeavor definitely to locate the Sioux. This reconnoissance will require two or three days' time.[50]

Davenport was busy writing, too, musing over the fact that the Sioux may have escaped into the Big Horn Mountains and still taking little jabs at Crook:

If the Sioux retreat into the mountains the campaign will probably be prolonged into the winter, and artillery will be necessary in the field. General Crook, however, has a peculiar prejudice against the utility of this arm of the service against the Indians, although in the battle of the Rosebud it certainly would have been of great avail.[51]

However, despite his concerns and criticisms, Davenport still held out hope that the coming weeks would see the fortunes of war shift in favor of the Big Horn and Yellowstone Expedition: "General Crook has now the benefit of experience and an accession of force to enable him to lead on to victory, and there is reason to hope that the month of August will witness a decided triumph, provided that the Sioux are still disposed to try the fortune of battle."[52]

If, as Wasson speculated, the Sioux had scattered into small parties or, as Davenport suggested, withdrew into the mountains, then the chance of a major victory against a large village was virtually nonexistent. In the meantime, Crook would wait for Merritt and the Fifth Cavalry. In

Winchester '76

Daily Colorado Chieftain,
July 26, 1876

"Where," asked an Omaha reporter of an officer in Crook's command, "do the hostile Indians get all their firearms and ammunition?" The officer's reply was:

"The agency people say they don't furnish them any, and the traders claim that they don't. They got some from Custer's command the other day; but the most of their arms are repeating Winchester rifles, and the troops are not furnished with that pattern. Now if they don't get them at the agencies or of travelers, it must be that the Indians manufacture them themselves, and the Winchester Company should prosecute them for infringing on their patent."

reviewing Crook's situation a few weeks later, Wasson reflected:

In view of the unsatisfactory results on the Rosebud, June 17, the Custer affair on June 25, and the grand clamor on the outside, Crook had no alternative left but to await the arrival of the Fifth Cavalry, and take the chances of the enemy breaking camp, scattering, etc. . . . Had he attacked the enemy with the force in hand, and not gained a decisive result, the outside world would have bounced him for inordinate rashness and ambition.[53]

On that note, let us give the final word to Crook. According to one of his subalterns, the general, responding to the criticism that he was not doing enough to defeat Sitting Bull, stated:

I could fight and satisfy this clamor, but what would be the results? A lot of my good people killed, and a few dead Indians. But I am not out here to make a reputation or satisfy a foolish personal pride. I am here to do my duty to others, and to knock the bottom out of these Sioux when I do hit them.[54]

The "foolish . . . pride" comment was clearly a reference to Custer and helps date this remark to sometime after July 10, which is the date two couriers, Louis Richard and Ben Arnold, arrived at Crook's camp on Goose Creek with dispatches from Fort Fetterman announcing the battle of the Little Big Horn.[55]

8

The "Army of the Yellowstone"

"The soldiers of Reno's command testify that the Indians fought well and bravely; and in the opinion of the cavalry officers who took part in the Little Big Horn battle the Sioux are the best irregular cavalry in the world. Sioux Indians also fought on foot hand-to-hand with the soldiers, and not infrequently were the victors."—Unknown, In Camp on the Yellowstone, July 4, 1876, *New York Tribune*, July 22, 1876

"The repulse of Crook, the disaster of Reno, and the massacre of Custer and his command are creating something of a panic in War Department circles, and some fear is expressed for our divided commands on the Plains."—[Signed] Moultrie, "The Tactics of the Sioux," *New York Daily Graphic*, July 8, 1876

"To the coolness and bravery and foresight of Captain Benteen, of the Seventh Cavalry, at the beginning of Reno's engagement, is due the salvation of Reno and the greater part of his command. He now occupies the very enviable position of idol in the esteem of those who were engaged with him and came out with their lives."—A sergeant in the Sixth Infantry, Yellowstone Depot, July 15, 1876, *New York Herald*, August 1, 1876

"When I saw Custer march out with his regiment I said there is men enough to whip the whole Sioux Nation. I thought so, Custer thought so, and so did every officer in the army, and there is no use therefore in blaming Custer, for every officer in the army in his position would have acted in the same manner he did."—Major James Brisbin, quoted by James J. O'Kelly, In Camp on the Yellowstone, August 3, 1876, *New York Herald*, August 11, 1876

"We were well on our way [to General Terry's bivouac], and every one's thoughts were turned toward the distant Big Horn, where the fates would mete out to each his predestined fortune."—James J. O'Kelly, On Board the steamer *Carroll* en route to the Rosebud, late July 1876, *New York Herald*, August 7, 1876

"The country is most uninviting, and all the romance of this Yellowstone region fades like the baseless fabric of a vision when viewed from a military camp, with its prospect of long and fatiguing marches through the sand hills and sage brush under the burning beams of a sun that scorches the very marrow of the bones, with alkali water for drink, and this sweet season of sleep made hideous by the howling of coyotes or the more terrible yell of the Indian savage."—James J. O'Kelly, Camp on the Rosebud, August 6, 1876, *New York Herald*, August 18, 1876

"There is no use trying to conceal the fact that the victory of the Sioux, so terrible in its completeness, has lowered the morale of our troops; . . . they no longer look upon victory as certain."
—James J. O'Kelly, Camp on the Rosebud, August 6, 1876, *New York Herald*, August 18, 1876

"Sitting on the banks of the Rosebud River I am reminded of the drawings of that stream published in some of the New York illustrated journals. In print it is a magnificent stream; here, in reality, it has the proportions of a ditch, with mud puddles of alkali water seen here and there in depressions of its bank; so it is with many other things in this region. Distance and imagination lend them importance."[1]

Such were the thoughts of James J. O'Kelly, the thirty-one-year-old correspondent for the *New York Herald*. At the time, O'Kelly was about one week into his new assignment (not including travel time to Terry's camp on the Yellowstone), reporting on the Terry-Gibbon campaign; he did not know it yet, but by the end of the campaign he would become one of the first, if not the first, to critically investigate the Little Big Horn controversy—that is, which individual or individuals, if any, were responsible for the disaster—a controversy that still exists.

About one month prior to O'Kelly's arrival, the steamer *Far West* had transported the wounded, about forty in number, back to Fort Lincoln, and General Terry had set up camp on the north side of the Yellowstone at the mouth of the Big Horn River. In a dispatch dated July 4, a correspondent from the *New York Tribune* explained that the "camp is situated on the north side . . . because the expedition would be shielded by its waters from the attacks of the hostile Sioux occupying the region south of the river."[2] How times had changed. For the last three months, Gibbon's command had been posted on the north side of the Yellowstone *to keep the Sioux from crossing over.* Back in the middle of May he even tried (unsuccessfully) to get his command across the river in order to attack their village. Now, some seven weeks later, the river was being used as a protective barrier from those same Indians.

On the night of July 7, a small party of Crows brought the Terry-Gibbon camp its first news of Crook's battle on the Rosebud some three weeks earlier.[3] Captain Walter Clifford, Seventh Infantry, thinking that Crook and Terry were soon to combine their commands, had high hopes for the future:

We are awaiting the return of the Far West. If it has been decided to renew the campaign we can muster a force of about 1,000 infantry and cavalry. . . . [Then we will] cross the river, march up the Rosebud, effect a junction with Crook, and the next time the Sioux offer battle clean them up so effectually that, as the soldiers say, it will take "four of them to make a shadow."[4]

Two days later, Clifford noted that Herendeen was sent on a mission to the Crows: "Scout Herendeen, the best one in the outfit, has gone today (July 9) to the Crow camp, about fifty miles above here [toward present Billings], and will return in about four days."[5]

A party of about sixty Crows arrived at Terry's camp on July 15, so it seems probable that Herendeen brought them in.[6] O'Kelly described

the Crows as "physically a fine lot of men, and in their wild costumes strikingly picturesque."[7]

Four days later, on July 19, a shot fired from within the camp brought investigation and sad news:

[Captain Lewis Thompson of the Second Cavalry] shot himself through the head. He had been suffering severely for some time past from sickness, the seeds of which were laid at the time of his confinement in a Southern prison during the war. Some years ago he had applied to be put on the retired list. Lately he had been on the sick list. We buried him on the bluffs to the west of the camp with due military honors. The funeral service was impressively read by Lieutenant Maguire,[8] and Col. Gibbon made a few appropriate remarks.[9]

There was a bit of excitement the next morning, too, when a party of Sioux attempted a bold horse stealing raid: "Early on the morning of the 20th we were startled by some heavy firing toward the camp of the 7th Cavalry, and it was ascertained that a war party of 30 Sioux had been near, and that some of their number had ridden into camp for the purpose of stealing horses."[10]

Then, five days later, the troops were happily surprised by the return of William Evans and Benjamin Stewart, two of the three privates who had volunteered to deliver dispatches to General Crook on July 9, and who had "long since [been] given up for dead."[11] They were accompanied by four Crow scouts who had been sent on the same mission July 17. The third trooper, James Bell, "remained with Gen. Crook, as his horse had given out."[12] Evans and Stewart informed Terry that Crook's command was camped on Goose Creek, a tributary of the Tongue, and also reported that "three miles from Custer's battleground . . . they saw 30 dead Indians." It was naturally assumed that these were casualties from the fight on the Little Big Horn who had died shortly afterward. They also reported seeing Indian trails "leading toward the Rosebud, with heavy smoke in that direction."[13]

On July 26, Terry, responding to reports that some of Custer's men were captured alive and tortured, composed a brief note to the editor of the *Helena Herald* in Montana:

Please publish the fact that there is not the slightest evidence that any one belonging to General Custer's command was captured alive and tortured by the Sioux. On the contrary, everything leads to the belief that every officer and man was killed while gallantly fighting. I deem it proper to make this statement to contradict the harrowing accounts given in some of the papers in regard to tortured prisoners.[14]

Terry's letter was certainly a case of damage control, intended to alleviate public concern and to promote the image that everyone who died did so "while gallantly fighting."

During the last few days of July, the command marched downriver from the Big Horn to the Rosebud, where it arrived just in time to welcome twelve fresh companies of infantry on the first two days of August: first to arrive were six companies of the Twenty-second, 229 men (including fifteen officers),[15] on the steamer *Carroll*, followed by six companies of the Fifth Infantry, 300 men,[16] on the steamer *Durfee*. Also on board the latter boat were two three-inch Rodman guns and some replacement horses for the Seventh Cavalry. The commanding officers were Lieutenant Colonel Elwell Otis, Twenty-second Infantry, and Colonel Nelson Miles, Fifth Infantry, respectively. Reporter O'Kelly had been a traveling companion of the former group. One of the first things that struck him was the look of the men at the bivouac:

The absence of regularity of costume among the troops gives the whole outfit, to use a technical term, a romance that would not easily associate with regular troops. Both the officers and men set the regulations at naught, and dress very much as their fancy or their purses direct. Some are content with the regulation pants and blue shirt; others, more stylish, afford white corduroy breeches and tall riding boots, with any kind of shirts. But the true dandy dons a buckskin shirt with an immense quantity of fringe dangling about in the wind, which gives him the wild, adventurous look that suits the Plains so well.[17]

As for their entertainment, O'Kelly observed: "Horse racing is the only form of amusement within reach, and we have daily two or three races on an excellent level grass course which is behind the camp."[18]

But clothing styles and horse racing were minor asides. O'Kelly wanted to know about the battle of the Little Big Horn, and by the end of his second day in camp, he had already interviewed the two surviving senior officers of the Seventh Cavalry and prepared his first report on the battle:

Considerable annoyance is felt by the officers who participated in Custer's fight, on account of the incorrect or garbled accounts published in some papers. They claim that a good many officers wrote a good deal about the fight who know nothing of it, and that they have perhaps unwittingly done their comrades serious injustice. Under these circumstances I thought it well to interview both Major Reno and Captain Benteen, who, by general consent, were the persons who could give the fullest account of the whole affair.[19]

Noting Reno's "swarthy complexion," strong physique and "frankness of manner," O'Kelly found himself favorably impressed with the Illinois-born officer:

Reno looks every inch a soldier, and judging from his appearance and temperament would be the last man to leave a comrade in a tight place without making an effort to save him. He is very much annoyed at the unfair criticism passed on the surviving officers of the Seventh by the people who know nothing of the battle.[20]

That last comment was specifically directed at railroad engineer Thomas L. Rosser, a former major general in the Confederate army and former classmate of Custer's at West Point, who was now one of Custer's staunchest defenders in death. Rosser, basing his opinion on early newspaper reports of the battle, had written a letter that somewhat incriminated Reno in the death of Custer. The letter first appeared in a Minneapolis-St. Paul newspaper on

July 8, and was reprinted in the *New York Herald* on July 11. In part, Rosser's letter said:

I am surprised and deeply mortified to see that our neighbor, the P. P. and T. [the *Pioneer Press and Tribune*], in its morning issue, had seen fit to adjudge the true, brave and heroic Custer as harshly as to attribute his late terrible disaster with the Sioux Indians to reckless indiscretion. From what I can gather from General Terry's instructions to General Custer it is quite evident that it was expected, if not expressed, that Custer should attack the savages wherever found, and as to the manner of attack, of course that was left to the discretion and judgment of General Custer, and viewing the circumstances of this fatal attack from my standpoint, I fail to see anything very rash in the planning of it or reckless in its attempted execution. On the contrary, I feel that Custer would have succeeded had Reno, with all the reserve of seven companies, passed through and joined Custer after the first repulse. It is not safe at this distance, and in the absence of full details, to criticize too closely the conduct of any officer of this command, but I think it quite certain that General Custer had agreed with Reno upon a place of junction in case of the repulse of either or both of the detachments, and instead of an effort being made by Reno for such a junction, as soon as he encountered heavy resistance he took refuge in the hills and abandoned Custer and his gallant comrades to their fate.[21]

"[T]he conduct of any officer of this command" was most certainly a reference to Reno. "I don't usually pay attention to what is written about me," Reno told O'Kelly, "but in this case I felt compelled to reply,

as much on behalf of the other officers of the Seventh as in my own."[22]
O'Kelly offered to print Reno's
response to Rosser in the pages of the
New York Herald, to which Reno
immediately agreed.[23] Reno's letter
was dated "Camp on the
Yellowstone, July 30, 1876," and
stated in part:

When I read the first part of your letter
. . . my thought was that your motive
had only the object of a defense of a personal friend—a gallant soldier against
whom you fought; but after reading all
of it I could no longer look upon it as the
tribute of a generous enemy, since,
through me, you had attacked as brave
officers as ever served a government, and
with the same recklessness and ignorance
of circumstances as Custer is charged
with in his attacks upon the hostile
Indians. Both charges—the one made
against him and the one made by you
against us—are equally untrue.[24]

Regarding Rosser's claim that
Custer and Reno had agreed upon a
place of junction if they were
repulsed, Reno declared:

My battalion was to the left and rear
when we approached the village, but was
brought to the front by Custer. The only
official orders I had from him were
about five miles from the village, when
Lieutenant Cooke, the Regimental
Adjutant, gave me his orders in these
words: "Custer says to move at as rapid a
gait as you think prudent, and to charge
afterwards, and you will be supported by
the whole outfit." No mention of any
plan, no thought of a junction, only the
usual orders to the advance guard to
attack by the charge. . . . As we
approached near their village they came
out in overwhelming numbers, and soon

the small command would have been
surrounded on all sides, to prevent
which I mounted and charged through
them to a position I could hold with the
few men I had.

You see by this I was the advance and
the first to be engaged and draw fire, and
was consequently the command to be
supported, and not the one from which
support could be expected. All I know of
Custer from the time he ordered me to
attack till I saw him buried is that he did
not follow my trail, but kept on his side
of the river. . . . The Indians made Custer
over confident by appearing to be stampeded, and undoubtedly, when he
arrived at the ford, expecting to go with
ease through their village, he rode into
an ambuscade of at least 2,000 reds. My
getting the command of the seven companies was not the result of any order or
prearranged plan.[25]

In conversation with the *Herald*
reporter, Reno declared that if he
"had not made the charge for the
bluffs my command would undoubtedly have been annihilated as Custer's
was." He believed that Custer's first
mistake was underestimating the
strength of the Indians, which Reno
estimated anywhere from two thousand five hundred to five thousand
warriors. "The Indians are the best
light cavalry in the world," he
declared. "I have seen pretty nearly all
of them, and I do not except even the
Cossacks."[26]

Describing the Seventh's brief foray
in the direction Custer was supposed
to have ridden, Reno stated:

[T]he whole command moved forward,
proceeding about a mile and a half.
During this time chopping shots were
heard. So numerous were the masses of

Indians encountered that the command was obliged to dismount and fight on foot, retiring to the point which had first been selected. It was a crest of hills which formed a depression, in which the pack mules and horses were herded, and men were put in these crests, sheltering themselves as far as they could behind a growth of sage brush. This was about half-past five p.m., and we had just taken up position when the Indians came on us in thousands. The fight was maintained in this position until night. About nine p.m. the Indians withdrew, and immediately the command was put to work making such rifle pits as the scanty implements at our command enabled us to do—mostly hunting knives, plates and canteens, a few axes and three spades. We were left undisturbed until half-past two on the morning of the 26th, when two sharp rifle cracks opened one of the heaviest fires I have ever witnessed, and which continued until half-past nine a.m., when the fury of the attack subdued. In the meantime they fired into the herd through the opening of the valley from a hill which was beyond the range of my carbines.[27]

As with Reno, O'Kelly's initial impression of Benteen was quite positive, although, because of the captain's gray hair, he thought Benteen was older. In fact, both Reno and Benteen were born in 1834. Characterizing Benteen, O'Kelly noted his newly acquired high standing among the Little Big Horn survivors and pointed out that his appearance was deceptive for anyone trying to prejudge his battlefield prowess: "[Benteen] has covered himself with glory in the fight, and is popularly known as the Saviour of the Seventh . . . and from the kindly,

gentle expression of his face, one would scarcely expect so much decision of character as he has shown on the field of battle."[28]

Assuming O'Kelly recorded Benteen's words accurately, much of what he had to say was a little confusing, his sentences twisting about without any apparent rhyme or reason. Perhaps Benteen had something to hide about his actions that day, perhaps not, but if obfuscation was his game, Benteen was an adept player.

I was sent with my battalion to the left to a line of bluffs about five miles off, with instructions to look for Indians and see what was to be seen, and if I saw nothing there to go on, and when I had satisfied myself that it was useless to go further in that direction to rejoin the main trail. After proceeding through a rough and difficult country, very tiring on the horses, and seeing nothing, and wishing to save the horses unnecessary fatigue, I decided to return to the main trail. Before I had proceeded a mile in the direction of the bluffs I was overtaken by the Chief Trumpeter [Henry Voss] and the Sergeant Major [William H. Sharrow] with instructions from General Custer to use my own discretion, and in case I should find any trace of Indians at once to notify General Custer.[29]

Having marched rapidly and passed the line of bluffs on the left bank of a branch of the Little Big Horn River, which made into the main stream about two and a half miles above the ford crossed by Major Reno's command, as ordered, I continued my march in the same direction. The whole time occupied in this march was about an hour and a half. As I was anxious to regain the main command, as there were no signs of Indians, I then decided to rejoin the main trail,[30] as the country before me was mostly of the same character as that I had already passed over, without valley and without water, and offering no inducement for the Indians. No valleys were visible, not even the valley where the fight took place, until my command struck the river. About three miles from the point where Reno crossed the ford I met a sergeant [Daniel A. Kanipe, Company C] bringing orders to the commanding officer of the rear guard, Captain [Thomas M.] McDougal[l], Company B, to hurry up the pack trains. A mile further I was met by my trumpeter [John Martin, Company H], bringing a written order from Lieutenant Cooke, the adjutant of the regiment, to this effect: "Benteen, come on; big village; be quick; bring packs." And a postscript saying, "Bring packs." A mile or a mile and a half further on, I first came in sight of the valley and Little Big Horn. About twelve or fifteen dismounted men were fighting on the plains with Indians, charging and recharging them. This body numbered about 900 at this time. Major Reno's mounted party were retiring across the river to the bluffs. I did not recognize till later what part of the command this was, but [it] was clear they had been beaten. I then marched my command in line to their succor.

On reaching the bluff I reported to Major Reno and first learned that the command had been separated and that Custer was not in that part of the field, and no one of Reno's command was able to inform me of the whereabouts of General Custer. While the command was awaiting the arrival of the pack mules a company was sent forward in the direction supposed to have been taken by Custer. After proceeding about a mile they were attacked and driven back. During this time I heard no heavy firing,

and there was nothing to indicate that a heavy fight was going on, and I believe that at this time Custer's immediate command had been annihilated.[31]

Over the next several weeks, O'Kelly quietly gathered details about the Little Big Horn affair, mostly through camp talk. Soon a picture began to emerge that laid the blame of Custer's death on two of his highest ranking subalterns. Putting together these details in mid-September, O'Kelly's findings, which were for the most part strongly worded insinuations, were published in the *New York Herald* on September 20. This follow-up article stood in stark contrast to its predecessor and is printed in full in the interlude later in this chapter titled "A full and searching investigation."

On August 5, O'Kelly reported on the death of scout William E. "Yank" Brockmeyer, killed three days earlier in a skirmish with some Sioux Indians near the mouth of the Powder River. Three companies of infantry had taken the steamer *Far West* to that point to retrieve several tons of forage that had been left behind on a previous trip upriver. They found the forage easily enough, some of which had been destroyed by the Indians, but they were shortly under the watchful eyes of the Sioux. Major Orlando Moore quickly introduced them to his twelve-pounder Napoleon gun, which had the desired effect and pushed the warriors back out of range. For some unknown reason, perhaps nothing more than an adventurous spirit, Brockmeyer, in company with Dave Campbell, the pilot of the *Far West*, and another scout named George W. Morgan, decided to ride downriver a short distance and have a look around. It was a foolish move. A band of Indians attempted to cut them off, which led to another shot from the Napoleon gun. This time it was not enough, and a few of the warriors refused to be deterred. Hearing about the story afterward, O'Kelly informed his readers of the fatal outcome:

[One of the Indians] rode up to within six yards of his victim [Brockmeyer] to deliver his fire, and such was the speed of his pony that he was unable to stop him in time to get off. The wounded man's comrades opened fire on the Indian, killing him. The wounded scout died about three hours after receiving his hurt, notwithstanding that every effort was made to save him by Dr. Porter, to whose gallantry at the fight on the Little Big Horn so many of our wounded men were indebted to for their lives.[32]

Upon hearing news of the Indians at Powder River, Reno and Miles had asked Terry's consent to head down that way:

The continued presence of Indians at Powder River has induced Major Reno and Colonel Miles to request permission to go down with their commands to see what force of Indians may be thereabout, and endeavor to inflict some punishment on them. The detachment would then cross over by the old trail from Powder River to the Rosebud to rejoin the main command. General Terry, however, has had enough of this kind of experiment and refused to divide up his command.[33]

James J. O'Kelly's Views on Indians and Indian Policy

New York Herald, August 7, 1876

(Probably written in late July, on board the steamer *Carroll*, en route to Terry's camp near the junction of the Rosebud and Yellowstone rivers.)

[The Indian's] code of morality is to be a great warrior. He despises every one who is not a brave. The peace policy has proved and will continue to prove an absurd failure. The Indian will not lay down his tomahawk and his rifle unless he is compelled to do so by force, and all pretended success in inducing him to is either the result of idiocy or knavery. . . . The present war gives Congress and the government an opportunity to deal in a sensible, practical manner with the Indian question, and set it at rest forever. The Indian should no longer be treated as a privileged person; he should be made responsible to the law for his acts, punished or rewarded according to his desserts. General Sheridan long ago asked to have the control of Red Cloud, Spotted Tail and Standing Rock agencies handed over to the military authorities to enable him to deal with the hostile Sioux, as it is notorious that it is through these agencies they obtained the rifles and bullets which killed Custer and his gallant comrades; yet this reasonable demand has never been attended to. It has been treated with contempt by the powerful Indian Ring, that most corrupt and infamous outcome of our political system.

Instead, with the arrival of Otis and Miles, it was now time for the entire force to renew operations, and, so far as Terry was concerned, that meant marching up the Rosebud:

Orders were issued last evening [August 2] to begin the forward march. The two steamers [*Josephine* and *Far West*] were detained to ferry the command across the Yellowstone to the mouth of the Rosebud. Colonel Gibbon's command, which is known here as the Montana Men, were assigned to the advance guard and began crossing the river this morning.[34]

O'Kelly considered Gibbon's movement to the south side of the Yellowstone as the start of a "new campaign." Conversely, he pointed out that some of the veterans thought the Sioux campaign was, in fact, already over:

Whether they are destined to reap many laurels is a question upon which much difference of opinion exists. The old campaigners assert that we will have no fight and that the forces of Sitting Bull and his chiefs will disperse in small parties, making it impossible to encounter them. . . . Unless the Indians want to fight there will be no battle of consequence.[35]

The ferrying of troops across the river continued for several days. On August 6, Major Brisbin reviewed the Second Cavalry. O'Kelly described them as "decidedly weather-beaten" and "travel-stained," explaining that they have been in the field since March.[36] The following morning, Reno reviewed the Seventh Cavalry, which, according to O'Kelly, then numbered 418 men. He commented:

"Some of the companies are very strong, while those that suffered most severely in the Custer fight are merely the skeletons of their former selves, and it was not considered advisable to fill them up immediately with new recruits."[37]

O'Kelly also noted the camp talk among the Seventh's officers who believed they were entitled to brevet rank:

There is a pretty general feeling that the surviving officers who were in the fight should receive brevet rank, in acknowledgment of their constancy and gallantry in one of the most terrible Indian battles that has ever taken place. The brevet ranks cost the country nothing, but it is esteemed by the soldiers as a mark of approval and commendation given by the country as a reward for service performed.[38]

One issue that struck a raw nerve with many survivors of the Seventh Cavalry was the disregard that three of the detached officers paid to Sheridan's directive to rejoin their regiment in the field:

One company in the Seventh, that of Captain Benteen, has two officers, Captains [Henry] Jackson and [James M.] Bell, who became captains by the death of their comrades in the Custer fight, who have not joined this command, though General Sheridan's order commanding them to immediately report to their regiment was issued on the 12th of July. Lieutenant [Charles W.] Larned also gained the position of first lieutenant, and has not come on. It is rumored he has received an appointment as professor at West Point, which in a few years will give the rank of lieutenant colonel, while men who have been in active service for twenty years remain simple captains with honorable scars. This appointment has caused a good deal of comment. It is thought here that it was due to honor and decency for every officer who wears the uniform of the Seventh to have immediately reported for service in the field, unless detained by what is known in the service as "legitimate detail," but the failure of the three officers named in General Sheridan's order of the 12th to put in an appearance has given rise to a good deal of unfavorable comment, and the fighting men of the command speak of them as "coffee coolers," which is the frontier term of contempt for stay-at-home soldiers.[39]

On the other hand, Lieutenant Ernest A. Garlington, who had just graduated from West Point that June, "threw up a four months' leave of absence and reported promptly for duty. He has in consequence become a favorite, and is voted one of the right sort."[40] Garlington filled the vacancy left by the death of Lieutenant Donald McIntosh of Company G.[41]

On one point in particular, O'Kelly's copy was inconsistent. He described the Second Cavalry as being in "good spirits and condition," but then followed this up with the fact that "there has been a good deal of sickness among the men and some tendency to scurvy" due to a lack of vegetables and fresh meat. Describing the soldiers' diet, he wrote:

No attempt was made by the Commissary Department to send the troops vegetables, although the river affords every facility. During the campaign they have had to subsist chiefly on pork and crackers, a diet that would, in a short time, make havoc with the stomach of an ostrich. During the present expedition we are promised one ration of fresh meat every four days, for which we are expected to be thankful.[42]

In addition to dietary issues, the men were struggling with the intense heat. From the *St. Paul Pioneer Press*: [The temperature has been] "hot beyond precedent: the mercury indicates from 108° to 115° in the shade, according to locality. Much apprehension is felt as to the effect of marching in such heat."[43]

Extreme heat and an inadequate menu aside, the troops were all ferried across the river by August 7, and the time for horse racing had come to an end:

Preparations are at last complete, and we march at daybreak tomorrow, the route being up the Rosebud, and the objective point the Indians, wherever and whenever they may be found. Primarily we expect to effect a junction with Gen. Crook, but no deviation from the main object will be made for that purpose.[44]

O'Kelly added:

The plan of the new campaign is that we will move along the valley of the Rosebud as far as the nature of the ground will permit, then cross over to the valley of the Little Big Horn and endeavor to form a junction with General Crook, if that General will permit us and Mr. Sitting Bull throws no insurmountable obstacles in the way.[45]

In another dispatch (dated August 7), he noted the latest smoke-fueled speculation on the eve of departure:

Smoky, fog-like clouds hang over the hills and the whole sky is obscured by a dark-brown haze. If the conjectures as to the cause of this phenomenon are correct we cannot be far from the Indians and may succeed in striking them in their retreat, though unless they are willing to fight us it will be a very difficult matter to compel them to combat.[46]

Reveille was set for 3 a.m., and "Forward" at 5 a.m.[47] This time out the newly refitted Terry-Gibbon column consisted of troops from the Seventh Cavalry, Second Cavalry, Fifth Infantry, Sixth Infantry, Seventh Infantry, and Twenty-second Infantry. In addition there were three pieces of artillery and about 225 wagons carrying thirty-five days' rations and reduced forage for the animals.

O'Kelly broke down the command as follows, based on the official totals received directly from General Terry:
Infantry: officers, 55; men, 922.
Cavalry: officers, 26; men 574.
Battery: officers, 2; men 40.
Scouts: 75.
Total: officers, 83; men, 1,611.[48]

As the "Army of the Yellowstone" marched south up the Rosebud on August 8, it left behind one company of the Seventeenth Infantry and 120 dismounted recruits from the Seventh Cavalry, under command of Captain Louis H. Sanger, Seventeenth Infantry, to protect the newly constructed supply depot, "humorously christened 'Fort Beans.'"[49] For added firepower, the makeshift garrison also had three Gatling guns. O'Kelly described the depot as "a breastwork of barrels filled with sand."[50]

Closing out his August 7 dispatch, the special correspondent for the *New York Tribune* simply stated:

Our adieux have been made with those who stay behind, and their last Godspeeds have been said. Last letters have been written home. . . . The command is in excellent spirits, and no fears need be entertained of its fate when communications cease.[51]

INTERLUDE

The Finale to the Reno-Rosser Feud

Reno's letter to Rosser (mentioned earlier in this chapter) was published in the *New York Herald* on August 8. Rosser's reply, written one week later, was published August 22. If his rejoinder was any indication, the ex-Confederate officer was quite the romantic. His letter was filled with flowery and chivalric language such as "a soldier's honor and reputation," "valiant band," "gallant knight," "bold dash," "worthy command," "noble friend," "honored grave," and "patriots and lovers of heroic deeds."[52] Seemingly forgetting how Custer's cavalry had chased him from the field at Tom's Brook some twelve years earlier, Rosser had no qualms about criticizing Reno's actions at the Little Big Horn. After starting off his second letter by telling Reno that he had not intended any "disparagement" in his original letter, Rosser went on to disparage Reno a second time, and this time it was even more blatant:

The errors which I believe you committed in that engagement were attributed to what I believed to have been a lack of judgment and a want of experience in

Indian warfare, as I understand you have seen but little service with your regiment on the plains; and, in looking over your plan of attack, I could see no good reason for your gently pushing a line of skirmishers down toward a mounted force of Indians when it was expected that you would attack vigorously with your entire command. The fact of your dismounting and taking to the point of timber to which you refer, was an acknowledgment of weakness, if not defeat, and this, too, when your loss was little or nothing. This was an act which I condemned. You had an open field for cavalry operations, and I believe that if you had remained in the saddle and charged boldly into the village, the shock upon the Indians would have been so great that they would have been compelled to withdraw their attacking force from Custer, who, when relieved, could have pushed his command through to open ground, where he could have maneuvered his command, and thus greatly have increased his chances for success.

Rosser, likely influenced by early fanciful reports of the battle and its terrain features, imagined that Custer had been trapped in a canyon:

You must remember that your situation was very different from the one in which Custer was placed. You had an open field in which you could handle your command, while Custer was buried in a deep ravine or canyon, and, as he supposed, stealthily advancing upon an unsuspecting foe, but was, by the nature of the ground, helpless when assaulted on all sides by the Indians in the hills above him.[53]

He also brought up the timing issue that has since become the focus of many students of the battle:

You do not state, but I have the impression from some of the accounts sent in from the field, that you began your skirmish with the Indians about half past twelve to one o'clock, and that you recrossed the river and occupied the bluff about two o'clock. Now, to the reporter of the New York Herald you state that you made a reconnoissance in the direction of Custer's trail about five o'clock. The Indians appear to have withdrawn from your front as soon as you recrossed the river. Why, then, could you not have gone in pursuit of Custer earlier? When you did go you say that you heard "chopping shots." Do you not think that, even then, by a bold dash at the Indians, you might have saved a portion, at least, of Custer's perishing command? I have no desire whatever of casting a shadow over you or any one else, that the name of Custer may shine brighter; and, if my criticisms of your conduct in this engagement are unmerited, I deeply regret it, for from the beginning I have never had a thought of doing you or any member of your worthy command an injury, and, on the other hand, perhaps I can never benefit my noble friend who on this field fell a victim to a few combinations of unlucky mishaps.[54]

Rosser's last line would make for a great book title: *The Battle of the Little Big Horn: A few combinations of unlucky mishaps.*

Interlude

"A full and searching investigation"

"Major Reno says that Custer and all of his men were probably dead when he joined forces with Captain Benteen on the north bank of the creek. He does not

consider himself any more responsible for the killing of Custer and his men than a man in New York would have been. On the other hand, he thinks that either the want of a definite plan of battle or the mistake of General Custer placed the attacking detachment in serious and to some extent unnecessary jeopardy."
—From an interview with Major Reno, Washington, DC, November 17, 1877, *New York Herald*, November 19, 1877

"History records no instance of a battle where a commanding officer was abandoned to death by his subordinates, as Custer was at the battle of the Little Big Horn, without an investigation into the cause of the disaster. Shall the blood of Custer and his brave men cry for justice forever? I trust not, for the honor of the American people. Let us have justice, no matter where it strikes."
—Frederick Whittaker, Mount Vernon, New York, November 21, 1877, *New York Herald*, November 24, 1877

One of the great tragedies related to the battle of the Little Big Horn was the untimely death of Thomas B. Weir, the captain of Company D, in New York City on December 9, 1876. Undoubtedly Weir took to the grave a host of valuable details concerning the battle, which, had he lived, he may have eventually shared with the public. In January 1879, at the time of the Reno Court of Inquiry, the *New York Herald* remarked:

Action has at last been taken in this serious matter; but, unfortunately, not before the most important witness—the man who saw with his own eyes the last sad scenes of the Custer massacre—had passed from this world forever.[55]

The Reno Court of Inquiry

Tired of being publicly accused of cowardice and blamed for Custer's defeat at the battle of the Little Big Horn, Major Reno had requested a court of inquiry to clear his name. The trial was held in January and February 1879, during which eighteen soldiers (including Reno) and five civilians offered their testimony, much of which was most certainly restrained to protect the image of the regiment. The court's conclusion was that although some of Reno's subordinates "did more for the safety of the command by brilliant displays of courage than did Major Reno," still, there was no particular reason to censure his actions.[56] According to then-Lieutenant Jesse M. Lee, who served as the court recorder at Reno's inquiry, Colonel Wesley Merritt had told him at the time, "We have politely cursed him (Reno) and whitewashed it over."[57]

The *Herald* then stated that, had the government acted promptly and investigated the battle of the Little Big Horn in 1876, "the gallant Captain Weir would have settled forever the question of responsibility in the terrible drama enacted on the Little Big Horn."[58] That is quite a teaser. What did Weir know? What could he have said? He must have had some very strong opinions, not to mention cold hard facts. Fortunately, thanks to correspondent James J. O'Kelly, we can get a glimpse at what Weir may have revealed if he had had the chance. O'Kelly had spent much of August and September in the camps of the Seventh Cavalry and, in addition to "confidential communications" made to him by Reno's "brother officers," he soaked up the camp gossip. The result was the first newspaper article of its kind to appear about the much-debated battle. And there can be but little doubt that Weir was prominent among those "brother officers."[59]

Here is O'Kelly's investigative and fiery article from the *New York Herald* in September 1876.[60] It is followed by an editorial that speaks further to the charges against Major Reno.

New York Herald,
Thursday, September 21, 1876

A REVIEW OF CUSTER'S LAST FIGHT ON THE LITTLE BIG HORN.

THE RESPONSIBILITY FOR THE DISASTER.

WAS IT RASHNESS OF THE DEAD OR PRUDENCE OF THE LIVING?

SEVEN COMPANIES INACTIVE WHILE CUSTER WAS SLAUGHTERED.

THE DEAD HERO'S LONGING EYES.

Fort Lincoln, D. T., Sept. 20, 1876,
via Bismarck, Sept. 20, 1876.
Now that the campaign is over no time should be lost in clearing up the causes which led to the great disaster that will ever be remembered in our history. No confidence can be placed in the official report of the battle of the 25th of June. It is full of inaccuracies, and has been read with something approaching astonishment by the men who took part in the fright [fight?]. If the public wants to know the whole truth about

THE CUSTER MASSACRE
there must be a full and searching investigation where the witnesses will have to answer on their oath. If such investigation should be held startling revelations may be looked for. The story of Custer's fight and death is still unwritten. Your correspondent has gleaned some important facts which must compel further investigations, but the officers of the regiment will give no information unless they are compelled to do so. From the day the Herald correspondent arrived in the camp of the Seventh Cavalry he sedulously sought such information as would enable him to place this grave question in its true light, and fix in a manner that should have no room for cavil or evasion, the responsibility of the disaster that beset our arms on the 25th of June. The task was not an easy one. It was beset with difficulties that could not be met and overcome in the ordinary way.

RETICENCE OF OFFICERS AND WHY.
Men were there who could tell the whole truth, but they were soldiers; it was their duty to be silent; they were obliged to speak the official language; they were loyal to their regiment; there was a secret and they felt themselves bound in honor to be silent. It was also [in] their interest. Was it not known that the men who had in life been the enemies of the dead Custer were more than ever his enemies now that he was dead? How, then, could a mere subaltern dare to express an opinion? He must speak official language or he must prepare to be jumped, that is, pounced upon at some unwary moment and treated with the full vigor of military law, driven from his profession and made a beggar upon the world after years of meritorious service. What wonder that men who know the whole truth refused to speak their own thoughts and merely

echoed the official language. But little by little the truth came out; words spoken at every unguarded moment and dropped in the heat of argument, simple questions answered by officers and men, and the whole joined together and connected, has produced the conviction that there was blundering, [a] want of soldierly sympathy—a failure on the part of men to do their duty or lukewarmness in supporting General Custer—that might be called by an ugly name. The whole truth of the Custer massacre will

Never Be Known

unless the American public demands a full and searching investigation, when every man who was in the fight on the 25th of June at the Little Big Horn will be compelled to tell what he knows. There is buried with the dead a terrible secret; but the witnesses still live, and the government can learn the whole truth if the government wants to know it. Then can be settled forever the question whether the massacre of the Little Big Horn must be charged to rashness of the dead or prudence of the living. The issue is a fair one and must not be evaded. Either Custer or the men who survived him must be made responsible for the lives lost on the Little Big Horn, and now, while the witnesses are alive, is the time to settle the question forever.

Custer's Attack Justified.

That Custer was justified in making the attack on the village will hardly be questioned by any officer who has had any experience of Indian fighting. On that point the opinion of officers of the Seventh Cavalry is unanimous. Even today they believe that had the 600 men who rode after Custer's flag come into contact, as a body, with the Indians, success would not have been doubtful for a moment. The question, therefore, hinges on the description of the troops in the

actual fight, and this naturally involves the consideration of how far Custer's plans were carried out by his subordinate officers and what amount of cooperation he received at their hands.

There is the story of

The Fight In The Bottom,

about which various versions are given even by those who happened to be engaged in it. An investigation would throw some curious light on the actions of prominent actors, and bring out in bold relief names that have scarcely been mentioned in connection with the fight or the rout, as one may choose to view it. According to the official report the three companies in the bottom under Major Reno were overwhelmed by a mass of Indians and compelled to take to the woods. A prominent actor in the fight assured me that when the skirmish line retired to the woods there were not fifty Indians actually engaged with Reno's command. It is extremely doubtful whether more than one man had been struck by a hostile bullet when the skirmish line retired to the woods.[61] Nearly all the men were killed while getting their horses or on the way to the ford. There was a great deal of confusion and the ride to the ford was something like a stampede, with Reno at the head. Opinions are divided also as to whether the position at the point of woods in the bottom was tenable or not. One cool-headed man assured me that fifty men could have held it against 500 Indians.

Indians In Reno's Front.

The mass of Indians who moved into the bottom took no part in the fight against Reno's command. As they moved out from their village they caught sight of Custer on the bluffs and turned off to meet him and prevent him falling on their women and children. The story that they first overwhelmed Reno and then turned to Custer is pronounced a fiction. Some of Reno's command fought with great bravery, especially Captain [Thomas] French, who was the last man to cross the ford in the retreat. He remained behind his company, and at times was completely surrounded by Indians. Major Reno led the run to the bluffs, as he tells us in his official report, but there it is called a charge, though there were no Indians between the bluffs and the retreating cavalry to charge. When the retreat began from the skirmish line only one man is known to have been wounded.

INDIANS ENGAGED.

The number of Indians actually engaged with troops at this point did not exceed sixty. All the men who were killed in this command fell while getting their horses and while they were retreating across the ford to the bluffs, except the wounded man, who was abandoned in the retreat. The handling of the troops on this occasion has been severely criticized. On entering the bottom they were first deployed as skirmishers and then mounted and dismounted several times within a few minutes without any apparent cause. The soldiers were withdrawn from [the] skirmish line after they had fired a few shots at the Indians who were a long way off, and there was no defense of the woods worthy of the name. All this conspired to

DEMORALIZE THE TROOPS

and the manner in which the retreat was conducted caused it to degenerate into a stampede. There is a strong impression that had a tougher fight been made in the bottom the Indians could not have overwhelmed Custer with their whole force. It must be kept well in mind that the whole Indian force withdrew and concentrated to attack Custer as soon as Reno had retreated to the bluffs. The

statement that the Indians remained in front of Reno's position firing dropping shots is absolutely contradicted by officers who were present. The Indians left Reno severely alone on his hill, and for an hour heavy firing was distinctly audible in the direction Custer had taken. According to Captain Benteen's own statement he arrived on the field at the moment when Reno's command were escaping up the heights, and immediately joined his forces with those of Major Reno. There were then six companies assembled on the hill, increased soon to seven by the arrival of Captain [Thomas M.] McDougall with the pack train; that is to say, there was a force more numerous than that with General Custer, and who can doubt that the dead hero's eyes were after turned backward along his trail watching for the cloud of dust that would tell him his troopers were coming like a whirlwind to his support.

RENO'S SUPINENESS.

But they came not, and no serious effort was made to reach him. When Reno's command took position on the hill the Indians disappeared and went over the range of lower hills that hid Custer and his gallant men from view of his seven companies that were drawn up upon the hill under Reno, with not an enemy in view; with not a soul to bar the way while the roll of the rifle volleys across the hills told that Custer and his men were fighting for their lives.

THE ADVANCE OF D COMPANY.

In the official report furnished by Major Reno, it is stated that Company D [under Weir] of the Seventh Cavalry was sent forward to open communication with General Custer. This statement is inaccurate. It is true that D Company, of its own accord and without orders, did move forward to the crest of the hill which hid Custer and the men who died with him from the rest of the command, but they did so only when tired with the inaction of Major Reno's command, while rifle volleys were telling that their comrades were being done to death. Yet 300 horsemen under Major Reno were standing on a hill not four miles away from where General Custer fell, with not an Indian opposing their advance. When D Company went forward without orders precious time had been lost, and the order sent after this company was delivered when the company was returning. Custer's force was then destroyed; but had the seven companies under Major Reno advanced when Captain Benteen's battalion came up there is no doubt that they could have arrived at Custer's battlefield in time to take part in the fight.

PERTINENT QUESTIONS.

If Reno thought it possible for one company to open communication with General Custer why did he not try to join with his seven companies? Why was the mass of horsemen, kept idle on the hill for a space of time calculated at two hours, not hurled into the fight when they first arrived? What were seven companies of cavalry doing gathered upon a hill when four miles away their comrades were fighting desperately for their lives? When some members of D Company reached the summit of a range of low hills, which hid Custer's command from the view of Major Reno's forces, they saw some two miles away crowds of Indians on a hill, which is now thought to be the hill on which Custer died. The Indians were riding hither and thither, and on the plains masses of mounted men were swaying back and forth and straggling shots were fired from time to time. It was the end of the tragedy. The last victims were being offered up. From this it is

clear that if seven companies, instead of halting on a hill, had advanced at a gallop to where the firing was heard, instead of halting an hour or two on the hill, they could have arrived in ample time to have cooperated with Custer. There was nothing to prevent them doing so. The fifty or sixty Indians who had stampeded Major Reno's command had gone to take part in the fight against Custer, and Major Reno and his command were left absolutely free until Custer's men had been massacred,[62] when the whole Indian force returned to attack the men who had been standing idle for two hours while these same Indians slaughtered their comrades. How this came to pass and who is the responsible person must be answered by a searching investigation.

CAPTAIN BENTEEN'S MOVEMENTS.

Captain Benteen also, who in defense of the hill won golden opinions for his great courage and coolness, will have, unfortunately, to explain why his battalion failed to appear at an earlier hour on the battlefield. He had returned to the main trail and was following in Custer's wake before the fight began and could not at any time during the fight have been more than seven or eight miles distant from where Custer fell. About seven miles from Custer's battlefield Captain Benteen watered his horses at a pool in the road.[63] While the battalion was halted Boston Custer rode up [from the pack train], spoke with several officers and then rode on to the front. He was found dead by General Custer's side about seven miles from this pool of water. Captain Benteen received

CUSTER'S LAST WRITTEN ORDER.

"Hurry up. Big village. Bring up the packs." That order was practically ignored. Captain Benteen and his battalion walked at the ordinary marching pace until the point was reached where Reno's retreating men were seen, then, in combined force, halted for two hours and took no further part in the battle until the Indians came back and attacked them. No effort was made to join Custer or to follow up the Indians, who withdrew from Major Reno's front to go to attack Custer. The same Indians who fought Major Reno in the bottom took part in the fight against Custer, and had the companies advanced when they assembled on the hill they could also have taken part in the fight and Custer might be living today. Why Major Reno's command failed to move to the assistance of the General remains to be explained. A searching investigation would bring to light other and equally startling revelations with regard to the conduct of some of the prominent actors in the fight of the 25th of June, and justice to the living as well as to the dead demands that such investigation should be ordered by the government.

New York Herald,
Monday, October 2, 1876

THE CUSTER MASSACRE—MUST THE RESPONSIBILITY REST ON THE LIVING OR THE DEAD?

Our special correspondent, writing from Bismarck on his return from General Terry's expedition, felt it his duty to make public serious charges, which had been privately circulated in camp, against an officer who had been prominent in the Little Big Horn fight. With or without reason, a large share of the responsibility of the Custer disaster was laid on the head of Major Reno by actors in the fight, both on account of his hurried retreat to the bluffs and his inaction after his junction with Captain Benteen.

Our correspondent felt it was his duty, under the circumstances, to take the responsibility of putting before the country the serious charges of indifference and inefficiency which have been whispered about the camp by the soldiers who accompanied the gallant Custer in his onslaught on the Indian village. In doing this our correspondent did only his duty. He no doubt wrote these grave charges with as much regret as we felt in publishing them. There could have been no private spleen to vent, no personal interest to subserve, but only the fulfillment of a duty toward the public, who look to the *Herald* for an impartial account of what is transpiring in the most remote corners of the world. The rumors and charges may be unfounded: they may be absolutely untrue, as we sincerely hope they may prove to be. Our correspondent does not vouch for the correctness of these statements; for none of the events came under his own observation. But we cannot doubt for a moment that the rumors were in circulation substantially as he reported them to the *Herald*; and finding them whispered from one to another with no one having the courage to rise up and speak so that the country should hear what the soldiers and officers were saying, he took the responsibility of putting plainly into print the charges that were persistently made against the conduct of some of the prominent actors in the Little Big Horn tragedy.

Nothing is more painful than the laying of accusations against army officers engaged in difficult and dangerous duty. They have a great deal to contend against, and when it can be shown that their misfortunes have resulted from mistakes of judgment they are entitled to be treated with all charity. But, unfortunately, in the present case there is an element of doubt as to whether certain officers did do their duty in such a way as the country and their comrades had a right to expect. We do not make this accusation, but it is freely made by brother soldiers speaking among themselves in confidence, and we only call attention to the serious nature of these camp rumors in order to allow those interested either to prove the truth or the falsity of statements that affect the honor and compromise the soldierly reputations of some holding high rank in the army. No soldier, no matter how brilliant his past record may have been, can afford to allow statements reflecting on his efficiency and courage to pass unchallenged, and we sincerely hope to see a demand for investigation into this Custer massacre put forth by the officers themselves. This will be the best reply to any unworthy slanders that may have been uttered through jealousy or from a desire of revenge. The country would like to know all the truth about the Custer massacre, and no officer who did his duty need have any fear to come before an investigating committee to answer for his conduct. Much that our correspondent writes confirms in an authoritative way the suspicion entertained vaguely by the public that Custer had not been fairly dealt with, and strengthens the idea that the blundering of subordinates had as much to do in bringing about the massacre in the Little Big Horn valley as had the rashness of General Custer, if not more.

No officer of the United States army can afford to remain silent under accusations of such gravity. They must be answered, and, if possible, shown to be baseless fabrications. It will give real pleasure to the Herald if the officers interested in telling the whole truth about the Custer fight can show satisfactorily that none of the living are responsible for the untimely death of their comrades on the 25th of June. There exists in the public mind a deep seated suspicion that some one blundered, and the vague rumors that were current in General Terry's camp show that the soldiers were not satisfied with the conduct of all who went into the fight under the gallant Custer. The officers of the army cannot afford to have this subject discussed in the columns of the Herald and talked about in the public places and by the firesides of the country without trying to disprove these rumors if they can be disproved. We shall be delighted to do the fullest justice to the accused parties. We go further, and wish that they may be able to prove clearly that they are wholly free from responsibility for the blood shed so uselessly in the Little Big Horn. Soldiers in Indian wars cannot be judged by the same standard we apply when dealing with a civilized foe: the conditions are wholly distinct. Indian fighting resembles more the warfare of the Middle Ages, when victory was decided by personal prowess rather than by the application of scientific rules of war. Many circumstances may yet be unknown which would explain positions that we are now prepared to criticize severely; but if any such circumstances exist they should be at once brought to light.

9

Advance Along the Rosebud

"If the men could take their choice, they would prefer a short, sharp, and bloody campaign—and good luck to the survivors." —Cuthbert Mills, Fort Fetterman, July 25, 1876, *New York Times*, August 6, 1876

"If Crook has one virtue in advance of all others it is patience, and a disposition to bide his time. The trouble in the first place was that the country cared nothing about the Sioux question, and then, when Custer's folly showed it up seriously, there was a general howl of indignation. This fierce desire of the people for a speedy and crushing revenge on the Sioux is disgusting enough to the men at the front."—Joe Wasson, Camp on Goose Creek, August 4, 1876, *New York Tribune*, August 17, 1876

"General Crook is a brave, faithful and competent officer. He has to keep his eye and ear open to every detail which may advance or retard his success, the country holding him responsible for the results of his campaign. If his success is proportionate to his ability and sagacity, the campaign will be a rebuke to his critics."—Joe Wasson, Camp on Goose Creek, August 4, 1876, *New York Tribune*, August 17, 1876

"In very hot weather bacon, even with hunger sauce, has not the relish it ought to have. . . . Gen. Crook's command is roughing it in the full sense of the term, and as this sort of thing threatens to continue until Sitting Bull is found and thrashed, or thrashes us, most of us are extremely anxious to interview him with the least possible delay." —Cuthbert Mills, Somewhere on the Rosebud, August 9, 1876, *New York Times*, August 27, 1876

Watching from the top of a small hill on August 3 as ten companies of the Fifth Cavalry filed across the bluffs and down to the river crossing at Goose Creek, General Crook was heard to utter, "Oh, if they had come before—if they had come before."[1] Crook's somewhat melancholy mood was understandable. His decision to wait for Colonel

Wesley Merritt had delayed his forward movement by more than two weeks, not to mention the month of virtual inactivity that preceded the Fifth's call to service. Then there was the talk, as reported by Joe Wasson back on July 23 (see the end of chapter 7), of a Sioux village at the confluence of Ash Creek and the Little Big Horn, some forty miles north of Crook's position.[2] But without Merritt, the general chose not to act. Scout Louis Richard afterward found this village of about five hundred lodges deserted.[3] On top of that, Crook had just received news that another sizable Indian village had been within striking distance until recently. Davenport's dispatch from Crook's camp on August 4 supplies further details on this latter circumstance:

On the morning of August 1 Thomas Cosgrove, the white chief of the Snakes, left the camp at the crack of day, with a few of his braves, to make a reconnaissance of the hills and valleys at the base of the mountains. A great pillar of smoke had stood above the horizon north of the camp for more than a week, while eastward signal wreaths had been continually rising, sometimes forming a long mystic colonnade of aerial architecture. Cosgrove directed his course toward this point, and reached it after a ride of fifteen miles. He found the deserted site of a Sioux village, around which the fire, still smouldering, had swept off the grass. The village had evidently contained only part of the Indians who were encountered by Custer, Terry and Gibbon. There were traces of few tepees, but many wicky-ups were standing, and the number of families who had been encamped there were estimated at about

600, containing 2,400 persons. The scouts examined the debris which remained on the ground, and found evidences that the villagers had suffered much from scarcity of food. No bones were found near the fire-holes where they cooked, except those of dogs, which they seldom eat except when destitute of game.[4]

While Crook reflected on lost opportunities and future prospects, some of the correspondents were busy expressing their admiration for Merritt's chief of scouts, William F. Cody. Wasson wrote that the celebrated scout "will be a command unto himself,"[5] to which Davenport added:

William Cody, the inimitable "Buffalo Bill," arrived with Colonel Merritt, and is undoubtedly alone a strong reinforcement of the intelligent efficiency of the force in the field. In the recent scout after the Cheyennes, who were attempting to join Sitting Bull, he displayed all the old bravery and deadly prowess which have made him a hero in the hearts of the worshippers of melodrama and tales of adventure. He and Frank Gruard [Grouard] are probably the finest scouts now in active service.[6]

Turning his attention to the oft-neglected rank and file, Wasson commented:

I have recently seen a published statement that General Crook's campaign is not likely to end gloriously; that there have been many desertions from the command, which is said to be composed of the riff-raff of the great cities, and cannot therefore be relied on for hard fighting. How easy it is to sit down on easy chairs and dash off such cheerful statements as these! . . . Today, the average makeup . . . [of the army] is morally and physically good enough for every purpose required of it. It is almost wholly composed of well-meaning men, not always of the brightest to begin with, but after a few months' drill fully up to all matters of routine. As to courage, the much-abused fellows take only too readily to the enemy's fire. The great trouble is to teach them the importance of taking care of themselves, instead of rushing uselessly into danger on every occasion.[7]

Writing on the same day as Wasson, August 4, Davenport noted the steadfastness of the troops:

The soldiers, on the eve of seeking another battle, with the terrible fate of Custer and his men so fresh in their memories, are by no means as gay as they were when they last started toward the Yellowstone. But there is a grim resolve evinced in their manner and their faces to seek vengeance for the slain of the Little Big Horn. The only question now to be solved is their management by their officers. If that is good they must do well. A nobler body of soldiers never marched to meet a foe.[8]

In a letter to the *New York Tribune*, one of those noble soldiers with the command remarked on the chances of having another fight with the Sioux:

There is much doubt expressed among the troops as to the probability of having any more fights with the Indians this summer. The Indians have been whipped notwithstanding the Custer massacre. . . . They have also ceased to molest our camp, and our Snake and Ute allies say that the Sioux are splitting up into small parties. . . . It is presumed, therefore, that we shall only have a picnic the rest of the summer.[9]

William F. "Buffalo Bill" Cody, circa 1875. (*Eastman Portrait Gallery*)

Although this anonymous soldier made no mention of scurvy, he did report that Crook's command, just like with that of their Yellowstone counterparts, was in need of an improved diet:

We are in excellent health, but feel the want of some vegetables and fresh meat, of which we have been deprived since June 15. The wagon train was so loaded that only a small supply of canned vegetables was sent to us, barely enough for two messes. Were it not for the fish we are able to get here, we should have had a very poor time of it. We have lived on salmon, trout and white fish all summer. There is plenty of game in the country, but so large a command cannot get near it, and small hunting parties are prohibited.[10]

With the addition of the Fifth Cavalry, Crook's strength had been bolstered considerably. He now had an impressive twenty-five companies of cavalry at his disposal: ten each of the Third and Fifth and five of the Second, totaling some 1,350 men. He also had ten companies of infantry drawn from the Fourth, Ninth, and Fourteenth regiments, and good for an additional four hundred men. The cavalry was under Merritt and the infantry under Major Alexander Chambers. Captain George M. Randall, Twenty-third Infantry, headed some 240 Shoshone and Ute scouts, described as "a gaudily tinted throng," and Major Thaddeus H. Stanton was in charge of about seventy-five citizen volunteers.[11] About this latter group, Davenport noted:

The civilian scouts were marshaled under Major T. H. Stanton, who then and thereafter attempted in vain to make of frontier ruffians soldierly volunteers. They knew no discipline or awe of authority, and straggled along in a very disorganized manner.[12]

The night before setting out, Wasson wrote that "Crook feels confident of meeting the Sioux within three days," or, at the latest, within the week. If not, then they must have scattered.[13] He also commented on the eagerness of the troops to meet their Indian foes: "If we have the luck to meet the Indians there will be a hot contest, for every one has 'blood in his eye,' and yearns for a chance to revenge his fallen comrades."[14]

Writing a few weeks later from Deadwood, in present-day South Dakota, Davenport dramatically recalled the evening of August 4, which followed a day marked by sprawling prairie fires:

The atmosphere was clouded by dense masses of foul smoke, hanging close to the earth and constantly augmented by the wind, which blew from the prairies, burning along the base of the mountains. The sun glowed like a sullen ember and sunk behind the ghostly peaks of snow in the west. In the strange twilight a score of figures appeared on a bench of land west of the stream. They were mounted and moved in silent order, but on reaching the crest of the eminence they suddenly paused, and turning with startling swiftness galloped away. They appeared to be clothed like soldiers, but their manner of riding was unmistakably Indian. Twice they were again seen on distant ridges and then vanished. A special picket stationed on the west bank of the stream had not observed the strange apparition, but were alarmed after they had first dashed away, by a small shower of bullets pattering on the ground among their horses' hoofs, probably fired by the red devils while running.[15]

When the fire reached the green cottonwoods, they "produced a dense, pungent smoke which oppressed every sense." That night the "sky was profusely black, like the ebon vaults of chaos, with a blackness which only found expression when relieved by the lurid streams of lightning flashing across the horizon. . . . Suddenly, near midnight, the rain fell as if the very heavens were dropping."[16]

The command was on the march at 5 a.m., sunrise, August 5. About their immediate destination, Cuthbert Mills, the twenty-eight-year-old *New York Times* correspondent who had recently arrived with Merritt's column, wrote:

Where the Indians are now is doubtful, but it is generally supposed the village has gone to the old ground on the Rosebud where the last fight with Gen. Crook took place, and there the orders are for the Army to follow them. It is not probable that the same ground will be fought over again, but perhaps the fight may happen near it.[17]

Wasson noted that the "campaign will be carried out on Spartan principles."[18] Specifically, each trooper was allowed one blanket, a change of underclothes, an overcoat, four days' provisions in the saddlebags (for the cavalry), and 150 rounds of ammunition. The pack train consisted of 300 to 350 mules carrying an additional fifteen days' of rations.[19] The Shoshones and Utes, in addition to their usual colorful paraphernalia, were wearing small white flags attached to their war bonnets or scalp locks, in order to distinguish them from enemy warriors in case of a battle.[20]

Left behind once again was the ponderous, slowing-moving wagon train (numbering 150), under guard of Captain Furey, the quartermaster, and two hundred teamsters and citizen volunteers.[21]

On August 7, they crossed from the Tongue to the Rosebud,[22] along which, the following day, the Indian scouts discovered a vast trail. In a dispatch to the *Chicago Inter-Ocean*, Lieutenant Frederick Schwatka, Third Cavalry, described the incident:

On the eighth, the command moved down the [Rosebud] river about five miles to good grass and bivouacked, awaiting some definite intelligence from the scouts, who returned about noon, reporting that an immense trail had been found seven miles distant down the river, which, following the river, eight miles farther turned eastward in the direction of the Tongue River. Orders were received to move at 6:00 p.m. and to march as far down the Rosebud as the point where the trail left it—fifteen miles. The trail was about five or six days old.[23]

By the ninth, correspondent Mills was starting to think less about Sitting Bull and more about the daily menu:

One spoonful of coffee per day, one spoonful of sugar, eight hard crackers, and enough bacon to be spread out, with great care, through two meals, represents the actual practical total of all the elaborate calculations of fourths, tenths, eighths, and sixteenths of a pound which figure in the make-up of a day's rations on the commissary return.[24]

And Mills was clearly missing the fine dining that New York City offered:

We have all heard of people who die for their country, and of other people who live for it, and much credit both classes have received for their several services. But what credit will the individuals of this command get for starving for their country? I will venture to say none; and yet what a strength, depth, height, and breadth of patriotic ardor it requires to fill the vacuum left in one's internal economy by short rations. How sweet the thought of Delmonico's, the Café Brunswick, or the Hoffman, when, with a constitution which seems hollow clear down to one's boots, one sits down to a meal consisting of three small pieces of fried bacon, some fragments of "hardtack," and half a pint of poor coffee, and this after a march of twenty-five or thirty miles?[25]

Davenport noted that the Indians were, in all probability, not eating much better than the troops:

The Sioux seem resolved on abandoning all the region south of the Yellowstone for the present season. The traces of their camps along the Rosebud show that their ponies have nearly starved, and that their own subsistence has been far from plentiful.[26]

Looking back a few weeks later, he added details about the remains of former Sioux and Cheyenne camping places:

On the 9th a march of eighteen miles was made through a burned region, where there were frequent indications of the former sites of the Sioux village and some of recent war encampments. Where the fire had not come the grass had already been entirely consumed by the ponies of the Sioux. The bones of animals recently eaten were found, excepting those of dogs and horses. Several equine carcasses were seen from which the savages had cut steaks. They are believed, however, to have been killed by Cheyennes, as the Sioux loath horseflesh as food and eat it only in the worst extremity.[27]

If the troops and the Indians were suffering in the gastronomical department, one group was getting along just fine—the mule packers. Lucky for Mills, he knew a couple of them from an exploring expedition to Colorado the previous year:

When the situation is serious, a council of war is held. We held one, and I was detailed for a foraging expedition to the packers' camp. There I had a couple of friends with whom I was out last year on the Hayden survey. The packers are noted for knowing how to take care of themselves. They are nearly all old frontiersmen, and up to every dodge for securing personal comforts in the field, which one learns by long living there. So to the packers' camp I rode, drew aside my old friend Shep Madera, and stated the case to him. We wanted bacon at any cost; $2 a pound would be considered cheap. "You shall have it, old boy," was the encouraging answer; "you shall have it—but not a cent," and nothing could shake his determination on this point.[28]

Mills noted that the extra supply of bacon lasted only two meals, after which "a relapse into semi-starvation followed."

Besides traversing deserted Indian villages, that day's march also took Crook's column through an area teeming with Indian burial sites, including the final resting place of several warriors who died as a result of the Rosebud and Little Big Horn fights. The Indian scouts and soldiers desecrated the graves. Davenport described the scene:

The valley of the Rosebud is a favorite cemetery of the wild Sioux. Many sepulchres loom along the banks of the stream. They are platforms, built of cottonwood poles and crutches, on which the bodies of the dead are placed, well wrapped in their costliest raiment. During our march many freshly occupied were found. The Shoshones desecrated all of them that were visible from the trail. They even pulled down the bodies of dead papooses and scattered half-decomposed fragments on the earth. At some of the oldest sepulchres I found evidence that they had once before been desecrated and that the bones had been afterward collected, tied up in a bag and hung from the upright poles of the platform, perfumed with fragrant herbs. Usually the skulls lay grinning on the grass, finely polished by exposure to the weather. Some corpses were found which were apparently those of Indians who were killed in the Rosebud and Little Horn fights. On one of these Captain Anson Mills found a costly quilt, adorned with beads, and a rich robe. Subsequently a soldier discovered in the same sepulchre a fine revolver, plated with nickel and having a butt of ivory, with a belt containing 100 cartridges. Old Washakie, of the Snakes, said that these tributes to the dead [warrior] indicated that his rank among the living was high. He believed him to have been an important chief.[29]

Another eyewitness to these Indian burial sites recalled:

While coming down the Rosebud through the deserted Sioux villages, I noticed the remains of a great many sweat or medicine tepees or lodges, which shows that the Sioux must have had a great many wounded in the Rosebud and Little Horn battles. Their treatment for sickness or wounds consists almost entirely in the sweating process, very much like our modern Turkish baths.[30]

Next, Davenport addressed the difficulty and frustration of trying to follow the Indian trail, even for the Indian scouts:

As we advanced down the valley of the Rosebud the scouts constantly changed their opinions in regard to the age of the trail. It was at first two weeks old, then ten days, then a week and then four days.[31]

On the morning of August 10, the column continued its march north down the Rosebud, and four miles later it came upon "the remnants of an immense Indian village."[32] Schwatka reported:

[The deserted village] was about two miles to two and a half long and probably filled the entire valley, about a mile and a half wide. Near the center of its length were the [remains] of a large amphitheater where the Sioux and Cheyennes had had a Sun Dance during the last spring.[33]

Our good friend and oft-quoted correspondent Reuben Davenport brings this chapter to a close:

[A]bout noon, General Crook's column halted about thirty miles from the mouth of the Rosebud. The scouts reported that the trail, a short distance ahead, diverged from the valley toward the east, spreading out like a fan, as if the Sioux were dispersing. Thirty fresh pony tracks lay above the myriad old ones, and were supposed to have been made by a party of rear spies of the Sioux. . . . [Shortly afterward dust] was seen toward the north, and Cody, who was the foremost scout returning from the advance, reported that from the top of a hill he had seen a body of troops. We were not sure they were not Sioux, however, until they drew nearer, when it was discovered that General Terry's command was approaching. Buffalo Bill galloped to meet them and found their whole force elaborately disposed for battle.[34]

It was a historic moment. Crook. Terry. The Rosebud. Two armies. Several hundred imaginatively decorated Indian scouts. Over three thousand five hundred men. Many came to view it as an unfortunate turn of events.

Aboard the steamer *Far West* near the mouth of the Powder River on August 15, 1876, James J. O'Kelly, wrote in a piece that would appear in the *New York Herald* on August 24, 1876, that:

The preparations made by the War Department to carry on operations against the Sioux were ridiculously inadequate and altogether unsuitable to the nature of the country. Huge wagon trains have been sent out that creep over the ground . . . instead of good mules, which could go anywhere cavalry or infantry could pass without delaying the column in making bridges and roads.[35]

The Army of the Yellowstone's first day's march along the Rosebud was not quite what Terry had hoped for. First, the terrain proved more difficult for the wagons to pass over than was expected, and Lieutenant Edward Maguire, of the Engineer Corps, was kept busy constructing bridges and improving parts of the trail. Second, the men and animals were battling the "overpowering" heat, the temperature rising as high as 116 degrees. The infantry, marching as flankers, "were obliged to sit sometimes for an hour in the sun." After toiling for ten miles in these conditions, it was "with real satisfaction that the troops received orders to pitch their tents for the night in a broad bottom surrounded by low hills." James J. O'Kelly made note of the gossip going around the camp that first night: "Some stupid fellows

started a rumor that a horse and dead soldier, belonging to Company C of the Seventh Cavalry, had been found by the pickets, but the rumor proved to be wholly groundless."

The next day, August 9, there was a "heavy downpour" and the temperature dropped by as much as sixty-five degrees. Continuing south, they passed over ground that had previously been home to several Indian villages. O'Kelly noted:

Our march now lay through a succession of abandoned Indian camps, showing that we were on a favorite hunting ground of the Sioux. The bleached bones of buffaloes and now and then the shaggy head of this monarch of the plains, testifying to the recent passage of Indian hunters, were met with from time to time, scattered among wickyups or temporary shelters made of saplings and tree branches, but so far no signs of the hostile Sioux were encountered. [However, our] picturesque but dirty Crow and Ree allies had brought in information of the near approach of the Sioux, and we were in hourly expectation that the savages would appear to dispute our progress.

Excitement followed a little later when the Crow and Arikara scouts came galloping up to the command during a temporary halt, yelling that "heap Sioux" were headed their way:

This our informant expressed clearly in [sign] language showing us the Sioux mounted and coming to cut our throats. The interpreter soon after arrived and confirmed us in our interpretations of the Indian sign language.[36]

Two companies of the Seventh Cavalry, under Captain French and Lieutenant DeRudio, were "sent forward to support the scouts in case of attack" while the remainder of the column "closed up" and made hasty preparations. Oddly, it turned out to be a false report.

The next morning, at about 11 a.m., the Indian scouts rushed into camp yet again, "uttering their unearthly screams" that the Sioux were coming. This time it was not a false alarm; indeed, indistinct "figures were discovered on the distant bluffs." O'Kelly described the ensuing action:

By general consent these were pronounced Sioux. The troops were immediately formed in line of battle, and the scene suddenly became animated in the extreme. One battalion of the Seventh Cavalry, under Captain Weir, formed a mounted skirmish line at full gallop, aided by the Second Cavalry, drawn up in column on their flank, under Major Brisbin, and Lieutenant Low's battery of three [ordnance] guns. The trains were closed up, and the companies of the Fifth Infantry, under Colonel Miles, the Sixth, under Major Moore, and Twenty-second, under [Lieutenant] Colonel Otis, were extended along the flanks, and moved in the rear as supports. For a few moments all was expectation and anxiety.

A single horseman advanced from the timber and there was a muttered exclamation from many mouths, "there they come." As we strained our ears for the report of the first gun the horseman advanced toward the skirmishers making signs of friendship and was allowed to approach. It proved to be Cody, the scout, better known as Buffalo Bill, dressed in the magnificence of border fashion. He announced that we were in front of General Crook's command and

might put off all bloodthirsty thoughts for that day.

In opposition to the beautiful cavalry charges as generally depicted in the movies, O'Kelly's description of Captain Weir's mounted skirmish line is rather astonishing:

It is worthy of note that, though not a shot was fired, Captain Weir's battalion of the Seventh Cavalry had twelve men dismounted in the gallop to form the skirmish line, and two men of one company had their legs broken. This result is in part due to the system of sending raw recruits, who have, perhaps, never ridden twenty miles in their lives, into active service to fight the best horsemen in the world, and also to the furnishing the cavalry young, unbroken horses, which become unmanageable as soon as a shot is fired. Sending raw recruits and untrained horses to fight mounted Indians is simply sending soldiers to be slaughtered without the power of defending themselves.

Next up, the Terry-Crook cavalcade.

IO

The Search for Sitting Bull

"Our warriors in the Sioux country have sense enough to leave their feathers and gold lace at home. General Terry wears a pair of corduroy pants, an old blouse and a stained, weather beaten, Panama hat. General Gibbon dresses even plainer, and General Brisbin covers himself with a suit of blue overalls."—News clipping, *Daily Colorado Chieftain*, August 22, 1876

"Everybody has grown dissatisfied with what they claim to be the continued mismanagement of the officers, and criticize the conduct of officers severely, and frankly express their disgust at having anything to do with a campaign, which is evidently based upon false theories."—Unknown correspondent, Terry's camp on the Yellowstone River, August 26, 1876, *Weekly Rocky Mountain News*, September 6, 1876

"Terry and Crook are much exercised over the newspaper attacks which pour in upon them with each mail, and are already bending their shoulders under the weight of public condemnation. All they say in reply is, 'I have done my best.'"—Unknown correspondent, Terry's camp on the Yellowstone River, August 26, 1876, *Weekly Rocky Mountain News*, September 6, 1876

"So innumerable and contradictory have been the rumors and statements, the orders and counter-orders, the movements and counter-movements up here during the past ten days that your correspondent confesses himself utterly bewildered by them and almost despairing of being able to narrate with any degree of satisfaction the news, doings and results of that period. It has been a period of anxious waiting-for-something-to-turn-up and of uncertainty of movement, painful to experience and yet inevitable in such a campaign as the present one."—James Joseph Talbot, Mouth of Powder River, September 1, 1876, *New York World*, September 17, 1876

"Poor Terry appeared to me more and more like a big, good-natured schoolboy—totally ignorant of the distracting conditions of Indian warfare; wanting to do something for his country, but not knowing, of himself, how to go about it."—Joe Wasson, Crook's Camp on Little Missouri River, September 4, 1876, *Daily Alta California*, September 17, 1876

"For a certain period, during which Gen. Crook's command was doomed to linger by the Yellowstone last month, there seemed to be a painful presence of a superfluity of brigadiers, and time proved the correctness of this view."—Joe Wasson, Fort Laramie, Wyoming Territory, September 25, 1876, *New York Tribune*, October 2, 1876

"What is the matter with Crook?" So reads one of the subheadings inside James J. O'Kelly's August 15 dispatch to the *New York Herald*. O'Kelly then goes on to criticize Crook for not coming forward to meet and greet General Terry when the two commands crossed paths five days earlier. After all, Terry was the senior officer, and Crook, having marched into Montana Territory, was now in Terry's military department.[1] O'Kelly wrote:

Some four miles from the point where we formed the line of battle General Crook was found encamped. He did not leave his camp to meet General Terry, a circumstance that caused no little comment. The conduct of this officer through the campaign has been, to say the least, peculiar. On consultation General Terry learned that Crook had been following for several days a heavy trail, supposed to be leading in the direction of Powder River.[2]

O'Kelly considered this last item another point of contention. Why had not Crook sent a courier to Terry alerting him of the movement of the Indians? If he had, Terry "could have easily moved down" from his position on the Yellowstone to "cut off the Indians' retreat northward."[3] Then O'Kelly suggested the reason behind Crook's behavior: "The fact that General Terry is a volunteer general and not a West Pointer, may, perhaps, have something to do with it."[4]

Whether or not these statements represented O'Kelly's opinions or reflected the views of Terry's staff was unstated.

Avoiding the issue of Crook's snub altogether, Cuthbert Mills focused on the visual aspect of the two generals' first conference:

Endless amusement was created in camp by an illustrated journal of New York, which contained a graphic picture of the meeting of Gens. Crook and Terry, wherein these two gentlemen appeared in full Brigadier Generals' uniform, with all their staff in full dress, and several Indian chiefs in gorgeous costume thrown in to give a picturesque effect to the whole. If any one ever saw Gen. Crook in the field wearing anything but a suit of ragged clothes, which might, boots and all, fetch $5 in a second-hand store, that person is unknown in this command.[5] Gen. Terry pays more attention to his personal appearance; but had the imaginative artist really seen the meeting of the two Generals he might have given the public a very vivid idea of the rough style in which we have lived this summer. He would have seen Gen. Terry and his staff dismounting in a patch of sage brush, near a clump of brush where stood Gen. Crook and staff, all as rough-looking and battered as their chief. Around them lay several small bundles of blankets which formed their beds, and a few yards off were scattered some tin plates, cups of the same material, a frying pan full of frizzling bacon, a pot of steaming coffee, and in the centre of the gorgeous layout a pile of hard tack. This was the dinner to which Gen. Terry was invited, but it did not seem that he or his staff were blessed that day with very vigorous appetites.[6]

With the two commands now together some thirty miles south of the Yellowstone and plans to follow the Indian trail that Crook had been following since the eighth, Terry realized a major error in his strategy. Other than the small force under Captain Sanger at "Fort Beans," the Yellowstone was virtually devoid of a military presence. What was to keep the Indians from crossing over and escaping into the British Possessions, assuming they had not already done so? To help remedy the situation, four companies of the Fifth Infantry—B, E, G, and H[7]—under Colonel Miles performed an about face:

At five p.m. the Fifth Infantry [with two Rodman guns] began its return march over a road cut up by the passage of a heavy train during the day and though the men were fatigued and worn out by the long day's march, it did not halt until some sixteen miles had been gone over. Here a short halt was made for a few hours, when the march was resumed. At ten o'clock in the morning [August 11] the head of the column reached Rosebud Creek.[8]

Miles was ordered to patrol the Yellowstone between the Tongue and Powder rivers from the deck of the *Far West*, "using the steamer as a kind of gunboat,"[9] and to place detachments on the north side of the river at those same points (and others) to keep the Indians from crossing over.[10]

On August 11, Terry and Crook crossed "the rough divide between the Rosebud and Tongue Rivers,"[11] a distance at that point of about twelve miles. To the dismay of those under Terry, Crook's method of campaigning was now *their* method of campaigning. In other words, when they marched out of camp that morning, it was good-bye to the ponderous and slow-moving wagon train and hello to frugal living. In the few hours they were together, Crook had managed to influence Terry on the proper way to chase Indians. Captain Burt wrote: "[By the night of the tenth] General Terry, taking a leaf out of General Crook's book, had stripped down from wagons to pack mules, from tents to bivouac, from luxuries to bacon and hardtack."[12]

O'Kelly, having had about two weeks to let the matter stew, and apparently distressed over the drastic change in his comfort level (in which he could not have been alone), let loose on Crook:

[General Crook, the] "distinguished Indian fighter" has a theory that if we want to fight Indians we must live like Indians. He does not permit his soldiers to carry their shelter tents, which are the most useful and important part of their equipment, and, in order to cap the climax of absurdity, he compels the men of his command to leave their cooking utensils behind, except one small tin cup. The result of this patent humbug campaigning is that the soldiers, exposed to the rapid atmospheric changes of this climate, and unable to cook properly the miserably insufficient food supplied to them by a generous government, are rendered incapable of supporting the fatigues incident to an Indian campaign in these deserts. General Terry unfortunately allowed Crook to influence him on this point and issued similar orders to his column. Fortunately the old Indian campaigners found means to partially evade the ill-considered order, much to the satisfaction of the good-natured General who, desirous of showing a good example, left his tent equipage at the Rosebud with the train, and as a result enjoyed sleeping in terrestrial rains for six nights. In the future operations this absurd order will be quietly disregarded and general and soldiers, abandoning theatrical campaigning, will sleep under canvas and cook their food, convinced that sound health and a well ordered stomach are no obstacles to the rapid marching of an army.[13]

Crook's biggest admirer, Reuben Davenport, also had quite a bit to say about the general's parsimonious method of Indian campaigning, calling him out for alleged duplicity:

A fact which I must not omit is characteristic of the leader of the expedition. It shows that the Spartan simplicity for which he had been celebrated by his sycophantic subalterns is wholly a miserable affectation. The soldier was expected to carry all of his bedding and shelter and subsistence for four days on his horse. The Brigadier General was ostentatiously lauded by his creatures for setting an example of self-denial. But it was observed that each evening, on making camp, a mule packer moved over to the headquarters with his arms loaded with hospital blankets and a wide tarpaulin, which contributed to the comfort of the terror of the Apaches. In the meantime bedding for the sick could not be carried by the pack train, which was mainly laden with ammunition, bacon and hard bread. The soldiers' fare was restricted to the four articles which I have before enumerated—bacon, hard bread, coffee and sugar; but the mule packers, exercising a sort of usurped prerogative, winked at by the general commanding, were supplied with flour, beans, tea, rice &c., on which they remained sleek, saucy and fat while the soldier[s] dwindled. The reader has probably guessed that the Spartan Indian fighter was often beholden to the civility of the packers for fare superior to that which his military subordinates must be content. General Crook invariably established his headquarters near the pack trains and lived a double life—one exhibited to his soldiers with calm vanity, but in which each one detected shams and flaws, and the other to his familiars and toadies, which was a consistent mirror of selfishness.[14]

In a newspaper interview in late October, Crook had a chance to respond to Davenport's accusations, not just on this charge, but others as well:

Every officer and man in the command knows the statement [by Davenport] to be untrue. I did not take a meal with the packers during the entire trip, principally because I was not invited to do so. Not that I think there would be anything improper in it. . . . The correspondents who accompanied the expedition were, with the exception of the *Herald* man, so far as I know, fair and thoughtful in their statements of its operations, but the representative of the *Herald*, for what reason I am unable to say, persisted to the last in misrepresenting it, and stating as facts things that never occurred or were utterly distorted and untrue.[15]

The grand combination continued down the valley of the Tongue River until August 14, when the trail turned east toward the Powder River, about five miles from a location Davenport referred to as "Tongue River buttes."[16] The fifteenth was spent navigating the terrain between the Tongue and Powder rivers, described by Davenport as "a rough and difficult country, the chief features of which were rolling hills, clad with pine trees and deep valleys, which rendered the march very fatiguing."[17] After a trek of twenty miles, they struck the Powder River about forty-three miles from its mouth. Two days later, on the seventeenth, within about ten to fifteen miles of the Yellowstone, the Indian trail yet again turned to the east. Clearly, the Indians wanted to avoid contact with the troops patrolling the river. Voicing what must have been the talk of the officers, Davenport commented:

[The trail leads in] the direction of the Little Missouri River, where the bands of Sitting Bull are in the habit of wintering. It is thought that they will try to escape from the troops either by crossing the Yellowstone and going north or by breaking into small bands and sneaking back to their reservations. They have burned the grass behind them so as to stop pursuit and the want of forage will render this measure very effective against our cavalry horses, which are already very much worn out. The scouts say the main trail is at least nine days old.[18]

With the grass burned off, the Indian trail estimated at more than one week old,[19] and the command in such close proximity to the Yellowstone, Terry deemed it best to continue on to the mouth of the Powder River to rest and refit, not just for the men, but for the horses too.

Wasson's pointed comments about the state of affairs at this time no doubt reflected Crook's feelings as well. The following is from Wasson's August 18 dispatch to the *Daily Alta California*:

When Terry cut loose from his elegant wagon camp [on August 11], he was in a miserable plight, and his shoulder-strapped equipage became a severe impediment to all concerned. It has caused a delay already in the pursuit of at least five days, while a succession of rainstorms has so completely obliterated the trail that it is altogether aggravating. To complete the picture of delay and disgust, after following the trail east over to Powder River and down that stream to within fifteen miles of its mouth, Terry insisted on moving the whole force down here, where he has a steamboat landing, and where we will lie at least today, and how much longer remains to be seen. Crook is hugely disgusted, and throughout his command there is a similar feeling. . . . [Crook's meeting up with Terry] came about accidentally, and, as it now appears, very unfortunately.[20]

Later in the same communication, Wasson came up with one of his wittiest lines; referring to the snail's pace speed of Crook and Terry's joint operations, he called it "the funeral procession in search of Sitting Bull."

For the next week, the two commands convalesced and waited for supplies to arrive, at the junction of the Powder and Yellowstone rivers. Davenport quipped that "General Crook's soldiers enjoyed needed repose, but meanwhile the great Sioux trail grew no younger." After three to four days of inactivity, Crook's "friendly Snakes and Utes had grown impatient of the absence of any achievement by the great white chief whom they had followed all the summer, and . . . departed toward their home." About the same time Terry's Crow scouts left too.[21]

Writing for the *New York World*, correspondent James Joseph Talbot voiced his opinion on the Indian scouts:

The first incident of importance that occurred . . . was the departure of the Indians for home on the 21st inst. Several small parties of them had left on various pretexts before, but as they were generally old men on worn-out ponies, or young "fortune hunters," who joined the expedition in hopes of plunder, and not finding any left in disgust, their departure was not regretted in the least. The remaining Indians, numbering 250 or 300 Utes, Snakes, Rees, Crows and Shoshones, finding that they had only

long marches, short rations and a hard time generally, with very little prospect of anything better in the future, finally became discontented with what was to them the unprofitable monotony of the campaign, and, after holding several "pow-wows" among themselves, resolved to return to their reservations, the resolve taking practical effect on the 21st, as before stated. And it might be said with equal truth in their case that their departure was not regretted. Contrary to the popular belief, they are of little value in a campaign. One or two dozen of them are always desired, and are invaluable as scouts, but a large number is only a nuisance.[22]

Adding his two cents on the scouts, Mills declared:

Over two hundred Snakes and Crows gave up the chase in despair and left us at the Yellowstone. They have been having an easy time of it compared with us, for they had their houses with them, and always killed enough game to make them independent of ration bacon. But they could not stand the everlasting march after an enemy who cannot be found, so they had a final war dance and howling match, and then went home, leaving the white men to continue the search.[23]

About the Crows in particular, Talbot added:

The Crow Indians are generally acknowledged to be the best and bravest Indians now on the plains. In an even fight, or with small odds against them, they have always whipped the Sioux, and it is only by their overpowering numbers that the latter have succeeded in driving the former out of this region, which rightfully belongs to them. Naturally, therefore, the two are, as they always have been, the bitterest enemies.[24]

It did not take long for the correspondents to take note of the marked contrast between the two commands. Davenport observed:

While idling in camp near the mouth of the Powder River the two armies exchanged civilities with a zest sharpened by the hardship undergone by one and the enthusiasm of the other. Terry's soldiers enjoyed comforts which seemed to Crook's weather-beaten veterans like Oriental luxuries. . . . Terry's legions . . . were ensconced in tents and attended by an immense train of wagons, loaded with supplies.[25]

As for Crook's command, Davenport wrote:

Since leaving Goose Creek no one in the southern column had been sheltered by canvas, unless in disobedience to strict orders. No man was supposed to have more than a single blanket to wrap about him when he slumbered. The food which was to afford the vigor requisite to sustain bitter hardships and the brunt of battle was simply bacon, hard bread, coffee and sugar.[26]

Wasson, too, noted the dissimilarity between the two commands, extending the comparison to the Indian scouts as well:

There was no comparison—it was all contrast. . . . Crook's ship was trimmed down to fast-sailing condition—every man's outfit complete in itself, and the pack-train on the Pacific Coast plan, better organized still. . . . Terry's scouting force is of no account whatever, while Crook's scouts have worn out their animals in keeping track of the trails, and so the case stands.[27]

If Wasson had a problem with Terry's skills as a commander,

O'Kelly was equally displeased with Crook. His dispatch from the Powder River on August 24 takes Crook to task for what O'Kelly considered to be the general's farcical method of Indian campaigning:

Only that Crook happened to meet General Terry he would long since have been compelled to turn back to Goose Creek, where he left his wagon train in accordance with the clever system of campaigning adopted on the Plains, which resembles nothing so much as a Chinese stage battle, where the combatants are constantly rushing in an excited manner after invisible enemies they never seem to catch, but who now and then manage to catch the pursuers.

To illustrate the system it is only necessary to suppose that General Crook left Goose Creek with twenty days' rations. This would enable him to march in pursuit of the Indians for ten days. At the end of that time Crook would have been compelled to march ten days back in order not to die of starvation, for this country is absolutely incapable of furnishing food to an army of white men. Having reached his supply train and refitted the General would have to march ten days to reach the point from which he first retreated, having thus lost twenty days, tired out his men and horses, accomplished nothing, and given the Indians twenty days to rest themselves and graze their ponies. It requires no special military education to know that a campaign conducted on such principles is little more than a farce, even if the General does sleep without a tent and grows fat on hard tack and alkali water.

That a man possesses an exceptional constitution and an ostrich-like stomach does not constitute him a great general, and the mere fact that soldiers sleep in the rain and get dysentery and rheumatism will not make them better Indian fighters. The sooner this sensational campaigning is put an end to the better it will be for the health of the army and the purse of the nation. If we cannot fight Indians as civilized men, let us adopt the essentials of Indian warfare, not the theatrical effects merely. If it is necessary to take away the soldier's tent why not take away his overcoat and blanket, which are less useful, and give him merely a breech-clout and war paint; but at the same time give him two or three ponies to ride, give him fresh buffalo meat and game to eat, but above all discharge the Brumagem [pretend] Indian chiefs, and give the command to real savages, who will not spend their time marching up hill and then down again, but will establish their supply camps or caches where it is possible to pick them up conveniently, while the chiefs go after their enemies with real, and not simulated, war whoops.[28]

Davenport also weighed in on the subject of Crook's tactics, more specifically his use of the wagon train. On August 18 he wrote:

General Crook has left his supply train entrenched on Goose Creek, where it is now practically useless. It is not always practicable to have the supply train accompany the column, but there is no good reason why it should not follow at some distance in the rear.[29]

By the time "Terry and Crook's cooperative society"[30] reached the Yellowstone, the men were so desperate for something to eat other than hardtack that when a trader's Mackinaw boat arrived from Fort Ellis on the seventeenth, loaded with goods, the men stampeded toward the water. Davenport captured the "ludicrous" scene:

No sooner had the Mackinaw come into sight than there was a grand rush of officers and soldiers to the water's edge, and confused shoutings assailed the ears of the boatmen. Before touching the bank, they were surrounded by horsemen who rode into the water. . . . Rank and degree were forgotten in the expression and attainment of a multiplicity of desires, which were burlesqued in the earnestness of the pleading. One individual wanted a "frying pan," another a "coffee pot," and everyone asked for canned fruits, with an avidity which met only with disappointment. This scene, which I have not attempted to describe, but merely to hint at, was repeated on the arrival of other boats. The privation of the troops was depicted in the contrast between their browned and wrinkled faces, overgrown with beards, and the smooth, well-content lineaments of the river traders who sold them a few of the most meagre necessities at enormous prices.[31]

Several days into their temporary stopover at the mouth of Powder River, Captain Burt of the Ninth Infantry jotted down the latest camp talk, half-joking that the troops would sooner be fighting hunger than Indians. Little did he know just how true that statement would soon prove to be:

The general impression is that we are to have no fight, that the Indians have gone to the agencies, and there is nothing to do but be getting nearer our quarters and something good to eat. "Belly battles" are the only ones seemingly in store for us, judging from the interesting campfire gossip.[32]

On August 23, having just returned from a trip upriver to the mouth of the Rosebud on the *Far West*, Mills wrote:

A thousand rumors are in circulation as to what the Indians are doing, what we shall do, and the probability of a fight. Cody leaves the command at this place. He declares that there is no chance of a fight so long as the forces in the field are kept together. It is too large a body for the enemy to make a stand against.[33]

Cody was right; there was not much chance of a fight if the two commands stayed together; the Indians would just avoid them. It was Wasson's opinion, dating back to his August 18 dispatch to the *Daily Alta California*, that Crook, having been reinforced by the Fifth Cavalry, "had all the force necessary to cope with the enemy," and that he should "cut loose from Terry" and try to "strike the enemy in the Little Missouri, where the trail appears plainly to lead."[34] Conversely, Wasson pointed out Terry's belief that most of the Sioux were already north of the Yellowstone:

Terry and his outfit, on the other hand, have insisted that the Sioux have crossed the Yellowstone toward the British Possessions, and yet there is not the slightest evidence of it. He has sent his steamboat, with a six-pound cannon, down the river to see what he can see. All this big outfit needs to perfect it is half a dozen brass bands and Herald correspondents. Perhaps James Gordon Bennett's fleet of yachts would be necessary.[35]

Whether the Indians had retreated north, south, or divided up between the two, one thing was for certain: the summer was quickly drawing to a close and with it the current military campaign. As things stood now, in late August, Terry and Crook had accomplished next to nothing, and Terry, short on supplies, planned to wrap things up by mid-September. Crook, too, had limited supplies and would have to trek back to Fort Fetterman or Fort Laramie before too long. In all probability, nothing decisive was going to occur in the next few weeks to prevent the necessity of another frigid winter expedition. Presenting to his readers what would likely be the government's last-ditch effort to salvage the predominately ineffective campaign, O'Kelly declared:

In case the great trail breaks up on the Little Missouri, as many believe it will, and that any considerable trail leads toward the agencies, General Terry will move his column along it and on arriving at the agencies will proceed to disarm the Indians and take away their ponies, if so instructed by the government. If this were done it would render a renewal of the war next spring impossible, for no matter what lying Indian agents may say, the warriors who slaughtered Custer and his men were chiefly the young bucks from the agencies. . . . There is not the slightest hope that the Indians can be forced to fight this year unless they choose to do so themselves, and they certainly will not fight unless they are in numbers so overwhelmingly superior that they may hope to destroy our column as they did Custer's. This is not probable, and the only chance of obtaining some adequate results for the fatigues undergone by the troops and the expenses incurred by the government is in adopting the policy of disarming the agency Indians, who are Sitting Bull's active reserves. With the disarmament of the young bucks of the Standing Rock,

Red Cloud and Spotted Tail agencies all danger of a renewal of a war next spring would be at an end. The spirit of the Sioux nation would be broken, and it would be possible to inaugurate a policy looking to the civilizing of these savages.[36]

As much as the Indians were refusing to make an appearance before the troops, the rain had other ideas. From the pen of Cuthbert Mills:

It rained before we got to the Yellowstone; it rained nearly every night while the command was camped there; it has rained nearly every night since. The suffering the men have undergone from this cause has begun to tell seriously on their health. Dysentery and diarrhea have become alarmingly prevalent, while the provision for the sick is of the scantiest description. Ambulances we have none, and of medicines an extremely limited stock. Such infantrymen as have become too sick to walk are mounted upon mules; the sick cavalryman has to stick to his saddle. Since leaving the Yellowstone only one man, to my knowledge, has gone so far as to have to be carried on the rude mule litters, of which two or three have been provided. That the general health of the command is as good as it is rather surprises our doctors, who have been expecting a much worse state of affairs from the poor food and bad weather we have had.

Quite a number of sick men and officers were sent away on the boats from our Yellowstone camp, and some few gentlemen who had accompanied the expedition as volunteers went with them. A dinner on the boat, a sight of the comfortable sleeping quarters there, and then a look at the wet camp on the hills, and the thought of bacon and hard tack, was more than their courage could stand. They fairly gave out and left us for home. Perhaps a great many more would have gone had they been free to do so, for the weather was terrible.

The evening before we started away [August 23] I had occasion to visit Gen. Crook's headquarters. It was raining, as usual, and pushing through the wet bushes on the bottom land drenched me completely. An immense fire of logs was hissing under the cottonwoods, where the little red and white flag indicated the commanding officer was to be found. The General stood under the trees, wrapped in his army overcoat; but some yards away was a large canvas shelter made out of an old hospital fly. This was a significant novelty. The rain had at last washed the enthusiasm out of the staff officers. I hope I do these gentlemen no injustice, but it had seemed to me there had been just a little tinge of ostentation in the extreme primitiveness of their style of living. It would have been as easy to carry half a dozen tin plates, forks, and spoons, as to carry one solitary specimen of each of them and pass it around the mess. In fact no mess was worse provided than the headquarters mess, and assuredly there was no absolute necessity for it. Other things were in the same style, but between using hard tack for plates and one fork for six people, and getting drenched out of one's blankets every night for weeks together, there is a vast difference. The solitary fork was from choice; the continuous rain was not, and under it the enthusiasm for simplicity had slightly washed out. So the pack train had been searched and this piece of canvas found. The General, however, had not surrendered yet.

We stood talking for some few minutes under the tree, and the rain poured down harder every moment. At last, as if the thought had just struck him, the General said:

"Why don't you get under the shelter, Mr. ——?"

"I had scarcely thought it worthwhile, General. A mere shower." (Indifferently.)

He was silent for a time, until a sudden gust of wind shook the tree, and it poured a perfect deluge on us. This brought a surrender.

"The rain is increasing. I think we had better get under cover," said the General, and he made tracks for the canvas lively, and I followed him. We bundled in among the officers who were crowded there, all heads and tails, each one trying to dodge the particular stream of water which made for him from above or below, for the canvas was not new and the ground was sloping. It was nearly dark, the rain showed no signs of abating, and it was kindly suggested that I should "bunk" in there. I thought of the mile-and-a-half walk to my quarters over the hill, the dreary night, the soaking blankets spread upon the muddy ground, the poor prospect for sleep under that pelting storm, and the welcome shelter offered here. Sore was the temptation to accept the General's offer. But no! Should it be said that I, a civilian, wilted in the presence of men of such Spartan severity of outfit? I started for "home," found a place to sleep under a fragment of canvas which Capt. Hayes[37] had rigged up on a carbine and a stick, and went to sleep. Both of us slept soundly while we did sleep, but were frequently wakened. Once the carbine fell down and hit the Captain on the nose. He gave a violent kick, which landed on me; but, luckily, it is his habit to sleep with his boots off. The kick did not disturb me, but the observations which the Captain made in refixing the carbine did. They were comprehensive and vigorous.

But we forgot our own sufferings in the sight of the misery of the men. By the number of the dark figures one could see outlined against the camp fires it seemed that few, if any, could be lying down at all. I believe the majority of the men sat up the whole night long. Then the wood gave out, and numbers of the poor fellows went off down to the river bank, a mile or so away, and built fires there where drift wood was abundant. Those who did not, gave way to exhausted nature, and toward morning stretched themselves beside the expiring embers of their fires, and slept from utter weariness. Still there is a comic element in such a misery. Long and weary as were the hours, they did not pass without an occasional laugh being heard, and more than once Capt. Hayes and I woke together and sat laughing at the utter wretchedness of our situation. At the first sign of day I was once more awakened, this time by someone whistling a tune. The Captain was sitting up and cheerfully whistling over our sea of troubles. The rain had ceased, but a heavy mass of clouds covered the sky, threatening more. "Get up, old fellow," said he, "don't you hear the little birds singing their praises." I got up and shook off the water, while the Captain inspected a small bundle carefully wrapped up in a corner of the canvas, and observed, with much satisfaction, that "the grub was all right." The three days' rations drawn the night before were stored in that bundle. While we sat there, uncertain what to do, another officer crawled out of a "wickyup" he had built, looking so utterly bedraggled, woebegone, and drenched, that to refrain from laughing was impossible. But it was no laughing matter to this unfortunate man. His night's experience put him on the sick list, and the only wonder was that dozens more were not put there. Altogether it was an awful sight, and, be it remembered, it was only the worst of many bad ones.[38]

After six days of idleness and Terry still waiting for additional supplies to arrive via steamer, Crook rationed his command for fifteen days with the usual hardtack, coffee, and bacon, and then backtracked up the Powder River on the morning of August 24, apparently without giving prior notice to Terry, his superior officer.[39] Soon he would turn east, hoping to catch up with at least some part of the Sioux. Terry followed along in the sodden earth the next morning, and after a march of seventeen miles was going into camp when "Buffalo Bill" Cody arrived with dispatches and news: two steamers, the *Josephine* and *Yellowstone*, were approaching the Powder River with additional supplies and troops on board (one of whom, Private Dennis Shields, Sixth Infantry, had been killed two days earlier when Indians fired on the latter boat), a supply base was to be constructed near the mouth of Tongue River to house troops during the winter,[40] and a large band of Indians had skirmished with soldiers at Glendive Creek. If that last item was true, Crook was headed away from the action. Taking Cody and a small cavalry escort, Terry rode ahead about eight miles to Crook's bivouac to discuss the situation. Davenport, O'Kelly, and Captain Burt each recorded the episode:

(Davenport:) [I]ntelligence was brought [to Terry] by Buffalo Bill that the Sioux, 300 in number, had appeared on the south bank of the Yellowstone, with the apparent intention of crossing, and had been engaged by one company of infantry under Lieutenant Rice.[41] They

had also fired into the steamer Josephine, which was bound for the mouth of the Powder River. On receipt of this news and a conference with General Crook, General Terry made a countermarch to the Yellowstone, and we saw his banners no more.[42]

(O'Kelly:) After consultation with General Crook it was decided that General Crook's force should move down the divide between the Yellowstone and Missouri rivers toward Glendive River, while the chief body of the troops of General Terry's column, under the command of Colonel Gibbon, should return to the Yellowstone, passing by way of O'Fallon's Creek—a stream midway between the Powder River and Glendive Creek—to clear the country of any Indians that might try to escape from General Crook's advance. General Terry's whole command will cross the Yellowstone at some point below the Powder River and try to head off the Indians, who are supposed to be going north.[43]

(Captain Burt:) On August 25 we [Crook's command] moved still further up Powder River. . . . In the afternoon, General Terry came to our camp with two of his staff, and we learned that Indians had made their appearance on the Yellowstone and had fired on the boats coming up. Here was a difficult question to decide. The Indians there— did it mean the whole village, or a party on a raid or a ruse de guerre [ruse of war] to cover a crossing of a few Indians going north with their families, stealing away from the main camp? General Crook, still being under General Terry's orders, could only suggest that the commands separate, one to keep the main trail and run it to a definite conclusion, and the other to go down the Yellowstone and engage any force of the enemy that might cross. This was accepted as the plan, and to us was given the difficult and arduous task of striking off eastward on the trail into a country with which, saving Frank Grouard, our guide, not one of the column was familiar.[44]

On August 27, at O'Fallon's Creek, the steamers *Carroll* and *Yellowstone* ferried Terry's troops to the north side of the Yellowstone River. Three days later, after some fruitless marching, O'Kelly wrote:

The expedition to the north bank of the Yellowstone in so far as the finding of hostile Indians is concerned has proved a failure. Trails have been found of small hunting parties, but apparently no large band of Indians have crossed the river, unless they have crossed at a point further east.[45]

On the same day, an unidentified correspondent recorded:

No Indians yet, and no prospect of finding any. . . . Notwithstanding the marvelous accounts of Sioux to be found by the thousand on this side of the river, we have not come across the track of even one, and consider it a foregone conclusion that further attempts to catch the wily savages will be useless for this year. Terry is considerably annoyed about some dispatches received from Sheridan concerning the new posts, on account of the peremptory tone and style that is used toward a Brigadier General. In one of them he is ordered to establish a winter camp at the mouth of Tongue River, where the regiments selected will halt until spring, when the work of building proper quarters at that place and the mouth of the Big Horn will be commenced at the earliest opportunity. . . . What our next move will be after reaching Glendive is unknown, and is really of

little importance, as it can result in nothing.[46]

Admitting that the campaign was all but over, O'Kelly's thoughts turned to the proposed Tongue River Cantonment, an important structure in a region where winter comes early and often hits hard:

It will be imperatively necessary for the troops who have been designated to remain in the cantonment during the winter to set to work preparing winter quarters, as the severity of the winter months renders living under canvas absolutely impossible. In this climate the mercury falls to 30 degrees below zero and a column caught in a severe winter storm would be almost certain to perish.[47]

On the morning of August 31, Terry received word about a "fresh trail" that had been discovered "of an Indian war party supposed to number 150 warriors." He ordered Reno to take the Seventh Cavalry, recently reorganized into eight companies, together with a few Indian scouts, and "make a circuit of forty miles to a point designated on the Yellowstone, with the object of determining whether any large body of Indians had crossed to the north bank of the Yellowstone." The next morning Terry learned the result of Reno's scout from a courier: there was no sign of Indians.[48]

Following this episode, another correspondent commented: "The whereabouts of any hostile band is a greater mystery today than at any previous time during the year, and in their endeavors to elude pursuit, they are exhibiting the marked superiority

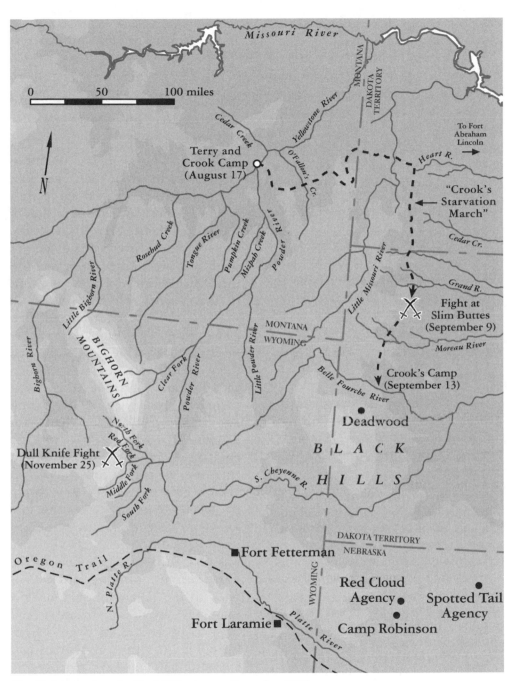

Crook's Advance into the Black Hills, August–September, 1876.

over our troops that has been shown throughout the campaign."[49]

Late on September 3, two Arikara Indians from Crook's command arrived in Terry's camp near Glendive Creek. Their news was dated only one day previous. O'Kelly reported:

Crook's command had reached the head waters of Beaver Creek, and was continuing its march in the direction of Sentinel Butte, near the Little Missouri. The heavy Indian trail which had been followed from the Powder River divided up near Beaver Creek, some of the minor trails going in the direction of the southern agencies, while the larger number led eastward. Although the trails indicate that the large band had broken up the bands may come together again before the [Little] Missouri is reached. General Crook is following up a fresh trail, which shows some 150 lodge poles.[50]

Two days later, September 5, the Irish-born journalist jotted down the finishing touches to the Dakota column's disappointing and lackluster summer:

General Terry this morning issued an order dissolving his operating column. Colonel Gibbon, with the Montana troops, leaves in the morning for Fort Ellis. Major Reno, with the Seventh Cavalry, and Major [Orlando] Moore's battalion of the Sixth Infantry will patrol the north bank of the Yellowstone, in order to prevent any band of hostile Sioux, that may be retreating before General Crook, crossing the river. Colonel Otis, with the Twenty-second Infantry, will remain at this point in charge of a subsidiary depot. General Terry and staff proceed to Buford by steamboat. The General will give his whole attention to the forwarding of

supplies to the new post on Tongue River. The campaign may be regarded as virtually at an end, so far as General Terry's column is concerned. Everybody in camp is delighted, as it has been evident for a long time that we were not likely to accomplish much good by remaining in the field.[51]

On the following day, an unknown correspondent from the *New York Times* likewise wrapped up events: Colonel Miles and ten companies of the Fifth Infantry were then on the way to Tongue River where "vigorous work will be required from them to build shelter before the severe storms of this region will have closed in upon them." He also stated that Miles was going to employ a number of experienced white scouts through the winter, keeping them "always on the go" and "further stimulating them by a reward of $500 if they find an Indian village." Lieutenant Colonel Otis was stationed with six companies of the Twenty-second Infantry at the supply depot at Glendive Creek.[52] They were living in "shelter-tents" and "cutting logs for huts." With the water level dropping at this time of year, Glendive was now the end of the line for the heavy steamers carrying tons of supplies up the Yellowstone. From now until next spring, all freight would have to be hauled in wagons from Glendive to the Tongue River Cantonment, about seventy-five miles west as the eagle flies.[53]

On the morning of September 8, aboard the steamer *Josephine*, Terry arrived at Fort Buford, at the confluence of the Missouri and Yellowstone

rivers. It was expected that by the fifteenth, all of his troops "will have
been withdrawn from the northern
country except the Twenty-second
Infantry [at the Glendive depot] and
the Fifth Infantry [at the Tongue
River Cantonment], containing 400
men."[54] Gibbon's men, "in the field
since March" and "poorly clad for
cold weather and fierce storms," must
have been particularly thrilled to be
going home.[55]

No doubt the Seventh Cavalry was
also relieved to be heading home.
However, as luck would have it, the
men still had one more mission to
run. Terry, hoping that Crook's presence south of the Yellowstone would
flush some of the Sioux to the north,
had ordered the Seventh Cavalry
under Reno, and a battalion of the
Sixth Infantry under Moore, to scout
the north bank of the Yellowstone on
their march back to Fort Buford
(from which point the Seventh
would return to Fort Lincoln). On
the morning of September 10, Reno
received a dispatch from Terry
informing him that a large number of
Indians were crossing at Wolf Point
on the Missouri, about eighty-five
miles west of Fort Buford. If Reno
hurried north, there might be time
for one last shot at the Sioux. A dispatch from an anonymous officer of
the Sixth Infantry, under date of
September 12, stated: "The Seventh
Cavalry and five companies of the
Sixth Infantry are en route to intercept the Indians and it is possible the
troops may engage them before their
crossing is completed or before they
have moved so far north as to make
pursuit useless."[56]

O'Kelly, who chose to stay with
Reno when Terry left for Fort
Buford, brings the Wolf Point detour
to its conclusion in his dispatch of
September 20:

Our sudden expedition to Wolf's Point
was caused by a report that Long Dog,
with some 150 followers, had crossed the
Missouri and that the river bank for a
mile was covered with Indians. [We]
reached Wolf's Point . . . on the afternoon of the 13th without encountering
any signs that would indicate the presence of an Indian force. On examination
it turned out that Long Dog and his followers had crossed the river and endeavored to procure ammunition from the
agent, Major Mitchell,[57] who held a long
conference with the chief, trying to per-
suade him to surrender. This he declined
to do, stating that Sitting Bull was on his
way to Fort Peck, and would compel the
agent to issue ammunition to his warriors. Long Dog's party stated that at one
time they were surrounded by the soldiers, and had to abandon their tepees
and other property in order to escape.
They were under the impression that the
soldiers were in pursuit of them,
although our column had no suspicion
of their presence. On finding they could
obtain no ammunition at the agency
they continued their march and are supposed to have gone into the Canadian
dominions [sixty miles to the north].
Pursuit was impossible, as the Missouri
at Wolf Point is not fordable.[58]

Terry showed up two days later, the
fifteenth, on the steamer *John M.
Chambers*, and "learning the exact
state of affairs, answered officially
that the campaign was at an end.
Next morning the return march [to
Fort Buford] began."[59]

Although the Sioux campaign had not yet produced the results expected, so far as defeating the Indians in battle and clearing the contested territory of all the "hostiles" was concerned, still, the multipronged military assault did have its value, especially upon the morale of the Indians. Unable to sustain itself en masse for any length of time, the Indian alliance was now scattered into smaller groups that could not hope to successfully fight the troops. Further, and more importantly, the military now had a foothold in their backyard, keeping them anxious and making it hard for them to rest or hunt. In Long Dog's case, it was easier to just get out of the country. Plus, he would be able to trade more freely in Canada.[60] The following statement by a Sioux Indian named Medicine Cloud, who returned to Fort Peck about the first of August, clearly reflected the situation that existed one month later: "The Sioux are living on meat, which they find it very difficult to procure, owing to the close proximity of the whites. . . . The Indians are in a constant state of alarm. There is no sleep in camp."[61]

For Terry's Dakota Column, the war was over, and Crook's Wyoming Column was on its last legs. Still on the trail of the Sioux, they were soon to learn the meaning of that old mountain man expression, "meat's meat."

We close this chapter with the words of an unknown officer who declared his disappointment that the soldiers did not get to even the score with Sitting Bull:

No one seems to know where Sitting Bull is. Some of the officers are inclined to think that he has disbanded his forces, and others are of the opinion that he is somewhere in the British Possessions with the best fighters of his army. The troops feel very much disappointed in not having met the slippery Indian on this last tramp, so that they could have had an opportunity to avenge Custer.[62]

II

The Relentless Pursuit

"Not an Indian has been killed since the Custer disaster, and nearly a fifth of the United States Army has been out here trying to kill some. . . . It is not our fault that no Indians have been killed. They have the [head] start and keep ahead of us in the race. We are stripped down to less baggage than the enemy carry, but it is hard catching an Indian in his own country when he does not want to be caught."—Cuthbert Mills, In Camp on Beaver Creek, Montana Territory, August 30, 1876, *New York Times*, September 14, 1876

"The country is too extensive and valuable to be given over longer to such a worthless set of vagabonds as the Sioux."—Joe Wasson, Camp on the Little Missouri, Dakota Territory, September 4, 1876, *New York Tribune*, September 15, 1876

"You cannot make war without hardship; put the command on half rations."—General Crook (as quoted by Cuthbert Mills), September 5, 1876, *New York Times*, September 28, 1876

After parting ways with General Terry, Crook made his way east toward the Little Missouri River, reaching that point on September 4, the same day that a "long, dark storm began."[1] It was to last for ten days. Scouting parties had been going out daily, but there was generally nothing to report other than scattered or insignificant trails. Referring to the daily marches, correspondent Cuthbert Mills stated simply, "[W]e are, so to speak, feeling out for the enemy, and looking for a trail."[2] On the morning of August 30, in the vicinity of Beaver Creek, scouts had brought word to Crook of a trail of thirteen lodges about two or three days old. But that was small game. Mills succinctly summed up the disappointment: "Trails of thirteen lodges only we are not looking for."[3]

Later that same day, scouts Frank Grouard, "Captain Jack" Crawford, and Louis Richard reported to Crook the result of another reconnaissance. Davenport wrote:

[The three scouts had] proceeded about thirty miles from camp, and reported on their return many scattering trails in the neighborhood of Beaver Creek. The large trail which we had followed from the Rosebud to the Powder River was undoubtedly dissipated.[4]

Not only had their quarry scattered and all but disappeared, but the scorched-earth policy of the Sioux was making Crook's pursuit rather difficult. Mills observed:

It is significant that as the command has moved east, it has everywhere found the country burned off. Had not the heavy rains quenched the fires, there would hardly be a blade of grass left. . . . It is perfectly clear the vast extent of country which we find burned over, has been burned for one of two purposes, or possibly both—first, to drive the buffalo eastward, and next, to prevent us following the trail from want of feed for the horses.[5]

Wasson added:

The Indians had burned the grass east of Powder River for fifty miles, and as wide as the eye could see. Doubtless they thought no troops would follow them.[6]

But Crook clung tenaciously to whatever hopes remained of finding the Sioux and stayed the course. This was in accord with what Captain Burt had stated back on August 23:

There is one man in the command who still has hope, who still thinks there is a chance to catch some, if not all, [of] the hostile Sioux. General Crook still believes we may have work to do before going into winter quarters, before we reach any agency; before, in fact, this campaign is over for us.[7]

With Grouard's discovery of a "principal" trail on Beaver Creek on September 2, it appeared that Crook's doggedness may well be paying off. Davenport noted, "General Crook determined to follow it as far as practicable, although then satisfied that the Sioux were no longer united to offer him battle."[8] But as they continued their march north along Beaver Creek, Davenport declared that even this trail had dispersed:

The trail was found to dwindle as we advanced, until it appeared that we were on the heels of but twelve lodges. We therefore abandoned it, and on September 3 moved about twenty miles eastward toward the Little Missouri River.[9] It was supposed, from the opinions given by the scouts, that the scattered bands might reunite there and fight.[10]

That same day, Crook sent two Arikara (Ree) couriers to Terry on Glendive Creek, informing him of the Wyoming Column's whereabouts and the scattered trails south of the Yellowstone. O'Kelly, with Terry's column, reported:

General Crook is following up a fresh trail, which shows some 150 lodge poles. This trail is thought to be no more than two days old. General Crook will continue the pursuit along this trail, and hopes to be able to overtake the Indians. His rations are nearly exhausted.[11]

On the night of September 3, some of Crook's scouts were involved in a minor scuffle with a small party of Sioux. Davenport supplied the most graphic of the accounts:

Eleven of the scouts, who had gone about nine miles ahead of the troops and halted to cook their supper, were surprised by eight Indians appearing on a hill and shouting to them in Dakota, "Are you Sioux?" Louis Richards was about to answer "Yes," when they said, "Speak or we will shoot!" Thereupon the other scouts discharged their rifles and were answered by the Indians. They fired again and the latter fled. In the morning when the column approached the spot the scouts discovered a wounded pony, which had been shot in the evening.[12]

The following day, September 4, the command marched about eighteen miles, trekking from a point along Andrews Creek to the east side of the Little Missouri, "over a very rough divide" and "through a deep and picturesque canyon walled with slate, clay, lignite and sandstone." Davenport wrote that the path was "covered with fresh trails of Indian ponies, and in the mud were the tiny prints of the feet of papooses."[13]

But the day's true significance centered on George Crook. The general was at a crossroads, having to face a situation that had been in the making ever since he left Terry at the Powder River Depot on August 24. The problem? He didn't have sufficient provisions for an extended march, exactly the type of peregrination he was then engaged in. With sunrise, the command would be down to three days' rations.[14] On top of that, the troops lacked proper clothing and bedding. "Not a man of the command is prepared for bad weather, so that should cold overtake us the suffering will be intense," wrote one cor-

Rabbit Hunting with Crook's Command

New York Times, September 14, 1876

In Camp at Beaver Creek, August 30, 1876.

Game of all kinds seems to be scarce, as if it had been driven away, for this is in other years a splendid game country. The enemy has, however, left us some, to wit, jack rabbits. An officer, speaking of what men will do, said that, after the longest kind of a march, if a rabbit starts up in camp the whole outfit will jump up and give chase in a moment. It happened this way in our last camp. A stretch of bottomland was found to be swarming with jack rabbits. When the men began to move about in the sage brush they started them out in all directions. A rabbit meant a full dinner of fresh meat—no light thing to men living as we do—and earnest indeed was the chase that followed a find. Shooting is strictly forbidden, but with anything that a blow could be given with the men rushed around, tumbling over each other and over the brush, wildly screaming and yelling at each frantic rabbit, who was the centre of a hurricane of stones, clubs, bridles, picket pins, lariats, canteens, hats, and miscellaneous articles generally. More rabbits got away than were caught, but of those that were [caught] there was nothing but their skins left when dinner was over. Sage hens are not scarce, but they can only be had by shooting, and they aggravatingly fly about our camps as if they knew all about the orders [not to shoot] which makes the place safe.

—Cuthbert Mills

respondent.[15] Crook had three options. He could: (1) continue south to the Black Hills settlements (which meant entering the Great Sioux Reservation), a trip estimated at seven days and 180 miles "according to the best authenticated map of the country,"[16] where he could purchase supplies and hope to close in on the Indians; (2) retire with his command to Fort Lincoln, perhaps a four-day/one-hundred-mile trip to the east,[17] for some much-needed R&R (rest and rations); or (3) send only his pack train to Fort Lincoln for supplies and wait for its return, at which time he could consider his next move. But the decision had to be made now.

Wasson, who described the general at this time as being "at sea in an open boat," "silent and determined," and "desperately resolved on 'doing something' with the means at hand,"[18] explained Crook's choice over the course of several dispatches (all written on September 5!):

New York Tribune, September 9, 1876: Including today there are only three days' rations for the command, and the General decided to make them reach six and take the chances, with what game could be killed, of reaching the Black Hills settlement[s]—certainly a distance of 150 miles. A courier goes to [Fort] Lincoln tonight[19] with an order via [Fort] Fetterman for the wagon train at old Fort Reno to move down toward Custer City to meet this column.[20] It is hoped that on the march from here some of the hostiles will be overtaken.

New York Tribune, September 15, 1876: All the Indian signs lead to the conclu-

sion that they have scattered in the direction of the Hills, and may be hovering about and harassing the people there, so that the situation justifies Gen. Crook in taking this step. To go to Lincoln and march back again, either taking the pack train or sending it thither and awaiting its return, will involve more hardships than will be encountered in marching to the Hills. Meantime word will be sent to Fetterman for the wagon train to move as rapidly as possible from old Reno by the nearest route toward Custer City.

Daily Alta California, September 17, 1876: The three days' full rations were to be stretched to six, and the Black Hills settlements our first resort for more. Everyone realizes that this is better than waiting and starving while the pack train goes to Fort Lincoln, on the Missouri River. . . . The bulk of the [Indian] sign goes toward the Hills, and it is not unlikely they will need looking after there-aways.

Davenport, writing from Deadwood on September 16, offered another view of Crook's verdict:

According to the best authenticated map of the country the distance from the camp on the Little Missouri to the Black Hills was 180 miles, to traverse which would consume at least seven days. . . . Nothing was apparently to be gained by moving on the Black Hills, except to the pride of the commander of the Department of the Platte, who would thus avoid being again under the tutelage of his senior brigadier [Terry] and would be nearer his own posts.[21]

When Finerty broached the subject with Crook at the end of the campaign, the general defended his decision:

To have taken the troops to Fort Lincoln to rest and recuperate would have been a very unfortunate move, in my judgment. The trail of a large body of Indians led toward the Black Hills, and there was none leading toward Fort Lincoln. It was impossible to tell what depredations these Indians might be committing on the miners and settlers, and I considered it my duty to march in that direction, notwithstanding the shortness of supplies. . . . Fort Lincoln is out of my own department and hundreds of miles from the points threatened by Indians. To have gone there would have been to abandon to the Indians the Black Hills settlements, the roads leading to them, and the frontier farther south.[22]

Closing out his September 4 dispatch to the *Daily Alta California*, Wasson voiced his displeasure with Terry's unhurried method of campaigning and declared that the burden of the campaign had fallen on Crook's Wyoming Column:

Crook is doing now what he would have done two weeks ago but for the junction with Terry and the delays. He would have followed up, rations or no rations, until the Indian "sign" determined a new plan of operations. . . . At all events, the Department of the Platte seems destined to do all the hard work for that of Dakota.[23]

For better or worse, on the morning of September 5, the command began its march toward the Black Hills on half-rations. Not exactly brimming with confidence, Davenport wrote, "We are marching on Deadwood City . . . and shall barely escape starvation before reaching there."[24] To be fair, Davenport was not the only one having doubts.

On the same day, scout Jack Crawford had written, "Starvation stares us in the face."[25] While hunger was a very serious issue, correspondent Mills pointed out another calamity for the troops:

To make the matter worse, the men had been unable to obtain any supplies of tobacco at the Yellowstone, and had now completely exhausted all the little stores they had husbanded. No one who knows what a life in the field is, and what a soldier's duties are there, but will understand how severe was this deprivation. It caused more actual suffering for the time being than even the shortness of food.[26]

The trail that day was "long and muddy,"[27] between twenty-six to thirty miles, to the headwaters of Heart River. According to Mills and Wasson, the command had now marched some four hundred miles since leaving Goose Creek on August 5.[28] But the big news was that for the second time in three days, the scouts encountered the Sioux. Wasson reported:

About 11 o'clock a party of twenty or thirty Sioux were discovered to the right by some of the scouts. There were about ten warriors; the rest were women and children. They had better ponies than the scouts, and were soon out of range, although it is reported that "Little Bat," one of the scouts, shot one of the warriors. The direction of the savages goes to confirm the general impression of their scattering toward the Black Hills.[29]

In another dispatch, Wasson added, "The campaign is again getting more interesting [in] every way, and I hope it will prove more decisive."[30] Mills added that the incident was "at least a small grain of consolation to see at last something of the enemy we had been so long in vain chase of."[31]

That night in camp, Davenport composed a letter to the *New York Herald* that made it into print just five days later. Readers back east could not have been too enthusiastic about a positive outcome after reading his report:

It is impracticable to further hunt the enemy with the troops now in the field, who are worn and weakened by exposure, starvation and hardship. They have been thirty-two days with no other shelter than one blanket for each man, in repeated cold storms of wind, rain and hail. Scurvy, fever and dysentery have prostrated about 300 soldiers, who have from time to time been carried on litters. Insufficiency of medical supplies is a still more alarming fact. Milder weather has been the Godsend which has prevented terrible mortality. In ten days later the average temperature of this climate will have become low, and the troops have yet to make a march of 300 miles southward, in summer clothing, with no tents. They have now only food for two [more] days.[32]

But Davenport also pointed out that the Indians were, in all likelihood, not faring any better than the troops:

Many fresh traces of hunting parties of the Sioux are found each day. Their condition is probably more destitute than that of the troops. Were General Crook now equipped to pursue them rapidly they must be forced to surrender. They must hunt or they starve, and hunting implies slow flight.[33]

Davenport was correct. Crook's only hope of contact lay in the "slow flight" of the Sioux.

12

The Starvation March

"Water and wood were neither plentiful nor convenient, and owing to cold rainstorms which prevailed constantly, camp life on half rations, and with no tents and little bedding, was extremely severe upon the men."
—Joe Wasson, Crook's Camp Near Slim Buttes, Dakota Territory, September 10, 1876, *New York Tribune*, September 18, 1876

"Consider the wretchedness of the men—so starving that they were eager to eat horse meat."—Cuthbert Mills, On the Belle Fourche, Dakota Territory, September 13, 1876, *New York Times*, September 28, 1876

"It was a race against the lean, lank legs of starvation, with the odds against us."—Reuben B. Davenport, Deadwood City, Black Hills, September 16, 1876, *New York Herald*, October 2, 1876

"I do not enjoy hardship, horse meat, and starvation more than other men, but when it is necessary to submit to these things, with the prospect of rendering adequate service to the country before me, I am ready to stand my chances."—George Crook, Red Cloud Agency, October 26, 1876, *Chicago Times*, November 4, 1876

On the sixth of September, Crook's order against hunting had been revoked and the day was marked by the "constant cracking of guns on the flanks" of the column.[1] According to Davenport, the men were firing away freely, hoping to obtain antelope steak for dinner. Perhaps sarcastically, he noted, "A horse was thus wounded. But little game was killed, however."[2] After a march of thirty-five miles, camp was made "in mist and rain around an isolated lake, on the summit of a wide rolling plain."[3]

Describing their unsatisfactory conditions, Davenport noted:

The water was salty and as thick as milk. There was no wood visible, not even a shrub. Some of us cooked a little coffee by building a fire of grass; but most had only raw bacon and brittle crackers for supper. To add to the forlornness of the situation, the commissary issued no bacon or sugar and only a meagre allowance of crackers and coffee. For days we had been unable to dry our clothing and we rolled ourselves up in reeking blankets and tried to sleep. The night winds grew chillier and chillier until morning, when we awoke with numbed and quaking limbs and a nervous sensation as if we had been set upon by a nightmare for ages.[4]

The few antelope killed were barely enough to stave off hunger, and the men of Crook's command were ravenous for something to eat. When some of the depleted horses were abandoned on the trail on the following day, the famished "soldiers broke from their ranks to kill them, in order to secure the meat."[5] Mills and Davenport described the scene:

(Mills:) Some horses dropped by the road utterly worn out. A man cut a piece from one after it was shot, and hung it behind him on his saddle for supper. His example was instantly followed by such a crowd of men that nothing was left of the carcass but the bones. Another horse a short way on suffered the same fate.[6]

(Davenport:) Some of the cavalry when they abandoned their horses shot them and took slices of the meat for their suppers, and men in passing the carcass afterward would fall out of the ranks and silently help themselves until nothing remained of it but the bones.[7]

Davenport would later recall another incident on this day:

In the advance the scouts chased about twenty Indians who appeared to be moving parallel to a tepee trail, over which it is supposed their families had just passed. It seemed a vexatious perversity of fate that we should come so close

upon the enemy, while, having exhausted our supplies, we were unable with prudence to engage them.[8]

It quickly became apparent to Crook that traveling en masse to the Black Hills was going to be too slow a process. A better plan would be to send a party ahead on the best horses to the nearest settlement to purchase supplies. In the meantime, the main column would continue limping south. Accordingly, on the night of September 7, on the north fork of the Grand River, at the northern edge of the Great Sioux Reservation, Captain Anson Mills, Third Cavalry, "was ordered to select 150 of the best mounted men of his regiment and start immediately to make a forced ride into the Black Hills, in order to send back relief as soon as possible."[9] Accompanying Mills were Lieutenants Emmet Crawford and Adolphus Von Luettwitz, battalion commanders; Lieutenant Frederick Schwatka, adjutant; Lieutenant John W. Bubb, Fourth Infantry, chief commissary officer; Thomas Moore, chief packer; Frank Grouard and Jack Crawford, guides; and correspondents Davenport and Strahorn. The pack train consisted of fifteen packers and sixty-one mules.[10]

Considering the miserable weather conditions of the past few weeks, it was only fitting that the relief party set out in a "thick mist," which made it difficult to see where they were going.[11] Davenport tagged along hoping to exchange "the privations of the field" for whatever civilization the Black Hills had to offer[12] and graphically described the first night's ride:

The storm had augmented in force since sunset, and the men were mustered in the most intense darkness. There was no danger, however, that any would shirk the duty, as there was an eagerness in the ranks to see a little of civilization again. . . . The mules brayed and the bell-mare shook her chimes, and there was much bustle and confusion until we started. At eight o'clock Frank Gruard rode out a hundred feet ahead and his figure was just dimly recognizable. The little column was in motion, the pack train carefully guarded to prevent the defection of any of the mules. It was impossible to know which was our proper direction, except by observations of the landscape, which had been made before dark. The mist circumscribed us so that our world seemed very small and beyond it dwelt the terror of the unknown. For two hours we moved in silence, the guide occasionally stopping to look at the compass by the flicker of a match. Suddenly there appeared a rent in the black heavens and the moon and stars looked through. By and by the North Star and the Dipper came forth. We verified our course. As suddenly the curtain was again drawn and the rain fell with fury. The air was more impenetrably black than ever. We rode on in rueful stillness until one o'clock and then halted for a sleep.[13]

By the morning of the eighth there was one thing that the soldiers wanted to find more than the Sioux, and that was food. Instead, some five weeks after setting out from Goose Creek, Captain Mills's small command finally found the Sioux. In the first of his two reports on the fight at Slim Buttes and the events leading up to it, Davenport simply wrote:

About thirty miles from the main column Gruard discovered indications of the proximity of an Indian village as we were approaching Slim Buttes, and we halted on the table land, concealed behind a knoll. The Indians were watched while they were herding their ponies, of which there were great numbers; but it was doubtful how many braves were in the party.[14]

His dispatch from Deadwood, written six days later, offered much more detail:

At daybreak [of September 8], groping through the damp obscurity, we saddled our horses and moved forward. When the light was broad enough to distinguish each other we were astonished at our muddy and haggard appearance. It still rained unrelentingly, and about eight o'clock a.m. we halted again in a small ravine where there was wood and a spring of water, in order to make a pretence of breakfasting. The kindling of a fire consumed an hour, and in another hour, having quaffed some black coffee and eaten a wee bit of venison, I was again mounted like my companions. The day continued gray and miserable. We passed grim and mysterious buttes whose names were unknown to us and whose outlines were but dimly defined in the universal mist. Our horses sank at every step deep into the slippery, slimy mud . . . and were perceptibly weakening with their constant toil. In the afternoon appeared in front the white forms of the Slim Buttes. We crossed the north branch of the Grand River and entered the foothills of this group of mountains. We had already, in the morning, crossed the trail of a small Sioux hunting party near their camp. Several hours later we found a place where they had again halted, and their trail lay directly in our course.

The mist seemed to close around us more grimly and to cling more coldly but closely to our beards and garments. We were quaking in our saddles about four o'clock, when, observing the conduct of Gruard who was ahead, we halted. He had dismounted just below the crest of a ridge and was kneeling just so that his eyes were on a level with the highest blades of grass. With his field glasses he was watching something beyond. It was a herd of ponies two miles below in the valley. Frank had been riding in advance, when he suddenly espied a white group of lodges behind a ridge, and he had turned and galloped back to concealment as quickly as possible. He had not been seen by anyone in the village. Presently a mounted Indian was seen by those who were peeping over the ridge, riding leisurely toward the herd, and then galloping off to a round bluff which overlooked our position. Our little party was speedily moved into a deeper hollow, and the savage, when he reached the point of observation, looked around with apparent satisfaction and then descended. Captain Mills, Lieutenant Crawford and Lieutenant Schwatka, in consultation with the guide, endeavored in vain by keeping a lookout over the ridge to ascertain the strength of the village. The herd of ponies numbered about 500. Frank believed that they belonged to a small but wealthy band of the Brule tribe, of which Roman Nose was the chief. . . . Shivering in a shallow hollow, near the summit of a table land, flanked by frowning buttes, the mist still falling and wrapping its clammy folds around us, we stood patiently, or impatiently, for two of the dreariest hours I ever passed. The wind was growing colder and our bodies shook with a horrible ague that seemed also to benumb our hearts. We wiped out the barrels of our guns and brightened our cartridges as best we could with shivering fingers. There seemed to be a common indifference as to whether we advanced or retreated; we were all sick with the suspense and the bitter discomfort of our condition. A dull apprehension of disaster reigned, but none knew what to do to dispel the dread.

It was determined at length to return on our trail about two miles and bivouac in a narrow pocket at the junction of two gorges. Here the animals were hidden so that they could only be observed from the edge of the depression. Fires were built of dead box elder wood, but did not much allay the misery produced by the rain, mist and cold. Supper for the soldiers consisted of a few fragments of hard bread and a few small scraps of bacon. The packers fared better, making an unctuous soup of flour and grease, which warmed while it nourished them. I accepted a little of their hospitality with an eagerness I never before could have conceived of. It was born of hunger and proved once more the philosophical truth that everything within our human knowledge is comparative. Our beds were the softest and most adhesive kind of mud and our covering wet blankets and greasy sheets of canvas, which had been used for months in protecting the cargoes of the mules from the weather. The fires burned sullenly in the canyon, and the glare which was created by the flames produced in the mist grotesque and unreal effects, which I observed and studied before I went to sleep. Hardly, however, were the wild and dreadful phantasies around me replaced by softer dreams, which came at the beck of Morpheus, than they were gone in an instant and I was aware of fierce tramping and snorting over my head. Some mules, bewildered, blinded and demented by the fantastic glare of the fires, had suddenly made a terrible rush, checked only by their lariats, and had nearly crushed me and my bedfellow beneath their hoofs. Once more during the night the same wild sound shook the ground, and my charger, "Nigger," broke loose and vanished in the black night. I searched for him in a rather desperate mood, and was delighted at last to find him standing passively near the camp. He rubbed his nose against me familiarly when I touched him, as if to declare that he knew it would be very ill-conduct to desert me in such an emergency as then beset me. One other alarm startled us—a shot fired by a picket at a shadow which he mistook for a Sioux. At one o'clock a.m. the camp was aroused by the guards and preparations made for the advance.[15]

It was then the early morning hours of September 9, and Mills's small command was about to strike out for the Wyoming Column's third substantial encounter with the Sioux since March. Barring any unforeseen complications, the plan was fairly straightforward. Lieutenant Schwatka was to charge through the village at the head of twenty-five mounted men, pistols blazing, and drive off the horses. The remainder of the troops, acting as infantry and divided into two battalions of fifty men each, under Lieutenants Crawford (right flank) and Von Luettwitz (left flank), were to form in skirmish line on either side of the village in order to catch the sleeping Indians in a deadly crossfire. As Wasson expressed it, "The object was to surround the enemy, stampede and capture their stock, and kill as many of the warriors as possible."[16]

Davenport continues as our trail guide, but now we switch to his dispatch written just one day after the fight:

At two o'clock all was in readiness, and the detachment formed ranks. In profound darkness, fog and rain it advanced slowly to the position of the previous evening, and there halting, the guide went forward to find the way to the village. After waiting half an hour he emerged out of the obscurity again, and we again moved. After a second halt the mules and horses, with about thirty men,[17] of whom I was one, remained behind [under charge of Lieutenant Bubb], while the main body advanced. At the first sound of firing we were to advance rapidly, but cautiously, and if the enemy proved too strong we were to secure and hold some favorable point until relieved. There was in these arrangements an anticipation of another disaster like that which befell Custer and his gallant Seventh. The waiting in the chill, wet darkness, straining the ear in vain for the sound of the fray, was full of dread, anxious suspense.

The dawn had not begun when a white soldier, patrolling a hill, espied a horseman coming at full gallop toward us. It at first appeared to be an Indian, but proved to be "Captain" Jack, the scout, who said the fight had begun, and we were to advance as rapidly as possible. We dashed forward through the mist and reached a round top of bluffs, from whence we saw flashes of guns a mile below, while now and again dull detonations reached us against the breeze. Here we met Gruard and a private, who brought an order from Captain Mills to despatch a courier to General Crook immediately, asking for reinforcements.[18] Two men volunteered for this service and galloped off to execute the order. We then advanced into the valley under fire.[19]

As Davenport and the rest of the command were soon to learn, the attack upon the village, which was "distributed along the edge of a little stream [Gap Creek] running from west to east,"[20] had been "accidentally precipitated."[21]

The success of the attack depended on the completeness of the surprise given the enemy. It was hoped by Captain Mills to place his troops in the best positions that could be selected before a single gun was discharged. He moved forward very cautiously, unable to see more than 100 yards ahead, and did not distinguish the village until he was close upon it. The first objects that were seen were the ponies who had snuffed our approach and were excited. The whole herd gave a bound and dashed straight through the village, only a few lodges of which were visible, the rest being hidden behind a ridge. No time was now to be lost. Frank Gruard called out "Charge!" and Schwatka plunged into the village with his twenty-five men.[22]

The setback was that Von Luettwitz was unable to get into position in time "and the effect of a cross fire, therefore, was not gained."[23] Still, from their position both north and northwest of the village, Crawford and Von Luettwitz "riddled the tepees [with gunfire] before the occupants were fairly awakened."[24] The Sioux, cutting their way out of the lodges,[25] turned the troops' failed plan into their avenue of escape, and "were seen scrambling up the steep banks and into the gullies, with yells of dismay."[26] Schwatka, who led the

initial charge, reflected, "Many were seen to fall, and in the approaching daylight, it was often hard to tell whether the burdens carried were children or the slain and wounded." Then he added, "The village was deserted sooner than it takes to relate the fact, and Captain Mills' command then held a large hill west of this place and overlooking it."[27] Wasson, who arrived on the scene later that morning, recorded, "Though the great majority of the Indians had scattered to the bluffs . . . a small party of them had taken possession of a little narrow ravine within 100 yards of the village."[28] This group of Indians was soon to become the center of attention.

Despite the fact that the Sioux "were completely surprised, and scattered out 'pell mell,' half naked," they quickly gained favorable positions on the bluffs south of the creek, where they "secreted themselves"[29] and began to fight back. It was at this time or shortly before that Von Luettwitz became one of the first soldier casualties, knocked out of the fight with a bullet to the right knee. Scout Crawford applied a tourniquet, and Sergeant John A. Kirkwood carried the wounded lieutenant from the skirmish line.[30]

Although Schwatka managed to capture a good part of the pony herd,[31] the Sioux were still able to retrieve their fair share of mounts, and some of them were seen riding off toward the west. Davenport wrote, "It was surmised they were going to raise the neighboring bands to their assistance, and preparations were strenuously made for a desperate defense of the position commanding the village until General Crook, with the column, should arrive."[32] Other warriors "mounted on such ponies as they had been able to catch made several daring dashes to recover those captured, and all around the ridge, held by our men, the quick flashing of guns was, in the morning twilight, like a festive pyrotechnic display."[33]

According to Davenport, it was about this time that Captain Mills displayed strong signs of uneasiness and wanted to withdraw from the village. Stirring the pot of discord once again, the *Herald* reporter declared:

Through the weakness of an officer [Mills] a terrible reverse was at one moment imminent, but the firmness of a subordinate and the spirit of his troops saved him. . . . [Mills] had apprehensions that the Sioux would develop greater strength and attack him. He seemed overpowered by this fear at the inception of the fight, and when the Indians first sent their bullets into our ranks [at which time Von Luettwitz was shot in the knee], he exclaimed, "Retreat, men! Retreat!" They were in no mood for retreat, however, and Lieutenant Crawford seconded their impulse by drawing his pistol and shouting, "I will shoot any man who tries to retreat!" This noble insubordination prevented a disaster.[34]

Because of Indian gunfire, the soldiers were having a hard time occupying the village. Davenport publicly praised two of the officers for their heroic bravery in helping to repel the Sioux at this time:

Sergeant John A. Kirkwood

New York Times, May 13, 1930

Hero Of Campaign Against The Sioux Dies At Age Of 79.

Pittsburgh, May 12—Sergeant John A. Kirkwood, United States Army, retired, a former Pittsburgh citizen, to whom was awarded the Congressional Medal of Honor for gallantry during a skirmish with Sioux Indians in Dakota Territory on September 9, 1876, died yesterday at the age of 79 years in the National Soldiers Home in Washington, according to word received here today. He was sergeant of Company M, Third United States Cavalry, and the last survivor of the Allegheny County veterans who held the Congressional Medal of Honor.

The act of gallantry was performed at Slim Buttes. The 150 cavalrymen, dismounted, had been ordered to reform on higher ground. Lieutenant Von Luettwitz had been shot in the kneecap and lay in front of the Indian camp. Sergeant Kirkwood was in the rear guard of the retreating line and heard the lieutenant's cry. Running to the wounded officer, he carried him up the ridge and out of danger.

Lieutenants Crawford and Schwatka made repeated charges which drove the Sioux from those points from which their fire was annoying. They both made rapid explorations of the hills to gather up stray ponies so that they should not be secured by the Indians. In these they had many pistol encounters with the Indians and forced them to retire repeatedly. The gallantry displayed by both of these officers was splendid.[35]

"Most of the fighting had ceased when the sun was up," Davenport wrote, bringing attention to the fact that the fighting thus far had been in the predawn hours with little light. "At four a.m.," he continued, "a second courier was sent back, mounted on a strong Indian pony, to hasten General Crook." Mills was anxious that more Indians were on the way and that his small force would be overpowered. Davenport had volunteered to be the courier, but a soldier was selected instead.[36]

Throughout the morning, the Indians were continually losing real estate around the battlefield. At one point they held a position "behind a crest, from which there came an occasional shot."[37] Captain Mills wanted them silenced.

Lieutenant Crawford was sent with nine cavalrymen to charge them . . . and while he was making a circuit through a hollow to escape observation they [the Indians] opened conversation with our interpreter [Grouard] by shouting overtures to a truce.[38]

One of them announced himself as Stabber, a head warrior, well known at the agencies. He said: "I am tired of fighting. I have had enough of it this summer. I want to go back to the agencies."[39]

He was still calling out when Crawford's "little band reached the crest with a yell, which was answered by cries of dismay from the Indians. A few hasty pistol shots, by which one of them was wounded or killed, and they fled into the ravines and out of sight. The village was now excellently commanded by our troops, but still an occasional bullet came from the ravine on the west side of the village."[40]

And one of those bullets shortly struck Private John Wenzel in the head, killing him instantly, when he ventured too close to the edge of the gulch. He was the first trooper killed. Two other men were wounded about this time, Sergeant Kirkwood (a slight flesh wound to the side) and Sergeant Edward Glass (severely wounded in the right arm). Just how many Indians were in the ravine was still a mystery, but as Schwatka noted, "[They] not only held us at bay, but made it unsafe to approach the northern end or head of the village."[41] For the time being there would be no further attempt to dislodge its inhabitants. That could wait for Crook's arrival.[42] In the meantime, Mills stationed sharpshooters to cover the area.[43]

Individual soldiers had been searching the village haphazardly all morning, "tumbling over the contents of the lodges," which numbered about thirty-five, in their search for food.[44] By late morning they had found that and a lot more, specifically items that once belonged to Custer's Seventh Cavalry. Davenport, in his September 10 and 16 dispatches, detailed many of the findings, including Custer's regimental guidon, cavalry saddles, the overcoat of a slaughtered Seventh Cavalry officer, ammunition, several thousand pounds of meat and fruits, thousands of "splendid robes," deer and elk skins, trinkets, feathered war bonnets, moccasins, pieces of flour sacks from Spotted Tail Agency, and various kitchen utensils.

In addition to these items, the soldiers discovered two letters whose purpose was to make it known that their owners were so-called good Indians. One was from Frank C. Boucher, "an illicit trader and brother-in-law of Spotted Tail," in reference to Stabber, and the other from E. A. Howard, the former Indian agent at Spotted Tail Agency, regarding Charging Crow.

When Crook, who had turned forty-eight the previous day,[45] finally arrived sometime between 11 a.m. and noon, it was none too soon for Captain Mills, who did not know whom to expect first—additional troops or an overwhelming force of Sioux seeking vengeance for their fellow tribesmen. As Davenport noted:

[The passing hours] were weighted with suspense, for early in the morning mounted Indians had been observed riding away over the buttes, and it was confidently expected that stronger bands than the one we had dispossessed would come to attack us. Being fully advised of our strength they would, like Indians, seek to overwhelm us with superior force, and certainly would not have much difficulty in succeeding should our reinforcements not arrive in time. The ridge that we held was not adapted for the defense of a small body of men.[46]

Lucky for Mills, the main column was closer than he expected, about fifteen miles back on the trail, and one or more couriers had reached it at 7 a.m. Crook immediately hastened forward with "sections from the cavalry," about 250 cavalrymen

and 17 officers.[47] One correspondent (possibly Strahorn) noted the general's mixed feelings about the fight: "Crook was very much disappointed because Mills did not report the discovery last night, as there was plenty of time to have got up the entire command, and so effectually surrounded the village that nothing could have escaped; but the General is also pleased, too, all things considered."[48]

Correspondent Mills added, "If the whole command had been on the ground not one Indian would have escaped from the village."[49]

One of the first orders of business was the gulch from which bullets had been whizzing throughout the morning, including the slug that killed Private Wenzel.[50] Davenport wrote:

A parley was first tried and an interpreter [Frank Grouard] shouted in the Dakota tongue to the supposed wounded brave that the white chief would spare his life if he would surrender. . . . [He] was checked by the loud detonation of a Spencer rifle and a bullet flew within a hair's breadth of his head.[51]

Grouard's offer rejected, Lieutenant William Philo Clark, Second Cavalry, "called for [twenty] volunteers to make an end of the enemy."[52] However, their firing attracted so much attention from the other soldiers and scouts that soon the twenty men turned into a throng. Wasson wrote: "There was for half an hour a rush of men, mob-like, and a grand fusillade. . . . With difficulty Lieutenant Clark got the men under discipline."[53]

When things calmed down "a second parley was attempted."[54] The response? Another bullet from the ravine. Davenport described the scene that followed:

The fire was renewed and the besiegers drew nearer. Soldiers pressed around and volunteers swelled their ranks, until a dense black crowd stood about the mouth of the ravine. Suddenly there was a volley, followed by rapidly repeated shots sent among them [the soldiers], a tragic fright and a frantic rush from what seemed the gate of death. A soldier remained upon the ground, mortally wounded. It now was realized that the ravine . . . was a nest of devils bent upon holding off capture or death until assistance should come from some neighboring band. . . . An unceasing fire was poured into the ravine for half an hour, and sometimes shrill cries of pain were heard.[55]

Davenport assumed that the Indians were refusing to surrender because of their complicity in the battle of the Little Big Horn: "They probably thought that the guilt of Custer's slaughter, proved . . . by what was found in the village, sealed their fate if they were taken alive, despite the promises of the white chief."[56]

Earlier Davenport had pointed out the bravery of Lieutenants Crawford and Schwatka in keeping the Sioux at bay. Now he singled out Lieutenant Clark for what can only be called a reckless show of daring:

While the other besiegers crawled forward on their bellies to obtain a view of the figures within at which they were firing, Lieutenant Clarke intrepidly stood up in the ravine and fired his piece as coolly as if he were shooting at a deer, exposing his whole person to the aim of the savages.[57]

If Davenport's pen was true, then Clark was not only brave, but damned lucky, for shortly after this, the scout known as "Buffalo Chips" uttered his last words after foolishly exposing himself to enemy fire coming from the ravine:

A scout known as Buffalo White [sic], who has long been a friend and ardent admirer of Buffalo Bill, was one of the most eager and daring of those who ventured to watch for an opportunity to fire. Suddenly, amid the rapid roar of rifles, a sharp thud was heard by those next to White, and the blood spurted from his breast. He fell backward with the cry, "Oh God, boys! Oh God!" and rolled to the foot of the bank.[58]

According to Cuthbert Mills, this incident was followed by a "furious and continuous" fusillade from the soldiers.[59] To the contrary, Davenport stated:

The firing for a time ceased and another squaw came out, bearing a wounded papoose. It was then renewed, the Indians replying but seldom.[60]

When Captain Samuel Munson, Ninth Infantry, accidentally "slipped and slid into the middle of the den," he didn't climb back out empty-handed but had somehow latched onto an old Sioux woman and a baby. Davenport wrote:

The poor woman was whimpering and quaking with indescribable fear as she appeared in the crowd of soldiers. "Kill them," said a voice; "the squaws would have killed us as well as the bucks." "No," was answered in an indignant chorus. "You don't know the American soldier," and the hardened recruit from a foreign clime hung his head before the manly reproof.[61]

Another incident of note occurred when Baptiste Pourier shot and scalped an aged warrior just before the latter man was about to fire his own weapon at the scout. When the fight was over, the old man was "unceremoniously hauled up by what hair remained and by a leather belt around the middle. The fatal shot had struck him under the ear, and shattered the whole base of the skull. . . . His features wore a look of rigid determination."[62] Before climbing out of the gulch, Pourier had "found himself suddenly encompassed by the arms of a squaw and her boy, who begged him not to kill them, and he pushed them roughly out of the hell before him."[63]

By midafternoon, the survivors in the ravine finally decided to accept Crook's offer of surrender and gave up their weapons, which, according to Cuthbert Mills, included a few carbines that had belonged to the Seventh Cavalry.[64] Davenport noted that "they seemed to expect immediate death."[65] Wasson, Mills, and Davenport all captured the tragic surrender scene:

(Wasson:) The first to take advantage of the terms offered was an old squaw who looked like one of Macbeth's witches in the play. She was very much frightened and clung to the General's arm with a tenacity both amusing and touching. Soon after other squaws came out, bring-

ing with them two children, one a very beautiful girl about four years of age. Altogether about 15 women and children came out, followed finally by three warriors, the chief, American Horse,[66] being one of them. He was mortally wounded.[67]

(Mills:) The General insisted on getting the women out. Nothing was done for an hour or two except to guard the place, and so rapidly does the interest change in such times as these, that during this space the existence of the Indians [in the ravine] seemed half forgotten by the camp. Excitement rose again when, after another negotiation with Big Bat, they all consented to come up. There was a general rush, but the guard kept the space clear. Up came Iron Shield, a Sans Arc chief, helped by two squaws, and shot mortally in the abdomen; then two bucks wholly unwounded; then some squaws and children. One of the squaws carried a dead child out; another a wounded one. Its foot was shot off, and it soon died. The prisoners were led off under guard, and half a hundred men jumped down to where they had come from, while several hundred lined the sides and top of the ravine.

One of the bodies was at first mistaken to be that of a white man. This was followed by calls for vengeance among the soldiers: "Drag him out!" "Cut him to pieces!"

(Mills:) There was no white man, however. When the body was dragged into the light, it proved to be that of a squaw whitened by death. She was frightfully shot. A bullet had torn half her neck away, three had gone through her breast and shoulder, and two through each limb. Her body and clothing were one mass of mud and coagulated blood. The woman seemed to have been killed instantly, for her face wore a smile of perfect peace. Another squaw was dragged out scarcely less shot up than the other. Both were quite pretty for Indians. . . . After this came still another squaw, also shot in several places. It seemed that the bodies of the women had been used by the survivors as defenses.

When they were all laid out, and the curiosity of the command had been satisfied by an inspection of an hour or so, an Indian scout came up,[68] calmly scalped the unfortunate women, and hung the inglorious trophies at his belt with as much apparent satisfaction as if they had been taken from warriors slain by his own hand. Yet this Indian was a brave man, and had proved himself to be such. The bodies of the slain were left where they had been dragged, and the crowd of soldiers dispersed, most of them to cook the dried buffalo meat which now formed our only food."[69]

(Davenport:) At length an old squaw volunteered to go into the ravine and advise the bucks to surrender. There remained only three, one of whom was horribly wounded in the abdomen. The errand proved successful, and the ravine was carried. The crowd rushed in and found there the mangled bodies of three dead squaws and one [dead] brave.

Three living braves were brought out, one of them dying, and a dozen squaws and papooses. Altogether the captives numbered twenty-one. They were a pitiable group. The women spoke with fear and the babies sobbed. One of the squaws had a great red furrow in her hand where a bullet had ploughed its way. Another on entering the village ran to the tepee that had been hers and found there the corpse of her dead child, shot in the fight of the morning. The picture of anguish which she presented was too harrowing for the pen, and some

soldiers wrapped the babe in blankets and robes and laid it under a wicker shelter to await burial. The aspect of the bucks was stolid as flint. The one who was dying and whom the interpreters recognized as the Northern American Horse or Iron Shield of the Brule band lay half recumbent supported by two squaws. His face had a yellow copperish hue and showed the rigid contraction produced by terrible pain, but no muscular quiver. The eyelids were closed and there seemed no sign of life. His bowels were protruding from the wound and Dr. McGillycuddy[70] with compassionate skill attempted to replace them but found it impossible. American Horse was told that he must die, but he said nothing. The group composed of the old chief and his women was one as intensely tragic and direfully pathetic as could be wished for by the classic sculptor.

The other bucks, one of whom is called Black Wolf, were conversed with by the interpreters, and said that Crazy Horse's band, with the Southern Cheyennes, were encamped beyond the Slim Buttes, and that those of their people who had escaped had gone to bring back a strong force of warriors to annihilate us. They said that most of the Sioux had determined to go to the agencies for the winter, but that Sitting Bull, with about 100 lodges, had gone across the Yellowstone.[71]

Shortly after, in the same dispatch, Davenport added:

One of the most disgusting and horrible spectacles I ever beheld was the ghastly group of dead lying in the ravine after its surrender. General Crook's scouts had used their knives upon the head of each corpse, and the skulls were bare where the scalps had been savagely torn away, and the clothing of the dead squaws was so disarranged as to indecently expose

Wounded man being transported in a stretcher following the fighting at Slim Buttes. (*Library of Congress*)

their mangled forms. My faith in the superiority of white humanity received a terrible shock.

While the fight at the ravine was going on, Crook's chief medical officer, Surgeon Bennett A. Clements, whose makeshift hospital consisted of the "largest tepee" found in the village, had determined that Lieutenant Von Luettwitz would have to lose his right leg above the knee. "His system had been too worn down by the hardships of the campaign," wrote Cuthbert Mills, "to permit anything but amputation, which was done."[72]

With the wretched affair at the ravine behind them, the men turned their attention to cooking dinner and sorting through the spoils of war, or as one correspondent expressed it, "The village was thoroughly ran-

sacked."[73] The 150 troopers under Captain Mills who participated in the original attack that morning "received as much booty as they could carry off without difficulty"[74] and were also granted the captured ponies. Davenport received a horse previously ridden by a member of the Seventh Cavalry. The rest of the men were free to pick through the leftovers. Whatever was not wanted or could not be carried away was set afire, including the thirty-five lodges, which had been "torn to pieces."[75] There was so much to burn that it took a dozen huge bonfires. About an hour later, all that remained were "smouldering heaps of embers."[76] The bonfires created a large amount of smoke and, as Wasson noted, a quite unpleasant "perfume."[77]

If the troops thought the day's fighting was over, they were wrong. "Scarcely had the camp plunder been sorted and the order issued to burn the refuse," Wasson remarked, "when twenty minutes after four [p.m.] lively picket firing began in front of Captain Mason's battalion of the Fifth Cavalry. It soon became apparent that the defeated villagers of the morning had returned to pay off Captain Mills."[78] Cuthbert Mills recorded:

Every man was engaged in his several occupation, mine being to take hasty notes of the events of the day, when half a dozen rapidly succeeding shots were heard off west of the camp, and the cry spread from man to man, "Indians! Indians! We are attacked by Indians."[79]

Davenport added that, with enemy Indians swarming over the buttes, "the last tribute of regret for Buffalo White [Buffalo Chips] was hastily curtailed."[80] This first assault of the Sioux resulted in the wounding of two men, Sergeant Edmund Schreiber, Fifth Cavalry, and Private Augustus Dorn, Third Cavalry.

"It was evident," Cuthbert Mills declared, "that reinforcements had been obtained from Crazy Horse's village west of us [toward the Little Missouri River], and they had come in expecting to find only the small attacking party of the morning."[81] Instead they found Crook's entire force, which, despite being as exhausted as it was, responded rather quickly to drive back the Sioux and Cheyennes. As Mills noted, "Hardship and starvation had apparently broken the command until the first hostile shots came in."[82]

Black Bear Speaks

Cheyenne Daily Leader,
November 1, 1876

The eldest of the Indians captured, called Black Bear,[83] says that he belongs to the Brule Sioux, now at Standing Rock Agency, formerly from Spotted Tail Agency. He left there with American Horse (a Brule sub-chief killed in the fight) last summer to trade ammunition with the hostiles in the field. They had just accomplished this, and were on the point of returning, when surprised in the village at Slim Buttes. The Indians who lost their village in this fight were Minneconjous, and not Brules, as heretofore reported, the mistake being due, probably, to American Horse's outfit, the only capture of live Indians made, being Brule. The fact is, in a measure, consolation, as the Minneconjous are, without doubt, the most persistently hostile of the Sioux nation, and, for their numbers, have done more mischief, especially when this nation was reckoned as at peace, than any other sub-tribe in it, unless it might be the cut-off Uncapapas under Sitting Bull himself. Their principal chief is Crazy Horse, and the band defeated [at Slim Buttes] was no doubt a dependency of his, and relied on him in the afternoon to recapture their village, but were sadly disappointed when they ran against the entire command of General Crook, then brought up. The chief's name was Bear Nose, and not Roman Nose, who, by the way, is an important Brule chief and [also] a Minneconjou.

"[The Indians] first dismounted behind the high points on the west and opened a slow fire," Davenport observed, "but they were gallantly dislodged" by four companies of infantry "led by Captain A. S. Burt."[84] In another dispatch, he added that these companies "gallantly carried several difficult points of the Buttes, charging the mounted Indians on foot and pouring from the crests which they gained a terrible fire upon them."[85] He said "about twenty" Indians were killed in this action, which, on the surface, sounds like an exaggeration.

At the start of the fight, the Indians had tried to cut off a small detachment under Lieutenant Sibley that was bringing up "some dilapidated horses."[86] They probably wanted the horses more than they wanted the soldiers, although wiping them out would have been a welcome bonus too. In the end, as Davenport related, it did not matter, because they could not find a way to break through the soldiers' line. "Skirmishers were advanced rapidly and forced the Indians to widen their circuit, so that they were obliged to cross deep gullies and steep banks. When they reached the rear they made a dash . . . but Lieutenant Sibley reached the camp just in time to escape. The Indians were disappointed."[87] It was Sibley's second close call in two months.

Closing out the encounter, Davenport wrote:

They were driven back on every hand, and gradually concentrated their whole strength on the right of our line, where they had first made the attack and could secure the higher ridges. The infantry, however, charged them afoot up the heights at double-quick pace and then poured volleys into them when they were running across the ravines behind. On the right, further toward the rear, the Fifth Cavalry, under the direction of Lieutenant Colonel Carr,[88] engaged them warmly. . . . The last considerable demonstration was made on the right, when the fire of the infantry silenced the Sioux and drove them away from their front. The battle of the afternoon lasted about two hours. The attacking force of Indians was about 500 in number and their loss about forty-five killed and wounded. Four soldiers were wounded. In the darkness the occasional flash of a gun was seen, but the pickets easily guarded the camp.[89]

Wasson differed greatly with Davenport on the number of Indian casualties, declaring, "The troops reported four of the enemy killed and several unhorsed, but of this there is nothing official."[90]

Regarding the significant role of the infantry, a detail Davenport also recognized, Cuthbert Mills stated:

I think there will be no more sneering at infantry in Indian campaigns, at least if they are all like the infantry we have with us. They have won the admiration of everybody, both in marching and fighting. They went into that little skirmish at the village in admirable style, and their long guns soon cleared the Indians from their front.[91]

Crook's column lost two soldiers killed (Wenzel and Kennedy), one scout killed (Buffalo Chips), and fourteen wounded, including Lieutenant Von Luettwitz.[92] Whatever the Sioux casualties were, one more was added to the list when American Horse died shortly after midnight.

Reflecting on the day's events about two weeks later, Cuthbert Mills wrote:

The general impression in this command is that we have not much to boast of in the way of killing Indians. They kept out of the way so effectually that the only band which was struck was struck by accident, and when, by the subsequent attack upon us, it was discovered that another and much larger village was not far off, the command was in too crippled and broken down a condition from starvation and over-marching to turn the information to any account.[93]

On the day of the fight, one correspondent (possibly Strahorn) remarked, "It is regretted that other of the larger villages were not surprised and destroyed." Then he championed Crook's strategy of relentless pursuit: "But this affair demonstrates the good policy of a stern chase after the Indians, even by the foot soldiers."[94]

INTERLUDE

The Brothers Von Luettwitz

On October 25, 1876, the *Cheyenne Daily Leader* printed the following letter from Lieutenant Adolphus Von Luettwitz to General Crook. Rather than mention the loss of his leg, he defends Crook's decisions in the late campaign.

Cheyenne Daily Leader,
Wednesday, October 25, 1876

LETTER FROM A BRAVE OFFICER.

HOW A GALLANT SOLDIER SPEAKS OF HIS COMMANDER.

Crook City, D. T., October 3—Lieutenant A. H. Von Luettwitz, Third Cavalry, who was wounded in the battle of Slim Buttes, D. T., Sept. 9, and was compelled to suffer the amputation of his right leg above the knee, writes to General Crook from Crook City, in the Black Hills, where he was left, as follows:

General, I am sorry to leave the army, and especially to be deprived of the pleasure of serving under such an able and energetic officer as yourself. I have been a soldier since my 17th year, having been educated at the Artillery and Engineer School of Berlin. Now it is all over.

Your march from Heart River to the Hills showed both your generalship and your duty as a true soldier. Seeing a large Indian trail going south towards your department, you considered it your duty to follow it and to protect your wards. You feared neither hardships nor privations, but shared both equally with us. Nobody can blame you that our campaign was not crowned with full success. Our forces were too small. The area of country passed over by your command extends from the North Platte to the Yellowstone, and from the Big Horn to the Little Missouri—an area more than twice the size of France. Eight hundred thousand Prussians could not successfully occupy France in 1870. How could 2,000 men be expected to control twice as large a country? Our Indian war will be at an end as soon as traders and speculators are prevented from selling arms and ammunition to the redskins, and as soon as the British government prevents their getting aid from and finding refuge in British North America.

I am, General, with the highest respect, your obedient servant,

A. H. Von Luettwitz, First Lieutenant, Third Cavalry.

The following day, the *Cheyenne Daily Leader* printed a letter from Crook to Von Luettwitz's brother in Germany:

Cheyenne Daily Leader,
Thursday, October 26, 1876

KINDLY WORDS FROM ONE SOLDIER TO ANOTHER—LETTER OF GENERAL CROOK TO BARON VON LUETTWITZ.

General Crook has written the following letter to a brother of Lieut. Von Luettwitz, Third Cavalry, concerning the manner in which the latter was wounded, September 9, in the battle of Slim Buttes:

Headquarters Dept. of the Platte, in the Field, Camp Robinson, Nebraska, Oct. 21, 1876.

Gustavus, Baron Von Luettwitz, Major 81st Infantry, Wiesbaden, Germany:

Dear Sir: Your brother, Lieutenant A. H. Von Luettwitz, Third U. S. Cavalry, has communicated to me your address, coupled with the request that I would apprise his family of the manner in which he received the wound from which he now lies disabled. I have, therefore, the honor to inform you that during our recent campaign against the large tribe of hostile Indians called Sioux, who roam through the country north of this, it became necessary to dispatch a small force of picked men under selected officers to the new mining town of Deadwood City, in the Black Hills, there to obtain supplies for the command. This advance guard encountered a vil-lage of the enemy, and in the skirmish ensuing the Lieutenant was so badly wounded in the knee-pan that amputation of the leg became necessary to save [his] life.

In this sad misfortune, incurred in the gallant performance of duty, your brother has the sincere sympathy of myself and all his associates, while we at the same time feel a pride in the distinguished gallantry with which he has sustained himself, not only on this, but other occasions. His conduct attracted my attention at the affair of the Rosebud, June 17. I write freely, knowing that as you are yourself a soldier, my motives will be appreciated.

Accept, my dear sir, the assurances of my regard and consideration.

George Crook, Brigadier General U. S. Army.

13

A War of Attrition

"The war of savage life and civilization is at its height in these mountains, and its nature is horribly desperate. Citizens do not limit their revenge to an imitation of the Indian custom of scalping, but when they kill a Sioux they cut off his head, exhibit and sell it at auction."—Reuben B. Davenport, Crook City, Black Hills, September 12, 1876, *New York Herald*, September 17, 1876

"It is not surprising that the Sioux were and are unwilling to give up the Black Hills country. It is altogether the most lovely section we have passed through on our seven weeks' march from Goose Creek."—Cuthbert Mills, Custer City, Black Hills, September 22, 1876, *New York Times*, October 12, 1876

"If the matter rested solely with Gen. Crook, there would be not a day's remission of field operations until the whole Sioux nation had been thoroughly subdued."—Cuthbert Mills, Near Custer City, Black Hills, September 25, 1876, *New York Times*, October 11, 1876

On the morning of September 10, some of the warriors from Crazy Horse's village humored themselves by taking long-range shots at the troops. It may have been annoying, but, as Davenport declared, their sharpshooting had "no effect."[1] Marching out of camp at 9 a.m.,[2] Crook made sure that the flanks were "carefully guarded against any attempt of the Sioux to recapture the prisoners and ponies."[3] All of the captives were brought along, except for a couple of women who were left behind "to carry Crook's compliments to the main body of the hostile Sioux, and to request them, for their own good, to go to the agencies and stay there and behave themselves."[4] The column was then about sixty miles north of the Belle Fourche River (also known as the North Fork of the Cheyenne River), which represented the northern boundary of the Black Hills. From there it was about a fifteen-mile march to Crook City, and an additional six and a half miles, as the crow flies, to Deadwood.[5]

About a dozen men had to be carried along on mule litters, including Von Luettwitz, who was suffering from the loss of his right leg. Without referring to the lieutenant by name, Cuthbert Mills had noted:

The unfortunate lieutenant who was shot in the capture of the Indian village and had his leg amputated, was twice thrown out of his litter on the forced march to the Belle Fourche. His screams and cries were terrible.[6]

The other wounded men, if well enough to ride, did so. "As long as a man could sit on a horse or a mule he sat there," observed Mills.[7] Wasson noted, "No other amputations and deaths are anticipated at present."[8]

With the front of the column out of sight, the Indians "incautiously made their appearance"[9] and began to skirmish with the rear guard, but they ended up getting the worst of it. Wasson described part of the action:

The command had hardly got out of sight of the village when the enemy began to come down in the rear, where a battalion of the 5th Cavalry, under Capt. [Samuel S.] Sumner, still lingered. Quite a batch of the enemy were cornered in a ravine . . . and several of the Indians were killed and a number unhorsed and disabled. Privates Foster of Company F and Madden of Company M were wounded in this last action.[10]

Another eyewitness was scout Jack Crawford, who related a different version of the same episode:

I was about starting for the front, when I noticed the maneuvering of Carr's command, and, sitting on my mule at a short distance off, I watched Lieutenant Colonel Carr. He mounted his cavalry on the brow, or near the top of the ridge. On the other side were the Indians. After the main column had got nearly a mile from him, he started, as if to join them, on the gallop. Then as soon as out of sight in the valley with the rear battalion, he dismounted every other man and sent them back on their hands and knees to the brow and awaited the Indians, who, seeing the head of the first battalion moving up opposite the hill, charged to gain the ridge to get a shot at the departing Fifth. As soon as they came within a hundred yards, "up boys, and at them," was the command, and in less time than it takes to tell it, eight good Indians were lying [dead] on the ground and several were wounded, while Carr lost but one man wounded, Madden, a private.[11]

As for that day's march, Davenport said they traveled twelve miles, Strahorn fifteen miles, and Cuthbert Mills wrote, "The command marched no more than ten miles today, on account of the wounded."[12]

In camp that afternoon, Wasson reflected on the past few weeks:

Gen. Crook's 40 days' march in mud and rain on bacon and hard tack, and little of that, is near its close. It is not the success desired and striven for, but it has [been] decided that it is only by such hard work and exposures that the hostile Sioux can be brought to terms; also that Gen. Crook has been on the right track ever since he left his wagons, and that his views as to the Indians' scattering were correct. It has been shown that the foot [soldiers] have overtaken the enemy on a stern chase, and have had to come to the relief of the men on horseback. The immediate effect on the troops is seen in their revived spirits. . . . Great knowledge of the hostile country and its characteristics has been acquired.[13]

On September 11, it was déjà vu as Captain Mills, once again, was sent ahead to purchase supplies. "The dried meat and fruit captured in the Indian village near Slim Buttes was not sufficient, as was supposed," Davenport wrote, "to sustain the column until it could reach the Black Hills."[14] This time Mills's relief party would be half the size as last time, twenty-five men from Company M of the Third Cavalry (his own), and fifty picked men from the Fifth Cavalry.[15] Along for a second time were Bubb, Grouard, Captain Jack, and Davenport. The new face was Lieutenant George F. Chase, Third Cavalry. Most of the men were mounted on the best of the ponies captured from the Sioux. Summing up, Wasson wrote, "Their purpose is to reach the Black Hills settlements and secure a change of diet for the command, which should arrive in three days more."[16] Davenport, having learned from the captured Indians that "many war parties were prowling near the Belle Fourche River," especially from Crazy Horse's band, dismally referred to the relief party as a "sort of forlorn hope."[17]

According to Wasson, that evening Crook's command, in addition to eating from the captured provisions, dined on "fifteen fat ponies." "All the bread is gone," he somberly noted, then, voicing his displeasure with the rotten weather, added, "It has been cold, wet, and windy for ten days in succession."[18] Echoing Wasson, Lieutenant Schwatka declared: "We camped that night on Owl Creek, half starved, with a diminished ration of jerked buffalo meat, horse meat without salt, and a pelting, cold rain to add to all our discomfits."[19]

The next day, Major John J. Upham, with Captains Edward Leib, Edward Hayes, and Julius Mason, led a "picked force of 162 men" of the Fifth Cavalry to investigate the trail of a village moving down Owl Creek.[20] Nothing came of the effort, and they were back with Crook on the fifteenth, but not before losing one trooper killed while hunting. His "scalped and mutilated remains were brought into camp and decently interred."[21]

With Captain Mills off for the hills and Major Upham off on his scout, the main column under Crook marched about thirty-five miles from Owl Creek to Willow Creek on the twelfth. "[It] was one of the worst [marches] of the campaign," Finerty recalled. "We were 'on the go' from daylight until after dark, leading our miserable horses most of the way."[22] Another correspondent added that it was "one of the most exacting [marches] that troops ever experienced."[23] Lieutenant Schwatka clearly shared their sentiments:

The march of the twelfth was one long to be remembered in the sufferings of American soldiery. With nothing to eat but pony meat, with no salt, a disagreeable, cold, rainy day, the weary and starved command launched itself over the miry alkali flats that separate Owl Creek from Crow Fork of the Belle Fourche—a long, long thirty-five miles. The horses fell out exhausted by dozens, the men were too weak to lead any distance, the halts were only sufferings taken at a standstill—far more annoying than the march, bad as it was. Camp was reached late at night, and weary and broken down, many a man slept that awful night as if he was but a drunkard in the slums of a city, prostrate on the wet ground. Stragglers continued to come in until late the next day.[24]

On the thirteenth they trudged seven more miles to the Belle Fourche and made camp, their stomachs anxiously awaiting the return of the relief party, desperate for a change of diet.

We now return to Captain Mills's advance mission to the Black Hills for provisions. Once again, we rely on Davenport's always descriptive narrative:

We left the column as it was about to encamp and rode all the night of the 11th, which was very dark and foggy. We several times lost the points of the compass and at midnight unsaddled our horses and lay down to snatch a little sleep. The morning was as gray and dreary as possible, but the mist seemed dryer than before and we began to hope for a cessation of the long storm. The vapor was dissipated and at nine o'clock the clouds began to melt and we saw the Black Hills in the distance. We entered the beautiful valley of the Belle Fourche in the afternoon [September 12], anxiously scanning its wide extent for some dreaded Sioux village, but were gladly disappointed. We halted on a small tributary for dinner. The guide had killed an antelope and its haunch was cut up and either fried or roasted by the officers, scouts and correspondents. The soldiers were content to butcher an Indian colt, which they cooked and ate and declared to be excellent "veal." We had discovered some very fresh pony tracks and were anxious to proceed, lest a war party of

the Sioux should come upon us. We rode rapidly toward the foot hills and were among them before the sunset. They form the most beautiful region that I have seen in Dakota, Wyoming or Montana. They are fertile and picturesque and luxuriously clothed in green. We found thickets loaded with ripened wild plums, and ate them with a keen relish.

We were uncertain that the Black Hills were still populated, fearing a concentration of the Sioux upon the settlements. The sombre mass called the Bear Butte, which stands detached from the range, guided us to the mouth of the Whitewood Canyon, which is a short distance west of it, and there, at sunset, part of our party was left in camp, while Captain Mills, Captain Jack, Frank Gruard and myself, with a guard of five soldiers, started to reach Crook City before midnight. We emerged from a dense oak thicket in the bottom of the canyon, to be challenged by three horsemen who had stopped in the middle of a well-worn road at the base of a mountain.

"Who are you?"

"White men."

There were then eager greetings. The horsemen explained that they were searching for cattle that they had lost, that Crook City was but five miles up the canyon, that the settlers were veritably besieged by the Indians and that the hills were full of food. All this information, quickly gleaned, satisfied our hungry minds for the present, but not our stomachs. Captain Jack, Frank and I dashed up the road at a gallop which we did not check until we were in Crook City. It need not be remarked that a banquet was the immediate order. Afterward we went to bed. General Crook's commissary, Lieutenant Bubb, arrived an hour later at Crook City and immediately took steps to send supplies to the starving troops in the morning.[25]

Riding into Crook's bivouac on the Belle Fourche on the morning of the thirteenth, Captain Mills and the rest of the relief party were met with loud cheers: "Hurrah for Crook! Hurrah for Mills!" the men shouted "like schoolboys."[26] "We were breakfasting on pony steak . . . when we heard the lowing of oxen, which then seemed sweetest music to our ears," Finerty recalled. "The effect on the troops was electrical." Lieutenant Bourke commented: "Down the hillside we saw fifty head of beef cattle coming as fast as men could drive them, while not a mile in the rear, canvass [sic] wagon sheets gleaming in a cloud of dust betokened the replenishment of our Commissariat."[27]

Finerty further described the joyous scene as hundreds of hungry men were gratefully reintroduced to fresh meat and other foodstuff:

The arrival of the beef herd, together with some wagon loads of crackers and vegetables from Crook City, on the edge of "the Hills," changed the aspect of affairs and made everybody feel happy. The beeves were speedily shot and butchered, and the soldiers were not long in satisfying their appetites upon the meat, which they roasted, in Indian fashion, on willow wands, that served the purpose of toasting forks.[28]

Cuthbert Mills captured the spectacle, too, vividly describing what occurred when a local merchant rolled into camp:

The first sutler who came into camp sold his bread at a dollar a small loaf, and a pound of crackers at the same price. At these prices, so wild had the men become for the food that they would have torn the wagon to pieces in their efforts to get it, and a strong guard had to be put around it, while four officers went into the vehicle and sold the articles. I knew an officer, who in ordinary times is of quite delicate appetite, to pick up a cracker which had been trodden under foot, and, with a small piece of bacon given him by a brother officer, sit down by the wagon and devour both with the greatest relish.[29]

Davenport, never short for words, thought that Crook's men looked like "an army of skeletonized ragamuffins,"[30] then added:

When bread was sent out to them they mobbed the wagons containing it, and had devoured the whole load a few moments after it reached the camp. For two days they had been subsisting on horses, having consumed all of the provisions found in the captured village.[31]

Summing up the existing situation, and still not shy to speak his mind on matters pertaining to General Crook, Davenport declared:

The condition of General Crook's column renders recuperation imperative, and only something akin to madness could prompt its return to the field at present. The infantry might endure further operations,[32] but 800 of the cavalry are dismounted, and the horses which have not already been abandoned are unfit for immediate service. A great number of government saddles have been left on the way and the whole loss of public property occasioned by the march to the Black Hills is enormous. Add to this the discontented mood of the soldiers, who will be ripe for desertion as soon as they receive their two months' pay, and you have a picture of a disorganized, tattered and demoralized army, such as history presents only at rare intervals.

The campaign outside of the agency reserves must be considered as closed, and it has been without palpable results. The reasons which I adduced in former letters for the failure of General Crook to justify his reputation as an Indian fighter still apply, and with redoubled force, to events which have happened since. I will not re-enter upon their discussion, but simply add that the ruthlessness with which he has subjected his army to needless suffering, hardship and privation, and has sacrificed the property of the army to the accomplishment of no adequate object, should provoke an inquiry which should be conducted in the light of martial law.[33]

With Crook's campaign unofficially over, and happy for something to eat other than a horse, Cuthbert Mills reflected on the hardships of the last six weeks, even throwing some credit his own way (though the reader may question his comment about taking part in any skirmishing):

Gen. Crook's campaign against the Sioux Indians ceases for the time with our arrival here today. So remote, so wild, so distant from any settlement have been the places we have been marching through since leaving the Yellowstone on the 24th of August that our camp here seems almost like home. Crook City is twelve miles away, and Deadwood about twenty. These infant settlements of the Black Hills are to us as important as New York or Boston. We are receiving supplies from them, and that is all we want. . . . Here we have come to rest, and never did troops more urgently need or more

thoroughly deserve both the rest and food they are promised.

All that the soldiers have done and suffered, I have done. I have marched with them, camped in the same camps, eaten the same food as they, slept as they have, ridden and walked as they have, and taken a hand in the little skirmishing they have had. . . . [S]ince leaving Goose Creek on the 5th of August last, I have endured more hardship, privation, and misery than ever I thought to have endured in my life. It is with a sincere feeling of thankfulness to Providence for bringing us safely through as much as we have suffered, that we sit beside our campfire tonight and partake of the first full meal we have had in three weeks.[34]

On the night of September 14, Crook received a dispatch from Sheridan "to proceed at once to Fort Laramie" "to arrange for a vigorous prosecution of the Indian war through the coming winter."[35] He would leave shortly. The next day camp was moved to Whitewood Creek, about five miles closer to Crook City. "All day long, wagons and vehicles of all sorts, heavily loaded with provisions, rolled in from Crook City and Deadwood," Lieutenant Bourke observed. "Evidences of sympathy and kindly appreciation were not lacking. . . . We were the recipients of all kinds of compliments, none the more grateful than the fresh vegetables."[36]

Lieutenant Schwatka reflected on the drastic change that had taken place in their fortunes from just a few days previous: "The line of sutler's wagons seemed to convert our encampment into a big county fair and formed a strange contrast to our camp a few days ago when we were half starving."[37]

Correspondent Finerty remarked: "The arrival of Crook's army in the neighborhood caused quite a flutter among such merchants as had supplies for military needs, and every kind of speculator, from a photographer to a three-card-monte man, was soon on the road to Whitewood Creek, where lay Crook's brigade."[38]

But for some, all of this food and kindness had a negative effect. A few days later, Cuthbert Mills was to write:

What with the long feeding on one unvarying diet, and, when this food gave out, the semi-starvation that followed, everybody became wild for food. All forms of farinaceous food were those for which there was most craving, and when the command was supplied with abundant food of all kinds, over-eating was the natural consequence, and the digestive apparatus was thrown into hopeless disorder. Many persons who had escaped trouble during the whole of what was called the starvation period succumbed to the period of plenty, and are not fairly off the sick list yet.[39]

Also on the fifteenth, a copy of the *Black Hills Tribune*, out of Crook City, was brought into camp. Mills found one story in particular to be "rather amusing reading":

[There was] a glowing account with startling headlines of the great engagement between Gen. Crook's army and the hostile Sioux under chiefs Roman Nose and American Horse. . . . [W]e found that a village of thirty-three lodges was attacked, that from seventy-five to one hundred Indians were killed, and that we had performed such deeds of valor as

would make heroes of us all. This, of course, was highly gratifying.[40]

On the morning of the sixteenth, Crook, accompanied by a small staff, correspondents Davenport, Finerty, Wasson, and Strahorn, and an escort of twenty men under Lieutenant Sibley,[41] departed the main column for the trip to Fort Laramie, about 155 miles southwest of Deadwood. Command of the Wyoming Column now devolved on Colonel Wesley Merritt, who was to continue as far south as Custer City at the southern end of the hills, there to "await new supplies of clothing and equipments."[42] After a brief stop in Crook City, the general hastened on to Deadwood, where he "was received with cheers and explosions of gunpowder," not to mention a petition "bearing more than 1,000 names, asking his protection from the Indians who infest the mountains."[43] However, their claim that more than one hundred white men had been killed by Indians in the past two months was most certainly a ruse to have the troops remain in the area. An army command in their backyard meant money in their pockets. In his dispatch six days later, Mills recalled how Crook had kindly turned down their request:

Under the circumstances Crook had to decline, expressed his regret, said he was glad to meet them, that their town was a model of enterprise, and would grow, and various other polite things. While he was with them there were grand doings and rejoicings, and Deadwood was made to howl.[44]

However, as Mills went on to explain, Crook's decision did not sit well with many of the Black Hillers, whose previous jubilation soon turned into angry condemnation:

Now [that] he is gone, nine men out of ten one meets in the hills are denouncing the General because he refused to disobey his orders and keep his broken down force here for their benefit. They declare that the coming of the army here is a calamity to them, since the Indians will swarm in worse than ever [once the army leaves],[45] and they sneeringly inquire what the military have done all this summer, after the enormous expense the taxpayers are put to. Indeed, a gentleman of the gambling fraternity, with a red nose and a brass-bound pistol, darkly hinted in my hearing that Crook's official days were numbered, a certain numerously signed petition of Black Hillers for his removal being on its way to Washington. This is pretty hard talk for men who have endured what we have to listen to with any patience. . . . The truth seems to be, however, that the largest amount of cursing and growling, of which we have heard so much, comes from the gamblers, horse thieves, and more knavish class of traders, who see in the departure of the Army their hope of profit gone. They care little or nothing about protection from Indians. . . . If the Army had stopped here for a couple of months some of these gentry would have made their fortunes on it, and some would have been strung up to trees.[46]

One morning, as the main column was making its way toward Custer City, some delinquent Black Hillers tried to pull a fast one on the troops. Mills described the ploy:

They tried to detain the column by getting up a bogus scare. A fellow came riding furiously after us with a story that within ten minutes after the command had left camp sixty Indians had run off a beef herd within a mile of the place; while the front of the column was met by other men with a story that the Montana herd of horses had been run off from another place. These ingenious alarms failing of their purpose, the disappointed thieves used what opportunity they had for stealing our horses, and some twenty or thirty head have been stolen during our march through the hills.[47]

Another dispatch illustrated the frontier justice administered to a couple of outlaws near Custer City:

Over 100 head of stock have been stolen from the command since we came into the Hills, and no effort has heretofore been made to recover the animals until this morning [October 13], when between twenty and thirty head were run off by a Mexican and a white man who have been following the command. Several teamsters and one of our scouts, Slim Jim Hilton, followed them. About 11 a.m. they returned with eleven head of the stock, but failed to bring the thieves back. They are both dead. The Mexican got behind a rock and fought hard for his life, but the boys meant business and he paid the penalty of his crimes.[48]

On the seventeenth, twenty-two miles south of Deadwood, Crook and his entourage met three companies of the Fourth Artillery seven days out of Red Cloud Agency, escorting a supply train of thirty wagons, the first official shipment of supplies for the Wyoming Column.[49]

Captain Harry C. Cushing, Fourth Artillery, recorded the following description of the general:

[General Crook was] a quiet, middle-aged man, habited in a suit of grey citizen's clothes and riding a sedate and businesslike white horse, who plodded along totally oblivious of his real rank among his equine comrades. The pantaloons of this General were stuffed irregularly in his boot legs, and his chapeau was a soft felt, of most modest and negligent appearance. The sandy, long beard appertaining to the Commanding General was ingeniously woven into two plaits, which, to say the least, gave him a very bizarre appearance. Across his saddle pommel lay a Springfield rifle and around his waist was strapped a prairie belt, plentifully garnished with central-fire metallic cartridges, calibre 45, ready for any emergency, aboriginal or sylvan. The countenance of this General was impressive.[50]

Of the others in the party, Cushing observed:

The staff followed, generally arrayed in butternut colored shirts and overalls, a style of dress peculiarly affected by the denizens of these parts; while in the rear of them came the escort chastely decked with a fine assortment of patches. Interspersed among the foregoing were several correspondents of Eastern papers regarding each other with professional animosity. . . . In rear of all rode an imperturbable Ute Indian [Ute John], the solitary representative of the race, while the extreme and final rear was composed of about 20 pack mules, who meandered through the adjacent thickets totally regardless of order and scornful of expostulation. To them a bell mule, mature and experienced, was law and prophet. At the tinkle of her bell they advanced or halted, and as her movements were controlled by one of the superior race his jerking her to a standstill brought this asinine mob to a state of rest.

General Crook arrived at Fort Laramie on the evening of September 21, having stopped briefly at Red Cloud Agency the day before. Sheridan, who had been waiting for Crook since the sixteenth, departed two days later.[51]

Correspondent Joe Wasson was at Fort Laramie on September 24 when Crook's wagon train rolled into view, the same one that had been left behind on Goose Creek about seven weeks earlier. After such a long and strenuous campaign, he found comfort in the sight of the wagons, as well as the fort's dwellings: "To meet here the dear old wagon train with its camp equipage, as well as to see a number of houses, was reassuring."[52]

Somewhat unbelievably, he stated that Sheridan departed Fort Laramie feeling "quite satisfied with the situation in the Department of the Platte." Almost certainly the lieutenant general of the army was being disingenuous (see the last paragraph to this chapter). The campaign had been going on, more or less, since the previous March, and other than the minor fight at Slim Buttes, the army had yet to win a resounding victory. On top of that, the Northern Indians, under Crazy Horse and Sitting Bull—the "hostiles"—had yet to be defeated, even if their morale was on the wane.[53] Still, despite the slow start, this was a war of attrition, and the victor was a foregone conclusion. Reviewing the late campaign, the *New York Herald* stated:

The first campaign ends in the Indians' being broken into small bands, flying in all directions, utterly demoralized, while more men are going daily to the Black Hills and our frontier settlements are steadily advancing.[54] So far as the killing of Indians was concerned the campaign just closed was undoubtedly a failure, but that the Indians are completely beaten and demoralized and rendered wretched by the operations there is not a doubt. The object sought to be attained by the campaign—viz, the breaking of the Sioux power, the safety of our miners and the securing of our frontier settlements—has been accomplished.[55]

Getting back to Sheridan, many of the officers (perhaps Crook among them) privately blamed him for the Wyoming Column's inconclusive results. After all, it was Sheridan who had redirected Merritt's cavalry back in mid-July to intercept the Cheyennes that bolted from Red Cloud Agency, a change in plans that they felt stood in the way of their success. It was the "what if" factor. What if the Fifth Cavalry had reached them earlier? Perhaps they would have trounced the Sioux. Recall General Crook's statement in a previous chapter when Colonel Merritt and the Fifth Cavalry finally arrived at his Goose Creek bivouac on August 3: "Oh, if they had come before—if they had come before."[56] On the subject of Merritt's July diversion, Wasson remarked:

Many of the officers say that if Sheridan kept [his] hands off the 5th Cavalry after Gen. Crook ordered them to Goose Creek in July, there would have been a different tale to tell long ere this. It is now considered by every one who is well informed that Merritt's raid against the Cheyennes [on July 17 at Warbonnet Creek] was a very trivial affair in comparison with the importance of striking the head and front of the great hostile band in the Big Horn country, where Gen. Crook had the gauntlet thrown in his face every day for a fortnight.[57]

Back in the Black Hills, the Wyoming Column under Merritt had departed Crook City on September 19 and arrived at Custer City four days later.[58] Here they remained for several weeks, resting and scouting. Cuthbert Mills reflected on what had been, for many of the men, long-time isolation from friends and family:

Of what has occurred in the outside world since we left Goose Creek on the 5th of August, we cannot know until our wagon train arrives from Fort Fetterman. We are told that there are two wagonloads of mail matter for us in the train, and scarcely an hour passes, or a wagon comes over the road into Custer City, but the most anxious inquiries are made respecting that mass of mail matter. Some of us have not received a letter or any communication whatever, either personal or official, since we left Medicine Bow or Cheyenne, in June last. Next to being out of rations the want of communication with friends is the most trying part of campaigning. Now we have enough food for our bodies, we are longing for something for our minds.[59]

On Tuesday, October 24, the Wyoming Column was back in familiar territory. A dispatch in the *Cheyenne Daily Leader*, October 26,

1876, announced their appearance at Red Cloud Agency: "The arrival of Colonel Merritt's command at Red Cloud Agency, Tuesday, signalized the closing up of the Big Horn and Yellowstone campaign, which will be succeeded by the Powder River expedition."

Continuing its summary of the spring-summer military campaign (with the focus on General Terry, but applicable to Crook, too), the *New York Herald* remarked:

Now that the Sioux campaign on the Yellowstone has been closed for the season and the troops sent to their posts we may sum up and see what has been accomplished by the operations during the past summer. Whatever may be said or thought about it by others, that portion of our Indian war intrusted to General Terry, so far as he was concerned, seems to have been conducted to the entire satisfaction of those engaged in it, who, after all, are perhaps the best judges of what should have been done. General Sheridan has hastened to express his approbation of General Terry's management, and when we remember what an eminent authority the Lieutenant General is on Indian fighting we feel like accepting his opinion as final. Certainly no man in the nation is more capable of judging what ought to be accomplished in an Indian campaign, and we have never yet known General Sheridan to bestow praise where it was not deserved or withhold a reproof when it was merited.[60]

In fact, the *Herald* writer sounds as if he was trying to convince himself of his own words. In any event, what Sheridan stated publicly and how he felt privately were two different matters altogether. His true feelings were revealed in a letter to Sherman written in February 1877:

The fact of the case is, the operations of Gens. Terry and Crook will not bear criticism, and my only thought has been to let them sleep. I approved what was done, for the sake of the troops, but in doing so, I was not approving much, as you well know.[61]

INTERLUDE

An Interview with "Buffalo Bill" Cody

Cheyenne Daily Leader,
Thursday, September 28, 1876

BUFFALO BILL ON THE SIOUX CAMPAIGN.

A reporter of the Chicago Times gives the following account of an interview with Buffalo Bill:

Everybody has heard of "Buffalo Bill," the daring scout of the plains, but William F. Cody is by no means so widely known, although they are one and the same person. The first title is used exclusively beyond the wild Missouri, but in "God's country" it is dropped for the more civilized cognomen of Mr. Cody. Mr. Cody arrived at the Tremont House on yesterday direct from Terry's command on the Yellowstone, and in the afternoon a Times reporter called to see him. A tall, slim, wiry man of perhaps 33 responded. From beneath a light-drab sombrero his brown hair fell in graceful waves around his shoulders. His face was covered with a thick growth of black, curly whiskers that clung closely to the skin as though afraid of getting left. What little of the complexion was visible was richly bronzed by exposure. For the rest, Cody wore a heavy velvet coat buttoned high, dark pants, and a pair of boots that many a society man would give a small fortune to be able to get into. Taken all in all he is rather a fine looking fellow, and considerably of the Custer order.

Cody had a double object in visiting Chicago. In the first place, he wished to consult with Gen. Sheridan with reference to a scheme which is on foot in the territories to raise a company of 100 frontiersmen for winter missionary work among the Sioux, with Cody at the head. Such a command the territorial governors argue, would be of more actual service to the settlers than a full regiment of regulars.

"Have you any intimation as to how Gen. Sheridan will consider the proposition?" asked the reporter.

"None at all. He is out of the city, and he is one of that kind of men who don't tell their staff all they know. I expect him back at three o'clock."

"What do you expect to do with your company provided you raise it?"

"Strike the redskins wherever I find them, and then get away before they get too thick."

"Do you regard the season's campaign as a success?"

"It has been more like a big picnic party than a campaign. As a general thing, instead of sending their cavalry out light to strike the Indians and amuse them until the infantry came up, the commanding officers have used the cavalry to prevent the Indians from attacking the infantry. The war department, whose duty it is to forward supplies, has managed that part of the campaign splendidly."

"As chief of scouts you were with all the commanding officers in the field at various times. Who is the best of them?"

"Lieut. Colonel Carr of the 5th Cavalry. He is brave and dashing, and cautious at the same time. He never rests until he has all the information possible, and spares himself no pains or labor to obtain it. He is by all odds the best Indian fighter of the outfit.[62] I started out with him early in the season, then was with Merritt, afterward with Crook and latterly with Terry, and I know them all. Custer was a good Indian fighter. They may talk about his recklessness, but I tell you nothing short of dash will do with Indians. When you find them you have got to strike instantly or get away. If you strike hard, the chances are in your favor, but you may go under. You have got to take the chances in order to win."

"Where is Sitting Bull?"

"He is hiding on the Big Horn River. He struck out to the east, doubled on his pursuers, got into the mountains, and broke his force up into hunting parties. Not more than 50 Indians have gone north toward British America."

"Have the commands fared pretty well?"

"For the last two or three weeks Crook's command has had a rough time of it. Their rations gave out, it has rained constantly, and horses and men are in a terrible shape. By the way, speaking of horses, Lieut. Colonel Carr can start out with a regiment, march it further, and have his stock in better order at the end than any other officer on the plains."

Interlude

An Interview with General Crook in the Black Hills

In an interview with Cuthbert Mills on the night of September 13,

General Crook "very frankly stated his views" about the Indian War then being conducted against the Sioux and Cheyennes:

New York Times,
Wednesday, October 11, 1876

"Our next objective point is Crazy Horse. He should be followed up and struck as soon as possible. There should be no stopping for this or that thing. The Indians cannot stand a continuous campaign. I cannot tell whether we can go on yet. That depends on our getting the things we want. The best time to strike Indians is in the winter. They cannot remain together in large bodies at that season. The necessities of subsistence compel them to separate, and then is the time to throw a large force on each band and crush them all in detail. If you strike one band now, it is never so far from others but these can concentrate on the attacking force if it is a small one, or they can communicate with each other and scatter if they want to run from a large one."

In reference to the hardships of the past campaign, Gen. Crook said they were not likely to occur again. "How could any one anticipate such a season of rain, when we had been lying idle all the summer without having a drop fall upon us? We had to go on when once we left Goose Creek, at any cost. The Indians were not where we expected to find them. Would it do to turn back again, after lying idle so long, with the old cry that our rations would give out or something else prevented our going on? This is an old trouble in Indian fighting. The system of moving without a wagon train is the only proper one for a campaign of this character. A mule train can go anywhere; there is no rear to protect at the cost of largely reducing your fighting force. Our train was not large enough. That will be remedied. We were unable to carry enough provisions to give us time to scout the country when we cut loose from our base. We had to make straight for another place as soon as we left the last, because our rations were not sufficient to allow us to wait on the way and search the country. Then we were almost without guides or scouts. I had no man I could depend upon except Frank Gruard, and he could not do all the work. The others were well enough, but they did not know the country, and they could not be got to go out any distance. If we had had Indians with us from the Yellowstone here we should not have had such trouble in crossing the country. I always try to get Indian scouts, because scouting is with them the business of their lives. They learn all the signs of a trail as a child learns the alphabet; it becomes an instinct. With a white man the knowledge is acquired in after life. You cannot be sure that an Indian is telling the truth; he will lie to you; so will the white man. But if you can make it to the Indian's interest to tell the truth you get correct information; a white man will lie intentionally, and mislead you unintentionally. Our two Indian bucks there (pointing to the campfire where the captives were gathered), I am trying to train for scouts. They would be of immense use. I told them it was to their interest to come in with us; that they should be fed, paid, and clothed, while as they were now they had not a thing in the world. I told them I did not want to kill them, or I would have had them burned out of their hole in that ravine. Frank has talked to them too, and they seem inclined to listen to reason. Some people say it is wrong to use the people of a tribe against itself, but pshaw! if I can kill one rattlesnake by making another bite him, I shall do it."

[To these statements Mills, somewhat humorously, added]: "That Gen. Crook is fully able to carry out his ideas in regard to the Sioux, I entirely believe; but at the same time I don't hanker after accompanying him in the execution of his plans. I rather doubt that about no repetition of the hardships of this campaign; and having passed through them without apparent damages, except that weeks of soaking may have sown the seeds of a future crop of rheumatism, I am inclined for the future to applaud Gen. Crook's methods of Indian campaigning from the safe distance of New York."

14

Red Cloud and Spotted Tail

"Orders have been issued from department headquarters [in St. Paul] for one company of infantry from Fort Snelling and another from Fort Abercrombie, to proceed immediately to Standing Rock Agency, in pursuance of orders received yesterday from Sheridan, taking military control of the Sioux agencies, and treating the absent Indians as enemies and to be disarmed and deprived of their ponies on coming in or endeavoring to go out, and be arrested and held as prisoners of war."—"More Troops to the Front," *Weekly Rocky Mountain News*, August 2, 1876

"We are a great people, a warlike people, full of men who, at a safe distance, can eat up a tribe of Indians before breakfast, and digest them in time for devouring a regiment or two of Hessians. But somehow we cannot whip Sitting Bull. That limping savage has won a year's campaign against us."—Editorial, "Our Indian Campaign," *Daily Alta California*, September 16, 1876

"This summer's campaign can scarcely be called a great success, but those who know Gen. Crook best have faith in his ability to subdue the Sioux as thoroughly as he did the Apaches of Arizona and other Indian tribes. The task is perhaps rather a heavier one than has hitherto fallen to him in Indian warfare; but it is pointed out that the General failed a good deal in Arizona, before he learned the way to success."—Cuthbert Mills, Near Custer City, Black Hills, September 25, 1876, *New York Times*, October 11, 1876

"I know the hostile Indians will not hold out much longer. What is termed the Indian War is nothing more than the same struggle that has been going on for the past 200 years. It began in New England, and has gradually edged westward. Each outbreak has the same ending. This Sioux difficulty will not last long enough to interfere a moment with the tide of westward migration."—"General Sherman's Views," *Cheyenne Daily Leader*, October 15, 1876

Back in late July, while Crook had been eagerly awaiting the addition of Merritt's cavalry reinforcements and Terry was straining his eyes downriver for steamers carrying more men and supplies, the Interior Department, after repeated urgings, finally transferred control of the troubled Sioux agencies to the military, the role of the agents now being superseded "by the officers of the War Department":

The Commissioner of Indian Affairs on Saturday evening [July 22] telegraphed to the Indian agents at Red Cloud and Spotted Tail agencies to turn over their respective charges to the military officers at Camp Robinson and Camp Sheridan, respectively. This was done by the Commissioner for the reason that he thought best, under the present condition of affairs in the Indian country, to have perfect harmony between the military and civil officers near the agencies, and thus prevent any possible controversy between the officers at this point and the agents.[1]

This was quickly followed by another communiqué from the commissioner of Indian affairs on July 26, the key words of which were "unconditional surrender":

Allow the military to so far control your Indians as to prevent any from joining the hostiles, and the latter and their families from coming in except on unconditional surrender. Aid in arresting, disarming and dismounting such. Issue no rations to such except as prisoners. Assure all peaceable Indians of full protection and kind treatment.[2]

Meanwhile, with the Fifth Cavalry having been called to reinforce Crook's Wyoming Column in mid-July, additional troops had been needed to fill the void in patrolling the roads south of the Black Hills. The *Cheyenne Daily Leader* announced the new troop replacements in an article on July 26: "Colonel McKenzie,[3] with six companies [of the Fourth Cavalry], has been ordered from the Indian Territory to Red Cloud Agency and vicinity . . . to take the place of Colonel Merritt, who has gone [north] with the Fifth Cavalry to join Crook."[4]

Mackenzie was a well known cavalry officer dating back to the Civil War. Described as being "considerable on the fight," he had been instrumental in defeating the Kiowas and Comanches on the southern Plains, the high point of which was his victory in Palo Duro Canyon (Texas) in September 1874. Now, at age thirty-six, he was the new commander of the District of the Black Hills.[5] Mackenzie's presence in the theater of the Sioux War was soon to have severe consequences, particularly for the Northern Cheyennes, all but putting the nail in the coffin to further resistance on the part of the nonreservation Indians.

With the agencies now under temporary military supervision, it was time to get an accurate census count. In an interview with Captain Frederick Mears, Ninth Infantry, correspondent Joe Wasson learned what many had suspected all along—that many of the Indians had left the reservation:

[O]n August 10, when the Spotted Tail Agency was turned over to Captain Mears' temporary charge, 9,135 Indians were reported as under its control. By actual count, including whites, squaw-men and half-breeds, only 4,700 were found. At the same time, on Captain [William H.] Jordan [Ninth Infantry] taking control of the Red Cloud Agency, 12,000 were reported and only 4,800 were found on actual count.[6]

The following month, after meetings with the Manypenny Commission,[7] Red Cloud and Spotted Tail were among seventy-two Sioux chiefs and headmen at their respective agencies who signed an agreement giving up the Black Hills country and the unceded territory; the agreement was also signed by six Arapahoes and five Cheyennes.[8] In October, 158 more signatures were collected at the other Sioux agencies, including Standing Rock and Cheyenne River. The Indians faced a dilemma: they were barred from leaving the reservation to hunt, but they were told that if they did not sign the agreement, they would not get further subsistence from the government. It was, as one writer expressed it, a "sign or starve" type of deal.[9] Payment for the Black Hills was not part of the agreement; however, by signing, they would receive rations (but with stipulations, such as having to cultivate the land), medical assistance, and schools. Additionally, all future goods were to be distributed at points along the Missouri River (where it was cheaper to feed them). That last detail implied that the Red Cloud and Spotted Tail Indians would have

to move closer to the Missouri River, a region they found less than pleasing. If they did not like that idea, it was suggested they could move to the Indian Territory.[10] Seemingly disgusted with the proceedings, one Indian named Fire Thunder, when it was his turn to sign, held his blanket before his eyes and touched his hand to the pen as if he were blindfolded.[11]

In conference with the Manypenny Commission, Spotted Tail had commented on the ongoing Sioux War and the lack of sufficient rations, and was anything but timid when it came to pointing the finger of blame for the current troubles:

This seems to me to be a very hard day; half of our country is at war, and we have come upon very difficult times. This war did not spring up here in our land; it was brought upon us by the children of the Great Father, who came to take our land from us without price, and who do a great many evil things. The Great Father and his children are to blame for this trouble. We have here a storehouse to hold our provisions, but the Great Father sends us very little provisions to put into our storehouse, and when our people become displeased with our provisions and have gone north to hunt, the children of the Great Father are fighting them. It has been our wish to live here peaceably, but the Great Father has filled it with soldiers, who think only of our death. Some of our people have gone from here in order that they may have a change, and others who have gone north to hunt, have been attacked by soldiers from this direction, and when they have got north have been attacked by soldiers from other directions, and now when they are willing to come back the soldiers stand between them and keep them from

Red Cloud, left, and Spotted Tail. (*Library of Congress*)

coming home. It seems to me there is a better way than this. . . . You have mentioned to me two countries. The Missouri River country I know. When we were there we had a great deal of trouble. I left hundreds more people buried there. The other country [Indian Territory] I have never seen, but I agree to go and look at it with fifty of my young men.[12]

According to one newspaper account, Spotted Tail was prodded into signing the agreement on September 23 by a white man living with the Sioux:

While outside [the council room] E. W. Raymond, a white man living with Spotted Tail's people the last twenty-seven years, told him if he did not sign the treaty Red Cloud would get ahead of him and derive all the advantages to be had from the treaty. Raymond then went to Red Cloud and Red Dog, of Red Cloud's Agency, who were outside of the council room, and told them to go in and urge Spotted Tail and his people to sign. They did so, making short but effective speeches, and then withdrew.[13]

In the end, what the whites had failed to take by force they seized by threats and imaginative paperwork.

With the signing over of the Black Hills to the U. S. government, the next matter of importance was disarming and unhorsing the reservation Indians who were aiding and abetting the "hostiles," most of which support was believed to be coming from Red Cloud Agency.[14] According to an unnamed officer, this strategy "had been resolved on last summer, as an absolute necessity to the successful termination of the war . . . but as Red Cloud and others were constantly asserting their friendship . . . it was found difficult to carry out the resolve of disarming them."[15]

If the "young bucks" were disarmed, correspondent James J. O'Kelly had written in late August, "the spirit of the Sioux nation would be broken." Continuing, he declared:

So long as they are permitted to go about armed to the teeth, and are supplied with the means of killing by the government and its agents, it is useless to expect them to abandon their savage state of semi-independence. Let the government send orders for the disarmament and we can lay the basis of a permanent peace.[16]

The long-anticipated action to disarm the agency Indians finally occurred on the morning of October 23 on Chadron Creek, about twenty-five miles east of Red Cloud Agency:

Last night [October 22] at dark Colonel Mackenzie was ordered to take all his available force of cavalry, consisting of six companies of the 4th and two companies of the 5th Cavalry, and march immediately upon the Indian encampment at Chadron Creek. This movement was executed with great secrecy and promptness, and at dawn of day the camp of Red Leaf was surrounded by Major [George] Gordon's battalion, and that of Red Cloud was surrounded by Capt. [Clarence] Mauck's battalion. Not a shot was fired. The troops closed in and completed the cordon, and these two pestiferous tribes, with all their women, children, ponies, and arms, were captured. The Indians were at once disarmed and dismounted, and the whole convoy is now on its way to the agency under charge of Colonel Mackenzie. This is the first move in the performance of a work that should have been done last spring.[17]

All told, the troops captured some five hundred men, women, and chil- dren; over seven hundred ponies; and about eighty guns.[18] Justifying his action, Crook declared that Red Cloud and Red Leaf had been living "a considerable distance from the agency and in quite intimate communication with the hostiles."[19] But Red Cloud and Red Leaf were not the only Indians told to put on their walking shoes. The same scene had been enacted at the Standing Rock and Cheyenne River agencies in the Department of Dakota by troops under General Terry. A dispatch in the *New York Times* on October 27 said, "It is believed that the Indians [at Standing Rock] hid most of their arms, as they had a day's warning, and only about two hundred stand have been found, including shotguns and revolvers. About six hundred ponies were surrendered, and a large number are yet to be brought in." The Indians were told that the ponies would be sold at auction and the money used to purchase cattle.[20]

Spotted Tail's followers were spared the same fate as Red Cloud's and Red Leaf's because of "Old Spot's" "unswerving loyalty" to the government.[21] Adding insult to injury for Red Cloud, Crook played Sioux politics and declared Spotted Tail head chief of all the Sioux at both Red Cloud and Spotted Tail agencies. In a dispatch to Sheridan on the twenty-third, Crook explained:

I had a satisfactory council with Spotted Tail, and am satisfied that he is the only important leader who has had the nerve to be our friend, and have therefore put him in charge as head chief of all. The line of the hostile and the peaceably dis-

Three Cheers For Crook

Cheyenne Daily Leader,
October 26, 1876

How The People Rejoiced Over The Good News From Red Cloud Agency.

Custer City, Oct. 25, 1876— Immediately on the reception of the news, last night, that General Crook had surrounded the Agency Indians, disarmed them and taken their ponies, etc., Judge Harlow called the citizens together by means of a large bonfire and the ringing of a bell through the streets, when the telegraph operator, Mr. James Halley, appeared, and by the light of the fire read the intensely interesting information to the expectant crowd. Three cheers were given for the telegraph, when Major T. M. Newson was called for, and was picked up bodily and placed upon a barrel. He spoke in congratulatory terms and praised Crook and the government for the action taken, when three rousing cheers were given for General Crook.

Brief speeches were made by others, when Mr. Halley, at the urgent request of the people, again read the news, and three tremendous cheers were given for him, which the mineral hills echoed and re-echoed for miles around. Everybody was happy; scalps were at a discount, and there is now a feeling of security never before felt in the Hills, as it has always been thought that it was more the roving bands of Agency Indians who have committed the numerous acts of violence against the whites than those belonging to the army of Sitting Bull. After the meeting in the street had adjourned, a very happy crowd congregated at the Custer House, where songs and dances crowned the closing hours of the day.

posed is now plainly drawn, and we shall have our enemies only in the front in future.[22]

Three days later, Crook explained the state of affairs at the above-named agencies to a reporter:

We have only taken away the ponies and guns from those who we believe to have been in sympathy with the hostiles, and it was all done without firing a shot. We believed at one time the Indians would prove troublesome, but we surrounded them at night while we thought they were about joining the hostiles, and we made prisoners of upward of eighty [men] of Red Cloud's and Red Leaf's bands. . . . We have made Spotted Tail chief of the Sioux nation. We think he is a good Indian if there is one, and, we must confide in some of them. We have taken no guns or ponies from his people. We only wanted to destroy a nucleus of supplies for the hostiles at Red Cloud Agency, and I think we have done so in taking away their arms and ponies from Red Cloud's and Red Leaf's bands. . . . We locked them up for a day and turned them out again last evening. They are now comparatively helpless, and without ponies cannot well get away to join their friends in arms.[23]

And what did Red Cloud think of being deposed? A few weeks later, after taking a few whiffs from a pipe, he told a reporter from the *Omaha Daily Bee*:

The Ogalallas still look to me as their chief, and the most of them know nothing of any change. My people would not obey a Brule chief, and will never look up to Spotted Tail as the head chief of this tribe. I lost fifty ponies myself, and my family fifty more, and the soldiers took all our arms. They even took an old knife from my squaw, and a small knife and some matches from my little boy. We had nothing but our fingers left to eat with. We took things coolly and let them go on, although we knew that we had done nothing. Sitting Bull ought to be punished, and not us. We do not want to be in a fight all the time, and would like to be peaceable, but they can fight him all they wish. The Great Spirit knows that my words are truth. We were told to move to within five miles of the agency, and said we would do so, but the weather was stormy so we could not. Next day [October 23] we were surrounded and captured by the troops. I am glad to have these things known; I have spoken enough.[24]

Surprisingly, Red Cloud had his defenders, as seen by this statement from the *Omaha Herald* in late October 1876:

The progress of wickedness towards these red men is both steady and merciless. It exemplifies the spirit of lawless power over a helpless and defenseless race and people, who have been robbed of everything but their courage and manhood in the course of the unceasing history of black wrongs and still blacker perfidy with which these Indians have been treated since our memory and knowledge runneth not to the contrary. The glory and shame of the treatment and capture of Red Cloud and his men, after driving him and them to despair of all hope of justice at the hands of bayo-

nets and power, belongs to those who revel in it. For our part, we think it the culmination of all the long list of wrongs and outrages that have been visited upon the Indians in the last ten years.[25]

One day after the action at Chadron Creek, Merritt and the Fifth Cavalry rode into Red Cloud Agency (recall they had been camped near Custer City in the Black Hills for a few weeks), thus bringing to a close the Big Horn and Yellowstone Expedition. On the same day, General Crook had offered them the following parting words:

General Orders, No. 8: The time having arrived when the troops composing the Big Horn and Yellowstone expedition are about to separate, the Brigadier General commanding addresses himself to the officers and men of the command to say:

In the campaign now closed he has been obliged to call upon you for much hard service and many sacrifices of personal comfort. At times you have been out of reach of your base of supplies; in most inclement weather you have marched without food, and slept without shelter; in your engagements you have evinced a high order of discipline and courage; in your marches, wonderful powers of endurance, and in your deprivations and hardships, patience and fortitude. Indian warfare is of all warfare the most dangerous, the most trying, and the most thankless. Not recognized by the high authority of the United States Senate as war, it still possesses for you the disadvantages of civilized warfare, with all the horrible accompaniments that barbarians can invent and savages can execute. In it you are required to serve without the incentive to promotion or recognition, in truth, without favor or hope of reward. The people of our sparsely settled frontier in whose defense this war has been waged, have but little influence with the powerful communities in the East; their representatives have little voice in our national councils, while your savage foes are not only the wards of the nation, supported in idleness, but objects of sympathy with large numbers of people otherwise well-informed and discerning. You may, therefore, congratulate yourselves that in the performance of your military duty you have been on the side of the weak against the strong, and that the few people there are on the frontier will remember your efforts with gratitude. If in the future it should transpire that the avenues for recognition of distinguished services and gallant conduct are opened, those rendered in this campaign will be recommended for suitable reward.[26]

With the summer campaign officially over and his farewell said, the unwavering general turned his gaze north once more.

15

The Dull Knife Fight

"The severe blow given to the Cheyennes by Mackenzie will create in the minds of those savages a feeling of disgust at being hostile."—Unknown, Fort Fetterman, December 30, 1876, *New York Tribune*, January 11, 1877

"[Mackenzie's] attack on the daring Cheyennes has taught them that they may not consider themselves safe from the avenging pursuit of the white man, even in their most remote and inaccessible fastnesses."—Jerry Roche, Fort Laramie, January 4, 1877, *New York Herald*, January 14, 1877

On November 5, twelve days after formally closing out the summer campaign, General Crook was on the road from Fort Laramie to Fort Fetterman, an eighty-mile trip. He arrived on the night of November 7. This was his third time on the warpath since March, and despite some down time following the battle of the Rosebud, the previous campaign still contained more than its share of rigorous marching, harsh weather, insufficient fare, and all-around hard times. An 1873 newspaper sketch of the general had described him as being "tough as a mule" and capable of "wearing out" many of the younger men of his command.[1] Perhaps this was true; even Davenport would have had to admit that Crook was virtually indefatigable.

The forthcoming campaign to defeat Crazy Horse, who was Crook's primary target, was officially dubbed the Powder River Expedition.[2] Mackenzie (who arrived at Fort Fetterman on November 9) was in charge of the cavalry, and Lieutenant Colonel Richard Irving Dodge, Twenty-third Infantry, was in charge of the infantry. The breakdown of Crook's command was:

FOURTH CAVALRY: 6 companies, 17 officers, 485 men.
FIFTH CAVALRY: 2 companies, 6 officers, 150 men.
THIRD CAVALRY: 2 companies, 5 officers, 135 men.
SECOND CAVALRY: 1 company (K) (detailed with headquarters), 2 officers, 55 men.[3]
FOURTH ARTILLERY (acting as

infantry): 4 companies, 9 officers, 147 men.

NINTH INFANTRY: 6 companies, 11 officers, 294 men.

TWENTY-THIRD INFANTRY: 3 companies, 8 officers, 111 men.

FOURTEENTH INFANTRY: 2 companies, 5 officers, 85 men.[4]

All told, there were 11 companies of cavalry totaling 30 officers and 825 men, and 15 companies of infantry totaling 33 officers and 637 men.[5]

Crook's staff included Lieutenant John G. Bourke, Third Cavalry, adjutant; Lieutenants Walter S. Schuyler, Fifth Cavalry, and William Philo Clark, Second Cavalry, aides-de-camp; and once again Captain John V. Furey was called upon as quartermaster. The supply train was extensive, consisting of 168 wagons and 400 pack mules, carrying supplies for thirty days. There were also seven ambulances. Attending the wagons and mules were 219 drivers and 65 packers.[6] In addition to thirty days' provisions, Crook brought along "150 head of fine beef-cattle."[7]

The corps of Indian scouts was impressive, and once fully organized numbered about 350. These included Sioux, Pawnees, Arapahoes, Cheyennes, and Shoshones (ninety-one Shoshones had preceded Crook to Cantonment Reno on October 27, and were awaiting his arrival). Although Lieutenant Clark was in overall command of the Indian scouts, the Pawnees were more likely to follow the direction of Frank North because of their long-time association with him, which dated

back to 1864.[8] One of the Sioux scouts was identified as Standing Bear, "the Indian captured in the American Horse fight."[9] It seems reasonable that Standing Bear was another name for Black Bear, the Brule warrior who later created a pictographic depiction of the battle of the Little Big Horn (see the end of chapter 6) and who was captured in the American Horse/Slim Buttes fight (see chapter 12).[10]

Including the Indian scouts (but not the civilians) the expedition numbered over eighteen hundred men. An anonymous dispatch to the *New York Tribune* remarked, "With this force General Crook proposes to play the return match with Crazy Horse and other recalcitrant savages."[11] Acknowledging the great strength of the column, a letter to the *Cheyenne Daily Leader* declared:

Nothing even bearing the remotest resemblance to a disaster need be apprehended. The column is too strong to suffer a repulse from any force that the Indians can possibly bring to bear at this season. The exciting rumors of defeat and massacre, so ripe during the last campaign, will be wanting in this. . . . Nothing but the flight of all hostiles north of the Yellowstone, or their ignoble surrender, can or will prevent the Powder River expedition from being a success of magnitude, if not the crowning mercy of this infernal war.[12]

In view of Crook's experience with Davenport over the summer, one would think that the general would have banned all future *New York Herald* correspondents from reporting on his expeditions. Such was not the case, but unlike the previous campaign, the Powder River Expedition hosted only one official correspondent, Jerry Roche, and, as luck would have it, his employer was the *New York Herald*. In addition to Roche there were the usual anonymous reports sent into various newspapers, such as the *New York Times* and *New York Tribune*. Just prior to leaving Fort Laramie for Fort Fetterman, Roche commented on the measures being taken against one of their most dangerous enemies—the weather:

Extensive preparations are on foot by all going who are in a condition to provide for themselves, to guard against the rigors of a winter which is expected to be very severe, and though it is said the campaign is not intended to be prosecuted on the Powder River much longer than two months the officers generally anticipate and are preparing for a more protracted struggle with the elements if not with the hostiles. It is enough to make one shiver to see the precautions that are being taken by knowing ones to avoid being frozen and to hear their terrible stories of camp life in a region where mercury freezes and one can take his iced whiskey in solid lumps. The troops will be fairly provided with covering, but in spite of all the precautions that may be taken I am inclined to believe that there will be considerable suffering on the trip and that more than a few will be found to have succumbed to the trials of the campaign before it is ended.[13]

Concerning their human enemies, Roche remarked:

That hostile Indians can be found in numbers large enough to engage the entire command there can be little doubt, if one may accept the surmises and conclusions of some of the scouts engaged on the expedition just concluded. The impression that they are still well armed and liberally provided with ammunition prevails here pretty generally, notwithstanding the recent action at the agencies.[14]

Another area of concern was with the Indian scouts, some of whom were known to be bitter enemies:

I find that several people here, who profess to be familiar with Indian affairs, apprehend difficulty between the Pawnee and Sioux scouts. The tribes have been a long time enemies.[15]

On a less serious note, Roche described the would-be "Buffalo Bills" hanging around Fort Laramie:

There is a queer lot of fellows here who hover about the post and hang on the ragged edges of the command. These are the long-haired, unwashed "Injun slavers" whose chief delight is to be looked upon as great scouts. Some of these fellows seem to think that all they need to do in order to be universally admired is to dress in an outlandish fashion, interlay their conversation with elaborate oaths and border superlatives, and become known to fame as "Grasshopper Jim" or "Jack Rabbit Bill." A good healthy Indian would scare half a dozen such frauds to death with one vigorous yell.[16]

For the most part, he shied away from writing anything controversial; perhaps it was not his style, or perhaps it was just that nothing controversial occurred. The closest Roche came to sounding like Davenport was the following remark concerning the inept marksmanship he witnessed among some soldiers shooting at various herds of antelope:

Judging by some scenes I witnessed a few days ago [this would be about the third week of October], I should say it was not to be wondered at that some of the troops suffered for food in the midst of a game country during the summer campaign. We saw several herds of antelope on the hills at either side, and some of the cavalry soldiers set out to hunt them, but invariably missed them, shooting at a distance of 400 or 500 yards. I asked some of the packers on the mule train how they fared on the march from Goose Creek to Deadwood, when rations were so far below zero with the main column and they said, "We never ate any horse meat; we had plenty of antelope. Herds crossed the road every day, and we had several good hunters with us who killed enough for all of us."

I have been thinking, if provisions run short on our winter campaign, General Crook should send the packers out hunting for the rest of the command. I have been thinking, too, that if a soldier can't shoot one antelope out of a dozen at 500 yards an Indian won't be in much danger from his carbine at 700 or 800.[17]

Accompanying Crook on his ride to Fort Fetterman were Company K of the Second Cavalry (the "Egan Grays"), Frank North and the Pawnees, and about 150 of the enlisted scouts from the Red Cloud Agency. Roche found nothing particularly interesting about the trip, other than the outlandish appearance and bizarre sounds emanating from the Indian scouts:

Nothing of moment occurred on the march hither, and we should scarcely have known that we had with us over 200 barbarians but for their weird howling and strange chanting at night and the picturesque manner in which they shrouded themselves in bright colored blankets as they rode along behind us. They have a way of building tents, too, peculiar to themselves. Their wickiup is like a huge Chinese lantern. It is broad at the base and tapers toward the top, which is open. In the centre they build their fire, and when wood is plentiful the blaze produces a pleasing illumination.[18]

On the eighth the Sioux scouts "sought a talk with the great white chief General Crook."[19] First up was Three Bears, who was anxious that his people at the Red Cloud Agency would be properly cared for in his absence:

I am talking in behalf of all my people left behind at the agency, and I want the beeves turned over to them the same as ever. . . . When the delegation that has gone down to the Indian Territory gets back I want the Indians to wait for me and not to go to Washington until we start together. I don't want them to start before that time. As soon as we get through with the business out here we can work together, and that's the reason I want them to wait for me. I want to ask [for] something now and then, and I want him (pointing to General Crook) to agree to it. When we travel together we should work together as one. A great many of our men back at the agency have guns. I wanted a note sent to both stores at the agency to have them sell ammunition for a couple of days, because the hostile Indians will come down from the north and raise trouble with our people while we are away. I want you to write right away, because if my young people don't cry for bread while I'm away I'll like you all the better when I come back. I have no one back there to do my business or talk for me now, and I don't know what they will do while I'm gone. We want some of the horses the Pawnees are driving along, so that we can do our work better. [Crook assented, after which Three Bears continued:] I want you to put that down on paper [that we got half the horses back]. If a man wants to get on in the world he must keep his ears straight and he won't get in trouble. We are going to listen to you after this and do all you tell us. If we get any money for our country (meaning the Black Hills), we don't want it taken away from us. We want it kept for us. I want the Great Father to hear me when I ask for wagons and sheep. I want them myself. I don't want the agent to take them for me. I am glad for those things you gave me today (meaning his uniform). We want shoes for our women and children when we draw annuity goods.[20]

Fast Thunder also expressed concern for those left behind on the reservation, and, like Three Bears, did not want any delegation to leave for Washington (to discuss where they would live) before he returned from the current campaign:

All the bucks you see here are from Red Cloud[,] and from Spotted Tail, there are seven of us. I want a letter sent there, too. I want my words to go to Spotted Tail Agency. A great many Indians went south with that delegation to the Indian Territory. We want the delegation to wait for us when they come back [before they go to Washington]. The Great Father sent us out here to do this business and told me to do it or die. I am going to do it. When we come back we want to pick out an agency, and when the other Indians come back we want to work together and tell the Great Father what we want. I have a band at my agency, and while I am away there is no one to look out for them. When you send a letter down I want you to tell the Great Father to treat my band right and give them their rations right. I want you to give the Spotted Tail Indians permission to trade for ammunition for one day. The Northern Indians will come down and make trouble for them when we are away. Some of these young men [with me] have no horses. We want you, when you divide the horses, to get us fast horses, so we can do whatever you tell us to do and catch whatever you send us after.[21]

Sharp Nose, a prominent warrior among the Arapahoes, spoke next:

These are all Arapahoes you see here now, and they are all your friends. They have been your friends a long time. They are getting like the white people, and want to fight for them. This place here was our country. The government never gave us any money for this post [Fort Fetterman], and we don't want any. We are going with you to fight the Northern Indians. When you came to the agency and asked us to help you to fight those Indians we said, 'Yes, we'll go with you.' When you asked the Sioux if they would go they wanted to talk over the matter. But we did not stop to talk over the matter. We said we'd go. The Sioux said they'd like to wait until springtime, when the grass is green, because the winters are very cold here. We did not want to talk. We said, 'Yes, we'll go,' and here we are. We want good arms, good horses and plenty of ammunition. We want to scout in our own way, but your men can go along the road. We will send five men one way and five another, and if they see game they will kill it, for they like fresh meat. If they see Indians they'll tell you where they are. We have been your friends a long time, and we want to travel the same road with you. While we are gone we want you to look after our families at the agency and see that our children don't suffer for want of food.[22]

To all these statements, Crook responded exactly as expected. He assured the scouts that their families would be taken care of and reinforced that all of the Indians needed to learn new ways in order to survive:

The General promised the Indians their families should not suffer during their absence and then gave them some advice. He told them about the white man's laws and how bad men are punished, and not permitted to go off to the hills like the hostiles when they have stolen cattle or killed men. He told them the white men did not wish to do them any harm but were coming to live in their country. The buffalo, they must have noticed, were all disappearing, and they must turn their attention to some other way of living. They should learn to keep cattle, till farms and live in houses like white people. The Indians seemed pleased with the talk and left seemingly satisfied.[23]

Roche had noted in his dispatch of November 3 that difficulty was apprehended between the Sioux and Pawnees, but by the time of his November 14 dispatch, the situation had reversed:

No apprehensions are now felt of disturbances between our Sioux and Pawnee soldiers. They have had a talk and a smoke among themselves and have stopped calling each other taunting names, as was their habit for a little time after our departure from Fort Laramie.[24]

Reminiscent of Davenport's description of the Shoshones back in June, Roche found the Pawnees to be well organized and soldierly, at the same time observing the awkwardness of the Sioux and Arapahoes in their new uniforms:

The Pawnees are a very orderly, well drilled and disciplined lot of soldiers, many of whom can speak and write some English. Thus far the Sioux and Arapahoes have been difficult to handle, but they are gradually being instructed and will soon present a tolerably good appearance. It was amazing to see their awkwardness when they first put on their clothes. They looked like those peculiar angular pictures of mailed knights of a few centuries ago, with their upper limbs very much in the way and their boots so unmanageable that at each step they cast their feet high in the air and grinned at the novelty experienced.[25]

Acknowledging that the temporary layover at Fort Fetterman was not too exciting, Roche turned to that old familiar standby, the weather:

Since our arrival here we have been busy procuring our supplies, furnishing and outfitting for the trip, and beyond the routine necessary for such preparation but little has transpired of any interest. . . . [On Saturday evening, the eleventh,] it commenced snowing and continued until Sunday afternoon. Then it cleared up cold, and continued to grow colder until midnight, when the thermometer recorded 17 degrees below zero. The cold snap came on so suddenly that we were unprepared for so severe an attack, and consequently there was little sleep in some of our tents that night. . . . The smoke of our camp fires mounts up from a white waste for three or four miles along the riverside.[26]

On the thirteenth, some of the scouts held another conference with Crook. Roche was on hand to capture the proceedings. "Most of the 'talks' were short and of no great account," he reported, "but Fast Thunder asked to have his talk taken down in writing and sent on to the Great Father."27

Last spring a year ago I was in Washington. When I was there the Great Father told me if there were any white men's horses stolen that I should go and get them and return them. When the Great Father told me that I knew it was right, because that is what the white men have to work with; and I did help to give some back that were stolen. Those Indians that stay at the [Red Cloud] agency now have never done any harm to the white people, and I think it very wrong to take away their horses. I wish you would tell the Great Father not to take away any more of the horses from these Indians. The reason I am going out to fight the Northern Indians is that the country up there was given to us by the Great Father, and I want to get it back. The Great Father and the Indians at the agency work together, and the young men are going to help you. You know who to pick out. You have good sense and good eyes, and you have selected men who will help you when you get out there. I want you to tell the Great Father to give us back the country where we were living at the agencies. The young men want this. We are your friends now, and we don't want you to take our horses away any more. We are going to stick by you. We don't know how to work yet. We want to have our horses so that we can sell them and buy cows, &c.

Now, you say you do not want us to fight but to find the northern villages and Indians, but they do not know this, and they will make hard work for us. We want to know if we capture the horses at the village if we can keep all we capture. We are going out to capture the Northern Indians. We want to take them to our agency and have them work for us. They won't have any horses and they won't have any guns; and they will learn after a while that we will do what is right with them. Everything you say is good, and whatever you have told us has been right, and you have all along done what you said you would do.

When we were north a good many of our women married the Northern Indians, and when we capture these Indians we will find a good many of our relations there; that is the reason we want to take them to our agency. This is all for me.28

Based on part of Fast Thunder's speech, it is clear that the Sioux were under the impression that if they helped Crook defeat the nonreservation Indians, he would return the favor and represent them in their quest to remain at their current agencies in the White River country of northwestern Nebraska. The problem, as they well knew, was that this region lay south of the actual Great Sioux Reservation. In his response, Crook explained why Red Cloud and Red Leaf had been treated so harshly a few weeks previous and stated that he did not know if the president would allow them to remain living where they were (of course, telling them that their case was virtually hopeless would not have been too beneficial to their willingness to track down Crazy Horse):

I have heard what . . . [you have] said. [S]ome time ago Red Cloud and Red Leaf were the head men at the agency and our people were feeding them at the time. They made a treaty and promised they would not steal stock from the white men. These men have been well treated and have been taken to Washington, and though they pretended to be the friends of the white men they were all the time acting in bad faith, stealing stock and killing white men. . . . [U]nder our government every man contributes to the support of the Indians on the reservations, and . . . the very men they killed were giving their share to feed them. . . . [T]he trails of the depredating Indians led to the Red Cloud Agency, and . . . we had only [the word of the Sioux] that they did not do the mischief. At last the government got angry and would not stand it any longer. During the past summer a great many Indians went north and joined the hostiles and killed our soldiers. The Red Cloud Indians were also supplying them with food and ammunition, and the reason those Indians recently captured at Red Cloud were captured was because the government wanted to keep them where it could see who were good and who were not. If the Indians behave themselves hereafter the government will protect them and will not take their ponies away. [I do] not know what the Great Father [will] do about letting [the Sioux] live where they are now on the agency. [I want] to bring the Northern Indians down to the agency, and that [is] the reason [I want the scouts] to go with [me]. When the white man does wrong his own people punish him, and [I want the Sioux] to punish such of their people as did not do right. Those Indians who have been East saw how well the white man lives, and [I want] those present to tell the rest of their people that the white man [wants] the Indians to live the same way.[29]

Three Bears, having been appointed a first sergeant in the scout corps, told Crook that when the time came, the scouts would "do what was right," and wanted to know if the enlisted Indians would be allowed to keep the horses they captured in the event of a fight. Crook consented, but wisely added that the scouts should not "rush in and alarm a village before it was surrounded, merely to capture ponies."[30]

On November 14, the command pulled out of Fort Fetterman and headed north for Cantonment Reno, a distance of about eighty-five miles. Prior to leaving, Roche took a few minutes to jot down some news items, including a rumor that Sitting Bull had surrendered:

Today we start for old Fort Reno, on our way in search of Crazy Horse's band. . . . News of the reported surrender of 400 lodges of Sitting Bull's Indians having come to us from the East some hopeful spirits among us predict in consequence a surrender of Crazy Horse's people and a probable early termination of our trip. I fancy that in most instances of this sort the wish is father to the thought, however, and from what I can learn our Indian auxiliaries are not very hopeful of so peaceful a settlement of our differences with the remaining northern hostiles under Crazy Horse and Sitting Bull.[31]

During the march to the cantonment, the column advanced "without much regard to order," Roche observed, "comfort and convenience taking precedence over discipline and appearance." Continuing, Roche noted:

Shoulder straps are at a discount here, and buckskins, buffalo hide and blanket shirts take the place of the natty uniforms seen East. The soldiers are pretty well supplied with warm clothing, and they will need all they have before their labors cease.[32]

Cantonment Reno, under command of Captain Edwin Pollock, Ninth Infantry, came into view on the morning of the eighteenth. It was established in October 1876 on the west bank of the Powder River, and its function was that of a supply base deep in Indian country.[33] One observer with the command referred to it as "the last evidence of civilization" in that neck of the woods.[34] The ruins of old Fort Reno, abandoned eight years earlier as part of the treaty of 1868, were about three miles north. Upon arriving, Crook sent out eight Sioux and six Arapahoes "to take a scout in the neighborhood of Crazy Woman's Creek [a tributary of Powder River] with four days' provisions, his intention being to move in time to meet them on their return."[35] Roche wrote:

[During the scouts'] absence two parties of miners moving outward from the Black Hills to prospect in neighboring hills arrived in our camp, and had a talk with General Crook about the Indian trails they had found in their wanderings. From this interview the General concluded that Crazy Horse's camp must be located somewhere on the Rosebud. He then determined, instead of moving at once toward Crazy Woman's Fork, to await the return of the scouts.[36]

When the fourteen scouts returned to the Powder River cantonment three days later, they had in tow an unexpected guest they had captured near Crazy Woman's Creek. An anonymous account in the *New York Times* reported:

On the evening of November 21 the scouting party returned, bringing a captive, a young Cheyenne brave who had unsuspectingly walked into their camp one night, supposing them his friends, and, as the interpreter inelegantly expressed it, "[he] was ketched before he knowed it." It seems that he had been traveling with a small party of Cheyennes, who were returning from a visit to Crazy Horse. They camped near old Fort [Phil] Kearny one night, and in the morning when about to move on, our prisoner, finding his horse missing, had gone out some distance in search of it. After securing his animal he returned to his camp only to find his comrades gone, he could not tell whither. Striking out alone, he took the direction of the village of his tribe in the Big Horn Mountains. At night he fell in with five lodges of Sioux, who were engaged in collecting meat for the winter. He remained with them one night and started in the morning to carry out his original idea. His horse gave out during the day, and after trudging some distance on foot, he arrived after dark in sight of what appeared to him the welcoming campfires of Indians on Clear Creek. He hesitated at first, dreading he knew not what, but finally walked boldly down to the fire and sat down. He found a mixed party of Sioux and Arapahoes. Upon asking them whom they were and where they were going, he was told that they were a war party from the agency going on a raid against the Shoshone. This according well with his ideas of propriety, he cheerfully told them all the news, including the present residence of Crazy Horse, and the whereabouts of the Cheyenne village. After gleaning all possible information, his entertainers, with grim humor leading him on to commit himself, finally offered him some food in the shape of hard tack and bacon. He then saw that he was betrayed, and his eyes filled with water. The Arapahoes now threw off their reserve, and, presenting their pistols, demanded the surrender of his gun, which was turned over without hesitation.[37]

Here is Roche's version of the incident:

In going out [from the cantonment on the eighteenth] our Indian scouts had left their soldier clothes behind them, and the captive wandered into their camp. Believing himself among friends, he told them that there were some Cheyenne lodges in a ravine on the south side of the mountain, near Crazy Woman's Creek, but that the main body of the tribe had crossed the mountains. After obtaining all the information the Cheyenne possessed they covered him with their pistols, held under their blankets and said—"We are white soldiers now and we want your gun; if you don't give it up you know what will happen." The surprised hostile submitted and was brought to Fort Reno [Cantonment Reno].[38]

The captured Cheyenne was named Many Beaver Dams.[39] Although Lieutenant Bourke referred to him as a "boy," the fact that he was out on his own, and was carrying a gun, indicates he was probably in his early teens.[40] After Crook questioned him further, it was determined that the column should strike out immediately after Crazy Horse, who was said to be camped on the Rosebud, near where the battle had taken place in June.[41] Roche again:

In pursuance of this determination we struck camp at Fort Reno [Cantonment Reno] at daybreak on Wednesday [November 22], and arrived at the Crazy Woman Creek late in the afternoon.[42] Immediately orders were promulgated to prepare for a ten days' march toward the Rosebud, with the pack train only, our wagons to be left where they were until our return. We got everything ready that night for an early start, determined to take with us only such clothing as we could wear, no tents, and a small allowance of bedding, two blankets each—rather cool covering for such nights as we have had of late, but still all that could be permitted with the transportation at hand. The camp was astir far into the night preparing for the morrow's march, but by sunrise on Thursday [November 23] all was changed.[43]

That morning a Cheyenne messenger named Sitting Bear approached Crook's camp waving a flag of truce. About two and a half weeks earlier, Mackenzie had sent him on a mission from Red Cloud Agency to warn the reservation holdouts "that they must come in and give up their arms and ponies, or the soldiers would pursue them and compel them to do so."[44]

(Roche:) Sitting Bear had left Crazy Horse's village several days before, and was slowly drifting back toward the agency. The day before his arrival in our camp he ascertained that the five Cheyenne lodges which our captive had spoken of had discovered our approach and set off toward Crazy Horse's camp. They would give him the alarm and doubtless set him also moving.[45]

With Crazy Horse likely warned of his approach, Crook altered his plans: first he would strike the Cheyennes, then he would track down the elusive Crazy Horse. Accordingly, a strike force under Mackenzie was quickly organized consisting of 10 companies of cavalry, about 750 men, plus the Indian scouts. Crook with the infantry, one company of cavalry, and the wagon train would remain behind.[46] Additionally, he sent out fourteen Pawnee and Shoshone scouts "with instructions to cross the mountains at the first pass they came to and search for trails or signs of Indians beyond." If they "discovered any evidence of the presence of the Indians they were to recross the mountain and meet us on the south side, along which we were to travel."[47]

The column was then on Crazy Woman's Fork of the Powder River. To the north about thirty-five miles lay the mouth of the stream, which empties into the Powder, the water then swirling its way into the Yellowstone, the Missouri, and the Mississippi. But Mackenzie's direction lay south, toward the head of the stream—toward the Cheyenne village and the end of their resistance in the Yellowstone country.

The march on the twenty-third was no more than twelve miles, after which camp was made "in mud" on a fork of Crazy Woman's Creek. That evening seven Sioux and Arapahoe scouts were sent out to search for the unsuspecting village with instructions to return the following night.[48] Sunrise Friday morning found the command in the saddle once more, the Indian scouts in the advance, the column marching southwest toward a break in the Big Horn Mountains known as Sioux Pass or Crazy Woman Pass.[49]

About 1 p.m., the head of the column halted in a "grassy vale" to allow the troops time to close up. Just as the pack train was pulling into camp, several of the scouts, who were posted on the nearby hills, brought attention to themselves by circling around on their horses "in a wild, excited sort of way."[50] Roche recounted:

A moment afterward a shrill Indian yawp went up from the farthest Indian on the hill in front. This was echoed by two or three of our Indians farther down toward us and then re-echoed a hundred times by our wild irregulars scattered through the valley.

Not knowing the cause of the alarm, the troops began to deploy for battle, rushing about anxiously and "throwing out skirmishers all along the hillside." Roche was particularly impressed with one company that had resaddled, mounted, and advanced toward the hills in less than three minutes from the time of the first alarm. There was just one thing missing to make the scene perfect— the enemy:

The hostiles were not approaching to attack us, as was apprehended, and the savage yell we heard merely indicated that some of the scouts we had sent out the night before were coming in, having discovered the location of the hostile village. They had communicated their discovery by signals from a distant hill to our outposts, and the howl we had heard was but a shout of triumph.[51]

Mackenzie soon learned from the scouts what he already knew, that the camp was some distance off:

Four of these soon came galloping in with the welcome intelligence that they had seen the herds and smoke of the hostiles in a cañon near Powder River and at a comparatively short distance, though as an Indian has no idea of miles, and can not make his expressions of distance very intelligible to a white man, except by comparison with some distance already marched, we could not make out whether the hostiles were 10 miles or 25 miles away.[52]

To which Lieutenant Bourke added: "'Heap ponies' is an expression too indefinite to serve as a basis for any strategic conclusions to be founded upon."[53] But even without specifics, Mackenzie knew the village had to be close by, within a day's march at maximum. He ordered the troops to prepare for a night march. If all went well, they would attack at dawn.

(Roche:) From this time forward extreme caution was observed, so as to guard as much as possible against alarming the village. Our pickets were sent out dismounted while we rested here, and no fires were permitted lest the smoke should betray our presence. After a cheerless meal of hardtack and cold bacon, and about three hours' rest, we started on our night march about four o'clock in the afternoon.[54]

(Anonymous:) From this time everybody's nerves were strung to the highest tension, all sanguine that our expedition would be a success, yet fearful of some accident which might frustrate our plans. To such an extent did this nervousness obtain that, when a picket, who

Colonel Ranald Mackenzie. (*National Archives*)

had seen one of our own Indians leading a pony up a hill to our rear, came galloping into camp in an excited manner and reported hostiles in sight, the whole force commenced preparations to repel an attack, several companies being deployed in front of the horses to protect the herds. The Indians mounted their war ponies and went scurrying over the hills in wild confusion, until the commander, whose experience in such matters was extensive, allayed the excitement by calmly investigating the cause.[55]

Upon exiting the valley they "entered a wildly picturesque pass in the mountains," and as they ascended the hills there was one in particular that offered an impressive view of the entire column. Roche described the scene:

The head of the column . . . wound about the base of a steep conical hill, then moved about an eighth of a mile through a deep red sandstone cut, then clambered up the side of another hill which commanded a full view of the entire command as it stretched out in double file behind. "What a splendid picture!" exclaimed all who saw the advancing column from this point. And so it was a pretty sight for the moment, but its form was changed and its beauty vanished as we passed the crest of the second hill.[56]

The landscape soon leveled off, and Sharp Nose, the Arapaho scout, "called attention to two black specks away to the left."[57]

(Roche:) Before any white man present could do more than barely discover their existence he told us they were the two Sioux scouts who had remained behind to learn something more about the village.[58] . . . In about twenty minutes they joined us and just as they reached us the pony ridden by Jackass, one of the Sioux scouts who was a little in advance of the other [whose name was Red Shirt], stumbled and fell over, completely exhausted. Jackass himself, who, by the way, is a brave, bright-eyed, handsome young Indian, was about as tired and hungry as the pony, and could not tell us what he had seen until after he had eaten a few mouthfuls of hard bread and bacon. Then, with flashing eyes and in eager haste, he said he had seen some of the ponies and counted eleven of the lodges from a hill overlooking the village. He said we could reach the village at midnight by marching onward steadily.[59]

The anonymous *New York Times* correspondent offered additional details in his November 30 dispatch:

These men reported that they had watched the village all day, observing many ponies, and getting in sight of eleven lodges, though they could not tell how many more there might be, the remainder being hidden by bluffs. They had taken copious mental notes of the country, and could guide us on, though they said that we should have to make a considerable detour and approach the village from the side opposite to us, there being a high mountain between us and it.[60]

Roche afterward recalled the difficulties of that night's march:

We continued our march along into the night, over jagged hills, through deep ravines, across rapid mountain streams miry and deep, but the sky was clear and cloudless and the moon rose to light up our narrow and difficult pathway. Before entering the roughest country on our road to the camp we passed through a beautiful valley about half a mile wide and over three miles long, level as a race course all the way. When we emerged from this we were obliged to move very slowly, and the cavalrymen had to dismount at least twenty times during the night and lead their horses in single file, passing through ravines with which the country lying between us and the mouth of the canyon where the camp stood was cut up and crossed in all directions. If we could have gone in a direct line from the point where we halted in the afternoon to the [Cheyenne] camp the distance would not have been over ten miles, but along the route we were obliged to move we must have marched over twenty miles, a march more difficult and exhausting than one covering three times the distance would have been in a tolerably level country. . . . Shortly after midnight [November 25] the moon set and left us to grope our way in comparative darkness through a part of our road where it was almost impossible to find or follow a trail. . . . Patiently and persistently we pressed along in this way until just before the dawn of day, when we approached the mouth of the canyon. At this time we knew the village was not far off.[61]

Lieutenant Clark then sent out several scouts to reconnoiter while the officers attempted to close up the column, which had become "strung out" due to the rough terrain. Additionally, the large contingent of Indian scouts was hurried forward in preparation of a "sweep through the village." Arrangements for the attack were still in progress when one of the advance scouts returned with essential news: the village was located on two sides of the Red Fork of Powder River; two, maybe three, pony herds had been located; and the Cheyennes "were having war dances in four places in the village." In other words, this was a sizable village. Concerning the concurrent war dances, the Cheyennes were, in fact, celebrating a recent victory over a Shoshone hunting party.[62] It may have been the very attack reported in the *Cheyenne Daily Leader* on November 30 (see sidebar, "Intertribal Warfare").

As observed by Roche, this latest report delivered by the Indian scout created no little stir among the rest of the scout contingent:

The Indian scouts were busy now casting off superfluous clothing and relieving their horses of every additional weight that threatened to check their speed or impair their usefulness in the field. This done they crowded forward all eager to have the foremost place, more like race horses coming to the score than warriors entering the field of battle.[63]

Intertribal Warfare

Cheyenne Daily Leader,
November 30, 1876

The Shoshones were making their usual fall hunt after buffalo, north of Owl Creek. The village was divided into several hunting bands, and one of these, numbering about fifty lodges, was attacked on the 30th of October, about thirty-five miles east of the mouth of Owl Creek, Washakie being at the latter place with the main village. The Cheyennes and Arapahoes began the attack early in the morning and the battle lasted all day. The Shoshones had their women and children to take care of and were outnumbered four or five to one. The Shoshones had the advantage of position; they had one man, three women, and two children killed, and three men wounded. Most of their horses were shot, and a fire occurred during the fight by which they lost nearly all of their property. The loss on the other side, as far as known, was nine killed and as many wounded. The Shoshones escaped during the night and reached Washakie the second day, with their dead and wounded, without food or clothing, horses or tepees. The Indian scouts report the hostile village still on the western slope of the Big Horn Mountains, and numbering from two to three hundred lodges.

With the impending battle fast approaching, Roche seems to have been unaffected, even moving out in front of the scouts to hear better the sounds emanating from the distant village: "While we rested a moment to make ready for the dash I dismounted, tightened my saddle girths, and, moving a little in advance of the Indians, I distinctly heard the drum and the war song of the hostiles."[64]

The sun was rising quicker than Mackenzie would have liked, but there was no turning back now. The *New York Times* correspondent vividly portrayed the circumstances and the anxiousness of the scouts:

The morning star was above the horizon, and it lacked but little of daylight, while we had still two miles to go. The order was given to move on, when it was discovered that the advance of the cavalry was obstructed by a deep fissure in the ground, the frozen sides of which had been worn so smooth by the unshod hoofs of the Indian ponies that they were as slippery as glass. This circumstance caused much delay, and the Indians, waiting a little distance in front, waxed impatient, their uneasiness increasing as the morning star rose higher and higher, and still the troops did not come on. They knew better than we that should we fail to reach our destination before daylight we should meet with a disagreeably warm reception. As the delay was prolonged these allies became more and more excited, as with flashing eyes and eloquent gestures they tried to convey to those in charge of them the reasons for their haste.[65]

When most of the cavalry had crossed the "last deep cut near the mouth of the canyon" (the "deep fissure" mentioned above), Mackenzie organized his troops. Major Gordon's battalion was placed at the head, and Captain Mauck's battalion was placed in reserve.[66] Sharp Nose

"rushed up to Colonel Mackenzie just before the order to charge was given, and, with flashing eyes and the impulsive gestures of a heroic leader, urged him to make haste."[67] Lieutenant Joseph Dorst, Fourth Cavalry, Mackenzie's adjutant, "was sent forward to Lieutenant Clark to tell him to let loose the Indians."[68] Bourke was likewise sent back to Major Gordon with the same order—charge! The village lay in a canyon to the west; the cavalry and scouts would be coming from the east.

The correspondent for the *New York Times* described the opening dash of the scouts and the bracing sounds of battle:

The Indians unslung their carbines and advanced at the head of the column in a compact mass, the ponies partaking of the excitement of the riders, prancing and curveting, eager to be let loose. We passed down through a narrow defile guarded on either side by overhanging rocks, crossed the small stream that flowed through it, and debouched into a basin which opened out before us. The scouts pointed to a sharp bluff about a half mile ahead, behind which was the village. The Arapahoes and Sioux, led by Lieutenants Clark and [Hayden] Delaney [Ninth Infantry], rode ahead, close behind them the Pawnees, then the cavalry. The Shoshones, under Lieutenant Schuyler, had been deflected to the left to occupy the heights which overlooked the field on the south. Gradually the pace was quickened, the Indians chafing under their detention like hounds on the leash. Suddenly a shot was heard in front, the Arapahoes bounded forward to secure the herds, the Shoshones let their horses out along the steep side-hill, and with demoniacal yells, shouting of war songs, and the dismal screech of war-whistles and tremolos, charged the height. Another shot from the village, a chorus of war-whoops and yells, a volley from the Shoshones, and the ball had opened.[69]

Roche was riding boldly with the advance, the screeching sound of a Pawnee's whistle indelibly etched in his memory:

We were now, though unaware of the fact, just about three-quarters of a mile from the nearest tepee, and we galloped forward with all the speed possible, wholly unacquainted with the ground we were entering, and not knowing what sort of a reception we should get. The Indian scouts swarmed about the field in front and on either flank of Colonel Mackenzie and staff, Lieutenants Clark and DeLany leading the Sioux and Arapahoes, Major North [leading] the Pawnees, and Lieutenant W. S. Schuyler [and Cosgrove] . . . at the head of the Shoshones. Our only music was furnished by a Pawnee Indian who blew on a pipe a wild humming tune that rose above all other sounds and smote the ear with strange effect. It reminded me forcibly of the prolonged shriek of a steam whistle. Added to this were the shouts of our foremost line of scouts as they dashed forward to run off the herds of ponies. Then there were a few flashes here and there in the dusk of morning, a few sharp rifle and carbine cracks, and, rising above all other sounds, the thunder of our advancing column resounded from the side of the canyon.[70]

"Sudden as was the attack," Roche remarked, the Cheyennes dashed into ravines and crept behind "convenient bluffs, rocks and bushes, where they fortified themselves to await until the soldiers rushed in. Day had not broken sufficiently to fully discover their movements to us, but the bulk of our advancing column gave them an excellent chance to fire at us with telling effect."[71]

Newspaper narratives of the Dull Knife Fight, as it came to be called, are rather scarce. Two of the best have been quoted from throughout this chapter: an anonymous (and largely unused) account from the *New York Times*, December 24, 1876, and Jerry Roche's account from the *New York Herald*, December 11, 1876. The battle segments of these two articles are reprinted below.

New York Times, Sunday, December 24, 1876

THE FIGHT WITH THE CHEYENNES.

A WARMLY CONTESTED AFFAIR—HAND-TO-HAND CONFLICTS—SOME CLOSE SHOOTING—THE INDIAN ALLIES—MARCHING TO THE ATTACK—THE CASUALTIES.

Powder River Expedition, Camp on Crazy Woman's Fork, Nov. 30, 1876. The village was situated on the southern side of a basin formed by the receding of the side walls of a cañon. The bottom of this amphitheatre was a plain of small extent, surrounded on all sides by almost impassable mountains, and cut up by numerous dry ravines, with steep cut banks, which not only greatly impeded the movements of our cavalry, but afforded good cover for the enemy. Overlooking the village on the south were some steep bluffs of considerable height, which the Shoshones fortunately occupied in time. From the upper end of the village a deep ravine led up to the mountain.

The alarm having been given, the hostiles commenced running into the last named gulch to gain a herd of ponies grazing near its head. A company of the Fourth Cavalry, commanded by Lieutenant John A. McKinney, was ordered to charge for this herd and capture it if possible. Ignorant of the nature of the ground in his front, the brave McKinney dashed ahead only to be met at the ravine by a withering fire poured in at close range by a number of Indians who awaited under cover of the bank the charge of the cavalry. Lieutenant McKinney, realizing that he could not pass this obstacle, wheeled his company by fours to the right, and continued up the bank of the ravine to fulfill the original order. He had not advanced many yards before the Indians delivered another volley, and McKinney fell, pierced by six bullets. Many men in the column were wounded, and the company, finding itself ambushed and bereft of its commander, retired in some disorder behind a small conical hill on its right. The Colonel, seeing this, instantly ordered Captain Hamilton's company to charge in support of the first. Captain Davis' company was also ordered to the right of the hill. The men of those companies having been dismounted advanced on foot and a sharp skirmish ensued with the Indians, who now, in considerable numbers, held the head of the ravine. Immediately after this Captain Taylor's company, Fifth Cavalry, was ordered to charge the village. In the execution of this movement Captain Taylor had four horses killed under his men, and one man killed and scalped by Indians lurking in the brush, which was very thick along the stream. This was the only man scalped during the whole

affair, and the perpetrator of the act was killed before he could carry off his trophy.

The Indians had now gotten into the rocks at the foot of the mountain, and numbers of them occupied all the small ravines opening into the main creek. They succeeded in getting their families into a bend of the creek about a mile above the village, and protected by a high bluff which they quickly fortified. The nature of the ground was such— resembling the lava beds of California— that this position could not be turned, though a vigorous attempt was made by Colonel Mackenzie to accomplish it.

The fight now resolved itself into sharpshooter practice, and continued without cessation until dark, when the enemy withdrew under the friendly cover of the night.

How severe this fire was may be seen from the fact that many of those killed and wounded on both sides were hit at over 600 yards range. There were, however, several instances of personal contests that were almost hand-to-hand. In one case, two soldiers became engaged with two Indians so closely that the men of each party seized the muzzles of the guns of the other. After struggling for some seconds, one soldier—a Corporal [Patrick F. Ryan, Fourth Cavalry][72]— was killed, his slayer being shot by the other soldier. The second Indian escaped unharmed. In one place, where a party of Indians had ensconced themselves in a cave, the assailants were so near them that the dead were powder-burned.

Captain Davis worked for a long time to dislodge a small party of Indians who had taken refuge in some rough cañons at the foot of the mountains, and at last succeeded by a ruse. He retired his men rapidly from the ridge on which they were posted, and put them in a small ravine to his former rear. The

Cheyennes, forgetting the nature of the country, thought the soldiers retreating and rushed after them with shouts of triumph, but quickly changed their tune, when, as they attained the crest of the hill, eight of their number fell dead.

This affair afforded a greater than usual number of opportunities for the exhibition of personal bravery, and many such occurred among both officers and men. There was one Indian who did great execution with a Sharps rifle, the report of which made the hills re-echo like a small field piece. Many attempts were made to get this man but it was only accomplished after the sun went down, and he had incautiously exposed himself more than usual.

Lieutenant Allison, Second Cavalry, in the afternoon found himself on a rocky hill under a severe fire. He bravely held his post after the two men on his right and left had been hit—the one killed and the other wounded.

While the fight was going on Colonel Mackenzie kept moving from point to point, directing affairs, and accompanied by his staff, composed of Lieutenants Lawton, Dorst and Bourke, the latter an aide of General Crook, and a volunteer. In crossing the centre of the field, which was without cover, these gentlemen were constantly exposed to a galling fire. In the evening the horses had to be sent across this space to water, and many of them fell victims to the accurate aim of the enemy. During the day the Indian scouts plundered and burned a portion of the village, which was found to consist of 173 lodges, and to be very well supplied with even the luxuries of life. Immense quantities of meat were destroyed and buffalo robes and blankets without number. Among the various articles picked up was the scalp of a white girl apparently about 15 years of age, and with golden hair. This had been elaborately ornamented with cloth of different colors. We also found three necklaces, decorated with pendants made of human fingers, trophies of past battles, and the hand of a Shoshone squaw.[73] Toward evening our pack train, which had stopped several miles back the night before, came into the village and was put into camp near a little hill, behind which the hospital was established. The train was very welcome, as it carried not only our rations, but our spare ammunition, which we now began to need.

As night fell the firing gradually ceased and the pickets having been posted, the troops were put into camp in and near the village, and everyone except the doctors retired to rest.

This village was composed of Cheyennes under the chief Little Wolf. Dull Knife and Roman Nose being subordinate to him. We know that forty lodges of these have participated in every fight that has occurred during the past year, and to verify this there were simple proofs found. There fell into our hands horses, saddles, arms and other matter acquired at the Custer massacre, and some trophies of General Crook's fight of June 17. One of the Seventh Cavalry guidons formed part of a pillow-case. We found also scalps of Shoshone squaws, gained in a recent fight with those people. The lodges were well provided with ammunition, both in the form of cartridges and the powder to refill them. These same Cheyennes are considered to be the bravest and best fighting Indians on the plains, and it is a question as to the probable result of their overthrow on the other hostiles. They are now comparatively harmless and without ammunition, without blankets, without food, and, almost naked as they are, the suffering among them during this cold weather must be intense.

During the fight Colonel Mackenzie sent forward interpreters to talk to them and give them an opportunity to surrender, but they rejected, with expressions of scorn and defiance, all such overtures, and even fired upon the envoys while they were talking. Owing to the lateness of our attack, the hostiles were enabled to secure many of their horses, but we succeeded in taking away about 600 head.

Some scalps were taken by our Pawnees and Shoshones, but our allies, as a rule, did not degenerate into any savagery. One of our Sioux scouts, Three Bears, distinguished himself by his bravery; having his horse killed under him in the centre of the village, he being the first man to penetrate that far.

Reveille was sounded early on the morning of the 26th, and preparations made to resume the fight, should it be necessary. But the scouts reported the enemy gone, and even penetrated his fastness of the previous night, finding one dead body and many pools of blood, an indication of his having numerous wounded. No sign of the Cheyennes could be seen, except the small campfire of a party of observation far off on the mountain. For two or three hours it snowed heavily, so as to render the landscape obscure, but at length it cleared off, and at 12 o'clock the demolition of the village being completed, the command got under way on its retrograde march.

In summing up the results of the engagement, we found that we had lost one officer and five soldiers killed, and twenty-six wounded, including one Shoshone Indian. The enemy lost more heavily, leaving upward of thirty dead in our hands, though their loss in killed will probably aggregate more than that. We marched that day about eight miles, the rear of the column reaching camp after

dark. On account of our wounded, who were conveyed on "travaux," we made easy marches, and reached the camp of our main column on Crazy Woman's Fork on the 29th.

Dispatches having been sent to General Crook during the fight, he started to join us with the infantry and artillery, but, finding us moving down, returned with his column. We had much snow on our return march, but owing to the completeness of our outfit no one suffered much. The wounded got along especially well, with one exception, Private McFarland, Company L, Fifth Cavalry, who died on the morning of the 28th inst.

The fourteen Shoshone [and Pawnee] scouts, who started out before we left the Crazy Woman, returned to us on the 27th, having followed the circuitous trail of the hostiles through the mountains until they accidentally encountered them as the latter were fleeing from the battlefield. Our scouts tried to steal some of their horses, but got worsted, and felt themselves lucky to have escaped with their lives.

One of the fallen, Private Beard [James Baird], Company D, Fourth Cavalry, was buried on the field.[74] The others were brought here for interment. A spot was selected where the river makes a bend, inclosing an elevated plateau of small dimensions, and here, in the heart of this wild but beautiful country, at the foot of the snow-covered mountains of the Big Horns, than which there is no grander range amid waving prairie grasses, in a land uninhabited save by the Indian and the buffalo, rest the five brave men who died on the battlefield.[75]

New York Herald,
Monday, December 11, 1876

General Mackenzie's Fight.

GRAPHIC DETAILS OF THE BATTLE AT CRAZY WOMAN'S FORK.

DISCOVERY OF THE INDIAN VILLAGE.

HOW IT WAS SURPRISED AND DESTROYED.

BRILLIANT AND SUCCESSFUL DASH ON THE HOSTILE CAMP.

DESPERATION OF THE SAVAGES.

[Written by Jerry Roche]

Camp on Crazy Woman's Fork of the Powder River, Thursday, Nov. 30, 1876. [It was the thundering of our advancing column] that first alarmed the hostile savages and made them cut short the war dance and the song of victory for the grim reality of war itself. On a big bass drum, afterward found in the village, which they had as a present from the great father in Washington, those already awake sounded the alarm in the village, and then fled through the ravines toward the hills with a rapidity born of mortal terror. We now found ourselves on a little plain running nearly parallel with the village and elevated about twenty feet above the bottom on which the lodges stood. The village was in a canyon running nearly east and west, the lodges, numbering nearly 200, ranging along both sides of a clear, rapid stream, that wound along close to the base of the range of hills forming the south wall of the canyon. The canyon was nearly four miles long and from about a third of a mile to a mile wide from base to base of the hills forming its side walls. It was narrowest at its eastern end and sloped downward considerably from this point, at which we entered it, for two miles or more to about the beginning of the village, which was fully three-quarters of a mile long. North of the village the ground rose a little, and about a third of a mile west of it the canyon terminated

in a succession of flat-topped hills, cut up by ravines, which ran in every direction. The lodges were completely hidden in thick brush. The northerly wall of the canyon was an almost perpendicular mountain, averaging some 800 to 1,000 feet in height for more than half its length.

Once after entering the canyon and before reaching the village we were obliged to cross the stream that ran through the village. Four or five dry ravines also intercepted our way before reaching the little plain overlooking the lodges. Between this plateau and the tepees were a low bluff and a red sandstone butte about thirty feet high, and nearly opposite these, about half a mile to the northward and a little in advance, were two single and one double red sandstone broken ridges under the shadow of the north wall. A few hundred yards west of these, and running irregularly from north to south, were several deep gulches, accessible from the village by intersecting ravines not quite so deep. This much I deem necessary by way of description before attempting an account of the fight.

OPENING THE BALL.

By the time Major Gordon's battalion had got on a line with the centre of the village the hostiles, in large numbers, had taken possession of the ravines in front of us, and had also secreted themselves behind the bluffs to the left of the village. The hill on the south side of the canyon terminates abruptly near the western end of the village, and is perhaps 500 feet high at the point where it ends. Lieutenant Schuyler went with the Shoshones to this point, and, sheltered by a few loose rocks, remained there all day and through the night. As the different companies of the First battalion arrived on the little plain parallel with the village they moved toward the ravines and were met by a heavy fire from different points behind the brush and rocks a few dozen yards in front. At this time the hostiles were trying to run off a herd of ponies from the plateau over the village, into which our men were trooping, and word of their intention was taken to Colonel Mackenzie, who sent an order to Lieutenant McKinney, by Lieutenant Lawton, Fourth Cavalry, to charge up toward the ravines and cut off the progress of the hostiles.

DEATH OF McKINNEY.

Lieutenant McKinney dashed forward with his company and the hostiles halted and, dropping into the ravine just ahead, waited until the company came up and then fired up, mortally wounding him and also wounding his First Sergeant,[76] five of his men and his horse. Before falling he exclaimed to his company, "Get back out of this place; you are ambushed." Subsequently he asked the doctor to tell his mother how he died. He lived about twenty minutes. As he fell the first fours of his company faltered, and Colonel Mackenzie, beside whom I stood, about fifty yards behind Lieutenant McKinney's company, seeing the break, ordered Major Gordon to send Captain Hamilton's company, then just behind us, forward to the same position.

In the charge two of Lieutenant McKinney's men got cut off from the company and were corralled in the rocks all day, being obliged to defend themselves as best they could until nightfall.

On receiving the order to advance Major Gordon himself went forward with Captain Hamilton, and as they advanced the breaking company reformed under Lieutenant Otis, returned to the spot, and drove the hos-

tiles from the ravine. The pony herd was split, each side getting a share. In this second dash Lieutenant Otis' cap was turned about on his head by a bullet from a fleeing hostile. Both companies then sheltered themselves behind a bluff to the right. Meanwhile Captain Hemphill's company was moving forward to take a position to the left, which they were subsequently obliged to abandon, and Captain Taylor was ordered to charge right through the village. He did so and had four of his horses killed. One man named Sullivan,[77] belonging to the other company, was killed and scalped on this dash. This was the only soldier scalped in the fight. While among the tepees a bullet passed through the lapel of Captain Taylor's coat, just over his heart. Captain Mauck's battalion was pouring into the field meanwhile, dismounting and running forward toward the west of the village and to the shelter of some bluffs on the left that commanded the ravines west of the village. All this while these ravines were full of hostiles, who had the advantage of the advancing troops to the extent of being in a position to fire at the approaching masses while comparatively secure themselves.

THE SCENE BY DAYLIGHT.

It was still the gray dawn of morning, and the moving figures of men and horses seen at any considerable distance appeared more like shadows than living things. But time sped quickly, and very soon broad daylight broke upon the busy scene. The engagement now became general, and no single spectator could possibly keep a record of the events in progress, although concentrated in a narrow space. I candidly confess I was wholly unequal to the task, especially as I found it necessary to discover some care for the safety of myself and my horse. For a while the fire of our men was deafening, and its roar reverberated along the hillsides with thunderous sound. From the rocks and ravines in front the hostiles answered back at first vigorously, but afterward with more caution, and always at an animated object. Many of our troops—among which were several recruits—were not paying much attention to what they fired at, so long as their fire was discharged in the general direction from which the balls of the hostiles came. Indeed, it very soon became apparent to those officers whose attention was not otherwise occupied that we were having a sad waste of ammunition on our side. This was no unimportant matter, viewed in the light in which we then contemplated the situation. We were not routing the hostiles as fast as was desirable. They had intrenched themselves in the hills in pretty secure nooks from 500 to 1,500 yards off, and were pegging away at our troops wherever they could get in a good shot. Any one who crossed the little plateau above the village was especially made a target of, as I found out more than once during the fight. When the battle had proceeded for an hour, or perhaps longer, the rapid and wasteful firing of our recruits was checked, for Colonel Mackenzie began to think, about this time, that he was in for a long fight. The nature of the country and the ferocity and stubbornness with which the hostiles contested for possession of every ridge and rock and ravine, naturally led to this conclusion. For a while Lieutenants Clark, Bourke, Lawton and Dorst were kept moving briskly from point to point to caution company commanders that they must not permit their men to waste any ammunition.

Tactics Of The Hostiles.

The hostiles were wasting none, and were continually shifting their position to try and bring our men within range of their long guns, as well as to go beyond the range of our carbines. It did not take them many minutes to determine the character and range of our weapons and to utilize the discovery to the best possible advantage. One of their tricks was ingenious in its way. A party of braves would creep behind some projecting ledge of rock or hospitable ridge far enough to get just beyond range of our guns, and then would make a wild charge forward howling savagely to draw out our men, from whose bullets they considered themselves safe, but whose exposure would give them the very chance they sought. A somewhat similar plan was once put into successful operation against them by Captain Davis. The Captain's company was suddenly withdrawn from a bluff fronting some rocks, behind which eight or nine hostiles were securely concealed. When they saw the men break and run away from them as they supposed, they jumped up and ran out after them, and in their excitement, familiar as they were with the ground, forgot for the moment that there was a deep, dry ravine just in the rear of the retreating men. Into this ravine the soldiers jumped and delivered a volley at the elated savages as they advanced, killing some and sending the rest back to the rocks in dismay. Some of them found shelter in a cave to the right, where they were pursued and killed, every one.

Taking A Hand In The Fight.

In my endeavors to watch and trace the course of action, I crossed the field I should say a dozen times during the first hour of the fight. I had carried my gun in one hand from the moment of entering the field, but had not discharged it once. I dismounted once during this time behind the red sandstone butte on the left, and in remounting discovered that my overcoat was considerably in the way. On getting into the saddle I galloped across once more to a ridge where Frank Grouard, Baptiste [Pourier], Billy Hunter[78] and one or two other scouts and interpreters were shooting at some hostiles on the hills to the left. There I shed my overcoat, attached a picket rope to my bridle and crept to the crest of the bluff next to Frank Grouard, who was evidently too much interested in the work in hand to pay any attention to fresh arrivals at his side.

"What are you firing at, Frank?" I inquired.

Without turning to see who spoke he opened the breech of his gun, pressed in another cartridge and answered my inquiry in the Sioux language. Again I asked him where the particular Indian was that he was trying to knock over, and again he replied in Sioux and kept on shooting. Then I reminded him that I didn't happen to understand the Indian tongue and should be obliged if he would answer me in English, and, suddenly recollecting himself, he laughed, and pointed to a hill 800 yards in front, from which bullets were coming in quick succession to the crest of the bluff we occupied. A moment afterward some one on my left knocked over one of the Indians on this ridge and the others crept to safer quarters. Frank did not get his man that time, but he did before the battle closed, and he now rejoices in the possession of a scalp of a hostile Cheyenne.

SCENE IN THE VILLAGE.

Frank and myself then rode across the field again to the village, and found that some of the lodges had been set on fire already. On entering the village we found the body of a squaw, just freshly scalped, lying near one of the lodges. A Pawnee scout was moving off from the prostrate body, bearing with him the dripping scalp. This unfortunate squaw had been found in the village hidden in a tepee after the troops had passed through it by Private Butler, of the Second Cavalry, who told the Pawnees, many of whom were then in the village, not to kill her. Butler's back was scarcely turned, however, before the old squaw was shot and scalped. We then walked through a portion of the village and counted about 175 lodges, and still had not counted all. We went into several, and found in every one two or three packages of dried meat. The lodges were mostly lined on the inside to the height of two or three feet with undressed hides, and everything remained as if the inmates had stepped out for a few moments. In some the fires were burning, and kettles of water stood on them, as if in preparation for the morning meal. A number of the Pawnees were systematically going through the village and securing large quantities of plunder. We were both very hungry now, and Frank Grouard helped himself to some of the meat. After a hasty glance through the village we returned to the field again, where the battle still progressed with considerable animation.

A DUEL.

A corporal [Ryan] and private had just had a close fight with two hostiles at an advanced position to the right. The men met within a few yards of each other. At the first fire the corporal fell. Then the private fired, killing the Indian who had killed the corporal, and the other Indian fled. I scoured through the field for some time again, and the fire still came from twenty different points in the hills beyond. Dead horses were lying about at different points, but the men were now all dismounted, and the horses securely sheltered from the fire in the ravines and behind the bluffs. The killed and wounded were now being taken to the right of the field where Drs. Wood and Le Garde [LaGarde] were attending to the wants of the living and sheltering the dead. Meantime the hostiles had gotten their women and children into the mountains, beyond the western end of the canyon. I came back again to the village and found a number of our Indians, some soldiers and civil employes of the expedition, going through the lodges searching for relics. At one point I met a soldier who told me he had just seen a silk guidon of the Seventh Cavalry, which was found in a tepee in use as a cover for a pillow. There were also found in the village a guard roster of Company G, Seventh Cavalry, saddles, canteens, nosebags, currycombs and brushes, shovels and axes, marked with the letters of different companies of the Seventh Cavalry, a memorandum book with a list of names of the three best marksmen at target practice in Captain Donald Mackintosh's [McIntosh's] company, Seventh Cavalry; rosters of other companies of the Seventh; a letter written by an enlisted man of the Seventh Cavalry to a young lady, the letter already stamped and directed. This letter will be forwarded. Several horses of the Seventh Cavalry were found among the herds captured. Photographs of several white men were also found, a gold pencil case, a silver watch, pocketbooks with sums of money, some gold pieces, the hat of First Sergeant William Allen, of Company I, Third Cavalry, killed in the Rosebud fight, with the company stamp and his initials on it;[79] an officer's overcoat of dark blue army cloth, an officer's rubber coat and two officers' blouses, a buckskin coat of American make, with a bullet hole in the shoulder, and supposed to be the coat worn by Tom Custer in the Little Big Horn fight; bullet moulds, field glasses, &c.

INDIAN TROPHIES.

Among the Indian trophies in the possession of our troops now are three beaded necklaces, ornamented with human fingers. One has depending from it ten fingers, one seven, and one shown me by Lieutenant Bourke has eight fingers strung round it.

We have a belt, found in the village, full of cartridges, with a silver plate marked "Little Wolf," given this doughty chief at Washington a few years ago.[80] We also found a pass for Roman Nose from Red Cloud Agency, giving him permission to leave the reservation a few days to search for his lost mules.

After going through the village the second time I again crossed the field and took shelter with Major Gordon, Captain Hamilton and some other officers behind the double bluff to the right. I had some broken hard tack in my saddle pockets, and I found some gentlemen here who gladly accepted the crumbs. It was no easy matter to arrive at or leave this point without getting hit, still some of the soldiers and some orderlies were continually passing back and forth, and Colonel Mackenzie made this point his headquarters for a while. The hostile fire came over this ledge from three points. Bullets came in just over our heads from the crest of the mountain on the north, from a mound almost directly in front, and others fell near our feet, shot from behind some rocks on the hills to the southwest of us. A soldier who tried to leave just after I arrived had his hat shot off. He calmly picked it up again, put it on, and as he moved slowly away looked very angry as he glanced toward the point from which the ball came. One soldier was lying dead on the side of the bluff just above us. Soon after I arrived the order was given to the men at this point to cease firing altogether. It was as well, for most of the Indians on the hills had crept beyond range of the cavalry carbines, and were watching their chances to pick our men off.

Arrival Of The Pack Train.

After I had been here half an hour or so—indeed, I cannot definitely say how long, for it is not easy to take note of time on such occasions—Lieutenant Bourke came up and said the pack train had arrived. Instantly I determined to risk another crossing, for I was getting very hungry. About the same time the horses of Captain Hamilton's company were ordered across to water, and most of them had been taken over before I mounted my horse. When I did so and moved out into the field I saw a soldier just ahead of me riding one horse and leading another. This man had not gone fifty yards from the bluff before his led horse fell, hit by a ball from the hills, and he was wounded himself. Before I had crossed the field, though going at full speed, at least a score of balls whistled past my ears. I found the pack train just camping in the willows, near the middle of the village, and soon was engaged in disposing of a late breakfast. It was about two o'clock now, I should judge, and the pack train had been in the canyon over two hours, but was only just going into camp. The mules had their packs on for twenty-three hours. It just occurs to me that most of us had been in the saddle about the same length of time.

As I arrived at the pack train Colonel Mackenzie was sending out a despatch to General Crook, then over two days march off by the shortest route, to bring up the infantry. This looked as if Colonel Mackenzie expected that the Indians would fight him from the hills until he was reinforced. My first despatch to the Herald was sent out about the same time that Colonel Mackenzie sent for the infantry. The extreme caution exercised

by the hostiles early in the fight in the use of ammunition indicated either a scarcity of the article or a determination to save it for a long battle. At first we did not know which way to interpret their action, but just after eating I learned that they had left nearly all their ammunition behind, and that considerable quantities of it were being destroyed in the lodges already set on fire. A keg of powder also exploded with a loud report in one of the burning tepees. Doubtless this deprivation made them all the more determined to make every shot tell.

An Indian Sharpshooter.

One Indian had found a secure place in the hills and played sharpshooter nearly all day with one of Sharps' long-range rifles. The gun must have shot a cartridge containing about 120 grains of powder. Every time he fired the report seemed to rend the very walls of the canyon, echoing like the roar of cannon from hill to hill. Late in the afternoon a cheer went up from some of our boys in front and the big gun was silent thereafter. I subsequently heard the fellow was killed by one of Captain Davis' men, but the other Indians near him got away with the gun. Gradually the Indian fire ceased until toward sundown when it had stopped altogether. All our killed and wounded but one man, who fell on an exposed bluff near the end of the canyon, had been got in before this time, and just after sundown his body was brought in. As twilight fell upon the scene some of our Indian soldiers kept popping away at hostiles, who in the cover of darkness were creeping from their hiding places in the rocks; but I do not think they fired with much effect. Numerous pickets were posted on the hills before nightfall, for we apprehended a renewal of the fight by sundown or a little afterward. But night fell upon our battlefield, and with it came peace and silence about the hostile village.

Our killed and wounded had been transferred from the north side of the field to the shelter of the bluff on the right, and here I found the extent of our loss was one officer and five men killed and twenty-five men and one Indian wounded. The small proportion of Indian scouts shot in the fight is trace-able to their familiarity with the manner of fighting of their own people and to the shrewdness with which they evaded fire on the field while fighting at times quite as well as our regulars. Their chief usefulness, however, consisted in their employment as scouts and in leading the first dash at the hostiles to capture their ponies and demoralize them by showing them that their own people were arrayed against them. They cannot be disci-plined to fight like white soldiers. Two of the Shoshones and one of the Sioux had horses shot under them and yet escaped unhurt. During the fight Three Bears had his horse shot under him and rode back past me mounted behind another Indian, in search of a pony on which to renew the fight.

Indian Scalps.

In the evening I saw some scalps that had been taken from the lodges, and among these was the scalp of a white girl. I saw also a number of blank books taken from the tepees, on the leaves of which had been sketched the exploits of several of the Cheyenne braves, after the manner of Sitting Bull, sketches of whose san-guinary career appeared in the Herald last summer. After nightfall an effort was made to count up the Indian loss, and the lowest figure at which it was placed was twenty-five killed outright. I saw the Pawnees parading six scalps early in the evening and two soldiers showed me two scalps they had secured. Frank Grouard

got a scalp, Lieutenant Allison killed an Indian, Captain Davis' company killed six or eight, the Shoshones killed four, a one-eyed frontiersman with one party of our Indians killed one and the Sioux and Arapahoes killed about a dozen, but did not take any scalps. Others, too, were killed and severely wounded, of which no account has yet been received, so on the whole I should say the hostiles had fully fifty killed and mortally wounded.

The Killed.

Lieutenant J. A. McKinney, com-manding Company M, Fourth Cavalry.
Corporal Patrick F. Ryan, Company D, Fourth Cavalry.
Private Joseph Menges, Company H, Fifth Cavalry.
Private Alexander Keller, Company E, Fourth Cavalry.
Private John Sullivan, Company B, Fourth Cavalry.
Private Beard [Baird], Company D, Fourth Cavalry.
Private Alexander McFarland, Company L, Fifth Cavalry (died on the 28th).

Wounded.

[There were twenty-two names on the wounded list, including a Shoshone scout named Anzi.]

A Decoy Flag.

Late in the afternoon I learned that one party of hostiles on a hill to the right showed a white flag three or four times during the fight, but would shoot at an exposed head after its exhibition just the same as ever.

When the fight was over, Colonel Mackenzie sent out some Indians with Roland,[81] the Cheyenne interpreter, to talk with the hostiles on the hills. They saw old Dull Knife in the distance, and he said to them that his three sons had been killed in the fight, and that he was willing to surrender, but the others were not. They had been told, he said, that the whites were coming to make a treaty with them, but instead they came and fired into their village, consequently they could not trust the whites. A heap of their people, he said, had been killed in the fight, and the rest were ready to die.

During the night the hostiles camped within four miles of the village and in the morning they were obliged to kill six or seven of their ponies for food. The carcasses were found by our Indians in the hills. The night was very cold and windy, and next day we were enveloped in a heavy snow storm. After burying Private Beard on the battlefield the rest of our killed and wounded were placed on litters, hitched at one end to mules and with the other end dragging on the ground, and we prepared to leave the canyon by noon on Sunday. Before starting the Colonel sent out the interpreters and Indians once more to talk with the hostiles, but they had "a big mad" on in the morning and their pride would not permit them to answer our men at all.

The Hostile Chiefs.

The principal chiefs of the hostile village, I have been told, were Dull Knife, Little Wolf, Roman Nose, Gray Head and Old Bear, and among the 200 lodges were forty that have been in all the recent fights with the troops.

Before leaving we burned everything in the village that our Indians did not want. There were 165 fires going in the hostile camp on Sunday morning, and in the blaze were consumed large quantities of dried meat, undressed skins, axes, saddles, tin ware, frying pans, snow moccasins, strychnine in large quantities, used to poison wolves; the tepees and tepee poles, medicinal herbs and, indeed, all the lares and penates of the reds. The destruction was complete—nay, even artistic. Not a pin's worth was left unburned. We captured between 500 and 600 ponies.

Sunday evening [November 26] we camped about eight miles from the canyon on our return to the supply camp, and next morning we learned that the infantry was on the way to join us, fully convinced that they would soon have to take a hand in the fight. They were turned back on Monday and arrived here Tuesday, the cavalry, with killed and wounded, getting back last night.

I find that Lieutenant McKinney's death, though he fell in action at the head of his command, as a soldier must be prepared to fall, is very generally regretted by the officers of the command. He was a dashing, brave young officer, whose manly qualities had endeared him to his comrades, and his death cast a shadow on our victory. His body, I understand, is to be forwarded to his friends.

The nature of the land about the hostile village would have enabled our savage foes to cut the head of the column to pieces if aware of our approach, and if we had not so thoroughly surprised them some one would have [had] to record a second edition of the Custer massacre. Had a smaller force, of whose approach the Indians had been apprised, attacked the village, not a man would have escaped.

16

The Powder River Expedition

"This will be a terrible blow to the hostiles, as these Cheyennes were not only the bravest warriors, but have been the head and front of most of the raids and deviltry committed in this [Powder River] country."—Dispatch from General Crook, *New York Times*, December 2, 1876

"No one who has had a taste of a winter campaign out here will fail to join with General Sherman in his wish that our success now may put an end to the hostiles. But I fancy our chances of catching Crazy Horse napping are not very good."—Jerry Roche, In Camp on the Belle Fourche, December 19, 1876, *New York Herald*, February 5, 1877

"The Cheyennes, whom Colonel Mackenzie defeated in the Sioux Pass of the Big Horn Mountains in November, had joined Crazy Horse at his camp at the mouth of the Powder River in a very destitute condition, having lost everything."—Dispatch, Red Cloud Agency, January 29, 1877, *New York Tribune*, January 31, 1877

"I never went to war with the whites. The soldiers began chasing me about, for what cause I do not know to this day. I dodged as long as I could and hid my village away, but at last they found it and I had no alternative but to fight or perish."—Hump, Tongue River Cantonment, May 10, 1877, *New York Herald*, June 4, 1877

Mackenzie's attack on Dull Knife's village was disastrous for the Northern Cheyennes and effectively removed them as a threat in the Sioux War. For a nomadic people who did not have the luxury to easily replenish their food stores and dwellings, the loss of these necessities, coming as it did during the inhospitable northern winter months, was especially damaging, and virtually impossible to overcome. Additionally, as one historian noted, lost in the flames of the lodges was "most of the old Northern Cheyenne material beauty. . . . Never again would Northern Cheyenne material culture reach the heights of richness and splendor that the people knew before that bitter day in the Big Horns."[1] Factor in the loss of life—upwards of forty men, women, and children, and a substantial number of horses—and their situation had to be rather bleak.[2] A few months later, a Cheyenne warrior named Hump told a correspondent:

As it was we were beaten and lost most of our lodges and bedding. We had to retreat over a hundred miles, and the weather was bitter cold. We almost perished, but at last reached Tongue River, where there was a big camp [under Crazy Horse].[3]

The Dull Knife fight was the second time in nine months that the Cheyennes suffered the loss of a village and practically all of their worldly belongings. It was also the second time in nine months that they sought refuge with Crazy Horse. Wooden Leg and nine other men were away on a raid against the Crows at the time of the fight but joined up with the survivors shortly afterward. Many years later, he recalled:

The Cheyennes had to run away with only a few small packs, as our small band had done on lower Powder River [after the attack in March by Colonel Reynolds]. The same as we had done, they had to see all of their lodges burned and most of their horses taken. Many of our men, women and children had been killed. Others had died of wounds or had starved and frozen to death on the journey through the mountain snow to Tongue River.[4]

On the surface, it appeared to be a replay of the Reynolds fight in March, albeit with a more favorable outcome for the army this time. However, there were a couple of key differences. The Reynolds attack took place in mid-March, and despite the fact that the harsh winter weather was still raging, warmer weather was just around the corner, and with it the Cheyennes had, relatively speaking, an easier time of refitting. But Mackenzie's attack came in late November, with some four months of fierce winter weather still staring them in the face. One reporter explained the Cheyennes' dire situation this way:

As Mackenzie's attack happened in the latter part of November, and as the winters in Wyoming are exceptionally severe, the sufferings and privations of the Cheyennes may be imagined better than described. . . . They could not procure food for their women and children, because much of their ammunition and many of their guns had fallen into the hands of the troops. They had been driven from their village at daylight, and very many of them had not saved even a blanket. They were encumbered with wounded, for whom they could provide nothing.[5]

Additionally, this latter attack came at the tail end of a long campaign in which the Sioux had seen the last of their ascendancy in the Powder River country and Yellowstone Basin expire. The government would no longer tolerate the summer roamers, and the winter roamers were going to be hounded into submission (besides the fact that the reservation leaders signed the land away in September and October). Already, supply bases had been set up on the Powder River and at the mouth of the Tongue, and troops, in company with fellow tribesmen, former allies, and enemy tribes, as witnessed in the recent battle against the Cheyennes, were scouring the country to destroy them. As if that were not enough, the reservations were now under military supervision and could no longer be used as a place of temporary refuge, support, or recruiting. The Cheyennes could try turning to Crazy Horse for assistance in getting through the winter, but come summer there would be no major gathering of the tribes, no return to splendor. Past glories were just that, and the summer of 1876 was a one-time deal.

As alluded to by Hump and Wooden Leg, the Cheyennes, downtrodden, traipsed to Crazy Horse's village, which they found on Beaver Creek, a tributary of the Tongue River. Wooden Leg recalled a generous welcome from their long time allies:

Eleven sleeps the tribe had journeyed when we arrived at the place on Beaver Creek. . . . Here we found the Ogallalas. The Ogalala Sioux received us hospitably. They had not been disturbed by soldiers, so they had good lodges and plenty of meat and robes. They first assembled us in a great body and fed us all we wanted to eat. To all of the women who needed other food they gave a supply. They gave us robes and blankets. They shared with us their tobacco. Gift horses came to us. Every married woman got skins enough to make some kind of lodge for her household. Oh how generous were the Ogallalas! Not any Cheyenne was allowed to go to sleep hungry or cold that night.[6]

However, Wooden Leg's recollection is at odds with what seems to be the general understanding of the whites at the time. Lieutenant Bourke, under date of April 4, 1877, noted in his journal:

The Cheyennes, with whom we had the fight in November, began to weaken. Three hundred and eighty-six [including Little Wolf] had already surrendered at Red Cloud [Agency] in February and March. . . . They had suffered terribly [in the Dull Knife fight] and were obliged to surrender or starve. They had first joined Crazy Horse, who was on Tongue River, but Crazy Horse wouldn't do anything more for them. The Cheyennes were very mad with Crazy Horse and didn't like the way in which he had acted towards them. . . . They claimed that the Northern Sioux had not behaved toward them with compassion. They expressed a desire to be enlisted as soldiers that they might go out to fight Crazy Horse's people.[7]

Moreover, a newspaper report in early May 1877, following the surrender of Dull Knife in late April, declared:

The Cheyennes complained with much bitterness of the unkindness of the Northern Sioux, who had not treated them with any generosity in the hour of their suffering. They wished to retaliate upon the Sioux by enlisting as soldiers in the ranks of the white man and going out to destroy Crazy Horse's village.[8]

Conversely, Short Buffalo, an Oglala Sioux, recalled: "There is nothing to that story. We helped the Cheyennes the best we could. We hadn't much ourselves."[9]

Short Buffalo's statement notwithstanding, the contemporary evidence does not bear out Wooden Leg's recollection, but there is no definitive answer to the question. On the one hand, it is hard to believe that the Sioux did not treat their long-time allies to the best of their ability; on the other hand, it is at least possible that Wooden Leg's memory mixed up the time after the Mackenzie fight with the time after the Reynolds fight.[10]

In the larger picture, the destruction of the Cheyenne village at this time illustrates not only the clash of two cultures, but the clash of two eras, and the Cheyennes on the Red Fork of Powder River were practically an anachronism, still caught up in intertribal warfare, in their old life, in their old feuds, even while a more dangerous enemy was knocking at their door. Recall that at the time of Mackenzie's attack upon the Cheyennes, the tribe had been celebrating a recent victory over the Shoshones and that Wooden Leg and nine other men had missed the battle being away on a raid against the Crows. The transcontinental railroad had been running for seven years, and the Wright brothers were only twenty-seven years away from making their first flight. Yet here in the Powder River country (and the Greater Yellowstone Basin) there existed several small tribes whose lifestyle was fast becoming extinct. The world was moving on, but the Powder River country was, for a brief moment, trapped in time.

✳

The Powder River Expedition remained in camp on Crazy Woman's Fork until the morning of December 2, tramping some twenty-five miles back to Cantonment Reno on the same day. Of their departure from Crazy Woman's Fork, an anonymous correspondent for the *New York Tribune* jested: "It cannot be denied that it was with a sensation of relief that the parting glance was taken of the cheerless hills, and that Crazy Horse was voted not such a bad fellow after all in that he had gone to the eastward."[11]

That night Roche sent off a brief dispatch to the *Herald* mentioning, among other news items, Crook's plan to search for Crazy Horse, and that the Shoshones were going home:

The Powder River expedition returned to Fort Reno today, and sets out after Crazy Horse's band in the morning. Our course will be in the direction of Little Powder River, [which is] northward from this point,[12] General Crook's impression being that Crazy Horse has left the Rosebud and is moving in the direction toward which we go.[13] We carry about thirty days' provisions. The Shoshones go home tomorrow. They found the hand of a Shoshone girl and several scalps of their people in a hostile village. More Sioux and Arapahoes from Red Cloud are expected to join us on our way out.[14]

Sometimes the story behind the story is more interesting. In this case, Roche's statement that the command would move out in the morning after Crazy Horse was incomplete, at least if you were to ask Lieutenant Colonel Dodge:

Genl Crook told me last night that we would probably remain at [Cantonment] Reno today—at all events would not start before 11 or 12 oclk. . . . I was lying in my bed about 7 waiting for my man to bring water when an orderly came to the tent door to say that the Genl wished me to get my Comd off as early as possible for Buffalo Springs. I was disgusted, but there is no use in being so with Crook's orders. He really does not know ahead what he intends to do. Makes up his mind at the last moment, & then acts at once—expecting everybody else to do the same. He has nothing to do but make up his mind. I have to take care of my men. I had clothing to draw & other things to attend to.[15]

Buffalo Springs, located on the Dry Fork of Powder River, was about fifteen miles south of the cantonment. Here Crook set up another supply base upon his arrival on December 3, then waited for further news on the whereabouts of Crazy Horse. Two days later, as noted by the *Tribune* correspondent, he was still waiting:

Here we have remained for two days momentarily expecting to move forward and momentarily being disappointed. Life is accompanied by so few comforts at this camp that I think I am warranted in saying the troops are burning for the fray. The Indians still continue to be subjects of uncertainty. It is, however, conceded that they are somewhere on or about the Powder River, or mayhap the Little Missouri, and perchance the Belle Fourche. Gen. Crook himself, in answer to my question as to the direction of his next march, waved his hand comprehensively over all the northeastern points of the compass.[16]

Skirmishing with Suppositious Sioux

New York Tribune,
December 25, 1876

In Camp at Buffalo Springs,
December 5, 1876.

When the command remains in camp for a day or so, the troops are exercised in skirmish drill to be the better prepared for fighting. These drills generally last about two hours, during which time the observer will see fifteen companies of foot [soldiers] dispersed in as many different directions on the surrounding hills, "picking off" suppositious Sioux or rallying into groups to repel imaginary charges. Fifteen bugles blow, fifteen company commanders yell admonitions at the fifteen stupids pertaining to the fifteen companies, and the unceasing click of the breech locks as they are closed and opened reminded me, as I gazed on the scene, of a sewing machine in a large family.

—Anonymous

While Crook's scouts were out looking for Crazy Horse's village, the homeless and weary Cheyennes had better luck, staggering into that war leader's encampment about December 6. In the meantime, every day that Crook remained bivouacked at Buffalo Springs was another day consuming his already limited supplies with nothing to show for it. Again, from the *Tribune* correspondent:

It will be impossible for the campaign to last over a month, as the rations will be eaten by that time and the animals cannot be fed. At this time no definite news of the hostiles has been received, and this has undoubtedly [been] a great influence against the expedition's forward march. Unless accurate information is received about the Sioux, it would be useless to start out after the savages in what Gen. Sherman regards as the most inhospitable country on the continent. It is not probable that Crazy Horse will run any risks of losing his village and ponies as long as he can help it, and the only way he can be gotten at is by a surprise. He is probably aware of our intentions, and the surprise will have to be a great surprise indeed. I am inclined to think that, like the typical policeman, Gen. Crook, even if he does not make any arrests, will at least make the savages "move on." . . . There may be even now a strong conservative element in the hostile camp who vote the war a failure, and are unable to see the constitutionality of Crazy Horse's war measures. Let us hope that it is so.

"This sort of war is not a bit like our October trainin'." It is excessively and disagreeably uncomfortable and unrelieved by the comfort of patriotism. It is purely a matter of business, and in that respect I think too much praise cannot be awarded to the troops who have thus far undergone so many hardships, and whose future 20 or 30 days is anticipated under the remark of one who knows the country—"nightly hell."[17]

The camp at Buffalo Springs was well supplied with wood, but there was little grass and "execrable water in very small quantities."[18] Therefore, on December 6, despite still being in the dark on Crazy Horse's whereabouts, Crook struck east toward the Belle Fourche River, leaving behind a

mixed detail of infantry and artillery to guard the supplies. Roche wrote:

We know nothing definitely of the location of Crazy Horse's village, and must be content to grope forward for a time. We sent scouts back to Red Cloud [Agency] to bring on other Indians, and these would not be back for several days, and we may not hope to learn anything to guide our future movements, except by accident, until their return. All that was left for us to do, then, was to press onward a little and seek a better camping ground.[19]

That day's march was ten miles to a point near Pumpkin Buttes (Wyoming) where, cheerful to find "good, pure water," some of the men named the springs "Grand Springs" in appreciation. On the downside, other than some sagebrush, "there was not a stick of wood anywhere." Luckily they had packed some along in the wagons for just such an emergency. The next morning they were on the move again, trudging along "in a thick, dreary snow storm, working on toward the head waters of the Belle Fourche."[20] Bourke described the weather that day as "a chilling storm of snow that beat down upon the column all day."[21] Finding water after a march of twenty-one miles, they settled down for the night. Despite the miserable weather, the Indian scouts cashed in with a successful hunt:

Game was plentiful along the line of our march that day and our Indians reaped a rich harvest by sales of deer and antelope killed on the way. They earned all they got, however, for the weather was so cold one could scarcely pull a trigger without risk of freezing his fingers.[22]

Although Roche did not see fit to mention his own hunting exploit that day, Bourke made note of it:

Mr. Roche shot a porcupine this afternoon and roasted it in the ashes. The meat is fat and has a greasy, rancid taste, something like pork.[23]

While Roche was busy roasting his *porkcupine*, Dodge was busy giving vent to his frustrations with the commanding general in his journal:

However good a soldier Crook may be, he has no administrative ability whatever. He well knows that this part of the expedition must be a failure, if for no other reason, because we cannot transport our supplies. His train is in wretched condition yet he does nothing to keep it in order. . . . Mules are the very first element of success in such an expedn as this—yet he seems to care nothing for his mules. The Cavy horses & Indian ponies are giving out every day, & by the time we reach the mouth of Little Powder, it will be a miracle if more than half of us do not have to walk back. Yet he pushes on. I would not say it out loud—but I think he is pushing on now simply from vanity. It will look well to go on—no matter at what cost of life or property.[24]

General Crook was busy that evening too, virtually admitting to the *New York Tribune* correspondent that he knew the campaign was over:

This is a tentative campaign on my part. One can't fight Indians until he finds them to fight, and when an Indian doesn't want to be found it is usually a matter of some difficulty to find him. I think I am warranted in making that assertion both from my own and others' experiences. It becomes a doubly difficult matter in a country like this. This is a big country. It is just as hard to conquer a few Indians as it is a great many, all things being equal, and I do not anticipate obtaining any great success for the balance of this campaign, measured by tangible results. But I do expect to so annoy and worry the hostiles as to make it evident to them that they are having the hot end of the poker and it does not pay to remain inimical to us. It may be brought home to them this winter, and it may take another campaign to do it, but it will be so eventually. I do not expect to surprise them, as the recent destruction of the Cheyenne village has put them on the alert, and I believe they know more of our movements than we do of theirs. But I intend to place my command in the heart of their country, and its mere presence will result in the breaking up of their winter homes, and thus generate a feeling of uneasiness and discontent. Of course, if I see a chance to strike them, I will avail myself of it. The country I am going to is the winter quarters of the hostiles, and has hitherto been exempt from attack during that season. When they see that it makes no difference to us, and that we will be after them in all seasons, they will begin to appreciate their status. The campaign will be necessarily short. Our animals cannot get along without forage, and the supply is limited, with no means of replacing it. We are too far from a railroad. Without animals it is impossible to campaign in this country, as the Indians have ten ponies to our one, and can go where they please, and we cannot catch them. But, for the time being, we can keep them going, and that will not please them. I cannot make the march I did last summer, for the horses would give out. There is no grass, little water, and less wood.[25]

The command moved along slowly, following the course of the Belle Fourche River northeast. On the ninth, Crook sent fifty wagons back to Buffalo Springs for supplies, during which time the column continued to advance by "slow degrees."[26] After going into camp on the twelfth, no further movements were made until the morning of the twentieth. During that long interval, wagons from Fort Fetterman arrived loaded with sutler's supplies, and the wagons returned from Buffalo Springs. Not that anyone with the command knew it at the time, but they were then about ninety miles north of Fort Fetterman. As noted by Roche on the nineteenth, last month's victory over the Cheyennes seemed so far removed from their current situation: "Slow as the world may be supposed to move with us out here in this 'most inhospitable section of the American continent,' our recent brush with the Cheyennes already seems a thing of the far distant past."[27]

While they were in camp, one or more couriers arrived from Cantonment Reno with news that two Sioux scouts had been sent from Red Cloud Agency (per Crook's instructions) to locate Crazy Horse's camp, after which they were to report directly to Crook. Additionally, Captain Randall was at Cantonment Reno with seventy-six Crow Indians. They were quite late in joining the command and had had a little skirmish with the Cheyennes, capturing forty ponies. "General Crook regards this little collision as a fortunate circumstance," Roche reported, "as it

will help to confirm the hostiles in the impression now becoming prevalent among them that they are nowhere safe from the assaults of the whites and their Indian allies."[28] His closing words in his dispatch of the nineteenth illustrated just how dependent the troops were on the Indian scouts:

Our Indian scouts have not yet returned from Red Cloud Agency, and there is some uneasiness manifested on account of the delay, of which they and the two spies sent to Crazy Horse are the occasion. We are wasting good weather and consuming our supplies here idly for want of knowledge of the enemy's whereabouts.[29]

On the twentieth, after seven days of rest, the column advanced only six more miles. It also turned out to be the end of the line for the Powder River Expedition. Roche's dispatch the following day explained Crook's decision to return to Fort Fetterman:

General Crook announced, at a council with our Indian scouts here today, that the expedition would start homeward in the morning. We have rations for twelve days, and half-forage for a week. Neither the Indians sent to locate Crazy Horse's village, nor those sent to Red Cloud, to bring out more Indian soldiers, have joined us yet; and our present meagre stock of supplies, with the limited amount of transportation at the posts which are nearest us, will not permit a further prosecution of the present campaign. Since our fight in the Big Horn Mountains small bands of Indian braves have been wandering about the country in our vicinity and keeping a watch on all of our movements, a fact which tends to make a surprise of the hostile Sioux by

Indians setting fire to prairie grass. (*Library of Congress*)

our troops a matter of extreme difficulty, if not wholly impossible; even if our stock were in better condition and supplies for the men and animals were more plentiful.[30]

In addition to the reasons outlined by Roche, Dodge noted in his journal that Crook was "in a terrible humor" at news just received concerning affairs at Red Cloud Agency. The friendly Indians were being disarmed and unhorsed by Major Julius Mason, Third Cavalry, the commander at Camp Robinson,[31] the same as if they were hostile Indians. This action was in direct opposition to Crook's modus operandi. After all, punishing the innocent and guilty alike was no way to gain the confidence of the Indians and certainly no incentive for them to cooperate with the whites. He believed that his effective policy was being negated, and he was helpless to do anything about it. Dodge wrote:

This [news] taken with the absence of all information in regard to his spies, has completely knocked the "Old Man" up. He told me that he did not sleep a wink last night, and pretended that he is sick. He is really only worried.[32]

The trip back to Fort Fetterman was made under some extremely frigid temperatures. From the correspondent of the *New York Tribune*:

On the 23d the thermometer sank to 20 degrees below zero, and all night long the uncomfortable mules, turned loose to pick up what grass they could find. . . . Early on the 24th the command started out for a long march to obtain water. It was colder than there is any necessity of describing; the animals were covered with hoar frosts; the creaking of the wagon wheels was fearfully suggestive of frigidity, and the muleteers slapped their fingers in a lively way to keep them warm. That night, Christmas eve . . . the mercury was frozen in the bulb. Water was simply ice, and one had to chop out with a hatchet the means of making his coffee. As for washing one's face, that was a refinement not thought of. Wind River Creek was reached on the 27th. . . . Two days more marching brought the troops here [Fort Fetterman]. The weather had moderated—true, yesterday morning it was 27 degrees below zero, but that was pure torridity.[33]

General Crook was back at Fetterman on the twenty-eighth, having moved ahead in an ambulance. The rest of the command trekked the final eleven miles the following day. Since turning south on the Belle Fourche on December 22, they had traveled 120 miles, an average of fifteen miles per day. From Fort Fetterman on December 30, the *Tribune* correspondent summarized events to date and looked ahead to the following spring:

Crazy Horse, with commendable alacrity, got away from the Powder, the Tongue, the Rosebud, and all other places where he ought to have been and retired to some secluded spot on the Little Missouri. In the mean time such material objects as corn and oats disappeared before the hunger of the mules, and it became evident to Gen. Crook that there was no use waiting any longer for something to appear. . . . The Powder River expedition therefore is a *fait accompli*. Gen. Crook is satisfied with the results. The severe blow given to the Cheyennes by Mackenzie will create in the minds of those savages a feeling of disgust at being hostile. Although Crazy Horse has not been struck yet, he has been made very uncomfortable. . . . Gen. Crook thinks of this campaign that its results will be seen in the spring. He believes that the friendly Indians and a small column of troops will finish the matter in another campaign. Everything

indicates that there will be no difficulty in raising a large force of Indians whenever wanted. The enlistment of Sioux from the agencies has proved successful. To their untutored minds, being placed upon an equality with white troops is very gratifying. No question of honor enters into their minds, but they will fight their red brothers as long as they can get their ponies. Gen. Crook thinks that the condition of affairs at the agencies will be much improved and that there will be no trouble there any more. From here the constitutional parts of the army separate. The cavalry go to Red Cloud Agency and the infantry and artillery to their proper stations.[34]

What appears to be Roche's final dispatch concerning the campaign was composed at Fort Laramie on January 4, 1877, and published in the *New York Herald* ten days later under the headline "The Powder River Expedition—The Progress and Finish of the Last Indian Campaign." Here are the highlights:

On the Dull Knife fight:

[The Powder River Expedition's] attack on the daring Cheyennes has taught them that they may not consider themselves safe from the avenging pursuit of the white man, even in their most remote and inaccessible fastnesses. That the punishment they received was severe no one will question who witnessed the battle, and yet there are very few, if any, even of those who participated in the fight that feel now that this chastisement was at all equal to their deserts or proportioned to what our power over them would have been under slightly different circumstances. Unaided as it was, the cavalry did well, though ignorant of the situation, to carry by storm and hold against their fierce enemies the village and all its contents, entering in the dim, uncertain light of the opening dawn as villainous a spot as nature could have afforded any band of savage outlaws for their fortress and hiding place.

On the Indian scouts:

When the expedition set out the surmises as to its probable effectiveness were not unmixed with a certain vague dread of disasters to be apprehended from the presence of so many Sioux, Arapahoe and Cheyenne auxiliaries. The column, it was generally admitted, was well organized. No better appointed command had ever started after hostile Indians in the territory we were to traverse. "But, but," surmise whispered, with a knowing wink, "those enlisted Indians will make trouble"; and, indeed, for a time it looked as if General Crook had placed too much confidence in their loyalty. Even among officers of the command one heard many murmurs of disapproval. With other Indians, it was said his confidence might be all right, but the treacherous Sioux were not to be trusted. If they failed to cut the throats of half the command they would at least quarrel with their old enemies, the Pawnees, also of the auxiliaries. The first meeting of the members of these two tribes tended a little to strengthen these notions. Among the representatives of both there were impetuous young braves, who, cherishing the traditional animosities of their respective people, indulged at first in little taunts and innuendoes. They soon learned, however, not only to avoid quarrels, but grew to be fast friends before they parted, even to the extent of presenting each other with horses and having friendly pow-wows while we camped on the Belle Fourche. . . . Their ideas of warfare are comprised in the general order "every man for himself,"

while at the same time all combine for a common purpose.

On the difficulties of the campaign during December:

Viewed at a distance our march along the Belle Fourche may seem aimless as contrasted with our progress to the Big Horn Mountains, and in a certain measure it was so, though we could but have done differently under the circumstances. General Crook judged that Crazy Horse, on hearing of our fight, would leave the Rosebud and move toward the bad lands at the head of the Little Missouri, a favorite resort of this chief when apprehending pursuit, and one which affords him opportunities of harassing the troops and also evading them by passes known only to the Indian. The best approach to these fastnesses was that selected for the expedition, but our advance was necessarily controlled by the elements, by the quantity of supplies on hand and capable of being forwarded, and the effectiveness of scouts sent out to determine the exact location of the hostile camp. As matters have turned out it would have been about as well for the column to have returned to the point of organization immediately after the Big Horn fight [that is, the fight in the Big Horn Mountains in November 1876]. But then no one could have foreseen all the difficulties that encompassed us. From old Fort Reno scouts were sent back to the Red Cloud and Spotted Tail agencies to enlist as many more Indians as would be found willing to join us. Word was sent also to Major Mason, post commander at Red Cloud, to despatch two Indian spies to ascertain the location of Crazy Horse's camp, with instructions to report back to General Crook where they found the hostiles. Meantime, arrangements were made by our quarter-

master, Captain Furey, to have forwarded additional supplies of grain for our
stock, and we moved by slow marches
along the Belle Fourche, stopping in
some places two or three days where we
could obtain a little grass and shelter for
our animals. Gradually the time passed
and the weather, we saw, would soon be
severe enough to test the endurance of
men and animals, even when most comfortably clad and liberally supplied with
food.

On the limited supplies for men and
horses, and no word from the Sioux
spies or additional Indian scouts:

Still but very scant supplies of grain
came to us, and we learned that the commanders of the frontier posts we had left
could neither procure at their stations
nor press into service any considerable
trains of wagons to forward supplies.
When this news reached us, about
December 20, we were some seven or
eight days' march from Fort Fetterman
by the most direct return route we could
select, with only half forage for about
that number of days and rations to the
1st or 2nd of January. We had not yet
heard from the guides sent to the agency
nor from the spies sent to Crazy Horse,
and so for the time being we were in
something of a maze. Soon hunger and
the weather began to tell on our animals,
and no inconsiderable proportion of
them looked as if about to lie down and
let their bare bones whiten on the lone-
some wilds after the wolves had picked
off them the last tough morsel of their
flesh. It was marvelous to see with what
avidity they devoured every shrub and
blade of grass they came upon, the bark
of the cottonwood boughs being a
choice morsel. We cut down hundreds of
these trees on our line of march and fed
the bark to our animals. When one finds

himself in the midst of such a country,
wholly dependent on his animals, he is
very glad of the opportunity to engage
himself for their benefit, and consequently wood chopping became for a
while quite a fashionable sort of entertainment, in which the best people in
our community assisted.

On Crook's decision to return to Fort
Fetterman:

With many of our horses in the condition described a week's hard travel after
the enemy, without increased forage,
would leave a very large proportion of
the command dismounted. To have gone
hunting for Crazy Horse's village, ignorant as we then were of its probable situation, might have entailed much more
than a week's march outward, not count-
ing for the return home. General Crook
concluded, therefore, to start homeward
at once, his situation compelling him to
take that course.

On marching in frigid temperatures
and Dr. Joseph R. Gibson's frozen
thermometer:

[The] cold and discomfort was intensi-
fied each successive march until the climax was capped on Christmas eve and
Christmas morning, when the mercury
froze in the bulb of Dr. Gibson's thermometer and of every thermometer on
the expedition. Building one's house at
night to pull it down the next morning is
cold work in such weather, but we were
glad to have the material for such an
abode as our tents afforded. It is not easy
to picture the intensity of such cold as
we then experienced. As a result, the
noses, ears, cheeks or fingers of nearly
one-half the command have been frost-
ed, not severely, it is true, but enough to
show unmistakably the imprint of the
fingers of old King Frost, who appears to

hold undisputed possession of the territory hereabouts; and, indeed, so far as most of us are concerned, he is quite welcome to do so. . . . To be sure, we return with peeled noses and cheeks indicative of our incursions into frigid latitudes, badges of our sufferings of which we should be proud perhaps, only there is so little poetry in savage warfare that one can put it all in his eye.

On Captain George M. Randall, the Crow scouts, and the value of friendly Indians in the hostile country:

Christmas night Captain George M. Randall, with about seventy Crow Indians, joined us, having left old Fort Reno two days previously. Captain Randall had a very trying march. From the first he was surrounded with difficulties not easy to surmount. The Crows had been frightened a good deal in the Rosebud fight and were not very eager for another contest with the Sioux. He had some trouble, therefore, in persuading them to join him for a winter campaign, and expected no less than a general desertion as he proceeded on his way toward us. There were a great many impediments, too, in the way of his successful progress in the direction he was obliged to take. The snow was very deep on the mountains, and, his supplies being limited, he was obliged to operate "long" on experience and "short" on provisions. Fortunately he had had some Indian experience, and was ready to devour his share of raw buffalo meat, hot, too—blood hot—when the animal was killed, and hunger taught him to scramble for first cut of uncooked liver, &c. Reviewing such an experience as Captain Randall has had one is very glad to be alive and is ready even to jest on past trials, however rough, though he may not crave to live over again the life just past. Marching through snow from one to five feet deep is not pleasant, no matter how bright the sun, if you are hungry and there does not happen to be a supply depot within 100 miles of you. Nor does a bivouac at night with scant wood beside a frozen stream help one much. To keep warm you must herd closely then, and Captain Randall did herd very closely, but—well, he has thrown away three suits of underclothing since. The Captain is with us, but the Crows have been sent back, and though they had no chance to fight with us their scout toward us was not without its advantages. Any movement of friendly Indians through the hostile country helps the work on hand.

The Powder River expedition was, indeed, a *fait accompli.*

17

The Surrender of
Crazy Horse

"The sufferings of Colonel Miles' command during the campaign were very great, but the successful result has fully repaid him for the hardships endured."—Anonymous, Tongue River Cantonment, December 21, 1876, *New York Herald*, January 16, 1877

"[The Cheyennes] are a fine looking race, the men being tall and soldierly and the children very bright in appearance. The women, who do all the drudgery about the lodges, are generally haggard and careworn. These people are entirely destitute, and haven't seen even the commonest necessaries of life. Their village was destroyed by General Crook's cavalry in November last."—Anonymous, Red Cloud Agency, May 2, 1877, *New York Herald*, May 11, 1877

"No one regrets that Crazy Horse is cantering over the happy hunting grounds. Many would be glad to have Sitting Bull feeding in the same pasture."—Editorial comment, *Cheyenne Daily Leader*, September 18, 1877

From his cantonment on the Tongue River, it was Colonel Miles's plan to allow the Sioux little rest through the cold winter.[1] As far as the Sioux were concerned, they simply wanted the troops out of the Yellowstone country so they could hunt in peace. The first real action was in October, on the north side of the Yellowstone. On the seventeenth, Miles departed the cantonment with all ten companies of the Fifth Infantry, some 450 men, and a Rodman gun, in search of an overdue supply train from Glendive Creek, seventy-five miles to the east.[2] The following day he met the supply train, about one hundred wagons, coming along near Custer Creek, with an escort of some two hundred men under Lieutenant Colonel Otis. The latter informed Miles that his small force had been skirmishing with the Sioux along the route; in fact, this was their second attempt to get through. The wagons first set out on the tenth but had to turn back one day later because of Sioux hostility and the capture of about forty of their mules.[3] Miles and Otis bivouacked for the night, then Otis continued on to the cantonment while Miles continued east after the Sioux. Two days later, he caught up with them at Cedar Creek.[4] For two days, October 20 and 21, Miles met with Sitting Bull under a flag of truce. It was the first such conference between a government representative and a "hostile" leader since the start of the Sioux War. At the end of the second meeting, with no agreement forthcoming—the Sioux wanted Miles out of the country, and Miles wanted the same for the Sioux—the Fifth Infantry, aided by the Rodman, drove some six hundred to eight hundred warriors from their village and from ridge to ridge in a running fight. One report said the troops pursued the fleeing Sioux for forty-two miles.[5] Two soldiers were wounded, while the Sioux left behind six dead on the battlefield. A report printed in the *New York Herald* from one of the officers present, possibly Lieutenant James W. Pope, Fifth Infantry, stated:

Six dead Indians were seen lying on the field; but as the Sioux had full opportunity to carry off their dead before they could be reached by the troops it is reasonable to believe a great number were killed. Whatever their loss in killed may have been, more severe was the loss of several tons of dried buffalo meat and a large amount of camp equipage. For this they had fought, and by the loss of the

fight the prestige of Sitting Bull was diminished. His punishment for the destruction of a gallant band of cavalry [Custer's Seventh] was accomplished by infantry alone, not a cavalry soldier or officer being on the field in this engagement. Colonel Miles displayed that superb handling of troops that so distinguished him during the war and on the Southern plains. The Indians were so completely baffled by the rapidity of his movements as to be unable to make any formidable opposition.[6]

An anonymous dispatch from the Tongue River Cantonment on December 31 further glorified Miles's victory and, more importantly, pointed out that many of the Sioux had become discouraged with continuing the conflict, no doubt based on the fact that five Sioux chiefs had surrendered to Miles a few days after the encounter:

[Colonel Miles] met in open fight the great leader of the hostile Sioux, defeated him, routed and demoralized him, and demonstrated not only to the entire satisfaction of the country but to that of the savage chief himself, that infantry soldiers can, when ably commanded, whip any number of Indians that dare to oppose them in open combat. It was the first decided victory of the Sioux war, and its result has been to completely dishearten and demoralize Sitting Bull and his following.[7]

This was the first large-scale fight of the Sioux War in which the Indians had to face artillery, even if it was just one piece, and no doubt much of Miles's success was due to its unexpected use.[8] Two months later, on December 18, three companies of the Fifth Infantry (about 110 men), under Lieutenant Frank Baldwin, with the aid of a howitzer, routed Sitting Bull once more. The scene of the fight was along Ash Creek (a tributary of Redwater Creek), about fifteen miles north of the fight with Miles on October 21. The village contained 122 lodges, 90 of which were left behind in their hurried flight. The soldiers took what supplies and trophies they wanted, along with sixty captured mules and ponies, and burned the rest. Only one Indian was reported killed.[9] A dispatch from the Tongue River Cantonment on December 31 praised Baldwin's triumph:

Lieutenant Baldwin did not lose a man in the engagement. The affair was a very gallant one, and Lieutenant Baldwin and his command deserve great credit for the courage and cool determination with which they charged upon and routed so large a camp of "hostiles," who they had every reason to believe would fight with the energy and fiendishness of despair.[10]

Sitting Bull, practically destitute after two attacks on his village in as many months, retreated to the south side of the Yellowstone for a short time before crossing into Canada in early May 1877.[11] For him the war was over. However, Miles still had Indians to conquer. Departing the Tongue River Cantonment on December 29 in search of Crazy Horse, Miles's command included five companies of the Fifth Infantry and two companies of the Twenty-second (436 officers and men), a handful of white and Indian scouts, plus a Napoleon gun and a three-inch Rodman—both masqueraded as

wagons.[12] The column moved south along the Tongue River's snow-covered landscape amid frequent subzero temperatures. On the afternoon of January 7, Miles's scouts captured seven Cheyenne women and children, and a boy about fourteen, after which the scouts and soldiers skirmished with an estimated 250 Sioux and Cheyenne warriors, many of the latter being survivors of Mackenzie's attack. The following morning more than six hundred warriors, Crazy Horse the most prominent among them, brought the fight to Miles's command. Newspaper coverage of the encounter—variously called the Battle of the Wolf Mountains, Miles' Battle of Tongue River, or the Battle of the Butte—was slim, but at least two reports made it into print, one in the *New York Herald* and the other in *Frank Leslie's Illustrated Newspaper*, both of which are excerpted here.

From the *Herald*, dateline Tongue River, January 19:

After proceeding some sixty miles up Tongue River Miles discovered signs of recent Indian encampments, and pushing on he struck their full force on January 7. On the evening of that day quite a heavy skirmish took place, and on the 8th the Indians, to the number of 1,000 warriors, well armed and plentifully supplied with ammunition, appeared on his front. They gave every indication of being confident of their ability to annihilate the troops. Colonel Miles attacked them, however, with his gallant little command, and by an admirable disposition of his force succeeded in gaining a decisive victory.

The loss of the Indians is hard to estimate, as they always carry their dead and wounded from the field; but it is known to have been very great. The battlefield was covered with traces of blood. The Indians fought with great desperation. The battle was contested on very rough and broken ground, where it would have been impossible for cavalry to ride. The Indians were entirely on foot, and charged the troops repeatedly.

Our officers and men displayed the greatest coolness and courage, and poured deadly volleys into the ranks of the "hostiles." Though outnumbered at least three to one they never once contemplated the possibility of defeat. For more than five hours the fight raged as terribly as ever was witnessed on a battlefield. A heavy snow storm prevailed during a portion of the fight.[13]

From *Frank Leslie's Illustrated Newspaper:*

After a march of eleven days through snow two feet deep—including a pursuit of eight days—several squaws and children were captured, one hundred and twenty head of beef cattle recaptured, and Crazy Horse had to fight. Our engraving,[14] from a sketch by an officer of the expedition, represents the battle on the 8th of January 1877, in the gorges of the Wolf Mountains, at the decisive moment when the Indians endeavored to flank the troops by occupying a high hill to the left and rear. Having failed to produce much effect on the line in the valley, the Indians, leaving a force dismounted in the timber in front, and on the other side of the river, sufficient to keep the troops in the valley occupied, moved their main force to the left, in rear of the hills on that side, with the intention of occupying the hills to the left and rear. [Captain James S.] Casey's company (A) was sent to drive them from the first hill to the left. He took the hill under a heavy fire, and had to fight hard to keep it; but he did so, and inflicted heavy loss on the Indians, killing their Great Medicine Man, Hi-no-ton-ka—or Big Crow—and one of the head warriors—a very brave and promising young Sioux, known to some of the scouts. Another body [of Indians] occupied a hill to the left of Casey, and [Lieutenant Robert] McDonald's company (D) was sent to drive them from it, which the soldiers did gallantly. Then the Indians massed in large numbers on the highest spur of the main ridge, which commanded the whole position, and took our line, artillery and all, in reverse. [Captain Edmund] Butler's company (C) was sent to take this—the key point of the position. The company crossed the plain, about half a mile wide, to the foot of the bluff, under a heavy and continuous fire, which was redoubled on the left, when, under the leadership of the captain, it moved up the first rise in double-time. Butler's horse was shot under him. The men, firing, advanced at a run, scaled the precipitous height through snow and rocks and fallen timber, and in a snowstorm took the bluff crowning the height. The Indians gave up the conflict. The Indian loss was 16 killed, including the medicine man and the chief. The number of wounded is not known, but in front of Butler and McDonald's companies on the hills there were heavy traces of blood on the snow. The subsequent march up the valley also showed traces of blood for miles. The loss of the troops in the expedition was three men killed,[15] eight wounded; three horses were killed, one horse wounded; two pack-mules wounded in the train. In this action the Indians were armed with magazine guns, Sharps rifles, etc. For people who were said to be short of ammunition, they used it quite freely. They expended more than the troops.[16]

"This engagement was unlike any other Indian fight I had ever witnessed," Miles remarked afterward. "It was fought on ground where it would have been impossible to have maneuvered cavalry. They [the Indians] fought entirely dismounted, not a single rifle being fired on horseback, their ponies being used only to carry them from one line of ravines . . . to others. They used loud shrill whistles to convey their orders. I have never seen [infantry] troops more steady, and I could not compliment them too highly for their fortitude."[17]

When Red Horse, a Minneconjou Sioux, surrendered at the Cheyenne River Agency in late February 1877, he explained the Indian side of the fight:

The fight happened in this way. Some Cheyenne women, moving along carelessly over hills with their lodges, were discovered by troops and captured. The two men who were behind came on to the main camp and reported what had happened. A war party went out to drive the troops back. The fight was on Suicide Creek [a.k.a. Hanging Woman Creek]. Some days before the capture of those women a plan was laid to send 50 Ogallallas and Cheyennes down to the post [Tongue River Cantonment] to draw the troops out. They were ordered to keep firing on them, to draw them on to the main camp, where some 1,000 lodges [warriors?] were waiting to receive them. This was a secret, and was not known to the women and children. The two men coming in and reporting the capture of the seven women, spoiled the plan, for a party immediately formed and went down, attacked the troops, and stopped them at Suicide Creek. I was in all the counsels. The plan as laid miscar-

ried. It was a failure. We expected to have a great battle.[18]

Estimates of Indian losses at the Battle of Wolf Mountains, some twenty miles north of the Montana line, vary widely. Wooden Leg stated that Big Crow was the only man killed, which appears to be rather improbable. Miles reported twelve to fifteen killed and twenty-five to thirty wounded. On the other hand, some of his officers put the number killed as high as twenty-three.[19] One thing is certain: this proved to be Crazy Horse's last fight against the whites. Although he didn't know it yet, his next battle would be against life on a reservation, not an easy task for a man used to his freedom.

Between the punishing campaigns of Miles and Crook that fall and winter of 1876–77, many of the reservation holdouts began to waver. The free life was no longer so free, and their former winter haven was no longer a safe place. In effect, they became the game animals of the Yellowstone Basin, and each time a village went up in smoke, so did many years of industry. Throughout the winter and spring, various bands went into the agencies and gave up their arms and ponies. Following are several newspaper excerpts detailing some of these surrenders:

New York Herald, March 15, 1877, "Hostiles Surrendering":

Chicago, March 14, 1877—[O]n the 25th of February 229 Sioux, belonging to the Minneconjou, Sans Arcs and Two Kettles bands arrived at the Cheyenne Agency from the main hostile camp on

Tongue River and surrendered, giving up their arms and all their horses—some 300 in number. The principal men of this party were Red Horse, Spotted Elk and White Eagle. The former, upon coming in at the Agency, told Colonel Wood that he and his people wanted to behave themselves in future, and then, upon close questioning, told what he knew of the battle wherein Custer's command was annihilated.

New York Times, April 18, 1877, "Surrender of the Sioux Bands":

Cheyenne, April 17—Advices from Camp Robinson . . . state that on the 14th inst. the village of Sioux previously mentioned as coming in with Spotted Tail, surrendered to Gen. Crook, at the Spotted Tail Agency. The village numbered about 1,000 persons, mainly Sans Arcs and Minneconjous, under Roman Nose and other chiefs. The Indians asked permission to approach the agency in the style commonly used by them upon entering a friendly village, which was granted them. About 10 o'clock the warriors, to the number of perhaps 300, made a regular charge on the agency from several directions, yelling and firing their pieces in the air. At 11 o'clock the main village filed past the post and went into camp on a spot designated by the agent. As the village was approached, about 30 principal chiefs and head men rode in a line into the fort, advancing slowly up the Parade to the commanding officer's quarters, where, wheeling to the left, they faced Gen. Crook, to whom they were presented by Spotted Tail. The son of Lone Horn first rode forward and, laying his gun on the ground, said, "I lay down this gun as a token of submission to Gen. Crook, to whom I wish to surrender." The chiefs all shook hands with Gen. Crook, and rode away to put their people in camp. On the 15th inst., a

council was held, in which the Indians were told what would be required of them by the Government. They said that their professions of peace were sincere, and this is fully credited by all who saw them. They turned over to the agent upward of 1,430 ponies and horses, also arms, the exact number of which could not be ascertained, but the collection embraced many carbines taken in the Custer massacre. They are believed to have brought in many relics of that affair, and Gen. Crook has given orders to spare no pains in the recovery of such things.

New York Times, April 22, 1877, "Surrender of More Indians":

Camp Robinson, April 21—Eighty lodges of Cheyennes, under Dull Knife and Standing Elk, surrendered to Gen. Crook at 11 a.m. today. The village comprises about 550 persons, 85 of whom are fighting men. They turned in 600 ponies, 60 guns, and about 30 pistols. They are completely destitute of all the necessaries of life, having lost everything when their village was destroyed in November last. They have no lodges, but simple shelters of old canvas and skins, very few blankets and robes, and no cooking utensils. Many are still suffering from frozen limbs. It is surprising that they have been able to hold out so long under these circumstances, and their doing so proves the fortitude of the American Indian under privation and hardship. This makes about 780 Cheyennes who have surrendered here since January 1.

New York Tribune, April 23, 1877, "Surrender of Hostile Cheyennes":

Red Cloud Agency, Neb., April 22— Yesterday morning the hostile Cheyennes came into this agency and surrendered. They approached the agency from the north, and, as they came over the hills into the valley, began singing and firing their guns. The warriors were formed in companies and maneuvered with as much apparent ease as companies of cavalry. The leading company carried a white flag, in front of which rode Standing Elk, Dull Knife, and other chiefs, these being preceded by Lieutenant [William Philo] Clark and interpreter Roland ["Bill" Rowland].

Dull Knife said he was glad to see the white chiefs, and that his people had heard what they said. He hoped this would be an everlasting peace. "When your messengers came to us," he said, "we listened to their words and came right in. From this time on, everything you say to my people will be heeded." Turning to Colonel Mackenzie, he said, "You are the one I was afraid of when you came here last summer." Standing Elk said they were glad they had come in and had been received so well. When they shook hands today, it meant an everlasting peace, so far as he and his people were concerned.

The band that surrendered yesterday are in a very wretched condition as regards tepees, clothing, and ponies. This is the band whom Colonel Mackenzie thrashed so soundly on the North Fork of Powder River on November 25 last. At that time they lost their entire village and over 500 ponies. They have therefore few tepees now, and even these are patched up from skins, gunnysacks, and scraps of canvas. A number of the Cheyennes are suffering from frozen limbs, the result of losing everything in the fight with Mackenzie. There are also many widows from the same cause. Altogether a more destitute and wretched lot of people is seldom seen. Colonel Mackenzie directed that supplies be issued, beginning with the

widows and wounded people. Some of the most badly wounded have been placed in the hospital at Camp Robinson. As fast as material arrives they will be placed in comfortable lodges and supplied with clothing and blankets. Some of those who came in under Little Wolf [in late February] were nearly famished, and one man actually ate till he died.

A more miserably poor band probably does not exist on the plains, yet they are among the bravest of all the northern Indians, none of the Sioux tribes surpassing them in power or endurance and personal courage. Their final voluntary surrender and disarmament removes one of the last serious obstacles to safety of travel and residence on this frontier. Up to this time there have surrendered at Spotted Tail Agency 1,221 hostiles in various bands of Sioux. At Red Cloud Agency there have surrendered, prior to this band, 400. Those arriving yesterday number 524, making an aggregate of over 2,000 at both agencies. Several thousand ponies and a large number of arms of all descriptions have been turned in. The last couriers from Crazy Horse report him still moving for this agency.

And then on May 6 came the biggest surrender of all, when Crazy Horse led about nine hundred followers into the Red Cloud Agency, including 217 men who were classified as warriors.[20] Six days later, on May 12, Crazy Horse was among a number of Oglalas who enlisted as army scouts.[21] He also became somewhat of a celebrity among the whites, many of whom wanted to meet the mysterious warrior whose bravery and leadership had been instrumental in the killing of Custer the previous June.[22] But all was not roses. The army believed he was planning to stir up trouble again, but the charges came from rival Sioux leaders and headmen who were jealous of the attention he was receiving. Four months later, on September 5, he was mortally wounded in an unfortunate scuffle while resisting arrest. The revered warrior died late that night. In hindsight it may have been for the best; his ultimate destination after the Camp Robinson guardhouse was to have been exile in the Dry Tortugas, seventy miles off the coast of Florida.[23] In the end, Crazy Horse survived the battle of the Rosebud, the battle of the Little Big Horn, and a host of other deadly conflicts during the period of intertribal warfare, only to die a victim of hearsay and reservation politics.

The last military action of any significance in the Sioux War occurred on May 7, the day following Crazy Horse's surrender, on a little known eastern tributary of the Rosebud River called Little Muddy Creek (today known as Lame Deer Creek). The troops had departed the cantonment on May 1, and after five days of marching had reached a point some sixty miles up the Tongue River. Here the scouts discovered an Indian trail heading west. Miles left his wagons under the protection of three companies of infantry and, taking supplies for six days, struck west toward the Rosebud. His command then consisted of four companies of the Second Cavalry (under command of Captain Edward Ball), a detachment of twenty-five mounted infantry, three companies of the Twenty-sec-

ond Infantry, and some scouts, including John Bruguier and the Cheyenne warrior Hump, both of whom "knew their business."[24] All told, Miles had more than three hundred men.

The scouts located the village on the sixth, some fifteen miles away as the eagle flies, and plans were implemented for the standard dawn attack. After a temporary halt to rest and eat, the mounted units of Miles's force continued on for a night march, while the three infantry companies were ordered to follow along at a slower pace. "Every one seemed anxious enough for the fight," wrote an unidentified officer. "Officers and soldiers alike seemed disposed to make the most of the opportunity, and felt the chance presented was a good one to distinguish themselves."[25] The officer continued:

The Indians had just turned out their herd to graze when they discovered our approach and made every effort to recover it or run it into the hills, but Lieutenant [Lovell H.] Jerome [Second Cavalry] with his company of [mounted] infantry and citizens [the white and Indian scouts] dashed down upon them, and drove them back, securing all the ponies.[26]

For Miles, the fight was almost his last. Early in the action he had called a stop to the shooting to have a parley with Lame Deer, after one of his scouts identified the Sioux leader among the fighters. Hump arranged the meeting, and a small party of whites and Indians advanced toward each other (apparently the whites remained on their horses). Lame

Deer laid down his carbine as requested and shook hands with Miles, but the situation was tense; a warrior named Iron Star, Lame Deer's nephew, was visibly agitated. Shortly afterward, scout Robert Jackson rode forward and pointed his gun at Lame Deer. At the same time a Cheyenne scout named White Bull was trying to wrest Iron Star's rifle away. At this point, Murphy's Law took over: the weapon discharged, and the bullet passed through White Bull's coat. Lame Deer, figuring he was about to be shot down, grabbed for his carbine and fired point blank at Miles. Miraculously, he missed. It was fortunate for Miles but unfortunate for the man behind him, his orderly, Private Charles Shrenger, Second Cavalry. He was hit in the chest and died instantly. All hell broke loose, and both Lame Deer and Iron Star were dead within a minute or two. Iron Star had almost escaped over a hill, only to run headlong into Company G, Second Cavalry, whose captain, James N. Wheelan, dropped him with a shot from his pistol.

How many Indians were killed in the assault that followed is unclear. Lieutenant Alfred Fuller, Second Cavalry, stated fourteen were found on the field, while another participant claimed forty-five Indians were killed and others carried off.[27] According to Jackson, Lame Deer was shot seventeen times. And to show just how much had changed since the summer of '76, the Sioux chief was scalped by White Bull, a former ally.[28] Besides Shrenger, three other soldiers were killed, and eight

or nine were wounded. Over two hundred Indians escaped into the hills, including Lame Deer's son, Fast Bull. Miles ordered the village burned; the survivors were destitute except for what few items they managed to carry away in their hasty flight:

The victory is one of the most complete that has ever been gained over any body of Indians on the Plains. The entire herd was taken, numbering fully five hundred as good ponies as I ever saw. The entire camp was burned with its contents, and the Indians who escaped are utterly destitute. They can never recover from their loss and gather together again what we have destroyed. The two chiefs in command of the village, Red Elk and Lame Deer, are both among the dead.[29]

Lieutenant Fuller, who had been "shot through the shoulder," was sent back to Bismarck, where he told a reporter that the troops had captured 450 horses and 54 lodges, among which were found "many new agency goods, and saddles, guns, officers' clothing, &c., taken from the 7th Cavalry in the Custer fight."[30]

While the attack on Lame Deer's village represented the last significant encounter of the Sioux War of 1876–77 it did not include the final gunshots of that war. So far as the author can tell, those came on July 7, 1877, and, in an odd twist, they appear to have been part of an entirely Indian affair, pitting Cheyenne scouts against Sioux diehards from Lame Deer's razed village. Major Henry M. Lazelle, First Infantry, reported the incident (and one that occurred three days earlier) in a communiqué dated September 5, 1877:

On the 4th of July I pushed the cavalry and scouts 40 miles to the northward into the big bend of the Little Missouri; the scouts encountered near here about 15 Indians, and they think that two or three of them were killed or badly wounded in the fight; but I ascertained that the Indians had crossed to the west bank of the Little Missouri. I crossed it on the 7th in a direction largely gaining on them; and availing myself of the presence of two Cheyenne Indians [scouts], I got them to go forward with the hope of spying out the Indian camp. They were, however, attacked by eight Sioux and driven back but killed one and got his horse and gun, themselves escaping unharmed. They had learned enough of the location of the Sioux camp to believe that they could guide me there that night. Leaving the train, I took six companies of infantry, the cavalry company, and scouts, starting at dark, and reached the Sioux camp at Sentinel Buttes at an early hour in the morning, after a march of 22 miles, to find it hastily deserted, apparently only a few hours before. A careful examination gave convincing proof that the Indians were a remnant of Lame Deer's band, whose camp had been destroyed by Colonel Miles, on the Rosebud, in April [May].[31]

By the beginning of September, the fugitives of Lame Deer's band had had enough of the refugee lifestyle. A dispatch dated September 4 reported that "Shedding Bear with fifteen lodges of Lame Deer's band, numbering about eighty persons," surrendered to Captain Daniel W. Burke, Fourteenth Infantry, at Camp Sheridan.[32] The dispatch further stated that Fast Bull (Lame Deer's son), with a band numbering four hundred to five hundred, would be arriving in a few more days. The dispatch continued:

These are the Indians that have been committing depredations in the vicinity of the Black Hills, and their coming in leaves that country and the Big Horn country entirely free of Indians.[33]

Six days later, September 10, Fast Bull's surrender was announced in a brief dispatch out of Camp Sheridan:

Lame Deer's band of Indians [under Fast Bull] arrived here today, which completes the surrender of all the hostile Sioux, clearing the Black Hills and Big Horn country [of Indians], as Sitting Bull and his party are in the British possessions. The number surrendering is between 300 and 400. About 175 of the band had previously arrived.[34]

With the death of Crazy Horse, the surrender of Fast Bull's band, Sitting Bull in Canada, and the army having gained permanent footholds in the disputed territory, the Sioux War was, for all intents and purposes, effectively over.

New York Tribune,
Monday, May 7, 1877

Surrender Of Crazy Horse.

He Brings In A Procession Of Indians Two Miles Long—A Brilliant Result—Over 3,500 Indians Surrender In Ten Weeks.

Red Cloud Agency, Neb., May 6—The entire Crazy Horse band, consisting of about 900 Indians, surrendered here today. Col. McKenzie [Mackenzie] trusted the management of the details of surrender to Lieut. Clark, 2d Cavalry. Riding out five miles from the Agency,

Crazy Horse and his band on their way to surrender to General Crook at the Red Cloud Agency, May 6, 1877. (*Library of Congress*)

the lieutenant met the savages and had a short preliminary talk. Crazy Horse was riding a few steps in advance of the leading chiefs, while some 300 warriors marshaled in six companies and advancing regularly in single line, followed. Though attired in purely Indian costume, there was a total lack of the usual pomp and parade manifested by the vanquished. The survey of the leader was evident upon every hand, and the perfect discipline of the warriors in their new sad role, with the quiet reigning throughout the vast cavalcade, was deeply imposing.

After ordering his followers to halt, Crazy Horse and his principal men dismounted, advanced to meet Lieut. Clark, and shook hands cordially. Mr. Clark briefly told the savages of the general desire for peace, and added that all bad feeling of the past must be buried.

Crazy Horse told his spokesman to convey his sentiments, as he would say nothing. The answer was in effect that the chieftain would make peace for all time, and that as he smoked the peace pipe he would invoke the Great Spirit to make it eternal. All of his things he said he had given to his brother-in-law, Red Cloud. Another chief, He Dog, advanced and placed his war bonnet and war shirt upon Lieut. Clark as a sign of his submission and good will. This ceremony completed, Crazy Horse ordered an advance and the vicinity of the agency was reached at 2 p.m.

As they entered the broad valley of White River, near the point selected for the camp, the warriors formed in five bands, 40 in each band, and filed across the stream, chanting songs suited to the occasion. Here the great train of camp equipage, with the ponies and the savages, formed a compact line two miles in length. The solemn peace chant echoed from front to rear and everything betokened utter submission of the once dreaded band. While the tepees were being pitched, the ponies, numbering over 2,000, were turned over to the Red Cloud band, to whom they are given as a reward for their cooperation in subduing the hostile bands [and thus they gained back the horses taken from them in October 1876]. Many excellent American horses and mules were noticed in the herd.

At 4 p.m. the warriors gathered in the center of the crescent shaped camp to surrender their arms. Crazy Horse, Little Big Man, He Dog, Little Hawk, and other chiefs laid their guns upon the green sward, and were closely followed by some fifty braves. Lieut. Clark then quietly informed them that every arm must be turned in; that now they could show their desire for peace in a conclusive manner. As they hesitated, he told them they could take their arms back to their tepees, and he would search every one singly until all weapons were found. The warriors quickly picked up their rifles and retired, when the lieutenant ordered up a thorough search of the village. Thus far he has secured one hundred and seventeen stands of arms. Crazy Horse surrendered three fine Winchester rifles. The Indians exhibited no objections to having the tepees searched, and the work has been accomplished with no trouble.

Crazy Horse is an Ogallalla Sioux, tall, slender, and about 37 years old. He has been at war for 12 years, having left Fort Laramie in 1865 upon the occasion of the murder of his brother. He exhibits two bullet wounds, one through the face, leaving an ugly scar. In his tribe he rules as a despot, and his people dread him while yet most worshipping him for his wonderful bravery. He has not uttered five words to his conquerors; in fact, he talks to no one. A coincidence worthy of notice is that Crazy Horse tonight took supper with the scout, Frank Gruard [Grouard], who two years ago was his prisoner, and who has since led Gen. Crook's forces unerringly to the great chieftain's haunts.

Chief Little Big Man is considered the worst of all the Indians. It was he who in [September] 1875 broke up the proceedings of the great Peace Commission by riding naked and armed to the teeth into the circle and declaring for war. Little Hawk wears a medal presented to his father by President [James] Monroe in 1817.

18

Last Rites and Last Rambles

"President Truman signed legislation today to pay $101,630 to Sioux Indians for ponies the Army took away from them after the Custer massacre. . . . The payments are to go to the Indians or their heirs."
—*New York Times*, July 4, 1945

"Every now and then something pops up in the day's news to remind us how short the period of American history is and how closely it is all tied together."—*New York Times*, July 24, 1946

Following the Sioux War of 1876 there was just one obstacle left to white settlement in the Yellowstone Valley: the large Crow Reservation that bordered the Yellowstone River. Although the Crow Indians have managed to hold on to a good-sized chunk of the eastern portion of their reservation, the outlook in the early 1880s was less than optimal that they would even have that section of land to show for their allegiance to the US government during its wars with the Sioux. In fact, over the next two decades, the Crow Reservation shrunk by intervals until by the early 1900s it was less than half its original size based on the 1868 treaty. Their cessions included all the land adjacent to the Yellowstone River. From the *New York Times*, April 4, 1880:[1]

While discussing the Indian problem in its relation to the Yellowstone Valley, I must not overlook the Crows. This tribe, which numbers about 900 or 1,000 warriors, is in many respects the most formidable tribe of Indians on our frontier. Their wealth in ponies is said to be almost incalculable, though 20,000 is probably a reasonable estimate of the size of the herd. The Crows, for some years, have been the warm allies of the whites, with whom they have gladly combined in hunting down their common enemy, the Sioux. By this association they have gained a knowledge of our tactics and methods of warfare which might operate to our disadvantage if they should ever go on the warpath against us. Besides this, they are excellently armed with the best patterns of breech-loading rifles manufactured in the United States, which they can use effectively, mounted as well as afoot. They are now on the friendliest terms with their paleface neighbors, and it is to be hoped that no question will ever arise to disturb the existing harmony. But clouds are beginning to appear on the horizon, the full import of which it is difficult to foresee. In the first place, the Crow Reservation is unquestionably the garden spot of the Yellowstone Valley, and as such it is exciting the envy of the white settlers. The reservation embraces all the territory west of the one hundred and seventh degree west longitude, south and east of the Yellowstone River and north of the Wyoming border, and includes 20,000 square miles of the most fertile and best-watered soil in Montana. There is an almost continuous chain of settlers along the north shore of the Yellowstone, from here to the Gallatin Valley, and the south shore would be quickly taken up also were it not for the Crow obstacle. The ranchmen on the north bank of the [Yellowstone] river opposite the reservation find themselves somewhat uncomfortably situated, from the fact that the northern buffalo herd, upon which the Crows depend for their food and their robes, and the hides to construct their tepees, or lodges, inhabits the upper portion of the Territory, and they are in constant danger of having their farms overrun by Indian hunting parties. . . . Meanwhile, the wave of civilization is washing the borders of the Crow country. Houses are constantly springing up on all sides. Valuable gold discoveries have been made on Clark's Fork, in Wyoming Territory, but [are] only accessible by the Montana route through the reservation. The great cattle men of Western Montana have no ready outlet for their herds except by crossing the Crow lands, and this privilege is sternly denied them. Too many influences are operating concurrently for the removal of the Crows to make it probable that they will much longer occupy their pres-ent home, and it will be well, for various reasons, if the present Congress takes action on the petition for their removal which was recently sent to Delegate [Martin] Maginnis, at Washington, after receiving the signatures of nearly every white resident of the entire Yellowstone Valley. It is not difficult to foresee what will be the result if the Indians are not induced to sell out their claim amicably, and when, as will otherwise be the inevitable consequence, they find the whites determined to push them off their reservation. I, for one, shall wish to be as close to a military post as is possible. The flurry might be brief, but it would be destructive. I am not sounding an idle alarm but am giving expression to the declared sentiment of many of the oldest and coolest settlers of this region, with whom I have conversed upon the subject.

On January 29, 1879, the secretary of war proclaimed the Custer Battlefield a national cemetery. By the early 1890s (if not sooner), advertisements started to appear in newspapers and magazines touting the battlefield as an exciting travel destination for the curious and adventurous. This advertisement appeared in the *Watertown (NY) Herald* on December 9, 1893:

A visit to this spot, which is now a National Cemetery, is extremely interesting. Here, seventeen years ago, General Custer and five companies of the Seventh U. S. Cavalry, numbering over 200, officers and men, were cut to pieces by the Sioux Indians and allied tribes under Sitting Bull. The battlefield, the valley of the Little Big Horn, located some forty odd miles south of Custer,

Montana, a station on the Northern Pacific Railroad, can be easily reached by stage. If you will write Chas. S. Fee, St. Paul, Minnesota, inclosing four cents in postage, he will send you a handsomely illustrated 100 page book, free of charge, in which you will find a graphic account of the sad catastrophe which overtook the brave Custer and his followers in the valley of the Little Big Horn, in June '76.

Jerome Stillson, who interviewed Sitting Bull in Canada in October 1877, died three years later, on December 26, 1880. He was about thirty-nine years old. His death was reported in the *New York Times* the following day:

Jerome B. Stillson, one of the best known journalists of this city, died at the St. Denis Hotel yesterday afternoon at 2:30. He had been suffering from Bright's disease of the kidneys since last June, and was confined to his room for three or four weeks past. His body was taken to Merritt's undertaking establishment, in Eighth Avenue, preparatory to its removal to Buffalo today. Mr. Stillson was born in Buffalo in 1841. During the latter part of the [Civil] war he became a special correspondent for the *New York World*, and rapidly rose to distinction as a journalist. When peace returned to the country he was made correspondent of the *World* in Washington, and in 1874 served as managing editor of that paper for a short term. He then became the Albany correspondent of the *World*, filling that position until 1875, when he went to Denver, Colorado, where he engaged in business in connection with Western lands. In 1877 he became attached to the staff of the [New York] *Herald*, his first notable productions in

this capacity being a series of letters from Utah describing the evils of Mormonism. While engaged in this work he was shot at and wounded in Salt Lake City. Since then he has remained on the *Herald* staff, his last work having been done in Indiana during the [political] campaign of last September. Mr. Stillson leaves no family. He was married about 10 years ago to Miss Bessie Whiton of Piermont, N. Y., but she died a few years after the marriage.

Although Stillson's obituary said he was to be buried in Buffalo, he was buried next to his wife in Piermont (Rockland County), New York.[2] Outside of Mark Kellogg, the reporter who died in the battle of the Little Big Horn, Stillson was the first of the Sioux War correspondents to die.

Correspondent Joseph Wasson was appointed U. S. consul for the Port of San Blas, Mexico, in early 1883, but died shortly after, on April 18, 1883. He was about forty-two years old.[3]

Frontiersman Frank J. North, who led the Pawnee scouts at the Dull Knife battle, later became a Nebraska rancher and also joined "Buffalo Bill's Wild West" show. While performing in Connecticut on July 31, 1884, he was badly injured in a fall from his horse:

During the exhibition of Buffalo Bill's Wild West Show at Charter Oak Park this afternoon a serious accident occurred to Major Frank North, the well-known interpreter of the Pawnee

Indians and a ranchman of Nebraska. The cavalcade of about 100 Indians, cowboys, and attachés had started at a signal on a wild chase down the track, and had proceeded but a short distance when Major North was thrown by the breaking of his saddle girth. Though followed by many running animals, all going at a reckless speed, the skill of the drivers prevented a general trampling upon him. One horse, however, planted his forefeet in his side and back and five or six ribs were broken. Four thousand spectators witnessed the accident, but it was not generally known till the whole performance was over that any one was seriously harmed. Major North was taken to the Oakwood Hotel, and is as comfortable tonight as could be expected. He has been for years a great sufferer from asthma and there may be internal injuries which will make his recovery doubtful.[4]

North never fully recovered. He died on March 14, 1885, at age forty-five.

In 1882, George Crook was sent back to Arizona to fight the Apaches. His 1883 campaign into the formidable Sierra Madre Mountains of Mexico was well-documented by Captain John Gregory Bourke (1846–1896) in his book *An Apache Campaign in the Sierra Madre*. When Geronimo escaped Crook's grasp in 1886, the long-time Indian fighter was criticized for his overdependence on Apache scouts and asked to be removed from command, telling Sheridan (1831–1888): "It may be that I am too much wedded to my own views in this matter, and as I

have spent nearly eight years of the hardest work of my life in this department, I respectfully request that I may be relieved from its command."[5]

His new assignment found him back in the Department of the Platte. His replacement in Arizona was Nelson Miles (1839–1925), whose use of artillery in 1876–77 was too much for the already wearied Sioux and helped put an end to the Great Sioux War. Miles became a brigadier general in December 1880, and lived long enough to see World War I and air warfare. The thought must have crossed his mind that fighter planes would have come in handy against Sitting Bull and Geronimo.

Crook was promoted to major general in April 1888 and placed in command of the Division of the Missouri. It was his last assignment. He died about two years later, at age sixty-one. From the *New York Times*, March 22, 1890:

Chicago, March 21—Major Gen. George Crook, United States Army, in command of the Department of the Missouri, died at the Grand Pacific Hotel, at 7:15 o'clock this morning, of heart disease. He arose shortly before 7 o'clock apparently in his usual health, and, in accordance with his custom, began exercising with the weights and pulleys connected with an apparatus for the purpose which he kept in his room. After a few minutes he stopped and laid down upon a lounge, saying that he felt a difficulty in breathing. A few minutes later he called to his wife: "Oh, Mary, Mary; I need some help. I can't get my breath." Dr. Hurlbut, who lives near by, was sent for. Everything possible was done, but Crook failed to rally. Mrs.

Crook and her sister, Mrs. Reid, were the only members of the family present at his bedside when he passed away. He had no children. Ever since he returned from his last trip to the Northwest he had been complaining of a bearing-down sensation in the neighborhood of the heart. In accordance with the wishes of Mrs. Crook it was arranged this afternoon that the funeral services shall be held on Sunday afternoon. The remains will then be put on board a special car, tendered by the Pullman Company, and will leave for Oakland, Md., at 3 o'clock, over the Baltimore and Ohio Road, escorted by the officers of the late General's staff and a small detachment of soldiers as a body guard. Adjt. Gen. [Robert] Williams, on behalf of the widow, has asked a number of prominent citizens to act as pallbearers. In the meantime the body will lie in state in the parlor of the Grand Pacific Hotel, with a body guard of soldiers.

Upon learning of Crook's death, Captain George M. Randall (1841–1918), of Crook's staff, told a newspaper reporter:

We have noticed for some time that Gen. Crook was not in his usual health. He was a man who never complained and said very little about his sufferings. At the theater last night [March 20] I saw that he was not feeling at all well and asked him if he was in pain. He said, "No," but I think that was the beginning of the end.[6]

In October 1877, General Terry met with Sitting Bull (then about forty-five years old) at Fort Walsh in Canada, but failed to convince the venerable and resolute chief to return

to the United States. Sitting Bull told him:

The part of the country you gave me you ran me out of. I have now come here to stay with these people, and I intend to stay here. I wish you to go back and to take it easy going back.[7]

"By 'taking it easy,'" correspondent Jerome Stillson explained, "Sitting Bull meant that the commission should take such a long time in going that it would never get back."

The Hunkpapa chief held out on Canadian soil for a few more years, but when he could no longer support himself by the hunt (the Canadian government did not supply rations to his people) he was forced to return to the United States. In fact, many of his followers had already preceded him. He surrendered to Major David H. Brotherton, Seventh Infantry, on July 20, 1881, at Fort Buford in present North Dakota, at the head of 187 followers. In his own way, he never surrendered; when it came time to hand over his Winchester rifle, he did so through his five-year-old son, Crow Foot. Three years later, the famed Sioux chief toured with "Buffalo Bill" Cody for a few months. In 1889, he became angry with his fellow Sioux leaders after they signed an agreement to sell some eleven million acres of land on the Great Sioux Reservation to the US government for white settlement. When asked by a reporter what effect he thought this would have on the Sioux, Sitting Bull was quoted as saying: "Don't talk to me about Indians; there are no Indians left except those in my band. They are all dead, and those still wearing the clothes of warriors are only squaws. I am sorry for my followers, who have been defeated and their land taken from them."[8] Sitting Bull was killed by Sioux Indian police while resisting arrest on December 15, 1890, on the Standing Rock Reservation, at the height of the Ghost Dance craze.[9] He was about fifty-nine.

General Terry had retired from the army in April 1888 and moved to New Haven, Connecticut. With Sitting Bull now dead, he could finally breathe easy. Instead, he stopped breathing entirely on December 16, 1890. He was sixty-three. Perhaps he read about Sitting Bull's death in the morning paper before passing. Well, it makes for a good story.

The grave and family plot of William C. Rawolle in the Green-Wood Cemetery, Brooklyn, New York. (*Author*)

Captain William C. Rawolle of the Second Cavalry (he was promoted from lieutenant in December 1880) was in all of the major fights of the Wyoming Column in 1876, from the Reynolds fight on Powder River through Slim Buttes. He was also one of the officers who brought relief horses out to Lieutenant Sibley's scouting party in early July 1876. His death was reported in the *Brooklyn Daily Eagle* on June 12, 1895:

Captain William C. Rawolle, United States Army, died suddenly of heart failure at the home of his brother, F. Rawolle, 263 Hicks Street, early yesterday morning [June 10]. Captain Rawolle was visiting Brooklyn on sick leave. His regiment is stationed at Fort Logan, Colorado. In the exercise of his duty a few months ago Captain Rawolle con-

tracted a severe cold, which developed into an attack of the grip. He partly recovered and obtained a leave of absence. He arrived in Brooklyn in April. Here he discovered that his sickness had affected his heart, which troubled him considerably. A few minutes after he had complained of a severe pain in the region of his heart yesterday he breathed his last. He was a native of Prussia and came to America, settling in New York City, with his parents, in boyhood. He was in his 55th year at his death. In 1861 the deceased enlisted in the army as a volunteer. He took part in seventeen fierce battles, including Fredericksburg, Chancellorsville and Antietam, during the war and came out unscathed. Most of the time he was on General Sturgis' staff. At the close of hostilities he was made a colonel. Then he entered the regular army and had been a captain for twenty-five years. Captain Rawolle was expecting a major's commission when he applied for a leave of absence. The deceased had seen much active service in Indian engagements since the close of the civil war, and was one of the reserve force sent to the assistance of General Custer in the latter's fatal encounter with the confederated Sioux on the Little Big Horn in 1876. Captain Rawolle and his fellow rescuers arrived a few hours too late to save the life of Custer and his companions.[10] The deceased subsequently helped capture Custer's slayers. Captain Rawolle's wife was with him at his death. His three children, who have not yet learned of their father's death, are at the military post at Fort Logan. The funeral services will be held this evening. The interment will be in Greenwood Cemetery [in Brooklyn].

Thaddeus H. Stanton, the long-time paymaster (since the Civil War) who participated in the Reynolds battle in March 1876 and was a correspondent for the *New York Tribune*, went on to become paymaster general of the United States in 1895. He retired in January 1899, and died in Omaha on January 23, 1900, just seven days short of his sixty-fifth birthday. From the *New York Times*, January 24, 1900:

Stanton had been ill for a long time. He was known as the "fighting Paymaster" because of his insistence on a place in the line during the Indian outbreaks. Gen. Stanton was born in Indiana [in 1835], but when a child his parents went to Iowa to live, and from that State he went, with hundreds of others, to join John Brown in Kansas in 1857. . . . In 1875 he went with Gen. Crook on the Black Hills expedition, and a year later

was chief of scouts for Gen. Crook, seeing hard service against the Indians then and in succeeding years. December 1890 found him in Omaha as Chief Paymaster of the Department of the Platte. . . . He often paid the troops in the field and courted danger rather than avoided it. He was appointed Paymaster General with the rank of Brigadier General in March 1895, succeeding General William Smith. Gen. Crook once said of Stanton: "His entire army life has been a period of unselfish, untiring, intelligent, and oftentimes heroic performance of duty."

Cuthbert Mills, the *New York Times* correspondent who spent the latter part of the summer of 1876 with General Crook's Big Horn and Yellowstone Expedition, died on February 15, 1904. His death was reported in the *New York Times* two days later:

Cuthbert Mills, a member of the banking firm of W. S. Lawson & Co. of 40 Exchange Place, and for years a well-known writer on financial topics, died Monday night in his apartment, in the Ansonia. He had been ill a short time with pneumonia. Until he entered the banking firm, for which he wrote a weekly financial letter, he was identified with the daily newspapers of this city, and for a while was on the staff of The New York Times. He was a member of the Metropolitan Museum of Art and the Municipal Art Society. Much of his time was spent in his Staten Island home, and he recently established a church in that neighborhood. He was about fifty-six years old.

John F. Finerty, the only correspondent who accompanied the Sibley Scout, went on to several interesting adventures, including a three-month trip through Mexico in 1879, and reporting on campaigns against the Utes (1879) and the Apaches (1881).[11] His death was reported in the *New York Tribune* on June 11, 1908:

Chicago, June 10—Colonel John F. Finerty, a well-known newspaperman, lecturer and Irish patriot, died at his home here early today, aged sixty-two years, from an ailment of the liver with which he had been suffering for six months.

Mr. Finerty left a wife and two children, John Finerty, Jr., assistant attorney for the New York Central Lines, and Miss Vera Finerty, a senior student in the University of Chicago.

John Frederick Finerty was a native of Galway, Ireland, where he was born on September 10, 1846. He was educated in the national schools of Ireland and with private tutors and came to this country in 1864. He served in the Union Army in the last year of the war. He also saw service in some Indian campaigns [as a correspondent]. In 1868 he became a reporter on "The Chicago Republican" and in 1871–72 he was city editor of that newspaper. He then joined the city staff of "The Chicago Tribune," where he remained three years. From 1876 to 1882 he was a war correspondent of "The Chicago Times," being engaged in reporting the Indian wars on the frontier. Returning to Chicago in 1882, he founded "The Chicago Citizen," and the same year he was elected to Congress as an Independent and served one term. He advocated the increase of the navy and

additional fortifications. In 1884 he was an ardent supporter of Mr. Blaine for President and acted thereafter with the Republican party until 1900, when he supported Mr. Bryan on the anti-imperialistic issue. He was a radical advocate of Irish independence and served seven times as president of the United Irish Societies of Chicago. For three terms he was president of the United Irish League of America. Mr. Finerty was a popular lecturer on historical subjects, American, Irish and cosmopolitan. He was the author of "Warpath and Bivouac" and "The People's History of Ireland," and edited "Ireland in Pictures." He was a member of the Grand Army of the Republic and the American-Irish Historical Society.

John V. Furey, Crook's quartermaster for the 1876 campaign, was made a brigadier general on February 24, 1903, and retired the following day. He returned to his birthplace, Brooklyn, New York, where he died on December 17, 1914, at age seventy-five. From the *New York Times*, December 18, 1914:

Furey is survived by his widow, who was Miss Georgianna C. Grosholz of Philadelphia. His brother was the late Robert Furey, an old-time Democratic politician in Brooklyn. When he died, in the early part of 1913, he willed his estate, said to be worth between one and two million dollars and assessed at $500,000, to John Morrissey Gray of Brooklyn, who had been his associate for eighteen years. The will cut off all relatives and Gen. Furey brought suit to have it set aside. The suit was compromised on Oct. 8, 1913, by Gray paying Gen. Furey $65,000.

James J. O'Kelly, the correspondent of the *New York Herald* who arrived at General Terry's camp at the mouth of the Rosebud on the first day of August 1876, moved back to the British Isles a few years later and eventually became a member of the House of Commons. He died December 22, 1916, and his death was reported in the *New York Times* on the following day:

Mr. O'Kelly was widely known for his adventurous career. He was one of Parnell's earliest recruits in Parliament, and went through the ritual of suspension and removal from the House which marked the early eighties. While still a member of Parliament he accepted a commission to go up the Nile during the Sudan campaign and interview the Mahdi, but Lord Kitchener barred that enterprise. Mr. O'Kelly fought in the Franco-Prussian war, having a commission in the French Army. His passion for adventure also found an outlet in the United States Army during the Indian campaigns of a generation ago. At the time of the Cuban revolt against Spanish rule he served as a correspondent for New York and London newspapers and distinguished himself by his daring. Mr. O'Kelly was born in Roscommon, Ireland, and was in his seventy-first year.

Italian-born John Martin (his birth name was Giovanni Crisostomo Martini) will forever be remembered as the last white man to see Custer alive and the soldier who delivered the famed general's last message. He retired from the army in 1904, after thirty years of service. On December 18, 1922, Martin was hit by a truck while crossing the street, his injuries being further complicated by a lung condition.[12] He died six days later, on the twenty-fourth, at age sixty-nine. His death was reported in the *Brooklyn Daily Eagle* on December 26, 1922:

John Martin, believed to be the last survivor of the Custer massacre on the Little Big Horn, died Sunday in the Cumberland Street Hospital, at the age of 69. . . . He is survived by his widow, his daughter, Mrs. Julia Jenson of 4218 5th Ave., three other daughters, Mollie, Jane and May, and four sons, George, John, Frank and Lawrence Martin. The funeral will take place tomorrow afternoon at 3 o'clock, from the home of Mrs. Jenson. Interment will be in Cypress Hills [Brooklyn], where the military honors will be accorded him.

Curly, the Crow guide who escaped death at the Little Big Horn by leaving Custer's command before it was too late to do so, lived forty-seven more years. He died on May 22, 1923, "of a fever which failed to yield to his primitive methods of treatment." He was about sixty-seven years old. His widow and son inherited his estate of over $11,000, "besides a yearly annuity from the Government in recognition of his services."[13]

✳

In 1888, Reuben Briggs Davenport made some headlines with his new book, *The Death-Blow to Spiritualism: Being the True Story of the Fox Sisters*. He also remained in the newspaper business for the rest of his life, eventually ending up in France as the chief editorial writer of the *New York Herald*'s Paris edition, a position he held from 1920 until he died in February 1932, at about age eighty.[14] Were Davenport's criticisms of General Crook during the 1876 Sioux Campaign accurate, or was he just trying to be controversial and somewhat antagonistic in order to sell newspapers and make a name for himself as a reporter in his early twenties? As of this writing, there seems to be no way to definitively answer that question. However, motives aside, the fact is that our knowledge of the Sioux War is all the richer through his descriptive and informative dispatches. No book on the Sioux War of 1876 can be complete without utilizing Davenport's many newspaper reports. The man also had a romantic side, as witnessed by the following poem:

A Mirage

I see her from the crowd,
Nor seek her fated glance;
How strange that we should meet
By this ignoble chance!

At times her eyes greet mine
With fire too quick reproved,
As if 'twere ages hence,
The hour when we first loved.

A little hour, alack!
So swiftly sped it then;
In vain to turn the glass
And count the sands again.
I stand beside the sea
And watch its wavering gleam,

And ask my dull despair
Whence rose so fair a dream.

A vision 'twas unreal,
A mirage of the shore;
The echo in my breast
Is but the ocean's roar![15]

Ohio-born Edward S. Godfrey, a lieutenant in Company K, Seventh Cavalry, in 1876, retired with the rank of brigadier general in 1907. He lived twenty-five more years, dying at age eighty-eight at his wife's ancestral home in Cookstown, New Jersey. From the *New York Times*, April 2, 1932:

Cookstown, N. J., April 1—Brig. Gen. Edward S. Godfrey, veteran of the Indian wars, died here tonight at the age of 88.

Indian fighter, Medal of Honor man and a veteran of the Battle of the Little Big Horn, in which General Custer and his troops were wiped out by the Indians, General Godfrey spent more than a third of a century in the service of his country. Besides taking an active part in the contests which wrested the West from the red men, he saw active service in the Civil War and in the Philippine and Cuban campaigns.

Born in Kalida, Putnam County, Ohio, Oct. 9, 1843, General Godfrey's military career began when he was 17 years of age. His father could not dissuade him from answering Lincoln's first call for volunteers, but he exacted a promise that his son return to school after his first enlistment of three months. The promise was kept, but in 1863 he won an appointment to West Point.

At his graduation as president of his class, he was commissioned a second lieutenant in the Seventh Cavalry, of which Lieut. Col. George A. Custer, Brevet General of the Civil War, was the commander. He became a captain [in December 1876] soon after the massacre at the Little Big Horn and had advanced to the grade of colonel by the time of the Spanish-American War. He then received a command of the Ninth Cavalry [June 26, 1901], a Negro regiment, which he led in the Philippines and in Cuba.

An officer of the Seventh Cavalry in the days when the West was won, Godfrey rode the plains for twelve years fighting Indians almost continually. General Godfrey received the Medal of Honor for conspicuous gallantry when, as a captain, he led his troop in action in the Bear Paw Mountains, Idaho [Montana], against the famous Chief Joseph of the Nez Perces on September 30, 1877.

General Godfrey was instructor of cavalry tactics at West Point from 1879 to 1883 and a pioneer in modern army equitation [horseback riding]. He was for a time commander of Fort Riley, Kansas, and of the school of application for cavalry and field artillery. Retired as a Brigadier General in 1907 he made his home at Cookstown in the pines of South Jersey in a colonial house which had been in the possession of Mrs. Godfrey's family for more than 200 years.

General Godfrey emerged from his retirement to take part in the fiftieth anniversary celebration of the battle of the Little Big Horn, in 1926, and the peace ceremonies on Custer Ridge, near Garry Owen, Montana. A former commander of the Kansas commandery of the Loyal Legion, he was also a past commander of the Department of Arizona, G. A. R. [Grand Army of the Republic];

a former commander and historian of the Military Order of Indian Wars, a former senior vice commander of the Military Order of the Loyal Legion, and commander of the Army and Navy Legion of Valor.

Shortly before the close of 1876, Elizabeth Bacon Custer received $4,750 from the New York Life Insurance Company, little compensation for the ill-timed loss of her husband. It would have been an even $5,000, but she had to pay a $250 "war premium."[16] She outlived her legendary husband by almost fifty-seven years. The three books she wrote about her life with George Custer have been reprinted ever since: "Boots and Saddles" (1885), "Tenting on the Plains" (1887), and "Following the Guidon" (1890). As a matter of fact, she fairly dedicated the rest of her life to the cherished memory of her husband, as exemplified by this 1896 article:

Gen. Custer's most faithful biographer has been his wife. It was nearly ten years after his death before Mrs. Custer could summon courage to give the story of her hero to the world. Writing of her initial effort in compiling "Boots and Saddles," Mrs. Custer says in a letter not hitherto published:

"I never should have had the courage at all to do the work if I had not longed to tell something of my husband's home life. It has always seemed to me that few men who compel the admiration of their country, lived so beautiful a social life as my husband. He was so unselfish, boyish and unaffected in his own home that it used to seem incredible that he was the

Elizabeth Bacon Custer and her husband.
(*Library of Congress*)

same man about whom admirers of his public career flocked whenever we left our home. His relations with his intimate friends, his family, his soldiers and his servants were worthy of a better pen than that of his wife in describing them, and so I told my story in describing him, without having it presume to be anything as difficult as a life. If I had not so grand a subject I would not now feel such humiliation that I could not do better.

"If I can only learn to write more of my hero and keep him before his country I shall not have lived after him in vain."[17]

Mrs. Custer died on April 4, 1933, four days short of her ninety-first birthday.

Massachusetts-born William E. Morris was a private in Company M at the Little Big Horn, where he was wounded in the left breast. He left the army in 1878, at age twenty, and went to New York, where he worked his way up the social ladder from waiter, to lawyer, to judge. He died on November 26, 1933, at age seventy-five. From the *New York Times*, November 27, 1933:

Municipal Court Justice William E. Morris of the Second District in the Bronx, who fought with Custer in the battle of the Little Big Horn, died yesterday of arterial sclerosis at his home, 2780 Pond Place, the Bronx, at the age of 75. Illness had prevented his holding court since last June. His son, William E. Morris, Jr., a civil engineer in the Bronx Sewer Department, survives.

When in 1878 he bade farewell to Indian fighting and the United States cavalry, Justice Morris came to New York. For a few years he made his living as a Bowery waiter and used his spare time in studying law. Soon after gaining admission to the bar he formed the firm of Morris, Kane & Costello, which developed a lucrative criminal practice. He also joined Tammany Hall and entered politics, serving one term in the State Assembly, and two terms as Alderman. For some years he held the Democratic leadership of the old Thirty-fifth Assembly District. He resigned this post when he was elected in 1911 for the first of three successive ten-year terms, as a justice of the Municipal Court. The final term will end on December 31, 1941.

When the battle of the Little Big Horn was fought in June 1876, William E.

Morris was 17 years old. He had advanced his age four years to obtain an enlistment in Boston, his birthplace.[18] At the same time of the battle his regiment, the Seventh United States Cavalry, was divided into three columns. Trooper Morris, in the one led by Major Reno, fought most of the engagement in the valley. Custer was on the other side of the hill. As he moved off with the Custer column, Byron L. Tarbox, half-brother of the justice, called out to him: "Look out for your scalp, Bill. The Indians don't like red-headed fellows." The justice had red hair in those days. But he lived to tell the tale and he never saw Byron alive again.

The Reno column reached the top of the hill after many losses. Justice Morris was wounded, but managed to entrench himself and spent the night firing at flashes below him. After two months in a hospital he served throughout the Nez Perce campaign. His son last night was reluctant to say that his father was the last survivor of the battle, but he knew of no other. He was a former captain in the Sixty-ninth Regiment, N. Y. N. G. [New York National Guard], a member of the Society of Indian Wars, Royal Arcanum and the Elks.

✳

Lovell H. Jerome was a lieutenant in the Second Cavalry in the fight against Lame Deer on May 7, 1877. He secured his place in history that October when he was taken prisoner by the Nez Perce and exchanged for Chief Joseph after that leader had been taken hostage by Colonel Miles during the Battle of the Bear Paw in northern Montana. Jerome resigned in April 1879 due to excessive drinking, then signed up again for a couple

of years in the Eighth Cavalry in the early 1880s. Once again, his love of alcohol brought an end to his army career. In his old age, Jerome looked back fondly on the good old days of cavalry versus Indians. From the *New York Times*, August 6, 1933:

These are dull days for an Indian fighter, "Colonel" Lovell Hall Jerome acknowledged yesterday. In 1877 the "Colonel" was fighting the Sioux; nowadays, he is fighting off boredom. And he is still a good warrior—means to keep right on fighting.

Today will be the "Colonel's" eighty-fourth birthday anniversary, but he does not intend to let that interfere with his customary program. He will spend most of the day in his familiar armchair, at 829 Park Avenue, just as he spent most of yesterday. At the proper time he will go out for his daily stroll and luncheon at a neighborhood restaurant, where he will order as many steins of beer as he happens to feel like drinking. No more, no less.

Sometimes, when he gets to thinking about it, the "Colonel" misses the frontier life, which was always spiced "with enough danger to make it interesting." In 1877 he was exchanged as a hostage by the Nez Perces tribe, and it was his troop, under Colonel John Gibbon's command, which arrived at the junction of the Big Horn and Little Big Horn rivers two days after the massacre of General Custer and his 264 men in 1876.

"Colonel" Jerome, whose title is honorary, since he was only a Lieutenant when he retired in 1879, is now old enough to get a special birthday card from the West Point Military Academy every year. And he looks forward to the day when he will be the oldest living graduate. But the trouble is how to amuse himself in the meantime.

He used to play a pretty good hand at auction bridge, but as soon as contract became the rage he gave it up, a little scornfully. "People have to devote their lives to that game," he said. Nowadays, he sticks to detective stories and euchre. He doesn't like motion pictures, can't sit still long enough to see one through, he explained. "Of course, they're wonderful things," he added, "for people who can stand 'em." He can't.

A New Yorker for eighty years, he misses the old-time "neighborly spirit." He remembers making the New Year calls for his family in 1872 when he was home on leave. In a sleigh, drawn by three horses, he called on more than a hundred families and only ten lived above Forty-second Street. He does not remember whether he took a drink at every house he visited, but thinks it very likely, as that was the custom.

"Colonel" Jerome goes motoring occasionally, but says he will never set foot in an airplane. He wouldn't mind it if he could trust the pilot to bring him back promptly, as soon as he'd had a chance to look around. But once in the air, he thinks a frivolous pilot might say to himself: "Now that I've got the old man up, I might as well pull a few stunts." The "Colonel" was never much afraid of Indians, but he's afraid of that, and he admits it.

Jerome died on January 17, 1935, at age eighty-six, with the distinction of being West Point's oldest living graduate at the time.

Charles A. Varnum was born in Troy, New York, in June 1849, and was a lieutenant in Company A, Seventh Cavalry, at the time of the battle of the Little Big Horn. Still with the Seventh Cavalry fourteen years later, he earned the Medal of Honor for his part in a fight with the Sioux on December 30, 1890, the day after the Wounded Knee Massacre. He died at age eighty-seven on February 26, 1936. He was the last surviving officer that rode with Custer to the Little Big Horn. From the *New York Times*, February 27, 1936:

On graduating from West Point in 1872 Colonel Varnum was commissioned a second lieutenant in the Seventh Cavalry. In the Battle of the Little Big Horn in June 1876, he was wounded while fighting with Reno's battalion, which, unlike the two [battalions] under Custer,[19] escaped annihilation. In all, he served thirty-two years in the Seventh Cavalry.

In June 1876, John M. Carnahan had been the telegraph operator in Bismarck. It took him twenty-two hours to transmit all the reports related to "the story of the Custer massacre on the Little Big Horn." He died in Missoula, Montana, on October 24, 1938, at the ripe old age of eighty-nine.[20] From the *New York Herald Tribune*, June 30, 1957:

Fifty thousand words later—and a "Herald" telegraph toll of more than $3,000—the East had been informed and shocked and filled with fury against the Sioux. Custer became a hero anew. The Sioux were forever damned. The story broke in "The Herald" on July 6, the same day a garbled report had been published in Wyoming and Montana. Many Eastern papers refused to print the Custer story because it appeared unrealistic. Then Gen. Sheridan issued a denial. "It comes without any marks of credence; it does not come from Headquarters—such stories are to be carefully considered," he said boldly.[21]

Following the Sioux War, correspondent Robert E. Strahorn wrote several propaganda-style books about the West and Pacific Northwest (unfortunately he did not include his experiences with General Crook during the Sioux War)[22] and was employed in the publicity department of the Union Pacific Railroad from 1877 to 1883. He was also one of the founders of the College of Idaho in the early 1890s. He lived through World War I and most of World War II, and outlived all of the other Sioux War correspondents. He died on March 31, 1944, at age ninety-one.[23]

The last surviving soldier of the Seventh Cavalry who participated in the Battle of the Little Big Horn was German-born shoemaker Charles Windolph of Company H. He was in Benteen's battalion and took part in the defense of Reno Hill where he was wounded in the posterior. More importantly, on June 26 he helped provide covering fire for other troopers who had to make themselves targets for the Indians in order to obtain water for the wounded. He was awarded the Medal of Honor in October 1878 for his valor during the Little Big Horn battle. He also received the Purple Heart on his ninety-fifth birthday for the wound he had received seventy years earlier.

Windolph died on March 11, 1950, at age ninety-eight. From the *New York Times*, March 12, 1950:

Born in Germany [on December 9, 1851], Mr. Windolph came to the United States when he was 19 years old, and two months later enlisted in the Army. He served for twelve years, leaving because his wife felt it was "not the place for a married man." Most of his Army career was spent in Dakota Territory. He was on the 1874 Custer expedition to the Black Hills, during which gold was discovered, leading to the gold rush of 1876. After leaving the Army [in March 1883], Mr. Windolph came to Lead [South Dakota]—then a frontier gold-rush camp—and worked for the Homestake Gold Mine until he was pensioned eighteen years ago.

Jacob Horner hailed from New York City and enlisted in the Seventh Cavalry at age twenty on April 8, 1876, about six weeks before the Terry-Custer column departed Fort Abraham Lincoln. He was assigned to Company K, but he was not assigned a horse (there were not enough to go around, least of all for new recruits) and found himself walking, along with seventy-seven other cavalrymen, when the Dakota Column marched west on May 17, 1876.[24] It turned out to be a lucky circumstance. Not having a horse, he was left behind at the Powder River Depot when Custer headed up the Yellowstone on June 15. Horner lived seventy-five more years after the famous battle, and when he died on September 21, 1951, about two weeks before his ninety-sixth birthday, he was the last living soldier of the Seventh Cavalry affiliated with the historic campaign of 1876. From the *New York Times*, September 23, 1951:

Bismarck, N. D., Sept. 22—Sgt. Jake Horner, who escaped the massacre at Custer's "Last Stand" because there was a shortage of horses, died here last night of pneumonia. He was 96 years old.

Mr. Horner was the last survivor of Gen. George Custer's Seventh Cavalry Regiment, cut down by the Indians in the battle of the Little Big Horn. He and a number of troopers who lacked mounts were left behind while Custer and his regiment rode off to their fatal engagement.

He was a veteran of a bitter battle against Chief Joseph and a valiant band of Nez Perce Indians [in 1877] and participated in Custer's 300-mile forced march to the Powder River.

Mr. Horner left the Army in 1880 "because I met a girl and married her." He retired from a prosperous meat business when he was 74, but acted as an adviser to film companies on frontier movie scripts.

And whatever became of Major Marcus Reno and Captain Frederick Benteen? Reno was court-martialed for "conduct unbecoming an officer and gentleman" in 1877 and 1879, and was finally dismissed from the army on April 1, 1880, after nearly twenty-three years of service. He died of cancer on March 30, 1889, at age fifty-four. From the *Dodge City Times*, April 4, 1889:

Washington, D.C., April 2—Major Marcus Reno, late United States Army, who served with General Custer in the Yellowstone Sioux massacre, died at Providence hospital. Major Reno about three months ago became afflicted with a cancer on the tongue. The cancerous portion was removed last week by Dr. John B. Hamilton. A few days ago erysipelas set in the right hand and there was pneumonia of both lungs, which brought about his death in a few hours.

Benteen went on to fight against the Nez Perce Indians in 1877, was appointed major of the Ninth Cavalry in December 1882. He was brevetted a brigadier general in February 1890 for his services at the Little Big Horn in June 1876 and against the Nez Perce at Canyon Creek, Montana, in September 1877. He was suspended from the army for one year in April 1887 for drunk and disorderly conduct and received a medical discharge in July 1888, after more then twenty-six years of service (he suffered from impaired vision, frequent urination, and neuralgia).[25] He died ten years later, on June 22, 1898, at age sixty-three. From the *New York Sun*, June 23, 1898:

Gen. F. W. Benteen, formerly one of the best-known officers of the regular army, died in Atlanta yesterday. His death resulted from a stroke of paralysis. Although a native of Virginia he joined the Union forces, and conducted himself so gallantly throughout the civil war that at its close he held the title "Colonel of 138th United States Infantry." He also made himself famous during the Indian wars. He also was one of the few survivors of Custer's fight. He had lived in Atlanta since 1888.

Both Reno and Benteen will forever be tied to Custer's controversial legacy, and while Custer's death may have been a foregone conclusion at the battle of the Little Big Horn even if they had tried to follow his trail without delay, the fact that they dug in on a bluff while gunfire was heard downstream has left their conduct under a cloud of suspicion from which they will likely never escape.

At the time of this writing, Charles St. George Stanley and Jerry Roche have disappeared into history.

INTERLUDE

"Wiggle-Tail-Jim and Scalp-Lock Skowhegan"

Some may recall fondly the classic TV series *F Troop* from the 1960s that poked fun at the Old West, particularly the cavalry-versus-Indians theme. In the episode "Old Ironpants," there was a scene in which Captain Wilton Parmenter (played by actor Ken Berry) said to George Custer (played by actor John Stephenson), "Good luck on your new assignment at Little Big Horn." If you just smiled (and I'd bet you did), then you will enjoy this next section. First up is a brief story about a practical joke Custer played on a friend who was visiting him from New York. It was printed in the *Colorado Transcript*, September 6, 1899. It is followed by a handful of

witty remarks and one-liners concerning the Great Sioux War and its participants.

Colorado Transcript (Golden City), Wednesday, September 6, 1899

CUSTER'S JOKE ON OSBORN.

The late Charles Osborn, the New York broker, and General Custer were intimate friends, and Osborn annually visited the general at his camp on the plains. During one of the Indian campaigns he invited Osborn and a party of friends out to Kansas, and after giving them a buffalo hunt, arranged a novel experience in the way of an Indian scare. As Osborn was lying in his tent one night, firing was heard at the outposts and the rapid riding of pickets. "Boots and saddles" was the order in the disturbed atmosphere of the night, and Custer appeared to Osborn loaded with rifle, two revolvers, a saber and a scalping knife.

"Charley," he said, in his quick, nervous way, "you must defend yourself. Sitting Bull and Flea-in-Your-Boots, with Wiggle-Tail-Jim and Scalp-Lock Skowhegan, are on us in force. I didn't want to alarm you before, but the safety of my command is my first duty. Things look serious. If we don't meet again, God bless you."

The broker fell on his knees. "My God, Custer," he cried, "only get me out of this! I'll carry 1,000,000 shares of Western Union for you into the firm to get me home. Only save me."

But Custer was gone, and the camp by shrewd arrangement burst into a blaze, and shots, oaths and war-whoops were intermixed, until suddenly a painted object loomed on Osborn's sight, and something was flung into his face—a human scalp. He dropped to the ground, said the Lord's prayer, backward, forward and sideways, until the noise died away, and there was exposed a lighted supper table, with this explanation on a transparency: "Osborn's treat!"

✳

"The Indians stripped Custer's men and [now] the Black Hillers and other citizens in the Sioux country will be able to buy army clothing from the post traders at very reasonable rates for some time to come."
—*Daily Colorado Chieftain*, July 14, 1876

"The 'friendly Sioux' are getting up a numerously signed protest against the practice of cutting the hair short so prevalent in the army. Inspector Vandever will present it to the Indian bureau and endeavor to get Secretary Cameron to issue an order against the practice as it detracts from the ornamental appearance and greatly injures the value of the scalp."
—*Daily Colorado Chieftain*, July 14, 1876

"A peace policy which swallows up a regiment of cavalry at a gulp is really not much of a success as a peace policy."
—*Daily Colorado Chieftain*, July 20, 1876

"The slaughter of Custer's command strengthens our belief that the only good Indians in this country are those standing in front of cigar stores."
—*Daily Colorado Chieftain*, July 21, 1876

"The Custer massacre has caused a marked increase in the sale of [James Fenimore] Cooper's novels."
—*Deseret News*, August 2, 1876

"The Indian is not a bad looking man. It's the war paint that makes him look ghastly and hideous. Nothing else in the world could give him the same awful appearance, unless it is a pair of linen pants."
—*Daily Colorado Chieftain*, August 6, 1876

"Sitting Bull has been badly defeated several times—in the newspapers."
—*Deseret News*, August 30, 1876

"Several men who were reported killed with General Custer have come to life again. They were not with his command."
—*Harper's Weekly*, September 2, 1876

This next news clipping was unintentionally humorous in its absurdity:

"One of the chiefs who led the Sioux against Custer on the Little Big Horn has unmixed white blood in his veins. He was born in Pike County, Missouri, his father being one of the pioneers of Missouri and a veteran of the Mexican war. He was captured by the Indians when a boy, grew up among them, and finally became their chief."
—*Harper's Weekly*, September 2, 1876

"The campaign against the Indians will shortly come to a close . . . and the official reports thereof may soon be expected to be sent in. Briefly they may be somewhat as follows—

Custer's—'We met the enemy and we were theirs.'

Reno's—'We met the enemy, but were sorry we did. We were almost theirs, but, thanks to help at hand, we escaped with the skin of our teeth.'

Crook's—'We met the enemy, but were glad to retire in good order.'

Terry and Crook's—'We have not met the enemy, so we are not theirs and they are not ours. We have not discovered the enemy, and we cannot find out whether there is any or not. We have seen a big trail, but have never caught a glimpse of the big trail-makers.'"
—*Deseret News*, September 13, 1876

"Buckskin Sam," the oldest guide in the State of Maine, and who was with General Custer at the massacre of the Little Big Horn in the Black Hills, was voted the prince of story tellers at the annual congress of the Tale Teller's Club last night at the Putnam House.
—*New York Times*, March 4, 1907

NOTES

Chapter One

1. For the fact that the government was planning to construct a new military post in the Black Hills, see "The Black Hills—Letter from the Secretary of War," *Daily Colorado Chieftain*, September 10, 1874. From this article we quote Acting Secretary of the Interior Benjamin R. Cowen and Secretary of War William W. Belknap. Cowen (September 8, 1874): "What is known as the late exploring expedition of Gen. Custer is merely a military reconnaissance for the purpose of ascertaining the best location, if in future it should become necessary, to establish there a military post." Belknap (June 22, 1874): "It is well known to the [War] department that at various times settlers in the adjacent country have contemplated expeditions to the Black Hills and the department has uniformly discountenanced such movements, but it has now become a military necessity that accurate knowledge should be possessed by the army, as to this portion of our territory and for that purpose only, is the present expedition taken [by Custer]." "grass roots" is from an untitled news clipping in the *Weekly Rocky Mountain News*, September 23, 1874. The Black Hills were so named because, when viewed from a distance, their numerous dark green pine trees gave them "a black appearance." Lieutenant Gouverneur K. Warren, "The Border of the Black Hills," printed in Lloyd McFarling, *Exploring the Northern Plains* (Caldwell, ID: Caxton Printers, 1955), 285.

2. See Davenport's report "The Black Hills" in the *Herald* on August 12, 1875; "The

Black Hills Gold-Fields," *New York Times*, October 18, 1875; Robert M. Utley, *Frontier Regulars: The United States Army and the Indian, 1866-1891* (Lincoln: University of Nebraska Press, 1984), 245; and Paul L. Hedren, *Traveler's Guide to the Great Sioux War* (Helena: Montana Historical Society Press, 1996), 32.

3. The Sioux Treaty of 1868, also known as the Fort Laramie Treaty of 1868, marked the end of about three years of fighting and hostility between the US government and various bands of Northern Sioux, Cheyennes, and Arapahoes, these tribes being loosely organized under Chief Red Cloud of the Oglala Sioux. Commonly referred to as "Red Cloud's War," the high point was the destruction of eighty men under Captain William J. Fetterman on December 21, 1866. As part of the treaty ending the war, the government agreed to abandon three forts—Reno, Phil Kearny, and C. F. Smith— built along the Bozeman Trail, an overland route created in 1863 that connected the Oregon Trail to the gold fields of Montana. The problem was that it also ran directly through prime Indian hunting grounds, including the Powder River Basin in present Montana. With the forts closed and the trail discontinued, the treaty looked like a victory for the Indians, though in reality it was really just a temporary concession on the part of the government.

4. The "Indians herein named" were specifically the following bands of Sioux: Brule, Oglala, Minneconjou, Hunkpapa, Blackfeet, Two Kettle, Sans Arcs, Yanktonai, Cuthead,

and Santee. Also signing were the Northern Arapahoes. The Northern Cheyennes signed a separate treaty, which gave them the choice to stay with the Sioux and Arapahoes on the Great Sioux Reservation in present-day South Dakota or move south to Indian Territory with their southern relatives. The first seven Sioux tribes named above (the Brule through the Sans Arcs) composed the Lakota, or Teton Sioux, nation. Because of their popular image in the media as the archetypal Plains Indians, the Lakota came to represent all the Plains Indians. In this book we use the name Sioux, to coincide with the popular phrase "Great Sioux War."

5. The Sioux Treaty of 1868 can be viewed at http://digital.library.okstate.edu/Kappler/.

6. This is based on article 11, which stated that "the tribes who are parties to this agreement hereby stipulate that they will relinquish all right to occupy permanently the territory outside their reservation as herein defined, but yet reserve the right to hunt on any lands north of North Platte [that is, the unceded territory] . . . so long as the buffalo may range thereon in such numbers as to justify the chase." Also see Hedren, *Traveler's Guide*, 32; Michael P. Malone, Richard B. Roeder, and William L. Lang, *Montana: A History of Two Centuries* (Seattle: University of Washington Press, 1991), 126; and "An Interview with General Custer, the Famous Indian Conqueror," *New York Herald*, May 22, 1875.

7. The town of Fort Smith was established near where Fort C. F. Smith used to stand.

8. These descriptions and distances were determined using Google Earth, http://www.google.com/earth/index.html.

9. Here is something else to consider: The Fort Laramie Treaty of 1868 was signed on April 29. The Crow Indians signed their treaty on May 7, eight days later. So, technically, the land may have rightfully belonged to the Sioux, et al. But the Crow Treaty was ratified by Congress on July 25, 1868, and the Fort Laramie Treaty was ratified on

February 16, 1869. That is about a six-month time difference. Legally, an argument can be made that the Crow owned the disputed land. Of course, the Sioux would argue it is grossly unfair that they should lose title due to the quirky workings of the US Congress. As a matter of historical record, it should be noted that the Sioux were relative newcomers to the Black Hills, displacing the Crows and Kiowas during the latter half of the 1700s and early 1800s, first pushing into the area around the same time that the thirteen British colonies were fighting for their independence from Great Britain. George B. Grinnell, *The Fighting Cheyennes* (Norman: University of Oklahoma Press, 1985), 37, and Stan Hoig, *Tribal Wars of the Southern Plains* (Norman: University of Oklahoma Press, 1993), 92.

10. Thomas B. Marquis, interpreter, *Wooden Leg: A Warrior Who Fought Custer* (Lincoln: University of Nebraska Press, 2003), 282–283. Wooden Leg was born in 1858 and died in 1940. Concerning the Indians' understanding of the 1868 treaty, one officer acknowledged "the inability to make the Indians understand anything of imaginary geographical lines. They knew nothing of such nice distinctions, but had a general idea that their possessions extended west as the crow flies, to the Wind River Mountains of Wyoming, and northwest through the eastern part of Montana to the British possessions." D. C. Poole, *Among the Sioux of Dakota* (New York: D. Van Nostrand, 1881), 33.

11. "The Black Hills—Thousands Searching for Gold," *New York Tribune*, April 27, 1876. Differing from this view was a dispatch in the *New York Herald* just a few days later, which said, "All the Big and Little Horn country is included in the Crow reservation, and game is plenty near the mouth of the Big Horn River, but the Sioux occupied the country and the Crows could not hunt." "The Sioux War—The Crows Going to Fight the Sioux," *New York Herald*, May 3, 1876.

12. "An Editor's Sentiments," *New York Herald*, May 20, 1876.

13. Also see Wayne R. Kime, ed., *The Black Hills Journals of Colonel Richard Irving Dodge* (Norman: University of Oklahoma Press, 1996), 4.

14. "The Disastrous Indian Campaign," *New York Herald*, July 7, 1876. Concerning the army's task being disagreeable, Davenport wrote: "Lieutenant Colonel Dodge . . . wrote to General Crook deprecating the intended expulsion of the miners and dreading the necessity of performing so disagreeable a duty if it should be required of him." "The Black Hills," *New York Herald*, August 18, 1875.

15. John S. Gray, *Centennial Campaign* (Norman: University of Oklahoma Press, 1988), 26 (Sheridan to Terry, November 9, 1875). Lieutenant General Philip H. Sheridan was in command of the Military Division of the Missouri (with headquarters in Chicago), and General Alfred H. Terry was in command of the Department of Dakota. At the time of the Great Sioux War, the Military Division of the Missouri included the departments of Dakota, Missouri, Platte, and Texas. It was in these departments that the Plains Indian Wars were fought.

16. "Gold Dust from the Black Hills," *New York Herald*, June 6, 1876.

17. "Black Hills," *Weekly Colorado Chieftain*, June 15, 1876.

18. "The Black Hills," *Brooklyn Daily Eagle*, March 1, 1876.

19. Untitled clipping, *Weekly Rocky Mountain News*, March 8, 1876.

20. "Editorial Notes," *Deseret News*, March 15, 1876.

21. Untitled clipping, *Brooklyn Daily Eagle*, July 3, 1876.

22. Untitled clipping, *Deseret News*, June 14, 1876.

23. Untitled letter, *Deseret News*, May 31, 1876.

24. "Report of General Crook" (labeled No. 6), printed in *[Annual] Report of the Secretary of War* (for the year 1876), vol. 1 (Washington: Government Printing Office, 1876), 498.

25. For example, on February 28, 1876, President Grant addressed a letter to both houses of Congress, stating in part, "A prolonged delay in furnishing provisions to . . . [the Indians at the Red Cloud Agency] will cause great distress, and be likely to provoke raids on white settlements, and possibly lead to a general outbreak of hostilities . . . and I recommend that the appropriations asked for be made at the earliest day practicable." "The Sioux Indians," *New York Times*, March 1, 1876.

26. Gray, *Centennial Campaign*, 309.

27. One newspaper reported in June 1876 that an estimated 183 whites had "lost their lives or been seriously maimed on the various routes to the Black Hills." Untitled clipping, *Daily Colorado Chieftain*, June 29, 1876. On June 24, 1876, the *Cheyenne Daily Leader* announced that "the Cheyenne route is now absolutely safe, being guarded by cavalry and infantry." For more on the Black Hills front, see Paul L. Hedren, *Great Sioux War Orders of Battle: How the United States Army Waged War on the Northern Plains, 1876–1877* (Norman: University of Oklahoma Press, 2011), 84–89. Incidentally, although the Black Hills were located within the Department of Dakota, under command of General Terry, the most-used roads leading thereto were in Crook's Department of the Platte. Consequently, the troops called on to protect these roads were from his jurisdiction. Charles M. Robinson, *General Crook and the Western Frontier* (Norman: University of Oklahoma Press, 2001), 161.

28. "How It Feels to Be Scalped," *Colorado Banner*, June 29, 1876, repr. from *Kansas City Times*. Ganzio's companions took him to Fort Laramie, where Drs. Adoniram J. Gray and Charles V. Petteys provided medical assistance. Paul L. Hedren, *Fort Laramie and the Great Sioux War* (Norman: University of Oklahoma Press, 1998), 138.

29. "For the Black Hills," *Colorado Banner*, February 3, 1876.

30. "General Sherman Has No Fears for the Safety of the Frontier Towns—Bad Whites Do the Killing," *New York Herald*, May 30, 1876.

31. Major Thaddeus H. Stanton, "The Big Horn Expedition," *New York Tribune*, March 9, 1876.

32. This is from a statement made by Bear-Stand-Up in "News from Sitting Bull's Camp," *New York Times*, July 15, 1876.

33. "A Soldier Murdered by Horse Thieves," *Weekly Rocky Mountain News*, March 8, 1876.

34. Untitled clipping, *Laramie Daily Sentinel*, August 10, 1876.

35. The article continues, "But while we build empires on his plains we should not kill him, we should not rob him, we should not treat him as a panther or a grizzly bear." In other words, let's take the Indian's land, but let's be nice about it.

36. "The Black Hills Bill," *New York Times*, June 4, 1876.

37. "The Upper Missouri Indians," *Weekly Rocky Mountain News*, June 10, 1874, repr. from the *Chicago Journal*. In addition to any spiritual attachment to the Black Hills that the Sioux and other tribes may have had, the region was also considered valuable for the lodge poles that were collected there.

38. Untitled letter of Geminien P. Beauvais to William F. Lee, *Cheyenne Daily Leader*, March 3, 1875. Beauvais (1815–1878) and Lee were frontier traders.

39. The government offered to buy the Black Hills outright for $6,250,000 in fifteen annual installments, or to lease the area for $400,000 a year for as long as necessary. "The Black Hills—Failure of the Negotiations for the Purchase of the Reservation," *New York Herald*, October 1, 1875. But the Sioux were not satisfied with either offer.

40. Untitled clipping, *Weekly Colorado Chieftain*, October 7, 1875.

41. As one historian pointed out, deal or no deal, the whites already held effective possession of the Black Hills. Utley, *Frontier Regulars*, 245.

42. Ibid., 242–243.

43. John M. Carroll, ed., *General Custer and the Battle of the Little Big Horn: The Federal View* (New Brunswick, NJ: Gary Owen Press, 1976), 5–6. About twenty-five thousand Indians lived on the Great Sioux Reservation at the time. Robert M. Utley, *The Indian Frontier of the American West, 1846-1890* (Albuquerque: University of New Mexico Press, 1984), 178.

44. Under date of February 27, 1876, Lieutenant John G. Bourke, Third Cavalry, wrote, "Arrived at Fort Fetterman last evening with Gen. Crook. . . . Our journey of two days' duration took us over some 80 miles of country." Charles M. Robinson, *The Diaries of John Gregory Bourke*, vol. 1 (Denton: University of North Texas Press, 2003), 209. If they were traveling for two days and arrived the night of February 26, then they had to have departed Fort Laramie on February 25.

45. The distance between Deadwood and Custer City is about forty-three miles by air. On the ground, the distance would be perhaps ten miles longer. About Deadwood, an early resident stated, "Ten thousand venturesome, excited gold seekers panned gold in the streams and crowded into the cabins in spite of orders from the United States Government to stay out of the Sioux reservation, and thus the outlaw camp of Deadwood was born." Estelline Bennett, *Old Deadwood Days* (Santa Barbara, CA: Narrative Press, 2001), 1.

46. The last section of this article has distinct similarities to a dispatch by correspondent Robert Strahorn that was printed in the Denver *Weekly Rocky Mountain News* on March 8, 1876, with a dateline of Fort Fetterman, February 29. As the *New York Times* was known to run some of Strahorn's articles during this period, the author's first

inclination was to think this was one of them. But the dateline for the article printed here was March 17, from Cheyenne, Wyoming, the same day Strahorn was covering Colonel Joseph J. Reynolds's attack on an Indian village on the Powder River in southern Montana, more than 260 miles to the north. Still, much of the final paragraph here was lifted from Strahorn's February 29 dispatch. For mention that Strahorn wrote for the *New York Times*, see Carrie Adell Strahorn, *Fifteen Thousand Miles by Stage* (New York: Knickerbocker Press, 1911), 2. Strahorn's dispatches to the *Rocky Mountain News* were generally signed "Alter Ego." An anonymous dispatch described Strahorn as being "about five feet nine in height, solid built, dark hair and whiskers, black eyes, regular features, and an American beyond no doubt . . . . As a correspondent, he ranks with the best, his letters being not only correct in detail, but also choice bits of literature, whether he essays the serious or lighter words." "Brief Personal Sketches of the Newspaper Correspondents with General Crook's Army," *Daily Rocky Mountain News*, August 8, 1876.

47. Fort Buford was built in 1866, and was located at the confluence of the Missouri and Yellowstone rivers. It was about three hundred river miles from Bismarck, North Dakota. "Montana's Rapid Growth," *New York Times*, June 23, 1879.

48. John "Portugee" Phillips (1832–1883), whose real name was Manual Felipe Cardoso, is remembered for his 236-mile ride from Fort Phil Kearny to Fort Laramie following the Fetterman battle, December 21, 1866, in order to obtain reinforcements for the besieged garrison.

49. The impression here is that the correspondent was unaware that President Grant had, in November 1875, withdrawn army resistance to whites entering the Black Hills. However, in the next column he correctly noted that the area was "no longer barred to the people."

50. Concerning the Red Cañon Massacre: On April 16, baker Charles Metz, his wife, and several companions were leaving the Black Hills, where Metz had recently sold his business for $3,000, when they were ambushed, killed, and mutilated. W. G. Felton, though wounded several times, managed to escape. It is possible that the outlaw "Persimmon Bill" joined with the Indians in the attack. Hedren, *Fort Laramie*, 76–77.

51. Hunton's body was discovered on May 5 by a party of men including frontier scout Baptiste "Little Bat" Garnier. Hedren, *Fort Laramie*, 83–85. Garnier was nicknamed "Little Bat" to distinguish him from another scout named Baptiste "Big Bat" Pourier.

52. Medicine Bow Station was a stop on the Union Pacific Railroad about eighty-five miles southwest of Fort Fetterman. It served as a distribution point for men and supplies for the army.

53. Established in southeastern Montana in August 1866 to protect the Bozeman Trail from Indian depredations, Fort C. F. Smith was abandoned two years later as part of the Fort Laramie Treaty of 1868. Robert W. Frazer, *Forts of the West* (Norman: University of Oklahoma Press, 1972), 84.

CHAPTER TWO

1. "Cheyenne and the Black Hills," *Denver Daily Times*, February 21, 1876.

2. "The Black Hills—What General Crook Thinks of the Situation," *New York Herald*, August 20, 1875.

3. Robert Strahorn, "General Crook's Expedition," *Weekly Rocky Mountain News*, March 1, 1876.

4. Technically, Sitting Bull and the other nontreaty chiefs did not have an agency to report to because they never signed a treaty. But that did not stop the government from issuing such an order. This was an important point that most newspapers did not pick up on. The *Daily Colorado Chieftain* was one that did: "As to any breach of treaty, the

Indians who are at the head of this war never made any treaty with the government of the United States, and to this day defy its power." "Another Philanthropist," July 23, 1876.

5. *Military Expedition against the Sioux Indians*, 44th Cong., 1st sess., Executive Document 184 (1876), 15.

6. One report stated that the message never even reached Sitting Bull because the messengers turned back out of fear, stating their hearts "were not big enough" to deliver such news to the Hunkpapa Sioux holy man. "Interesting Sketch of the Indian Leaders," *New York Herald*, August 9, 1876.

7. *Military Expedition against the Sioux Indians*, 26.

8. Paul Andrew Hutton, *Phil Sheridan and His Army* (Lincoln: University of Nebraska Press, 1985), 302.

9. Companies A, B, E, I, and K of the Second, and A, D, E, F, and M of the Third.

10. Stanton, "The Big Horn Expedition."

11. Strahorn, "General Crook's Expedition."

12. In addition to being chief of scouts, Stanton (1835–1900) was also accompanying the expedition as a reporter for the *New York Tribune*.

13. Stanton, "The Big Horn Expedition."

14. Strahorn, "General Crook's Expedition." Another correspondent wrote, "While apparently frank with all who approach him, he is never communicative, except occasionally to his aids. To all others he is a Sphinx." John F. Finerty, "Expedition Excerpts," *Cheyenne Daily Leader*, July 23, 1876.

15. Ibid.

16. See General Orders No. 1 in Robert Strahorn, "The Big Horn Expedition," *Weekly Rocky Mountain News*, March 8, 1876.

17. Ibid.

18. Ibid.

19. Robert Strahorn, "The Indian War—The Movements of the Big Horn Expedition," *Weekly Rocky Mountain News*, March 29, 1876.

20. "An Indian War Anticipated," *New York Times*, March 13, 1876. Though unsigned, the author believes this was written by Strahorn.

21. Strahorn, "The Indian War—The Movements of the Big Horn Expedition."

22. Ibid.

23. Ibid.

24. J. W. Vaughn, *The Reynolds Campaign on Powder River* (Norman: University of Oklahoma Press, 1961), 45 and 158; and Robinson, *Diaries of John Gregory Bourke*, vol. 1, 220. Writing on June 8 from Tongue River, Strahorn mentioned that one man had been "fatally wounded" during Crook's winter campaign; no doubt he was referring to Jim Wright. Robert Strahorn, "Crook—Letter from His Camp on Tongue River," *Weekly Rocky Mountain News*, June 28, 1876.

25. Robert Strahorn, "General Crook in the Wake of the Plundering Sioux," *Weekly Rocky Mountain News*, April 12, 1876.

26. Ibid.

27. Ibid.

28. Ibid.

29. Ibid.

30. Ibid.

31. Ibid. It should be noted that Strahorn described Crook's meeting as if it occurred on the night of March 7. However, Lieutenant John G. Bourke, Third Cavalry, Crook's aide-de-camp, placed the event on the night of March 6, and that is where it is placed in the narrative. Robinson, *Diaries of John Gregory Bourke*, vol. 1, 229.

32. These details are from a combination of Bourke, Strahorn, and Stanton.

33. Strahorn, "General Crook in the Wake of the Plundering Sioux."

34. A Kanaka was someone of Hawaiian or Polynesian descent. In Grouard's dictated autobiography, he claimed that he was born in September 1850 on the island of Ana in the South Pacific and that his father was a missionary and his mother Polynesian. Joe DeBarthe, *The Life and Adventures of Frank Grouard, Chief of Scouts, U. S. A.*

(Alexandria, VA: Time-Life Books, 1980), 21–22.

35. Four hundred miles north of Cheyenne would place the command slightly north of the Yellowstone River at a point near O'Fallon's Creek. In other words, it was more than one hundred miles too far. Reynolds's battle on Powder River (about to be described) was about 285 miles due north of Cheyenne.

36. According to Reynolds's official report, the command camped on Red Clay Creek, about ten miles south of the mouth of Otter Creek. Based on the miles traveled each day, this would be correct. Vaughn, *Reynolds Campaign*, 206.

37. Bourke recorded in his journal that Crook badly wounded one buffalo but it got away. Robinson, *Diaries of John Gregory Bourke*, vol. 1, 243.

38. Companies E, F, and M of the Third Cavalry, and E, I, and K of the Second Cavalry. Vaughn, *Reynolds Campaign*, 60. Vaughn numbered the attack force at 300 men, while Gray stated there were 359 men plus 15 officers. Gray, *Centennial Campaign*, 53. A dispatch to the *New York Times* (printed later in this chapter) stated that Reynolds's force contained 330 men, including officers.

39. Stanton was mistaken on this point. The village contained mostly Cheyennes under Old Bear; Crazy Horse was not present. Thomas B. Marquis, *Custer on the Little Bighorn* (Algonac, MI: Reference Publications, 1987), 53; and Vaughn, *Reynolds Campaign*, 123, 127–129. According to a report by Lieutenant William Philo Clark in September 1877, the village contained "about sixty lodges of Cheyennes under Old Bear and fourteen Sioux under He Dog." Charles M. Robinson, *The Diaries of John Gregory Bourke*, vol. 2 (Denton: University of North Texas Press, 2005), 491.

40. Another account states that only one man was killed and an old woman captured. Stanley Vestal, *Warpath: The True Story of the Fighting Sioux, Told in a Biography of Chief White Bull* (Lincoln: University of Nebraska Press, 1984), 178. According to an unnamed half-breed scout who was present, the Indian casualties totaled one old woman and two children. Regarding the size of the village, he said the troops destroyed about forty lodges. "The Starving Indians," *New York Times*, April 23, 1876.

41. Listed as Lorenzo Ayres in the *New York Tribune*, March 27, 1876, and Lorenzo Ayers in the *Weekly Rocky Mountain News*, April 12, 1876.

42. On March 17, Bourke noted in his journal that "Mr. Strahorn acted like a veteran and was of great use to Capt. Egan during the fight." Robinson, *Diaries of John Gregory Bourke*, vol. 1, 254.

43. The Society Islands are in the South Pacific and include Tahiti and Bora Bora.

44. According to Strahorn's wife, "The forty-seven brave troopers [under Egan] surely did awaken the camp on that terrific charge. Teddy Egan's horse was shot in the neck, Lieut. John G. Bourke's bridle rein was shot out of his hand, Hospital Steward Bryan's horse was killed under him, and in a few minutes troopers were being killed and wounded, and Bob's stampeded mount fell over a precipice and broke its neck." Strahorn, *Fifteen Thousand Miles*, 3.

45. As noted previously, the casualties were probably much lower than those stated here.

46. Wooden Leg told his biographer that a Cheyenne named Bear-Walks-on-a-Ridge shot a soldier in the back of the head, after which Bear-Walks, along with Two Moons and Wooden Leg, rushed forward and stabbed the soldier to death. Marquis, *Wooden Leg*, 167. This unfortunate soldier was likely McCannon. Vaughn, *Reynolds Campaign*, 132. McCannon was in Company F, Third Cavalry (see Stanton's article earlier).

47. Hospital steward William C. Bryan received the Medal of Honor for his brave conduct in this battle. The medal was issued June 15, 1899. http://www.army.mil/medalofhonor/citations3.html.

CHAPTER THREE

1. Wooden Leg recalled circa 1927: "[Following the destruction of our village we] kept going eastward and northward. We forded the Little Powder River and went upon the benches beyond. Three nights we slept out. Only a few had robes. There was but little food, only a few women having little chunks of dry meat in their small packs. There was hard freezing at night and there was mud and water by day. . . . Early on the fourth day we arrived at where we had aimed, a camp of Ogallala Sioux far up a creek east of Powder River. . . . The Ogallalas received us hospitably, as we knew they would do. Crazy Horse was their principal chief. . . . . They fed us to fullness and gave us temporary shelter and robes. At night a council was held by the chiefs of the two bands. At the council our people told about the soldier attack. It was decided that the Ogallalas and the Cheyennes should go together to the Uncpapa Sioux, located northeastward from us. The next forenoon all of us set out in that direction." Marquis, *Wooden Leg*, 169–170.

2. "spiritual leader," Thomas B. Marquis, "Forcing of Tribe from Black Hills Country Provoked Trouble," printed in the Montana *Billings Gazette*, July 17, 1932; "distinguishing characteristic" and "unrelenting hostility," "Interesting Sketch of the Indian Leaders," *New York Herald*, August 9, 1876. In regard to Sitting Bull's status among the Indians, one historian stated that his "counsel commanded . . . attention and respect," even among the Northern Cheyennes and Northern Arapahoes. Utley, *Frontier Regulars*, 236–237.

3. "The Fight with Crazy Horse: An Abridged Synopsis," *Weekly Rocky Mountain News*, April 12, 1876 (reprinted in the previous chapter).

4. Robert Strahorn, "The Indian War—Gen. Crook Has a Battle with the Sioux," *Weekly Rocky Mountain News*, March 29, 1876. This was the first of two battles in 1876 in which the Cheyennes were dealt a severe blow to their material culture. The second was the destruction of Dull Knife's village in late November by troops under Colonel Ranald Mackenzie.

5. Ibid.

6. Colonel Reynolds noted in his official report, "Two of the killed, Dowdy and Schneider, were brought off the field and left [as in permanently?] on the Hospital ground, there being no available means of burying them or transporting them. The other two, McCannon and Ayers, were not brought from the Picket line, nor seen by their Company Commanders at all when or after they were killed." Vaughn, *Reynolds Campaign*, 213.

7. The possibility of a wounded man being left on the battlefield was mentioned by both Stanton and Strahorn in the previous section, "Newspaper accounts of the Reynolds battle on Powder River."

8. It should be noted that afterward, Reynolds wondered why Crook had not supplied him with pack mules if he wanted the captured provisions hauled away. Vaughn, *Reynolds Campaign*, 177.

9. Thaddeus H. Stanton, "Destruction of a Sioux War Camp," *New York Tribune*, March 27, 1876, and Thaddeus H. Stanton, "The Big Horn Expedition—Partial Failure of Its Object," *New York Tribune*, April 7, 1876.

10. Stanton, "The Big Horn Expedition—Partial Failure of Its Object."

11. Coincidentally, about fifty or sixty of these horses were afterward recaptured by Crook, who, while on his way to meet Reynolds, happened to cross paths with the Cheyennes. The general, known as a good marksman, wounded one of the Indians, who was carried away by his companions. "Matters Pertaining to the Close of General Crook's Campaign," *Weekly Rocky Mountain News*, April 19, 1876; Robinson, *Diaries of John Gregory Bourke*, vol. 1, 257–258; and Martin F. Schmitt, ed., *General George Crook: His Autobiography* (Norman: University of Oklahoma Press, 1986), 192.

12. Schmitt, *General George Crook*, 192.

13. Vaughn, *Reynolds Campaign*, chapter 10, passim.

14. Ibid., 103, 106, 111, 166–169, 223, and Hedren, *Fort Laramie*, 80–82.

15. Stationed at Fort Shaw, John Gibbon (1827–1896) was in command of the District of Montana in 1876. He was colonel of the Seventh Infantry from March 1869 to July 1885, when he was promoted to brigadier general.

16. General Terry's headquarters were in St. Paul, Minnesota, thus the confusion.

17. Joe Wasson, "Gen. Crook's Campaign—Outline of Future Movements," *New York Tribune*, June 2, 1876.

18. Charles D. Collins, Jr., *Atlas of the Sioux Wars*, 2nd ed. (Fort Leavenworth, KS: Combat Studies Institute Press, 2006), text accompanying Map 14, "Sheridan's Campaign Plan."

19. "Interview with Sherman," *New York Herald*, July 7, 1876.

20. In February 1876, scout Frank Grouard told a reporter that, "if whipped, the Sioux would join their brethren in the British possessions." "General Crook's Chief Scout," *Weekly Rocky Mountain News*, August 2, 1876, repr. from the *Kansas City Times*.

21. Editorial, "The War on the Hostile Sioux," *New York Herald*, May 18, 1876.

22. In terms of leeway to the commanders in the field, this reads very much like Terry's final instructions to Custer on June 22, just before he set off on his last campaign.

23. *Military Expedition against the Sioux Indians*, 53–54.

24. These totals do not include Indian scouts, packers, and others who routinely accompanied military expeditions. The figure of 196 cavalry for Gibbon comes from James H. Bradley, *The March of the Montana Column*, ed. Edgar I. Stewart (Lincoln: University of Nebraska Press, 1991), 50. The other totals are derived from various sources.

25. Editorial, "Strong Enough to Whip the Sioux," *New York Herald*, July 11, 1876.

26. These totals are based on a study by the author that included data from over one hundred newspaper reports. The more extravagant totals were dismissed as sensational tales. Sitting Bull's name is used here as synonymously representing all of the "hostiles."

27. "The Big Horn Expedition," *Cheyenne Daily Leader*, May 27, 1876.

28. "The Indian War—The Commander and the Expedition Against the Sioux," *New York Herald*, May 20, 1876.

29. Reuben Davenport, "Going to the War," *New York Herald*, June 9, 1876. By campaign's end, Davenport would have reason to question the humanity of the whites too. Following a fight in September, he wrote, "My faith in the superiority of white humanity received a terrible shock." Reuben Davenport, "Crook's Campaign," *New York Herald*, October 2, 1876. Davenport accompanied Crook's military expedition from May through September 1876. The writer of an anonymous dispatch guessed that he was about thirty-five. It was humorously observed among Crook's men that Davenport had conspicuously marked all of his gear—saddle, bridle, haversack, canteen, etc.—"New York Herald," practically everything but his horse, "but he has got him so he looks like a Herald horse." Characterized as being hungrier for news than for food, it was stated that some of the stories given him by the soldiers were "whoppers." "Brief Personal Sketches of the Newspaper Correspondents with General Crook's Army." In fact, Davenport was a gifted writer, and his dispatches remain a great source of knowledge about the Sioux War.

30. Davenport, "Going to the War."

31. Ibid.

32. Ibid.

33. Reuben Davenport, "The Big Horn," *New York Herald*, May 29, 1876.

34. Reuben Davenport, "Sitting Bull's Band," *New York Herald*, May 30, 1876. A report in the *New York Tribune* on May 18,

1876, stated, "Gen. Crook's plan to get Indian scouts from Red Cloud's band was defeated by the intervention of Agent [James S.] Hastings and Inspector [William] Vandever, notwithstanding the fact some of the most friendly desired to go and fight the hostile Indians." "The Crook Expedition," dispatch possibly written by Joe Wasson. Regarding this incident, Crook told a correspondent: "A considerable number [of Sioux] were willing to go [with me] and so expressed themselves, but the agent and inspector, by means of bribes and threats, prevented them. My plan was to test the pretended friendship of these people whom the government was feeding, and by enlisting them against the hostiles, to draw the dividing line so distinctly that the agency could no longer be used as a base of supply for those on the warpath." John F. Finerty, "The Fellows in Feathers: An Interview with General Crook," *Chicago Times*, November 4, 1876, printed in Peter Cozzens, ed., *The Long War for the Northern Plains* (Mechanicsburg, PA: Stackpole, 2004), 386.

35. Davenport, "Going to the War." This story came to Davenport via the half-breed scout Louis Richard.

36. "A 'Close Shave' for Crook," *Weekly Rocky Mountain News*, May 24, 1876, and Robinson, *Diaries of John Gregory Bourke*, vol. 1, 285.

37. Robert Strahorn, "Indian Matters," *Weekly Rocky Mountain News*, May 31, 1876.

38. "The Surrendered Hostiles," *New York Herald*, May 11, 1877.

39. Reuben Davenport, "Army of the Big Horn," *New York Herald*, May 28, 1876.

40. Robinson, *Diaries of John Gregory Bourke*, vol. 1, 293.

41. Davenport, "Army of the Big Horn."

42. Strahorn, "Indian Matters," and "The Indian Country," *New York Times*, May 28, 1876.

43. Davenport, "Army of the Big Horn." Vliet and Crawford's guide was Baptiste "Big Bat" Pourier. Marc H. Abrams, ed. and

comp., *"Crying for Scalps": St. George Stanley's Sioux War Narrative* (Brooklyn, NY: privately printed, 2010), 39.

44. The cavalry and infantry totals include men and officers, and are from Neil C. Mangum, *Battle of the Rosebud* (El Segundo, CA: Upton & Sons, 1987), 46. In a dispatch written on May 29, Strahorn stated there were 900 cavalry and 250 infantry. "Running Down the Redskins," *Weekly Rocky Mountain News*, June 7, 1876. However, these totals were likely too high. The other details are from Strahorn's article.

45. Davenport, "Going to the War."

46. Strahorn, "Running Down the Redskins."

47. Reuben Davenport, "The Warpath," *New York Herald*, May 24, 1876.

48. "The Indian War—The Commander and the Expedition Against the Sioux."

49. Strahorn, "Running Down the Redskins."

50. Ibid.

51. Strahorn, "Crook—Letter from His Camp on Tongue River."

52. James E. H. Foster, "From Fort Fetterman to the Rosebud," *Chicago Tribune*, July 5, 1876, printed in Cozzens, *Long War*, 265.

53. According to Davenport, following Crook's winter campaign, in which Richard had participated as a scout, he was hated by the Sioux. They are "yearning for his scalp, and it is certain that only the sentiment of kinship and not one of friendliness for the whites impelled his four dusky cousins to guard him safely to Fort Laramie. He brought with him the remnant of his herd of ponies and cows, his squaws and children, and evidently had bidden adieu to his old home near the agency. His deep Indian stoicism permitted no betrayal of regret." Davenport, "Going to the War."

54. Strahorn, "Crook—Letter from His Camp on Tongue River."

55. Ibid. The white man "who speaks the Sioux tongue" was dispatch carrier Ben

Arnold. Although the soldiers thought this late-night visitor was a prying Sioux, it was discovered several days later that he was, in fact, a Crow scout. John F. Finerty, *War-path and Bivouac*, ed. Milo M. Quaife (Lincoln: University of Nebraska Press, 1966), 100.

56. Strahorn, "Crook—Letter from His Camp on Tongue River."

57. Ibid.

58. Ibid.

59. Among the newspapers represented by Joe Wasson (1841–1883) during the Sioux War of 1876–77 were the *San Francisco Daily Alta California* and the *New York Tribune*. A fellow correspondent said of him: "Crossing the Great Plains to California when a mere boy, he has wandered around on the Pacific Coast as an editor, miner, and correspondent; thence back to the States, and across the sea to Europe. He is by nature, inclination, and education a model Bohemian. . . . [He] is a clear, able writer; he gives you facts, boiled down and in language that can be easily understood." "Brief Personal Sketches of the Newspaper Correspondents with General Crook's Army." Wasson's dispatches to the *Daily Alta California* were signed "Jose."

60. Charles St. George Stanley certainly is a mystery. According to the caption of an illustration in *New Mexico Magazine*, November–December 1972 (see page 23), St. George Stanley was a "British-born" painter who "arrived in Denver in 1867 after studying at the Royal Academy of Art in London." It says Stanley "covered military action against the Sioux for *Harper's Weekly* and [Frank] *Leslie's*." After reading this, I contacted the Royal Academy of Art and received an e-mail response from research assistant Andrew Potter on January 28, 2011, which said that a man named Charles Stanley had registered at the academy in December 1839 at age 17 "to study painting." This coincided perfectly with information from Edna Robertson and Sarah Nestor, *Artists of the Canyons and Caminos* (Layton,

UT: Ancient City Press, 2006). Those authors quoted a newspaper article that described Charles St. George Stanley as a "dashing and debonair" Englishman. If this information is accurate, then St. George Stanley would have been about fifty-four in 1876. However, other news clippings about him were recently brought to my attention by researcher Chris Penn of England that suggest that St. George Stanley was much younger. A news item in the *Colorado Banner* on November 9, 1876, referred to him as "the young and yet good scenic painter," and a news item in the *Colorado Transcript* on December 19, 1877, said one of Stanley's recent paintings of Gray's Peak in Colorado "would be a credit to the brush of many older artists."

61. Captain William J. Fetterman, Captain Frederick H. Brown, and Lieutenant George W. Grummond.

62. Frances Grummond.

63. This should read "the night *of* our arrival here," which was June 7.

64. Thomas B. Burrowes, Andrew S. Burt, and Samuel Munson.

65. Anson Mills, Joseph Lawson, Alexander Sutorius and William H. Andrews. At the time Lawson was a lieutenant with the brevet rank of captain; he was promoted to captain on September 25, 1876.

66. These were Sergeant John Warfield, Third Cavalry, and Private Emil Renner, Second Cavalry. Mangum, *Battle of the Rosebud*, 40.

67. Edgar B. Robertson, Ninth Infantry.

68. Thaddeus H. Capron.

69. William L. Carpenter.

70. Frank Grouard, Baptiste Pourier, and Louis Richard.

71. Concerning the dangerous duty of the couriers, Strahorn declared: "The private courier is expected to ride the 190 miles from this point [Crook's camp on Goose Creek] to Fort Fetterman, in from forty to fifty hours, while the bearer of official dispatches is usually allowed twenty-four hours

longer. Owing to the whole region traversed being overrun by the hostile Sioux, nearly all of the riding is done at night, and during daylight horse and rider are secreted in some out-of-the-way gully or thicket. About $200 is the maximum price paid to government couriers for each ride, while correspondents find it necessary to give from $300 to $500 to secure desired haste." "The Big Horn—How We Get the News from the Front," *Weekly Rocky Mountain News*, July 12, 1876, dispatch dated "Big Horn Expedition, Camp Cloud Peak, June 28, 1876."

72. This article is printed in full in Abrams, *"Crying for Scalps."*

73. Finerty also acknowledged this warrior, writing, "One fellow wore what seemed to be a tin helmet, with a horse-hair plume." Finerty, *War-path and Bivouac*, 95.

74. "Sitting Bull Talks," October 1877 interview with Jerome B. Stillson, *New York Herald*, November 16, 1877.

75. Ibid.

76. "Abbot Martin's Visit to Sitting Bull," *New York Herald*, December 5, 1877.

77. "President Grant—The Indian War," *New York Herald*, September 2, 1876.

Chapter Four

1. Robinson, *Diaries of John Gregory Bourke*, vol. 1, 305.

2. Grinnell, *The Fighting Cheyennes*, 328–329.

3. Joe Wasson, "The Sioux War—Gen. Crook's Expedition," *New York Tribune*, July 1, 1876.

4. When the Crows did arrive, they were under the leadership of Old Crow, Medicine Crow, Good Heart, and White Forehead. Reuben Davenport, "Looking for Sioux," *New York Herald*, June 21, 1876.

5. This differs from another report that says the Indian scouts were lent firearms by the government. Reuben Davenport, "Battle of Rosebud Creek," *New York Herald*, July 6, 1876, reprinted in this chapter.

6. The Shoshones that arrived on June 15 were under the leadership of Wesha/Weesaw, a.k.a., Louissant (a mixed-blood French-Canadian), Nawki, and Tom Cosgrove, an ex-Confederate cavalry officer, employed as chief of scouts at the Shoshone Agency in Wyoming. Davenport, "Battle of Rosebud Creek"; Finerty, *War-path and Bivouac*, 102–103; and Robinson, *Diaries of John Gregory Bourke*, vol. 1, 317. Although Washakie, the aged and revered Shoshone chief, was expected to be with the scouts at this time, he did not join the campaign until July 11.

7. Colonel Gibbon's command had been in relatively close proximity to the Sioux for about two weeks in the latter part of May. On the seventeenth, the same day he received word that the Sioux village was within striking distance on the Tongue River, he tried in vain to cross his troops to the south side of the Yellowstone near the Rosebud. Much to the disgust of the Crow scouts, the troops found the river to be an "insuperable obstacle." After several hours with barely any headway, four drowned horses, and a party of Sioux warriors watching the ordeal, Gibbon called the whole thing off. As one officer put it, "And so we failed to march against the foe." Bradley, *March of the Montana Column*, 104–105.

8. Wasson, "The Sioux War—Gen. Crook's Expedition."

9. Robert Strahorn, "The Battle of Rosebud," *New York Times*, July 13, 1876. This article was unsigned, but the text contains a clue about the author's identity. In a dispatch to the *Weekly Rocky Mountain News* dated June 8, 1876, Strahorn used a similar expression in describing the Sioux around the time of Red Cloud's War, ten years prior. He wrote, "To be an Indian then 'was better than to be a king.'" Considering that the *New York Times* printed several of Strahorn's Sioux War articles and that both instances of the expression were used within several weeks' time, it can be assumed that this was one of his reports.

10. Davenport, "Looking for Sioux."

11. Strahorn, "The Battle of Rosebud."

12. Ibid. What Crook didn't know was that the Crows were wrong. The Indians were then making their way up the Rosebud before crossing over to Reno Creek, a confluence of the Little Big Horn. By June 17, the day of the big battle with Crook, their village was located about twenty-two miles to the northwest. This is illustrated in Gray, *Centennial Campaign*, map titled "Crook's Rosebud Campaign and Reno's Reconnaissance." In his official report written on June 20, Crook stated: "The Crow Indians were under the impression that the hostile village was located on Tongue River or some of its smaller tributaries, and were quite positive that we would be able to surprise it. While I hardly believed this to be possible, as the Indians had hunting parties out, who must necessarily become aware of the presence of the command, I considered it would be worthwhile to make the attempt." "Sub-report of General Crook" (labeled No. 6B), printed in [*Annual*] *Report of the Secretary of War* (for the year 1876), vol. 1, 504.

13. Davenport, "Battle of Rosebud Creek," and Robinson, *Diaries of John Gregory Bourke*, vol. 1, 316.

14. Robert Strahorn, "Crook—Letter from His Camp on Tongue River," *Weekly Rocky Mountain News*, June 28, 1876. For use of the term "walk-a-heaps," see "Crook's Campaign," *Cheyenne Daily Leader*, August 5, 1876, and Finerty, *War-path and Bivouac*, 74.

15. Strahorn: "The Battle of Rosebud."

16. Ibid.

17. "Sub-report of General Crook" (labeled No. 6B), printed in [*Annual*] *Report of the Secretary of War* (for the year 1876), 504. Scout Frank Grouard offered another story for the change of plans: "The General asked me . . . from my trip to the village of the friendly Crows, if I had any idea where the Sioux camp was. From all signs I had seen I supposed they were on the Rosebud, and I so informed him." Then he added, "[Two days later,] Camping on the Rosebud, we ran onto a scouting party of Sioux just before reaching the river, but from the direction they took I was satisfied the camp was on the Rosebud, down the stream." DeBarthe, *Life and Adventures of Frank Grouard*, 223–224. Captain William S. Stanton of the Corps of Engineers simply stated, "June 16—At 6 a.m., General Crook, with all the cavalry, and the infantry mounted on mules, headed for the Rosebud." McFarling, *Exploring the Northern Plains*, 366. In any event, they marched from the Tongue to the Rosebud.

18. Reuben Davenport, "The Indian War—Big Fight with the Sioux on Rosebud Creek," *New York Herald*, June 24, 1876.

19. Joe Wasson, "The Sioux War—A Battle on Rosebud Creek," *New York Tribune*, July 6, 1876. According to another report, the soldiers had been shooting the buffalo too. Strahorn, "The Battle of Rosebud." Bourke stated that thirty buffalo were killed that day, although he is vague about who did the killing. Robinson, *Diaries of John Gregory Bourke*, vol. 1, 325.

20. "The Indian War—Crook's First Fight," *Daily Alta California*, July 13, 1876. This article contains parts of dispatches from two or more correspondents, none of whom are mentioned by name, and sometimes it is unclear which one is being referred to. However, this quote is most certainly from John F. Finerty, as it was clearly identified that the writer was the correspondent of the *Chicago Times*.

21. Ibid.

22. Ibid. In his book, Finerty altered his story slightly about the Indian allies refusing to go on the scout. In that latter version, some of the Shoshones agreed to go, led by Tom Cosgrove and Frank Grouard. Finerty, *War-path and Bivouac*, 120–122.

23. Finerty implies as much in his book.

24. Reuben Davenport, "The Battle of Rosebud Creek," *New York Herald*, July 13, 1876.

25. Strahorn, "The Battle of Rosebud."

26. On the topic of infantry versus cavalry firearms, an unknown correspondent noted: "Short arms in Indian warfare [that is, the cavalry carbine] are entirely inefficient. The long infantry rifle is the thing to lift the Indian off his feet, wherefore the Sioux dread the 'walk-a-heaps,' terribly armed and unembarrassed by scary horses, much more than they do our showy cavalry. Had the latter 'the long rifle' they would be twice more effective than they are. It is objected that the infantry gun would be 'unhandy.' I don't think so. General Crook always carries one on his saddle, and surely any trooper can do the same. The carbine is a pretty weapon, but compared with the musket of the foot soldier it is a mere military toy, excellent for dress parade, but damnable for active service." "Crook's Campaign," *Cheyenne Daily Leader*, August 5, 1876. Another correspondent was to write: "The short carbine of the cavalry I do not consider good for much except at uncomfortably close quarters, and the conditions favorable to its effective employment seldom present themselves in Indian fighting. . . . It would seem that the Indians' favorite method of fighting is to surround the enemy as they would a herd of buffaloes, and in this style of fighting a long range gun is of inestimable value." Jerry Roche, "The Winter Expedition on the Eve of Departure," *New York Herald*, November 10, 1876.

27. Captain Azor H. Nickerson, Twenty-third Infantry.

28. This differs from Davenport's account: "Captain Nickerson, aide and acting assistant adjutant general, was despatched at full gallop to check Captain Mills' advance, and overtook him only after a chase of five miles, during which he was accompanied by a solitary orderly." Davenport, "Battle of Rosebud Creek."

29. Lieutenant George F. Chase, Third Cavalry.

30. Captain George M. Randall, Twenty-third Infantry.

31. This is a reference to an incident during the battle when an Indian named Humpy saved Sergeant John Van Moll of the Third Cavalry. A dispatch printed in the *Cheyenne Daily Leader* on December 21, 1877, offered a colorful account of the episode: "The Shoshones made a brave stand, but were soon overwhelmed and compelled to retreat. They were all mounted, but Van Moll fought on foot, his horse being held back with those of the rest of the regiment, in rear of the heights. When the Crows and Shoshones drew off, the gallant sergeant found himself alone with the Sioux, who came on with fierce yells to scalp him. He retired, firing as he went, and several soldiers started to his rescue. They would have been too late, however, for the hostile savages were close upon him. At this critical moment a solitary Indian warrior of the Shoshones, distinguished by the nickname of 'Humpy,' turned back from the mass of his retreating comrades, and rode like a streak of greased lightning down toward the imperiled sergeant. The Sioux bullets flew like hail around him, throwing up the dust in little clouds; but the heroic savage never heeded them. Bending low on his war pony's neck, he rode right up to Van Moll, who was becoming exhausted, halted his horse, turned him, and cried, 'Jump.' The sergeant leaped up behind his dusky deliverer, and, although chased by a dozen Sioux, the twain arrived safe in the army lines amid the cheers of the whole battalion. It was one of the most thrilling episodes of the Sioux war. Gen. Crook recommended 'Humpy' for a medal, which, it is believed, was granted by the government. Van Moll was recommended by some of the officers for a commission, and his name was on file for a lieutenancy at the war department." According to St. George Stanley, Humpy was a "Shoshone by birth, but has been adopted by the Crow nation." Abrams, *"Crying for Scalps,"* 119. Van Moll was killed by a drunken soldier on December 14, 1877. "Whisky's Work," *Cheyenne Daily Leader*,

December 16, 1877. The author is unaware that Humpy ever received a medal for his brave deed.

32. This military-style discipline displayed by the Shoshones was of long standing. At the 1851 Treaty of Fort Laramie (also known as the Horse Creek Treaty), Corporal Percival G. Lowe, First Dragoons, had been impressed with, "The attitude of the Snakes, the cool, deliberate action of the chief, the staunch firmness of his warriors." Continuing, he recalled: "The scene was impressive, as showing the faith that band of warriors had in each other; the entire confidence of their families in them; the self-reliance all through. It was a lesson for soldiers who might never again see such a grand display of soldierly manhood, and the lesson was not lost. Every dragoon felt an interest in that tribe." Percival G. Lowe, *Five Years a Dragoon* (Norman: University of Oklahoma Press, 1991), 67. In this case, their military bearing was due to the work of Tom Cosgrove, the former Confederate cavalry officer who was one of their leaders.

33. Lieutenant James E. H. Foster, Third Cavalry. Foster's account of the battle of the Rosebud follows this one.

34. To say that the Indians "murdered the poor soldiers" is certainly a strange choice of words.

35. This trooper may have been Private Gilbert Roe, Third Cavalry. Mangum, *Battle of the Rosebud*, 81.

36. Captain Avery B. Cain, Fourth Infantry.

37. To read another of Foster's articles about the Sioux War, see James E. H. Foster, "From Fort Fetterman to the Rosebud," *Chicago Tribune*, July 5, 1876, printed in Cozzens, *Long War for the Northern Plains*, 265–281 (particularly pages 276–281).

38. This differs from Henry's account: "A rifle-bullet had struck me in the face, under my left eye, passing through the upper part of my mouth, under the nose, and out below the right eye." Guy V. Henry, "Wounded in an Indian Fight," *Harper's Weekly*, July 6, 1895.

39. Captains Elijah R. Wells and Thomas B. Dewees, and Lieutenants William C. Rawolle and Samuel M. Swigert.

40. As mentioned in a previous note, the Indian who saved Van Moll was named Humpy.

CHAPTER FIVE

1. "The Recent Fight with the Sioux," *New York Times*, June 26, 1876.

2. This estimate refers only to the number of Indians confronting the troops under Royall. Foster's account is reprinted in the previous chapter.

3. Strahorn, "The Battle of Rosebud." Strahorn's estimate seems reasonable. By this time the combined village likely had a substantial number of visitors from the agencies, which would have increased their numbers. In fact, according to a Sioux man named Bear-Stand-Up, the visitors were not allowed to leave: "After the troops got into the country I could not get away. Indians were made soldiers to watch the camp and keep the people together." Bear-Stand-Up returned to Spotted Tail Agency on June 25, so he may have been in the village at the time of the Rosebud fight, or in the fight itself. If so, he was smart enough to leave that detail out of his interview. "News from Sitting Bull's Camp," *New York Times*, July 15, 1876.

4. Editorial, "Details of General Crook's Battle with the Sioux," *New York Herald*, July 6, 1876.

5. Davenport, "The Indian War—Big Fight with the Sioux on Rosebud Creek." As a companion piece to Davenport's first dispatch about the battle, the *Herald* justly observed: "There is no necessity to lay blame at present upon General Crook, whose decision not to pursue the Sioux into a dangerous country was probably the best under the circumstances. Whether he blundered in the fight we do not presume to say until he has been heard from at length." However, by the next day the *Herald's* tone began to change, wondering why trained troops could not do

more than hold their own against a band of "savages" with whom it was believed they were, more or less, evenly matched.

6. Davenport, "Battle of Rosebud Creek."

7. Davenport, Ibid. In support of Davenport's view, an unknown eyewitness wrote: "The Second Cavalry and the infantry were only temporarily exposed to the enemy's fire. Henry's and Mills' battalions [under Royall] did most of the fighting." "Why the Column Fell Back," *New York Times*, July 13, 1876.

8. On that same day the *Herald* commented that Davenport "was present in the thick of the battle, [and] became himself a combatant by the force of circumstances in one stage of the engagement." "Details of General Crook's Battle with the Sioux."

9. Robinson, *Diaries of John Gregory Bourke*, vol. 1, 382.

10. Mangum, *Battle of the Rosebud*, 142–143 (Royall's official report). All told, the five companies under Royall totaled about 225 men. Ibid., 67.

11. Ibid., 68.

12. Robinson, *Diaries of John Gregory Bourke*, vol. 1, 383-384.

13. Reuben Davenport, "Crook's Command," *New York Herald*, August 3, 1876.

14. Bourke offered an alternative view regarding the military drills. Writing in his diary on July 17, he noted, "Cavalry and Infantry Battalions drilling in school of the skirmisher and school of the company and exercising their horses, morning and afternoon." Robinson, *Diaries of John Gregory Bourke*, vol. 1, 377.

15. Which was, of course, Crook's position.

16. "The Indian War—Crook's First Fight." This article contains parts of dispatches from two or more correspondents, none of whom are mentioned by name, and sometimes it is unclear which one is being referred to. However, this quote is most certainly from John F. Finerty, as it was clearly identified that the writer was the correspondent of the *Chicago Times*.

17. Robert Strahorn, "Crook—The Battle of Rosebud," *Weekly Rocky Mountain News*, July 5, 1876, reprinted in the previous chapter.

18. For instance, see the *Cheyenne Daily Leader*, June 27, 1876, and the *Weekly Rocky Mountain News*, July 5, 1876. In the latter account, Strahorn wrote that Crook allowed the cavalry to unsaddle, despite the fact that the Crow scouts had just reported Sioux in the area, because he supposed they were merely a small hunting party.

19. "A Montana Account of Crook's Defeat," *New York Herald*, July 12, 1876, repr. from the *Helena Independent*, June 30, 1876, from a Fort Laramie dispatch dated June 25. The story also said that when officers at Fort Laramie heard details about the battle, they spoke in "unmeasured condemnation" of Crook's falling back to his supply camp "in the face of the savage enemy," a charge the officers of the post afterward vehemently denied. See "A Base Slander Refuted," *Cheyenne Daily Leader*, July 20, 1876. While some details of the story may be true, or based in truth, the idea that the Crows called General Crook a "Squaw Chief" after the fight is hard to believe.

20. For example, Strahorn, "Crook—The Battle of Rosebud." A report in the *Cheyenne Daily Leader* on June 24, 1876, said, "The Indians completely surrounded our command, forming a circle fully five miles in circumference, from every point on which they poured in a galling fire."

21. Strahorn, "The Battle of Rosebud," This description matches perfectly with the reminiscence of Wooden Leg, a Cheyenne warrior who fought in the battle of the Rosebud when he was about eighteen. Describing the fight many years later he said, "[We] fought and ran away, fought and ran away. The soldiers and their Indian scouts did the same. Sometimes we chased them, sometimes they chased us." Marquis, *Wooden Leg*, 200. Also, recall Davenport's description of the skirmish at Tongue River Heights in an earlier chapter: "They seemed bold and confident,

and when a feint of retiring was executed by the troops they quickly changed their retreat to an advance." "An Indian Battle," *New York Herald*, June 16, 1876.

22. Strahorn, "The Battle of Rosebud."

23. Ibid.

24. Ibid.

25. "Why the Column Fell Back."

26. Joe Wasson, "Crook's Command," *Daily Alta California*, August 1, 1876.

27. Strahorn, "The Battle of Rosebud." Regarding the pursuit, or chase, of the Indians at the close of the battle, Strahorn wrote, "they were completely routed and driven seven miles into the rough timbered country and the firing entirely silenced." Robert Strahorn, "Indian Matters—Crook Has a Battle with the Sioux," *Weekly Rocky Mountain News*, June 28, 1876. According to one historian, the Sioux and Cheyennes weren't so much driven from the battlefield as much as they were just tired and hungry, "having ridden all night and fought most of the day." In other words, they didn't care to continue the fight any longer and withdrew by choice. Peter J. Powell, *People of the Sacred Mountain* (San Francisco: Harper & Row, 1981), 998. However, as no source is given, it is unclear whether this is the author's opinion or a statement based on oral testimony.

28. Strahorn, "The Battle of Rosebud."

29. Davenport, "Battle of Rosebud Creek."

30. Joe Wasson, "The Sioux War—A Battle on Rosebud Creek," *New York Tribune*, July 6, 1876.

31. He seems to have forgotten about the Crow and Shoshone scouts.

32. John Finerty, "The Fellows in Feathers: An Interview with General Crook," *Chicago Times*, November 4, 1876, printed in Cozzens, ed., *Long War for the Northern Plains*, 385.

33. "The Recent Fight with the Sioux."

34. Robinson, *Diaries of John Gregory Bourke*, vol. 1, 329, 334–335. Bourke's killed total apparently included one of the slain Shoshone scouts.

35. For instance, the *New York Herald* on June 24, 1876, the *Weekly Rocky Mountain News* on July 5, 1876, and the *New York Times* on July 13, 1876. According to Indian accounts, one report stated they lost thirty-six killed and sixty-three wounded, while another account raised both totals: eighty-six killed and one hundred wounded. "The Custer Fight," *Colorado Banner*, June 21, 1877, repr. from the *Chicago Times*, and "The War on the Big Horn," *New York Tribune*, July 21, 1876, respectively.

36. Strahorn, "Indian Matters—Crook Has a Battle with the Sioux," and Strahorn, "Crook—The Battle of Rosebud."

37. Finerty, *War-path and Bivouac*, 141.

38. Strahorn, "Crook—The Battle of Rosebud."

39. One of the headlines in the *New York Herald* on June 24, 1876, read, "Thirteen Sioux Scalps." For mention of the eight scalps, see Davenport, "Battle of Rosebud Creek." A statement by Crook makes it sound like the majority of these scalps were taken while the Indians were in retreat from the battlefield: "The command finally drove the Indians back in great confusion, following them several miles, the scouts killing a good many during the retreat." "The Recent Fight with the Sioux."

40. A few weeks later, some of these same Crow scouts visited Terry's camp and said they had left Crook because "he does not fight to suit them—that is, he did not have his full force in the fight." Captain Walter Clifford, "From Terry's Camp—An Officer's Diary of Events at the Camp on the Big Horn," *New York Herald*, July 29, 1876. An interesting side note: according to one little-known book, there were eight Crow warriors still living in 1928 who had fought in the battle of the Rosebud: Plenty Coups, Bell Rock, Cuts-the-Bear's-Ear, Big Nose, Bear Crane, The Crane, Coyote-That-Runs, and Finds-and-Kills-Him. Another warrior named Little Fire died in September 1927. Coe Hayne, *Red Men on the Bighorn* (Philadelphia: Judson Press, 1929), 109.

41. Davenport, "The Battle of Rosebud Creek."

42. "Why the Column Fell Back."

43. Abrams, *"Crying for Scalps,"* 87–88.

44. Robinson, *Diaries of John Gregory Bourke*, vol. 1, 330.

45. Davenport, "The Indian War—Big Fight with the Sioux on Rosebud Creek."

46. "Why the Column Fell Back."

47. Robinson, *Diaries of John Gregory Bourke*, vol. 1, 340.

48. Abrams, *"Crying for Scalps,"* 93.

49. Strahorn, "The Battle of Rosebud."

50. They arrived at Fort Fetterman on June 27. "Arrival of the Wounded Men at Fort Fetterman," *New York Herald*, June 28, 1876.

51. Crook's request for infantry is stated in his letter to General Robert Williams, A. A. G., June 19, 1876. "The Chase after Indians," *New York Daily Graphic*, June 24, 1876. Also see his letter to Sheridan on the same date. "The Recent Fight with the Sioux."

52. Wasson, "The Sioux War—A Battle on Rosebud Creek."

53. Joe Wasson, "Skirmishes of General Crook's Force," *New York Tribune*, July 27, 1876. When it came to cavalry, Wasson wrote that Crook believed one Sioux on horseback was equal to two cavalrymen, "considering that it requires at least one in four of the latter to hold horses." Ibid.

54. Strahorn, "The Big Horn—How We Get the News from the Front."

Chapter Six

1. In retrospect, 1876 was quite an eventful year. In addition to witnessing the Great Sioux War and the Centennial Exposition, Jack London, author of *White Fang* and *Call of the Wild*, was born; James Butler "Wild Bill" Hickok was killed in Deadwood, in present-day South Dakota, while enjoying a game of poker; the James and Younger gang members, which included the notorious brothers Frank and Jesse James, were almost wiped out in the streets of Northfield, Minnesota, when their plans to rob a bank did not quite go as expected; Colorado became the thirty-eighth state; and *The Adventures of Tom Sawyer*, by Mark Twain, whose real name was Samuel L. Clemens, was first published.

2. "Interview with Sheridan," *New York Herald*, July 7, 1876.

3. Ibid.

4. This is an unofficial designation commonly used by historians to refer to the Terry-Custer column.

5. Frontier, "The Expedition against the Sioux," *New York Daily Graphic*, May 29, 1876. Interestingly, reporter Mark Kellogg was known to write under the pen name "Frontier" in the early 1870s. Sandy Barnard, *I Go With Custer* (Bismarck, ND: Bismarck Tribune Publishing, 1996), 47. However, he is not known to have submitted any articles to the *New York Daily Graphic* during the Great Sioux War.

6. Mark Kellogg, "The Hostile Sioux—Three Columns Moving Against the Bad Dakotas," *New York Herald*, May 18, 1876.

7. Almost no two accounts agree on the number of men, horses, mules, wagons, etc. These numbers come from various sources, including Gray, *Centennial Campaign*, 97, and "The Hostile Sioux—Three Columns Moving Against the Bad Dakotas."

8. "The Indian War—General Terry's Column Moving Toward the Yellowstone River," *New York Herald*, June 19, 1876 (possibly written by Custer). Stanley's Stockade was a supply depot left over from 1873, when troops under General David S. Stanley served as a military escort for the Northern Pacific Railroad's surveying teams.

9. "Opinions of the Press," *New York Herald*, May 10, 1876. Custer was (and still is) frequently referred to as a general, which refers to his brevet rank from the Civil War. Regarding Secretary Belknap, he resigned from office on March 2, 1876.

10. "Custer and Grant," *Brooklyn Daily Eagle*, May 6, 1876. Custer was called to testify on March 29 and April 4. Robert M. Utley, *Cavalier in Buckskin* (Norman: University of Oklahoma Press, 1988), 159.

11. These headlines are all from the *New York Herald*, May 6, 10, and 11, 1876, respectively.

12. "President Grant's Latest Mistake—Custer Punished," *New York Herald*, May 6, 1876.

13. "Opinions of the Press."

14. Ibid.

15. "President Grant's Latest Mistake—Custer Punished."

16. "Grant and Custer," *New York Herald*, May 12, 1876.

17. Ibid.

18. "Opinions of the Press."

19. Utley, *Cavalier in Buckskin*, 162–163.

20. "who always make mischief" is from "After Twenty Years," *New York Times*, January 21, 1896.

21. "The Outrage on General Custer," *New York Herald*, May 10, 1876.

22. Utley, *Cavalier in Buckskin*, 163.

23. "The Big Horn Expedition—Preparations for Its Departure from Fort Lincoln," *New York Herald*, May 9, 1876. Some readers may think this dispatch was written by Mark Kellogg, but by his own words, he first joined the expedition at Fort Lincoln on May 14. "Off for the Big Horn," *Bismarck Tribune*, May 17, 1876.

24. "The Big Horn Expedition—Preparations for Its Departure from Fort Lincoln."

25. Kellogg, "The Hostile Sioux—Three Columns Moving against the Bad Dakotas," dispatch dated "Fort Lincoln, Dakota, May 17, 1876." The number of miles was obtained using Google Earth.

26. Letter from Lieutenant Colonel Daniel Huston, Sixth Infantry, to General Alfred H. Terry, January 16, 1876. *Military Expedition against the Sioux Indians*, 43–44.

27. Kellogg, "The Hostile Sioux—Three Columns Moving against the Bad Dakotas."

28. Ibid.

29. Frontier, "The Expedition against the Sioux."

30. Ibid.

31. "Gen. Terry's Expedition—No Signs of Indians Found," *New York Times*, June 18, 1876.

32. "The Indian War—General Terry's Column Moving Toward the Yellowstone River." Having only four companies, it is clear that Custer was not really expecting to find any Indians, at least not in substantial numbers. Writing a letter to his wife that night, he told her he went on the scout "to determine the truth of the many rumors . . . to the effect that the hostile Indians were gathered on the Little Missouri River, with the intention of fighting us here." Elizabeth B. Custer, *Boots and Saddles* (Norman: University of Oklahoma Press, 1987), 267.

33. "The Indian War—General Terry's Column Moving Toward the Yellowstone River."

34. "After Sitting Bull," *New York Herald*, June 27, 1876.

35. The village "some distance up the Rosebud" is from Gray, *Centennial Campaign*, 85. Gray reprints Gibbon's letter to Terry. The other details are from "After Sitting Bull."

36. The column under Gibbon consisted of six companies of infantry and four of cavalry. They had been moving east down the north side of the Yellowstone in an effort to keep the Sioux from crossing over and escaping toward the Missouri River.

37. Bradley, *March of the Montana Column*, 99, 124.

38. Regarding the several steamers then in service by the army on the Yellowstone River (including the *Far West*, *Josephine*, *Yellowstone*, *Benton*, *Carroll*, and *Silver Lake*), the government was paying $350 a day for their use. Charles S. Diehl, *Chicago Times*, August 16, 1876, printed in Cozzens, ed., *Long War for the Northern Plains*, 399.

39. Most details in this paragraph from "After Sitting Bull."

40. According to an untitled dispatch in the *New York Daily Graphic* on May 25, 1876, dated "Fort D. A. Russell, Wy. T., May 20," Reynolds, "the celebrated Sioux scout," was earning two hundred dollars a month for his services.

41. "After Sitting Bull."

42. Ibid.

43. Unknown to the two couriers, the Indians they had seen were likely friendly Crow scouts attached to Gibbon's command. Bradley, *March of the Montana Column*, 138.

44. "After Sitting Bull."

45. Ibid.

46. "Gen. Terry's Expedition—The Yellowstone River Reached," *New York Tribune*, July 3, 1876. Lieutenant Kinzie, in charge of the Gatling gun, was in the Twentieth Infantry.

47. "After Sitting Bull."

48. Ibid.

49. "Gen. Terry's Expedition—The Yellowstone River Reached," *New York Tribune*.

50. "Before the Battle," *New York Tribune*, July 11, 1876.

51. Gray, *Centennial Campaign*, 133–134.

52. Both quotes are from the *New York Herald*, July 11, 1876: George Custer, "A Voice from the Tomb," and an editorial, "Antecedents of the Little Horn Massacre," respectively.

53. Custer, "A Voice from the Tomb."

54. Ibid.

55. Major James S. Brisbin, "Custer's Death," *New York Herald*, July 8, 1876. No one seems to have entertained too seriously the idea that the Indians could have backtracked toward the Black Hills. Although Major Brisbin, Second Cavalry, is credited with writing the article quoted here, research shows that it passed through the hands of Clement Lounsberry, editor of the *Bismarck Tribune*, on its way to the *New York Herald*. C. Lee Noyes, "A Dispatch from the Battlefield," *Research Review: The Journal of the Little Big Horn Associates* 18 (Summer 2004): 19. It is very likely that Lounsberry added a few details to the narrative. Regarding Reno's insubordination, one historian wrote: "The fact is, Terry's plan was doomed from the start. Reno's violation of orders led to securing the proof of the plan's futility. Reno thereby saved Terry from an ignominious goose chase, and at the same time handed him some intelligence upon which to build a better plan. It was not Reno's disobedience, but the intelligence it uncovered, that made Terry *want* to discard his plan." Gray, *Centennial Campaign*, 137.

56. It was on February 22 that four troops of the Second Cavalry, under Major Brisbin, departed Fort Ellis to rescue the settlers at Fort Pease, at the mouth of the Big Horn River, who were under siege by the Sioux. "The Siege of Fort Pease," *New York Herald*, March 8, 1876. On March 16, they arrived safely in Bozeman, Montana, about three miles from Fort Ellis. "The Fort Pease Disaster," *New York Herald*, April 6, 1876.

57. Brisbin, "Custer's Death."

58. Edward J. McClernand, "Journal of the Marches Made by the Forces under Colonel John Gibbon," *Annual Report of the Secretary of War on the Operations of the Department for the Fiscal Year Ending June 30, 1877*, vol. 2, part 2 (Washington: Government Printing Office, 1877), 1370.

59. About 150 troopers had been detached since June 10, most at the Powder River Depot. Gray, *Centennial Campaign*, 290.

60. In other words, the rations were expected to last Custer until July 6.

61. Custer, "A Voice from the Tomb."

62. "Mr. Kellogg's Last Letters," *New York Herald*, July 11, 1876.

63. Charles House, "How the Herald Revealed Custer Massacre," *New York Herald Tribune*, June 30, 1957.

64. "Mr. Kellogg's Last Letters."

65. Ibid. One can almost see Custer feeding Kellogg the lines and Kellogg asking him to

slow down while he writes. Perhaps the most telling part of the portrayal was, "*a man to do right, as he construes the right.*"

66. Some versions of Terry's orders change the word "space" to "distance."

67. "General Terry . . . had notified him [Custer] he would be at the mouth of the Little Horn on the 26th and would expect couriers from him." Brisbin, "Custer's Death."

68. Edward S. Godfrey, *Custer's Last Battle* (Golden, CO: Outbooks, 1986), 16, and "The Disastrous Campaign," *New York Tribune*, July 7, 1876.

69. John Gibbon, "Last Summer's Expedition against the Sioux and Its Catastrophe," in Alan Gaff and Maureen Gaff, eds., *Adventures on the Western Frontier: Major General John Gibbon* (Indianapolis: Indiana University Press, 1994), 131. It is this writer's opinion that Gibbon's words, "by sending a scout down the valley of Tullock's Fork," should not be taken literally. If Herendeen (1846–1918) had actually followed Tullock's Creek cross country to the Big Horn, he would have been practically back at the Yellowstone River. The author thinks he was supposed to scout part way down the creek, then cut across toward the mouth of the Little Big Horn. And this makes sense because Gibbon's column was supposed to scout the lower end. The amount agreed on for Herendeen's extra compensation was two hundred dollars.

70. Herendeen's later account was written in response to renewed interest in Custer's last battle brought about by the Reno Court of Inquiry then being held in Chicago. This was an inquiry demanded by Reno to clear himself of charges of cowardice and wrongdoing at the battle of the Little Big Horn. Although the court ruled in his favor, it was barely so, and the overall tone of the witnesses' testimony was not exactly flattering.

71. Godfrey, *Custer's Last Battle*, 18.

72. One historian supplied a (one-sided) conversation that took place between Custer and Herendeen about the scouting of Tullock's Creek. According to this story, Herendeen said, "General, this is Tullock's, and here is where I leave you to go see the other command." Custer never responded, and after a few minutes, Herendeen simply fell back in with the column. Fred Dustin, *The Custer Tragedy* (El Segundo, CA: Upton & Sons, 1987), 97. Did it happen this way? Maybe, but Dustin did not provide his source.

73. The first quote is from the editorial "Gen. Custer's Death," *New York Times*, July 17, 1876, and the second quote is from the editorial "The Slaughter Near the Little Horn River—Death of General Custer," *New York Herald*, July 7, 1876. It was also the *Herald*'s opinion that "General Custer was a man whose mental organization made him peculiarly vulnerable to the sting of disgrace." Ibid.

74. At the time of Custer's attack, the village contained seven camp circles, six of which were Sioux: Oglala, Hunkpapa, Sans Arc, Minneconjou, Brule, and Blackfeet. The seventh camp was composed of Northern Cheyennes.

75. Another eyewitness recorded: "Presently two or three Indians came rushing back on their wiry ponies, their long black hair streaming on the wind, and reined up in front of our idolized leader. The words they said were few, but they filled him with delight, and there was the old gleam in his eyes as he called his officers around him. The village was just ahead and we were sure it could not get away." Unknown eyewitness, "Another Account of the Battle," *New York Herald*, July 30, 1876. According to Red Horse, a subchief of the Minneconjou Sioux, on the day of the battle an Indian who was on his way back to Red Cloud Agency discovered a dust cloud rising several miles from the village. He then "turned back and reported that a large herd of buffalo was approaching the camp." "Custer's Battle—A Hostile Indian's Graphic Story of the Fight," *New York Herald*, March 15, 1877.

76. Some twenty years later, one of the officers recalled that "Benteen was directed to take his [battalion] out of column, and proceed with it across the hills to the left, which turned out to be small mountains, and reach the valley of the Little Big Horn as soon as possible. If Indians were found trying to escape up the valley, we were to intercept them and drive them towards the village." Captain Francis M. Gibson, "The Custer Massacre—Captain Gibson's Share in the Fight as Told by Himself," *New York Evening Post*, February 20, 1897. Differing from the standard "scout to the left" story (as it is popularly phrased), one correspondent wrote that Custer "ordered Benteen to make a detour to the left with three companies, *and instructed him to go as far as he could into the Indian camp*" (italics mine). Special correspondent, "Custer's Last Battle," *New York Tribune*, July 13, 1876. Whether the correspondent personally heard this story from one of the officers or was making an educated guess was not stated. As Custer did not yet have precise knowledge of the location or size of the village, this scenario does not hold much weight.

77. It was at this time that Fred Gerard, the Arikara interpreter, informed Custer that the Indians were "running like devils." Utley, *Cavalier in Buckskin*, 183.

78. Lieutenant Charles DeRudio, "A Thrilling Tale," *New York Herald*, July 30, 1876.

79. "The Terrible Sioux," *New York Herald*, July 11, 1876. Whether or not Reynolds said this, it makes for good copy. In any event he was killed soon after. One newspaper account of his death stated that he "fell by the side of his horse, making a breastwork of him. He must have died in a hand-to-hand conflict, for he had a revolver open and empty in his hand." Another version stated that his "horse was shot and fell upon his legs, and being unable to extricate himself, and having dropped his gun, was killed without firing a shot." "Private Dolan's Story,"

New York Herald, July 23, 1876, and "The Sioux Campaign—Story of the Fight by Captain John W. Smith," *New York Herald*, October 13, 1876, respectively. Keep in mind that both of these statements were made by people who had not seen the event.

80. From Wooden Leg's account: "Suddenly the hidden soldiers came tearing out on horseback, from the woods. I was around on that side where they came out. I whirled my horse and lashed it into a dash to escape from them. All others of my companions did the same. But soon we discovered they were not following us. They were running away from us. They were going as fast as their tired horses could carry them across an open valley space and toward the river. We stopped, looked a moment, and then we whipped our ponies into swift pursuit. A great throng of Sioux also were coming after them. My distant position put me among the leaders in the chase. The soldier horses moved slowly, as if they were very tired. Ours were lively. We gained rapidly on them. I fired four shots with my six shooter. I do not know whether or not any of my bullets did harm. I saw a Sioux put an arrow into the back of a soldier's head. Another arrow went into his shoulder. He tumbled from his horse to the ground. Others fell dead either from arrows or from stabbings or jabbings or from blows by the stone war clubs of the Sioux. Horses limped or staggered or sprawled out dead or dying. Our war cries and war songs were mingled with many jeering calls, such as: 'You are only boys. You ought not to be fighting. We whipped you on the Rosebud. You should have brought more Crows or Shoshones with you to do your fighting.'" Marquis, *Wooden Leg*, 220–221.

81. From Reno's official report, July 5, 1876: "I soon found myself in the near vicinity of the village, saw that I was fighting odds of at least five to one, and that my only hope was to get out of the woods, where I would soon have been surrounded, and gain some high ground. I accomplished this by mounting

and charging the Indians between me and the bluffs on the opposite side of the river. In this charge, First Lieut. Donald McIntosh, Second Lieut. Benjamin H. Hodgson, Seventh Cavalry, and Acting Assistant Surgeon J. M. DeWolf, were killed. I succeeded in reaching the top of the bluff, with a loss of three officers and twenty-nine enlisted men killed and seven men wounded." Ronald H. Nichols, *Men with Custer: Biographies of the Seventh Cavalry* (Hardin, MT: Custer Battlefield Historical & Museum Association, 2000), 388–389.

82. Lieutenant James E. H. Foster: "Battle of the Rosebud," *New York Daily Graphic*, July 13, 1876. Foster would have agreed with the following remarks made by an Indian Wars historian: "The ability of troops to suffer reverses in combat and still retain their discipline is one of the severest tests to which a military unit can be subjected. Regulars who were ambushed or surrounded by superior numbers depended as much on their mettle as soldiers as they did on their weapons. A unit fighting for its life had to maintain discipline, sometimes at the forceful insistence of its officers." Don Rickey, Jr., *Forty Miles a Day on Beans and Hay* (Norman: University of Oklahoma Press, 1972), 297.

83. Ascending the opposite bank was no easy task. Dr. Henry Porter informed a correspondent that the "side of the bluff was so steep that men were compelled to cling to the necks of their animals to prevent sliding from their backs." "Dr. Porter's Account of the Battle," *New York Herald*, July 11, 1876.

84. Brisbin, "Custer's Death." On Hodgson's death, Dr. Porter stated: "While in the river Lieutenant Hodgson was wounded and his horse killed. He received another shot just as he reached the bank and tumbled back into the river dead." "Dr. Porter's Account of the Battle."

85. Gibson, "The Custer Massacre—Captain Gibson's Share in the Fight as Told by Himself."

86. At least one historian has tried to make a case that Kanipe was a fraud and had deserted Custer's command, then made up the fact that he was a courier. Vern Smalley, *Little Big Horn Mysteries* (Bozeman, MT: Little Buffalo Press, 2005), chapter 8. If true, an argument can be made that it was the best decision Kanipe ever made.

87. Utley, *Cavalier in Buckskin*, 186.

88. Gibson, "The Custer Massacre—Captain Gibson's Share in the Fight as Told by Himself." Reno's statement (per Gibson) about seeing Custer on "the crest of the hill we were then on" was a reference to the time when his battalion had been in a skirmish line on the other side of the Little Big Horn, prior to retreating back across the river.

89. While hiding out in the brush and timber, DeRudio witnessed several Sioux women "at the revolting work of scalping a soldier who was perhaps not yet dead. Two of the ladies were cutting away, while two others performed a sort of war dance around the body and its mutilators." Writing to a friend on July 5, he declared: "I cannot find words sufficiently expressive to describe my many thoughts during those six or seven hours of suspense. Many times I asked myself if it was possible that I should end my life in so barbarous, inglorious and obscure a manner. Sometimes I would answer myself that it could not be; I had gone through so many dangers, had made so many sacrifices for my adopted country, I could not think I should die in such a way. I could not believe I had been preserved so long to end in so unjust and obscure a manner." DeRudio, "A Thrilling Tale." DeRudio rejoined the command on Reno Hill after midnight on June 26.

90. "Custer's Battle—A Hostile Indian's Graphic Story of the Fight."

91. "Another Account of the Battle."

92. In his July 1876 account, Herendeen merely stated: "When the shooting below began to die away I said to the boys, 'Come, now is the time to get out.' Most of them did not go, but waited for night. I told them the

Indians would come back and we had better be off at once. Eleven of the thirteen said they would go, but two stayed behind."

93. Unknown to Herendeen, Reno was then trying to catch up with Company D, under Captain Thomas Weir, who, having heard gunfire to the north and believing it must be coming from Custer's battalion, had advanced without orders (or against orders, depending on the version). Well, no one can accuse Weir of lacking *esprit de corps*. The troops advanced to a high point now called Weir Peak, where they could see, through the smoke and dust, Indians astride horses shooting at objects on the ground. The Indians soon turned their attention to these onlookers, pushing the troops back to Reno Hill. In his official report, Reno offered his own version of the affair: "We had heard firing in that direction and knew it could only be Custer. I moved to the summit of the highest bluff, but seeing and hearing nothing, *sent* [italics mine] Captain Weir, with his company, to open communication with him." Nichols, *Men with Custer*, 389. From the available evidence, Reno's version is further from the truth. Lucky for Reno, Weir died in December 1876 and was unable to take part in Reno's court of inquiry in January and February 1879.

94. Horace Ellis, "A Survivor's Story of the Custer Massacre on American Frontier," *Journal of American History* 3, no. 2 (April 1909): 227–232.

95. Gibson, "The Custer Massacre—Captain Gibson's Share in the Fight as Told by Himself."

96. Years later Sergeant Daniel A. Kanipe would write: "We had supposed that he [Custer] and his men were corralled at some other point, as we were at this one." "A New Story of Custer's Last Battle," *Contributions to the Historical Society of Montana* 4 (1903): 282.

97. This was Private Michael Madden, Company K, Seventh Cavalry.

98. One company of infantry was left behind to guard supplies at the mouth of the Big Horn.

99. Lieutenant Bradley stated eight days' rations, and Lieutenant Alfred B. Johnson, Seventh Infantry, stated six days. Bradley, *March of the Montana Column*, 147, and Lieutenant Alfred Johnson, "Custer's Battlefield," *New York Herald*, July 26, 1876, respectively.

100. Bradley, *March of the Montana Column*, 153.

101. Ibid., 154.

102. Brisbin, "Custer's Death."

103. "The Sioux War," Terry to the Adjutant General of the Military Division of the Missouri, Chicago, June 27, *New York Herald*, July 9, 1876.

104. "Another Account of the Massacre," *New York Herald*, July 8, 1876, and special correspondent, "Custer's Last Battle," respectively.

105. Some fifteen years later, Roe recalled: "As soon as we had moved up the valley two miles we saw a lot of Indian ponies. Then we saw a man riding down the valley toward us at a very rapid pace. It was Bosby [scout Henry Bostwick]. 'If you're looking for Indians,' he yelled, 'there are lots of 'em right ahead.' Then I was ordered to the front as advance guard and right flank. We rode on the run, and at the top of the hill we saw, away across the ravine, two men. One wore a light buckskin suit and the other the uniform of an army officer. Next we saw fourteen Indians go through the brush in single file, and ten minutes later, as though literally springing out of the ground right ahead, appeared a complete skirmish line of Indians, in rear of whom were 300 or 400 mounted men, with a cavalry guidon flying. I thought the men with the uniforms were officers of our army, but their behavior was peculiar, and so I sent the First Sergeant [Alexander Anderson] and two men ahead with a handkerchief tied to a carbine for signaling purposes. Just then pop! pop! went the rifles of the skirmish line, and back came

the Sergeant pell-mell. We were confronted with hostile Sioux, wearing the clothing of Custer and his men. Then we fell back to Gen. Terry's command." "Gen. Custer's Last Fight—The Discovery of the Battlefield and Its Victims," *New York Times*, March 22, 1891. Roe resigned from the army in January 1888. About this incident, Lieutenant Johnson wrote: "Toward evening we could see Indians on the bluffs in large numbers, flying around and watching every movement made by us. . . . One company of cavalry was sent on a side hill to watch their movements, and when the Indians saw them they yelled out, or rather some white man in their column did, 'Come on, damn you; we are ready for you!'" Johnson, "Custer's Battlefield." Speaking of white men among the Indians, Johnson was not alone on this point; Reno had stated there were white men among the Indians too. Writing to the adjutant general in Chicago on June 27, General Terry declared, "Major Reno is very confident that there were a number of white men fighting with the Indians." "The Sioux War." Despite these comments, it is not likely that there were any white men fighting side by side with the Indians at the Little Big Horn; more likely these statements were just imaginations running wild, aided by a disbelief that white troops could have been so badly defeated by Indians alone.

106. Brisbin, "Custer's Death."

107. "An Officer's Diary," *New York Herald*, July 13, 1876.

108. Ibid. Another reporter noted: "The Crow scouts had not lied to us. It was the awful truth. Faces paled, eyes moistened, teeth were set. An advance was now ordered. At every step we found tokens of the dreadful carnage." Special correspondent, "Custer's Last Battle." The Porter referred to was Lieutenant James E. Porter, Company I, Seventh Cavalry.

109. Brisbin, "Custer's Death."

110. It should be noted that at least two accounts mention finding agency goods among the hastily discarded items: Lieutenant John Carland, "Another Account of Custer's Fight," *New York Herald*, July 14, 1876, and "Custer's Death Trap," interview with Thomas Harrington, *New York Herald*, August 21, 1876.

111. Brisbin, "Custer's Death."

112. "An Officer's Diary."

113. That is, the ground traversed during Reno's retreat/charge from the woods to the bluffs across the Little Big Horn River.

114. Brisbin, "Custer's Death."

115. Special correspondent, "Custer's Last Battle."

116. Ibid.

117. "Another Account of the Battle."

118. Under date of August 23, 1876, a few days after having met surviving officers of the Seventh Cavalry, Lieutenant Bourke noted in his diary: "Reno saved, more by good luck than good management, the remnant of the 7th Cavalry at the Custer Massacre. He saw enough at that fight to scare him for the rest of his life. He will never make a bold movement for ten years to come." Robinson, *Diaries of John Gregory Bourke*, vol. 2, 83.

119. Brisbin, "Custer's Death."

120. The number of survivors in Reno's command is from "Another Account of the Massacre." Among those who died with Custer were four of his family members: his brothers Tom and Boston; his nephew, Harry Reed; and his brother-in-law, James Calhoun. Boston and Harry were civilians.

121. Major James S. Brisbin, "Custer's Last Fight," *New York Herald*, July 26, 1876.

122. "Another Account [from Scout Muggins Taylor]," *New York Herald*, July 6, 1876.

123. Brisbin, "Custer's Death."

124. George Herendeen, "Narrative of a Scout," *New York Herald*, July 8, 1876.

125. "Indian Tribes Uneasy," *New York Times*, July 9, 1876.

126. "Custer's Death Trap."

127. "An Officer's Diary."

128. Johnson, "Custer's Battlefield."

129. Carland, "Another Account of Custer's Fight." Regarding Lieutenant William W. Cooke, he was known for his long Dundreary-styled sideburns. By coincidence, Wooden Leg told his biographer that he scalped a trooper who had "a new kind of scalp." He "skinned one side of the face and half the chin, so as to keep the long beard yet on the part removed," after which he tied the strange scalp to the end of an arrow shaft. This trooper may have been Cooke. Marquis, *Wooden Leg*, 240–241.

130. "Gen. Custer's Last Fight—The Discovery of the Battlefield and Its Victims," statement of Charles F. Roe, *New York Times*, March 22, 1891.

131. Kanipe, "A New Story of Custer's Last Battle."

132. Quote from special correspondent, "Custer's Last Battle."

133. Brisbin, "Custer's Death."

134. Johnson, "Custer's Battlefield."

135. Special correspondent, "Custer's Last Battle."

136. "An Officer's Diary."

137. "Details of the Battle," *New York Times*, July 7, 1876.

138. Carland, "Another Account of Custer's Fight."

139. "Custer's Terrible Defeat," *New York Tribune*, July 7, 1876.

140. "Gen. Custer's Last Fight—The Discovery of the Battlefield and Its Victims," statement of Charles F. Roe.

141. Jeffry D. Wert, *Custer: The Controversial Life of George Armstrong Custer* (New York: Simon & Schuster, 1996), 355, and James Welch, with Paul Stekler, *Killing Custer* (New York: Norton, 1994), 175.

142. "Another Account of the Massacre."

143. Ibid. Captain George W. Yates had been a lieutenant colonel of volunteers during the Civil War, and Lieutenant William W. Cooke, the regimental adjutant, was a brevet lieutenant colonel.

144. Special correspondent, "Custer's Last Battle." The dispatch was dated "Camp at Mouth of the Big Horn, M. T., July 3." This same article may have been the first, or one of the first, to mention twenty-eight men killed in a ravine on Custer battlefield: "The line of retreat led through a deep gully, at the mouth of which 28 men were killed. They fought desperately, but the Indians had surrounded them and there was no escape."

145. Carland, "Another Account of Custer's Fight."

146. "Another Account of the Massacre." As a point of interest, Herendeen estimated there were six thousand Indians, including three thousand warriors. Herendeen, "Narrative of a Scout."

147. On the topic of horse holders, one correspondent noted: "Arriving upon the scene of action of Indian warfare, the cavalry do not fight as cavalry, but dismounting become infantry, armed, however, with a carbine, not the long range rifle of the infantry soldier, with its greater accuracy; according to the tactical books twenty-five per cent of the effective force [is] absent at the moment of conflict—number four of each group of four men being detailed to hold the horses of numbers one, two and three—in reality one man can and does hold eight or ten horses; at best a large per cent is lost from the action." "The Sioux Campaign—Virtual Suspension of Offensive Operations," *New York Times*, September 16, 1876.

148. Subtracting the horse holders leaves a fighting force of 450 men, or slightly more if each man holds more than four horses.

149. "Dr. Porter's Account of the Battle."

150. Carland, "Another Account of Custer's Fight."

151. "Dispatches from Gen. Terry," *New York Times*, July 7, 1876.

152. Johnson, "Custer's Battlefield."

153. This ford was at the bottom of Medicine Tail Coulee (a ravine running from the bluffs down to the Little Big Horn River).

154. Special correspondent, "Custer's Last Battle."

155. The first quote is from an anonymous correspondent; the second quote is from the *Tribune's* editor.

156. Curley left Custer's command near Medicine Tail Coulee and thus survived the battle.

157. Brisbin, "Custer's Last Fight." In another article, Brisbin stated, "It was evidently Custer's intention to attack the village at both ends and have the forces work toward each other." Brisbin, "Custer's Death."

158. "Another Account of the Massacre."

159. "The Custer Fight."

160. "Another Account of the Massacre." Davenport, based on a dispatch from Terry to Crook, wrote: "Terry caused a reconnoissance made southward on June 28, and a very large Sioux trail was found diverging from the one followed by Custer in his advance. Capt. [Edward] Ball, of the Second Cavalry, is of opinion that the enemy, after leaving the valley where the village was, was divided into two bands, one going toward the mountains and the other going southwest." Reuben Davenport, "Crook Safe," *New York Herald*, July 16, 1876.

161. Hedren, *Great Sioux War Orders of Battle*, 211.

162. "The Sentiments and Opinions of Sitting Bull," *New York Herald*, August 19, 1876.

163. "The Sioux Campaign—Story of the Fight by Captain John W. Smith."

164. "The Custer Fight."

165. "The Terrible Sioux." As for Custer attacking forty-eight hours too early, that was nothing more than misinformation. As stated previously, Terry had verbally informed Custer that Gibbon's column would be at the mouth of the Little Big Horn on June 26, but this had nothing to do with a predetermined time of attack.

166. "Details of the Battle."

167. As explained by one historian, "The notion that Terry meant for Custer to attack on June 26 arose only after the offensive ended in disaster." Utley, *Cavalier in Buckskin*, 176.

168. "Dispatches from Gen. Terry." Oddly, this dispatch differs from the official version held in the National Archives, which contains a different ending than the one printed here. It goes as follows: "I do not tell you this to cast any reflection upon Custer. For whatever errors he may have committed he has paid the penalty and you cannot regret his loss more than I do, but I feel that our plan must have been successful had it been carried out, and I desire you to know the facts. In the action itself, so far as I can make out, Custer acted under a misapprehension. He thought, I am confident, that the Indians were running. For fear that they might get away he attacked without getting all his men up and divided his command so that they were beaten in detail." Lloyd J. Overfield, *The Little Big Horn, 1876* (Lincoln: University of Nebraska Press, 1990), 36–38.

169. "Interview with Sheridan," *New York Herald*, July 7, 1876.

170. Ibid.

171. "The Slaughter Near the Little Horn River—Death of General Custer."

172. "Sheridan on the Situation," *New York Daily Graphic*, July 8, 1876.

173. "Another Account of the Massacre."

174. Lieutenant George D. Wallace: "A Letter from the Field of Battle," *New York Daily Graphic*, July 13, 1876.

175. Johnson, "Custer's Battlefield."

176. Although Custer had his long hair cut short before setting out on the campaign, the image was hard to escape, especially when your nickname was "Long Hair."

177. Recall an earlier quote: "They must have known that their hour had come," "Custer's Last Battle."

178. "Indian Chief as an Artist—Black Bear's Deerskin Painting of the Details of the Custer Massacre," *Indian Advocate* 14, no. 2 (February 1902): 40–41.

179. Ibid.

180. Describing the battle of Tom's Brook in the Shenandoah Valley, Virginia, October 9, 1864, one participant recounted: "Rosser's

cavalry was drawn up within plain sight of our lines. Custer formed his cavalry for the charge, and then rode out toward Rosser, slowly, all alone. Rosser was an old friend at West Point. Custer was a very striking figure, with his long yellow hair floating over his shoulders, his red neck-tie, his dashing hussar jacket, and a wide-brimmed, bandit-looking hat thrown backward on his head. He rode slowly out, entirely clear of his command, toward Rosser, many yards to the front, then halted and lifted his hat and made a royal cavalier salute to Rosser, dropping his hat to the horse's side. He then rode slowly back, placed himself at the head of his command, and ordered the charge. The charge was so sudden and impetuous that Rosser was swept before it like the wind. . . . If Custer is gone, the Army has lost its most impetuous and daring cavalryman." "Gen. Custer—Gen. Sheridan's Opinion of Him," *New York Times*, July 9, 1876.

181. Lieutenant James Calhoun, Seventh Cavalry.

182. Captain Walker and Calhoun, then a sergeant, served together in the Twenty-third Infantry during part of 1866 and 1867. Francis B. Heitman, *The Historical Register and Dictionary of the United States Army* (usually referred to as *Heitman's Historical Register*), vol. 1 (Washington: Government Printing Office, 1903), 274, 996.

183. Apparently Phillips was not too popular with the *Daily Colorado Chieftain*, which printed on August 2: "Mr. Phillips should be sent to the front to bring the Sioux into harmony with sentimental philanthropy. If we cannot win Sitting Bull, we may at least lose Wendell Phillips, and that will end the controversy."

184. "Custer's Death Trap," interview with Thomas Harrington.

185. The battle of Brice's Crossroads, June 10, 1864.

CHAPTER SEVEN

1. "cold and stern" is from Robert Strahorn, "The Big Horn," *Weekly Rocky Mountain News*, July 12, 1876; "rumors reach us here" is from Reuben Davenport, "Crook's Camp after the Retreat," *New York Herald*, July 13, 1876.

2. Davenport, "Crook's Camp after the Retreat."

3. Ibid.

4. Ibid.

5. Strahorn, "The Big Horn."

6. Davenport, "Crook's Camp after the Retreat."

7. Ibid., also contains the quote, "Sioux spies."

8. Joe Wasson, "Letter from Our Correspondent with General Crook's Command," *Daily Alta California*, August 1, 1876.

9. Davenport, "Crook's Camp after the Retreat."

10. Reuben Davenport, "The Big Horn Mountains—A Trip to Places Never Before Visited by Man," *New York Herald*, August 1, 1876.

11. Strahorn, "The Big Horn."

12. Details gleaned from Davenport, "The Big Horn Mountains—A Trip to Places Never Before Visited by Man," and Robinson, *Diaries of John Gregory Bourke*, vol. 1, 345–346.

13. Davenport, "The Big Horn Mountains—A Trip to Places Never Before Visited by Man."

14. Ibid.

15. Wasson, "Letter from Our Correspondent with General Crook's Command."

16. Davenport, "The Big Horn Mountains—A Trip to Places Never Before Visited by Man."

17. Unknown to Finerty, White Antelope (also known as High Bear or Tall Bear) had been shot in the head and instantly killed during the clash with Sibley's scouting party. "Kill Eagle's Story of His Stay with the

Hostiles," *New York Herald*, September 24, 1876.

18. This was the first official word of the Custer battle to reach Crook's camp since the rumor reported by Davenport on June 27.

19. Reuben Davenport, "Movement of General Crook's Army," *New York Herald*, August 18, 1876. One officer remarked, "The scalp song commenced with a low guttural, measured cadence . . . [and] soon swelled to a fearful chorus that no pen, nor musical scales, with all its sharps and flats, could dare describe or portray." Lieutenant Frederick Schwatka, *Chicago Inter-Ocean*, August 16, 1876, printed in Cozzens, ed., *Long War for the Northern Plains*, 352–353.

20. "Kill Eagle's Story of His Stay with the Hostiles."

21. Reuben Davenport, "Crook Safe," *New York Herald*, July 16, 1876.

22. Washakie was probably older by ten or more years at this time.

23. Davenport, "Crook's Command." Under date of July 17, 1876, Bourke wrote: "Wash-a-kie, the Shoshonee chief, ascends the hills around camp, every morning at sunrise and every evening before the pickets are withdrawn to the valleys, and gazes with searching glance through his field glasses over the land in all directions. He then reports to General Crook the result of his observations." Robinson, *Diaries of John Gregory Bourke*, vol. 1, 377.

24. Davenport, "Crook's Command."

25. Davenport, "Crook Safe." These three men were all in Company E of the Seventh Infantry. In a dispatch dated July 16, Captain Walter Clifford, their commanding officer, wrote, "They are all brave men, but know nothing of this country, and I fear very much for them." Clifford, "From Terry's Camp—An Officer's Diary of Events at the Camp on the Big Horn."

26. Robinson, *Diaries of John Gregory Bourke*, vol. 1, 365–367.

27. In fact, just a few weeks later Wasson would write: "Terry was anxious to cling to Crook's coat-tails and thus divide up the responsibility of a successful or unsuccessful campaign, as much as possible." "Crook's Command," *Daily Alta California*, September 17, 1876.

28. "General Crook's Report to General Terry," *New York Herald*, August 8, 1876.

29. Related to this, Wasson noted, "Since the news was received from Gen. Terry of Gen. Custer's disastrous defeat, criticism of Gen. Crook's retreat from the Rosebud River has ceased in this camp." Joe Wasson, "Skirmishes of General Crook's Force," *New York Tribune*, July 27, 1876.

30. Davenport, "Crook's Command."

31. Ibid.

32. "Camp Cloud Peak," *Daily Alta California*, August 7, 1876. Though unstated, this dispatch was likely written by Strahorn, as it matches closely another dispatch known to have been written by him; from "A Newsy and Interesting Letter from the Big Horn Expedition," *Weekly Rocky Mountain News*, July 26, 1876: "The lariats of the horses were severed by a stroke of the scalp knife, and one of the animals was relieved of a pair of patent hobbles which no Indian was supposed to understand or to be able to unfasten."

33. The new supplies were expected to last through mid-September. "A Fuller Account of the Situation at Camp Cloud Peak." *Daily Alta California*, July 24, 1876.

34. James Willert, *March of the Columns* (El Segundo, CA: Upton & Sons, 1994), 44.

35. Reuben Davenport, "Crook's Camp—Arrival of Provisions and Reinforcements," *New York Herald*, July 23, 1876. Among the reinforcements was Lieutenant Frederick S. Calhoun, Fourteenth Infantry, the younger brother of James Calhoun, who was killed with Custer.

36. Wasson, "Letter from Our Correspondent with General Crook's Command."

37. "Dispatch from Gen. Crook," *New York Times*, July 18, 1876.

38. "General Crook's Report to General Terry."

39. The number of warriors is from a dispatch written by Captain William H. Jordan, Ninth Infantry. Paul L. Hedren, *First Scalp for Custer: The Skirmish at Warbonnet Creek* (Lincoln: Nebraska State Historical Society, 2005), 21.

40. Hedren, *First Scalp for Custer*, 28.

41. Captain Charles King, *Campaigning with Crook* (Norman: University of Oklahoma Press, 1989), 34.

42. "Reports from the Agencies," *New York Herald*, July 20, 1876.

43. "'Buffalo Bill' Taking an Indian Scalp," *Colorado Banner*, August 17, 1876.

44. Paul L. Hedren, e-mail exchange with author, June 1, 2011.

45. "The War on the Plains—Colonel Merritt's Movements," *New York Times*, July 20, 1876.

46. Cuthbert Mills, "Scenes at Fort Fetterman—The Campaign against the Sioux," *New York Times*, August 6, 1876.

47. Ibid.

48. Davenport, "Movement of General Crook's Army."

49. "News from Crook," *New York Herald*, July 25, 1876.

50. Joe Wasson, "Crook's Expedition—A Sharp Pursuit of the Sioux," *New York Tribune*, July 27, 1876.

51. Davenport, "Crook's Command."

52. Ibid.

53. Joe Wasson, "Hunting the Sioux," *Daily Alta California*, September 26, 1876.

54. Andrew Burt, *Cincinnati Commercial*, September 11, 1876 (dispatch dated August 14), printed in Cozzens, ed., *Long War for the Northern Plains*, 371.

55. Henry W. Daly, "The War Path," *American Legion Monthly* (April 1927), printed in Cozzens, ed., *Long War for the Northern Plains*, 255.

Chapter Eight

1. James J. O'Kelly, "General Terry's Movements," *New York Herald*, August 15, 1876.

2. "The Sioux War—General Terry's New Camp," *New York Tribune*, July 22, 1876.

3. Clifford, "From Terry's Camp—An Officer's Diary of Events at the Camp on the Big Horn."

4. Ibid.

5. Ibid.

6. John Gibbon, "Hunting Sitting Bull," in Gaff and Gaff, *Adventures on the Western Frontier*, 155–156, and Edgar I. Stewart and Jane R. Stewart, eds., *The Field Diary of Lieutenant Edward Settle Godfrey* (Portland, OR: Champoeg Press, 1957), 23.

7. James J. O'Kelly, "Terry Moves—Arrival of Miles' Command at Terry's Headquarters," *New York Herald*, August 11, 1876.

8. Edward Maguire of the Engineer Corps.

9. "The Sioux War—Gen. Terry's Camp," *New York Tribune*, August 14, 1876.

10. Ibid.

11. Ibid.

12. Ibid.

13. Ibid. The following day, July 26, Terry thanked the three privates in General Field Order No. 5, which stated in part: "In making this public acknowledgment of important services, voluntarily rendered by these soldiers at imminent risk of their lives, the Department Commander desires to express his deep regret that at present it is not in his power to bestow the substantial reward which was so well earned; but he is confident that an achievement undertaken in so soldierly a spirit and carried so gallantly to a successful issue will not be permitted to pass unnoticed. I wish to establish in the public mind a higher and more just estimate of the character of the United States soldiers. The Department Commander in his own behalf, and in behalf of the officers of this command, desires thus to publicly thank privates William Evans, Benjamin F. Stewart and

James Bell, of Company E, Seventh Infantry, for a deed which reflects so much credit on the service." James J. O'Kelly, "After the Sioux," *New York Herald*, August 13, 1876.

14. "Custer's Fallen Braves Not Tortured by the Sioux—They Died Fighting," *New York Herald*, August 13, 1876.

15. O'Kelly, "General Terry's Movements." The fifteen officers were Lieutenant Colonel Elwell S. Otis; Captains Charles J. Dickey, Francis Clarke, Charles W. Miner, DeWitt C. Poole, Mott Hooton, and Archibald H. Goodloe; Lieutenants William Conway, William Campbell, Ben C. Lockwood, Oskaloosa M. Smith, James E. Macklin, William H. Kell, Edward W. Casey, and William N. Dyckman. James W. Howard, "A Trip to the Front," *New York Herald*, August 7, 1876, repr. from *Chicago Tribune*, July 26, 1876. Of the reinforcements from the Twenty-second Infantry, O'Kelly observed: "Considering the disastrous result of the former expedition, which had left Fort Lincoln full of confidence in its ability to sweep from its path any force the savages could muster to oppose its march, it was marvelous to watch the careless manner with which the recruits start off on their first military venture, manifesting all the sturdy confidence of youth and its contempt of danger. Their first experience of campaigning is not destined to be over agreeable. . . . With all their sturdy indifference to the danger that attends their undertaking, unless the Indians should break up into insignificant parties, there is a certainty that many of the men who step so gallantly over the steamer's side are going to their death. They seem, however, wholly unconscious of the fact, though they cannot be ignorant of it." James J. O'Kelly, "Trip of the Steamer Carroll En Route for the Big Horn River," *New York Herald*, August 7, 1876.

16. O'Kelly, "Terry Moves—Arrival of Miles' Command at Terry's Headquarters."

17. Ibid.

18. Ibid.

19. James J. O'Kelly, "Garbled Statements Corrected by the Officers of the Seventh," *New York Herald*, August 8, 1876.

20. Ibid.

21. "Rosser's Tribute to Custer," *New York Herald*, July 11, 1876.

22. O'Kelly, "Garbled Statements Corrected by the Officers of the Seventh."

23. An editorial in the *New York Herald* on August 8 stated, "[W]e are almost glad that Reno was goaded into making these statements, else we might have missed a valuable part of history."

24. O'Kelly, "Garbled Statements Corrected by the Officers of the Seventh." It is this author's opinion that Rosser's charges were directed solely against Reno, who, perhaps in an effort to garner support from his fellow officers, tried to make it sound as if Rosser had criticized all of them.

25. Ibid.

26. Ibid.

27. Ibid.

28. Ibid. With regard to Benteen's "Saviour" status, an unknown soldier on Reno Hill declared that "Benteen's gallant conduct filled us all with a new courage and evidently alarmed the enemy." "Another Account of the Battle."

29. Both Sharrow and Voss returned to Custer, with whom they died. Regarding the structure of this paragraph, it makes more sense if you flip the second and third sentences.

30. This is the second time in the first two paragraphs that Benteen has decided to rejoin, or return to, "the main trail."

31. O'Kelly, "Garbled Statements Corrected by the Officers of the Seventh." As a matter of record, in his official report, dated July 4, 1876, Benteen described his valley hunting episode as follows: "The directions I received from Lieutenant Colonel Custer were, to move with my command to the left, to send well-mounted officers with about six men who should ride rapidly to a line of bluffs about five miles to our left and front, with

instructions to report at once to me if any-thing of Indians could be seen from that point. I was to follow the movement of this detachment as rapidly as possible. . . . The bluffs designated were gained, but nothing seen but other bluffs quite as large and pre-cipitous as were before me. I kept on to those and the country was the same, there being no valley of any kind that I could see on any side. I had then gone about fully ten miles; the ground was terribly hard on [the] horses, so I determined to carry out the other instructions, which were, that if in my judg-ment there was nothing to be seen of Indians, valleys, &c., in the direction I was going, to return with the battalion to the trail the command was following. I accord-ingly did so, reaching the trail just in advance of the pack-train." "Report of Captain Benteen," printed in *[Annual] Report of the Secretary of War* (for the year 1876), vol. 1, 479.

32. James J. O'Kelly, "Colonel Moore's Reception of Foreign Stores," *New York Herald*, August 11, 1876, dispatch dated "Camp on Yellowstone, August 5." A dis-patch in the *New York Times* on August 18, 1876, "From Gen. Terry's Command," stat-ed that the carbine taken from the dead war-rior "was one of the new Springfield model, of forty-five caliber which had been captured in Gen. Custer's fight."

33. O'Kelly, "After the Sioux." In a dispatch about ten days later (dated August 15), and with the wisdom of hindsight, O'Kelly pointed out that it would have been better to go after the Indians near Powder River than to march south with the uncertainty of find-ing them at all. James J. O'Kelly, "The Sioux War—Sketch of Army Movements on the Powder and Yellowstone Rivers," *New York Herald*, August 24, 1876.

34. O'Kelly, "Terry Moves—Arrival of Miles' Command at Terry's Headquarters."

35. Ibid.

36. O'Kelly, "General Terry's Movements."

37. Ibid. The number 418 was stated in

O'Kelly, "Terry Moves—Arrival of Miles' Command at Terry's Headquarters."

38. O'Kelly, "General Terry's Movements." In a related story, on July 28, Sheridan received a document containing the signa-tures of over two hundred survivors of the Seventh Cavalry that was dated July 4 and requested that "the vacancies among the commissioned officers be filled by the pro-motion of Major Reno to the Lieutenant Colonelcy, of Captain Benteen to the Majority, and that the other vacancies be filled by officers of the regiment according to seniority." "A Petition from 230 Brave Men," *New York Times*, July 29, 1876. In later years, the document's authenticity was called into question, and in 1954, the FBI deemed many of the signatures to be forgeries.

39. O'Kelly, "General Terry's Movements." Both Jackson and Bell reported for duty in September. Larned resigned from the regi-ment that same month in order to retain his position at West Point. James B. Klokner, *The Officer Corps of Custer's Seventh Cavalry, 1866-1876* (Atglen, PA: Schiffer, 2007), 44, 73, 75.

40. O'Kelly, "General Terry's Movements."

41. Klokner, *Officer Corps*, 63.

42. O'Kelly, "General Terry's Movements." In another dispatch, O'Kelly remarked that a diet "dependant on pork, crackers and cof-fee, [is] a diet that would ruin any stomach." O'Kelly, "The Sioux War—Sketch of Army Movements on the Powder and Yellowstone Rivers."

43. "Terry on the March," *New York Tribune*, August 15, 1876, repr. from *St. Paul Pioneer-Press*, August 14, 1876 (based on internal statements, the dispatch was written on August 7).

44. Ibid.

45. O'Kelly, "Trip of the Steamer Carroll En Route for the Big Horn River."

46. O'Kelly, "General Terry's Movements."

47. Special correspondent, "Terry's March," *New York Tribune*, August 19, 1876.

48. O'Kelly, "General Terry's Movements."

The Indian scouts consisted of Crow and Arikara Indians.

49. "Army of the Yellowstone" is from "The Indian Campaign—March of the Yellowstone Army," *New York Times*, August 21, 1876; "Fort Beans" is from "Terry's Plans," *New York Tribune*, August 16, 1876, and O'Kelly, "General Terry's Movements."

50. O'Kelly, "After the Sioux."

51. Special correspondent, "Terry's March."

52. "A Criticism by General Rosser of Reno's Tactics," *New York Herald*, August 22, 1876.

53. Ibid.

54. Ibid.

55. "Custer's Death—Was the Gallant White Chief Abandoned by his Subordinates?" *New York Herald*, January 14, 1879.

56. "Major Reno Exonerated," *New York Times*, March 7, 1879.

57. This was stated in a 1912 interview with historian Walter M. Camp. Richard G. Hardorff, ed. and comp., *On the Little Big Horn with Walter Camp* (El Segundo, CA: Upton & Sons, 2002), 191.

58. "Custer's Death—Was the Gallant White Chief Abandoned by his Subordinates?"

59. The quotes "confidential communications" and "brother officers" are from ibid.

60. O'Kelly's article was reprinted in the *Herald* again on January 14, 1879.

61. At the time Reno decided to fall back to the woods, perhaps no more than two men had been killed: Sergeant Miles F. O'Hara, shot in the chest, and Private George E. Smith, whose horse carried him into the Indian village. Sergeant Henry Charles Weihe, a.k.a. Charles White, may also have been wounded at this time. All three men were in Company M. Nichols, *Men with Custer*, 251, 308, and 349.

62. In October 1877, Sitting Bull told an interviewer, "There were none but squaws and papooses in front of them [the men on Reno Hill] that afternoon." Later he added, "There was no need to waste warriors in that direction. There were only a few soldiers there in those intrenchments, and we knew they wouldn't dare come out." Jerome Stillson, "Sitting Bull Talks," *New York Herald*, November 16, 1877. Also, recall the words of Red Horse in a previous chapter, that when the warriors perceived the new threat (Custer), they all raced in his direction and left Reno's men alone on the hill.

63. The distance between the morass (watering place) and a landmark now known as Battle Ridge is about eleven miles—measured by the approximate route Custer followed. Thanks to Frederic C. Wagner III for providing this detail.

CHAPTER NINE

1. Cuthbert Mills, "Seeking an Indian Fight," *New York Times*, August 18, 1876.

2. Wasson, "Crook's Expedition—A Sharp Pursuit of the Sioux."

3. Lieutenant Frederick Schwatka, *Chicago Inter-Ocean*, August 16, 1876, printed in Cozzens, ed., *Long War for the Northern Plains*, 351.

4. Davenport, "Movement of General Crook's Army."

5. Joe Wasson, "The Sioux War—Gen. Crook's Advance," *New York Tribune*, August 9, 1876.

6. Davenport, "Movement of General Crook's Army." Correspondent Cuthbert Mills, who met Cody a few days earlier at Fort Fetterman, characterized him and the other scouts with Merritt this way: "A great feature of the expedition is the corps of scouts. There are some eleven or twelve of them and their chief is Cody, better known as 'Buffalo Bill.' . . . As a class, these men have rather a bad reputation—most of them being dangerous and good-for-nothing rascals, who take to their risky business because it pays well. Cody, however, is an exception, and stands high in the estimation of those he serves." Cuthbert Mills, "The Indian Campaign—From Fetterman to Goose Creek," *New York Times*, August 17, 1876.

7. Joe Wasson, "Crook's Expedition—Starting on a Vigorous Campaign," *New York Tribune*, August 17, 1876.

8. Davenport, "Movement of General Crook's Army."

9. "Gen. Crook's Command—Letter from a Soldier," *New York Tribune*, August 18, 1876.

10. Ibid.

11. Except for the number of infantry, all of these totals are from Joe Wasson, "The Indian War—Merritt's Cavalry Join the Command," *Daily Alta California*, August 9, 1876. In Davenport's summary of the campaign, written in mid-September, he said there were 1,250 cavalry and 400 infantry (the author believes his total for the infantry, which matches Lieutenant Schwatka's estimate, to be closer to the mark than the 500 stated by Wasson). Davenport, "Crook's Campaign," which is also the source for "a gaudily tinted throng."

12. Davenport, "Crook's Campaign."

13. Wasson, "The Indian War—Merritt's Cavalry Join the Command."

14. Ibid.

15. Davenport, "Crook's Campaign."

16. Ibid.

17. Mills, "Seeking an Indian Fight." On this point Davenport added, "Frank [Grouard] advised General Crook that he believed the Sioux had again occupied the country from which we failed to drive them on June 17." Davenport, "Movement of General Crook's Army."

18. Wasson, "The Indian War—Merritt's Cavalry Join the Command."

19. These details are a combination from various newspaper accounts. Interestingly, Lieutenant Bourke wrote, "Of ammunition, we had two hundred and fifty rounds to the man; one hundred to be carried by the cavalrymen on their persons or in the saddlebags, the rest to be packed on the pack-mules, of which we had three hundred and ninety-nine." Robinson, *Diaries of John Gregory Bourke*, vol. 2, 46. According to Mills, the infantry packed rations for one day only, the rest being carried on the pack mules. Cuthbert Mills, "The War with the Indians—Hunting for Sioux Savages," *New York Times*, August 27, 1876.

20. Joe Wasson, "Superior Condition of General Crook's Command," *New York Tribune*, August 11, 1876, repr. of a dispatch to the *Chicago Tribune*.

21. Wasson, "The Indian War—Merritt's Cavalry Join the Command."

22. That night they camped about eight miles north of the Rosebud battlefield. Lieutenant Frederick Schwatka, *Chicago Inter-Ocean*, September 11, 1876, printed in Cozzens, ed., *Long War for the Northern Plains*, 355.

23. Ibid., 357. Regarding the trail of the Indians, Davenport wrote, "Shortly after the column entered the valley the theory that the Indians had in a body gone northeastward was confirmed by the great proportions of the main trail, after numerous converging paths from tributary valleys and hollows had united with it." Davenport, "Crook's Campaign."

24. Mills, "The War with the Indians—Hunting for Sioux Savages."

25. Ibid.

26. Reuben Davenport, "The Sioux War—Junction of Crook's and Terry's Commands," *New York Herald*, August 21, 1876.

27. Davenport, "Crook's Campaign."

28. Mills, "The War with the Indians—Hunting for Sioux Savages." Madera helped Mills again in September during what came to be known as the "The Horsemeat March": "I went to my old friend Shep Medera . . . and not only got a luxurious supper of roasted antelope, sugared coffee, and hard bread, but the cook gave me a piece of ribs for our mess." Cuthbert Mills, "The Pursuit of the Sioux," *New York Times*, September 28, 1876.

29. Davenport, "Crook's Campaign."

30. "Indian Sweating Treatment," *Daily Alta California*, October 20, 1876.

31. Davenport, "Crook's Campaign."

32. Schwatka, *Chicago Inter-Ocean*, September 11, 1876, printed in Cozzens, ed., *Long War for the Northern Plains*, 357–358.

33. Ibid.

34. Davenport, "Crook's Campaign."

35. All quotes and details from this point to the end of the chapter are from James J. O'Kelly, "The Sioux War—Sketch of Army Movements on the Powder and Yellowstone Rivers," *New York Herald*, August 24, 1876.

36. O'Kelly was unaware of the fact that in the Indian sign language of the Great Plains, the Sioux were designated by the hand sign for cutting one's throat. William P. Clark, *The Indian Sign Language* (Lincoln: University of Nebraska Press, 1982), 341.

CHAPTER TEN

1. Regarding military jurisdictions, by the beginning of September, Wasson was to complain that the "Platte Department ought to have extended at least to the Yellowstone River, which is the natural base of supplies of a campaign against the hostile Sioux. General Crook's operations have all been outside of his own department so far." Joe Wasson, "The Sioux War—General Crook's March," *New York Tribune*, September 15, 1876.

2. O'Kelly, "The Sioux War—Sketch of Army Movements on the Powder and Yellowstone Rivers."

3. If Crook had sent a courier, it probably would not have changed a thing. The Indians were already more than a few steps ahead of the pursuing troops.

4. O'Kelly, "The Sioux War—Sketch of Army Movements on the Powder and Yellowstone Rivers."

5. Regarding Crook's manner of dress, an article printed shortly after his death in March 1890 said: "When Gen. Crook is around his headquarters he rarely wears enough uniform to designate his high rank, and when in the field he dresses more like a rough cowboy than a general officer, but when he starts east, or comes to Washington on business, Mrs. Crook takes him in hand and makes him wear good clothes—well fitting and becoming ones, too—and a high silk hat replaces the broad brimmed slouch he loves so well." "A Lewis County Boy," *Journal & Republican* (Lowville, New York), April 24, 1890, repr. from the *National Tribune*, Washington, D.C.

6. Cuthbert Mills, "The Indian Campaign—The Part Taken by General Crook's Command," *New York Times*, October 11, 1876.

7. Hedren, *Great Sioux War Orders of Battle*, 118.

8. O'Kelly, "The Sioux War—Sketch of Army Movements on the Powder and Yellowstone Rivers."

9. Ibid.

10. Under date of August 14, 1876, Lieutenant Godfrey included the following update in his diary regarding the goings-on with Colonel Miles: "A courier came from Genl Miles saying Indians had not crossed Yellowstone—one company at Tongue, two at Powder River and one on St. boat [steamboat] patrolling river." Stewart and Stewart, eds., *Field Diary of Lieutenant Edward Settle Godfrey*, 36.

11. Burt, *Cincinnati Commercial*, September 11, 1876 (dispatch dated August 14), printed in Cozzens, ed., *Long War for the Northern Plains*, 371.

12. Ibid.

13. James J. O'Kelly, "Operations of the Combined Columns under Terry and Crook," *New York Herald*, September 12, 1876.

14. Davenport, "Crook's Campaign." On the other hand, near the close of the campaign, Cuthbert Mills remarked, "Officers and men have been all on equal footing. Few in this command had any advantage in living over the mass, and, be it said, that the commander of this little army has lived exactly as the poorest soldier in it." Cuthbert Mills,

"The Pursuit of the Sioux," *New York Times*, September 28, 1876. Additionally, an anonymous trooper with the Fourteenth Infantry was to reminisce twenty-five years later: "[General Crook] was an unassuming man, nothing vain or haughty in his make-up; in fact in those days we did not have that kind of men in the West. His dress was more like that of a packer instead of a general in the army. When on the march he wore a canvas suit, with a cartridge belt containing 100 rounds of ammunition, a plain sombrero—we had no regular field hat—his face covered with a thick beard, and a fine Springfield rifle swung across the pommel of his saddle. You could always see him riding at the head of the column accompanied by his adjutant, Capt. J. G. Bourke and Frank Gourard [Grouard], his chief of scouts. No matter how fiercely the bullets rained about him he would never lose his head, and more than that, he never asked a man, be he private or officer, to do something which he, Crook, wouldn't do himself. Many a night, upon this very expedition . . . I saw him with a blanket thrown over his shoulder sitting by the blazing camp fire, his frame outlined against the dark night, with a piece of bacon on a spit, cooking it over the fire for his supper." "A Campaign with Crook—Fighting Indians in the Seventies Under 'Old Grey Fox,'" (Washington) *Times*, February 17, 1901.

15. John Finerty, "The Fellows in Feathers: An Interview with General Crook," *Chicago Times*, November 4, 1876, printed in Cozzens, ed., *Long War for the Northern Plains*, 389.

16. Davenport, "Crook's Campaign."

17. Reuben Davenport, "General Terry's March to the Yellowstone," *New York Herald*, August 24, 1876.

18. Ibid.

19. Regarding the Indian trail at this time, Gibbon wrote, "There were no indications leading to the belief that we were anywhere close to them." Gibbon, "Hunting Sitting Bull," in Gaff and Gaff, *Adventures on the Western Frontier*, 163–164.

20. Wasson, "Hunting the Sioux." If Crook's meeting up with Terry was accidental, it appears to have been the reverse for Terry. Under date of August 5, while still on his journey to Terry's Rosebud camp, correspondent Charles S. Diehl had written, "But little is definitely known concerning the proposed movement of the command, beyond the fact that General Terry will follow the course of the Rosebud south until a junction is formed with Crook." Charles S. Diehl, *Chicago Times*, August 16, 1876, printed in Cozzens, ed., *Long War for the Northern Plains*, 394.

21. Davenport, "Crook's Campaign." The correspondents lacked agreement on precisely when the Indian scouts left Crook and Terry; the dates range from August 20 to 22.

22. James Joseph Talbot, "Camping with Crook—The Fruitless Marches and Countermarches," *New York World*, September 17, 1876.

23. Cuthbert Mills, "Wearying Drag of the Pursuit," *New York Times*, September 14, 1876, dispatch dated "In Camp, Beaver Creek, August 30, 1876."

24. Talbot, "Camping with Crook—The Fruitless Marches and Countermarches."

25. Davenport, "Crook's Campaign."

26. Ibid.

27. Wasson, "Hunting the Sioux." This dispatch was written prior to the departure of the Indian scouts; it was dated "Camp at Junction of Yellowstone and Powder Rivers, Montana, August 18, 1876."

28. O'Kelly, "Operations of the Combined Columns under Terry and Crook."

29. Davenport, "General Terry's March to the Yellowstone."

30. Quote from Wasson, "Crook's Command."

31. Davenport, "Crook's Campaign."

32. Burt, *Cincinnati Commercial*, September 11, 1876 (dispatch dated August 23), printed in Cozzens, ed., *Long War for the Northern Plains*, 372.

33. Cuthbert Mills, "Steaming up the Yellowstone," *New York Times*, September 12, 1876. On August 19, Mills had accompanied Captain Burt of the Ninth Infantry on his mission to secure about 250 Crow Indians to serve as scouts. About the venture, Mills recorded: "At the last accounts received of them the Crows were pow-wowing after their usual manner on the question of whether they should or should not go into the campaign against the Sioux; and from his long acquaintance with this tribe, Captain Burt was selected as the proper man to convince them that it would be to their profit in ponies and scalps to come in and join their brother Indians already with the 'Gray Fox' [Crook]." From his closing statement, it is clear that Burt was then unaware that the other Indian scouts had just abandoned the expedition. As for the outcome of Burt's undertaking, Mills bluntly stated, "Our Crow expedition was a failure." Ibid.

34. Wasson, "Hunting the Sioux."

35. Ibid. James Gordon Bennett was the publisher of the *New York Herald*.

36. O'Kelly, "Operations of the Combined Columns under Terry and Crook." It was O'Kelly's opinion that "Terry can be trusted to carry out the disarmament without undue severity, and yet with firmness. All his instincts are on the side of humanity, and if it is possible to accomplish this necessary work without bloodshed he may be relied upon to do it."

37. Edward M. Hayes, Fifth Cavalry.

38. Mills, "Wearying Drag of the Pursuit." At the end of the campaign, Mills noted that it had been an "unprecedented rainy season." Mills, "The Pursuit of the Sioux."

39. Gray, *Centennial Campaign*, 230. About the Wyoming Column's departure, Talbot wrote, "They had one week's rest (for three days of which they had a limited supply of forage), but they were so utterly worn out by the hard, continuous marching of the previous month, and many of them much longer, that even one week's rest could not wholly

recuperate them." Talbot, "Camping with Crook—The Fruitless Marches and Countermarches." Crook afterward told a reporter, "I was perfectly satisfied to serve under General Terry as long as the public interests could be benefited thereby. When it was considered expedient to divide the commands, they were divided." Finerty, "The Fellows in Feathers: An Interview with General Crook," *Chicago Times*, November 4, 1876, printed in Cozzens, ed., *Long War for the Northern Plains*, 388. Regarding their time in camp on the Yellowstone, Lieutenant Bourke confided in his journal that a description of one day would just as well answer for the others. Robinson, *Diaries of John Gregory Bourke*, vol. 2, 67. About the delivery of supplies via steamer, Bourke wrote: "[W]e had been grievously disappointed in not finding on the Yellowstone the amount of supplies expected and in having to fritter away a whole week's time until this steamer brought up forage and that steamer brought down shoes. The administration of the supply corps on the Yellowstone was unsatisfactory." Ibid., 96.

40. This cantonment, temporarily designated Post No. 1, was renamed Fort Keogh in November 1877. It was one of two military posts for which Sheridan received $200,000 from Congress to build in the Yellowstone country in the wake of the battle of the Little Big Horn. As one correspondent pointed out in early July, "Summer campaigns against Indians in this country, until permanent supply posts are established, will amount to nothing." "The Indian War—Crook's First Fight." This quote may be from an unnamed correspondent of the *Helena* (Montana) *Herald*. The second fortification, Post No. 2, was established in July 1877, at the mouth of the Little Big Horn. It was officially designated Fort Custer four months later. The Tongue River Cantonment was high priority for Sheridan, who had declared that "the Yellowstone country must be occupied at all hazards." "Latest from Terry and Crook," *New York Times*, September 5, 1876.

41. Lieutenant Edmund Rice, Fifth Infantry.

42. Davenport, "Crook's Campaign."

43. James J. O'Kelly, "The Sioux War—General Terry and Crook in Hot Pursuit of the Indians," *New York Herald*, September 5, 1876.

44. Burt, *Cincinnati Commercial*, September 14, 1876 (dispatch dated September 5), printed in Cozzens, ed., *Long War for the Northern Plains*, 375.

45. James J. O'Kelly, "The Sioux Campaign—The Expedition to the North Bank of the Yellowstone," *New York Herald*, September 8, 1876.

46. Dispatch from General Terry's camp near the Yellowstone, August 30, *Deseret News*, September 27, 1876.

47. O'Kelly, "The Sioux Campaign—The Expedition to the North Bank of the Yellowstone."

48. James J. O'Kelly, "The Sioux War—Terry's Movement along the Yellowstone," *New York Herald*, September 12, 1876. Around this time, Benteen left the expedition, being assigned to recruiting duty in the East. James J. O'Kelly, "General Terry after the Indians," *New York Herald*, September 5, 1876. However, shortly after, he asked to be relieved of that duty, which was granted. He was replaced by Captain Weir. Charles K. Mills, *Harvest of Barren Regrets* (Glendale, CA: Arthur H. Clark, 1985), 285–286. It was to be Weir's last assignment. He died in December 1876, and was buried in Cypress Hills National Cemetery in Brooklyn, New York. There is little doubt that Weir took a lot of valuable information about the battle of the Little Big Horn to the grave.

49. Charles S. Diehl, *Chicago Times*, September 12, 1876, printed in Cozzens, ed., *Long War for the Northern Plains*, 406.

50. James J. O'Kelly, "Crook Following Up an Indian Trail," *New York Herald*, September 12, 1876.

51. James J. O'Kelly, "Terry's Operating Column Dissolved," *New York Herald*, September 12, 1876. Another correspondent noted, "Now that all active operations have been abandoned for the year, the utter failure of the campaign is felt by everyone. The humiliation of defeat is shared by the soldiers and officers alike." Charles S. Diehl, *Chicago Times*, September 16, 1876, printed in Cozzens, ed., *Long War for the Northern Plains*, 409.

52. On September 11, two of these companies left the Glendive Depot to join Miles at Tongue River. Jerome A. Greene, *Yellowstone Command: Colonel Nelson A. Miles and the Great Sioux War, 1876-1877* (Lincoln: University of Nebraska Press, 1994), 61.

53. "The Sioux Campaign—Virtual Suspension of Offensive Operations." The number of miles between Glendive and the cantonment was estimated using Google Earth. The land route with wagons would have been slightly longer.

54. "Terry's Command Divided Up and Returning Except Two Regiments," *New York Times*, September 16, 1876, repr. from the *Chicago Times*, original dispatch dated September 8, at Fort Buford. Originally, Sheridan had intended for some part of the Fifth Cavalry to spend the winter on the Yellowstone, too, but by mid-September, acknowledging the difficulty in keeping them properly supplied, he countermanded the order.

55. Ibid.

56. "The Uncapapas Sioux Moving Toward Canada—Troops in Pursuit," *New York Herald*, September 19, 1876. Another source stated that Moore's battalion consisted of three companies. Ronald H. Nichols, *In Custer's Shadow: Major Marcus Reno* (Norman: University of Oklahoma Press, 2000), 233.

57. "Major" Thomas J. Mitchell was the agent at Fort Peck, at the confluence of the Milk and Missouri rivers in Montana.

58. James J. O'Kelly, "The Campaign Officially Announced at an End—A Futile Pursuit of Indians Closes It," *New York Herald*, September 21, 1876. The author

reversed the first two sentences of this dispatch from their original sequence. As for the troops not being able to cross the Missouri at Wolf Point, it did not seem to stop the Indians.

59. Ibid.

60. For more on the Sioux in Canada in the wake of the Great Sioux War, see David Grant McCrady, *Living with Strangers: The Nineteenth Century Sioux and the Canadian-American Borderlands* (Lincoln: University of Nebraska Press, 2006). Useful here was page 66.

61. "The Sentiments and Opinions of Sitting Bull," *New York Herald*, August 19, 1876.

62. "What Returned Officers Say," *Deseret News*, September 27, 1876.

Chapter Eleven

1. Davenport, "Crook's Campaign."

2. Mills, "Wearying Drag of the Pursuit."

3. Ibid.

4. Davenport, "Crook's Campaign."

5. Mills. "Wearying Drag of the Pursuit."

6. Wasson, "The Sioux War—General Crook's March." In another dispatch, Wasson added, "When the Indians saw the pursuit extended east of their burned belt of grass, this side of Powder River, they seem to have become stampeded—fleeing in every direction." Wasson, "Crook's Command."

7. Burt, *Cincinnati Commercial*, September 11, 1876 (dispatch dated August 23), printed in Cozzens, ed., *Long War for the Northern Plains*, 372.

8. Davenport, "Crook's Campaign." Beaver Creek runs south to north until it joins with the Little Missouri. Crook was then camped along the southern reaches while the scouts were advancing to the north searching for trails.

9. Lieutenant Bourke was more precise. Under date of September 3 he wrote, "Marched twenty miles to Andrews Creek, near Sentinel Buttes." Robinson, *Diaries of John Gregory Bourke*, vol. 2, 94. This was

about where the Dakota Column had camped on June 1, 1876, on its outward march from Fort Abraham Lincoln.

10. Davenport, "Crook's Campaign."

11. O'Kelly, "Crook Following Up an Indian Trail."

12. Davenport, "Crook's Campaign."

13. Ibid.

14. About the diminishing rations, Wasson declared: "The diet of bacon and hard tack and sugar and coffee is monotonous, and most every one says his hunger is not appeased thereby, however much he may eat. The soldiers say there is a disproportionate amount of hard bread—not enough for the bacon—and that the army board should remedy the matter." The good news was that they were finding large quantities of "ripe choke cherries and buffalo berries," which will "serve to fend off scurvy, which occasionally crops out." Wasson, "The Sioux War—General Crook's March."

15. "Crook's Command in a Bad Way," *Deseret News*, September 27, 1876. Sounding a bit like Davenport, Wasson wrote: "The troops of this command and all connected with it have already suffered considerably on account of limited bedding, clothing, &c. Cool nights have prevailed, interspersed with a good many wet ones. . . . Today [September 4] . . . a cold rain storm set in, and it promises to hold out. Many of the men left their overcoats in the wagon train, and nearly every man of the command brought no change of underclothing, and no soap to wash what they had." Wasson, "The Sioux War—General Crook's March."

16. Davenport, "Crook's Campaign." Regarding the uncertainties of the march, Cuthbert Mills declared, "None of our scouts had ever been over the country, and our maps were not encouraging or trustworthy." Mills, "The Pursuit of the Sioux."

17. Davenport, "Crook's Campaign."

18. Wasson, "Crook's Command."

19. Rather than a lone courier, Crook had sent two Arikara Indians with dispatches. Mills, "The Pursuit of the Sioux."

20. The wagon train, under command of Captain Furey, had since been moved from Goose Creek to old Fort Reno, about 250 miles southwest of Crook's current position north of the Black Hills. For mention of the wagon train having been moved, see Cuthbert Mills, "The Hostile Savages—The Campaign against the Sioux," *New York Times*, September 9, 1876.

21. Davenport, "Crook's Campaign."

22. Finerty, "The Fellows in Feathers: An Interview with General Crook," *Chicago Times*, November 4, 1876, printed in Cozzens, ed., *Long War for the Northern Plains*, 388–389.

23. Wasson, "Crook's Command."

24. Reuben Davenport, "The Hostile Sioux—Crook's March," *New York Herald*, September 10, 1876.

25. Reuben Davenport, "The Indian Campaign Virtually Over," *Deseret News*, September 20, 1876, repr. from the *Omaha Daily Bee*.

26. Mills, "The Pursuit of the Sioux."

27. Wasson, "Crook's Command."

28. Mills, "The Hostile Savages—The Campaign against the Sioux," and Wasson, "The Sioux War—General Crook's March."

29. Wasson, "The Sioux War—General Crook's March." Concerning the statement that the Sioux had better ponies than the scouts (who were therefore unable to give pursuit), an unknown correspondent wrote, "This column is in an unserviceable condition, utterly unfit to do more than act as infantry. The horses are too poor and broken down for active pursuit of the enemy." "Crook's Command in a Bad Way."

30. Wasson, "Crook's Command."

31. Mills, "The Pursuit of the Sioux."

32. Davenport, "The Hostile Sioux—Crook's March."

33. Ibid.

Chapter Twelve

1. Davenport, "Crook's Campaign."

2. Describing a previous night's dinner of antelope that he was lucky to partake in, Davenport wrote, "No banquet spread on silver and illumined with diamonds had the relish of this savage repast, for such it was, and its recurrence was imbued with greater zest by the long intervals during which ill luck restricted us to the bacon and 'hard tack' of the soldier." Ibid.

3. Ibid.

4. Ibid.

5. Reuben Davenport, "Crook's Victory," *New York Herald*, September 17, 1876.

6. Mills, "The Pursuit of the Sioux."

7. Davenport, "Crook's Campaign."

8. Ibid.

9. "north fork of the Grand River" is from Lieutenant Frederick Schwatka, *Chicago Inter-Ocean*, October 4, 1876, printed in Cozzens, ed., *Long War for the Northern Plains*, 361; "to send back relief" is from Davenport, "Crook's Campaign."

10. These numbers come from Captain Mills' official report of the Slim Buttes affair, printed in Greene, *Slim Buttes*, 132. For the record, Wasson said there were forty mules, and Davenport said fifty-one.

11. Davenport, "Crook's Victory."

12. Davenport, "Crook's Campaign."

13. Ibid.

14. Davenport, "Crook's Victory." According to Mills, it was later learned that these Indians were returning to the Standing Rock Agency. Cuthbert Mills, "The Indian Campaign—Attack upon a Camp of Sioux," *New York Times*, September 17, 1876.

15. Davenport, "Crook's Campaign."

16. Joe Wasson, "Capture of the Village." *New York Tribune*, September 18, 1876.

17. In his official report, Captain Mills said twenty-five men were left behind to guard the horses.

18. According to Davenport, Crook "was supposed to be on the march about twenty miles in our rear." Davenport, "Crook's Campaign."

19. Davenport, "Crook's Victory."

20. Mills, "The Pursuit of the Sioux." Regarding the name of the stream: In his official report, Captain Mills called it Rabbit Creek (a tributary of the Moreau River). However, as afterward discovered by Walter M. Camp, an Indian Wars historian who searched the area for the battle site, the fight took place on Gap Creek, which is a tributary of Rabbit Creek. Jerome A. Greene, *Slim Buttes, 1876: An Episode of the Great Sioux War* (Norman: University of Oklahoma Press, 1990), 143. For a map of the battlefield, see Greene, *Slim Buttes*, 62.

21. Davenport, "Crook's Victory."

22. Davenport, "Crook's Campaign."

23. Davenport, "Crook's Victory."

24. Ibid. Schwatka wrote, "The dismounted men followed up the mounted charge rapidly with a deadly fusillade into the village." Schwatka, *Chicago Inter-Ocean*, October 4, 1876, printed in Cozzens, ed., *Long War for the Northern Plains*, 363.

25. Regarding the Indians having to cut their way out of the lodges, Schwatka explained, "The night having been very rainy, the Indians had securely fastened the openings in their lodges, and it was with evident impediment that they made their exits." Schwatka, *Chicago Inter-Ocean*, October 4, 1876, printed in Cozzens, ed., *Long War for the Northern Plains*, 363.

26. Davenport, "Crook's Victory."

27. Schwatka, *Chicago Inter-Ocean*, October 4, 1876, printed in Cozzens, ed., *Long War for the Northern Plains*, 363.

28. Wasson, "Capture of the Village." Lieutenant Schwatka stated that the ravine was located at the "head of the village." The statement is vague but implies a very short distance. Schwatka, *Chicago Inter-Ocean*, October 4, 1876, printed in Cozzens, ed., *Long War for the Northern Plains*, 364. Describing the ravine, Captain Burt wrote, "[It] is only about thirty feet long and a few feet down at its deepest; so narrow and insignificant one could cross it without

thinking it was the grave of eight beings in the end." Burt, *Cincinnati Commercial*, September 17, 1876 (dispatch dated September 9), printed in Cozzens, ed., *Long War for the Northern Plains*, 376. Lieutenant Bourke stated the ravine was about ten feet wide and fifteen to twenty feet deep. John G. Bourke, "The Battle of Slim Buttes," printed in Cozzens, ed., *Long War for the Northern Plains*, 381.

29. "pell mell" is from "Another Account of the Encounter," *New York Herald*, September 17, 1876 (the author believes this dispatch was written by Robert Strahorn); "secreted themselves" is from Davenport, "Crook's Victory."

30. Greene, *Slim Buttes*, 60–61. Kirkwood received the Medal of Honor in October 1877 for bravery in action this day, but it was not for helping to save Von Luettwitz. Instead it was for valor in trying to dislodge a party of Sioux Indians from a ravine.

31. Wasson stated that they captured 140 ponies. Davenport put the number at 200.

32. Davenport, "Crook's Victory."

33. Davenport, "Crook's Campaign."

34. Ibid. As Davenport had not yet arrived on the battlefield with Lieutenant Bubb, this incident was related to him by Frank Grouard. The story was published in the *New York Herald* on October 2, 1876, and was soon after found out by Mills and his subordinates. Schwatka, Crawford, and Bubb all declared the story false and sent out counterstatements. In June 1878, Davenport rebutted his own story in a letter to Mills, apologizing for too easily believing Grouard (whom he did not mention by name). These details are from John D. McDermott's introduction to Anson Mills, *My Story* (Mechanicsburg: Stackpole, 2003), xvi–xvii. Grouard mentioned this incident with Mills in his biography (dictated to Joseph DeBarthe in 1891) but used language far less inflammatory. The story may well have been based on some scrap of truth but exaggerated in Grouard's telling to Davenport, or by

Davenport himself. In any event, Anson Mills's solid reputation survives intact.

35. Davenport, "Crook's Victory."

36. Ibid. Cuthbert Mills, who arrived on the scene later that day, said that the initial fighting lasted about thirty minutes. Mills, "The Pursuit of the Sioux."

37. Davenport, "Crook's Campaign."

38. Davenport, "Crook's Victory."

39. Davenport, "Crook's Campaign."

40. Ibid.

41. Schwatka, *Chicago Inter-Ocean*, October 4, 1876, printed in Cozzens, ed., *Long War for the Northern Plains*, 364.

42. Mills's official report.

43. Davenport, "Crook's Campaign."

44. Ibid. Surprisingly, or perhaps not surprisingly, the correspondents lacked unanimity on the number of lodges. Davenport said thirty-five, Strahorn forty-one, Cuthbert Mills thirty-three, and Wasson forty. Based on these numbers, the number of warriors could have been anywhere from fifty to one hundred.

45. On September 8, Lieutenant Bourke pensively noted in his journal: "General Crook celebrated his [forty-eighth] birthday this evening. He drew out from the breast-pocket of his coat, a pint flask of whiskey which he had concealed there the day before we left the Yellowstone, and passing it around to the members of his mess and the other officers present—Colonel Evans and Colonel Chambers, called upon them to drink [to] his health. There were (13) or fourteen in the group and the flask held a little short of sixteen ounces, making just a taste for each one. Then those of us who had a piece of cracker in their pockets ate them; those who had none, went without. Take it for all and all, it was decidedly the 'thinnest' birthday celebration I have ever attended." Robinson, *Diaries of John Gregory Bourke*, vol. 2, 102.

46. Davenport, "Crook's Campaign." At the time, Davenport was under the impression that the ravine at the head of the village contained only one man.

47. "sections from the cavalry" is from "Another Account of the Encounter"; the number of men that advanced with Crook is from Lieutenant Colonel Carr's official report of the fight, dated September 15, printed in Greene, *Slim Buttes*, 136. Also see Greene, *Slim Buttes*, 68.

48. "Another Account of the Encounter."

49. Mills, "The Indian Campaign—Attack upon a Camp of Sioux."

50. It should be noted that the sequence of events at Slim Buttes is somewhat vague, as no two accounts match up precisely. In the end, it comes down to interpretation.

51. Davenport, "Crook's Campaign."

52. Wasson, "Capture of the Village."

53. Ibid.

54. Davenport, "Crook's Campaign."

55. Ibid. The "mortally wounded" soldier may have been Private Edward Kennedy, Fifth Cavalry. His leg had to be amputated, and he was dead before morning. Mills, "The Indian Campaign—Attack upon a Camp of Sioux." Another soldier, Private J. W. Stephenson/Stevenson, Second Cavalry, was shot in the ankle; despite being seriously wounded, he survived the battle.

56. Davenport, "Crook's Campaign."

57. Ibid.

58. Ibid. This man's real name was Jonathan White. In August, Cuthbert Mills had written about him: "A great feature of the expedition is the corps of scouts. There are some eleven or twelve of them and their chief is Cody, better known as 'Buffalo Bill.' Like all great men, he has his imitators. One of the fellows in the corps has obtained the sobriquet of 'Buffalo Chips,' because he acts as 'striker' to Bill, and wears his hair long, after the fashion of that famous individual. 'Chips' is not a bad scout, and probably dreams of the time when he, too, shall go East, and as the great scout of the Big Horn pocket his thousands from nightly crowded houses. He killed the first buffalo seen on the march, but it was an awfully tough old bull."

Mills, "The Indian Campaign—From Fetterman to Goose Creek."

59. Mills, "The Pursuit of the Sioux."

60. Davenport, "Crook's Campaign."

61. Ibid. About this incident, Lieutenant Bourke recorded: "I don't know how it happened but Captain Munson and myself found ourselves in the ravine on one side, while similarly, Big Bat and another guide, Cary, occupied the other. Alongside was a pile . . . of squaws and little papooses, covered with dirt and blood and screaming in a perfect agony of terror. The oaths and yells of the singing soldiers, pressing in behind us made the scene truly infernal. Just in front, three or four dead bodies lay stretched, weltering in their own gore. . . . [I]n response to Bat's encouraging call of Washte-helo ('All right' or 'Very good'), the women and children came up to us, [and] it did not take much time to get them out, following down the bends of the ravine." Robinson, *Diaries of John Gregory Bourke*, vol. 2, 109–110.

62. Mills, "The Pursuit of the Sioux."

63. Davenport, "Crook's Campaign."

64. Mills, "The Indian Campaign—Attack upon a Camp of Sioux."

65. Davenport, "Crook's Victory."

66. Regarding this man's identity, Davenport, in three dispatches, stated he was known by two different names: American Horse and Iron Shield. Lieutenant Schwatka noted, "The tribe was that of Roman Nose, Brule Sioux, with American Horse in direct command." Schwatka, *Chicago Inter-Ocean*, October 4, 1876, printed in Cozzens, ed., *Long War for the Northern Plains*, 364. According to a Hunkpapa Sioux named Has Horns, the fatally wounded man was a Sans Arc Sioux named Iron Shield. Richard G. Hardorff, *Lakota Recollections of the Custer Fight* (Spokane: Arthur H. Clark, 1991), 162n9. Also, see the sidebar titled "Black Bear Speaks."

67. Wasson, "Capture of the Village."

68. The scout was a Ute Indian called "Ute John." Regarding this incident, Finerty wrote: "Ute John, the solitary friendly Indian who did not desert the column, scalped all the dead, unknown to the General or any of the officers, and I regret to be compelled to state a few—a very few—brutalized soldiers followed his savage example. Each took only a portion of the scalp, but the exhibition of human depravity was nauseating." Finerty, *War-path and Bivouac*, 289.

69. Mills, "The Pursuit of the Sioux."

70. Valentine T. McGillycuddy (1849–1939) held various jobs in the West, including topographer, doctor, and Indian agent. He was the attending physician at Camp Robinson when Crazy Horse was killed in September 1877.

71. Davenport, "Crook's Campaign." Wasson wrote that the Indian prisoners told Crook that Sitting Bull had gone "down east and north to Antelope Buttes to trade with peaceable Indians." Joe Wasson, "Sent ahead for Supplies," *New York Tribune*, September 18, 1876.

72. Both quotes are from Mills, "The Pursuit of the Sioux." For more on Von Luettwitz, see the interlude, "The Brothers Von Luettwitz."

73. "Another Account of the Encounter."

74. Davenport, "Crook's Campaign."

75. Ibid.

76. Ibid.

77. Wasson, "Capture of the Village."

78. Ibid.

79. Mills, "The Pursuit of the Sioux."

80. Davenport, "Crook's Campaign." Cuthbert Mills wrote that the scout's body was "lying muffled up in a buffalo robe," and that one of his fellow scouts had been digging his grave. Mills, "The Pursuit of the Sioux."

81. Mills, "The Indian Campaign—Attack upon a Camp of Sioux." About this incident, Captain Burt stated: "They think probably to find only Mills' command of one hundred and fifty men. Mistake, for doughboys are up, and lots of critterback. The matter is soon settled, and the Indians are driven off,

wiser men." Burt, *Cincinnati Commercial,* September 17, 1876 (dispatch dated September 9), printed in Cozzens, ed., *Long War for the Northern Plains,* 377.

82. Mills, "The Indian Campaign—Attack upon a Camp of Sioux."

83. This appears to be the same Black Bear who described his pictographic representation of the battle of the Little Big Horn at the end of chapter 6.

84. Davenport, "Crook's Campaign."

85. Davenport, "Crook's Victory."

86. Davenport, "Crook's Campaign."

87. Ibid.

88. Eugene A. Carr (1830–1910).

89. Davenport, "Crook's Campaign."

90. Wasson, "Capture of the Village."

91. Mills, "The Indian Campaign—The Part Taken by General Crook's Command."

92. Davenport listed the names of the wounded in his September 16 dispatch: Lieutenant Von Luettwitz, Third Cavalry; William B. Dubois, Third Cavalry; Sergeant Edward Glass, Third Cavalry; Charles Foster, Third Cavalry; Edward McKiernan, Third Cavalry; Sergeant John A. Kirkwood, Third Cavalry; August Dorn, Third Cavalry; J. M. Stevenson, Second Cavalry; Sergeant Edmund Schreiber, Fifth Cavalry; Daniel Ford, Fifth Cavalry; Michael H. Donnelly, Fifth Cavalry; William Madden, Fifth Cavalry; George Cloutier, Fifth Cavalry; Robert Fitz Henry, Ninth Infantry. Davenport, "Crook's Campaign." This list includes the names of two or three men who were wounded in a skirmish on September 10. *Heitman's Historical Register* shows that Von Luettwitz retired May 5, 1879, and died on March 29, 1887 (see page 989).

93. Cuthbert Mills, "Among the Black Hills." *New York Times,* October 12, 1876.

94. "Another Account of the Encounter."

Chapter Thirteen

1. Davenport, "Crook's Victory."

2. Greene, *Slim Buttes,* 93.

3. Davenport, "Crook's Victory."

4. Joe Wasson, "Off for the Black Hills," *New York Tribune,* September 18, 1876.

5. These distances were determined using Google Earth.

6. Mills, "The Indian Campaign—The Part Taken by General Crook's Command."

7. Ibid.

8. Wasson, "Off for the Black Hills."

9. Davenport, "Crook's Campaign."

10. Wasson, "Off for the Black Hills." Davenport stated that seven of the Indians were killed. Davenport, "Crook's Campaign."

11. "General Carr's Strategy," *Cheyenne Daily Leader,* October 1, 1876. Although this dispatch was unsigned, Crawford, by his own admission, rode a mule, at least for part of the campaign (he mentions this in "The Story of a Scout Bearing the Herald Despatches," *New York Herald,* September 18, 1876). This detail and the fact that he served as a correspondent for the *Omaha Bee* make it fairly certain that this description came from his pen.

12. Davenport, "The Indian Campaign—Attack upon a Camp of Sioux." To add to the confusion, Lieutenant Bourke's journal entry for the day states, "We made some eighteen or twenty miles across a rough trail, bivouacking on a branch of what I should call the north fork of Owl Creek." Robinson, *Diaries of John Gregory Bourke,* vol. 2, 114.

13. Wasson, "Off for the Black Hills."

14. Reuben Davenport, "A Forlorn Hope," *New York Herald,* September 17, 1876.

15. Greene, *Slim Buttes,* 98, and Joe Wasson, "Sent Ahead for Supplies," *New York Tribune,* September 18, 1876.

16. Wasson, "Sent Ahead for Supplies."

17. Davenport, "A Forlorn Hope."

18. Wasson, "Sent Ahead for Supplies."

19. Schwatka, *Chicago Inter-Ocean,* October 4, 1876, printed in Cozzens, ed., *Long War for the Northern Plains,* 364.

20. Mills, "The Pursuit of the Sioux."

21. Schwatka, *Chicago Inter-Ocean,* October 4, 1876, printed in Cozzens, ed., *Long War for the Northern Plains,* 365. Also see

"Movements of Crook's Command," *New York Herald*, September 19, 1876. The dead man's name was Miller or Milner.

22. Finerty, *War-path and Bivouac*, 304.

23. "Movements of Crook's Command."

24. Schwatka, *Chicago Inter-Ocean*, October 4, 1876, printed in Cozzens, ed., *Long War for the Northern Plains*, 364–365.

25. Davenport, "Crook's Campaign."

26. Finerty, *War-path and Bivouac*, 307.

27. Robinson, *Diaries of John Gregory Bourke*, vol. 2, 120.

28. Finerty, *War-path and Bivouac*, 307. About Crook City, Mills was to write: "Crook City receives the main portion of its supplies from Bismarck and Fort Pierre. Prices are not at all unreasonable. I had an excellent dinner in a very neat restaurant for seventy-five cents, and other meals at the same rate. Shaving costs twenty-five cents, and cigars . . . , the same price." Mills, "Among the Black Hills."

29. Mills, "The Indian Campaign—The Part Taken by General Crook's Command."

30. Davenport, "Crook's Campaign."

31. Ibid.

32. Regarding the infantry, Cuthbert Mills remarked: "On the march they may be said to have actually walked down the cavalry. They only want some rest, and new boots, to be ready for the field again. I remember the jeer that a long-legged infantryman threw out as the cavalry column passed at the close of a long day's march. 'Two days more of this,' he shouted, in reference to some soldier's witticism from the mounted men, 'two days more of this and we'll fetch the whole lot of you.'" Mills, "The Indian Campaign—The Part Taken by General Crook's Command."

33. Davenport, "Crook's Campaign."

34. Mills, "The Pursuit of the Sioux."

35. "to proceed at once to Fort Laramie" is from Mills, "Among the Black Hills"; "a vigorous prosecution" is from "Sheridan on the Way to Meet Crook," *New York Herald*, September 15, 1876.

36. Robinson, *Diaries of John Gregory Bourke*, vol. 2, 129.

37. Schwatka, *Chicago Inter-Ocean*, October 4, 1876, printed in Cozzens, ed., *Long War for the Northern Plains*, 366.

38. Finerty, *War-path and Bivouac*, 320-321.

39. Mills, "The Indian Campaign—The Part Taken by General Crook's Command."

40. Mills, "Among the Black Hills."

41. Details are from Willert, *March of the Columns*, 594; Finerty, *War-path and Bivouac*, 313; and Robinson, *Diaries of John Gregory Bourke*, vol. 2, 130. For mention that all four correspondents departed with Crook, see Oliver Knight, *Following the Indian Wars* (Norman: University of Oklahoma Press, 1993), 280.

42. "Movements of Crook's Command," and "Movements of the More Prominent Officers Engaged in the Recent Campaign," *New York Herald*, September 28, 1876.

43. Reuben Davenport, "Crook's Command in the Black Hills," *New York Herald*, September 21, 1876. According to Mills, "Among the Black Hills," Deadwood's population was then about two thousand, which would mean that close to half of them signed the petition. However, according to Bourke, the petition contained 713 names. Robinson, *Diaries of John Gregory Bourke*, vol. 2, 135.

44. Mills, "Among the Black Hills."

45. Ibid. Later in the same dispatch, Mills followed through on this subject: "As to the Indians coming in [to the Black Hills] worse than ever after the departure of the Army, it is all nonsense. From what we can hear of the matter, it is supposed that there are some forty or fifty Indians, scattered in small bands around the outskirts of the Hills, who have been stealing and killing whenever they could do so with safety. This has been going on all the summer, while the mass of the Sioux nation were up in the Powder River country. Small parties and individuals have been attacked and killed on the roads leading

to the Hills, but the settlements themselves have never been in danger."

46. Ibid.

47. Ibid.

48. "The Indian Campaign," *New York Herald*, October 15, 1876.

49. Details from "A Supply Train for Crook's Command," *New York Herald*, September 12, 1876, and Captain Harry C. Cushing, "In the Black Hills," *Daily Alta California*, October 2, 1876.

50. Cushing, "In the Black Hills."

51. "Generals Sheridan and Crook in Council," *New York Herald*, September 22, 1876.

52. Joe Wasson, "Gen. Crook's Campaign— His Arrival at Fort Laramie," *New York Tribune*, October 2, 1876.

53. For more on how the multipronged military campaign had affected the Indians, see the end of chapter 10.

54. "Frontier settlements" was a euphemism for "illegal gold-mining towns."

55. Editorial, "Terry's Sioux Campaign," *New York Herald*, October 2, 1876.

56. Mills, "Seeking an Indian Fight."

57. Wasson, "Gen. Crook's Campaign—His Arrival at Fort Laramie."

58. Jerome A. Greene, *Morning Star Dawn: The Powder River Expedition and the Northern Cheyennes, 1876* (Norman: University of Oklahoma Press, 2003), 11, and Greene, *Slim Buttes*, 110. The distance between Crook City and Custer City is about forty-seven miles, as the eagle flies.

59. Mills, "The Indian Campaign—The Part Taken by General Crook's Command."

60. Editorial, "Terry's Sioux Campaign."

61. Robinson, *Diaries of John Gregory Bourke*, vol. 2, 126. On October 15, 1876, the *Cheyenne Daily Leader* printed some outtakes from an interview between General Sherman and a Chicago newspaperman. In the piece, the *Leader* quoted Sherman as saying, "I am sorry that I can't express an opinion regarding the summer campaign against the Indians, but you understand that as a

public man I am not at liberty to tell all I think or know. It wouldn't do for me to begin to criticize Crook or Terry." Of course, that last sentence more than expressed his opinion.

62. Describing Carr's marksmanship on the trip from Fort Fetterman to Crook's camp on Goose Creek in late July and early August, Cuthbert Mills had written: "Another hunter is old Gen. Carr, Lieutenant Colonel of the Fifth Cavalry, who until we got into very dangerous country has been trotting about the flanks of the column and banging away with a double-barreled shot-gun at sage hens and rabbits with uniform non-success. Indeed, the old gentleman could not apparently hit a barn door, but he shoots and shoots as if something dropped at every discharge, while most of the time the only effect has been to make nervous people jump in the saddle when they hear the reports." Mills, "The Indian Campaign—From Fetterman to Goose Creek."

CHAPTER FOURTEEN

1. "by the officers of the War Department" is from "President Grant—The Indian War," *New York Herald*, September 2, 1876; "and thus prevent any possible controversy" is from "Indian Agents Directed to Turn Over Their Charges to the Military," *New York Herald*, July 25, 1876. The civilian agent at Red Cloud was James S. Hastings, and the civilian agent at Spotted Tail was E. A. Howard. Also on July 22, Congress approved building two new posts in the Yellowstone country (these were to become Forts Keogh and Custer).

2. "Reply to Criticism on the Action of the Indian Office," *New York Herald*, July 31, 1876.

3. Colonel Ranald Slidell Mackenzie, Fourth Cavalry.

4. "Troops for the Agencies," *Cheyenne Daily Leader*, July 26, 1876.

5. "considerable on the fight" is from Jerry Roche, "The Winter Expedition on the Eve

of Departure," *New York Herald*, November 10, 1876; *District of the Black Hills* is from "The War Against the Sioux," *New York Tribune*, August 24, 1876.

6. Joe Wasson, "Interview with Captain Mears, Direct from the Indian Country," *Daily Alta California*, October 6, 1876.

7. George W. Manypenny, a well-known humanitarian, headed the government commission that was sent to the Sioux reservations to gain, what one historian called, "fictive legal title" to the Black Hills. Jeffrey Ostler, *The Plains Sioux and U. S. Colonialism* (Cambridge, England: Cambridge University Press, 2004), 66.

8. Although the 1876 agreement was deemed official by the US government, it lacked the minimum number of signatures required in article 12 of the Sioux Treaty of 1868, specifically three-fourths of all adult male Indians on the Great Sioux Reservation. To read the 1876 agreement and see the list of signatories, see "Report of the Sioux Commission," in *Annual Report of the Commissioner of Indian Affairs to the Secretary of the Interior for the Year 1876* (Washington: Government Printing Office, 1876), 349–357. Use of the term "agreement" instead of "treaty" is intentional; the act of making treaties with the Indian tribes was terminated by an act of Congress in March 1871.

9. Ted Morgan, *A Shovel of Stars: The Making of the American West* (New York: Touchstone, 1996), 307. Also see Hedren, *Fort Laramie*, 155–158.

10. Concerning a move to Indian Territory (present Oklahoma), the locals were not exactly waiting with open arms, as expressed in this news item: "Speaking of the proposed removal of the Sioux to the Indian Territory, the Oklahoma *Star* cries, 'Save us from our friends!'" Untitled, *Deseret News*, November 1, 1876.

11. "The Council at Red Cloud," *New York Times*, September 23, 1876. For more on these proceedings, readers can see James C.

Olson, *Red Cloud and the Sioux Problem* (Lincoln: University of Nebraska Press, 1975), 224–230.

12. "The Treaty Consummated with the Sioux at Spotted Tail Agency," *New York Herald*, September 27, 1876.

13. "The Treaty Signed—Hesitancy of the Indians Overcome Through the Influence of a Squaw Man," *New York Herald*, September 27, 1876. Whether Enoch Raymond (1824–1909) had an ulterior motive in getting Spotted Tail to sign the agreement or was truly looking out for the best interest of the Sioux was unstated.

14. In fact, Red Cloud's son, Jack, had joined the northern holdouts for a time and fought in the battle of the Rosebud, in which he lost a prized rifle that his father had received on a trip to Washington in May–June 1875. Richard E. Jensen, *The Indian Interviews of Eli S. Ricker, 1903–1919* (Lincoln: University of Nebraska Press, 2005), 84 (interview with William Garnett).

15. "Gen. Crook's 'Gleam of Light,'" *Daily Alta California*, October 27, 1876. On the topic of Red Cloud's faithfulness to the government, one news clipping stated that "old Red Cloud has been 'carrying the water on both shoulders' all summer. While his actions have been peaceable and he has been guilty of no overt act, yet he could undoubtedly have stopped many of his young men from joining the hostile bands, as Spotted Tail did." Untitled, *Cheyenne Daily Leader*, October 27, 1876.

16. O'Kelly, "Operations of the Combined Columns under Terry and Crook."

17. "Gen. Crook Heads Off a New War," *New York Tribune*, October 25, 1876. Gordon was in the Fifth Cavalry and Mauck in the Fourth. Details from the lead-in sentence also from the *New York Tribune*.

18. The first two items are from "The Late Capture a Large One," *New York Tribune*, October 26, 1876; the number of captured guns, which sounds a bit too low, is from an October 26 interview with Crook in "The

Indian Question—A Correspondent's Travels to the Seat of War," *New York Herald*, November 4, 1876, dispatch dated "Fort Laramie, Wy. T., Oct. 27, 1876."

19. Roche, "The Winter Expedition on the Eve of Departure," quoting Crook's report. In an interview several years later, Major Thaddeus Stanton, in response to whether or not Red Cloud had joined the "hostiles," said, "He was on his reservation but early in the campaign indubitable evidence was received by General Crook that Red Cloud, although making professions of friendship, was furnishing all his young men and all the materials of war that he possibly could to Sitting Bull and the hostile tribes to carry on their war against the government." "Red Cloud's Ponies—Why They Were Seized and Sold by Command of General Crook," *Omaha Daily Bee*, February 14, 1883.

20. Regarding the sale of the horses, a dispatch to the *New York Herald* on November 3, 1876, said: "Over 350 of the ponies captured at Red Cloud were sold at auction yesterday, and averaged about $5 each. They were mostly a poor half-starved lot, but were not dear at the price to ranchmen and others who could turn them out to grass for a while and give them a chance to improve. But they will need close watching, or the Indians will steal them back again. About 300 of the most serviceable ones were picked out before the sale for the enlisted Indians [the Pawnees], and will be given them before we start. The money received for those sold will be turned in to the Department of the Interior and applied in some way to the benefit of the former owners of the animals. Among the captured lot were found several American horses stolen from ranches about here. These were identified by their owners and turned over on proof of ownership. This is an instructive commentary on the 'honest Injun' professions of Mr. Red Cloud's braves." Roche, "The Winter Expedition on the Eve of Departure."

21. Use of the term "Old Spot" is from "Spotted Tail's Mission," *New York Herald*,

February 23, 1877; "unswerving loyalty" is from "Red Cloud and His Band [Made] Prisoners," *Daily Colorado Chieftain*, October 25, 1876.

22. "Gen. Crook's Report," *New York Tribune*, October 25, 1876.

23. Jerry Roche, "A Correspondent's Travels to the Seat of War," *New York Herald*, November 4, 1876.

24. "What Red Cloud Says," *Deseret News*, December 6, 1876, repr. from *Omaha Daily Bee*, dateline Red Cloud Agency, November 12.

25. "Red Cloud Captured at Last," *Deseret News*, November 15, 1876, repr. from the *Omaha Herald*, October 26.

26. "Gen. Crook's Address to His Men," *New York Times*, November 22, 1876.

Chapter Fifteen

1. "Sketch of General Crook," *New York Daily Graphic*, May 7, 1873.

2. Concerning Crazy Horse, recall what Crook told Cuthbert Mills in an interview on September 13 (Interlude: "An Interview with General Crook in the Black Hills"): "Our next objective point is Crazy Horse. He should be followed up and struck as soon as possible." Mills, "The Indian Campaign—The Part Taken by General Crook's Command." Crook revealed the official name of the expedition in an interview in late October. Roche, "A Correspondent's Travels to the Seat of War."

3. These details are from Jerry Roche, "March of the Powder River Expedition under General Crook," *New York Herald*, November 27, 1876.

4. Ibid.

5. Greene has slightly different numbers than those given by Roche, stating there were 61 officers, 790 cavalry and 646 infantry. Greene, *Morning Star Dawn*, 28–29.

6. Details on the supply train are from Roche, "March of the Powder River Expedition under General Crook." Roche noted that there were supplies for an addi-

tional seventeen days waiting for them at Cantonment Reno.

7. "Crook's Campaign," *Cheyenne Daily Leader*, November 28, 1876.

8. Usually referred to as "Major" Frank North, in deference to an honorary rank he held in 1867, his rank for the current campaign was captain. Accompanying him was his younger brother Luther, with the rank of lieutenant. Greene, *Morning Star Dawn*, 15–16, 85. Like his brother, Luther also had a long history with the Pawnees. Donald F. Danker, *Man of the Plains: Recollections of Luther North, 1856–1882* (Lincoln: University of Nebraska Press, 1961). For the Shoshones preceding Crook to Cantonment Reno, see Greene, *Morning Star Dawn*, 77.

9. Roche, "March of the Powder River Expedition under General Crook." Interestingly, it was previously written of Crook, "He will capture a 'hostile,' and, with the offer of good food, clothes, gun, horse, &c., in addition to authority, will buy him into turning against his own household. This is the grand secret of Crook's universal success." "Sketch of General Crook."

10. Lieutenant Bourke stated that this man's name was Charging Bear and that he was an Oglala Sioux. The name difference may be nothing more than an alternate translation, and the tribal affiliation may be an error on Bourke's part. Robinson, *Diaries of John Gregory Bourke*, vol. 2, 110n and 154 (for the Oglala reference).

11. "The Indian War—Conflicts with the Savages," *New York Tribune*, December 23, 1876.

12. "Crook's Campaign."

13. Roche, "The Winter Expedition on the Eve of Departure." Some of the items that Crook requested for the expedition were sealskin caps, overshoes, blankets, woolen mittens, ponchos, and shelter tents. Greene, *Morning Star Dawn*, 31.

14. Roche, "The Winter Expedition on the Eve of Departure."

15. Ibid.

16. Ibid.

17. Roche, "A Correspondent's Travels to the Seat of War." Commenting on Roche, Bourke wrote, "[Mr. Roche is] a far more presentable, scholarly and genial gentleman than his predecessor, Mr. Davenport." Robinson, *Diaries of John Gregory Bourke*, vol. 2, 177. Bourke's comment must have come before he read what Roche had to say about the soldiers' marksmanship.

18. Jerry Roche, "Our Indian Allies—Crook's Talk with his Red Soldiers," *New York Herald*, November 16, 1876. Although Roche referred to the Indian scouts as barbarians at this time, less than two months later his opinion had softened: "Of their conduct . . . nothing can be said but in praise. They put forth every effort to aid us and indulged in every scheme known to their crafty and untiring natures, and from first to last were wholly and zealously faithful. . . . All were eager as our own men to make the surprise complete." Jerry Roche, "The Powder River Expedition—The Progress and Finish of the Last Indian Campaign," *New York Herald*, January 14, 1877, dispatch dated "Fort Laramie, Wy. T., Jan. 4, 1877."

19. Roche, "Our Indian Allies—Crook's Talk with his Red Soldiers."

20. Ibid.

21. Ibid. As things turned out, the trip to Washington did not take place until September 1877.

22. Ibid. Sharp Nose was known for his battlefield prowess and his distinctive appearance. On a visit to New York in 1877, he was described as "by far the noblest Indian of them all in appearance . . . his face is more expressive and intelligent than those of his associates." "Farewell to the Braves—The Sioux and Arapahoes Go Home," *New York Times*, October 6, 1877.

23. Roche, "Our Indian Allies—Crook's Talk with His Red Soldiers."

24. Roche, "March of the Powder River Expedition under General Crook."

25. Ibid. About the Shoshones, Davenport had stated that they were "regularly disciplined in imitation of the white soldiers." Davenport, "Battle of Rosebud Creek." Davenport's dispatch is reprinted in chapter 4.

26. Roche, "March of the Powder River Expedition under General Crook."

27. Ibid.

28. Ibid.

29. Ibid. The text has been edited for ease of reading and to eliminate references by *New York Herald* correspondent Jerry Roche in the article in which it appeared. As for the Spotted Tail and Red Cloud Indians being allowed to continue living outside the bounds of their reservation, both agencies were relocated in 1878 to within present-day South Dakota, where they were renamed Rosebud and Pine Ridge, respectively.

30. Ibid.

31. Ibid.

32. Ibid.

33. On August 30, 1877, Cantonment Reno was upgraded to fort status and renamed Fort McKinney. Frazer, *Forts of the West*, 182.

34. "The Indian War—Conflicts with the Savages."

35. The quote is from Jerry Roche, "General Mackenzie's Fight," *New York Herald*, December 11, 1876; the number of scouts is from Robinson, *Diaries of John Gregory Bourke*, vol. 2, 170.

36. Roche, "General Mackenzie's Fight."

37. "The Fight with the Cheyennes," *New York Times*, December 24, 1876.

38. Roche, "General Mackenzie's Fight."

39. Jensen, *The Indian Interviews of Eli S. Ricker*, 23 (interview with William Garnett), and Greene, *Morning Star Dawn*, 81. Sometimes he is referred to as just Beaver Dam. The Arapahoes let him escape on a horse before the upcoming battle; he then returned to the vicinity of the Cheyenne village while the battle was in progress, only to be accused of scouting for the soldiers. But he was able to talk his way out of it. Grinnell, *Fighting Cheyennes*, 377–378.

40. Robinson, *Diaries of John Gregory Bourke*, vol. 2, 177.

41. Ibid., 177.

42. According to Lieutenant Bourke, the distance to Crazy Woman's Creek was twenty-three miles. Robinson, *Diaries of John Gregory Bourke*, vol. 2, 178.

43. Roche, "General Mackenzie's Fight."

44. Ibid.

45. Ibid.

46. The company of cavalry that remained behind with Crook was Company K of the Second. Greene, *Morning Star Dawn*, 85.

47. Roche, "General Mackenzie's Fight."

48. "in mud" is from "The Fight with the Cheyennes"; other details are from Roche, "General Mackenzie's Fight."

49. "The Fight with the Cheyennes."

50. Roche, "General Mackenzie's Fight."

51. Ibid. Another eyewitness recorded: "It seems that among the Sioux, whenever one has discovered the enemy, or any certain sign of him, he gives, upon coming in sight of his friends, an imitation of the howl of the prairie wolf. Our allies, therefore, instantly comprehended that their scouts were returning with news of the village." "The Fight with the Cheyennes."

52. "The Fight with the Cheyennes."

53. Robinson, *Diaries of John Gregory Bourke*, vol. 2, 181.

54. Roche, "General Mackenzie's Fight."

55. "The Fight with the Cheyennes."

56. Roche, "General Mackenzie's Fight."

57. Ibid.

58. It was perhaps because of this incident that Roche later remarked: "That the Indian can discern and distinguish distant objects better than a white man is an undoubted fact of which the slightest experience will convince any unprejudiced observer." Roche, "The Powder River Expedition—The Progress and Finish of the Last Indian Campaign."

59. Roche, "General Mackenzie's Fight." The *New York Times* correspondent also commented on the collapse of Jackass's

horse: "As they were approaching, one of their horses stumbled slightly and toppled over from sheer exhaustion. His rider, however, treated his fall as a good joke, coming up in good humor." "The Fight with the Cheyennes."

60. "The Fight with the Cheyennes."

61. Roche, "General Mackenzie's Fight."

62. Ibid. On November 24, a Cheyenne man named Sits-in-the-Night was out looking for his horses not too far from the village and saw indistinct figures driving them away. He also heard a "rumbling noise" in the distance and for some reason concluded that soldiers were nearby. When he went back to the village and reported what he had seen and heard, Crow Split Nose, the chief of the Crooked Lances, a Cheyenne military society, feared an attack. He suggested that the women take down the lodges and that the tribe build breastworks in a nearby cut bank. However, Last Bull, chief of the Fox soldiers, a rival military society, refused to allow these precautions to take place. Instead, he insisted that everyone stay up and dance all night. It was this dancing and drumming that some of Mackenzie's scouts heard just hours before the attack on the morning of the twenty-fifth. Grinnell, *Fighting Cheyennes*, 374.

63. Roche, "General Mackenzie's Fight."

64. Ibid.

65. "The Fight with the Cheyennes."

66. "last deep cut" is from Roche, "General Mackenzie's Fight." For mention of Mauck's battalion in reserve, see Greene, *Morning Star Dawn*, 109.

67. Roche, "The Powder River Expedition—The Progress and Finish of the Last Indian Campaign."

68. Roche, "General Mackenzie's Fight."

69. "The Fight with the Cheyennes."

70. Roche, "General Mackenzie's Fight."

71. Roche, "Mackenzie's Victory," *New York Herald*, December 1, 1876.

72. Corporal Ryan is identified in Greene, *Morning Star Dawn*, 126.

73. From "After the Battle," *Cheyenne Daily Leader*, December 29, 1876: "Besides some fresh Shoshone scalps found in the lodges there was also discovered a little buckskin bag filled with children's right hands. A Shoshone Indian found these horrible trophies, and believing them to be the hands of some of the children of his people burned them and the scalps at once."

74. It's not certain why Baird was the only soldier buried on the field. According to one soldier's reminiscence (sixty-four years later), the burial was a mistake. Greene, *Morning Star Dawn*, 247–248n1.

75. McKinney's body was sent back to his home in Memphis, Tennessee. Ibid., 158.

76. Sergeant Thomas H. Forsyth, Company M, Fourth Cavalry. His head was grazed by a bullet. Greene, *Morning Star Dawn*, 111.

77. Private John Sullivan, Company B, Fourth Cavalry. Ibid., 119.

78. Also known as William Garnett.

79. Sergeant Allen's death was detailed in Lieutenant James E. H. Foster, "Battle of the Rosebud," *New York Daily Graphic*, July 13, 1876, reprinted in chapter 4 (fourth from the last paragraph).

80. Little Wolf visited Washington, DC, in 1873.

81. Willis "Bill" Rowland. Greene, *Morning Star Dawn*, 35, 121.

Chapter Sixteen

1. Peter J. Powell, *Sweet Medicine: The Continuing Role of the Sacred Arrows, the Sun Dance, and the Sacred Buffalo Hat in Northern Cheyenne History*, vol. 1 (Norman: University of Oklahoma Press, 1969), 166–167.

2. A report dated "Red Cloud Agency, Neb., May 2, 1877," from an anonymous correspondent said, "Thirty of their warriors were killed and forty wounded, while next only to that in severity was the loss of nearly two-thirds of their herd of ponies killed, wounded and captured by the troops." "The Surrendered Hostiles." Lieutenant Colonel

Dodge wrote, "How they can exist in this bitter weather without anything is a problem for them to solve." Wayne R. Kime, ed., *The Powder River Expedition Journals of Colonel Richard Irving Dodge* (Norman: University of Oklahoma Press, 1997), 95. Dodge missed the fight, having stayed behind with Crook and the infantry, but based on the number of lodges, he estimated there were about six hundred warriors in the village. That sounds like too many, but he considered all men from the age of twelve to be warriors. Ibid., 96.

3. "The Sioux War—Hump, the Cheyenne Chief," *New York Herald*, June 4, 1877. According to the reporter, Hump (or, more likely, Buffalo Hump) had previously said, "Alas! for my race; it is passing away from among the peoples of the earth, and the last of the red men will soon perish under the setting sun." Ibid. Admittedly, it sounds like a line out of *The Last of the Mohicans*, but perhaps it was true to Hump's sentiments.

4. Marquis, *Wooden Leg*, 287.

5. "The Surrendered Hostiles."

6. Marquis, *Wooden Leg*, 287–288.

7. Robinson, *Diaries of John Gregory Bourke*, vol. 2, 250–251.

8. "The Surrendered Hostiles."

9. Eleanor H. Hinman, interviewer, "Oglala Sources on the Life of Crazy Horse," *Nebraska History* 57 (Spring 1976), 39, interview from 1930.

10. For the view that the Sioux were as generous as they could be, see Harry H. Anderson, "Indian Peace-Talkers and the Conclusion of the Sioux War of 1876," *Nebraska History* 44 (December 1963), 245–246n24. Anderson stated that the Cheyennes under Little Wolf who surrendered in mid-March 1877 made negative statements against the Sioux because they were bitter toward Crazy Horse for trying to prevent them from surrendering.

11. "The Sioux War—Gen. Crook's Winter March," *New York Tribune*, December 25, 1876.

12. In fact, this turned out to be inaccurate. The expedition moved south before turning east then north down the Belle Fourche. Any plans for going to the Little Powder River, now or later, never materialized.

13. Crook was mistaken in thinking that Crazy Horse had moved his village to the east. The Cheyennes had found him camped along a tributary of the Tongue River, and Colonel Miles was to find him along that same river, about twenty miles north of the Montana line, in early January.

14. Jerry Roche, "Return of General Crook—The Command to Set Out after Crazy Horse's Band," *New York Herald*, December 6, 1876.

15. Kime, ed., *Powder River Expedition Journals*, 103–104.

16. "The Sioux War—Gen. Crook's Winter March."

17. Ibid.

18. Jerry Roche, "Powder River Expedition," *New York Herald*, February 5, 1877. This dispatch was dated "Camp on Belle Fourche, Dec. 19, 1876," but was very late in reaching the office of the *Herald*. What may have been Roche's last dispatch on the Crook-Mackenzie campaign had already been printed some three weeks earlier.

19. Ibid.

20. Ibid.

21. Robinson, *Diaries of John Gregory Bourke*, vol. 2, 202.

22. Roche, "Powder River Expedition."

23. Robinson, *Diaries of John Gregory Bourke*, vol. 2, 202.

24. Kime, ed., *Powder River Expedition Journals*, 113–114.

25. "Conflicts with the Savages—A Force of Two Thousand to Be Kept Harassing the Indians," *New York Tribune*, December 23, 1876.

26. Roche, "Powder River Expedition."

27. Ibid.

28. Ibid.

29. Ibid.

30. Jerry Roche, "General Crook's Return to Fort Fetterman," *New York Herald*, December 26, 1876.

31. Julius Mason was previously a captain in the Fifth Cavalry.

32. Kime, ed., *Powder River Expedition Journals*, 131–132. As a point of interest, the two Sioux spies arrived at Fort Fetterman on January 1. "They had been on the Rosebud and Tongue rivers, and saw no signs of hostiles at either place." "The Powder River Expedition," *New York Herald*, January 4, 1877 (this dispatch consisted of one short paragraph, probably written by Roche).

33. "Gen. Crook at Fort Fetterman," *New York Tribune*, January 11, 1877. Bourke noted that there were considerable cases of frostbite, but that only "one poor fellow will have to lose his toes." Robinson, *Diaries of John Gregory Bourke*, vol. 2, 232.

34. "Gen. Crook at Fort Fetterman."

CHAPTER SEVENTEEN

1. For a thorough study of Colonel Miles's campaign against the nonreservation Sioux and Cheyennes, see Greene, *Yellowstone Command*.

2. The seventy-five miles was measured using Google Earth. One contemporary dispatch stated that the distance between the two points was about one hundred miles and described the route as "running partly along the Yellowstone bottom and partly back over the high prairies and through the mauvaises terres [bad lands] of the Yellowstone." "Attack of Redskins on a Supply Train," *New York Herald*, November 27, 1876.

3. "Sitting Bull—Operations of the Hostiles against Military Convoys," *New York Herald*, November 6, 1876.

4. Cedar Creek is a northern tributary of the Yellowstone, joining the latter river about ten miles east of the mouth of the Powder River.

5. "After Sitting Bull—Good Work of the Fifth Infantry in Driving the Sioux," *New York Herald*, November 30, 1876.

6. "Sitting Bull—Operations of the Hostiles against Military Convoys."

7. "General Miles' Chase of the Hostile Indian Bands through Montana's Snows—Sitting Bull Forced to Retreat," *New York Herald*, February 19, 1877. On the other hand, the Sioux do not seem to recall anything special about this fight. For instance, see Vestal, *Warpath*, 222–223.

8. Also see Greene, *Yellowstone Command*, 103 and 266n21.

9. Ibid., 136–144.

10. "General Miles' Chase of the Hostile Indian Bands through Montana's Snows—Sitting Bull Forced to Retreat."

11. Joseph Manzione, *"I Am Looking to the North for My Life": Sitting Bull, 1876-1881* (Salt Lake City: University of Utah Press, 1991), 36.

12. The scouts included Luther Sage "Yellowstone" Kelly, Thomas Leforge, and Buffalo Horn, a Bannock. Greene, *Yellowstone Command*, 157–158. Four of the seven companies had preceded Miles into the field, three on the twenty-seventh and one on the twenty-eighth. Ibid., 157. Mention of the wagons being disguised is in ibid., 157–158, and Miles's official report dated "Cantonment on Tongue River, Montana, January 23, 1877," printed in *Annual Report of the Secretary of War on the Operations of the Department for the Fiscal Year Ending June 30, 1877*, vol. 1 (Washington: Government Printing Office, 1877), 495.

13. "General Miles' Victory," *New York Herald*, February 6, 1877.

14. This engraving can be found in Greene, *Yellowstone Command*, 167.

15. Three men did die on the expedition, but only one died in the fight on the eighth, Corporal Augustus Rathman. Private William H. Batty was killed by Indians on January 3 while herding oxen, and Private Bernard McCann died on the twelfth of a wound received at the fight. All three men were in the Fifth Infantry. Greene, *Yellowstone Command*, 171, 162, 178, respectively.

16. "General Miles' Expedition against Crazy Horse," *Frank Leslie's Illustrated Newspaper*, May 5, 1877. All of the officers named were in the Fifth Infantry.

17. See Miles's report dated "Cantonment on Tongue River, Montana, January 23, 1877," printed in *Annual Report of the Secretary of War* (for the year 1877), vol. 1, 495.

18. "The Custer Massacre—An Indian Chief's Account of It," *New York Times*, March 15, 1877.

19. These details from Greene, *Yellowstone Command*, 176.

20. For newspaper coverage of Crazy Horse's surrender, see "Surrender of Crazy Horse," *New York Tribune*, May 7, 1877, at the end of this chapter.

21. Crazy Horse's enlistment paper can be viewed at http://www.american-tribes.com/Lakota/BIO/CrazyHorse.htm. Accessed November 29, 2011.

22. Thomas R. Buecker, *Fort Robinson and the American West, 1874–1899* (Norman: University of Oklahoma Press, 2003), 104.

23. Lieutenant Henry R. Lemly, "The Death of Crazy Horse," *New York Sun*, September 14, 1877, and Jesse M. Lee, "The Capture and Death of an Indian Chieftain," *Journal of the Military Service Institution of the United States* 54 (May–June 1914), 339.

24. John F. McBlain, "The Last Fight of the Sioux War of 1876–77," *Journal of the United States Cavalry Association* 10 (June 1897). Other details are from Greene, *Yellowstone Command*, chapter 9, and, "The Little Muddy—Details of General Miles' Last Brilliant Victory," *New York Herald*, June 11, 1877.

25. "The Little Muddy—Details of General Miles' Last Brilliant Victory."

26. Ibid.

27. "A Band Defeated by General Miles on Little Muddy Creek," *New York Tribune*, May 30, 1877, and "The Little Muddy—Details of General Miles' Last Brilliant Victory," respectively.

28. Greene, *Yellowstone Command*, 210.

29. "The Little Muddy—Details of General Miles' Last Brilliant Victory."

30. "A Band Defeated by General Miles on Little Muddy Creek."

31. Major Henry M. Lazelle's report, dated "Camp on Yellowstone River, near Tongue River Cantonment, September 5, 1877," printed in *Annual Report of the Secretary of War* (for the year 1877), vol. 1, 574; also Greene, *Yellowstone Command*, 221–222.

32. *Deseret News*, September 12, 1877, untitled dispatch dated "Camp Robinson, September 4."

33. Ibid.

34. "Surrender of Lame Deer's Band," *New York Times*, September 13, 1876. Also see Thomas Powers, *The Killing of Crazy Horse* (New York: Knopf, 2010), 510n2, and Charles M. Robinson, *The Diaries of John Gregory Bourke*, vol. 3 (Denton: University of North Texas Press, 2007), 507.

Chapter Eighteen

1. This excerpt is from an article headlined "Montana's Indian Puzzle," written by Thompson P. McElrath, a newsman and former soldier. His father, Thomas McElrath, was a partner with Horace Greeley in the *New York Tribune*. Thompson McElrath died in December 1898. "Death List of a Day," *New York Times*, December 11, 1898. Thanks to Paul L. Hedren for identifying McElrath as the writer of this article from the initials T. P. M.

2. "Funeral of Jerome B. Stillson," *New York Times*, December 30, 1880.

3. Knight, *Following the Indian Wars*, 32, and California State Mining Bureau, *Third Annual Report of the State Mineralogist for the Year Ending June 1, 1883* (Sacramento, 1883), 18.

4. "Six Ribs Broken," *New York Times*, August 1, 1884.

5. "A Soldier's Career," *New York Times*, March 22, 1890.

6. "Maj. Gen. George Crook Dies of Heart

Disease," *Fort Worth Daily Gazette*, March 22, 1890.

7. Jerome Stillson, "Sitting Bull—Graphic Picture of the Powwow at Fort Walsh," *New York Herald*, October 23, 1877.

8. "Gall Signs the Treaty—Sitting Bull's Band Grunt Disapproval," *New York Times*, August 7, 1889.

9. The Ghost Dance was a harmless religious dance that generated a deadly overreaction from the US government and resulted in the Wounded Knee Massacre on December 29, 1890.

10. Of course, this story was untrue. However, it is interesting to note that just about everybody west of the Missouri River and east of the Rockies in late June 1876 *almost* rescued Custer on the Little Big Horn River (whether by their own word or some newspaper editor's years later, as in this case).

11. Dan L. Thrapp, *Encyclopedia of Frontier Biography*, vol. 1 (Lincoln: University of Nebraska Press, 1991), 491.

12. These details are from a twenty-one-page PDF document at http://www.littlebighorn.info/Articles/Martino.pdf.

13. "Custer's Last Scout Dead," *New York Times*, May 25, 1923.

14. Knight, *Following the Indian Wars*, 319, and Thrapp, *Encyclopedia of Frontier Biography*, vol. 1, 377.

15. *St. Paul Daily Globe*, July 8, 1886.

16. These monetary details are from "Custer's Life Insurance," *New York Herald*, July 16, 1876, and *Colorado Mountaineer*, December 20, 1876.

17. "The Custer Massacre—Memories of the Terrible Little Big Horn Battle," *Nebraska Advertiser*, June 26, 1896.

18. Morris enlisted on September 22, 1875, and gave his birth date as May 1, 1854. Nichols, *Men with Custer*, 235.

19. Custer's five companies were divided into two battalions, one each under captains Keogh and Yates.

20. Quote and date of death from "John M. Carnahan—Telegrapher Flashed the News of Custer Massacre in 1876," *New York Times*, October 25, 1938.

21. Charles House, "How the Herald Revealed Custer Massacre," *New York Herald Tribune*, June 30, 1957.

22. Strahorn wrote to a friend circa 1878, "I could write a book about our trials and tribulations on those marches [in 1876], and sometime in the future the half-formed fancy of the present moment may take shape." Robert Vaughn, *Then and Now; or, Thirty-six Years in the Rockies* (Minneapolis: Tribune Printing, 1900), 307. Whether Strahorn followed through and wrote about his time with Crook in 1876 is unknown; if he did, it has not come to light.

23. Knight, *Following the Indian Wars*, 323–324, and Dan L. Thrapp, *Encyclopedia of Frontier Biography*, vol. 3 (Lincoln: University of Nebraska Press, 1991), 1376.

24. The seventy-seven men statistic is from Nichols, *Men with Custer*, 155.

25. Mills, *Harvest of Barren Regrets*, 367.

BIBLIOGRAPHY

Books, articles, and official documents

Abrams, Marc H., ed. and comp. *"Crying for Scalps": St. George Stanley's Sioux War Narrative.* Brooklyn, NY: privately printed, 2010.

Anderson, Harry H. "Indian Peace-Talkers and the Conclusion of the Sioux War of 1876." *Nebraska History* 44 (December 1963): 233–254.

Annual Report of the Commissioner of Indian Affairs to the Secretary of the Interior for the Year 1876. Washington: Government Printing Office, 1876.

[Annual] Report of the Secretary of War (for the year 1876). Vol. 1. Washington: Government Printing Office, 1876.

Annual Report of the Secretary of War on the Operations of the Department for the Fiscal Year Ending June 30, 1877. Vol. 1. Washington: Government Printing Office, 1877.

Barnard, Sandy. I Go With Custer. Bismarck, ND: Bismarck Tribune Publishing, 1996.

Bennett, Estelline. *Old Deadwood Days.* Santa Barbara, CA: Narrative Press, 2001.

Bradley, James H. *The March of the Montana Column.* Edited by Edgar I. Stewart. Lincoln: University of Nebraska Press, 1991.

Buecker, Thomas R. *Fort Robinson and the American West, 1874–1899.* Norman: University of Oklahoma Press, 2003.

California State Mining Bureau. *Third Annual Report of the State Mineralogist for the Year Ending June 1, 1883.* Sacramento, 1883.

Carroll, John M., ed. *General Custer and the Battle of the Little Big Horn: The Federal View.* New Brunswick, NJ: Gary Owen Press, 1976.

Chun, Clayton K. S. *US Army in the Plains Indian Wars.* Oxford, England: Osprey, 2004.

Clark, William P. *The Indian Sign Language.* Lincoln: University of Nebraska Press, 1982.

Collins, Charles D., Jr. *Atlas of the Sioux Wars.* 2nd Ed. Fort Leavenworth, KS: Combat Studies Institute Press, 2006.

Cozzens, Peter, ed. *The Long War for the Northern Plains*. Mechanicsburg, PA: Stackpole, 2004.

Custer, Elizabeth B. *Boots and Saddles*. Norman: University of Oklahoma Press, 1987.

Danker, Donald F. *Man of the Plains: Recollections of Luther North, 1856–1882*. Lincoln: University of Nebraska Press, 1961.

DeBarthe, Joe. *The Life and Adventures of Frank Grouard, Chief of Scouts, U. S. A.* Alexandria, VA: Time-Life Books, 1980.

Dustin, Fred. *The Custer Tragedy*. El Segundo, CA: Upton & Sons, 1987.

Ellis, Horace. "A Survivor's Story of the Custer Massacre on American Frontier." *Journal of American History* 3, no. 2 (April 1909): 227–232.

Finerty, John F. *War-path and Bivouac*. Edited by Milo M. Quaife. Lincoln: University of Nebraska Press, 1966.

Frazer, Robert W. *Forts of the West*. Norman: University of Oklahoma Press, 1972.

Gaff, Alan, and Maureen Gaff, eds. *Adventures on the Western Frontier: Major General John Gibbon*. Indianapolis: Indiana University Press, 1994.

Godfrey, Edward S. *Custer's Last Battle*. Golden, CO: Outbooks, 1986.

Gray, John S. *Centennial Campaign*. Norman: University of Oklahoma Press, 1988.

Greene, Jerome A. *Morning Star Dawn: The Powder River Expedition and the Northern Cheyennes, 1876*. Norman: University of Oklahoma Press, 2003.

———. *Slim Buttes, 1876: An Episode of the Great Sioux War*. Norman: University of Oklahoma Press, 1990.

———. *Yellowstone Command: Colonel Nelson A. Miles and the Great Sioux War, 1876–1877*. Lincoln: University of Nebraska Press, 1994.

Grinnell, George B. *The Fighting Cheyennes*. Norman: University of Oklahoma Press, 1985.

Hardorff, Richard G., comp. and ed. *Lakota Recollections of the Custer Fight*. Spokane: Arthur H. Clark, 1991.

———, comp. and ed. *On the Little Big Horn with Walter Camp*. El Segundo, CA: Upton & Sons, 2002.

Hayne, Coe. *Red Men on the Bighorn*. Philadelphia: Judson Press, 1929.

Hedren, Paul L. *First Scalp for Custer: The Skirmish at Warbonnet Creek*. Lincoln: Nebraska State Historical Society, 2005.

———. *Fort Laramie and the Great Sioux War*. Norman: University of Oklahoma Press, 1998.

————. *Great Sioux War Orders of Battle: How the United States Army Waged War on the Northern Plains, 1876–1877.* Norman: University of Oklahoma Press, 2011.

————. *Traveler's Guide to the Great Sioux War.* Helena: Montana Historical Society Press, 1996.

Heitman, Francis B. *Historical Register and Dictionary of the United States Army* (usually referred to as *Heitman's Historical Register*). Vol. 1. Washington: Government Printing Office, 1903.

Henry, Guy V. "Wounded in an Indian Fight." *Harper's Weekly,* July 6, 1895.

Hinman, Eleanor H., interviewer. "Oglala Sources on the Life of Crazy Horse." *Nebraska History* 57 (Spring 1976): 1–51.

Hoig, Stan. *Tribal Wars of the Southern Plains.* Norman: University of Oklahoma Press, 1993.

Hutton, Paul Andrew. *Phil Sheridan and His Army.* Lincoln: University of Nebraska Press, 1985.

"Indian Chief as an Artist—Black Bear's Deerskin Painting of the Details of the Custer Massacre," *Indian Advocate* 14, no. 2 (February 1902): 40–41.

Jensen, Richard E. *The Indian Interviews of Eli S. Ricker, 1903–1919.* Lincoln: University of Nebraska Press, 2005.

Kanipe, Daniel. "A New Story of Custer's Last Battle." *Contributions to the Historical Society of Montana* 4 (1903): 277–283.

Kime, Wayne R., ed. *The Black Hills Journals of Colonel Richard Irving Dodge.* Norman: University of Oklahoma Press, 1996.

————, ed. *The Powder River Expedition Journals of Colonel Richard Irving Dodge.* Norman: University of Oklahoma Press, 1997.

King, Charles. *Campaigning with Crook.* Norman: University of Oklahoma Press, 1989.

Klokner, James B. *The Officer Corps of Custer's Seventh Cavalry, 1866–1876.* Atglen, PA: Schiffer, 2007.

Knight, Oliver. *Following the Indian Wars.* Norman: University of Oklahoma Press, 1993.

Lee, Jesse M. "The Capture and Death of an Indian Chieftain." *Journal of the Military Service Institution of the United States* 54 (May–June 1914): 323–340.

Lowe, Percival G. *Five Years a Dragoon.* Norman: University of Oklahoma Press, 1991.

Malone, Michael P., Richard B. Roeder, and William L. Lang. *Montana: A History of Two Centuries.* Seattle: University of Washington Press, 1991.

Mangum, Neil C. *Battle of the Rosebud*. El Segundo, CA: Upton & Sons, 1987.

Manzione, Joseph. *"I Am Looking to the North for My Life": Sitting Bull, 1876–1881*. Salt Lake City: University of Utah Press, 1991.

Marquis, Thomas B. *Custer on the Little Bighorn*. Algonac, MI: Reference Publications, 1987.

———, interpreter. *Wooden Leg: A Warrior Who Fought Custer*. Lincoln: University of Nebraska Press, 2003.

McBlain, John F. "The Last Fight of the Sioux War of 1876–77." *Journal of the United States Cavalry Association* 10 (June 1897): 122–127.

McClernand, Edward J. "Journal of the Marches Made by the Forces under Colonel John Gibbon." *Annual Report of the Secretary of War on the Operations of the Department for the Fiscal Year Ending June 30, 1877*. Vol. 2, part 2. Washington: Government Printing Office, 1877.

McCrady, David Grant. *Living with Strangers: The Nineteenth Century Sioux and the Canadian-American Borderlands*. Lincoln: University of Nebraska Press, 2006.

McFarling, Lloyd. *Exploring the Northern Plains*. Caldwell, ID: Caxton Printers, 1955.

Military Expedition against the Sioux Indians. 44th Cong., 1st sess., Executive Document 184 (1876).

Mills, Anson. *My Story*. Mechanicsburg, PA: Stackpole, 2003.

Mills, Charles K. *Harvest of Barren Regrets*. Glendale, CA: Arthur H. Clark, 1985.

Morgan, Ted. *A Shovel of Stars: The Making of the American West*. New York: Touchstone, 1996.

Nichols, Ronald H. *In Custer's Shadow: Major Marcus Reno*. Norman: University of Oklahoma Press, 2000.

———. *Men with Custer: Biographies of the Seventh Cavalry*. Hardin, MT: Custer Battlefield Historical & Museum Association, 2000.

Noyes, C. Lee. "A Dispatch from the Battlefield." *Research Review: The Journal of the Little Big Horn Associates* 18 (Summer 2004).

Olson, James C. *Red Cloud and the Sioux Problem*. Lincoln: University of Nebraska Press, 1975.

Ostler, Jeffrey. *The Plains Sioux and U. S. Colonialism*. Cambridge, England: Cambridge University Press, 2004.

Overfield, Lloyd J. *The Little Big Horn, 1876*. Lincoln: University of Nebraska Press, 1990.

Poole, D. C. *Among the Sioux of Dakota*. New York: D. Van Nostrand, 1881.

Powell, Peter J. *People of the Sacred Mountain*. San Francisco: Harper & Row, 1981.

———. *Sweet Medicine: The Continuing Role of the Sacred Arrows, the Sun Dance, and the Sacred Buffalo Hat in Northern Cheyenne History*. Vol. 1. Norman: University of Oklahoma Press, 1969.

Powers, Thomas. *The Killing of Crazy Horse*. New York: Knopf, 2010.

Rickey, Don, Jr. *Forty Miles a Day on Beans and Hay*. Norman: University of Oklahoma Press, 1972.

Robertson, Edna, and Sarah Nestor. *Artists of the Canyons & Caminos*. Layton, UT: Ancient City Press, 2006.

Robinson, Charles M. *The Diaries of John Gregory Bourke*. Vol. 1. Denton: University of North Texas Press, 2003.

———. *The Diaries of John Gregory Bourke*. Vol. 2. Denton: University of North Texas Press, 2005.

———. *The Diaries of John Gregory Bourke*. Vol. 3. Denton: University of North Texas Press, 2007.

———. *General Crook and the Western Frontier*. Norman: University of Oklahoma Press, 2001.

Schmitt, Martin F., ed. *General George Crook: His Autobiography*. Norman: University of Oklahoma Press, 1986.

Smalley, Vern. *Little Big Horn Mysteries*. Bozeman, MT: Little Buffalo Press, 2005.

Stewart, Edgar I., and Jane R. Stewart, eds. *The Field Diary of Lieutenant Edward Settle Godfrey*. Portland, OR: Champoeg Press, 1957.

Strahorn, Carrie Adell. *Fifteen Thousand Miles by Stage*. New York: Knickerbocker Press, 1911.

Thrapp, Dan L. *Encyclopedia of Frontier Biography*. Vols. 1 and 3. Lincoln: University of Nebraska Press, 1991.

Utley, Robert M. *Cavalier in Buckskin*. Norman: University of Oklahoma Press, 1988.

———. *Frontier Regulars: The United States Army and the Indian, 1866–1891*. Lincoln: University of Nebraska Press, 1984.

———. *The Indian Frontier of the American West, 1846–1890*. Albuquerque: University of New Mexico Press, 1984.

Vaughn, J. W. *The Reynolds Campaign on Powder River*. Norman: University of Oklahoma Press, 1961.

Vaughn, Robert. *Then and Now; or, Thirty-six Years in the Rockies.* Minneapolis: Tribune Printing, 1900.

Vestal, Stanley. *Warpath: The True Story of the Fighting Sioux, Told in a Biography of Chief White Bull.* Lincoln: University of Nebraska Press, 1984.

Welch, James, with Paul Stekler. *Killing Custer.* New York: Norton, 1994.

Wert, Jeffry D. *Custer: The Controversial Life of George Armstrong Custer.* New York: Simon & Schuster, 1996.

Willert, James. *March of the Columns.* El Segundo, CA: Upton & Sons, 1994.

NEWSPAPERS

Billings Gazette
Bismarck Tribune
Brooklyn Daily Eagle
Cheyenne Daily Leader
Colorado Banner
Colorado Mountaineer
Colorado Springs Gazette
Colorado Transcript
Daily Alta California
Daily Colorado Chieftain
Daily Rocky Mountain News
Denver Daily Times
Deseret News
Dodge City Times
Fort Worth Daily Gazette
Frank Leslie's Illustrated Newspaper
Harper's Weekly
Journal & Republican (Lowville, New York)
Laramie Daily Sentinel
Nebraska Advertiser
New York Daily Graphic
New York Evening Post
New York Herald
New York Herald Tribune
New York Sun
New York Times
New York Tribune

New York World
Omaha Daily Bee
St. Paul Daily Globe
(Washington) *Times*
Weekly Colorado Chieftain
Weekly Rocky Mountain News

INDEX

Gen. George Crook. (*Carly Sacks*)

Acknowledgments

I would like to thank Douglas W. Ellison (North Dakota) for his friendship and for writing the excellent foreword; Paul L. Hedren (Nebraska) for his friendship and support, for helping to keep me on track (even if he did not know it), and for reading the initial version of several chapters and offering insightful suggestions that helped make this a better book; Steve Schwartz (New Jersey) and Gary Leonard (England) for reading some early versions of various chapters and offering helpful feedback and suggestions; Jerome A. Greene (Colorado) for his friendship and support; Bob Brown (New York), correspondent for ABC News from 1977–2010, and writer extraordinaire, for his friendship, support, and shared interest in Charles St. George Stanley; Chris Penn (England) for sharing his findings on St. George Stanley; Phil Rothman for the Custer books; Carly Sacks for the fine sketch of George Crook; my editor, Ron Silverman, for helping me fine-tune the narrative; Trudi Gershenov, designer, for the eye-catching cover; Tracy Dungan, cartographer, for his wonderful maps; publisher Bruce H. Franklin for making this book a reality; the civilian and military newspaper correspondents who risked life and limb, and braved all kinds of weather, to make this book possible; my mom for always lending a helping hand in life's daily struggles; and my wife, Jodi, and son, Aaron Lakota, for their love and support. As for the book, any shortcomings are mine alone.